ANOTHER GOSPEL

Other Books by Ruth Tucker
From Jerusalem to Irian Jaya
Daughters of the Church (with Walter L. Liefeld)
First Ladies of the Parish
Guardians of the Great Commission
The Christian Speakers Treasury
Sacred Stories: Daily Devotions from the Family of God

ANOTHER GOSPEL

Alternative Religions and the New Age Movement

Ruth A. Tucker

Academie
Books Grand Rapids, Michigan
Zondervan Publishing House

ANOTHER GOSPEL
Copyright © 1989 by Ruth A. Tucker

ACADEMIE BOOKS is an imprint of Zondervan Publishing House,
1415 Lake Drive, S.E., Grand Rapids, Michigan 49506.

Library of Congress Cataloging in Publication Data

Tucker, Ruth, 1945-
    Another gospel : alternative religions and the new age movement
/ Ruth A. Tucker.
       p.   cm.
    Includes index.
    Bibliography: p.
    ISBN 0-310-40440-1
    1. United States—Religion.   2. Cults—United States.   I. Title.
BL2525.T82   1989
291'.0973—dc19   89-5628
                                                                  CIP

All Scripture quotations, unless otherwise noted, are taken from the HOLY BIBLE: NEW INTERNATIONAL VERSION (North American Edition). Copyright © 1973, 1978, 1984, by the International Bible Society. Used by permission of Zondervan Bible Publishers.

Edited by Leonard G. Goss

Printed in the United States of America

89 90 91 92 93 94 / DH / 10 9 8 7 6 5 4 3 2 1

To
my son
Carlton
who has encouraged and challenged me
on this project
from beginning to end

CONTENTS

PREFACE

Authors of books covering a wide-ranging topic such as this one are inevitably heavily dependent on those scholars and writers who immerse themselves in one segment of the topic. I am no exception. The work that Jerald and Sandra Tanner have done on the subject of Mormonism is an example of such scholarship. They have given their adult lives to jointly researching the topic and have pored over thousands of primary sources from the vast archives relating to the history, theology, and current controversies of that religious movement. I am deeply grateful to them for their commitment to the truth and to scholarly research.

There are dozens of other scholars whose work has also played an important role in this volume. These scholars are in some cases members or former members of the religious organizations they have researched. In other instances, they have done their digging entirely from the outside. In all cases, it is greatly appreciated. Fawn Brodie, Donna Hill, Linda Newell, and Klaus Hansen are among those who have done significant research on Mormonism. Gary Land and Walter Rea have made valuable contributions in the area of Seventh-day Adventist studies. Raymond Franz, James Penton, and the Bottings have made similar contributions regarding the Jehovah's Witnesses. Three individuals stand out in their research on Christian Science: Stephen Gottschalk, Robert Peel, and Julius Silberger. Other writers whose work I found very helpful include James Freeman on the Unity School of Christianity, J. L. Williams on The Way International, Deborah Berg Davis on the Children of God, Larry Shinn on the Hare Krishnas, and J. E. Esslemont on Baha'i.

Although this book is not one that contains personal reflections, much of the material is presented in light of my own discussions and interviews with members of alternative religions and the New Age Movement. I have also had the privilege of having members of such religions as the Mormons, Jehovah's Witnesses, The Way International, the Hare Krishnas, Baha'i, and the New Age Movement speak to the seminary and college classes I teach on this subject.

In addition, I have had the opportunity to tour the United States, visiting cult centers and interviewing members at key locations, including the Christian Science headquarters in Boston; the Watchtower complex in Brooklyn; the Unification Seminary in Barrytown, New York and the Unification headquarters in New York City; the Hare Krishna commune in Philadelphia and the Golden Temple in West Virginia; the Baha'i Temple in Wilmette, Illinois; the compound of Rajneesh in Antelope, Oregon; the Worldwide Church of God in Pasadena; the Mormon Temple and tabernacle in Salt Lake City; the Unity School of Practical Christianity in Lee's Summit, Missouri; the Reorganized Church of Latter-Day Saints in Independence, Missouri; The Way International in New Knoxville, Ohio; and Scientology centers in both Los Angeles and Clearwater, Florida.

I have also been privileged to work closely with my editor at Zondervan, Len Goss, and to benefit from both his library and his expertise in the area of alternative religious movements.

Despite all the help I have received from the writings of other scholars, and from both the years of teaching I have done in this field and the personal interaction I have had with members of alternative religious movements, I offer this book with a solemn recognition of my own limitations. Yet, it is my hope that the reader on completing this volume will have grasped the essence of these movements and will be stimulated to dig deeper into this fascinating subject.

INTRODUCTION

Bob is a high school science teacher and the father of three teenagers who manages to spend time in his off hours working with disadvantaged youth in his community. His quick wit and genuine concern for others was apparent from the first time I met him—the very type of individual I would feel good about being one of my son's teachers. He has been in my home on different occasions, and I always feel challenged by his sharp mind.

Dolores is a black woman in her late forties and lives a few blocks from my home. Her two children are out of school and working. She is prim and proper, in comparison to her laid-back and slightly scruffy husband. She is easy to talk with and eager to help, but I'm not always sure she is being straight with me. I sometimes ask myself, what is her hidden (or not so hidden) agenda? Yet, I like her, and we've had some good times together.

Janice is a college student I became acquainted with a few years ago. We spent much of a weekend together and talked about a lot of things that we cared deeply about. She was real—the type of person I knew I would enjoy spending more time with. When we said "good-bye," we hugged, with tears in our eyes. It was the last time we saw each other.

Bob, Dolores, and Janice are the kind of ordinary people that you would expect to meet on an airplane, at an adult education course, or at a church social. But to many people they are not ordinary. They are *cultists*. Bob is a Mormon. Dolores is a Jehovah's Witness. Janice is a "Moonie."

In attempting to understand the Mormons, the Jehovah's Witnesses, or the "Moonies," it is imperative that we get to know adherents of these movements as individuals—as people. If we perceive them only as nameless faces who are part of a movement or organization, we have failed to take the first and necessary step of reaching out to them in a meaningful way.

In cross-cultural evangelism overseas, missionaries are admonished not to ridicule other religious beliefs or practices. When a missionary visits a sacred shrine where shoes are to be left at the door, it would be unconscionable to defy the custom. Yet, these "cross-cultural" courtesies are often blatantly ignored when they pertain to situations within our own culture. We often ridicule or mock the unorthodox religious beliefs of people in our own communities, because *cultists* do not deserve respect. The Jehovah's Witnesses are called "intellectual hillbillies" by one prominent writer, and a film expose of Mormons depicts their beliefs in tactless comic cartoon characters.

People—Bob, Dolores, and Janice—are, and ought to be, preeminent in any discussion of variant religions. Of course, doctrine is the determining factor in judging whether or not a movement is unorthodox, but it is the personal touch that is the determining factor that prompts an individual to become an active member of such a movement. Studies have repeatedly shown that people do not join a religion on doctrinal grounds. Rather, they join because they have found caring people and warm fellowship.

People are important from a historical perspective as well. It is crucial to know who the *people* were who founded and developed these religious movements. What were their character traits? What claims did they make to visionary experiences? Were there inconsistencies between teachings and practice? How have their teachings compared with Scripture?

The lives of the founders of any religious movements are important for study, but far more so in the case of the "cults" or variant religious movements. Unlike Luther, Calvin, or Wesley, the founders of these groups have invariably claimed special revelation from God. Luther's doctrine is affirmed only so far as it corresponds with the Bible. That he claimed to have had personal encounters with the devil is regarded with interest or amusement but is not incorporated into a creed or a body of belief. The same, however, cannot be said for Joseph Smith. A significant portion of his doctrine is not confirmed in Scripture, but is openly declared to be new revelation for "latter-day saints." Thus his claimed experiences with the angels or heavenly personages are regarded by his followers as far more than an amusing episode in his life.

The only "new" revelation that Christians, who hold the Bible as their only source of authority, claim is valid is that which is found in Scripture itself. Jesus certainly came with a "new" message. His followers were dubbed "the cult of Jesus," and with good reason. They were the followers of a "prophet" who had a radically different message to proclaim. Why should a Jew—or much less a Gentile—have accepted his message? What basis do Christians today have for accepting the message of Jesus? One important basis is his very life and character. Jesus himself is his own best claim to deity. He had authority within his very person to access the throne of God the Father and to offer "new" revelation.

Jesus is the focus of any true Christian belief system, and his life and ministry is open for scrutiny. This is well illustrated by the evangelistic focus of E. Stanley Jones, the great Methodist missionary to India. "I defined Christianity as Christ," wrote Jones, in reference to a debate with a Jain scholar. "If you have any objections to make against Him, I am ready to hear them and will answer them if I can." On another occasion when being challenged by a Hindu, he responded, "My brother, I am the narrowest man you have come across. I am broad on almost anything else, but on the one supreme necessity for human nature I am absolutely narrowed by the facts to one—Jesus."[1]

Is it not fair to put the lives and ministries of others who claim new revelations and teachings to the same test? Indeed, some leaders in variant religious groups have suggested that very notion themselves. Joseph Fielding Smith, a historian and one-time presiding prophet of the Mormon church, made this very challenge concerning Joseph Smith: "Mormonism . . . must stand or fall on the story of Joseph Smith. He was either a prophet of God divinely called . . . or he is one of the biggest frauds this world has ever seen. There is no middle ground."[2]

This same challenge must be made about prophet-founders of all the variant religious movements who claim new revelations and authoritative writings. Indeed, there is no middle ground. This does not mean that they must be judged by the very standard of sinless perfection that characterized Jesus, but it does mean that their lives and ministries should be above reproach.

An unfortunate aspect of studying the lives of these men and women is that in the past there has been a severe want of historical objectivity. Among the followers there has been a predilection to treating these prophet-founders as supersaints who could do no wrong, and among the opponents the very opposite approach was taken. The Joseph Smiths, the Ellen G. Whites, the Charles Taze Russells, and the Mary Baker Eddys were viewed across the board by many critics as degenerate scoundrels and tools of Satan who were utterly incapable of honorable deeds. Joseph Smith, for example, was deemed to be "entirely destitute of moral character" by an early writer, and that assertion has been repeatedly quoted as fact in books on Mormonism by contemporary writers on cults.

Such unwarranted slurs are inappropriate. With all his character flaws and heretical beliefs, Smith had, at least outwardly, many redeeming qualities. And it is important for the student of alternative religions to realize this. What was it in his personality and character that impelled so many people to be drawn to him? What can be learned from his life and outreach that can help explain why modern "prophets" and charismatic leaders draw so many followers? In making these judgments, the modern writer is aided immensely by the vast amount of solid historical research that has been done by scholars in recent years—especially scholars within the movements or in some instances ones who have recently come out. Mormons, especially, are to be highly commended for their honest scholarship, and it behooves "cult" researchers to pay close attention to their contributions to the field.

To some scholars the only appropriate text on "cults" is one that is theologically oriented, which this is not. The purpose of this volume is to present a historical and contemporary overview of alternative religious movements. It is not an apologetic for orthodox Christianity. That endeavor is left to the theologians. There are occasional responses to particular variant beliefs in the text, and a synopsis of the cardinal doctrines of the faith with biblical references is presented in an appendix, but such is not intended to be a definitive defense of traditional orthodoxy.

Nor is this text sociologically oriented. Commendable studies have been done on alternative religions from a sociological perspective, but these studies do not correspond with the characteristics that determine whether a movement is a "cult" or alternative religion from an orthodox Christian perspective. Indeed, from a sociological perspective, Mormonism today would be far less cultic than many fundamentalist fringe churches, which subscribe to historic orthodoxy. Yet, there are sociological features that are common to variant religions—features that are particularly prominent in the developmental stages of such movements. These are noted where applicable throughout the text.

This book then is a volume that tells the story of the development of alternative religions, focusing on key individuals, important events, and doctrines and practices that deviated from historic orthodoxy. It also brings these movements up to date by presenting significant current issues and controversies, and it recounts how many of these groups have expanded worldwide and sought to enter the mainstream of "respectable" religion.

Chapter 1

Cults, Sects, Denominations, World Religions: Definition of Terms

The Cults Are Coming, The Cult Explosion, The New Cults, Those Curious New Cults, Understanding the Cults, Dealing with Destructive Cults. All are recent book titles that grab our attention. Other books on the same subject offer an even more menacing warning: The Youth Nappers; The Mindbenders; Youth, Brainwashing, and the Extremist Cults, and Let Our Children Go. The very word "cult" conjures up images of kidnappers and brainwashers who are out to get us. The word "cult" has unfortunately become a pejorative term that sometimes reflects more on the speaker's attitude than on the subject being spoken about, and it is a word that is of questionable value in studying religious groups that have developed in recent generations outside the beliefs of historic Christian orthodoxy. Nevertheless, it is a word that has become part of our vocabulary and it is difficult to deal with the subject of unorthodox religious movements without making use of it.

Defining a Cult

What is a cult? A cult is someone else's religious group that does not agree with mine. That may be a light-hearted definition, but it does have a ring of truth to it. Because religion is so personalized it is often difficult to objectively sort out what is true and what is false. There are many variable factors to consider in determining whether a religious group ought to be categorized as a cult, a fundamentalist fringe movement, a sect, a denomination, or an entirely different world religious tradition, and there are unavoidable inconsistencies. Some religious groups that are frequently categorized as cults (e.g., Seventh-day Adventists) are far less "heretical" than religious groups not generally placed in that category (e.g., Unitarians). There is a need to classify unorthodox belief systems, but it is unfortunate that some groups have been stigmatized as cults, while other groups are graced with more respectability by being classified as denominations or world religions, when their orthodoxy is equally or even more highly questionable.

Because of the indecisive nature of the term, some observers have refused to use it entirely. J. Gordon Melton, who has served as the director of the Institute for the Study of American Religion, takes this position: "I no longer break groups into cults, sects, and denominations. I find myself saying, 'This is a New Thought religion,' 'This is an occult religion,' and 'These are Hindu-type religions.' In lumping them together, we assume that all cults have similar characteristics, and they don't."[1]

Yet the term "cult" is one that is widely used in the media and in religious circles, and is no doubt a part of our vocabulary that will not quickly die. When asked if the term should be dropped from usage, Jim Sire of InterVarsity Press responded, "We should if we could, but we can't; I think we're stuck with it."[2] Indeed, it is a word that is here to stay, and for that reason it needs at least a provisional definition—a definition that can be derived in part from the features that many cults have in common.

A "cult" is a religious group that has a "prophet"-founder called of God to give a special message not found in the Bible itself, often apocalyptic in nature and often set forth in "inspired" writings. In deference to this charismatic figure or these "inspired" writings, the style of leadership is authoritarian and there is frequently an exclusivistic outlook, supported by a legalistic lifestyle and persecution mentality. There are many other "cult" characteristics, but the above would fit such groups as

the Mormons, the Jehovah's Witnesses, the Seventh-day Adventists, Christian Science, the Unification Church, and The Way International. But even with groups that exhibit these characteristics there are significant differences in their "cultic score meter." This is determined largely by the extent of heresy that is found in the "inspired" writings. Ellen White's writings, for example, would be considerably less heretical than would Joseph Smith's. It is even true that, except for her defense of such doctrines as the Investigative Judgment, many would not view them as heretical at all.

Others have offered definitions of cults that are worth considering. Jim Sire defines a cult as "any religious movement that is organizationally distinct and has doctrines and/or practices that contradict those of the Scriptures as interpreted by traditional Christianity as represented by the major Catholic and Protestant denominations, and as expressed in such statements as the Apostles' Creed."[3]

Sociologists have tended to define cults more in terms of lifestyle, proselytizing practices, and authoritarian leadership, rather than in terms of belief or by any standard of orthodoxy. This means of identification, however, can be very misleading, as Brooks Alexander of the Spiritual Counterfeits Project contends:

In the first place the concept of "cult" should not be equated with the intensity of commitment or involvement which is characteristic of the so called high demand groups, religious or secular. Nor is aggressiveness or proselytizing cultish in itself. Both of these qualities—in one form or another—

are basic to authentic Christianity. . . . These two qualities in particular are worth singling out because they have apparently been the basis for mislabeling some groups as cults. Two groups which have occasionally been the target for such mistaken identification are "Jews for Jesus" and Campus Crusade for Christ.[4]

The difficulty of defining "cultists" was demonstrated very passionately in a debate in the Ontario, Canada Legislature over a proposed bill that was designed to deal with members of cults. One member of that body made a compelling speech in opposition to singling groups out as cults:

I know people, friends of mine, who did what I thought were irrational acts when they were 16 or 17 years of age. They went off to convents and seminaries. They renounced worldly goods. They took a vow of poverty. They gave up the automobiles and the hockey sticks and the football games that I wanted and thought were important. They didn't want to go out with girls. They wanted to go into a seminary. How strange, I thought. How can they do that?

They wore funny clothes. They had values the rest of the society didn't have. Were they a cult? No, they were Jesuits. I think, quite frankly, the Jesuit order in Canada and in the world has proved its value to our society.[5]

According to sociologist and cult researcher Ronald Enroth, there are "at least three basic approaches in defining *cult:* a sensational or popular approach, a sociological approach and a theological approach." While virtually no one utilizes one approach exclusively, these are effective categories to consider. "A sensational approach to cults is built on journal-istic accounts in the popular press which frequently focus on the dramatic and sometimes bizarre aspects of cultic behavior. A sociological definition includes the authoritarian, manipulative, totalistic and sometimes communal features of cults. A theological definition involves some standard of orthodoxy."[6] The approach used in this book is weighted toward the theological, with consideration of the sociological and sensational approaches as well.

Fundamentalist Fringe Movements

The type of movement most closely identified with cults (and often termed a cult) is the fundamentalist fringe movement. Sociologically these groups fit very closely into a cult category, but doctrinally they are essentially orthodox, believing in the authority of Scripture, the Trinity, the deity of Christ, and other cardinal tenets of historic Christianity. In methodology and practice, however, these groups are generally authoritarian and led by domineering leaders who maintain strict control over their followers' personal lives.

An example of such a group is the Faith Assembly, located primarily in Indiana and other midwestern states. This Pentecostal fringe movement was founded and led by Hobart Freeman, who had been active in mainstream evangelical circles until he established his own church and religious movement. He received graduate theological degrees from Southern Baptist Theological Seminary in Louisville and from Grace Theological Seminary in Winona Lake, Indiana, where he was employed as a professor until he was fired on theological

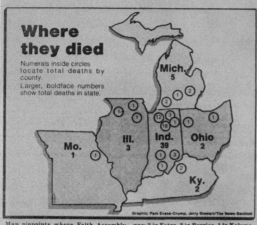

The News-Sentinel

FORT WAYNE, INDIANA   MONDAY, MAY 2, 1983   25 CENTS

52 Deaths Tied To Sect

Where they died

Numerals inside circles locate total deaths by county.
Larger, boldface numbers show total deaths in state.

Mich. 5

Ill. 3   Ind. 39   Ohio 2

Mo. 1

Ky. 2

Graphic: Pam Evans-Crump, Jerry Stewart/The News-Sentinel

Map pinpoints where Faith Assembly members and children have died. Indiana county deaths were 18 in Kosciusko, 12 in Elkhart, 3 in Noble, 3 in Wayne, 1 in DeKalb, 1 in Marion and 1 in Johnson. Michigan: 2 in Eaton, 2 in Berrien, 1 in Kalamazoo. Illinois: 1 in DeKalb, 1 in Stephenson, 1 in Winnebago. Kentucky: 2 in Shelby County. Ohio: 1 in Mansfield, 1 in Mercer. Missouri: 1 in Ralls.

Medical help refused for babies, children

By JIM QUINN
and BILL ZLATOS
© The News-Sentinel, 1983

At least 52 people — most of them babies and children — died while they or their parents were following the teachings of the Faith Assembly, a new, rapidly growing church that teaches members to avoid doctors.

The Rev. Hobart Freeman, founder and leader of the Faith Assembly, was preaching to a small circle of followers in a barn 10 years ago.

Since then his church has grown explosively, and so has the number of deaths among those adhering to his doctrine.

The News-Sentinel has learned:

• There have been twice as many medically unattended deaths as previously reported among those adhering to Freeman's teachings.

• Only a small fraction of the 52 known victims were old enough to understand the teachings of the Faith Assembly.

• An even smaller fraction made their own decision to shun medical treatment.

One victim asked for a doctor a few hours before her death, but no doctor arrived because her husband and friends decided prayer was best for the woman. They prayed for her for hours after she had died.

• Routine medical procedures could have prevented many of the deaths.

• Faith Assembly deaths were found in Indiana, Illinois, Ohio, Kentucky, Michigan and Missouri.

• Seven families suffered more than one death. The families accounted for 18 of the 52 deaths. Two of the families lost three members each.

"You can't fool with Mother Nature and you can't fool with bodies the way these people have," said Barbara Clouse, the public health nurse in Kosciusko County and an outspoken critic of the church. The church has many members in Kosciusko County.

Before The News-Sentinel's research, Clouse kept the most accu-

Faith Assembly:
The 52 who died
■ First in a series

More stories inside

■ When a baby boy died of asphyxiation after a home birth, a grand jury called the parents' and midwife's behavior "callous, reckless, negligent and stupid."
More cases of infant deaths on Page 8A

■ Little Dustin Gilmore turned sick, then deaf, then blind. His parents suspected fumes from a faulty chimney. Instead, he had a type of meningitis. He died without seeing a doctor.
More child deaths on Page 5A

■ Bonnie Jo Vargo wouldn't see a doctor, and her last two pregnancies ended in stillbirths. A month after the second, she too died of blood poisoning.
More mothers' deaths on Page 7A

■ Faith Assembly member Arthur Graham, a diabetic, had taken insulin since childhood. Then he stopped the injections. He died 4 days later.
More adult deaths on Page 6A

TOMORROW

■ The beliefs and the rules of the Faith Assembly.

Newspaper reports of deaths in Faith Assembly

---

grounds. His headquarters and mother church were located in the "Glory Barn" in a small town near Fort Wayne, Indiana, and it was there in 1983 that reports began surfacing about an inordinate number of deaths within his congregations. The Fort Wayne *News-Sentinel* reported that "At least 52 people—most of them babies and children—died while they or their parents were following the teachings of the Faith Assembly, a new rapidly growing church that teaches members to avoid doctors."[7]

Faith healing was not the only controversial aspect of this fringe group. In an article entitled "Faith Assembly Rejects Dissent," reporters Jim Quinn and Bill Zlatos write that "Members are taught there is a powerful reward for those who follow the rules and a powerful punishment for those who disobey. . . . Those who stumble risk exposure by other members, ridicule before the congregation, excommunication and eternal punishment in hell." Members were not only expected to avoid doctors, but to "discard eyeglasses and hearing aids," "shun birth control and sexual foreplay," and "cancel insurance policies." Conformity, according to a former member, was insured by "spies in the land" and "a Gestapo mentality," with "people checking up on each other." By the late 1970s the movement had become exclusivist. According to a former member, "It ended up with him (Freeman) saying, 'This is it. This is the place. You can not be saved anywhere else' "[8]

Freeman practiced what he preached. When he became ill in 1984, he refused to see a doctor or to take any form of medication. He died in December of that year. The cause of death: bronchopneumonia and heart failure. His movement continues on without him.[9]

Other authoritarian and isolationist fundamentalist fringe movements include the University Bible Fellowship, the Fundamentalist Army (founded by R. L. Hymers and based in Los Angeles), Maranatha Christian Churches (founded by Bob Weiner and known also as the Maranatha Campus Ministries), Community Chapel (founded by Donald Lee Barnett and based in Seattle), Northeast Kingdom Community Church (based in Island Pond, Vermont), and the First Community Church of America (founded by Robert Taylor).[10]

From Heresy to Orthodoxy and Vice Versa

Another complicating factor in attempting to define a movement as a cult, a sect, or a denomination is that religious movements often change over the years, both in doctrine and in practice, and thus what might have been viewed a "cult" in previous generations might now be regarded a sect or denomination. In some instances, the change of category is warranted, as is true of Seventh-day Adventists, but in most cases the movements were wrongly labeled by contemporary antagonists, who feared the fragmentation of religion. Examples of religious groups that were often characterized as cults by contemporaries are the Quakers, the Methodists, and the Salvation Army. Today, in North America, with the seemingly limitless variety of new denominations and parachurch organizations, the appearance of such religious groups would go almost unnoticed, but prior to the mid-nineteenth century—especially in England where anything that deviated from the Anglican tradition was viewed as cultish—such groups were regarded as aberrations that ought to be eliminated.

It is inaccurate for some of the contemporary cultic groups, such as Mormons, to point to these Christian groups of an earlier era as having a common heritage—that of being characterized as a cult and rejected by the established churches. There is very little commonality. Though the Quakers, the Methodists, and the Salvation Army dared to defy teachings and practices of the Anglican church, they did not offer new Scriptures or deny the cardinal doctrines of the Christian faith.

It is highly unusual when a cult actually develops into a denomination, and in such instances it can usually be assumed that the cultic nature of the movement was only marginal to begin with—as in the case of Seventh-day Adventists. The reverse trend, however, is really more common—that of being a one-time orthodox denomination moving in a cultic direction doctrinally by denying historic Christian orthodoxy. The term "cult" might not be deemed appropriate in such situations, but in actuality the move from denomination to cult is what has taken place.

Sects

It is not always easy to differentiate a cult from a "sect." John Gerstner's book *The Theology of the Major Sects* includes chapters on Jehovah's Witnesses, Mormonism, Christian Science, and other groups typically classified as cults. His rationale for using the term "sect" was presumably a well-meaning effort to avoid using the term "cult," but such terminology only serves to further confuse the issue. The word "sect" derives from the Latin *sequi* (to follow). Its historical meaning has been clarified by Ernst Troeltsch. His conception of a "sect" is that of "a religious group which is gathered or called out of some natural organic group or state church on positively anticonformist grounds, sometimes by a charismatic leader, but as often by some principle of greater strictness, more single-minded dedication, or more intense abnegation of the world and its attractions. Often, even usually, the

sect has as its main principle some aspect of the orthodox faith which is being lost or neglected." Groups that historically have fit into this definition include the Quakers, the Mennonites, the Salvation Army, the Plymouth Brethren, and the Pentecostals—all of which have today moved to the more "respectable" classification of "denominations."

Denominations

A denomination is a branch of institutionalized Christianity that has established a reputation of stability and credibility. Most of the major denominations are rooted in orthodoxy, though many have significantly deviated from their traditional heritage. In many instances, one denomination grew out of another, such as the Methodists who developed out of the Anglican church. Religious groups that fit this classification include Roman Catholic, Lutheran, Presbyterian, Methodist, and Baptist.

World Religions

World Religions are religious movements that have attained a status recognized worldwide for their embodiment of particular sacred traditions. Many world religions were initially sectarian movements with "prophet"-founders that grew out of another world religion. Christianity, which came out of Judaism, and Buddhism, which developed out of Hinduism, are examples. Religious movements that are classified as world religions include Hinduism, Buddhism, Jainism, Shintoism, Judaism, Christianity, and Islam. At what point a sect or cult becomes a world religion is undefined, but some scholars have suggested that Mormonism is approaching a size and worldwide influence that would qualify it one day to be classified as a world religion.

Categories of Cults

Once a working definition of the term *cult* is established and is distinguished from fringe movements, sects, denominations, and world religions, it is important to more closely define the term by breaking it down into specific categories. As with defining the term, this is not easily accomplished because there are so many variations of cults. Here again Ronald Enroth is helpful. He offers six basic categories: (1) Eastern-mystical, (2) aberrational-Christian, (3) psychospiritual or self-improvement, (4) eclectic-syncretistic, (5) psychic-occult-astral, and (6) institutionalized or established.[11]

Many cults could fit into more than one category, but in most cases there would be a primary category that would most adequately represent the movement, as the following examples indicate: Eastern mystical cults (Hare Krishnas, Transcendental Meditation, and the Rajneesh Ashram); aberrational Christian (Children of God, The Way International, Church of the Living Word); psychospiritual or self-improvement (Scientology, est, Silva Mind Control); eclectic-syncretistic (Unification Church); psychic-occult-astral (New Age Movement, Church Universal and Triumphant, Eckankar); institutionalized or established (Mormons, Jehovah's Witnesses, Christian Science).

Moving Into the Mainstream

From the earliest centuries of the church down to the present time, cultic movements have been scorned, persecuted, and censured by society at large and by church and government officials. The response of the groups has most commonly been one of two extremes: either to fight back and become even more extreme in beliefs and practices, or to accommodate themselves to acceptable standards that blend in with the religious landscape. In many instances, these two extremes can be equated with two stages of development. Mormonism is a good example. Early persecution only intensified the scandalous activities of the movement. The mob murder of Joseph Smith for his vigilantism and rumored polygamy paved the way for Brigham Young, who openly trained his own paramilitary force and brazenly demonstrated plural marriage with his dozens of wives. But by the 1890s, Mormon leaders were beginning to change their strategy and to accommodate to some of society's standards. And by the mid-twentieth century the movement was engrossed in an intense search for respectability. Through very effective publicity efforts, Mormons have presented themselves as the epitome of good citizenship—moral, ethical, hard-working, humanitarian, God-fearing, flag-waving Americans.

One of the most common gimmicks to gain credibility is to utilize "stars" to promote or represent the movement. To be sure, cults do not have a corner on this tactic. Evangelicals are also eager to flaunt their "stars." But, it has been this method that has been extraordinarily effective in conferring respectability on cultic movements. The Osmonds—especially Donnie and Marie—have been a show piece for Mormons, and singer John Denver and actress Shirley MacLaine have represented various facets of the New Age Movement. Sports figures, politicians, and beauty pageant winners as well as educational and cultural programs have also served to give credibility to cultic groups. The promotional value of the athletic program at Brigham Young University in this respect is immense. So too the cultural activities offered by the late Herbert W. Armstrong at his Ambassador College in Pasadena—especially those featuring the nation's top musical artists.

In recent years, one of the most effective and all-encompassing efforts of a cult to seek to move into the mainstream of American religion has been that of the Unification Church. Through scientific, philosophical, and religious conferences offered free of charge to ministers and educators at posh resorts, the organization has been able to win influential friends that would never otherwise have offered support.

In some instances, the association with "stars" can create embarrassment. This was true when *Time* magazine's cover story disclosed that rock singer Michael Jackson was a "God-fearing Jehovah's Witness" who, according to his mother, was faithful in "his door-to-door field service" which "he does twice a week maybe for an hour or two" and "attends meetings at a Kingdom Hall four times a week."[12] There was no doubt a sigh of relief among many straight-laced Jehovah's Witnesses, who regard rock music as from the devil, when Jackson later quietly disassociated himself with the movement.

Traditional Cults vs. New Cults

One of the reasons that alternative religions have sought so intensely to enter the mainstream of religion is to shed the "cult" image that has inevitably surrounded them. That image was intensified during the 1960s when numerous "new" cults appeared on the scene with rituals and practices which were perceived to be a threat to public welfare. The Moonies and the Hare Krishnas, for examples, were widely viewed as a danger to American youth—far more so than the Jehovah's Witnesses, whose door-to-door witnessing was only seen as a neighborhood annoyance.

It is dangerous to make generalizations about cultic movements, but in most instances the older a movement is, the less dangerous and psychologically threatening it is from a sociological perspective. The Mormons, for example, have moved into the mainstream and no longer promote polygamy or paramilitary organizations. The Jehovah's Witnesses and Christian Scientists have likewise moved toward the mainstream, though the former continues to practice a psychologically excruciating form of shunning former members, and the latter continues to emphasize prayer for healing over medical cures. Nevertheless, it is the newer cults—the Children of God, the Unification Church, the Hare Krishnas—and the fundamentalist fringe movements that are most often charged with bizarre behavior. They are frequently guilty of various forms of abuse and manipulation—especially among the most vulnerable segments of society. But even among these newer cults there is reason to believe—especially in the case of the Unification Church—that there has been a maturing process and the tactics are less threatening than they were a decade or two ago.

Taking Advantage of Vulnerable People

Children and young people have been, in many cases, the ones who have suffered the most from the duplicity and fraudulent tactics of many of the cultic movements that have appeared on the American scene in recent years. The complaints often have a ring of familiarity:

> Among the most frequent criticisms of the cults' methods are that the cults deliberately seek out likely prospects, "loners" or young people going through a transitional stage; that they do not fully inform potential members of who they are or what they are about until the recruits are "hooked"; that the recruits are showered with flattering attention, subjected to grinding lectures or incessant chanting (often at remote locations), and rarely left alone to think things out for themselves; and that recruits and converts are denied sufficient sleep and fed a low-protein, high-carbohydrate diet.[13]

In many instances, the grievances involve far more than the lack of full disclosure or poor nutrition. Indeed, instances of slavery and severe physical abuse are often recounted by former members, as are instances of blatant exploitation. It would be difficult to exaggerate the anguish

that many young women caught in the prostitution ("flirty fishing") of the Children of God have suffered.

And there has been untold agony suffered by children. In an article entitled "The Children of the Cults," the author points out that while "it is a matter of debate how much choice the young adult cultists are capable of asserting . . . there is an increasing visible group of individuals who are unequivocally without choice: small children."[14] In some cases, these are children whose parents have been unable to release them from the grips of the Hare Krishnas or Children of God, after one or both of them have forsaken the cult. And worse yet has been the physical abuse and death of children in such cults as the House of Judah, located in southern Michigan, where a young boy was beaten to death.

A similar tragedy occurred in Wolf Point, Montana, when a five-year-old boy whose parents were involved in the River of Life Tabernacle Church was beaten to death because he would not eat his supper. The newspaper headlines read: "Nine Members of Religious Sect Charged in Beating Death of Boy."[15]

Duping people out of money is another common complaint against the newer cults and fringe movements. This is a practice that frequently occurs among senior citizens, whose life savings is sometimes liquidated in a matter of days by the crafty charm of a charismatic religious leader. News stories have reported a significant increase of such incidents in recent years. How can such deception and corruption occur? In many instances, the root of the problem is a charlatan leader, blindly committed recruiters, and a vulnerable following. From Joseph Smith to "Moses" Berg and L. Ron Hubbard, magnetic individuals with a dedicated corps of disciples have been able to dupe ordinary citizens into believing their messages are the exclusive embodiment of the truth.

Prophet-founders

It is the attribute of a prophet-founder that very distinctly separates cults from denominations. Most denominations have a revered founder, such as Martin Luther or John Wesley, but extrabiblical revelations or writings are not ascribed to them. On the other hand, most of the prophet-founders of cults have been radical nonconformists who renounced the institutionalized church in favor of what God had revealed to them was the "true" church. As was true of Joseph Smith, Mary Baker Eddy, Sun Myung Moon, David Berg, Victor Paul Wierwille, L. Ron Hubbard, and Jim Jones, prophet-founders testify of visions or revelations or spirit guides or audible voices from heaven giving them and them alone the truth for this age. In some instances, these individuals may have been mentally deranged, but in most cases they simply had a unique ability to present themselves as believable and sincere.

The attribute most commonly associated with cult leaders is that of a profiteering charlatan who lives in palatial splendor. The much publicized instances of Rajneesh and Maharaj Ji may give that impression, but in most instances cult leaders live no higher than other comparable figures. While it is true that Sun

Myung has lived in a beautiful home on a large estate in New York, it is safe to say that it is no more lavish than the one-time luxury mansion of Jim and Tammy Bakker or of many other television evangelists. In some instances, cult leaders have lived in austerity, a prime example being that of Swami Prabhupada, the founder of the Hare Krishnas.

In the vast majority of cases, the prophet-founders of variant religious movements have been men. This is to be expected. Men have had more access to leadership positions than women in virtually all areas of life, including that of religion. They have wielded more power in the church in general than women have, and they have founded the vast majority of sectarian movements, denominations, and world religions.

Women as "Cult-makers"

Despite the historical evidence that would prove otherwise, the myth that women are the cult-makers has been propounded over the years by various churchmen, including some respected scholars. Walter Martin, one of the best known authorities on cults, writes: "It is one of the strange historical peculiarities of the saga of cultism that some cults were either started by women or were influenced in a major way by the allegedly weaker sex." Of the several women he cites, only Mary Baker Eddy was a prominent cult founder. Myrtle Fillmore had an important role in the founding of Unity, but her husband was the far more influential public speaker and writer. Martin also lists Marie Russell, who could hardly be viewed as a founder or major influence behind the Jehovah's Witnesses. And he cites two women who were merely devotees to their male authority figure, Father Divine, leader of a small cultic group known as the Peace Mission Movement.

Martin goes on to quote 1 Timothy 2:11–14, which admonishes women to "learn in silence" and not to "teach, nor to usurp authority," and which refers to Eve being deceived. His own commentary on the passage follows:

> It can be clearly seen from the study of non-Christian cults, ancient and modern, that the female teaching ministry has graphically fulfilled what Paul anticipated in his day by divine revelation, and brought in its wake, as history tells us, confusion, division, and strife. This is true from Johanna Southcutt to Mary Baker Eddy to Helena Blavatsky and the Fox sisters, all of whom were living proof of the validity of our Lord's declaration that "if the blind lead the blind, both shall fall into the ditch" (Matt. 15:14b).[16]

Is the female sex more prone to deception? This view is unthinkable in light of the apostle Paul's admonition for women to teach other women and children. It would be preposterous to assume that Paul would want those prone to deception to teach others who had the same defect, and worse yet to teach little children whose minds are so impressionable. Yet women have been subjected to this perversion of Scripture over the generations. An interesting example of this occurred in the 1920s soon after the Open Bible Standard Churches were founded. Women were denied ministry on this basis. The contemporary account is fascinating. One of the male leaders

of the church "told Mrs. Harrison that women had led people astray in religion. He named Mary Baker Eddy, etc. However, Mrs. Harrison retorted by saying that ten times as many men had led people astray, and she quoted from church history all the men who had led people astray, and won her point."[17]

Satanic Involvement

If women have not been the cult-makers, the second most likely suspect in many minds is Satan. Searching for Satanic involvement in cults has been a popular speculative pastime for many cult-watchers, but it is a difficult inquiry to document. Orthodox Christians who hold to biblical teachings on Satan accept that there is a Satanic or demonic influence in everything that is evil or false. And this influence would appear to be more pronounced in occultic religions (and, of course, Satanism itself) that are based on a belief in the powers of the unseen spirit world. But it is false and dangerous to assume that Satan is working more fervently with cultists than with Christians or that he has necessarily chosen one particular cult over another in which to establish his world dominion.

Failure of the Church

In the minds of many Christian leaders, the increase in cult membership is a direct result of a failure on the part of the church. Are cults, as J. K. Van Baalen has suggested, "the unpaid bills of the church?" Many religious observers would respond in the affirmative. J. Gordon Melton, a member of the United Methodist Church, gives a pointed example of this, reflecting on his own denomination. If a teenager "walked into the pastor's study and said, 'I committed myself to Jesus last night; I'd like to tell the congregation about it on Sunday,' the pastor wouldn't know what to do with him." Would the cults? "These groups do. They do best with people moving from adolescence to adulthood. That's what the mainline churches do worst—that and providing a sense of community. Large impersonal churches on the corner don't give most teenagers a sense of belonging."[18]

One of the appealing aspects of the new religions during the 1960s was the apparent rejection of materialism. While cult leaders sometimes lived splendidly, the message they offered was often one of sacrifice, self-denial, and rejection of the middle- and upper-class values of a capitalistic and decadent society. This was a quality not found in the vast majority of Christian churches where the gospel of wealth was taught (albeit often subtly) in one form or another. Jack Sparks offers further insight on the failure of orthodoxy:

> . . . much of what we call the Church has failed—often miserably—in carrying out its role before God, itself, and the world. Though it is still loved and even protected by the Lord, it has moved an embarrassingly great distance away from its original foundations. . . . No doubt this apostasy has been a contributing factor to the spiraling sizes of these modern cults with their faulty saviors and practices.[19]

In his book *The Chaos of Cults*, Van Baalen gives reasons why he believes

"the cults are the unpaid bills of the church." Among other things, Christianity has been diluted through "intermarriage between people of different national and religious backgrounds" which has resulted in "a type of smallest common-denominator faith that has left little to be believed and less to be taught." This has not been nearly as prevalent among Mormons and Jehovah's Witnesses who are strongly admonished not to marry outside the faith. Another factor, according to Van Baalen, has been the "dread of the 'social gospel' that was widely acclaimed a generation or two ago" which "contributed considerably to the fear of passing off the Christian religion as a 'this-world' affair." Indeed, many cultic movements have far surpassed evangelical Christianity in their concern for humanitarian causes. Still another factor has been "extreme Dispensationalism with its times and seasons," which has "left the impression that 'this old world' is tottering near the brink of destruction, and all we are expected to do is to snatch what little may be saved from the imminent universal conflagration." Such an ideology can foster the position that cultic movements are a sign of the apostasy of the end times, and that little can be done to counter them.[20]

Extremes in Response to Cultic Movements

How should Christians respond to cults or alternative religions? That is not an easy question. If all aberrant religious groups conducted themselves in a similar manner, it would be a simpler task to develop an appropriate response.

Deprograming

Virtually no one today would suggest that a Mormon ought to be deprogramed or run out of town. Whatever their religious beliefs may be, Mormons by and large are law abiding citizens who freely practice their faith. The response to Rajneesh and his devotees, however, might call for strong action. Innocent residents of the tiny town of Antelope, Oregon, where the cult group had settled, were threatened and terrorized, and indigents from the streets of Los Angles were bussed into the settlement in order to throw the balance of the local elections in favor of the cult. It is true that there is a danger in overreacting to these nontraditional religious movements, but there is also a danger in seeking to be too tolerant and thus fail to protect the victims of some of these movements.

Deprograming is not the answer, and, as it will be shown in later chapters, often fails to accomplish its desired results. Yet, mild forms of deprograming or "exit counseling" have been effective and can be used with caution. For this reason, it is difficult to identify fully with the strong position that J. Gordon Melton takes on the issue: "I feel about deprogrammers the same way I feel about rapists. I think they both ought to be tossed into jail. Anti-cultism can be as heretical as any cult."[21]

Deprogramers are by no means identical in their methods. In some instances, secular deprogramers such as Ted Patrick and others who have employed even more extreme methods (including rape, as some who have been deprogramed have charged), have committed worse offenses than the cults themselves. Those who have approached the procedure from a Christian perspective, however, are often more misguided in their efforts than criminal. Ronald Enroth, who himself opposes deprograming, concedes that sometimes he feels as though he almost has "to come to the defense of the deprogramers because of the inflammatory rhetoric of anti-anticultists." He points out that many deprograming experiences are not as reprehensible as opponents have claimed they were: "Many who have gone through deprograming insist that they have not been subjected to violence: the lights have not been on 24 hours a day. Some have told me they slept more during deprograming than during their whole cult experience. They have been fed and treated rather well."[22]

There are many others besides J. Gordon Melton who argue that there has been an extreme overreaction to the cult phenomena in America. In their book *Strange Gods: The Great American Cult Scare*, David Bromley and Anson Shupe take this position, claiming that the anticult movement is a serious threat to religious liberty. They argue that the cults which emerged in the 1960s such as the Moonies and the Hare Krishnas are not nearly so large as fearmongers have led people to believe, and that the leaders are not in all cases fraudulent profiteers. They likewise maintain that much of the anticult literature written by the so-called "victims" of cults consists of "sensational exposés," little of which "has merit as non-fiction."[23]

Deprograming, many observers contend, is a serious threat to religious liberty, especially when it has the endorsement of state and local governments and civil authorities. By the early 1980s several states had considered "anti-conversion" legislation that would have vastly increased the rights of concerned family members and deprogramers. The essence of the proposed legislation was to establish a procedure whereby a guardian would be placed in charge of an adult who was judged unfit or "brainwashed" by a cultic group. Due to strong opposition from individuals and organizations such as the Christian Legal Society, these legislative bills have had little success. Speaking for this organization, Thomas Brandon writes: "While the Christian and religious community must deal with the issue of new religions, the government is forbidden from interfering or abridging individual or organizational religious liberties. The anti-conversion legislation proposed by various states does in fact intrude upon the very core of individual liberties and religious freedom."[24]

An Objective Response to Cults

Among the targets of Bromley's and Shupe's fierce criticism are family-based groups, deprogramers, and "a rather autonomous set of fundamentalist Christian organizations." Indeed, they make stinging allegations about the integrity of some of the Christian cult-watcher groups that ought to be seriously considered. They question whether these groups honestly represent the data or whether they sometimes exaggerate the situation in order to rouse emotions among fellow Christians.

This very issue flared up in the spring of 1988 when Jerald and Sandra Tanner publicly denounced the irresponsible cult-bashing of various individuals who were making their case against Mormonism by claiming that the god of Mormonism is Lucifer. In an article entitled "Who is the god of Mormonism?" former Mormon elder James R. Spencer writes, "But there is one name he goes by which is not revealed to Mormons. It is the name by which he is known to most angels, fallen angels, and men. That name is Lucifer—the Angel of Light." Spencer goes on to lament the fact that a "dark cloud" has arisen because "Jerald and Sandra Tanner have mounted a relentless attack on this work."[25]

Jerald and Sandra Tanner in many ways stand out from among the so-called fundamentalist anticult organizations. They both have a long heritage in Mormonism and came out of that religion after much soul searching and after doing extensive research. Soon after they left Mormonism they established the Utah Lighthouse Ministry which is largely a research organization that has won the respect of non-Mormons and Mormons alike. Their style is one of careful and objective research; they disdain the all-too-common treatises against Mormonism that are based on rumor and hearsay.

At issue in the controversy between the Tanners and Spencer is one William Schnoebelen who claims to have been a Roman Catholic priest in the 1960s and an occult practitioner—involved in witchcraft, Satanism and voodoo—in the 1970s. Then in 1980, he and his wife were baptized into the Mormon church, even though some Mormons were aware that their occult involvement continued in the years that followed. Schnoebelen's story of his priesthood ministry so impressed the Mormons that he became the subject of a chapter in a Mormon book entitled *From Clergy to Convert*. In 1984, Schnoebelen testified that he had been converted to orthodox Christianity. He quickly won an audience with ex-Mormon groups, and he began telling his story of the covert Satanism being practiced in the highest inner circles of the Mormon church. The Tanners have challenged his testimony and his claim to have had access to inside information, and in the process they found many inconsistencies in his story regarding various clerical and occultic activities. Their fear is that unsubstantiated charges against the Mormons, such as those Schnoebelen has made, will only damage the cause of solid research that has been so effective in alerting Mormons to the truth about their church.[26]

There have been other instances in which evangelical Christians have been less than responsible in presenting the beliefs of the cults, one of the most blatant being the widely distributed film and video which was introduced in 1983 and entitled "The God-Makers." While most of what is presented is true to fact, the most disturbing element of the film is the manner in which it is presented. Mormon doctrine—especially that relating to the physical nature of God, the Adam/God theory, the council in heaven, and the future life of Mor-

mon men on planets with their eternally pregnant wives—is presented in cartoon animation. Cherished beliefs of Mormons—no matter how false and objectionable they may be—should not be maliciously ridiculed. In some ways, it is probably as offensive to a Mormon to view the depiction of their faith in *The God-Makers* as it would be for Christians to view an animated cartoon depicting a doctrine such as the virgin birth of Christ.

Dangers in Criticizing Cultic Movements

There are dangers involved in criticizing cultic movements—a danger that was highlighted recently when Jack Sparks, author of *The Mindbenders*, was brought to court by the Local Church for including that movement in his book and exposing its cultic nature. Another individual who has faced considerable opposition in his work is Ronald Enroth, a sociologist from Westmont College in California. He has done substantial scholarly research on various cultic movements and has come under fire—not so much from groups that are clearly outside the orthodox framework, but from groups such as the Fundamentalist Army on the fringe of the church. There have also been lawsuits and other opposition brought against those who have pursued research on the Church of Scientology, including death threats and suspicious bombings in several instances. Hazards certainly do exist in researching and writing about cults—so much so that a major Christian publisher not long ago turned down a manuscript on the basis that it might elicit a lawsuit.

The Benefits of Cults

How can there possibly be any benefits from unorthodox religious movements? Is there anything to be gained by the upsurge of contemporary cults? This can be answered in part through historical reflection, particularly by contemplating the situation in the early church when unorthodox challenges to Christian doctrine were commonplace. In that era, apologists arose and refuted the heresies—and in the process more clearly defined the boundaries and intricacies of Christian truth. Without the heretics, the foundations of Christianity might possibly have crumbled during the often-troubled times that plagued the medieval church. In the same sense, cults can challenge the church today. Bromley and Shupe speak to this issue:

> On balance the new religions have strengthened Christian solidarity. Every time a new religion appears or there is another sectarian split the question arises whether the new group is *really* Christian. On such occasions the established churches pause in their denominational squabbles and reflect upon what it is that they have in common so that the true Christian churches can be distinguished from the pretenders. Ironically, then, it is exactly the kind of challenge posed by the new religions that creates unity among the established churches. Furthermore, such challenges are a source of revitalization for the major denominations.[27]

Orthodox Christianity has much to learn by observing cultic movements—particularly in their ability to reach out and meet the deep human needs of people who are suffering and dejected. The fourth-century Roman emperor Julian, who disdained the "cult of Jesus" and referred to Christians as "atheists" because they did not believe in the Roman gods, nevertheless recognized their ability to effectively minister to people. His words could apply to a Christian's reflection on some of the modern day cultic movements. "Atheism has been specifically advanced through the loving service rendered to strangers, and through their care for the burial of the dead. It is a scandal that there is not a single Jew who is a beggar, and that the godless Galileans care not only for their own poor but for ours as well; while those who belong to us look in vain for the help that we should render them."[28]

Chapter 2

Historical Heresy: Unorthodox Movements of Past Centuries

The stereotype of a "cultist" as a glassy-eyed, half-crazed visionary with no concern for practical matters and society at large would not have fit the reputation and lifestyle of John Chapman. Chapman became a well-known figure on the American frontier in the early nineteenth century. His life is a fascinating footnote in the history of alternative religions and demonstrates how effective an "all-American" patriot can be in disseminating unorthodox beliefs. "Never married, vegetarian, friend of pioneer, Indian, and animal, he was something of a native American saint, and there grew up around him the folk legends suitable to a popular holy man." Children's books for generations have told the story of this man who helped change America's landscape—a man known simply as "Johnny Appleseed," whose impact on future generations was significant in many ways. "He carried his apple-seed business as far west as Ohio, providing an item of greatest economic importance to the pioneers.

But in the frontier cabins he left not only apples, but also Swedenborgian literature, especially chapters of Swedenborg's *Heaven and Hell.* 'Good news fresh from heaven!' he called it."[1]

The sterotype of a cultist as a wild-eyed religious extremist is quickly put to rest when reflecting on Johnny Appleseed, and on others who have also become known as great American heroes. Another individual who was involved in Swedenborgianism was Helen Keller, the blind and deaf writer who inspired millions with her determination and faith.

Swedenborgianism, officially known as The Church of New Jerusalem, was a mystical and occultic religion founded by Emmanuel Swedenborg, who was born in Sweden in 1688. He wrote more than thirty religious books that sought to correlate Christianity with messages he purportedly received from spirit guides. It was an eclectic theology (see Appendix A) that found adherents among free thinkers in Europe and the United States, through the evangelistic efforts of such individuals as Johnny Appleseed.

Chapman's "missionary" work paved the way for other brands of unorthodoxy that, in turn, helped pave the way for an acceptance of—and almost eagerness for—new religions of all kinds that soon dotted the spiritual landscape. Indeed, America has been fertile soil for alternative religions from its earliest days. The fantasy of a land offering religious freedom prodded not only the persecuted Pilgrims and Puritans to leave the Old Country for the unknown, but it also spurred Quakers and Moravians and other sectarian refugees who quickly discovered that religious freedom was very limited at best. Quakers were hanged in Boston Square, and Moravians were pushed back on the frontier, but hard-headed perseverance and Founding Fathers who were committed to religious liberty combined to secure a nation uniquely susceptible to new religions—and to the opposition they inevitably engendered. In many cases, victims of religious persecution became the persecutors just as soon as they themselves became part of the establishment. And persecution often only served to strengthen the faith of the victims.

The American frontier, with its free-wheeling individualism and spirit of democracy, served as an incubator for countless new religions that could not have thrived elsewhere. The unique character and spirit of this country was captured by a nineteenth-century Danish observer who became disillusioned with Mormonism.

It is significant that Mormonism first appeared in America. Enlightenment and national freedom for the most part should go hand in hand, [but] they often stand in striking contrast with each other—as is well known—and consequently the mass of the American people are almost always inclined to go in for any kind of humbug at all with incredible heedlessness and are willing to work in the service of the humbug with the "Yankees" own perseverance and energy. In a country where weeds or vices can rear their heads and call themselves "Freedom and Equality," that is where Mormonism may first be rightly understood and perceived. That which in other lands must be regarded as something unheard of and incredible appears here as something perfectly natural, as something which belongs to the order of the day.[2]

The Early Church

It is true that America has offered new religions a healthy environment in which to thrive, but it would be incorrect to see cult activity as a product of the modern era. From New Testament times to the present, Christianity has been fragmented by sectarian and cultic splinter movements that have in some cases faded away, and in other cases moved back into the mainstream of Christianity or lived on in opposition to orthodoxy.

In some instances, these movements have been identified as cultic primarily by doctrines considered unorthodox by the prevailing religious leaders of the day. The Arian heresy of the fourth century, which did not acknowledge the Son as coequal with God the Father (and which several modern-day cults draw on), is an example of this. Arius was an old man by the time he stirred up the biggest controversy that the early church had yet faced. He was a presbyter in Alexandria and a theologian—certainly not the stereotypical guru-like figure who wanted to start a new religious cult. His motivation, rather, seems to have stemmed from his concern "to preserve the monarchy of the Father" and his fear "that the orthodox doctrine was making the Son into a second God." As a result of action taken at the Council of Nicea, Arius was deposed from his office and exiled from Alexandria. His influence continued in the decades that followed, but not in the form of a separate religious movement.[3]

In other instances, these movements have been identified primarily by a charismatic leader who was able to capture an independent following—an individual who may or may not have veered from biblical orthodoxy. For example, Peter Waldo and the Waldensians—often considered forerunners of the Reformation— were viewed as dangerous "cultists" and persecuted by Roman Catholic authorities.

In the New Testament, there are numerous instances of heresy mentioned, but in most cases this unorthodox teaching was not associated with a cultic movement per se. Rather, the variant beliefs had infiltrated the church. Many scholars, for example, believe that Paul's letter to the Galatians was written in part to refute the Judaizers—those who sought to make Jewish law an essential element of the Christian faith. Other epistles, particularly Ephesians, Colossians, and 1 John sought to counteract other heresies—particularly Gnosticism and its influence on Christian communities. In his letters to Timothy, Paul strongly opposed those who "teach false doctrines" and "devote themselves to myths and endless genealogies," as well as those who "abandon the faith and follow deceiving spirits and things taught by demons." He named specific individuals such as "Hymenaeus and Philetus who have wandered away from the truth. They say that the resurrection has already taken place. . . ."[4] But in none of these cases does there seem to be a cultic movement that formed to promote the heresy. In the generation following the close of the New Testament period, however, sectarian movements developed—some of which were more heretical than others.

Montanism

Montanism was one of the first sectarian movements during the postapostolic period to attain notoriety for its divisiveness within the church. Was it a cultic movement or was it a reform movement that became a forerunner of modern Pentecostalism? The debate on this issue is long standing and continues to the present. It is true that Montanism was the earliest Christian movement in the postapostolic period that openly manifested charismatic gifts, but many historians and theologians argue that the movement went beyond the bounds of orthodoxy in the areas of prophecy and eschatology.

Montanus, a new convert to Christianity, arrived on the scene during the last half of the second century. He began his preaching ministry in

Phrygia in Asia Minor—an area that had always been characterized by enthusiastic forms of religion. Almost immediately this self-appointed prophet of the end times became involved in apocalyptic speculation, claiming that a new age of the "Spirit" had dawned. He divided history into three dispensations: the Old Testament dispensation of the Father, the New Testament dispensation of the Son, and the dispensation of the Spirit, which he believed began with his ministry. He viewed himself as the mouthpiece of the Paraclete—which was a role of monumental significance. "The coming of the Paraclete was the immediate prelude to the second advent of Christ and the establishment of the New Jerusalem in one of the towns of Phrygia."[5]

The belief that the "Spirit was manifesting Himself supernaturally . . . through entranced prophets and prophetesses" was a particularly important aspect of the Montanist movement. It was this aspect as much as any other that aroused opposition from outsiders. Montanus, who prior to his conversion had been a priest in a Phrygian mystery cult, was himself given to ecstatic trances. According to Eusebius, "he was carried away in spirit and wrought up into a certain kind of frenzy and irregular ecstasy, raving, and speaking, and uttering strange things, and proclaiming what was contrary to the institutions that had prevailed in the church." He also "excited two others, females and filled them with the spirit of delusion, so that they also spake like the former, in a kind of ecstatic frenzy, out of all season, and in a manner strange and novel."[6]

The two women were Prisca and Maximilla, who left their families and joined with Montanus, serving as prophetesses. Believing they were demon possessed, local churchmen sought to exorcise them, but without success. Their prophetic revelations called for an ascetic lifestyle, which included fasting, celibacy, and a willingness (and perhaps eagerness) to be martyred for the cause.[7]

From other early sources, it is apparent that the Montanists committed to writing some of their prophecies. Indeed, some scholars "have suggested that Montanists went so far as to suppress the New Testament writings in favor of their own scriptures." In doing so, they were not only challenging the biblical basis of Christianity, but "the form of ecclesiastical authority which was developing in the wider church," and for this reason, perhaps more than any other, the church reacted very negatively to Montanism.[8]

Montanism spread out from Asia Minor into neighboring areas and as far as North Africa where it found its most noted convert, Tertullian. He left the church in A.D. 212 and joined with the Montanists (the "men of the Spirit," as he referred to them). He was apparently attracted to the group by their disciplined lifestyle and their depth of spirituality. He referred to Montanists as elite or "spiritual" Christians, and regarded other Christians as being on a lower spiritual level. In defending their prophecy, he pointed to their acknowledgment of other sign gifts: "For seeing that we acknowledge spiritual *charismata*, or gifts, we too have merited the attainment of the prophetic gift." Epiphanius, fourth-century Bishop of Salamis, maintained that the difference between the Montanists and the wider church was that "they claim that we, too, must receive the charismata."[9]

Marcionism

Another second-century movement that veered even further away from orthodoxy than Montanism was Marcionism. Marcion, like many cult leaders today, was brought up in orthodoxy. Indeed, his father was a bishop of Sinope in Pontus. He was raised in a port city on the Black Sea and became a prominent merchant. As a young man, he was a zealous Christian and donated large sums of money to the church, but his fervency did not last. His own father excommunicated him from the church, apparently on the grounds of doctrinal heresy, though some early writers suggested the action stemmed from "his seduction of a consecrated virgin." Soon thereafter he left Pontus and went to Rome where he studied under the Gnostic teacher Cerdo, "who gave him some speculative foundation for his practical dualism."[10]

Through his philosophical and biblical study, Marcion became convinced that the Old Testament and New Testament could not be reconciled. In his view, the god of the Old Testament, the *demiurge*, was a subordinate god who created the material world and ruled it. But this god was clearly inferior to God the Father of Jesus, who was the God of the New Testament, and whose concern was in the spiritual realm. "Paul was Marcion's hero and the one from whom (he thought) he derived his

doctrine. His canon of sacred writings consisted of ten Pauline epistles (minus the Pastorals and the Hebrews) and the third gospel, both appropriately edited to suit his teachings." Marcionism had many of the components of a modern-day cult—especially with regard to its heretical doctrine and its separatist factions. Marcion brought his followers out of established churches and organized a movement that flourished for more than two centuries.[11]

The Medieval Church

Besides Montanus and Marcion there were many other individuals in the early church who veered away from orthodoxy on doctrinal and practical issues and some of these individuals led movements that were outside the boundaries of Christian orthodoxy. This trend continued into the medieval era, but as the centuries progressed the distinction between orthodoxy and heresy became more and more clouded. The Roman Catholic Church considered any separatist movement heretical, even though movements outside the institutionalized church were frequently more orthodox than the church itself. And, within the established church, cultic movements developed and were sometimes allowed to flourish, the cult of the Virgin Mary being the most prominent. These cultic movements often focused on martyred saints, including relatively obscure saints such as Margaret of Antioch, a fourth-century martyr, "who at fifteen preserved her chastity from violation by jumping off a building." She "became the subject of a medieval cult" and "was one of the voices heard by Joan of Arc."[12]

Albigensians (Cathari)

One of the largest cultic movements to arise outside the established church during the medieval period was one known as the Albigensians or Cathari—a movement that was also related to the Bogomiles in Eastern Europe. So dangerous were the Albigensians perceived to be that a Crusade was waged against them in France during the early thirteenth century, which virtually eradicated the movement. Like the Marcionites, they held to gnostic concepts of dualism—a New Testament god of light and an Old Testament god of darkness. They were divided into two classes, the Perfect and the Believers. The Perfect were those who had received the "consolamentum," a laying on of hands that conferred "spiritual baptism," a rite that could not be repeated in a person's life time. The person was to thenceforth be sinless, and the rite was his passport to heaven. Many delayed the rite until their deathbed, and sometimes that death came through "endura," a suicidal death brought on by fasting. Only the Perfect had sufficient holiness to pray directly to God.[13]

"What distinguished Catharism from traditional Christianity was its radical otherworldliness," writes Harold O. J. Brown. "Despite repeated attempts at reform, corruption was rife in the established church; even the monastic communities were by no means untainted. What the established church seemed unwilling or unable to provide—enthusiasm, a sense of religious exaltation, and personal purity—some of the heretics appeared to offer." The high standards required of the spiritual or perfect class met the needs of those who shunned corruption and desired to live on a higher level, and at the same time the rank-and-file believers were allowed to live essentially guilt-free while participating in the corruption. "Thus it was possible for some to be attracted to the heresy because they were disgusted by the worldliness and corruption they saw in the leaders of the church, while others embraced it because it permitted them a license the church in principle forbade."[14]

Beghards

Another Perfectionist group during the Middle Ages was known as the Beghards. In the twelfth century, Amalric of Bena taught that no one who was filled with the Holy Spirit was capable of committing sin. Also known as the Beguines and the Brethren of the Free Spirit, they were Perfectionists who renounced formal worship. They were often accused of antinomianism, in that they believed that when an individual was perfected he was above the law. Reports of promiscuity and nudism followed them, thus bringing down the wrath of the church and civil government. *The Book of Nine Rocks*, one of their works, clearly enunciates an antinomian perspective: "If therefore it be the will of God that I should commit sin, my will must be the same, and I must not desire even to abstain from sin."[15]

Romuald

Besides the various heretical movements that arose during the early centuries and medieval era of the church, there were individuals who were leaders of personality cults. One of the strangest figures in the history of the church was the wandering tenth-century monk Romuald, founder of a number of hermit communities in Italy. He was born into a wealthy family, but as a young man, after seeing a vision of a saint, turned his back on luxury and began a lifelong pilgrimage in search of personal holiness. His biography, written by his contemporary Peter Damiani, vividly describes this unending struggle, which included prolonged conflicts with the devil. "The devil would come striking on his cell, just as Romuald was falling asleep, and then no sleep for him. Every night for nearly five years the devil lay on his feet and legs, and weighted them with the likeness of a phantom weight, so that Romuald could scarcely turn on his couch."[16]

Romuald was not only concerned for his own soul, but for the souls of others, and he believed that anything less than perfection was of the devil. When he received word that his father (whom he believed to be under the influence of the devil) was leaving a monastery to return to the world, Romuald returned to Ravenna from Gaul. "There finding his father still seeking to return to the world, he tied the old sinner's feet to a beam, fettered him with chains, flogged him, and at length by pious severity so subjugated his flesh that with God's aid he brought his mind back to a state of salvation. . . . It was soon after he brought his father back to the way of holiness that the old man saw a vision and happily yielded up the ghost."[17]

For a time his search for perfection led him to a solitary existence in a swamp. After a while, however, "the poisonous air and the stench of the marsh drove him out; and he emerged hairless, with his flesh puffed and swollen . . . not looking as if belonging to the *genus homo;* for he was as green as a newt."[18]

After coming out of the swamp, Romuald set out as a traveling preacher, setting up hermit communities wherever he went. "From all directions men began to pour in for penance, and in pity to give away their goods to the poor, while others utterly forsook the world and with fervent spirit hastened to the holy way of life." His powerful speaking was often accompanied by uncontrollable weeping—a phenomena that has occurred among others in church history who were intensely seeking holiness. "Often, while speaking, a vast contrition brought him to such floods of tears that, breaking off his sermon, he would flee anywhere for refuge, like one demented. And also when travelling on horseback with the brethren, he followed far behind them, always singing Psalms, as if he were in his cell, and never ceasing to shed tears."[19]

Romuald continued throughout his life to claim visions and direct revelations from God. On one occasion, while on his way to Mass, "he became rapt in ecstasy, and continued speechless for so long a time that all present marvelled." When later asked about the incident, he responded, "Carried into heaven, I was borne before God; and the divine voice commanded me, that with such intelligence as God had set in me, I should write and commend for us a Commentary on the Psalms. Overcome with terror, I could only respond: so let it be."[20]

Romuald often physically abused his followers, as he had his father, and for that reason as well as others, his own very life was in danger from dissidents. If he were living today under the investigative eye of the news media, he would probably be categorized somewhere in between a Jim Jones of the Peoples Temple and a William Alexander Lewis of the House of Judah, who justified the beating death of a child as an act of God. But during the Middle Ages, his insanity was mistaken by many for spirituality.

Deprograming

Along with the various cults of the medieval period came opposition to those cults and to others perceived to be in cultic movements—sometimes from the institutionalized church and sometimes from individuals. Kidnapping and attempts at deprograming, often thought to be an innovation of recent decades, was not entirely uncommon in earlier centuries. This phenomenon occurred twice in the thirteenth century with two individuals who later were recognized as great saints of the church. Thomas Aquinas, born and raised in a wealthy noble family from Naples, was abducted by his brothers after he joined the Dominicans. They sought to tempt him away from his celibate vows by enticing him with a prostitute, but he held firm. In similar circumstances, Francis of Assisi was kidnapped by his father, who questioned his son's sanity after he forsook his wealth to serve the poor. It was not until after the local bishop became involved that Francis was released.[21]

During the Reformation era Protestants were not averse to the concept of deprograming, and they applied the procedure to various individuals whom they believed to be improperly detained in monasteries and convents. One such situation occurred in the convent of St. Clara at Nurnberg during the turbulent decade following Luther's posting of his *Ninety-five Theses.* Charitas Perckheimer, the abbess, recounted the ordeal:

Many powerful and evil-minded persons came to see the friends they had in our cloister, and argued with them and told them of the new teaching, how the religious profession was a thing of evil and temptation in which it was not possible to keep holy, and that we were all of the devil. Some would take their children, sisters and relatives out of the cloister by force and by the help of admonitions and promises of which they doubtless would not have kept half. This arguing and disputing went on for a long time and was often accompanied by great anger and abuse. . . .[22]

The Reformation Era and Following

During the Reformation era the accusations of heresy within Christianity were at an all time high. Protestants were accusing Catholics of heresy and vice versa. Wars were being waged in defense of the faith, and the Inquisition was revitalized and became an even more terrorizing force in society than it had been in previous generations. But in addition to fighting each other, Protestants and Catholics were condemning heresy in their own camps. Servetus was burned at the stake in Protestant Geneva because of his anti-Trinitarian beliefs, and Anabaptists were drowned in Zurich because of their uncompromising defense of believer's baptism and their opposition to infant baptism. Among the Roman Catholics, Madame Guyon and others were imprisoned for their nonconformity and refusal to submit to the church hierarchy. A heresy that alarmed both Protestants and Catholics was that which became known as the "Polish Brethren," a sixteenth-century unitarian movement that gradually spread into Western Europe and made lasting inroads on orthodoxy.

In many instances, the sectarian individuals and movements which rose in the post-Reformation era did not have large followings able to fight back against the established church, and many of them were unable to withstand the strong opposition they faced. This was not true of the Quakers, a movement that was widely perceived as a cult in seventeenth-century England.

Quakers

In 1650, a judge sentenced young George Fox, who later founded the Society of Friends, to six months in prison for preaching a blasphemous message in the form of his own testimony in which he claimed that he was free from sin. Fox's Pendle Hill vision later reinforced his belief in perfectionism. His vision was that of "a people to be gathered to the Lord," who would be freed from the power of sin in their lives. There was a strong apocalyptic theme to Fox's messages. He believed that the world had entered the "New Age of the Spirit" (similar to what the Montanists had taught). Indeed, his testimony implied that he was ushering in the millennial age himself: "Now was I come up in spirit, through the flaming sword, into the paradise of God. All things were new, and all the creation gave another smell unto me than before, beyond what words can utter. I knew nothing but pureness, innocency, and righteousness, being renewed up into the image of God by Christ Jesus, so that I was come up into the state of Adam, which he was in before he fell."[23]

Fox emphasized the uniqueness of his perfectionist beliefs: "Of all the sects in Christendom ... I found none that could bear to be told that any should come to Adam's perfection, into that image of God, that righteousness and holiness that Adam was in before he fell; to be clean and pure without sin, as he was." Indeed, he viewed as his mission in life bringing people out of the carnal sects and into a "spirit-filled" life: "I was to bring them off from all the world's fellowships, and prayings, and singings, which stood in forms without power; that their fellowship might be in the Holy Ghost, and in the Eternal Spirit of God; that they might pray in the Holy Ghost, and sing in the Spirit, and with the grace that comes by Jesus."[24]

Tongues speaking was reported among the Quakers as was a wide variety of religious excitement. Fox himself believed that he had power to work miracles and discern spirits, and his followers claimed similar charismatic gifts. Unrefuted evidence in court gave the following description of Quaker enthusiasm: "Men, women, and little children at their meetings are strangely wrought upon in their bodies and brought to fall, foam at the mouth, roar and swell in their bellies." Richard Baxter, a leading Puritan churchman, gave a similar account. "At first they did use to fall into violent Tremblings and sometimes Vomitings in their meetings, and pretended to be violently acted by the spirit; but now that is ceased. . . ."[25]

Ranters

Another mid-seventeenth-century English sect, very similar in some respects to the Quakers, was the Ranters—a group that held to a radical perfectionism. They believed that there was no need to read the Scriptures or listen to sermons, because they were possessed by the Father, Son, and Spirit, and thus were above the laws and written words of Scripture. This led to an extreme antinomianism—that sin did not exist and that every act of a true believer was a holy one.[26]

Richard Baxter, a well-known Puritan preacher who condemned "enthusiasm" of all stripes, was particularly critical of the Ranters: "They conjoined a Cursed Doctrine of *Libertinism*, which brought them to all abominable filthiness of life. They taught as the *Familists* that God regardeth not the Actions of the Outward Man, but of the Heart, and that to the pure all things are pure

(even things forbidden)." Other contemporaries accused them of having secret meetings similar to a witches' sabbat where they danced naked in the night, and of teaching there was no difference between God and the devil. The Ranters left no writings or doctrinal creeds and the movement was short-lived, but it made an indelible mark on society—enough to be considered a serious threat to the church.[27]

Nineteenth-Century America

Many of the movements in England and on the Continent regarded as heretical, and consequently persecuted, looked to America in the hope of finding religious freedom. The Quakers and other sectarian movements quickly discovered that colonial New England was no less intolerant than was Mother England. But despite opposition, religious diversity became a part of colonial life and even increased after religious freedom was guaranteed in the Constitution. One of the sectarian movements to emigrate from England and enjoy the freedom America offered was the "United Society of Believers in Christ's Second Appearing," more commonly known as the Shakers.

The Shakers

The Shakers were among those sectarian and revivalist movements that flourished in the burned-over district of Western New York state—a region periodically swept over by the flames of revival fires. In fact, the movement established a community only a day's walk from Palmyra, where Mormon leader Joseph Smith

Depiction of the Shaker Mountain Meeting, a feast in 1842. From *Two Years Experience Among the Shakers* by David R. Lamson.

grew up. The Shakers, founded and led by Ann Lee, emphasized communal living and celibacy, the latter being a doctrine that had grown out of visions which "convinced Ann Lee that lust was indeed the root of all evil and corruption in the world—not only in religious matters, but also in economic, social, and political affairs as well. Only by renouncing all 'carnal' desires . . . and by deciding to live a life of 'virgin purity' could mankind be restored to God." This viewpoint and practice resulted in a separation from her husband. According to her own testimony, "The man to whom I was married was very kind, according to his own nature; he would have been willing to pass through a flaming fire for my sake, if I would but live in the flesh with him, which I refused to do."[28]

The Shakers began in England in 1772, and eight years later Mother Ann Lee led a small contingent of her followers to America, where she soon established a community in New Lebanon, New York. Ann Lee was an uneducated woman whose early religious inclinations resulted in a prison term in 1770, in Manchester, England, for disturbing the peace. Her crime was involvement in "pentecostal religious activities, which included singing, shouting, and ecstatic dancing." While in prison she had a powerful "open vision" of "the very act of transgression committed by Adam and Eve in the Garden of Eden," which convinced her that such was the sin that resulted in the fall of man—a situation which could only be reversed through sexual abstinence. Another vision convinced her that she was divinely selected to spread this message throughout the world.[29]

It was after this that she immigrated to America and became the leader of a highly charismatic, perfectionist, and millennial movement that fed off the camp meeting revivals. Because of the ecumenical, nonsectarian spirit of the revivals, with unity based much more on experience rather than doctrine, it was not uncommon for certain ministers and revival leaders to look favorably upon the Shakers. In fact, in some instances Shakers were actually allowed to participate as speakers at the revival meetings. Barton Stone and others, however, denounced them as "wolves in sheep's clothing" and insisted their followers have nothing to do with them. The most controversial aspect of the Shaker movement related to Ann Lee's role. Many of her followers "came to believe that in her the spirit of God had been incarnated in female form, just as they believed that in Jesus the spirit of God had been incarnated in male form." But, whether Ann Lee herself ever claimed such quasi-divinity is open to question, writes Lawrence Foster. "Her frequent ecstatic utterances . . . are open to such an interpretation, particularly when she talked about walking with Jesus as her Lord and lover, or described herself as his Bride." Yet, she reportedly forbade her devotees from kneeling before her, and "she once confessed that she was afraid to go in to talk with young Believers because they assumed that whatever she said on any subject came directly from On High."[30]

The Shakers, even more than the Quakers, viewed on-going revelation from God as the supreme source of authority. Revelations, visions, and ecstatic trances became the religious norm. This paved the way for a liberal theology that paid little heed to traditional orthodoxy, and it also opened the door to conflict and struggles after Ann Lee's death over whose revelation was to be accepted as the legitimate message from God. The leadership of Frederick Evans, "a radical, and at first a materialist, deist, and free-thinker," stirred controversy for a time as did the leadership of others who sought to make their mark on this movement which seemed doomed to factionalism and dissension almost from the start.[31]

Universal Friends

Another sectarian movement that created a stir in the burned-over district near Palmyra, New York, was known as the Universal Friends, headed by Jemima Wilkinson. In 1776, at the age of eighteen, she reportedly died of the plague. "Her body grew cold and stiff. But then it became warm again, rose up, and began to speak." The voice, however, denied that it was that of Jemima. She had "left the world of time," and her body was now being used as a vessel to speak forth from the Spirit of God and to be known as "The Publick Universal Friend." For more than forty years "The Friend" preached a doctrine that, according to Robert Ellwood, "was generally orthodox enough, save for a lack of respect for lawful marriage, for she often persuaded followers to leave spouses who were not equally dedicated to The Friend, and came more and more to counsel complete chastity." Her manner was striking:

> Hers was a dramatic presence well able to lure the hearts of impressionable

followers from earthly bonds. Strikingly tall, with ample dark hair, passionate eyes, and lovely coloring, she wore a low white beaverskin hat and a full white robe. She was accompanied by two associates: Sarah Richardson, who was alleged to be "the prophet Daniel operating in these latter days in the female line," and James Parker, who, dressed in prophet's robes, gave voice to the spirit of Elijah. At The Friend's open meetings, these persons would declaim, fall to the ground in rapture, or describe visions of heaven as the Spirit gave them utterance, and The Universal Friend would stand between them to plead the love of God with graceful gestures and winning voice.[32]

Despite (or perhaps because of) her eccentricities, she won a large following—including wealthy individuals who lavishly favored her with gifts. She was not averse to displaying her opulence, which included riding around in "an open coach, shaped like an upturned half-moon, with seats of gold tapestry and both on the front panels and over her head were engraved the letters U. F." Many of her followers viewed her "as none other than the returned Christ, an opinion she neither affirmed nor denied."[33]

Isaac Bullard

There were many religious eccentrics who followed the frontier West during the early decades of the nineteenth century—many of whom have hardly merited a footnote in American religious history. One such curious character was Isaac Bullard of Woodstock, Vermont, who wore "nothing but a bearskin girdle and his beard." His eccentricity was demonstrated in other ways as well.

"Champion of free love and communism, he regarded washing a sin and boasted that he had not changed his clothes in seven years." He left Vermont in 1817 with a contingent of his followers, who were known simply as "Pilgrims," and, blazing a trail that Joseph Smith would later follow, settled first in New York state, then in Ohio, and finally in Missouri.[34]

John Humphrey Noyes

Many of the cultic movements that thrived during the early decades of the nineteenth century were sex oriented, and it may be no more than coincidence that those founded by women such as the Shakers and the Universal Friends championed the practice of celibacy, while those founded by men such as the Mormons, the Pilgrims, and the Oneida Community promoted plural marriage, free love, and "complex" or "community" marriage.

John Humphrey Noyes' religious pilgrimage from orthodoxy to cultic activity is significant from a historical perspective, because in some ways it parallels the experiences of cult leaders today. The founder of the Oneida Community, he grew up in New England and was converted during a revival in 1831. Initially, his search for true religion was apparently sincere and without any sort of perverse sexual motivation. Following his conversion he entered Andover Seminary, but became disenchanted with the curriculum that he believed emphasized the mind and knowledge over the heart and piety. He also was depressed by the fact that there was too much levity and too much disputing over Scripture.[35]

Noyes later described his search for holiness: "During the autumn of 1833 my spirit rapidly increased in strength. By constant fellowship and conversation with Boyle, Dutton and other zealous young men of the 'new measure' school who had recently joined the seminary, by reading such books as *The Life of J. B. Taylor* and Wesley's *Christian Perfection*, as well as by much study of the Bible and fervent prayer, my heart was kept in steady and accelerating progression toward holiness." While he was at Andover, Noyes wrote to his mother of his struggle: "The burden of Christian perfection accumulated upon my soul until I determined to give myself no rest while the possibility of the attainment of it remains doubtful."[36]

In his struggle to attain holiness, Noyes finally concluded that he had to get away from the sinful atmosphere of Andover, so he transferred to Yale. Here he studied under the school's most famous young professor, Nathaniel William Taylor, who had discarded much of Edwards' theology for what became known as the "New Divinity" or New Haven theology (which modified Calvinism and paved the way for Noyes' later perfectionist theology). It was Taylor along with such men as Lyman Beecher and Samuel Hopkins, according to Timothy Smith, who "transformed Calvinist dogma into a practical Arminianism, without having to jettison Calvinist verbiage."[37]

Taylor did not hold to the doctrine of original sin, and thus believed that man had the ability within himself to overcome sin. Noyes used this as a starting point in his own search for sinlessness. As he studied the Bible

he became convinced that the Second Coming of Christ had already occurred—in A.D. 70, at the time of the destruction of Jerusalem, when Christ established a covenant that was free from the law. This paved the way for the perfection of the saints apart from any form of legalism. He believed that "spirit guidance" was above the word of Scripture, and that true Christians were free from sin. Though such a theology would seem to open the door to unadulterated antinomianism, Noyes lived a very regimented lifestyle. He spent between three and four hours each day in prayer and meditation and the remainder of his twelve to sixteen waking hours in Bible study. He often denied himself meals for days at a time in order to sustain himself solely on spiritual food, while his "body became weak and pined away." His sister wrote: "He is certainly a remarkable person. I never knew anyone so self-denying, so divested of any worldly feeling"—hardly the description of the stereotypical cult leader.[38]

During his time at Yale, Noyes spent many hours discussing perfection with fellow students, which created considerable controversy, but in the summer of 1833 he received his license to preach along with his classmates. In 1834, less than a year later, he publicly testified that he believed himself to be morally perfect. So incensed were church officials by his audacity that his Congregational minister's license was rescinded.[39]

Noyes' declaration of sinlessness came while he was preaching a sermon entitled "He that committeth sin is of the devil." He left the meeting exhilarated by the fact that he had finally been able to take a public stand. That same night, alone in his room, he received further confirmation of his position. "Three times in quick succession a stream of eternal love gushed through my heart." All his doubts had vanished and he had a sense of overwhelming joy. Those who had heard Noyes' sermon were astonished, and within a week he was asked to appear at Yale to defend his position. His most vocal opponent was Nathaniel Taylor, who accused him of holding to nothing more than "the old Wesleyan scheme that had failed." He sarcastically suggested that the only support Noyes would ever find would be "among women and ignorant people, but not among the intelligent."[40]

The accusations and denunciations from his professors and classmates plunged Noyes into a deep depression, and he began doubting his own salvation. He became convinced that since he was not in communion with God, he must be in league with Satan. After a time he completely renounced God and became engulfed in "darkness and atheism."[41]

Noyes eventually came out of his depression and disbelief, and almost immediately began an itinerant evangelistic ministry preaching his perfectionism wherever he was permitted to speak. Wherever he went, scandal of sexual irregularities surfaced. Though he himself was not implicated, many who heard him assumed that his theology, like that of the New York Perfectionists, would automatically lead to "free love." Noyes at first tried to distance himself from such a philosophy, but that was no longer

possible after his notorious "Battle-axe Letter" surfaced. Here Noyes argued that God had set men and women apart as couples in the conventional marriage relationship during the time of apostasy that began in A.D. 70. In a state of perfection, however, such marriage barriers were not needed. He envisioned the ideal society as one where "base passions such as exclusiveness, jealously, and possessiveness were out of character." Indeed, he saw no more reason why "sexual intercourse should be restrained by law, than why eating and drinking should be—and there is as little occasion for shame in the one case as in the other."[42]

In 1841, four years after he wrote the letter, Noyes established a community for his followers. It was not until several years later in 1846, however, that he instituted community marriage. Noyes began the practice of "complex marriage" himself, and not surprisingly problems quickly arose—particularly with the husband of the wife whom Noyes sought to "share." The situation worsened as others began practicing "complex marriage," but nevertheless, Noyes was convinced it was a success and announced in 1847 that the Kingdom of God had arrived.[43]

Noyes' community continued on for more than three decades, but not without problems. There was always outside opposition as well as internal dissension, particularly from those couples or individuals who were not permitted by the ruling committee to have children. There was also opposition from individual members who had lesser status, and whose sexual activities were therefore severely limited. The Oneida Community was not

John Humphrey Noyes. From *John Humphrey Noyes* by George W. Noyes.

simply a "free love" situation, but was rather a community marriage experiment that was strictly limited by those in power. It was a social experiment that became very secularized, but in the words of Noyes himself, "Our fundamental principle is religion."[44]

The Strangites

Organized religions often die in infancy or soon thereafter. Indeed, as is true in other realms of life, the law of survival of the fittest often applies—at least in the sense of having a charismatic leader who is able to offer beliefs and practices that appeal to large numbers of people and can be perpetuated in future generations. Mormonism could be characterized as such. It survived while other move-

ments died. One such movement that was unable to survive was a rival of the Brigham Young branch of Mormonism after Joseph Smith died. It was led by James Strang, a colorful figure who claimed that he had received a letter from Smith shortly before his death urging him to carry on and "plant a stake of Zion" in Wisconsin. Strang also maintained that on the day of Smith's death he received a vision of an angel who anointed him the successor to the fallen prophet.

Then in 1845 Strang was instructed to dig up from under a tree on a Wisconsin hill an account of an ancient people, true believers who, like Smith's Nephites, were extinct but were to be revived in the person of the Mormons. Taking several men to the spot, Strang stood far away while they extracted from the earth a clay box holding three plates. . . . Four of the six sides of the plates contained characters in a language only Strang knew. The other two sides had drawings.[45]

Soon Strang had some two thousand followers residing at his community at Voree, Wisconsin, including William Smith, the brother of Joseph. William was lured to the Strang faction by a promise of "a coveted position as patriarch if William brought with him his mother, with the mummies and papyrus (the purported source of the Mormon Book of Abraham), together with the dead bodies of Joseph and Hyrum. William realized he could not move his brothers' bodies without alienating Emma, but he tried to manage the rest."[46]

Although Strang's following was smaller and less committed to the cause than was Young's, there were estimates that he had as many as ten thousand followers by 1846, compared to fifteen thousand for Young. Strang soon proved to be too much of a charlatan for some of his followers, and there were desertions from the highest ranks of leadership, including William Smith. After that, Strang moved his followers to Beaver Island in Lake Michigan, where he crowned himself king. In 1852, he was elected to the Michigan legislature, where he sought to use his position to build his own self-governed Mormon territory.[47]

In 1856, Strang was assassinated by some disgruntled members of his own movement. "He left behind five pregnant grieving widows and a crumbling kingdom." The movement dwindled in the years that followed and became little more than a curiosity to outsiders. "There are very few Strangites today," writes Latayne Scott. "They deny the virgin birth, the atonement of Christ, and the authority of the Utah Mormon prophets. They worship on Saturday, and attempt to keep the Law of Moses by, among other things, circumcising their males and by offering animal sacrifices."[48]

The Christadelphians

Despite the scandalous publicity surrounding such movements as the Mormons, the Shakers, and the Oneida Community, not all of the cultic movements that arose during the first half of the nineteenth century were communalistic and sex-oriented. Some were traditional in practice and deviated only in their doctrinal tenets. The Christadelphians are an example. The movement was founded by John Thomas, a medical doctor who emigrated from England to America in 1832. For a time he associated with Alexander Campbell of the Disciples of Christ, but by 1848 he started his own movement which, he was convinced, genuinely represented primitive Christianity. He established local assemblies of believers, and they soon became known as the Christadelphians or "Brethren of Christ."[49]

The Christadelphians have been regarded by some as forerunners of the Jehovah's Witnesses because of the many doctrinal similarities between the two groups, but there are apparently no direct links between them. Like the Jehovah's Witnesses, they believe that their movement is the only true form of Christianity and that all other professing Christians are deceived. Likewise, they reject the doctrine of the Trinity. They "adopted the old heresy that Jesus was the son of God but not God the Son. Jesus 'had two sides: Deity and humanity. The man was the Son whose existence dates from the birth of Jesus; the deity dwelling in Him was the Father.'" Other doctrines that parallel those of the Jehovah's Witnesses relate to the mortality of the soul and salvation that is dependent on works—particularly baptism by immersion.[50]

The Christadelphians, unlike the Jehovah's Witnesses and Mormons, did not flourish on American soil. Indeed they have been regarded as little more than a historical curiosity until recently when they seemed to suddenly reappear. "Visitors at last summer's Michigan State Fair," wrote Wesley Walters in 1984, "may have encountered a group believed to have been extinct—the Christadelphians. Importing most of their free promotional literature from Australia, the group appears to be trying a comeback in its native country."[51]

Contemplating the Future with a Historical Perspective

Unlike the Strangites and Shakers, whose short-lived success has long since vanished, the Mormons flourished. Along with such movements as the Jehovah's Witnesses and Christian Science, Mormons have weathered the storms of opposition and built powerful organizations during the early decades of the twentieth century. But religious movements sometimes move forward and then recede with changing times. There is no sign of decline among the Mormons and the Jehovah's Witnesses, but the size and influence of Christian Science has dwindled in recent decades. In the meantime, other alternative religions have arisen, but the future is uncertain. Will The Way International, the Children of God, and the Unification Church still be religious movements to be reckoned with in the twenty-first century, or will they be historical curiosities, even as the Shakers and Strangites are today? Will the New Age Movement be remembered as a passing fad of an affluent generation of the late twentieth century, or will it be the dominant religious force throughout the world? These are questions on which futurologists speculate and on which historians must wait to reflect.

Chapter 3

Mormonism:
The Legacy of
Joseph Smith

Mormonism, officially known as the Church of Jesus Christ of Latter-Day Saints, is the largest of the alternative religions that has sprung up on American soil. As is true with the members of almost all such movements, there is a feeling on their part of indignation at being excluded from the confines of traditional orthodoxy. Mormons claim to be true Christians and are disturbed when they are not regarded as such. But the Mormons have excluded themselves. Their prophet-founder testified to a vision which showed him that all the Christian creeds were wrong, that they were an "abomination" in God's sight. In that vision, he claimed that he was forbidden to join any of the "sects"—a reference to the various Protestant denominations that were prominent at that time. He maintained that God was speaking through him, and as a result three new scriptures (authored or compiled by him and his associates) were given a status equal to or greater than that of the Bible.

So, while the Mormons hold to many beliefs that may be Christian in origin, they also hold to many beliefs that are entirely distinct from the Christian tradition. The Mormon church is not merely a denomination that differs with other denominations on secondary or peripheral doctrines or practices; rather, it is a new religious movement which differs from Christianity on primary and essential doctrines and that stands alone with additional scriptures and beliefs that have never been a part of historic Christianity.

It is said that there is a new LDS member every four and one-half minutes. Because of the movement's rapid growth and influence, it is crucial that the background, doctrinal beliefs, and current practices of the Mormons be examined—and not only from sources written by their critics, but from their own scriptures and writings and from the scholarship of their own people. Mormons and non-Mormons must investigate these issues with an open mind and in light of the Bible and Christian tradition.

Joseph Smith

It is impossible to truly understand Mormonism without having a clear grasp of the personality and character of its founder, Joseph Smith. And to understand him, it is necessary to become acquainted with his family and his surroundings during the early decades of the nineteenth century.

Heritage and Early Life

Smith was born in Sharon, Vermont, on December 23, 1805, the fourth child of Joseph and Lucy Smith. His youth was spent in the small western New York town of Palmyra, his family having migrated from Vermont in 1816. The family was poor—more so than were most of their neighbors. One of these neighbors later commented about their status: "I knew the Smiths . . . but they were too lowly to associate with." Biographer Donna Hill has written that, "For a family of pride, this was a hard burden, especially for Lucy. Joseph Jr. too was made ashamed, and one of his lifelong concerns would be to raise the status of his family."[1]

Religion was an important influence in western New York, a region often referred to as the "burned-over" district, having been swept over so frequently by the fires of revival. The Smiths, like most of their neighbors, were religious people, but their religion was not of a conventional sort. They did not initially join a local church, a decision that was influenced in part by young Smith's paternal grandfather, Asael, who rejected with a passion the institutionalized church and its creeds. This suspicion and spurning of organized religion was passed down from father to son to grandson, and became an integral aspect of Mormonism from its very inception. But if organized religion was rejected, personalized religion was warmly embraced. Both Lucy and Joseph Smith, Sr., experienced dreams and visions that fortified their belief in the supernatural. Lucy's experiences were not particularly extraordinary, but her husband's are worth noting, especially in light of the much publicized visions their son would later have. Donna Hill relates the details in her biography of Joseph Smith:

Lucy says that in the first of seven visions he had, her husband was traveling through a field of dead timber with a spirit who told him this represented the world without religion, but that Joseph would find a box of food that gave wisdom. Joseph was happy, though he was kept from eating the food by horned beasts. Lucy says the dream confirmed her husband's belief that the preachers of their day knew no more than anyone else about the kingdom of God, thereby echoing the conviction of his father, Asael.[2]

The dreams and visions of his father and the religious piety of his mother were combined with another important influence in young Smith's life—the climate of superstitious beliefs that so permeated the region during the early nineteenth century. Legends of great Indian civilizations and of buried treasures abounded, and many people were caught up in the excitement. "Hundreds of burial mounds dotted the landscape, filled with skeletons and artifacts of stone, copper, and sometimes beaten silver," writes Fawn Brodie. "It would have been a jaded curiosity indeed that would have kept any of the boys in the family from spading at least once into their pitted surfaces, and even the father succumbed to the local enthusiasm and tried his hand with a witch-hazel stick. Young Joseph could not keep away from them."[3]

"Money-digging," as the activity was commonly referred to, became an avid pastime for young Smith, who used a "peep stone" to detect buried treasure. Even before he had reached the age of twenty he had acquired a reputation heralded enough to draw the attention of a farmer from many miles away to secure his services to locate mineral wealth believed to be situated on his property. He was unsuccessful in this instance as he apparently was in others, for in 1826, he was brought to trial for misrepresenting his ability to locate buried treasure—on the charge of being a "disorderly person and an imposter."[4]

Early Visions

It is in light of this backdrop, then, that Joseph Smith six years later told of visions during his youth that led to his digging up gold plates on the Hill Cumorah—plates that when translated contained the Book of Mormon, God's record for the Latter-Day Saints. The most widely-circulated version of the first vision has become part of Mormon scripture. In this account, Smith tells that he "retired to the woods . . . on a beautiful, clear day, early in the spring of eighteen hundred and twenty." His purpose was "to inquire of the Lord . . . which of all the sects was right." He "kneeled down" and "was seized upon by some power which entirely overcame" him. "Thick darkness gathered around" and then a "pillar of light" appeared over his head "above the brightness of the sun, which descended gradually until it fell upon" him. It was then that he "saw two Personages, whose brightness and glory defy all description." One of the two "personages" then called him "by name and said, pointing to the other—*This is My Beloved Son, Hear Him!*"[5]

There is no indication in Smith's testimony that he fell on his face and worshiped, as might be expected of one who suddenly comes face to face with God the Father and his Son, Jesus. Rather, from his account he seems to have taken the introduction in stride, and, amidst all the splendor, had the presence of mind to ask the question that was on his mind, "which of all the sects was right" and "which should I join?" The answer was that "they were all wrong." That conclusion, and the remainder of the message, would not have been unfamiliar to young Smith's ears. It sounded as though it could have come from the lips of his own father or grandfather:

The Personage who addressed me said that all their creeds were an abomination in his sight; that those professors were all corrupt; that: "they draw near to me with their lips, but their hearts are far from me, they teach for doctrines the commandments of men, having a form of godliness, but they deny the power thereof."[6]

Smith recalled his second vision some years later. This vision constituted his call and instructions regarding the gold plates, and occurred three years after the first one. He was in his bedroom asking God for forgiveness for his sins—"not great or malignant sins" but sins of "levity" and associating with "jovial company" ("sins" he would never overcome).

> While I was thus in the act of calling upon God, I discovered a light appearing in my room, which continued to increase until the room was lighter than at noonday, when immediately a Personage appeared at my bedside, standing in the air, for his feet did not touch the floor.
>
> He had on a loose robe of most exquisite whiteness. . . .
>
> He called me by name, and said unto me that he was a messenger sent from the presence of God to me, and that his name was Moroni; that God had a work for me to do. . . .
>
> He said there was a book deposited, written upon gold plates giving an account of the former inhabitants of this continent. . . .[7]

Smith was not permitted immediately to dig up the gold plates, and in the meantime he received other messages. The "personage" not only gave young Smith instructions regarding the treasure he would find buried but also regarding the woman he would marry. After courting Emma Hale against her father's wishes, Smith returned from Pennsylvania to his home, where in the fall of 1826, he again visited the Hill Cumorah. There the "personage" told him he could at last see the buried plates "if he brot with him the right person." Who was that person? Joseph "looked into his glass and found it was Emma Hale Daughter of old Mr Hale of Pensulvany." In January of 1827, he returned to Pennsylvania and proposed to Emma and they eloped without the consent of her parents.[8]

Finding and Translating the Gold Plates

The gold plates dominated the Smiths' early married life. According to Lucy Smith, Joseph's mother, her son and daughter-in-law went to the Hill Cumorah one night in the early autumn of 1827 and unearthed the treasure and brought it home. During the next two years that followed, they moved frequently and were preoccupied with translating the golden plates. "Perhaps in the beginning," writes Fawn Brodie, "Joseph never intended his stories of the golden plates to be taken so seriously, but once the masquerade had begun, there was no point at which he could call a halt. Since his own family believed him (with the possible exception of his cynical younger brother William), why should not the whole world?[9]

The process of translating was slow and filled with interruptions. Because Smith was a poor writer himself, he utilized the services of a "scribe." Emma and her brother initially both served him in that capacity, and others followed. According to Emma, Smith read the inscriptions on the gold plates at first by means of Urim and Thummim (special eye glasses that Smith supposedly dug up with the plates), and then switched over to a small stone. She often sat for hours writing the messages he dictated to her "with his

Joseph Smith. Courtesy of the Church of Jesus Christ of Latter Day Saints.

face buried in his hat, which had the stone in it."[10]

In the months after Smith claimed to have dug up the gold plates, they were not guarded or well hidden from potential thieves. According to Emma, "they lay in a box under our bed for months" and sometimes they were kept on a living room table, "wrapped in a small linen table cloth," and she had to move them each time she dusted. Although she "never felt at liberty to look at them," she felt through the linen cloth and found them "to be pliable like thick paper" that "would rustle with a metallic sound when the edges were moved by the thumb."[11]

Smith's seemingly casual attitude about the gold plates was further demonstrated in the summer of 1828, when he lent his only copy of the initial translation to a friend and benefactor, Martin Harris, who then lost it (or was the victim of a thief). Smith had to begin again, but he wisely received instructions from "Moroni, who explained that he was not to retranslate the same material but use a second account to avoid being trapped by inconsistencies."[12]

Losing the manuscript was a painful ordeal for Smith, for it meant he had to begin again at what had been a laborious process. This time, however, he had a new associate, Oliver Cowdery, who proved invaluable to him in producing the *Book of Mormon* and in establishing the church. "Oliver claimed some prophetic and divining powers of his own, and had brought with him a 'rod of nature,' perhaps acquired while he was among his father's religious group in Vermont, who believed that certain rods had spiritual properties and could be used in divining." He began his work as a scribe in the spring of 1829, but Joseph was anxious to elevate him to the position of "translator," since he had been doing the translation work entirely by himself. Any natural reservations that Cowdery had about assuming such a role, Smith no doubt speculated, could be handled with a revelation: "You shall receive a knowledge concerning the engravings of old records. . . . Yea, behold, I will tell you in your mind and in your heart, by the Holy Ghost, which shall come upon you." But despite the revelation, the words simply did not come to Cowdery, and Smith finally conceded the failure, and received another revelation for him: "it is not expedient that you should translate now."[13]

One of the more curious details of Smith's life during the years between his first vision, which confirmed that all sects were wrong, and the founding of the Mormon church, was his joining with the Methodists in 1828. After he "presented himself in a very serious and humble manner" to the local circuit preacher, his request that his name be added on the class roll of the church was granted. Soon after his membership became known, however, there were objections by some who "thought it a disgrace to the church to have a practicing necromancer" in the membership. Joseph and Emma were barred from attending services until Joseph agreed to renounce "his fraudulent and hypocritical practices." Nevertheless, his name remained on the church roll for several months.[14]

Despite that detour in his life, on May 15, 1829, Smith and Cowdery went into the woods together. They later reported that there they had received a message from John the Baptist, who appeared to them in a vision. He conferred on them the "Priesthood of Aaron," and then instructed them to baptize each other. Although the church itself would not be formed until the following year, this event marked the beginning of its organizational structure. As the entire foundation of the new movement was based on the authenticity of the gold plates, Smith's closest associates (Oliver Cowdery, David Whitmer, and Martin Harris) began to press him for the privilege of seeing them. With that prodding, Smith received a revelation for them: "Ye shall testify that you have seen them, even as my servant Joseph Smith, Jun., has seen them, for it is by my power that he has seen them, and it is because he had faith."[15]

This revelation was clearly as important to Smith as it was to his associates. He needed witnesses who would support his claim. But their testimony was not that Smith had in fact shown them the actual gold plates, but rather that while they were "in the woods" (a common location for early Mormon visions), the plates were shown to them "by the power of God, and not of man." Indeed, according to the testimony, "an angel of God came down from heaven, and he brought and laid before our eyes, that we beheld and saw the plates, and the engravings thereon."[16]

The *Book of Mormon*

After the *Book of Mormon* was completed, the next big hurdle was to finance its printing. Martin Harris had offered to sell property for that purpose, but his wife so strongly opposed it that he reneged on the offer. Once again Smith received a revelation—this time for Harris: "I command you to repent—repent, lest I smite you by the rod of my mouth, and by my wrath, and by my anger, and your sufferings be sore. . . . And again, I command thee that thou shalt not covet thine own property, but impart it freely to the printing of the Book of Mormon. . . ."[17]

Ancestry of American Indians

Once the *Book of Mormon* was published in 1830, it was advertised and sold by Harris and other Smith associates for $1.25 per copy. It was not an immediate bestseller, and for good reason. It is more than five hundred pages long and very laborious reading. It is the story of Lehi and his family, who migrated from Jerusalem in 600 B.C. to Central America. The story is more fanciful than real. The migration, which consisted of no more than twenty people, immediately "began to prosper exceedingly, and to multiply in the land." Very soon after they arrived, Nephi says that he taught his people to "build buildings, and to work in all manner of wood, and of iron, and of copper, and of brass, and of steel, and of gold, and of silver, and of precious ores, which were in great abundance." Then he reports that he "did build a temple; and . . . did construct it after the manner of the temple of Solomon." This all happened in less than thirty years after they left Jerusalem.[18]

By way of comparison, Old Testament scholar Gleason Archer has pointed out that it took more than one hundred and fifty thousand people over eight years to build Solomon's temple. "It is difficult to see," he writes "how a few dozen unskilled workers (most of whom must have been children) could have duplicated this feat even in the nineteen years they allegedly did the work. Nor is it clear how all kinds of iron, copper, brass, silver, and gold could have been found in great abundance (2 Nephi 5:15) for the erection of this structure back in the sixth-century B.C. America."[19]

After the temple was built, Nephi's authority began to be challenged, and God cursed those who were in defiance by causing "a skin of blackness to come upon them"— people who had been "white, and

exceedingly fair and delightsome" now became "loathsome."[20]

The *Book of Mormon* is a narrative of military conflict and political affairs. Some five hundred years after the migration from Jerusalem, King Mosiah decided that henceforth judges should rule the people instead of kings, and Alma became the first judge. Many battles and rebellions follow. The most significant event of all—prophesied and then fulfilled—is the appearance of Christ in America: "For behold, Nephi was baptizing and prophesying, and preaching, crying repentance unto the people, showing signs and wonders, working miracles among the people, that they might know that the Christ must shortly come." When Christ did come, he commissioned twelve apostles and repeated the Sermon on the Mount.[21]

Borrowings from the Bible

Many of the stories in the *Book of Mormon* were, as Fawn Brodie and many others have shown, borrowed from the Bible. The daughter of Jared, like Salome, danced before a king and a decapitation followed. Aminadi, like Daniel, deciphered handwriting on a wall, and Alma was converted after the exact fashion of St. Paul. The daughters of the Lamanites were abducted like the dancing daughters of Shiloh; and Ammon, the American counterpart of David, for want of a Goliath slew six sheep-rustlers with his sling.[22]

The majority of the *Book of Mormon* was written by Mormon—if the testimony of the book is to be taken at face value. Portions were also written by Nephi, a first generation immigrant from Palestine to America in the seventh century B.C., and by Moroni, the son of Mormon and the last Nephite chronicler to survive. Mormon himself was the military leader of the Nephites for nearly sixty years during the fourth century, when that civilization was waning. He was chosen of God at age fifteen, and he led his people through battles until he himself was killed at the age of seventy-three—always admonishing his followers that they would not prosper unless they kept the commandments of the Lord.[23]

Solomon Spaulding Theory of Authorship

Who really wrote the *Book of Mormon?* That very question has been taken up in many books and is the title of one book. It has has been an issue of controversy for more than a century and a half. No one except a professing Mormon believes the book actually came from gold plates bearing an accurate historical record, so from the earliest days theories were propounded as to what the source of the book actually was.[24] One of those theories was that Smith had plagiarized one Solomon Spaulding, a retired minister who had allegedly written two fictional narratives about the early inhabitants of America. The major problem with this theory is that the narrative from which the *Book of Mormon* was supposedly copied has been lost. This missing volume, known as *Manuscript Found*, was, as the theory goes, left in a print shop where it was stolen by Sidney Rigdon, a close associate of Smith in the early days of Mormonism. Spaulding died in 1816, fourteen

years before the *Book of Mormon* was published, but his stories had not been forgotten. He was the proprietor of a nonalcoholic temperance tavern, and, according to later witnesses, had told stories of the migrations of Nephi and Lehi to his customers. These same stories, then, found their way into the *Book of Mormon* through the stolen copy of *Manuscript Found*.[25]

The Mormons have discredited this theory, largely on the basis of the discovery of Spaulding's other narrative known as *Manuscript Story* (now at Oberlin College Library). They do not accept the theory that Spaulding wrote two novels, and they point out that the existing manuscript bears little resemblance to the *Book of Mormon*. It does, however, tell a fictionalized version of the origins of the American Indians, and has some similarities to Smith's version. Whether Smith may have been influenced by this volume is impossible to determine. Whether there was another volume and whether Smith plagiarized it is still an open question. The Solomon Spaulding theory is a theory that emerged in the 1830s and was given new life in 1976, when researchers studying the evidence claimed they found a page containing Spaulding's handwriting in an original copy of the *Book of Mormon*—handwriting that was verified by handwriting experts.[26]

Ethan Smith Influence

It seems more likely that the *Book of Mormon* was based in part on a book by Ethan Smith entitled *View of the Hebrews; or, The Ten Tribes of Israel in America.* The belief that the

American Indians had Hebraic origins was widely held. Indeed, "America's most distinguished preachers—William Penn, Roger Williams, Cotton Mather, Jonathan Edwards—had all espoused the theory." But it was Ethan Smith's book, published in Vermont in 1823, that probably had the greatest impact on the *Book of Mormon*. Its claims sound very similar to those in the *Book of Mormon:* "Israel brought into this new continent a considerable degree of civilization; and the better part of them long laboured to maintain it. But others fell into the hunting and consequently savage state; whose barbarous hordes invaded their more civilized brethren, and eventually annihilated most of them, and all in these northern regions!" According to Fawn Brodie, "It may never be proved that Joseph saw *View of the Hebrews* before writing the *Book of Mormon*, but the striking parallelisms between the two books hardly leave a case for mere coincidence."[27]

Smith's Fertile Imagination

But the similarities between these two works do not explain the origin of the *Book of Mormon*. While Smith may have been aware of this work and other works, such as Spaulding's, the simplest and most obvious conclusion is that it originated primarily in the mind of Smith himself. His mother's recollections of his youthful imagination would tend to support that theory, and would likewise tend to refute the belief in the divine origin of the book:

> During our evening conversations, Joseph could occasionally give us some of the most amusing recitals that could be imagined. He would describe the ancient inhabitants of this continent, their dress, mode of traveling, their buildings, with every particular; their mode of warfare; and also their religious worship. This he would do with as much ease seemingly, as if he had spent his whole life among them.[28]

Early Organization of the Church

Less than two weeks after the *Book of Mormon* went on sale on April 6, 1830, the church was officially organized as the Church of Christ. The meeting took place at the farmhouse of Peter Whitmer in Fayette, New York. There were six charter members who agreed to accept Smith and Cowdery as their leaders. Besides the necessary business matters, there was prayer and a communion service. The most significant aspect of that organizational meeting was Smith's revelation regarding the leadership of the new church. The revelation specified that this leader would be "a seer, a translator, a prophet, an apostle of Jesus Christ, an elder of the church through the will of God." The newly formed congregation was admonished in this revelation from God to accept "his [Smith's] word . . . as if from mine own mouth, in patience and faith."[29]

One of the most significant and long-lasting developments that occurred with the organization of the church was the commissioning of missionaries. Armed with the *Book of Mormon*, missionaries traveled to neighboring villages and soon there were converts and inquirers visiting Smith, wanting to know more of his new religion. The missionaries also traveled West in an effort to convert

Emma Hale Smith. Courtesy of the Church of Jesus Christ of Latter Day Saints.

Indians. It was on one of these journeys that Sidney Rigdon, a minister of a small congregation that had at one time been associated with the Disciples of Christ, was brought into the fold. Rigdon proved to be an important addition to the church and had a powerful influence on Smith. Indeed, it was through his urging that Smith received a revelation that would constrain the scattered "saints" to move to Kirkland, Ohio.[30]

More Revelations

One of the pivotal doctrines of the Mormon religion is the belief in continuing revelation—that God "will yet reveal many great and important things pertaining to the Kingdom of God."[31] Without this doctrine, Smith would have been devoid of the au-

thority he needed to control his fledgling church and even his immediate family.

It was very important to Smith that he have the full support of Emma in his religious activities. Although she was absent for the initial organizational meeting of the church, and was not baptized until two months later, from all outward appearances she strongly supported her husband in the early years. There is speculation, however, that she may have at least privately questioned some of his activities and perhaps even the very claim that he actually possessed gold plates. That may have prompted what has become known as the "E-lect Lady" revelation. Following the opening salutation, "Hearken unto the voice of the Lord your God while I speak unto you, Emma Smith, my daughter," it designated her as "an elect lady, who I have called" and then proceeded to give her a solemn warning: "murmur not because of the things which thou has not seen for they are withheld from thee and from the world."[32]

Of all the "revelations" Smith received, he was bound to be wrong at times—especially when predictions of future events were involved. An example of this was when he sent two of his associates on business to Toronto, where they were to meet a man who would offer them what they had come for. When they "returned empty-handed and disillusioned . . . they confronted Joseph." How did he explain such discrepancies in his prophetic powers? It was simple. "Some revelations are of God, some are of man, and some are of the devil."[33]

One revelation that could be categorized as being "of man"—or more specifically "of woman"—was the Word of Wisdom, which admonishes Mormons not to partake of "wine or strong drink," "tobacco," and "hot drinks."[34] What prompted this "revelation" in 1833, is a fascinating footnote in Mormon history. While the Smiths lived in Kirkland, they were constantly being put upon by travelers and immigrants who needed lodging, and Emma's tiny house was often overcrowded. To make matters worse, many of her lodgers and visitors had annoying and vulgar habits. According to David Whitmer, a close associate of Smith's, "Some of the men were excessive chewers of the filthy weed, and their disgusting slobbering and spitting caused Mrs. Smith . . . to make the ironical remark that 'It would be a good thing if a revelation could be had declaring the use of tobacco a sin, and commanding its suppression.'" At first the comment was treated as a joke, but many of the women supported Emma and there developed apprehension among some of the men that their wives might be taken seriously by Smith. In a clever effort to respond, "one of the brethren suggested that the revelation should also provide for a total abstinence from tea and coffee drinking, intending this as a counter dig at the sisters." Although the Word of Wisdom was not closely adhered to in the early years—even by Emma—it made its way into Mormon scripture and has been an important tenet of the faith ever since.[35]

Kirkland, Ohio, Years

It was a "revelation" that prompted Smith in 1831, less than a year after the church was founded, to direct the entire membership to leave their homes and move some three hundred miles to Kirkland, Ohio. It meant hardship for many people who had to sell their property at a loss. For Emma, who was pregnant, the mid-winter journey was almost unbearable. She had moved seven times in the four years that she had been married, and there was no promise that this would be the last. According to the revelation, this would be "a land of promise, a land flowing with milk and honey. . . . Wherefore, for this cause I gave unto you the commandment that ye should go to the Ohio; and there I will give unto you my law; and there you shall be endowed with power from on high."[36]

Despite this promise of "power from on high," there were grave problems for Smith and his followers from the beginning of their sojourn in Kirkland. Smith sought to deal with the internal problems with revelations. Indeed, during his first two years in Kirkland, he received forty-nine revelations, most of them pertaining to practical matters that would have been difficult to resolve without Smith's claim that the solutions were from God. Some of Smith's followers questioned the revelations—often because they disagreed with the content, but also because they were concerned about the wording. On one occasion when some of them sought to correct his grammar while he was pronouncing the revelation, he "rebuked them, saying that every word of that revelation had been dictated by Jesus Christ." In an effort to substantiate the revelations, they were collected and published in the *Book of Commandments* in 1831, and at that time the poor grammar "dictated by Jesus Christ" was corrected.[37] The official book of revelations has since become known as the *Doctrine and Covenants* and contains one hundred and thirty-five of Smith's revelations and pronouncements.

Lynching by Dissidents

With the publication of the *Book of Commandments*, Smith might have hoped to settle the conflicts that had been brewing, but they continued and actually escalated, as some of his followers became so embittered that they left the church. Francis Gibbons, a Mormon biographer of Smith, gives the following account:

> The spirit of apostasy and opposition that had been festering in Ohio came to a head in the spring of 1832, producing the first and only act of overt violence against the Prophet or the Church in Ohio. For weeks before the tragic event occurred, the Prophet saw ominous signs of its coming. The ranks of the apostates were swelled with a number of embittered former members. . . . The Prophet's enemies and detractors outside the Church rallied around this small center of apostates, joining in their blind hatred of him and feeding on false stories and innuendos.
>
> The storm finally broke on a spring evening as Joseph dozed while tending one of the twins. . . . The first sign of danger was a light tapping on a windowpane. Shortly afterwards the front door burst open and within seconds the room was filled with a horde of angry, shoving men, who grabbed the Prophet and carried him outside. . . .
>
> At this point the mob seemed uncertain as to what they should do. . . . Finally he was stripped naked, except

for his shirt collar, and his body was scratched all over by a man who fell upon him like a wild animal. Then he was tarred and feathered, beaten senseless, and left for dead.[38]

The exact cause of this mob violence is debated, but some historians have suggested that the beginnings of Mormon polygamy can be traced to this time. ". . . Rumor and insinuation fed the fury of the mob that tarred and feathered him. When the Johnson boys joined the mob that entered their own home, they clearly suspected an improper association between Joseph and their sixteen-year-old sister, Nancy Marinda."[39]

Even prior to this attack, Smith had begun to look elsewhere for a permanent home for his followers. In 1831, only months after their arrival in Kirkland, Smith and some of his associates traveled to Missouri, and were soon followed by a larger group who would settle there in the land of "Zion," where he dedicated a temple site near Independence. He then returned to Kirkland, where he would preside over a tiny church whose two congregations were now separated by some eight hundred miles.[40]

The Book of Abraham

In Kirkland, as elsewhere when Smith was present, life was never routine. It was there that Smith was visited by a man who was traveling with an exhibit of Egyptian artifacts, and who had heard of Smith's reputation for translating the gold plates. The Mormon prophet, he hoped, could assist him in translating some ancient papyri. Fascinated by the prospect of actually proving his which Smith returned to the custody of the angel Moroni."[41]

Dedication of the Temple

One of the most important events to occur during the years that the Mormons resided in Kirkland was the building and dedication of the first Mormon temple. In March of 1836, after nearly three years of planning and construction, hundreds of people gathered to celebrate its completion. According to Mormon historian Gibbons, there was "a spiritual outpouring almost unmatched in ecclesiastical history." Smith himself later wrote a detailed description:

> A noise was heard like the sound of a rushing mighty wind, which filled the Temple, and all the congregation simultaneously arose, being moved upon by an invisible power; many began to speak in tongues and prophesy; others saw glorious visions; and I beheld the Temple was filled with angels, which fact I declared to the congregation. The people of the neighborhood came running together (hearing an unusual sound within, and seeing a bright light like a pillar of fire resting upon the Temple), and were astonished at what was taking place. This continued until the meeting closed at eleven P.M.[42]

Marker in an empty lot in Independence, Missouri, where Joseph Smith prophesied the building of a temple.

translation ability, Smith purchased the papyri (for more than two thousand dollars), and then proceeded to develop an "Egyptian alphabet and grammar," which was confirmed by "direct inspiration from Heaven." This translation became known as the *Book of Abraham*, and it became a part of Mormon scriptures. The original papyri were believed to have been destroyed in the Chicago fire, but turned up at the Metropolitan Museum in New York in 1967. A translation quickly established that they were "rather common funerary documents bearing absolutely no relationship to the Book of Abraham." For Mormon scholars, the finding proved to be an embarrassment. The papyri were authentic and there was no denying the actual translation— quite "unlike the golden plates,

It was during this dedication meeting that some of the temple rituals were initiated. Men and women were separated, and according to one of the men present, "The Lord poured out his spirit upon us and gave us some little idea of the law of anointing, and conferred upon us some blessings." The segregated nature of the meeting apparently was a source of contention and suspicion for some of the women. The testimony continues: "He told us to wash ourselves, and *that* almost made the women mad, and they said, as they were not admitted into the temple while this washing was being performed that some mischief was going on."[43]

Banking Ventures

The apparent distrust of the church leadership was evident in other facets of life in Kirkland as well. In 1836, Smith and some of his associates organized their own bank. Although it was denied a charter, Smith went ahead and printed currency notes—though they technically were not "bank" notes because they were issued under the title of "anti-banking" notes. Yet, they were widely circulated, and after a short time, fearing a run on the bank, Smith and his associate resigned as officers and the whole scheme collapsed. Many people—including faithful Mormons—believed that Smith had concocted the scheme for personal profit. As a result his life was endangered and he went into hiding, leaving Emma to struggle alone. She wrote to him complaining that "the situation of your business is such as is very difficult for me to do anything of any consequence."[44]

Missouri—the Land of Zion

Apostasy and financial problems were besetting the church in Kirkland, and for these and other reasons some of Smith's followers moved West to Missouri—the Land of Zion. But the problems were far more than a matter of simple geography. From the beginning, the Mormons had had serious problems in the "promised land." The lifestyle and beliefs of the Mormons roused controversy wherever they went, and this was particularly true in Missouri where settlers with a bent toward independence and individualism were naturally suspicious of neighbors who were a community unto themselves. "Many of the causes of these difficulties," writes Francis Gibbons, "lay in the rapid influx of Mormons, their distinctive religious beliefs, their aggressive proselytizing, and their cohesiveness, which some outsiders interpreted as clannishness. Perhaps more disturbing to the old settlers than almost anything else was the belief of the Latter-day Saints that Missouri was their promised land."[45]

Mob Violence

It was this fear of the Mormons, fanned by rumors of their secret military units, that more than anything else initiated mob violence against the early Mormon immigrants. "We are daily told," an old settler lamented, "that we (the Gentiles), of this country are to be cut off, and our lands appropriated by them for inheritances. Whether this is to be accomplished by the hand of the destroying angel, the judgments of God, or the arm of power, they are not fully agreed among themselves."[46]

All the grievances against the Mormons were summed up in a manifesto that was circulated among the old settlers in the summer of 1833. It was a warning for the Mormons to leave peaceably or to be driven out forcibly. A mass meeting in Jackson county that was called to discuss the matter was disrupted by the fury of the mob.

"The mob whipped some of the elders while the women and children ran off in terror to the nearby woods and fields." In many instances, the Mormons fought back, but in this case they were heavily outnumbered and agreed that their leaders and some of their families would vacate the county. This temporary arrangement by no means signaled the end to the violence. Some of the Mormons left, only to return to find their homes burned and to be met with more violence.[47]

When news of the mob violence reached Smith, he promptly received a revelation: "Behold, I say unto you, the redemption of Zion must needs come by power; Therefore I will raise up onto my people a man, who shall lead them like as Moses led the children of Israel. . . . Mine angels shall go up before you, and also my presence, and in time ye shall possess the goodly land."[48]

Zion's Camp

Within weeks Smith was preparing his followers for a military excursion to Missouri, and in May of 1834 they set out on the one thousand mile trek that would take them forty days. There were fewer than two hundred men, and they were poorly trained and equipped. Word of their coming preceded them, and the Missouri settlers were armed and waiting. Support from the governor did not materialize, and after a "series of anticlimaxes," including a cholera outbreak, Zion's Camp disbursed and the men were sent home, less than three weeks after their arrival. Some of the men were outraged by what they viewed as a colossal failure.

Wrote William McLellin: "Thousands of dollars by this wild expedition had been swallowed up, valuable lives lost, much human suffering endured, and many, very many privations undergone, as well as months of precious time spent worse than in vain." Perhaps the most significant outcome of this failed expedition was the stature Brigham Young gained through the experience—experience that would serve him well later when he would lead his followers to Salt Lake City.[49]

Most of the Mormons who remained in Missouri had been run out of Jackson county and were concentrated largely in Clay county, where they initially found some sympathetic supporters. But as their numbers increased there, so did hostilities. By the summer of 1836, the situation was becoming tense, and once again the Mormons were on the move to a less settled region.[50]

Fleeing Kirkland

By January of 1838, the situation in Kirkland, Ohio, had deteriorated to the point that Smith and his closest associate, Sidney Rigdon, got away "on the fastest horses they could find." Just a month before, Smith's leadership had been challenged to the point that a rival church was established. Only six of the early leaders of the church (the Twelve Apostles) remained loyal to Smith. Oliver Cowdery and the Whitmers led the dissidents. No longer could Smith maintain control of the Kirkland church, so despite the violence and bloodshed in Missouri, he and his followers had no real choice but to head West.[51]

With Smith and the vast majority of his followers now in Missouri, there was increased conflict. It was during this period that the paramilitary organization known as the Danites was formed. Its leader challenged the troops to "waste away the Gentiles by robbing and plundering them of their property, and in this way we will build up the kingdom of God." Though Smith himself was not directly involved with this group, and later spoke against it, the Danites became a feared segment of the Missouri Mormons. Compounding the apprehension of the non-Mormons were the vitriolic sermons of Sidney Rigdon, his most famous being his "salt sermon," which called for the extermination of apostates. As was true in Kirkland, the most troubling opposition for Smith and his followers were dissidents. Oliver Cowdery and other former close associates of Smith had also fled to Missouri, and they continued for some time to be a source of deep contention.[52]

Extermination Order

Opposition to the Mormons in Missouri reached a peak in the fall of 1838, when Governor Liliburn Boggs issued an order declaring that "The Mormons must be treated as enemies and *must be exterminated* or driven from the state." The state militia was called out and the Mormons were forced to lay down their arms. Smith and other Mormon leaders were taken prisoner and incarcerated in the Liberty, Missouri jail. With that turn of events, Brigham Young led the Mormon settlers back across the Mississippi where they would settle on its banks in a village in Illinois that became known as Nauvoo. Smith joined them the following April, following his jail term.[53]

Settling in Nauvoo

It was in Nauvoo, where Smith would spend the remainder of his short life, and where the most controversial aspects of Mormonism would come to light. Nauvoo grew quickly due to an influx of refugees fleeing hostile neighbors in Missouri and due to intense missionary work in England. Nearly three thousand "converts" had immigrated from England by 1843, most of them seeking economic security. The credit for this rapid influx of foreigners was due to the tireless efforts of Brigham Young, who was already gaining a host of loyal followers.[54]

It was in Nauvoo where Smith had time to develop church theology to a much greater extent than he had previously done. He delineated the thirteen articles of faith, which have become the standard creed of the church (See Appendix B). The articles contained standard Christian doctrine, except for the mention of the *Book of Mormon*, the emphasis on continuing revelation and the conviction that New Jerusalem will be built on the American continent. The articles did not contain any reference to polygamy which was then becoming an accepted practice nor was there any reference to temple rituals such as baptism for the dead.[55]

Plural Marriage

It was the issue of plural marriage—more than any other—that engendered controversy among the

Mormons themselves and drew criticism from the outside during the Nauvoo years, and this controversy and criticism continued until the practice was officially prohibited in 1890.

The practice of polygamy had actually begun many years earlier in 1831, shortly after Smith moved with his family and followers to Kirkland. According to close associates who testified years later, Smith "inquired of the Lord [if] the principle of taking more wives than one is a true principle, but the time had not yet come for it to be practiced." From the events that would soon come to light, it is not difficult to surmise that Smith was seeking to justify adultery—repeated sexual relationships with women other than Emma, his wife. It was in 1831, that he told Mary Rollins, who was then twelve, that she "was the first woman God commanded him to take as a plural wife." She eventually did become one of his wives, but she was not the first. That distinction was given to Fanny Alger, "a varry nice & Comly young woman," who at nineteen had come to live with the Smiths to help Emma with household tasks.[56]

Sordid Rumors

That a religious movement would justify polygamy is not in itself so astonishing. Indeed polygamy was practiced in the Old Testament, and has been practiced in various cultures throughout the world. What made Mormon polygamy so scandalous was the sordid nature of it, especially during the early decades. In the case of Fanny Alger, the "sealing" allegedly occurred in a hay mow.

Emma found them there at least once, and forced Fanny to leave when it was learned she was pregnant. When Oliver Cowdery learned of the matter, he was incensed, castigating Smith for the "dirty, nasty, filthy affair of his and Fanny Alger's."[57]

As rumors spread, some of Smith's associates sought to take matters into their own hands. While Smith was on a trip in 1835, the general assembly voted on an "Article on Marriage" to be added to the *Doctrine and Covenants.* It was simple and direct: "Inasmuch as this church of Christ has been reproached with the crime of fornication, and polygamy; we declare that we believe, that one man should have one wife; and one woman but one husband, except in case of death, when either is at liberty to marry again." Interestingly, that article was not removed until 1876, long after polygamy had officially been instituted by the church.[58]

Emma Smith's Opposition

It was in Nauvoo in the early 1840s when the issue of polygamy came to a head both personally and publicly for Smith. On the personal level, it was abundantly clear that Emma bitterly opposed the practice. Her opposition was such that Smith felt he needed a revelation in an effort to settle the matter: "And let mine handmaid, Emma Smith, receive all those that have been given unto my servant Joseph, and who are virtuous and pure before me; and those who are not pure, and have said they were pure, shall be destroyed, saith the Lord." The revelation not only confirmed that Smith could take additional wives, but it contained a death threat for Emma: "And I command mine handmaid, Emma Smith, to abide and cleave unto my servant Joseph, and to none else. But if she will not abide this commandment she shall be destroyed, saith the Lord; for I am the Lord thy God, and will destroy her if she abide not in my law."[59]

The revelation did not silence Emma, however, as Francis Gibbons relates in his laudatory biography of Smith:

> . . . . She rejected it and fought bitterly against it. In her moments of anguish, she was greatly influenced by prominent but weak men who had rejected the doctrine. Torn between her knowledge and better instincts and the basic jealousy of her nature, Emma oscillated between joy and despair, outgoing love and suspicion, depending on whose company she was in. Thus was manifested in her character a gross inconstancy that was both reminiscent of her agnostic father and prophetic of the wavering course she would follow once the steadying influence of her husband was gone.
>
> . . . . The thought of sharing her husband with another woman was an extremity Emma was not prepared to face. After her first violent reaction to the idea, she moderated even to the extent of participating in the selection of other mates for her husband, but her basic insecurity then dominated, and she returned to her original stance of unyielding opposition. It was in this rigid mold that her attitudes were finally cast, and so inflexible did they become that after the Prophet's death, she refused even to admit that he had ever taken another wife.[60]

It is not difficult to understand Emma's mixed reactions to her husband's escapades. On the one hand she was seeking to protect his image as the "prophet," and in that capacity she played the role of a facilitator. On the other hand, she was deeply hurt and angered by his attraction to other women and his obvious insensitivity to her. "Polygamy caused Emma long and agonizing doubts," writes Donna Hill. "Her Puritan ethics were affronted by plural marriage; she felt that her status was undermined and her prerogatives as a wife were threatened. She wondered if Joseph could be right in every other respect regarding the restored gospel and yet be led astray by overpowering sexual desires."[61]

The most oft-repeated story of her outrage is her confrontation with Eliza Snow. The accounts vary, but Eliza, who was pregnant by Smith, was either beaten with a broom handle or pushed down a stairway, injured to the point of miscarrying the child. Another incident that may reflect Emma's inability to accept plural marriage involved the poisoning of her husband. Smith "became suddenly sick at dinner and vomited so hard that he dislocated his jaw and 'raised fresh blood.'" That same day, according to one of his close associates, he accused Emma of trying to kill him. On one occasion after that it was reported that she demanded her husband renounce his other wives, threatening suicide if he did not.[62]

Smith's Wives

Historians differ on the precise number of women "married" to

Smith. Andrew Jensen arrived at the number twenty-seven, from actual testimonies from the women involved or from witnesses. Fawn Brodie calculated the number at forty-eight, and Stanley S. Ivins at eighty-four. It is believed that Emma knew of at least seven of these women and perhaps more, and that Smith had children by at least four of these women—though they were not publicly regarded as his children.[63]

Kingdom on Earth

It was the issue of polygamy that ended Smith's life. By 1842 rumors were rife about the rampant illicit sexual practices in Nauvoo, fueled largely by one John C. Bennett, who served as mayor and then had a falling out with Smith and others. Bennett published lurid inside stories of the Mormon leaders at Nauvoo, and outside opposition mounted. There were fears also among non-Mormons in the region concerning the potential military and political capabilities of the Mormons. Smith did nothing to ease those fears. In 1844, he became a candidate for President of the United States. Even before this, as Fawn Brodie writes, Smith was "fully intoxicated with power and drunk with visions of an empire of apocalyptic glory."[64]

It was this intoxication with power that prompted Smith in the spring of 1844 to establish a special governing council among his followers, a council that would be prepared to preside over the non-Mormon world and to install himself as "king." George Miller, the Presiding Bishop of the Church and one of the members of

that council, gave the following account:

> Joseph said to me . . . we will call together some of our wise men and proceed to set up the kingdom of God by organizing some of its officers. And from day to day he called some of the brethren about him, organizing them as princes in the kingdom of God, to preside over the chief cities of the Nation, until the number of fifty-three were called. In this council we ordained Joseph Smith as King on earth.[65]

It was this same intoxication with power that convinced Smith that he did not have to tolerate opposition from his enemies—even when it came in the form of newsprint. Publicly Smith and his loyal followers denied that polygamy was being practiced, even though it was widely practiced by his closest associates in Nauvoo. According to Klaus Hansen, he "apparently realized that polygamy could tear Mormonism asunder," and "he was intelligent enough to foresee the consequences if he would openly admit the existence of polygamy, given the climate of opinion in Illinois."[66]

Martyrdom of the "Prophet"

Having thus publicly denied his involvement and advocacy of polygamy, Smith was incensed when some of his own followers, in an effort to make reforms in the church, turned against him. They purchased a printing press and published a newspaper, the Nauvoo *Expositor*, exposing the gross immorality that was being practiced so widely among church members. These men were loyal Mormons themselves, professing to "know of a surety, that the religion of the Latter Day Saints, as originally taught by Joseph Smith . . . is verily true." But there was no openness to reform—at least not in the mind of Smith or his closest associates. He ordered the press to be destroyed, and his henchmen dutifully "dumped the press, type, and printed sheets into the street. Joseph blessed them 'in the name of the Lord' and promised that not a hair on their heads should be hurt."[67]

With that violent action, events moved quickly. On the following day, June 11, 1944, a large crowd of people gathered in Carthage and vowed to "exterminate . . . the wicked and abominable Mormon leaders." On June 12, Smith and seventeen other men involved in the destruction of the press were arrested and incarcerated in the nearby Carthage jail, where they remained for more than two weeks. Then almost without warning the local militia and town residents turned into a violent mob, and within a short time it was over. Smith and his brother Hyrum were shot.[68]

What was the effect of the murder of Smith and his brother Hyrum? A contemporary supporter summed it up by saying that the killers "did not realize that they were removing [them] to a sphere of far more extended usefulness, where they could more effectively help . . . to roll forward the designs of God in relation to this latter dispensation."[69]

Brigham Young and the Exodus to Utah

At the death of Smith, there was no automatic line of succession in place to prevent rival claims to power. Sidney Rigdon, who had opposed Smith on the issue of polygamy, had for many years been Smith's closest aid and was viewed as a natural choice by many. But others were determined that the mantle should not fall singly on the most charismatic leader, but rather on the church governing body—the Quorum of Twelve. Brigham Young, as the president of the Twelve, most forcefully made this claim. "I tell you in the name of the Lord," he admonished the crowd, "that no man can put another between the Twelve and the Prophet Joseph. . . . If the Twelve be the men to counsel you to finish the great work laid out by our departed Prophet, say so, and do not break your covenants by murmuring hereafter." After this appeal, his succession to power was made official by an assembly of the faithful in August of 1844.[70]

Opposition to Young's Leadership

There was opposition to be sure— from Sidney Rigdon and from others who believed God had placed his hand of approval on them. Following the death of Smith, it was written that "the Saints have divided into a surprisingly large number of sects, each of which claims to be carrying out the true intentions of its founder, who is believed to lead it in the world beyond." But it was Young who prevailed. In many ways, he lacked the winning personality of Smith, but he had leadership skills that proved indispensable in the stormy years that were on the horizon. To many he was the natural choice as successor to Smith, and on that August day

A drawing of the westward movement of Mormons to Utah. Courtesy of the Church of Jesus Christ of Latter Day Saints.

"many of those in attendance suddenly thought that they heard the voice of Joseph and saw the face of the deceased prophet instead. To the believing Saints it was a miracle. Joseph has personally placed his mantle on Brigham."[71]

The most intense opposition to the leadership of Young and the direction the church was taking came from Emma, Smith's widow. Almost immediately after his death, she found herself in financial straits with little help from the church. The church leaders even took possession of much of her husband's property, including his desk and personal papers. But the issue above all others that separated Emma from Young and the leadership of the church was polygamy. She bitterly opposed the practice while her husband was alive, and sought to suppress his part in it

after his death.[72] She and her followers refused to follow the leadership of Young, and they later settled in Independence, Missouri, which became the headquarters for the Reorganized Church of Jesus Christ of Latter-Day Saints. (See Appendix A.)

The death of Smith did not lessen the fears and apprehensions of the non-Mormons in Illinois and those in nearby Missouri, and tensions continued to flare. To avoid further violent opposition, Young and others began making plans to move further West, and in February of 1846, less than two years after Smith's death, the first migration of Mormons began. Their destination was uncertain except that they planned to settle in a territory where settlers were few and land was plenty. Their journey was slow and arduous, and there were extended encampments along the way. Not until the summer of 1847 did they arrive at the Great Salt Lake. This was their promised land, Young proclaimed as he approached the valley from the mountains: "This is the place where I, in vision, saw the ark of the Lord resting; this is the place where on we will plant the soles of our feet, and where the Lord will place his name amongst his people."[73]

It was Brigham Young who would wield his powerful leadership in unifying the Mormons as they settled in the Great Basin in the three decades that followed until his death in 1877. He became "Prophet, Seer, and Revelator," as Smith had been, though he felt somewhat uncomfortable with those "charismatic" expectations at first. He was an organizer, and it was in that realm that his greatest contributions were made. He was very unlike Smith in many ways. According to Lawrence Foster, "Young exercised real power, and he felt little need to promulgate formal revelations to bolster his authority. Instead, Young simply told the Saints what to do and expected them to obey."[74]

As the head of the growing religious settlement in Utah, Young served in many capacities. During his earliest years in the Great Basin, he supervised the massive influx of immigrants, charted new settlement areas, and sought to create a new economic order of self-sufficiency. He worked closely with the militia leaders to secure the defense of the region, and he served as a judge of sorts. He was frequently forced to function as an arbitrator in financial and property matters, and family disputes were an ever present drain on his emotional well-being. When

problems flared up in polygamous marriages, he was expected to have solutions—an expectation he often refused to accept: "When men have wives and cannot, or do not, live happily, and throw their family troubles, disputes, and cares upon me, or take a course by which their wives do so," he complained, "I think it wise for them to exercise a little patience and strive to learn wisdom in the conduct of those matters, that I may not be so frequently troubled with family difficulties."[75]

Opposition from Settlers and the Military

The most pressing concerns of Young and the Mormon settlers were the same as they had been in Ohio, in Missouri, and in Illinois—violent confrontation with their neighbors and law enforcement agencies. Indeed, the U.S. Army was ordered into the region in 1857, much to the indignation of Young, who declared martial law to repel the invasion "by a hostile force, who are evidently assailing us to accomplish our overthrow and destruction." What followed has been termed the Mormon War of 1857–58, and newspapers sought to sensationalize the hostilities and verbal threats. There were no real battles and the "war" was mainly a retreat of Mormon settlers who feared the Army presence.[76]

Mountain Meadows Massacre

The most deplorable atrocity to occur during the years of Utah settlement was what has become known as the Mountain Meadows Massacre of 1857. "Young did not order the butchery, but with fiery speeches he . . . encouraged it." There are many conflicting stories as to exactly what happened at Mountain Meadows, but when it was all over more than one hundred Arkansas immigrants had been slaughtered. John D. Lee, the highest ranking Mormon at the scene, initially blamed the crime on Indians, but prior to his execution in 1877 for his part in the atrocity, he gave an entirely different account— one of bloodthirsty revenge against non-Mormons that involved the "butchering all of the men and women and all but seventeen of the children."[77]

When Lee gave Brigham Young the news of the slaughter, Young reportedly "wept like a child." But the next day, after seeking God's guidance, he told Lee that he was convinced that "not a drop of innocent blood" was shed. "I have direct evidence from God that the act was a just one," he insisted, "that it was in accord with God's will. . . . Never tell any one, and write me a long letter laying all the blame on the Indians." Young could justify such a reaction by his strong commitment to blood atonement, the belief that shedding guilty blood allows souls a chance at salvation before the last resurrection:

I have seen scores and hundreds of people for whom there would have been a chance (in the last resurrection there will be) if their lives had been taken and their blood spilled on the ground as a smoking incense to the Almighty, but who are now angels to the devil until our elder brother Jesus Christ, uses them up-conquers death, hell and the grave. I have known a great many men who have left this church for whom there is no chance whatever for exaltation; but if their blood had been spilled it would have been better for them. The wickedness and ignorance of nations forbid this principle's being in full force, but the time will come when the law of God will be in full force.[78]

Widely-recognized Leader

Young was an imposing figure, widely recognized outside the Mormon community as a political and religious leader to be reckoned with, as Stanley Hirshon relates:

From the corners of the earth great and famous men journeyed to Salt Lake City to view him. Generals like Ulysses S. Grant and William T. Sherman; statesmen like William H. Seward and Schuyler Colfax; journalists and literary figures like Ralph Waldo Emerson, Horace Greeley, Mark Twain, and Samuel Bowles; explorers and adventurers like Richard F. Burton and Grenville M. Dodge; and showmen like P.T. Barnum came to see and talk to him. For Brigham Young was a marvel of his age: the husband of seventy wives, the father of fifty-six children, the colonizer of vast areas of the West, the Yankee prophet of God, the Moses of the modern children of Israel, the religious imperialist bent upon conquering the world.[79]

When Young died in 1877, he left behind a highly structured social order. Through his unflagging organizational and economic efforts, he administered the settlement of more than three hundred Mormon communities. "He championed the cause of the poorer saints and inveighed tirelessly against domination by outside economic forces and against what one church epistle described as 'the growth of riches in the hands of

Brigham Young. Courtesy of the Church of Jesus Christ of Latter Day Saints.

a few at the expense of many.'" Yet, "he himself became one of the territory's wealthiest businessmen.... Life among the Mormon elite in Salt Lake City in the time of Young took on the grand style he followed with his fancy homes, carriages, and entourage of bodyguards and attendants."[80]

Significant changes occurred in the church following the death of Young. Indeed, his death "marked the end of the period in which church affairs were dominated by a Mormon version of the cult of personality. Under the new leaders the various levels of the hierarchy grew and became more significant."[81]

The 1890 Manifesto

One of the most traumatic upheavals to occur in Mormon history was the discontinuance of polygamy in 1890. Opposition had been mount-

ing, and in 1887, the Edmunds-Tucker Act passed congress, which in effect dissolved the church and prohibited those who refused to sign a pledge to obey the laws from voting or holding office. The law was appealed, but in May of 1890, the Supreme Court upheld the law. With no other real alternative, President Wilford Woodruff issued the now-famous Manifesto a few months later that banned polygamy. Privately, Woodruff viewed the Manifesto as a temporary measure to appease the government, and polygamy continued to be widely practiced by Mormons in the years that followed.[82]

The personal and public ramifications of the 1890 Manifesto were enormous. The polygamous wives had mixed emotions. The first wife stood to gain by the decision, but the other wives often lost everything. That loss is reflected in the testimony of one such wife: "I was there in the tabernacle the day of the Manifesto, and I tell you it was an awful feeling. There President Woodruff read the Manifesto that made me no longer a wife and might make me homeless. I sat there by my mother and she looked at me and said, 'How can you stand this?'" This new pronouncement was also devastating to men. How could they suddenly renounce this central doctrine of their faith? Brigham Young had been determined that no one would ever tamper with the doctrine of plural marriage. His language was explicit: "Now if any of you will deny the plurality of wives and continue to do so, I promise that you will be damned.... Take this revelation ... and deny it in your feelings, and I promise that you will be damned."[83]

A polygamous family in the early days of settlement. From *"Tell It All": The Story of a Life's Experience in Mormonism* by T.B.H. Stenhouse.

For all of Mormon society, an old era had passed and a new era was beginning. This tumult is summed up by Robert Gottlieb and Peter Wiley:

Eighteen-ninety proved to be the most dramatic watershed in the history of the church, although it took another six years for Utah to gain statehood. Some historians would later argue that the history of the original Mormon church came to an end at this time. Others would refer to the Manifesto of 1890 as the great capitulation or, simply, the surrender. The attempt to build a separate nation ended with the Utah War and the triumph of the federal government in the Civil War. Joseph Smith's call to revolutionize the world through the establishment of the Kingdom of God by means of the secret Council of Fifty gradually gave way to the pleas for statehood and John Taylor's defense of republican principles. The great cooperative experiments championed by Brigham Young as a means to economic independence collapsed of internal discord and external pressure. And now the Saints were being called upon to give up celestial marriage. The Saints no longer anxiously awaited the millennium. . . .

Mormonism's most distinctive features gradually faded into the past and became the stuff of history. Henceforth, the Saints would concentrate on building up their church as a purely religious body as they came to identify more and more with the America of Main Street and the Model T.[84]

Gone were the days of larger-than-life personalities, and gone were the days when doctrine was changing almost daily. "In the modern church, there was little room for doctrinal innovation. There was no room for new visions. Instead, the teachings of Joseph Smith were being systematized by such theologians as James E. Talmage, while some of the rough edges were pared away and cleaned up for public presentation."[85]

Church Structure and Authority

One of the most striking features of the modern church has been its highly organized structure. Mormon congregations are known as wards and they ideally range in size from two hundred and fifty to five hundred. When a ward reaches the upper limit it splits to form two wards, with the hope that they each will double in size and split again. Generally two or three (or more) wards share facilities in populated areas—staggering their services and weekly meetings so as to accommodate the various congregations. The various wards in a geographical locality form a stake, headed by a stake president. Bishops preside over the wards. "All authority in the Mormon Church comes directly from the top; that is, the prophet who expects (and generally gets) obedience to his edicts. Much of the high leadership of the church has for its 150 years of existence been in the hands of about twenty families—the Smiths, Romneys, Kimballs, Cannons, Richards, Bensons, and others."[86]

General Conferences

Although the church is run from the top down, there is a sense of congregationalism at the local level. Twice annually the church meets in General Conference, which permits representatives from the local congregations to feel they have a part in the function of their church as a whole. Indeed, the high-ranking members of the general quorums (the First Quorum of the Seventy, The Presidency of the First Quorum of Seventy, the Council of the Twelve, and the First Presidency) are assigned to their positions "by higher authorities," but "must be sustained in their positions by the vote of the people over whom they preside." In some respects, these votes are little different than votes taken for one slate of officers in a totalitarian state. "With the routine dispatch born of frequent practice," writes Jan Shipps, "they [the conferees] handle matters of ecclesiastical business, voting at every General Conference, usually unanimously, to sustain the general officers of the church and, when necessary, forming themselves into constituent assemblies to accept new revelation as 'the will of the Lord.' "[87]

The Priesthood

The priesthood is central to Mormonism. It was instituted by God even before the church was actually founded, according to official Mormon tradition—though there is other evidence that would suggest that it was initiated later by Sydney Rigdon.[88] The Mormon version documents the "restoration of the priesthood" as occurring on May 15, 1829, near Harmony, Pennsylvania, along the Susquehanna River. Here John the Baptist appeared as an angel to Joseph Smith and Oliver Cowdery and said: "Upon you my fellow servants, in the name of Messiah I confer the Priesthood of Aaron, which holds the keys of the ministering of angels, and of the gospel of repentance, and of baptism by immersion for the remission of sins; and this shall never be taken again from the earth, until the sons of Levi do offer again an offering unto the Lord in righteousness."[89] The higher Melchizedek Priesthood was given soon after this by Peter, James, and John. Mormons from childhood hear these stories and recently have been able to view a dramatized recreation of the "Restoration of the Priesthood" on a professionally produced home video.

Whatever the origin of the priesthood was in Mormonism, it quickly became the authority base of the church. The Melchizedek priesthood "directs all the affairs of the church (general, stake, ward and mission). It has its various quorums, namely, the High Priest's Quorum, the Quorum of the Seventy, and the Elder's Quorum (in descending order of authority)." The lower Aaronic Priesthood handles responsibilities that correspond with its particular quorums: "the Priests, Teacher's, and Deacon's Quorums. Every male member of the church who is over twelve years of age ... has the privilege of being ordained to some office in the priesthood, if he lives 'worthily.' "[90]

Women are not permitted to enter the priesthood in the Mormon church, which means that a woman who has served faithfully for many years can be suddenly surpassed in authority by her adolescent twelve-year-old son. But the place of single women in the church is no better. Latayne Scott, in her book *The Mormon Mirage*, reflects on the role of women in Mormonism from her own experience:

> I was once sitting in a Relief Society meeting when the speaker made an attention-getting remark. In explaining the relationship of husband and wife she said, "Women are the doormats upon which men wipe their feet before going in to God."
>
> I was stunned. I looked open-mouthed at my friends in the room. Surely someone else was as outraged about this as I! But all around me young women were nodding in contemplation and agreement.
>
> This is an extreme example of an extreme attitude. But it is reflected in the Mormon beliefs that a woman can't be resurrected without a man to call her temple name to raise her from the dead, and that she can't be "exalted" without a husband. The supreme role of men and their priesthood in Mormonism is underlined by the continued emphasis of woman's dependence on man.[91]

It may be surprising to some that women are among the strongest opponents of opening the priesthood up to their sex. "We don't need the priesthood," insists Jaynann Morgan Payne, a former beauty queen. "I have all I can handle as it is." Besides, she argues, "A woman holds the priesthood through her husband." But there have been dissenting voices to this viewpoint, the most outspoken and widely publicized being Sonia Johnson. She "was a practicing Mormon, holding down three church positions, paying her full tithing, and regularly attending ward meetings"—and a strong supporter of the Equal Rights Amendment. She and other Mormon feminists spoke out against discrimination in their own church as well as in society at large. Many women were offended that twelve-year-old boys with the Aaronic priesthood had authority in the church that was denied them. This controversy created such tension in the church that in 1979, Johnson was excommunicated, a story that is told in her book *From Housewife to Heretic.*[92]

Women are not the only segment of the church who have been denied the priesthood. Until 1978, blacks were also excluded as well. The rationale for this was based on the Book of Abraham, which states that through Ham "sprang that race which preserved the curse in the land"—the curse being that "as pertaining to the Priesthood."[93] In the 1960s, during the early years of the Civil Rights Movement, there were rumblings in the church about the policy on blacks. This was aggravated when, because of this policy, missionaries were denied permission to enter Nigeria. Protests by the NAACP and other groups were organized in Salt Lake City, but the hierarchy was slow to move. "Ezra Taft Benson, the most politically outspoken member of the quorum of the Twelve [since promoted to the position of Prophet], saw the 1965 demonstrations . . . as a sign that there were traitors in the church and that communists were 'using the civil rights movement to promote revolution and the eventual takeover of this country.' "[94]

By the 1970s, it was apparent that the controversy over race would not go away, especially after Jerald and Sandra Tanner published material discrediting the Book of Abraham. Mormons were taking the issue into their own hands, and in one instance a Mormon elder himself ordained a black to the priesthood. The ordination was regarded as invalid and the elder involved was dismissed from the church. Finally the pressure became so great that the church reversed its position—or rather, God changed his mind, according to the Mormon account. On June 9, 1978 a new revelation was received by Spencer W. Kimball, the Prophet of the church, and the announcement of that was made public:

> . . . We have pleaded long and earnestly in behalf of these, our faithful brethren, spending many hours in the upper room of the Temple supplicating the Lord for divine guidance.

> He has heard our prayers, and by revelation has confirmed that the long-promised day has come when every faithful, worthy man in the church may receive the holy priesthood, with power to exercise its divine authority, and enjoy with his loved ones every blessing that flows therefrom, including the blessings of the temple. Accordingly all worthy male members of the church may be ordained to the priesthood without regard for race or color.[95]

Worship and Religious Observances

Mormons, like members of other religious faiths, vary in their levels of commitment. Some zealously practice and promote their faith, while others are more passive in their involvement, and still others are Mormon in name only—"jack Mormons," as they are referred to.

Ward Meetings

Mormons are expected to participate in two weekly religious meetings—the sacrament meeting on

Sunday and the Family Home Evening, which is an evening (usually Monday) set aside for family activities that "vary from outings like ice skating to popping corn and hearing a spiritual lesson presented by a family member."[96]

The degree of commitment among Mormons on the local level is generally measured by enthusiastic involvement in ward activities, rather than on deep personal piety or charismatic religious enthusiasm. Indeed, weekly religious meetings are often dull and with little evidence of fervor. Fiery sermons or gripping testimonies are virtually nonexistent. The meetings are "modest" and "informal affairs," according to Jan Shipps:

> Without a professional clergy to plan and carry out Sunday services, Mormon Wards have programs planned and carried out by the Saints themselves, a practice that leads to considerable variation from meeting to meeting and week to week. Ritualized in that the sacrament is always served and hymns are always directed by a choral leader from the stand, and in that on Fast Sundays, the first Sunday of every month, testimonies are always borne and babies are sometimes blessed, these local Latter-Day Saint Sunday programs are distinguished from conventional worship patterns by an absence of liturgy and classic sermonizing. In many local Mormon meetings, moreover, movement in the chapel provides a contrapuntal accompaniment to the proceedings on the stand. As teenaged Aaronic priesthood holders pass the sacramental bread and water to all who are in the congregation including babes-in-arms, as latecomers arrive and early departers leave, and as Saints too young to have developed meeting-length attention

spans move constantly to and fro, these local gatherings sometimes seem alive with sound.[97]

Word of Wisdom and Tithing

The Word of Wisdom or health code of the Mormons was instituted in the early years of the church, and its specifications are found in the *Doctrine and Covenants*, Section 89. Here the Word of Wisdom is offered "not by commandment or constraint" and is "given for a principle with promise, adapted to the capacity of the weak and the weakest of all saints." Indeed, in the early years—perhaps because of opposition—it was a suggested rule of life. Today, adhering to the Word of Wisdom is required of all those who would participate in temple rituals. Restricted substances include "wine or strong drink," "tobacco," and "hot drinks."[98] Strict Mormons also abstain from hot chocolate (and chocolate altogether) and from soft drinks—particularly those with caffeine. It is safe to assume, however, that vast numbers of Mormons disregard the Word of Wisdom even as Roman Catholics disregard restrictions against birth control.

Another practice among Mormons that has been observed since the depression of the 1930s is that of food storage. Mormons are expected to keep a two year supply of nonperishable food items. They are likewise expected to contribute to the church welfare program by donating such things as farm products and household supplies that assist families in need. Mormons are also expected to tithe, a directive that was instituted at the turn of the century. "The interpretation of the law of tithing as a strict ten percent of one's gross income is the reason that the Utah church is so much wealthier than the Reorganized church, which requires ten percent of one's 'increase'—what is left over after living expenses." According to Latayne Scott, "a rough estimate of the amount that a faithful Mormon will give annually, including tithe, ward quotas, contributions to welfare projects, and the cost of sending children on missions would average about twenty-six percent of his income." The majority of Mormons, however, do not even pay a full tithe.[99]

Temple Ceremonies

Mormon temple ceremonies are secretive rituals that have been copied to a large extent from Masonry. Freemansonry is an international fraternal organization with its earliest origins in the twelfth century. It is based on secretive, symbolical and allegorical religious concepts, and places a heavy emphasis on humanitarian activity. The movement began flourishing in nineteenth-century America and had a powerful influence on early Mormonism. In Mormonism, only worthy members are permitted to participate in the secret temple ceremonies and they are admonished not to reveal the nature of them to others. Of these rituals performed in the temple, the celestial marriage is the one that is most treasured by Mormons. Only through a temple marriage can a Mormon receive the highest exaltation in the after life. "If you want salvation in the fullest, that is exaltation in the kingdom of God, so that

you may become his sons and his daughters," wrote Joseph Fielding Smith in *Doctrines of Salvation*, "you have got to go into the temple of the Lord and receive these holy ordinances which belong to that house which cannot be had elsewhere." Later on in that same volume he wrote "Civil Marriage Makes Servants in Eternity," and "Celestial Marriage Makes Gods in Eternity."[100]

Temple ceremonies require special garments to be worn during the ritual itself and following the ritual a special undergarment is to be worn at all times. This practice originated with Joseph Smith himself, and the pattern was considered so sacred that the design could not be changed. For years "Mormon leaders vigorously maintained that the 'garments' must be 'worn as intended, down to the wrist and ankles, and around the neck,' and that they could not be altered from 'the very pattern in which God gave them.'" But despite their efforts to enforce conformity, the garments were "mutilated" from the earliest times, and in recent years, to accommodate stylish fashions, abbreviated modifications have been permitted.[101]

Most of the temple ceremonies are for the benefit of Mormons now living, but beginning in the 1870s, "the Saints earnestly began their work for the dead." The ordinance was initiated by Smith himself, who was deeply distressed by his brother Alvin's death which occurred in 1823, some years before the founding of the church. How could Alvin be given the opportunity to embrace the new religion? "The solution to the problem was the doctrine of baptism for the dead, to be performed vicariously in

Early photo of Salt Lake City Temple. Courtesy of the Church of Jesus Christ of Latter Day Saints.

this world. This is one major reason why Mormons diligently seek out the genealogies of their ancestors, for whom they are then baptized in specially consecrated temples." Baptism for a deceased individual does not automatically turn them into Mormons. "In keeping with the principle of free agency the deceased spirits are free either to accept or reject the work done in their behalf—to be either saved or damned."[102]

Because of the Mormon teaching that a great apostasy developed in the early church and continued until the time of Joseph Smith, the practice of baptizing for the dead quickly became a means of reclaiming people who had died generations and even many centuries earlier. Mormon president Wilford Woodruff, who is remembered for his revelation banning polygamy in 1890, gave a testimony which illustrates this determined effort to win celebrated figures of history to Mormonism:

> . . . two weeks before I left St. George, the spirits of the dead gathered around me, wanting to know why we did not redeem them. . . . These were the signers of the Declaration of Independence, and they waited on me for two days and two nights. . . . I straightway went into the baptismal font and called upon brother McCallister to baptize me for the signers of the Declaration of Independence, and fifty other eminent men, making one hundred in all, including John Wesley, Columbus, and others; I then baptized him for every President of the United States, except three; and when their cause is just, somebody will do the work for them.[103]

Some years ago a wealthy woman from the East Coast traveled many times to Salt Lake City for the express purpose of being baptized for the dead. She was baptized some thirty thousand times for deceased friends and relatives and such notable figures as Alexander the Great, Nebuchadnezzar, Julius Caesar, Napoleon, and Cleopatra. A Mormon elder later gave his appraisal of her work: "I believe that this lady saved more souls than Jesus."[104]

The actual saving of souls, however, was left to Mormons who had died. According to Brigham Young, these were "just as busy in the spirit world as you and I are here. They are preaching, preaching all the time, and preparing the way for us to hasten our work in building temples here and everywhere." Indeed, this underworld of "spirits in prison" was viewed as a most productive mission field.[105]

Doctrinal Distinctives

Mormon doctrine is extremely difficult to grasp, if for no other reason than it is filled with inconsistencies. Early teachings are very different than those of the Brigham Young era, which differ significantly from beliefs today. They not only differ, but in many cases they blatantly contradict each other. Yet, the words of Joseph Smith and the prophets who succeeded him were said to have come from God. What is most apparent even at a cursory glance at Mormon doctrine is that it is very far removed from historic Christian orthodoxy. Mormon doctrine is not merely a distortion of basic Christian doctrine, as would be true of Jehovah's Witnesses doctrine. It is rather an altogether new religion, couched within the Christian framework but far removed from biblical truth. It should also be noted that the *Book of Mormon*, thought to be the "bible" of Mormons, contains virtually no Mormon doctrine. That is to be found in later writings of Smith and other prophets of the church.

The Godhead

One of the most blatant Mormon heresies relates to the doctrine of the Godhead. The teaching on God is an example of how significantly Mormon doctrine changed even during the lifetime of Joseph Smith. The *Book of Mormon* presents a Trinitarian view of God. An example is 3

Nephi 11:27. Here Jesus is speaking: "... verily I say unto you, that the Father, and the Son, and the Holy Ghost are one; and I am in the Father, and the Father in me, and the Father and I are one." Mosiah 15:2 amplifies this in speaking of the incarnation and deity of Christ: "And because he [Jesus] dwelleth in flesh he shall be called the Son of God.... And thus the *flesh* becoming subject to the Spirit, or the Son to the Father, being one God...." If there was any doubt about the number of gods ruling the universe, the issue is settled in Alma 11:28–29, when the question is asked, "Is there more than one God?" and the answer is an unequivocal "no."

These verses, however, are not viewed as definitive on the teachings of the Godhead. They were superceded by Joseph Smith himself in later writings. By 1844, God was no longer perceived as a singular being, as Smith made clear to his followers when giving a funeral message (known as the King Follet Discourse), later published in the Mormon newspaper:

> First, God himself, who sits enthroned in yonder heavens, is a man like unto one of yourselves, that is the great secret.... I am going to tell you how God came to be God. We have imagined that God was God from all eternity... God himself; the Father of us all dwelt on an earth the same as Jesus Christ himself did... You have got to learn how to be Gods yourselves.[106]

Brigham Young expanded on this teaching when he declared that "He [God] is our Father—the Father of our spirits, and was once a man in mortal flesh as we are, and is now an exalted being. How many Gods there are, I do not know. But there never was a time when there were not Gods.... God has once been a finite being."[107] He also claimed that "we are created ... to become Gods like unto our Father in heaven" and that "man is the king of kings and lord of lords in embryo."[108] This teaching is summed up in the Mormon eternal law of progression: "As man is, God once was; as God is, man may become."

The whole of Mormon doctrine and ritual is hinged on the concept of the plurality of gods. "Indeed, this doctrine of plurality of Gods is so comprehensive and glorious," writes Mormon theologian Bruce McConkie, "that it reaches out and embraces every exalted personage. Those who attain exaltation are gods." For a Mormon, salvation is exaltation, which comes through the "gate" of celestial marriage, and, according to McConkie, it is "eternal life, the kind of life which God lives."[109]

As a man, God has the physical features of a man. This is made clear in *Doctrine and Covenants:* "The Father has a body of flesh and bones as tangible as man's; the Son also; but the Holy Ghost has not a body of flesh and bones, but is a personage of Spirit. Were it not so, the Holy Ghost could not dwell in us."[110] If God was once a man, who was he? Brigham Young taught that he was Adam, which would be a logical conclusion in light of the Mormon teaching that men become gods and with their wives propagate the planets. "When our father Adam came in the garden of Eden," declared Young, "he came into it with a celestial body, and brought Eve, one of his wives, with him. He helped to make and organized this world. He is MICHAEL, the Archangel, the ANCIENT OF DAYS! about whom holy men have written and spoken. He is our FATHER and our GOD, and the only God with whom we have to do."[111]

Although, the Adam-God teaching of Young is no longer officially embraced by Mormons, the essentials of the basic doctrine are still intact. Polytheism is at the very core of Mormon teaching, which maintains that the planets in the universe are each ruled by a different god. Elohim is the god of this planet, and he had a wife who bore his offspring as the Eternal Mother. Milton Hunter, a high Mormon official, has written, "The stupendous truth of the existence of a Heavenly Mother, as well as a Heavenly Father, became established facts in Mormon theology."[112]

The greatest of Elohim's offspring was Jesus, as James Talmage, a Mormon Apostle, has written in *The Articles of Faith:*

> Jesus Christ is the Son of Elohim both as spiritual and bodily offspring; that is to say, Elohim is literally the Father of the spirit of Jesus Christ and also of the body in which Jesus Christ performed His mission in the flesh. . . . That Jesus Christ, whom we also know as Jehovah, was the executive of the Father, Elohim, in the work of creation. . . .[113]

As the literal physical son of God, Jesus was conceived naturally, according to Mormon teaching, through sexual intercourse between God and his wife—it would be blasphemous to imagine that God committed adultery. That being the case, who was his wife? The Eternal Mother spoken of by Milton Hunter? Apparently not. "The fleshly body of Jesus required a Mother as well as a Father," argued Mormon Apostle Orson Pratt." Hence the Virgin Mary must have been, for the time being, the lawful wife of God the Father."[114] As to the doctrine of the Virgin Birth, the Mormons deny it. "The birth of the Savior was a natural occurrence unattended with any degree of mysticism, and the Father God was the literal parent of Jesus in the flesh as well as in the spirit."[115]

Despite their obvious polytheism, Mormons maintain they are Trinitarians. This was not always the case. According to the 1835 edition of *Doctrine and Covenants* there are "two personages in the Godhead," the Holy Spirit being the "mind" of the Father and the Son. "The Mormon leaders now teach that there are three personages in the Godhead— the Father and the Son both being personages of tabernacle and the Holy Ghost being a personage of spirit."[116]

Preexistent Spirit Life

Mormons believe that all human beings preexisted as spirits prior to their birth in physical bodies. "We were all created untold ages before we were placed on this earth," wrote Joseph Fielding Smith. "Man, animals and plants were not created in the spirit at the time of creation of the earth, but long before."[117] This belief is taken largely from *The Pearl of Great Price.* In the Book of Moses, it states, "For I, the Lord God created all things of which I have spoken, spiritually, before they were naturally upon the face of the earth."[118] In the Book of Abraham, the Lord says to Abraham "I rule in the heavens above and in the earth beneath, in all wisdom and prudence, over all the intelligences." Abraham responds: "Now the Lord had shown unto me, Abraham, the intelligences that were organized before the world was."[119]

This concept of preexistence presents a picture of a parent-child relationship between God and every human being. "All men and women," wrote Joseph Fielding Smith, "are in the similitude of the universal Father and Mother, and are literally the sons and daughters of Deity." The preexistent spirits were the "offspring of celestial parentage."[120] In *Articles of Faith*, James Talmage compares man's preexistence to that of Christ's: "Yet Christ was born a child among mortals; and it is consistent to infer that if His earthly birth was the union of a preexistent or antemortal spirit with a mortal body such also is the birth of every member of the human family."[121]

Eschatology

Mormon eschatology, like such apocalyptic movements as the Seventh-day Adventists, the Jehovah's Witnesses, the Worldwide Church of God, and the Unification Church, is based on special revelation for a very exclusive group of people and is qualified by geographical or chronological limitations. For the Mormons, the prophetic declarations came by "a Revelation of Jesus Christ unto his servant Joseph Smith," in 1832, while he was still living in Kirkland. In this instance, according to Smith, Jesus foretold a future "gathering of his saints to stand upon Mount Zion, which shall be the city of New Jerusalem . . . which is appointed by the finger of the Lord, in the western boundaries of the State of Missouri." Here a temple was to be built, marking the place where Christ would return at his second coming.[122]

Christ's second coming marks the beginning of the millennium, at which time the dead and living Mormons will be "caught up to meet him," and then they will return to earth to live in a thousand-year period of peace. At the beginning of the millennium, the wicked will be 'burned as stubble,'" and at the end they will be raised and given a second chance. After that there are four levels of final destiny. At the top is the Celestial Kingdom, a glorious realm on the earth, for those who have been married in the temple and have received full exaltation. Here they "shall dwell in the presence of God and his Christ forever and ever." The Terrestrial Kingdom, located in some other sphere, is the second highest level which is reserved for Mormons who were not faithful enough to attain the Celestial Kingdom and non-Mormons who lived righteous lives. Those consigned to this realm will "receive the presence of the Son, but not the fullness of the Father. The Telestial Kingdom is for the unrighteous, while hell is reserved only for a relative few—the sons of perdition—the devil and his angels as well as those individuals who are hopelessly unrepentant."[123]

To many the future dwelling place of the Mormons is confusing because those who enjoy exaltation, as a result of their temple marriage, will enter the Celestial Kingdom, but exalted Mormon men are also promised that they will reign as gods on their own planets. So while "the

Celestial Kingdom will be located on the sanctified earth . . . it will seem to all celestial beings that they are in the presence of God, even though He will be on his own planet, Kolob."[124]

Worldwide Expansion

One of the most striking aspects of Mormonism is its rapid increase worldwide since beginning in 1830. From a tiny band of zealots this movement expects to reach a membership of ten million by the year 2000. Although the expansion has surged in recent decades with new temples being built at an alarming rate, the missionary impulse was strong from the earliest years. Mormons left their homes and carried out missionary work among Indians on the frontier and also went into European countries. They went in teams and entered communities in an attempt to saturate the area, family by family, with the "restored gospel." A common practice then (and now) was to try to win professing Christians to their point of view. An example of this occurred in Denmark, one of the Mormons' most productive mission fields. In 1850, Erastus Snow and three others opened up the work there by becoming part of a local Baptist church. One of the early Mormon converts, who later left the movement, wrote of how the converts were won:

> One Sunday we saw . . . four strangers enter the meeting hall and sit down near the doorway. No one paid any further attention to them or had any slightest inkling as yet regarding their intentions. But the sober, almost deferential piety which they showed, in common with all Americans, at reli-

gious services, gave rise to a favorable opinion of them. They came frequently, made the acquaintance of the pastor and many members of the congregation, and gained admission to their homes, and then began little by little to speak about their mission, and they preached their new gospel. Their narrations concerning the miraculous call of the new prophet and his revelations naturally awakened great interest and discussion, and so Pastor Mönster proceeded to an investigation of the matter. But Apostle Snow handled him so cleverly that he himself, without actually becoming a Mormon, seemed for a time to be altogether drawn in that direction and convinced of the divine calling of the new prophet. . . .

> The teachings of the missionaries found a fruitful soil among the Baptists. There was even talk of entire congregations going over to Mormonism, with Pastor Mönster at their head. It did not actually go that far, but many did convert to the doctrine of the new apostle, and a new denomination was speedily organized under the name of "The Church of Jesus Christ of Latter Day Saints."[125]

The work in Denmark grew rapidly. In 1851, the *Book of Mormon* was translated into Danish. By 1853, the outreach had expanded to the point that the converts were divided into six branches. The work has continued unabated, and by the mid-1960s there were nearly two hundred missionaries assigned to the country.[126]

Short-term Missions

The recent surge in missionary outreach began in 1973 under the late President Spencer W. Kimball's administration. During a twelve year period the number of countries with mission bases increased from fifty to ninety-six, and the missionary force had reached thirty thousand by 1981. The vast majority of the missionaries are young men who have volunteered for two-year assignments, to fulfill an obligation to their church. In the words of Kimball: "Every boy and many girls and couples should serve missions. Every prospective missionary should prepare morally, spiritually, mentally, and financially all of his life in order to serve faithfully, efficiently and well in the Great Program of Missionary work. . . . A mission is not only a privilege and an opportunity but a solemn duty and obligation."[127]

Mormon missionaries. Courtesy of the Church of Jesus Christ of Latter Day Saints.

Despite the short-term nature of the missionary endeavors, the work is concentrated and the number of converts reported is impressive. According to Mormon missiologist R. Lanier Britsch, "Most Mormon missionaries proselyte full-time, i.e., 60 to 70 hours a week. Proselyting missionaries use several methods or combinations of methods in establishing contacts or teaching situations. House-to-house tracking, that is, knocking on doors and leaving printed information, is the most common approach."[128]

To accommodate the influx of converts worldwide, there has been a corresponding increase in the translations of the *Book of Mormon* and the building of temples. In 1985, a Mormon publication reported the completion of the seventieth translation. By 1986, there were forty temples worldwide, sixteen of which had been dedicated in the previous three years.[129]

Weak Commitments

Behind the facade of flawless success, however, are some serious problems. There are more dropouts in the missionary force than the church would like to admit—partly due to the intense pressure for each missionary to win at least six converts a year. This pressure leads to shortcuts that reduce long-lasting results. In investigating Mormon missionary methods, Kenneth Woodward found that "the number and duration of conversions are highly ephemeral." He interviewed a former zone leader in Bolivia who admitted that dozens of Indian families were baptized by a Mormon missionary and later rebaptized by the next missionary on the circuit. Another problem he found was that of "Dolly Baptisms—teen-age girls who are more attracted by the missionaries than by the Holy Spirit and hope to come to the United States as wives."[130]

Contemporary Issues

Despite its efforts to maintain a highly respectable public profile, the Mormon church has been plagued with numerous instances of negative publicity in recent years.

The Hofmann Case

One of the most publicized Mormon scandals in recent years has involved Mark Hofmann, a former Mormon missionary who forged Mormon documents and sold them for exorbitant prices. The most sensational of his forged documents was what became known as the "Salamander Letter," written by Martin Harris, an early church leader who gave a detailed account of Joseph Smith's money digging and his involvement in the occult. The letter speaks of Joseph Smith seeing "Spirits . . . with great kettles of coin money," and gives an interesting version of his digging up the gold plates:

> In the fall of the year 1827 I hear Joseph found a gold bible I take Joseph aside & he says it is true I found it 4 years ago with my stone but only just got it because of the enchantment the old spirit come to me 3 times in the same dream & says dig up the gold but when I take it up the next morning the spirit transfigured himself from a white salamander in the bottom of the hole & struck me 3 times & held the treasure & would not let me have it . . . .[131]

Though forged, the letter was entirely believable—so much so that church officials conceded its authenticity. In seeking to explain its contents, the letter was printed in the *Deseret News*, a church newspaper, cautioning readers to view it in light of the times: "Members should realize this letter was written very early in the Church, long before the restoration of the gospel was complete. At that point, it was logical that the religious folklore of the time was prevalent, and had not been replaced with the language of the gospel."[132]

Hofmann's forgeries were by no means limited to this one letter. He had forged more than one hundred documents, and had promised to sell the church some "priceless" documents—the McLellan letters—that would reveal other hidden secrets of early Mormon history. With no McLellan letters to offer, he became caught in a web between two prospective buyers, one who had given him a $150,000 advance. So desperate did he become that he determined that murder was his only way out of the tangle. During the early morning hours of October 15, 1985, he delivered homemade bombs to two homes resulting in the deaths of Kathleen Sheets and Steven Christensen—both fellow Mormons. "He later confessed to killing Christensen to avoid being found out and planting the bomb for Sheets to cast suspicion on disgruntled investors in a troubled business venture in which the two victims had been partners." In 1987, Hofmann "pleaded guilty to two counts of second-degree murder and two counts of fraud involving documents."[133]

Polygamist Fundamentalists

A continuing source of embarrassment for the Mormon church is the

President Ezra Taft Benson, current prophet of the church. Courtesy of the Church of Jesus Christ of Latter Day Saints.

not infrequent newspaper accounts of Mormon polygamists or "fundamentalists," as the media likes to name them. These are individuals, numbering some twenty thousand in Utah alone, who regard polygamy as a fundamental belief of the church and who for generations, since the Manifesto of 1890, have refused to acquiesce to the church or the government ban on it. An example of this is that of Alex Joseph, who became the mayor of Big Water, Utah in 1984. The husband of ten wives, Joseph defended his polygamous marriages, as private contracts that "his wives are free to withdraw from . . . at any time." Although he subscribes to traditional Mormon beliefs, he is regarded by the church as an apostate. "He formed the Church of Jesus Christ in Solemn Assembly after he was ex-

communicated from the Mormon Church because of his polygamy."[134]

Dissidents

One of the most serious problems the Mormon church is facing today is the challenge to its authority by its own people. Mormon anthropologists, historians, philosophers, and intellectuals of every stripe have in recent years been disputing their own traditions from every angle. They have challenged their present-day leaders as well as the writings and revelations of their forebears. In 1980, Ezra Taft Benson, who was then President of the Council of the Twelve Apostles and has since become the Prophet of the church, warned against dissent by arguing that the words of the living prophet are "more vital to us than the standard works." In some respects, he was reflecting earlier admonitions given to local lay or ward teachers:

> Any Latter-Day Saint who denounces or opposes, whether actively or otherwise, any plan or doctrine advocated by the prophets, seers, and revelators of the Church is cultivating the spirit of apostasy. . . . Lucifer . . . wins a great victory when he can get members of the Church to speak against their leaders and to do their own thinking. . . .
>
> When our leaders speak, the thinking has been done. When they propose a plan—it is God's plan. When they point the way, there is no other which is safe. When they give directions, it should mark the end of the controversy.[135]

Despite such warnings, Mormons are challenging their leaders and their traditions through published research and lecture forums at an increasing rate, much to the chagrin of the leadership.

Reaching Out to Mormons

One of the difficulties in reaching out to Mormons is finding common ground in terminology. Terms that are typically understood to have a particular meaning within the context of historic Christianity are used in an entirely different sense in a Mormon context. This is illustrated in a letter from the Director of Public Affairs at the church headquarters in Salt Lake City, responding to a charge that Mormonism was "nonorthodox": "We do believe in the Trinity—God, the Eternal, and His Son, Jesus Christ, and the Holy Ghost—and in the divinity of Jesus Christ. We're grateful whenever anybody accepts Christ as their Savior and tries to follow Him. That is what we're trying to do."[136] Such claims to Trinitarian belief and the deity of Christ are meaningless if the historic definition of terms are to be taken at face value.

But despite efforts to present an orthodox disguise, there is a concern among Mormon leaders that the distinction between evangelicals and Mormons not become too blurred. In 1982, in a sermon at Brigham Young University, Bruce McConkie, one of the Twelve Apostles, criticized a movement on campus among students to develop a "personal relationship" with Christ. He condemned the "creeds of Christendom" (the Apostles' and Nicene creeds) as "what Lucifer wants so-called Christian people to believe about deity in order to be damned." He referred to specific doctrines that teach God's na-

ture as spirit and triune as "lies about God." As far as Jesus is concerned, McConkie, insisted, "We worship the Father and him only and no one else."[137]

It is this very lack of emphasis on Jesus Christ that can serve as a catalyst in prompting a Mormon to reevaluate church teachings. This was true with Sheila Garrigus, who as a Mormon was struggling with her faith on various levels, but was most disillusioned by the fact that she could attend regular religious services week after week, without ever hearing the name of Jesus and how He was able to change lives.[138]

In recent years, there has been a growing number of Mormons who have become disillusioned and left the church. The vast majority of these, however, do not accept Christian orthodoxy as an alternative. Indeed, many profess agnosticism, having had the very ground of faith pulled out from under them when they realized that their own beliefs were unfounded. Others who leave Mormonism and are brought into the Christian faith are not able to make a clean break from the past, and it is not uncommon for them to hold dear to the *Book of Mormon* following their conversion to Christianity.

There is a long history among evangelicals in reaching out to Mormons with the gospel. In the late nineteenth century, Fredrik Fransen, the founder of The Evangelical Alliance Mission, made a concerted effort to reach out to Utah Mormons. He had been active in the Scandinavian Free Church before he immigrated to America, and became particularly concerned about the thousands of Mormons who left Sweden and

Denmark to make their homes in Utah. He himself spent time in Utah in 1879, and in the years following he sent missionaries of Scandinavian descent to work among the Mormons there. Most of these missionaries were single women who reached out to women immigrants who were "disillusioned and unprepared for the polygamous aspect of the cult. . . . They were able to visit these women in their homes and even hold services there. Each Mormon wife had her own 'home' and seemed to know when it was safe to have a meeting." One of these women was so effective that her work was castigated in a Mormon publication, "which said she would undoubtedly meet a gruesome death because she had raged against the latter day saints with a fervor which almost defied withstanding."[139]

Jerald and Sandra Tanner

An effective means of reaching out to Mormons has involved challenging Mormon doctrine and tradition through publishing and scholarly research. The most effective outreach in this arena is a husband-wife team, Jerald and Sandra Tanner, who have been characterized as "two of the most influential apostates of the 1960s." Both grew up as faithful Mormons, but both began to have doubts in their late teens about the truth of their religion. Jerald's misgivings began to surface after reading a historical document written by a close associate of Joseph Smith:

I can remember that the first time I saw David Whitmer's pamphlet "An address to all Believers in Christ," I threw it down in disgust. Afterward I began to think maybe that wasn't the right way to face the problem. If David Whitmer was wrong in his criticism of Joseph Smith, surely I could prove him wrong. So I picked up the pamphlet and read it through. I found that I could not prove him wrong, and that the revelations Joseph Smith gave had been changed. I later went to Independence, Missouri and saw a copy of the original *Book of Commandments*, which confirmed David Whitmer's statement.

Sandra's doubts began in college when she enrolled in the Mormon Institute of Religion class: "I started asking questions in class, trying to find answers to my doubts. But one day my institute teacher took me aside and told me to stop asking questions. There was a girl attending the class who was thinking of joining the church, and I was disturbing her with my questions."[140]

It was this questioning and concern to obtain the facts, even if it meant endless research, that propelled the Tanners into what became a full-time ministry. They work out of their home in Salt Lake City, organized under the name of the Utah Lighthouse Ministry. Here they print and distribute their more than fifty publications, the most exhaustive of which is *Mormonism—Shadow or Reality?* Although they receive hate mail and fierce criticism, they are admired by some Mormon scholars for their careful research and their objectivity. "Unlike some other individuals and groups critical of the Mormon church such as Saints Alive, Ex-Mormons for Jesus, and author/professor Walter Martin, the Tanners consider their research and methods dispassionate." According to Sandra Tanner, they make a concerted effort to avoid cynicism and ridicule: "We have tried to stay away from derogatory words or hostile terminology that may be offensive or belittling. Certainly our literature is meant to be hard-hitting in attacking the claims of Joseph Smith, but we've tried not to use loaded words.[141]

Thelma "Granny" Geer

Besides the very effective and scholarly methods of the Tanners, there are other means of reaching out to Mormons, and in most instances those who most easily gain an audience are those—like the Tanners—who have been on the inside themselves. "Saints Alive" and other organizations serve as a link between such individuals, but in many cases these people are individualists and activists who have developed their own styles. An example of this is Thelma "Granny" Geer, whose book *Mormonism, Mamma, and Me*, tells the story of her pilgrimage from Mormonism to evangelical Christianity. She was described as "a charming, if eccentric, witness to Mormons" in a 1982 article in *Christianity Today:*

> Thelma Geer dubs herself Granny Geer and—clad in an ankle-length skirt and pioneer's sun bonnet—spreads tracts in Mormon country supermarkets. She has been seen at airports dropping tracts on suitcases as they circulate on the baggage conveyor. Indefatigable even at 66, Geer once lectured 37 times in 16 days. Her 72-year-old husband makes their livelihood on a 10-acre watermelon and cantaloupe farm while she travels 240 days out of the year.[142]

Through her testimony, many Mormons have been converted to Chris-

tianity. Indeed, Mrs. Geer's fruitful ministry demonstrates that persistence, strong arguments, and genuine concern for Mormons and their eternal destiny can be effective ingredients for productive evangelism among Mormons.

Moving into the Mainstream of Religion

Since its founding in 1830, the Mormon church has moved away from being a bizarre fringe movement and into the mainstream of religion. This is due in part to a very conscious effort by the church to present an image of respectability to the outside world. The doctrines of the church have remained essentially the same, but certain practices, such as polygamy and banning blacks from the priesthood, have been eliminated, thus removing some of the prime targets of criticism. The rapid growth of the movement has likewise increased its stature. Mormons have spread out far beyond the borders of Utah, and the one-time clannishness of the movement is no longer as pronounced as it once was.

With the increase in size has come wealth and prestige. The church itself owns assets totalling billions of dollars, and individual church members, such as J. Willard Marriott, own giant corporations and wield enormous power in the nation's financial sector. The political influence of the Mormons has also grown dramatically in recent decades. The Mormons make up a powerful voting block, and many of their members have held important elected and appointed offices: George Romney, former Governor of Michigan; Stuart

Udall, former Secretary of the Interior; David Kennedy, former Secretary of the Treasury; and Ezra Taft Benson, former Secretary of Agriculture (and current President of the church). Also bringing prestige to the church is the reputation of Brigham Young University, both in academics and sports, and the high visibility of such personalities as the Osmond family.

Respectability has also been attained through the various humanitarian efforts the Mormon church has been involved in. This was particularly evident during a time of severe flooding in Utah in the mid-1980s, when Mormons were highly visible in community service—helping fellow Mormons and non-Mormons alike.

All of these factors have served to elevate the status of the Mormon church and at the same time obscure the distinctions between orthodox Christianity and Mormonism. Mormons have entered the mainstream and they speak of themselves as Christians, but their doctrines and their added scriptures speak for themselves. Indeed, Mormonism today is as far removed from Christian orthodoxy as it was in the early nineteenth century when Joseph Smith reported that a visionary personage—none other than Jesus himself—told him that all the Christian creeds were "an abomination in his sight."

Chapter 4

Seventh-day Adventism: Eschatological Confusion

It could easily be argued that a survey of Seventh-day Adventism does not belong in a book of this nature. Indeed, the controversy has raged for decades as to whether this religious group is a "cult" or an evangelical Protestant denomination. Such authorities on the subject as Anthony A. Hoekema, J. K. Van Baalen, and John R. Gerstner, have argued forcefully that the movement is cultic, while Walter Martin, among others, has taken the opposite view. Part of the problem is the use of the term "cult." No reputable scholar would claim that the Seventh-day Adventists are "cultic" to the same degree as the Mormons, for example. Yet, the history, and even present-day doctrine, of this group could be said to have cultic characteristics.

It is true, however, that Seventh-day Adventist believers are for the most part warm Christians and their churches are far more orthodox in their theology than churches in some of the mainline Protestant denominations. The vast majority of Seventh-day Adventists would subscribe to the cardinal doctrines of the faith including the virgin birth, and the deity and the bodily resurrection of Christ, and they would view the Bible as the inspired Word of God. Yet, there are some areas of doctrine where the Seventh-day Adventists deviate from historic orthodoxy. These doctrinal problems resulted from a false prophecy of Christ's return in 1844, and were then reinforced through "inspired" prophecy made by Ellen G. White. Some might argue that the contemporary church should not be held accountable for errors of the past, but the present-day leadership of this movement has soundly sustained these errors by excommunicating those from within who have struggled to make reforms.

The significance of Seventh-day Adventism and its relationship to unorthodox religious movements in America lies mainly in its historical development and its emphasis on eschatology and the resulting doctrinal error. In this sense, the move-

William Miller

William Miller. From *A History of the Origin and Progress of Seventh-day Adventists* by M. Ellsworth Olsen.

ment is similar to the Jehovah's Witnesses. The common elements have been their proclivity for setting dates for the return of Christ and speculation on His particular activities in the heavenly realm during the present era. Closely related to this is the exclusive claim to truth. For the Seventh-day Adventists, this truth was revealed through Ellen G. White; for the Jehovah's Witnesses, the truth has come through the Watchtower organization.

In many respects, William Miller might be labeled the forerunner of Seventh-day Adventism, though he himself was not connected with the movement. It was his date setting, however, which roused the curiosity of Christians and contributed to the widespread spirit of prophetic speculation in the 1830s and early 1840s.

William Miller was born in Pittsfield, Massachusetts, in 1782, the oldest of sixteen children. His meager education, which involved only a few years of formal schooling, was augmented by his delight in reading. He was reared in an atmosphere of deep religious piety, but as a youth he went his own way. He was a skeptic who made sport out of ridiculing the simple faith and pious mannerisms of family members. It was not until he was in his mid-thirties that Miller himself was converted—a result of his avid study of Scripture. But for Miller, committing himself to God was only the first step in his religious pilgrimage. He began studying the Bible verse by verse using only a Cruden's Concordance as an aid, and from that study he soon concluded that the main thrust of the biblical message related to the end times. He became convinced that a literal interpretation of key passages would reveal the point in history when Christ would return.[1]

Pinpointing Christ's Return

In addition to his Bible study, Miller kept abreast of current events, and it was a combination of these two interests that led him to conclude that the return of Christ was near: "Finding all the signs of the times and the present condition of the world, to compare harmoniously with the prophetic descriptions of the last days, I was compelled to believe that this world had about reached the limits of the period allotted for its continuance." But Miller was not satisfied simply with the certainty that his was the generation of the end times. He searched out prophetic passages for specific clues that would pinpoint the Lord's second coming. His conclusions were drawn largely from the Old Testament book of Daniel.

> From a further study of the Scriptures, I concluded that the seven times of Gentile supremacy must commence when the Jews ceased to be an independent nation, at the captivity of Manasseh, which the best chronologers assigned to B.C. 677; that the 2,300 days commenced with the seventy weeks, which the best chronologers dated from B.C. 457; and that the 1335 days, commencing with the taking away of the daily, and the setting up of the abomination that maketh desolate, Dan. 12:11, were to be dated from the setting up of the papal supremacy, after the taking away of pagan abominations, and which according to the best historians I could consult should be dated from about A.D. 508. Reckoning all these prophetic periods from the several dates assigned by the best chronologers for the events from which they should evidently be reckoned, they would all terminate together, about A.D. 1843.[2]

This conclusion was made without consulting Bible scholars or theologians, and it was deduced over a relatively short period of time, as Miller himself testified: "I was thus brought, in 1818, at the close of my two years' study of the Scriptures, to the solemn conclusion that in about twenty-five years from that time all the affairs of our present state would be wound up." For Miller, the truth that he had discovered was too compelling to keep to himself: "The question came home to me with mighty power regarding my duty to the world, in view of the evidence. . . . If the end were so near, it was important that the world should know it." Miller had expected that Christians would eagerly accept his conclusions, but, he writes, "To my astonishment, I found very few who listened with any interest. Occasionally, one would see the force of the evidence; but the great majority passed it by as an idle tale."[3]

Itinerant Preaching

In 1833, Miller became a licensed Baptist minister, and that launched him into his itinerant preaching ministry. By 1835 his fortune was beginning to change. No longer were his words of prophecy being rejected, but rather he could write, "The Lord opens doors faster than I can fill them." Many of these engagements were week-long conferences which allowed him opportunity to fully expound his biblical theories. Often the response was one of "great excitement," and the fear of the impending return of Christ often resulted in "a great breaking down, and much weeping." In 1839, he wrote, "There has been a reformation in every place that I have lectured . . . and the work is progressing in every place rapidly. The meeting-houses are crowded to overflowing. Much excitement prevails among the people."[4]

In 1839, Miller's message gained an important adherent in the person of Joshua V. Himes, the well-known pastor of the Chardon Street Chapel in Boston. "Himes was a born publicist and a lover of crowds and camp meetings. After 1839 he became Miller's promoter" and "a great organizer of millennial fear and fervor."[5]

In an effort to counteract the scoffing and negative publicity that was increasing in direct proportion to the crowds and the excitement that was generated, Himes agreed to initiate a publicity campaign with a sympathetic slant to his message. The first such effort was a Boston-based newspaper, *The Sign of the Times*, followed in 1842 with the New York-based *The Midnight Cry.* "Within two years journals were flourishing in Philadelphia, Rochester, Cincinnati, and elsewhere. Under Himes' directions tracts, pamphlets, and books streamed from the press and were shipped literally to the ends of the earth. It was Joshua V. Himes, far more than William Miller, who made the Adventist cause a national phenomenon."[6]

As the clock ran down on Miller's momentous year, excitement began to build. Miller opened the year with a rousing New Year's Day message, proclaiming that "this is the last year that Satan will reign in our earth." There was no doubt in his mind that 1843 had been calculated correctly. "This year—O blessed year—the captive will be released, the prison doors will be opened, death will have no more dominion over us, and life, eternal life, be our everlasting reward. This year—O glorious year!—the trump of jubilee will be blown. . . . This year! the long-looked-for year of years! the best! it is come!"[7]

The "Great Disappointment"

The original calendar year of 1843 was extended on into 1844—to March 21, the vernal equinox. It was a let down when the day passed uneventfully, but Miller refused to give up. A few days later he wrote: "The time, as I have calculated it, is now filled up; and I expect every moment to see the Saviour descend from heaven." Six weeks later, however, his demeanor had changed: "I *confess my error* and acknowledge *my disappointment.*" A few weeks after that, he publicly admitted his error at the Annual conference of Adventists which was being convened in Boston.[8]

Miller was not the only one disappointed. Many of his followers were deeply troubled and sought desperately to come to terms with their shattered expectations. Others sought to compensate for the error by appending new criteria for their prophetic timetable. Indeed, a "Seventh Month Movement" emerged that proclaimed Christ would return on the tenth day of the seventh month of the Jewish calendar of that same year—October 22, 1844. Miller himself did not initially subscribe to the new date-setting scheme, but as public enthusiasm escalated he joined the swell of anticipation—no doubt not wanting to be standing at the sidelines as a skeptic, should the Lord actually return on that day. But, again the date passed. "I have been twice disappointed," wrote Miller, "and although surrounded with enemies and scoffers, yet my mind is perfectly calm, and my hope in the coming of Christ is as strong as ever."[9]

It would be difficult to comprehend the depth of disappointment and humiliation that the Millerites endured immediately following the "Great Disappointment," as it has been commonly referred to. Joseph Bates, who would play a significant

Hiram Edson. From *A History of the Origin and Progress of Seventh-day Adventists* by M. Ellsworth Olsen.

role in the founding of Seventh-day Adventism by contributing the idea of seventh-day worship, wrote how people ridiculed him the following day when he went to the market, saying "I thought you were going up yesterday." His reaction was one of utter dejection: "With these taunts thrown at me, if the earth could have opened and swallowed me up, it would have been sweetness compared to the distress I felt." Miller wrote of similar experiences:

Some are tauntingly inquiring, "Have you not gone up?" Even little children in the streets are shouting continually to passers-by "Have you a ticket to go up?" The public prints, of the most fashionable and popular kind, in the great Sodoms of our country, are caricaturing in the most shameful manner the "white robes of the saints," Rev.

6:11, the "going up" and the great day of "burning." Even the pulpits are desecrated by the repetition of scandalous and false reports concerning the "ascension robes."[10]

Hiram Edson and the Sanctuary Theory

The Great Disappointment did not end the speculation concerning Christ's return, nor did it silence those who would seek to reinterpret the events of that very uneventful day. On October 23, the morning after the Great Disappointment, Hiram Edson, a zealous "Millerite" from western New York, went out to his barn with a friend to pray and ask God to reveal to them the meaning and purpose of what had happened—or, rather, what had not happened. After their time of prayer, they felt a sense of assurance and left to share it with some fellow believers. Edson later recounted what took place:

We started, and while passing through a large field I was stopped about midway of the field. Heaven seemed open to my view, and I saw distinctly and clearly that instead of our High Priest coming out of the Most Holy of the heavenly sanctuary to come to this earth on the tenth day of the seventh month, at the end of the 2,300 days, He for the first time entered on that day the second apartment of that sanctuary; and that He had a work to perform in the most holy before coming to this earth.[11]

With this vision, Edson and his friend, O. R. L. Crosier, turned the disappointment into a celebration of fulfilled prophecy. Of course they recognized Miller's error, but it was an error of geography and not of timing. He had taught that after 2,300 years the sanctuary would be cleansed, the assumption being that sanctuary cleansing would be the return of Christ to earth. But that was an assumption Edson and Crosier were unwilling to accept—especially considering the fact that the earthly event had failed to take place. They reinterpreted the prophecy and located the cleansing in the heavenly sanctuary, where Christ moved from the outer apartment into the Holy of Holies. In doing this, according to Edson and Crosier, Christ reflected the ministry of the Old Testament priests. Since his ascension, He had been doing the daily ministry of the priest, which offered forgiveness to people, but on October 22, 1944, Christ entered the Holy of Holies, where his ministry has been to "blot out" the sins of believers who have died. This interpretive effort to reconcile the Great Disappointment with the Bible was further developed and eventually became the doctrine of the "investigative judgment."[12]

Joseph Bates and the Seventh-day Sabbath

The most widely known characteristic of the Seventh-day Adventists is not their doctrine of investigative judgment, which so distinctively gives the movement cultic attributes, but their practice of worshiping on Saturday—an issue that is regarded by most Christians as a nonessential matter, so far as faith is concerned. That practice became an important aspect of the movement almost immediately following the Great Disappointment. Credit for initiating seventh-day worship is generally given to Joseph Bates who wrote a forty-eight page treatise in 1846, defending the regulation. Previously, however, some New Hampshire Adventists influenced by a Seventh-Day Baptist woman, Rachel Oakes, had changed their day of worship, and their practice, combined with Bates' written defense, set the stage for widespread acceptance.[13]

The title of Bates' defense was *The Seventh-day Sabbath, a Perpetual Sign*, which summed up his viewpoint. The seventh-day Sabbath was inaugurated by God by his very plan of creation and was committed to Adam and Eve in the Garden, and reaffirmed by Moses when he received the Ten Commandments on Mount Sinai. Bates later expanded his defense to include warnings for the future. He applied Revelation 14:6–12, which speaks of those in the end times who will receive a mark on their forehead for worshiping the beast and his image, to those people who would follow the Papacy (the beast) in Sunday worship. He argued that the Sabbath had been changed to Sunday by the Roman Catholic Church. In conjunction with this, "Bates drew the conclusion that the 'remnant' who keep the commandments of God—in other words, the faithful Adventists—would number only 144,000," a position that has not become dogma of the Seventh-day Adventist church.[14]

The "Spirit of Prophecy"

Another distinctive feature of Seventh-day Adventism is its reliance on the "spirit of prophecy"—specifically coming through the visions of Ellen G. White. The "spirit of prophecy" terminology is taken from Revelation

19:10, and was taken literally to refer to White. "Adventists believe that in the last days special counsels from God are to be revealed, which neither add to nor contradict Scripture, and that these counsels are primarily for the Seventh-day Adventist denomination. And while following these counsels, they claim they always test them by the Word of God."[15]

The claim that White's prophecies were tested by the Bible has been challenged by her opponents through the years. One critic, in fact, enumerated several of her claimed visions and sought to debunk them. Referring to one of these visions, he wrote, "she discovered that women should wear short dresses with pants and she and her sister followers dressed this way for eight years. But the ridiculous custom has now been abandoned." Two other visions related to slavery:

> In a vision in 1847, she saw that Christ would come before slavery was abolished and that it would be abolished when He came. But slavery has been abolished and Christ has not yet come. . . . In a vision of January 4, 1862, she had it revealed to her that slavery "is left to live and stir up another rebellion." But it did not live and it did not stir up another rebellion.[16]

Ellen G. White

Ellen G. White was not a likely candidate for charismatic leadership and greatness. She was poorly educated and unattractive, and outwardly had few qualities that would have compelled people to follow her. She was utterly unlike the fun-loving charismatic Joseph Smith and the attractive and appealing Mary Baker

Eddy—both contemporaries who were also born in New England. Yet, White had a powerful influence on American religion and culture—an influence that she personally wielded for several decades. "At the time she was born in Gorham, Maine," writes Rene Noorbergen, "John Quincy Adams 'reigned' as the country's sixth President, but when she died, Woodrow Wilson, the twenty-eighth President of the United States, lived in the White House."[17]

Early Life

Ellen Harmon and her twin sister Elizabeth were born in 1827 into a devout Methodist family. Her early life was routine, except for two incidents that would change the course of her life. On her way to school one morning she found a flyer that predicted the imminent return of Christ. "I was seized with terror," she recalled later; "the time seemed so short for the conversion and salvation of the world." Soon after this, she was the victim of a malicious assault, when a youth threw a rock at her, hitting her in the face. She was so seriously injured that it was initially feared she would not survive. "Her facial disfigurement—so bad that her own father could scarcely recognize her—caused frequent embarrassment and made breathing through her nostrils impossible for two years. Frayed nerves rebelled at simple assignments such as reading and writing. Her hands shook so badly she was unable to control her slate marks . . . and dizziness would overcome her."[18]

It was a few years after this in 1840, when Ellen was approaching adolescence, that William Miller came to nearby Portland to conduct a series of meetings on the soon return of Christ. His preaching made a deep impression on her as it did on many others. "Terror and conviction," she later wrote, "spread through the entire city." At the close of the service she, along with other "seekers," made her way to the "anxious seat," beginning a search for faith that was later climaxed at a Methodist camp meeting. Yet, she continued to struggle with self-doubt and depression. It was in this context that she began to experience dreams in which she was consoled by Jesus.[19]

Not long after this in 1843, during the increased excitement over Miller's prophecy of Christ's return, Ellen's family was expelled from the Methodist church. Their enthusiasm for Miller's views and their lax attendance at class meetings stirred conflict in the congregation, and as a result they were forced to leave. This turn of events identified them even more closely with the Adventists, and as October 22, 1844 approached, they looked with certainty to the glorious coming of Christ. For all the "Millerites" and assorted Adventists who had singled out that specific day, there truly was a "great disappointment," but for Ellen it caused heartbreak that few could appreciate. Her dreams had confirmed to her that Jesus was indeed real, and with His apparent blessing she had committed herself to the Miller prophetic timetable.[20]

Dreams and Visions

For the seventeen-year-old Ellen Harmon, however, the Great Disap-

pointment was short lived. Two months later in December, she experienced the first of her visions that would confirm the Adventist beliefs. During a small home prayer meeting in Portland, Maine, she later testified that she began "rising higher and higher, far above the dark world," where she looked down and saw the Adventist believers on the road to heaven. Those who doubted the Adventist truth fell back into "the wicked world below which God had rejected." Her next vision, some two months later, expanded the first and has been a source of controversy among Adventists since. Dissention broke out among some of Miller's followers over the shut-door question. "Had God really closed the door of salvation to sinners on October 22?" The answer came to Ellen again when she was with a small group of Adventist believers. She fell to the floor writhing in anguish during which time she received God's message that indeed the door had been closed.[21]

Ellen's next significant vision confirmed the seventh-day sabbath that Joseph Bates was promoting. As had been true in the previous incidents where she emerged with an answer from a vision, this was a controversial issue among the Adventist believers. She herself initially rejected the concept, but after meeting with Bates personally, she had a vision in which she testified that Jesus showed her the Ten Commandments on tables of stone. The fourth commandment addressing the sabbath had "a soft halo of light encircling it." An angel explained to her that the Adventists must keep the seventh day as a prerequisite to the

Lord's second coming. In making this claim, "Ellen placed herself in direct opposition to the moderate wing of Millerites, who . . . had officially condemned . . . visions, the shut door, and the seventh-day Sabbath. For the next few years she and the small band of fellow believers . . . were designated the 'sabbatarian and shut door' Adventists."[22]

Ellen married James White, a lay Adventist preacher, in 1846. At that time she had already acquired a reputation for her prophetic gifts—a quality her fiancé found appealing and one that would intensify his own ministry, as he later wrote:

When we first met, we had no idea of marriage at any future time. But God had a work for both of us to do, and He saw that we could greatly assist each other in that work. As she should come before the public, she needed a lawful protector; and God having chosen her as a channel of light and truth to the people in a special sense, she could be of great help to me.[23]

From the beginning, Mrs. White's visions were controversial. They were regarded by many to be characteristic of what was perceived to be the lunatic fringe of the Adventist movement. Joshua Himes, who had so effectively promoted Miller only a few years earlier was distressed by the "visionary nonsense" that was affecting so many, and summed up the situation with the terse appraisal, "Things are in a bad way at Portland."[24]

How did White rise above the rest of these self-ascribed prophets and sustain a loyal following? Her secret, it seems, lay in the fact that she offered divine confirmation to individuals who needed their positions strengthened. It was apparently not because her visionary style was any more authentic than that of others. From testimony of contemporary observers, she sank to the floor in a swoon that extended anywhere from a few minutes to hours. "She often uttered words singly, and sometimes sentences which expressed to those about her the nature of the view she was having, either of heaven or of earth. . . . When the vision was ended . . . she was then limp and strengthless, and had to be assisted to her chair." The content of her visions varied. On one occasion she saw Satan, whose "countenance is full of anxiety, care, unhappiness, malice, hate, mischief, deceit, and every evil." She went on to describe his physical features in detail:

His eyes were cunning, sly, and showed great penetration. His frame was large, but the flesh hung loosely about his hands and face. As I beheld him, his chin was resting upon his left hand. He appeared to be in deep thought. A smile was upon his countenance, which made me tremble, it was so full of evil, and Satanic slyness. This smile is the one he wears just before he makes sure of his victim, and as he fastens the victim in his snare, this smile grows horrible.[25]

Because of the criticism leveled against Mrs. White regarding her visions, her husband, who was editor of the *Review and Herald* and was considered by many to be the head of the early Seventh-day Adventist movement, backed away from his strong endorsement of her. In 1951, he discontinued publishing the testimonies of her visions, and four years later he harshly responded to critics by demanding, "What has the RE-VIEW to do with Mrs. W.'s views. . . . Its motto has been, 'The Bible, and the Bible alone, the only rule of faith and duty.'" The grassroots support for his wife, however, was stronger than he may have realized, and soon after that editorial he was asked to step down from his position and later to apologize for his depreciating his wife's visions. From then on Mrs. White had virtual full reign in disseminating her visionary messages.[26]

Health and Dietary Issues

In 1855, the Whites moved the headquarters for their movement to Battle Creek, Michigan, and several years later the church was officially organized. In the following years, Mrs. White concentrated her energies heavily on health matters—particularly preventative medicine. She traveled widely, in the decades that followed, lecturing on diet and health care, as well as on temperance. Indeed, "it was as a temperance speaker that she drew some of the largest crowds ever recorded in the 1860s and 1870s."[27]

In her visions and testimonies relating to health, most medical specialists today would recognize Mrs. White as being ahead of her time in some areas. Like other religious leaders of her day, she spoke out against the use of tobacco and alcohol. But she went far beyond this, repudiating the use of all stimulants (including tea and coffee), and before it was generally accepted, she was urging a diet of more vegetables and grains and less meat. But good health was dependent on more than a proper diet:

The more we exercise, the better will be the circulation of the blood. More people died for want of exercise than through overfatigue; very many more rust out than wear out. . . . We are more dependent on the air we breathe than upon the food we eat. . . . You should lower the temperature in your room . . . nothing can be worse than an overheated atmosphere.[28]

Admonitions for Christian Living

Much of Mrs. White's writings involve admonitions for her followers to live proper Christian lives. Health advice was only one particular aspect of this. She admonished pastors to "become Bible students," and to visit families and "converse with all the members of the family, whether they profess truth or not." These visits were not to be social times: "All lightness and trifling is positively forbidden in the word of God." But such solemnity was not limited to pastors: "Both brethren and sisters indulge in too much jovial talk when in each other's society. Women professing godliness indulge in much jesting, joking and laughing. This is unbecoming, and grieves the Spirit of God."[29]

Sexual Decorum

Mrs. White was especially concerned about childrearing and behavior among young people. This is graphically illustrated in her horror of masturbation and the harmful effects it was having on the health of Christian youth. "It is a sin that is destroying souls . . . in sabbath-keeping families," she wrote. "It is practiced to an alarming extent, and brings on disease of almost every description. Even very small children, infants, being born with natural irritability of the sexual organs, find momentary relief in handling them. . . . These children, generally puny and dwarfed, are prescribed for by physicians, and drugged; but the evil is not removed." Who was to blame for this problem? "In very many cases the parents are the real sinners. They have abused their marriage privileges, and by indulgence have strengthened their animal passions."[30]

Mrs. White's abhorrence of "sexual perversion" within marriage was a powerful theme in her inspired testimonies, and she was speaking the mind of God on this controversial issue. "The marriage covenant covers sins of the darkest hue," she wrote. "Men and women professing godliness debase their own bodies through the indulgence of the corrupt passions, and thus lower themselves beneath the brute creation. . . . Many do die prematurely, their lives sacrificed in the inglorious work of excessive indulgence of the animal passions. Yet because they are married, they think they commit no sin." No man could truly respect a wife if she submitted to such sinful behavior. He would tire of her and seek someone else "to arouse and intensify his hellish passions." As for the wife, "if she possess true love and wisdom, she will seek to divert his mind from the gratification of lustful passions to high and spiritual themes by dwelling upon interesting spiritual subjects."[31]

Dependence on Husband

Although it is Mrs. White who is generally given credit for solidifying the scattered Millerites and Adventists into a cohesive denomination, she would have been ineffective without the behind-the-scenes efforts of her husband. "Without him," writes Ronald Numbers, "her career as a prophetess would probably never have gotten off the ground. Since the 1840s, publishing had been his passion—and the key to her success. In those early days, it was he who insisted on printing her visions, after patiently correcting her grammar and polishing her style." His reluctance to deem her visions as church authority notwithstanding, his role in promoting her cannot be overdrawn.[32]

Organization of the Church

An organized denomination did not emerge naturally out of the prophecies of Mrs. White and the publishing of her husband. Indeed, in the early years there was strong opposition to any type of formal church organization. One early Adventist gave an ominous warning: "I discover that the 'organization' fever is fairly up again. Brethren, beware! Would to God that the huge monster had grasped and expired in death at its birth. My prayer is, Lord cripple the monster. Amen." Another leader wrote, "Take care that you do not seek to manufacture another church. No church can be organized by man's invention but what it becomes Babylon the moment it is organized."[33]

As a result of such opposition, it was not until 1863—nearly two decades after the Great Disappointment—that the Seventh-day Adventists were organized as a church. This took place at a General Conference in

Ellen G. White and her husband James White. From *A History of the Origin and Progress of Seventh-day Adventists* by M. Ellsworth Olsen.

Battle Creek, Michigan, bringing together some four thousand Adventists under one organizational umbrella. James White, the most prominent man in the early organizational efforts, was nominated to serve as the first president, but he declined in an effort to placate his opponents. Later, however, he served for ten years in that post.[34]

The Role of Women

As has historically been true of loose religious movements that become officially organized, women tend to lose status. Although Ellen G. White would maintain her prominence as a prophetess and evangelist, women in general were not encouraged to have a public profile. In 1881, out of concern for the need for more full-time ministers, a resolution was made at the General Conference, proposing "that females possessing the necessary qualifications to fill that position, may with perfect propriety, be set aside by ordination to the work of the Christian Ministry." The matter was taken up by the executive committee, where no action was taken on it, giving "the idea its most effective possible burial."[35]

Itinerant Evangelism

In the two decades that followed the formal organization of the church, the membership increased fivefold to twenty thousand. Much of this increase was a result of itinerant evangelistic campaigns that resembled in every way the frontier evangelism of the Methodists and Baptists and other evangelical churches. George Butler, who served as president for more than ten years in the 1870s and 1880s, described one such "melting meeting," in Iowa in 1885:

> I think I never felt freer in my life. A good many were in tears quite a portion of the time. When we came to call them forward for prayers, about one hundred and fifty came forward without much urging, and seemed ready to speak, and many good testimonies were given. Indeed, we really had a blessed season. . . . some who had been long out of the truth broke all down and wept freely. All felt that it was a very profitable day.[36]

External and Internal Dissension

Like the Jehovah's Witnesses who would develop out of their movement, the Seventh-day Adventists were frequently the victims of persecution as a result of their distinctive beliefs. In an effort to revive religious morals in the late nineteenth century, there was a renewed emphasis on keeping the "Sabbath"—an ideal that would not on the surface backfire on Seventh-day Adventists. But a *Sunday* Sabbath is what the National Reform Association, the Women's Christian Temperance Union, and the American Sabbath Union Party had in mind. Laws were enacted that prohibited Sunday work and activity, and as a result, dozens of Seventh-day Adventists were arrested for breaking the Sabbath. In some instances, they were treated like hardened criminals and forced to work in chain gangs. It was their protest against such laws that for the first time brought them into the political arena. Initially, Adventists were passive in their protest to the Sabbath-law discrimination. But by the late nineteenth century the General Conference was involved in "an energetic lobbying and publicity campaign" that stirred support from outside their ranks and brought an end to the widespread arrests.[37]

The Righteousness by Faith Issue

During the late nineteenth century, as the Seventh-day Adventists were struggling with opposition and persecution from the outside, they were also struggling with theological differences among themselves. Some of the younger men from California were challenging the traditional emphasis on the necessity of keeping the moral law and focusing on "righteousness by faith." Opposing the "Westerners"

were President Butler and other old-line conservatives, who feared there would be a laxity in moral standards if the former emphasis on the law was neglected. Ellen G. White did not hesitate to enter the fray, convinced that this emphasis was "just what Seventh-day Adventists needed, and she was determined to use her considerable influence to get this new emphasis on righteousness by faith before the members." She claimed that this emphasis "was what she had been trying to get across for over forty years," and she began publishing books in support of the position.[38]

Perfectionism and Competing Visionaries

Following her husband's death in 1885, Ellen White's role in church affairs continued to expand. As in the debate over righteousness by faith as opposed to works, she utilized her magnetic influence to calm the waters. This occurred in many petty controversies as well as in major clashes that created deep divisions in the movement, as in 1900 when many Seventh-day Adventists were being influenced by a form of perfectionism referred to as the "holy flesh" or "cleansing message." This was a notion that promised perfection in the form of new flesh so that an individual could be translated directly to heaven instead of having to die an ordinary death. She spoke at the General Conference and helped smooth over the differences of the opposing parties. But despite her mediating role, she herself came under fire—in many cases by those who opposed her stance and denied her unique prophetic function. Even more threatening to her position, however, was the emergence of competitors.

As early as 1884, Anna Garmire of Petoskey, Michigan, claimed visions that she said revealed, among other things, that the earth's probation would close in October 1884. Mrs. White rejected Anna's "inspiration," suggesting that it came principally from her father; but the Garmires persisted. Although they did not succeed in convincing many Adventists, their influence smoldered until as late as 1900, when it had a brief flare-up in Arkansas.

More troublesome was the case of Anna Phillips Rice, a young religious worker in Ogden, Utah, who began having "visions" in 1891, shortly after Mrs. White left America to be in Australia for nearly a decade. Rice appeared to be an earnest Christian, and soon her "visions" and "testimonies" were accepted by . . . leading Adventists . . . . Eventually, word from Ellen White convinced these leaders that Anna was sincere and well-meaning, but mistaken. . . .

Around the end of the century, Fannie [Frances E.] Bolton, a former literary assistant of Ellen White's, began to claim divine revelations. . . .[39]

Problems of Arianism and Pantheism

One reason that the Seventh-day Adventists have often been categorized as a "cult" is due to the divergent theology present in the movement during the early decades. This was due in part to the claims of visionary revelations that confirmed beliefs with no biblical base, but it was also due to the fact that individuals from a wide variety of backgrounds were drawn to the millenarian concepts of the Adventists. According to Richard Schwarz, a Seventh-day Adventist historian, "Most Adventist laymen were probably unaware of the fact that many of their prominent ministers had long held unorthodox Arian or semi-Arian views of the Godhead," a view rejecting the full deity of Christ. Another drift toward heresy that arose during the late nineteenth century was "a pantheistic or semipantheistic current of thought . . . that God was in all men and all objects in nature."[40]

In both of these instances, Ellen G. White used her powerful influence to steer the movement toward orthodoxy. In the controversy over pantheism, she "wrote letters that pointedly denounced the ideas," and when these letters were read at a crucial council meeting, several of the original proponents of the heresy "indicated acceptance of Ellen White's words as counsel from God that must be adopted." Problems continued to plague the movement for some time, but "the crises of these years of theological turmoil," writes Schwarz, "resulted in moving Seventh-day Adventists closer to traditional Christianity," and it was Ellen White "who played a key role in resolving these issues."[41]

Challenging the Authority of Ellen G. White

From the beginning there were challenges to Ellen White's place of prominence in the movement, and there were even objections to her visions and testimonies. It was not until the early twentieth century, however, that these challenges became so forceful that they threatened grave consequences on the otherwise thriving movement. Alonzo T. Jones, an influential church leader, was her most vocal critic during these years. In a booklet entitled *Some History, Some Experiences, Some Facts*, he charged that there were contradictions and errors in White's testimonies and gave examples to prove his claims. Recognizing her popularity among lay people and leadership alike, he was very careful not to discredit these testimonies entirely. "I use the Testimonies and the other writings of Sister White," he wrote, "for my own private study, in the study of the Bible, and in my family worship. But to use them on other people as a test of *their* orthodoxy or heresy, or as a club to bring them under or drive them out, I do not, and I will not. . . . I shall preach only the Bible."[42]

Divine Inspiration on Personal Matters

Jones and others were most disturbed about how White was using her testimonies as a vehicle to gain the upper hand in personality conflicts and political infighting. She was also accused of allowing her son William to influence the content of her testimonies. Criticism mounted, and more attacks were made against her in print, including a detailed chart that showed altered and plagiarized testimonies in parallel columns with testimonies that showed the contradictions in the original source. Even with such evidence, there were few who were willing to discredit Ellen White's testimonies altogether. John Harvey Kellog, the well-known Seventh-day Adventist doctor who headed the Battle Creek Sanitarium, is an example. He was not particularly disturbed by her apparent contradictions and plagiarisms, because he believed there were "principles for distinguishing her inspired from her uninspired writings." But he was distressed that other church leaders were manipulating her:

> If they would let her alone to deal with the great principles of truth, righteousness, temperance and reform, it would have been a wonderful thing; but they have got her tangled up with all the little personal affairs of business and a lot of other things that the Lord has not given her any information about or any light about, and have made her to do business with the sale of books or to settle church quarrels and such things. And the Lord has never authorized any such use at all of the wonderful gifts He gave her.[43]

Comparing Prophecies with Scripture

The old-guard leadership of the church was quick to respond to any efforts that were being made to discredit Ellen White. They sought to refute the accusations of errors and plagiarism, but the thrust of their argument was that from the very beginning "this denomination has believed in the spirit of prophecy." It was thus as much a matter of tradition as anything else. "It is an integral part of the beautiful system of truth which we call the third angel's message; so much is this so that those who have given up their faith in this part of the truth have invariably lost their spiritual perception, and eventually given up the whole message." Interestingly, another point that was made in defense of White was a comparison of the "liberals" in Adventism with the "liberals" in the Protestant church: the critics of Ellen White were distinguishing between her inspired and uninspired writings just as the higher critics of the Bible were distinguishing between what was inspired and uninspired.[44]

Such arguments only created further debate in the church because many people were uncomfortable with placing Ellen White's writings on the same plane as the Bible. Francis Wilcox, who edited the *Review and Herald* for more than three decades, however, seemed to have no difficulty with the comparison, and his influence helped to elevate the stature of her writings. "Wilcox argued that White served God the way Samuel, Elijah, and John the Baptist did. . . . Furthermore, her writings 'constitute a spiritual commentary upon the Scripture, a divine illumination of the word.' "[45] But despite such endorsements, the underlying misgivings about her writings continued to plague the church in the generations after her death in 1915.

The Great Controversy

What in fact was the source of Ellen White's testimonies? Did God instruct her through revelatory messages that a wife should shun the sexual advances of her husband? Critics might view such testimonies as merely the words of an overworked wife of the mid-nineteenth century. But much of Mrs. White's writing, which she claimed came through visions, was historical or theological. *The Great Controversy*, for example, is a lengthy religious history of the western world from the early church to the end times. Like her other works, it was viewed with skepticism almost as soon as it was published. Did it come from God, or was it taken from someone else's writings? How, it was asked, could an uneducated woman produce such voluminous yet factual manuscripts?

The long-held suspicions about Mrs. White's writings came to a head again in the 1970s when a number of scholars began writing books discrediting her. The most strident of these was entitled satirically *The White Lie*. In this volume, Walter Rea, Seventh-day Adventist minister, charged that Mrs. White "copied and borrowed almost everything" in her fifty-three books. In his research, he cited one example after another of her direct quoting, without acknowledgement, from the original source. The following is an illustration, the first taken from White's *The Great Controversy* and the second taken from James A. Wylie's *The History of Protestantism*, which was published eleven years before White testified that God gave her the words while she was in Switzerland:

> Zurich is pleasantly situated on the shores of Lake Zurich. This is the noble expanse of water enclosed with banks which swell upwards, clothed with vineyards and pine forests, from amid which hamlets and white villas gleam out. . . .

> Zurich is pleasantly situated on the shores of the lake of that name. This is a noble expanse of water, enclosed within banks which swell gently upwards, clothed here with vineyards, there with pine-forests, from amid

which hamlets and white villas gleam out. . . .[46]

Defending Plagiarism

That she used other sources without acknowledgement was not in itself viewed by critics as a serious crime. Such "plagiarism" was not uncommon in the nineteenth century. But what some Adventist leaders found particularly disturbing was that "she utilized the words of prior authors in describing words she heard spoken while in vision. In a few instances, she uses the writings of a 19th-century source in quoting the words of Christ or of an angelic guide." This concern threw a shadow over the very foundation of the Seventh-day Adventists, but the highest officials of the church strongly defended their founder/prophetess. "President Neal Wilson," according to a *Time* magazine article in 1982, "holds to the position that a prophet's thoughts can be divinely inspired even though they are not original." At the denomination's General Conference in 1980, Mrs. White was confirmed as a prophetess whose "writings are a continuing and authoritative source of truth."[47]

Opposing Opinions Not Tolerated

As an "authoritative source of truth," Ellen White's writings are not subject to criticism the way the writings of other church leaders or theologians would be. This was a major complaint of D. M. Canright, who knew Ellen White personally, but left the movement after twenty-eight years because he could no longer accept her testimonies as inspired

from God. In a book entitled *Seventh-day Adventism Renounced,* he harshly criticized the total confidence the church placed on her writings:

There is not a doctrine nor a practice of the church, from the observance of the Sabbath to the washing of feet, upon which she has not written. That settles it. No further investigation can be made on any of these matters, only to gather evidence and construe everything to sustain it. How, then, can their ministers or people be free to think and investigate for themselves? They can not, dare not, and do not.[48]

Recent Debate Over the Investigative Judgment

Of more concern to many contemporary Adventist scholars than the precise nature of the "spirit of prophecy" bestowed on Ellen White is the doctrine of the Investigative Judgment. The two tenets of the church are closely tied together because the latter was confirmed by one of White's early visions, and if questioned it would cast doubt on her entire prophetic ministry. Yet, because the teaching of Investigative Judgment cannot be supported by Scripture and because it diminishes the effect of Christ's atonement for sin and the doctrine of justification by faith alone, it has become a divisive controversy in the church. This doctrine, it is argued, denies the finished work of Christ on the cross by emphasizing his continuing atoning work. Unlike White's charismatic gift of prophetic utterings and "Testimonies," this teaching can easily be examined against the texts of Scripture, and that is precisely what some Adventist theologians have sought to do. In challenging that tradition, however, they have been ostracized from the very church they sought to reform.

The Findings of Desmond Ford

The most prominent of these theologians is Desmond Ford, an Australian, who along with more than one hundred other teachers and pastors, was forced out of the church. In his case, his ordination was "annulled" in 1983, after he denied that the year 1844 had any biblical significance and offered eighty "implicit" Seventh-day Adventist teachings on the doctrine of Investigative Judgment that could not be supported by Scripture. In responding to the fierce opposition from church leaders, Ford was conciliatory: "We're not antagonistic to the church," he maintained. "We just want to see it come into full harmony with Scripture. The big problem is that administrators are not well informed. Seventh-day Adventists scholars haven't been teaching or writing on the investigative judgment for decades."[49]

The Doctrine Explained

What is the Investigative Judgment? Many Seventh-day Adventists would be at a loss to answer this question, and many pastors would admit that they rarely, if ever, preach the doctrine. Yet, a significant portion of the denomination's Statement of Beliefs is devoted to this doctrine. Article twenty-three of the 1980 revision of this Statement affirms that "in 1844, at the end of the prophetic period of 2,300 days," Jesus "entered the second and last phase of His atoning ministry"—that being "a work of investigative judgment which is part of the ultimate disposition of all sin. . . ." In addition to this, "the investigative judgment reveals to heavenly intelligences who among the dead are asleep in Christ and therefore, in Him, are deemed worthy to have part in the first resurrection. It also makes manifest who, among the living are abiding in Christ, keeping the commandments of God and the faith of Jesus. . . ."[50]

This investigative judgment began in 1844 and is still continuing today. As Ellen White explained in *The Great Controversy*, it is a judgment for "all who have believed on Jesus . . . beginning with those who first lived upon the earth." Jesus serves as an advocate for these professing believers. As their names come before him, their good and bad deeds, as chronicled in the "books" spoken of in Revelation 20:12, are "closely investigated." During this time of judgment, "names are accepted, names are rejected." Those rejected are ones who "have sins remaining upon the books of record, unrepented of and unforgiven." Those accepted are "all who have truly repented of sin, and by faith claimed the blood of Christ as their atoning sacrifice. . . and their characters are found to be in harmony with the law of God." Only those will have their sins "blotted out, and they themselves will be accounted worthy of eternal life."[51]

The "Finished Work" of Christ and the "Blotting Out" of Sin

To biblical scholars, one of the most objectionable aspects of the investigative judgment is its apparent

An early depiction of the Investigative Judgement. From *A History of the Origin and Progress of Seventh-day Adventists* by M. Ellsworth Olsen.

denial of Christ's "finished work" on the cross. In this distinctive Seventh-day Adventist doctrine, a clear distinction is made between the forgiveness of sin and the blotting out of sin. Christ's atonement was sufficient for the forgiveness of sin, but not the blotting out of sin. This position is explained in *Questions on Doctrine:* "The actual blotting out of sin, therefore, could not take place the moment when a sin is forgiven, because subsequent deeds and attitudes may affect the final decision. Instead, the sin remains on the record until the life is complete—in fact, the Scriptures indicate it remains until the judgment."[52]

Even after the name of a completed life has gone before the investigative judgment and been accepted, however, the sin is still not entirely blotted out. That does not happen until Jesus places the sins "upon

111

Satan, who, in the execution of the judgment, must bear the final penalty" because he is "the originator and instigator of sin. The scapegoat, bearing the sins of Israel was sent away . . . so Satan, bearing the guilt of all the sins which he has caused God's people to commit, will be for a thousand years confined to the earth."[53] This "scapegoat" theory is taken from Leviticus 16:8, and is not considered to be sound biblical interpretation by most students of Scripture.

In summarizing the tenets of this doctrine, Anthony Hoekema argues that "the Seventh-day Adventist view of the atonement of Christ contains conflicting emphases. While insisting . . . that the vicarious death of Christ was sufficient for the redemption of a lost race, they have supplemented this pivotal doctrine of historic Christianity with their teaching on the investigative judgment and the placing of sins on Satan." This teaching "that the sins of all men are to be laid on Satan," he maintains, "assigns to Satan an indispensable role in the blotting out of sin, thus detracting from the all-sufficiency of Christ."[54]

Fear of Tampering with Traditions

For many Adventist leaders it made no difference what biblical arguments Desmond Ford and others offered to refute the idea of the investigative judgment. It was considered a distinctive aspect of Adventist tradition that could not be tampered with, as an editorial in the *Adventist Review* argued:

> These landmark doctrines are to be received and held fast, not in formal fashion but in the light of divine guid-

ance given at the beginning of the movement and made our own. Thus we become part and parcel with the movement, and the beliefs that made the original Seventh-day Adventists make us Seventh-day Adventists too.[55]

Reconciliation with Evangelicals

It is the doctrine of investigative judgment more than anything else that separates Seventh-day Adventists from mainline evangelicals, and the dismissal of Desmond Ford and other reformers within the church has widened the gap. Yet, the spirit of animosity between the two camps has diminished considerably in recent decades, since a series of meetings in the 1950s which opened up various doctrinal differences to forthright discussions. Evangelicals, including Donald Grey Barnhouse, Russell Hitt, and Walter Martin, met with Adventist leaders, and from that interaction there was general agreement that the two sides were much closer than had previously been thought. While it was generally agreed upon by the evangelicals that the Adventists taught justification by faith, there remained some significant points of disagreement: "conditional immortality; the seventh-day Sabbath; the investigative judgment and priestly work of Christ in the heavenly sanctuary; and, finally, the concept of a special people for a special message for a special time."[56]

Seventh-day Sabbath and Other Distinctive Doctrines

The distinctive that Seventh-day Adventists are most readily identified with is their Saturday worship and rest. Most evangelicals would consider Saturday worship a less important emphasis, and not an issue that would necessarily have "cultic" connotations. Indeed, before there were Seventh-day Adventists there were Seventh-day Baptists.

Distinction Between Moral and Ceremonial Law

The basis for keeping the Sabbath is not in conjunction with the Jewish ceremonial law, but rather with the moral law. Adventists make a sharp distinction between the two. Seventh-day Adventists believe that "these eternal moral principles are unchanged and unchangeable" and that "these basic principles are found in the Decalogue—Ten Commandments, or the moral law." In reference to the fourth commandment, they argue that "the Sabbath springs from creation week, and is likewise permanent and eternal." They further argue that "as the Sabbath was instituted at creation, before the entrance of sin, it was an inseparable part of God's original plan and provision for man."[57]

In response to their distinction between the ceremonial and moral law, Walter Martin argues that "although there are both moral and ceremonial aspects of the law in the Pentateuch, as well as civil and judicial, nowhere does the Bible state that there is any such juxtaposition of ceremonial with moral law. In fact, the whole Bible teaches that 'the law was given through Moses' (John 1:17) and that it is essentially a *unit*."[58]

Historical Arguments for Sabbath

From a historical perspective, Seventh-day Adventists maintain that the seventh-day Sabbath was practiced in the early church, and that "the first ecclesiastical writer known definitely to teach that the observance of the Sabbath was transferred by Christ to Sunday was Eusebius of Ceasarea . . . in the second quarter of the fourth century." They, likewise, cite Augustine of Hippo, a fifth-century bishop who spoke of Christians fasting on the seventh day. How did the change from Sabbath to Sunday come about? "We, as Adventists, believe there has been a wholly unauthorized, unwarranted, and presumptuous change in the Sabbath by the Catholic, or great Roman, apostasy, as prophesied by Daniel. . . ."[59]

Most biblical scholars and church historians would refute the Adventist claim that the early church preserved a seventh-day Sabbath until it was changed by the Roman Catholic Church in the fourth or fifth century. J. K. Van Baalen writes that in the New Testament era "there is a gradual, almost imperceptible change from the seventh day to the first day of the week." This begins when the resurrected Christ comes to his disciples on the first day of the week, and later when Paul met "on the first day of the week to break bread" with the believers in Troas. Paul, likewise, encouraged the Corinthian church to collect an offering for needy Christians on the first day of the week. Following the New Testament era, "the early writings of Church Fathers contain a large number of references to Sunday as the Sabbath day observed in their time. And these citations . . . range all the way from *The Epistle of Barnabas* (A.D. 100) to Eusebius (A.D. 324)." These sources indicate that both Saturday and Sunday were observed by Christians "just as at first the Jewish church kept circumcision and baptism, but gradually it was realized that the one had come in the place of the other."[60]

Soul Sleep

The belief in "soul sleep" is another aspect of Adventist doctrine that is often challenged by Bible scholars outside the movement. Defenders of the position maintain that their position is biblical and logical— that the soul as well as the body is in a state of unconsciousness: "Death is really and truly a sleep," writes Carlyle Haynes, "a sleep that is deep, that is unconscious, that is unbroken until the awakening at the resurrection." He goes on to argue that "the language of the Bible makes clear that it is the whole man which sleeps, not merely a part. No intimation is given that man sleeps only as to his body, and that he is wakeful and conscious as to his soul. All that comprises the man sleeps in death."[61]

Eternal Punishment

Seventh-day Adventists also deviate from many traditional theologians who hold that the Bible teaches a conscious and everlasting punishment of nonbelievers in hell. In *Questions on Doctrine*, a volume first published in 1957 to answer questions of some leading evangelical churchmen, five reasons are given for this position:

1. Because everlasting life is a gift of God (Rom. 6:23). The wicked do not possess this—they "shall not see life" (John 3:36); "no murderer hath eternal life abiding in him." (1 John 3:15).

2. Because eternal torment would perpetuate and immortalize sin, suffering, and woe, and contradict, we believe, divine revelation, which envisions the time when these things shall be no more (Rev. 21:4).

3. Because it seems to us to provide a plague spot in the universe of God throughout eternity, and would seem to indicate that it is impossible for God Himself ever to abolish it.

4. Because in our thinking it would detract from the attribute of love as seen in the character of God, and postulates the concept of a wrath which is never appeased.

5. Because the Scriptures teach that the atoning work of Christ is to "put away sin" (Heb. 9:26)—first from the individual, and ultimately from the universe. The full fruition of Christ's sacrificial, atoning work will be seen not only in a redeemed people but in a restored heaven and earth (Eph. 1:14).[62]

Worldwide Outreach

Although the Seventh-day Adventists can hardly be considered a cult in the same sense as the Mormons and Jehovah's Witnesses, yet they have been considered outside the evangelical fold by many mission societies. Thus, the church's vast missionary enterprise is often viewed as a threat to Christian missions. Recent statistics show that the movement is active in nearly two hundred countries (almost equal to the Jehovah's Witnesses) and is evangelizing in nearly six hundred languages.

The strong emphasis on missions

is not of recent origin. Ellen G. White wrote extensively on missions and exhorted her followers to make missions a priority in the church. "It is the duty of every Christian," she wrote, "to strive to the utmost of his ability to spread abroad the knowledge of the truth. Christ has commissioned His disciples to go forth into all the world and preach the gospel to all nations." Why? Because "the enemies of God are daily plotting for the suppression of the truth, and the enslaving of the souls of men." And what truth was being suppressed? "They are seeking to exalt the false Sabbath" was the specific issue to which she was referring.[63]

Despite Mrs. White's concern for worldwide expansion, the Seventh-day Adventists were slow to become involved in foreign missionary outreach. Finally in the 1890s the work began in earnest, but it was during the first two decades of the twentieth century, under the presidency of Arthur G. Daniells, the church's first missionary to New Zealand, that foreign missions became the focal point of the movement and launched the church into a massive worldwide outreach that circled the globe with evangelistic zeal and health services.[64]

The most striking aspect of Adventist missions is the humanitarian emphasis. Medical work has always been closely associated with the mission outreach, and in recent years other nonevangelistic services have been added. Worldwide, the church operates nearly one hundred and fifty hospitals and sanitariums and more than two hundred and fifty clinics and dispensaries.[65] In Japan, in addition to hospitals, there is a

health-food factory, a college, and several English language schools conducted by student missionaries who take a year out of their college education in America to work with Japanese students. Yet, despite this enormous expenditure, the Adventist church in Japan remains small, with fewer than one hundred churches and a total membership of some ten thousand.

One of the more unique medical missionary programs conducted by the Seventh-day Adventists has been a boat clinic service on the Amazon River. This endeavor was begun in the 1930s by Jessie and Leo Halliwell, a nurse and an electrical engineer. With their thirty-foot houseboat/clinic they traveled up and down the river, ministering in primitive areas where malnutrition, smallpox, syphilis, hookworm, leprosy, malaria, and other tropical diseases took their toll. After twenty-five years of service, the Halliwells "retired" to begin a new work in Rio de Janeiro, supervising the ministry of all the Adventist medical launches in South America. Before their retirement, however, many others had joined them in their work, and the Amazon was almost becoming crowded with floating clinics.[66]

It would be erroneous to imply that the Adventist missionary program is largely humanitarian in nature. Evangelism is a primary emphasis—an emphasis that was expressed by the movement's president in 1982, as he launched a worldwide blitz to bring a million more people into the fold. In an article entitled "Time for Reaping," President Neal Wilson wrote: "If you have been keeping abreast of activities in the Seventh-day Adventist Church you are certainly aware of the plan that calls for the whole church to engage in one thousand days of reaping. . . . Every one of us is needed and should be involved. As a result of our unified emphasis on public and personal evangelism, and claiming the blessing of the Holy Spirit, we have adopted a prayer objective of an average of 1,000 new souls a day for one thousand days."[67]

Though doctrinally they are in many respects similar to Protestant evangelicals, the Seventh-day Adventists have had to endure the stigma of being classified as a cult for more than a century, and this characterization has tarnished their image both at home and abroad. Yet, their missionary program has far exceeded that of most other Protestant denominations and continues to grow despite the doctrinal controversies over the credibility of Ellen G. White and the validity of the investigative judgment that have raged in the highest levels of the church.

Cult or Protestant Denomination?

An overview of Seventh-day Adventism seems to indicate that the determining factors on whether a religious movement is a "cult" or not are not always black and white. There are gray areas, and this movement would fall into such an area as an ambiguous category—its historical roots being more "cultic" than its

present-day perspective. But even its present-day perspective is clouded by the recent forced resignations of individuals who called into question the authority of Ellen White's writings and the validity of the doctrine of investigative judgment. Yet, it is difficult to evaluate Seventh-day Adventists because individual members themselves often profess a faith that would be difficult to distinguish from mainline evangelicals. Their church services, likewise, are similar or even identical to those of evangelical churches—with hymns and sermons that would sound very familiar.

"Do we look like cult members? Do we look like the kind of people who have strange beliefs?" asked Martha Fox, the pastor's wife to a visiting reporter. "If people would just come and worship with us they'd see we're mainstream Protestants. We're not far out. We're good, Christian people." This concern was reiterated by a history professor at Andrews University: "We see ourselves as being in the same Protestant stream as Lutherans, Methodists and Calvinists. If you understand what we believe, you'll see that we're not such odd ducks."[68]

Indeed, when the distinctive doctrines of the Seventh-day Adventists are not strongly emphasized, most Protestant evangelicals would probably find themselves far more at home in an Adventist church service than in a liberal mainline Protestant one.

Chapter 5

Jehovah's Witnesses: A Religion of Protest

Religious movements do not arise out of a vacuum. There are many societal factors that have an impact on their emergence and acceptance at a particular time and place in history. This is true of virtually any type of religious movement, but seems to be especially characteristic of millenarian sects—sects that emphasize end-time themes. In an article entitled "Hermeneutics or *Zeitgeist* as the Determining Factor in the History of Eschatologies?," Stanley N. Gundry has demonstrated that *zeitgeist* (the spirit of the times) has had a profound influence on the millenarian outlook at any given time.[1]

A striking example of a religious movement influenced by *zeitgeist* is the Jehovah's Witnesses, officially known as the Watchtower Bible and Tract Society. The movement arose in the late nineteenth century as an offspring of Adventist teachings. It was a time when there was much talk about the imminent return of Christ. "Speculation on this subject," writes Alan Rogerson, "was rife and the latter half of the nineteenth century saw a continual succession of people prophesying a date for Jesus' return and the end of the world."[2]

Another factor that influenced the emergence of the Jehovah's Witnesses during this period in American history was Populism, a protest movement against big business and big government. In 1872, at the very time that Charles Taze Russell was initiating the movement that became known as the Jehovah's Witnesses, some one million Americans ratified a political platform that set forth the Populist position. In it, the government was portrayed as a corrupt system controlled by the wealthy class, and it was claimed "that the fruits of the toil of millions are boldly stolen to build up colossal fortunes for a few unprecedented in the history of mankind; and the possessors of these in turn despise the Republic and endanger liberty."[3]

As the Jehovah's Witnesses developed a cohesiveness they began to view the outside world as the enemy—represented most explicitly by the institutionalized churches, human government, and big business. The Roman Catholic Church was regarded with particular anathema—another factor that no doubt was influenced by the spirit of the times. The late nineteenth and early twentieth centuries witnessed a widespread aversion for immigrants of Irish and Southern European descent, and for Roman Catholics in general, as was evidenced by the popularity of the Ku Klux Klan and nativist groups. It was this spirit of the times, in part, that offered fertile soil for the Jehovah's Witnesses. In summing up their outlook, Sydney Ahlstrom writes:

> In its early years, the group embodied a vehement, thoroughgoing protest against the prevailing order. The bold, even law-breaking, "publishers" of its message proclaimed that Satan's three great allies were false teachings in the so-called churches, the tyrannies of human governments, and the oppressions of business. They also attacked the pretensions of orthodox Christianity and questioned its two most central doctrines, the deity of Christ and the depravity of man. They appealed to the poor, outraged middle-class communities by violating their Sabbath quiet laws, and shocked "human governments" by refusing pledges, salutes, and military service to the devil's cohort.[4]

In many respects, the early Jehovah's Witnesses were similar to the Millerites (the followers of William Miller) and early Seventh-day Adventists, but unlike most other millenarian movements, they did not moderate their views as they came of age.

"In an important way," writes M. James Penton, "Jehovah's Witnesses are unique; they have preached millenarianism longer and more consistently than any major sectarian movement in the modern world."[5] This effort to safeguard that tenet of their faith has at different times both aided and injured their cause.

Charles Taze Russell

Charles Taze Russell, the founder of the Jehovah's Witnesses, has been one of the most vilified religious leaders of the past century, and for that reason it is very difficult to sort out the truth from the falsehood. In comparison to Joseph Smith and other cult leaders and founders, however, his personal life was certainly far more circumspect. The primary reason for his tarnished reputation is that he was married to a woman who was unwilling to tolerate the role that was generally accorded to and accepted by women at the turn of the century, and she later became his harshest critic. He had other critics as well. In 1912, during the heyday of his ministry, one Rev. J. J. Ross wrote a booklet entitled *Some Facts and More Facts about the Self-Styled "Pastor" Charles T. Russell.* "By thousands," writes Ross, "he is believed to be a religious fakir of the worst type, who goes about like the Magus of Samaria enriching himself at the expense of the ignorant."[6]

Russell was born in Pittsburgh in 1852, into a family of strict Presbyterians. As a youth he joined his father in the clothing business, and soon "amassed a sizable fortune." Business, however, was not his primary interest. He was preoccupied with spiritual matters, and at the age of seventeen, following a period of doubt and skepticism, he took a step that thrust him on a religious pilgrimage that would continue the rest of his life: "Seemingly by accident," he later recalled, "one evening I dropped into a dusty, dingy hall, where I had heard religious services were held, to see if the handful who met there had anything more sensible to offer than the creeds of the great churches. There, for the first time, I heard something of the views of the Second Adventists."[7]

During the years that followed this memorable night, Russell studied with a number of different individuals with varying degrees of Bible knowledge. One of these was a widely known preacher, George Storrs, who had been an avid champion of William Miller and later edited Adventist publications and helped to found an Adventist group known as the Life and Advent Union. The individual who had the greatest impact on Russell during the 1870s was Nelson Barbour, who taught the concept of the "second presence" of Christ which had begun in 1874. Russell offered financial support to Barbour who edited millennial publications, but as time revealed, he was more inclined to be a leader than a follower. He "was an avid student and began to develop his own doctrinal system based upon a close examination of the Scriptures, various Bible commentaries, and ideas common to much of nineteenth-century American Protestantism." In 1879, Russell initiated his own publication, *Zion's Watch Tower and Herald of Christ's Presence.*[8]

Early Organizational Efforts

Russell's "discovery" in 1875, that Christ had returned invisibly the previous year had had a powerful impact on him. No longer could he invest his life in merchandising. "Up to then his religious beliefs had been a 'spiritual hobby' but now he decided to use his substantial fortune to finance the advertising of the Second Advent." His publishing ventures that began on a small scale quickly expanded as a result of his intense commitment to the cause and his extraordinary advertising skills in promoting his viewpoint.[9]

By the late 1870s, Russell and a few loyal followers had established more than two dozen study groups in seven states between Ohio and the eastern seaboard. He was the acknowledged "pastor" of these congregations, and he was loved and respected by his disciples. His following grew steadily, and in 1884, he officially organized his movement under the name of Zion's Watch Tower and Tract Society. In the early years, as Russell himself was searching for religious truth, he was tolerant of other viewpoints. Issues such as water baptism and other "nonessentials" were a matter of individual preference. But by the 1890s, Russell was strongly urging his followers to study only his teachings, and eventually he was claiming that his *Studies in the Scriptures* "were practically the Bible topically arranged."[10]

Still, Russell retained a high popularity among his followers and his image outside the movement increased. The movement saw a steady increase, largely as a result of his personal magnetism. He made a pro-

Charles Taze Russell. From *Faith on the March* by A. H. Macmillan.

found impact on people wherever he had opportunity to lecture:

> His natural charm, his seeming broad-mindedness, his devotion to the Bible, his extreme claims, all won him devotees in the early years. Russell was always willing to meet people and talk with them. . . . In later life, his long white hair gave him the appearance of a modern patriarch. In speech, both public and private, his professionalized style marked him as a "spell-binder."[11]

Marriage to Maria Ackley

Russell's marriage to Maria Frances Ackley in 1879 was on the surface a happy occasion to celebrate the union of two individuals committed to a common purpose. She was a well-educated, intelligent woman who had been one of his Bible students. Initially, she was his strongest supporter. In fact, she went so far as to propound the theory that her husband was the "faithful and wise servant, whom his lord hath made ruler over his household," mentioned in Matthew 24:45. This was an effort to boost his authority in the face of opposition among his followers. Russell was reluctant to openly make such claims for himself, but according to Penton, "he was doubtlessly flattered by the new and enhanced role that she, by her exegesis, had created for him. Thus he accepted the logic of her interpretation, and his own writings began to make only slightly veiled statements to the effect that he was 'that servant.' "[12]

In the years immediately following their marriage, their relationship appeared to be one of mutual support. She edited her husband's writings, coauthored books with him, spoke to women's groups, and when Zion's Watch Tower Society was formed, she became the secretary-treasurer. Beneath the surface, however, trouble was brewing—trouble that had been germinating even before they repeated their wedding vows. "When they were married," writes Penton, "they had entered into an agreement that their union should not be consummated at that time, nor would they cohabit in the future. . . . Russell seemed to have no problem, for he evidently had little interest in a physical relationship. He simply 'preferred to live a celibate life.' "[13]

As late as 1895, six years after their marriage, Maria was publicly defending her husband from his critics, arguing that he was the "faithful and wise servant," and claiming to have a model marriage. "Our home," she declared, "so far from being a discordant one, is the very reverse—most happy." It was that very year, however, that Russell requested a separation, promising her the house if she would dutifully go along with the arrangement. Russell's motivation for separating from Maria was based on their overall "incompatibility" and that she was wielding too much influence over the ministry. He complained of being "continually harassed with suggestions of alterations of my writings." Moreover, she wanted to publish her personal opinions in Watch Tower publications without being censored and to speak her mind publicly. Regarding the latter concern, she bitterly complained that he had humiliated her in a public meeting.[14]

What followed in the next several years could be described variously as a circus, a soap opera, or a comedy of errors. In 1896, Maria reversed her stance on Matthew 24:45–47, that she had argued pointed to her husband as the "faithful and wise servant," and claimed rather that he had changed into the "evil servant," spoken of in the verses that immediately followed. The following year she called a committee together to settle the matter, but Russell, not to be outdone, mustered his own forces in defense of himself. There was for a time a short reprieve in this public marriage breakdown, but after Maria gained influence over the women's meetings, Russell directed certain individuals that they were "not to receive or harbor or entertain my wife under your roof under any pretext whatsoever." Soon after, Maria moved into a separate residence, and in 1899, they again called a truce, but it did not last. Maria's next major tactic was "to publish a tract which was an account of her relations with her husband over the years and another bitter attack on him. In it, she published correspondence between them and attempted, with some success, to paint him as an arrogant tyrant." These were sent to all the Watch Tower Bible students and others who had an interest in her husband's character. In retaliation, Russell and some of his loyalists went to her residence and removed all her personal possessions and those of the other tenants in the boarding house—an action which promptly provoked a lawsuit.[15]

Legal Separation and Court Trials

In 1903, Maria filed for a legal separation, which was followed three years later by a widely publicized court case. Her charges against him were primarily related to complaints of "conceit, egotism, and domination." She also, however, did not miss the opportunity to interject some ambiguous charges regarding her husband's relationship with the opposite sex. She accused him of being alone in the bedrooms of their adopted daughter and a hired maid and taking indiscretions with both of them on different occasions. She did not accuse him of adultery and, in fact, stated that she did not believe he was guilty of that crime. Nevertheless, that charge was made by critics and has followed him long beyond the grave. Russell denied any wrongdoing, and later took a vow to never again be alone in a room with a someone of the opposite sex.[16]

Russell's vow may have been prompted in part by the very negative publicity he was receiving in the press. The court record had included a quote from his adopted daughter, who alleged he had said to her: "I am like a jellyfish. I float around here and there. I touch this one and that, and if she responds I take her to me, and if not I float on to others." The veracity of this strange statement was impossible to prove, but more than any other aspect of the trial, the "jellyfish" story was sensationalized, and Russell was "soon pegged as the 'Jellyfish Pastor' and the name stuck with him to his death." A 1906 issue of the *Washington Post* is an example of the scathing slander that was put in print:

> The Rev. Russell says he's like a jellyfish; that he floats about touching his lady parishioners. . . .
>
> But, upon the whole, this new faith, "the Russellite," seems to possess a great many of the elements of popularity. Sooner or later, of course, the higher officials of the church, and perhaps a few of the more adventurous gentlemen of the congregation, may conclude that with a little practice they might become pretty active jellyfish themselves, and that would inevitably lead to dissension. . . . The great truth remains that the Rev. Jellyfish Russell has opened up a mighty attractive pathway to the higher life, and that, barring unforeseen catastrophes, he will get there with enviable frequency.[17]

His marital problems were not the only public embarrassments Russell endured during the years of his expanding ministry. There was also the "Miracle Wheat" scandal, which was no doubt exaggerated out of proportion by his critics outside the movement. Russell's most merciless opponent was the *Brooklyn Daily Eagle*, a tabloid that repeatedly maligned him

both in his personal and public life. In citing those articles about him, Walter Martin quotes lengthy segments "to authenticate beyond doubt the true history of Russell."[18] No newspaper should be used "to authenticate beyond doubt" the truth of a particular allegation, and that principle particularly holds true with the *Brooklyn Daily Eagle*, which was known for slanted reporting and vindictive stories about individuals who represented minority opinions.

The "Miracle Wheat" scandal that the *Brooklyn Daily Eagle* sensationalized in front-page stories in January of 1913, related to Russell's advertising the product for one dollar a pound—a real bargain if as claimed by the promotional hoopla that it would yield five times more than any other brand of wheat. That Russell intentionally sought to deceive is unlikely. His amazing claims for the wheat were made in the pages of the *Watch Tower*, and thus the only people affected by the sham were followers or potential converts— hardly the sort of people he would have chosen to alienate.

Bible Teaching and Writing

While such scandals have been magnified by Russell's critics, their actual impact on his career were negligible. His reputation was built largely on his Bible teaching and his writing, and by the time of his death in 1916, his six-volume series, *Studies in Scripture*, had more than thirteen million copies in circulation. These volumes were more than mere study helps in the eyes of Russell and his followers. In a 1910 issue of *Watch-*

tower magazine, he set forth his own estimation of them:

Not only do we find that people cannot see the divine plan in studying the Bible by itself, but we see also that if anyone lays the *Scripture Studies* aside even after he has used them, after he has become familiar with them, after he has read them for ten years—if he lays them aside and ignores them and goes to the Bible alone, though he had understood his Bible for years, our experience shows that within two years he goes into darkness. On the other hand, if he had merely read the *Scripture Studies* with their references and had not read a page of the Bible as such, he would be in the light at the end of two years, because he would have the light of the Scriptures.[19]

In many instances, Russell's interpretations were taken from others—his unitarianism and denial of Christ's full deity, for example, being little more than a warmed over Arianism of the fourth century. It was his eschatology, however, that was viewed as the most innovative of his teachings, and the aspect of his writings that was most eagerly read.

Date-setting Eschatology

Even more than the Millerites who preceded him, he was known for date-setting. Initially 1874 was seen as a crucial date. This was not original with Russell, but rather it came largely from others to whom he was indebted for his early millenarian concepts. The date "marked the end of 6,000 years of human history and they had expected Christ's return in that year. When it passed they felt disillusioned," but then the idea was advanced "that Christ had indeed returned in 1874 but invisibly."[20]

The year 1914 became the next crucial prophetic date to watch for. The date was arrived at by a contrived interpretation of Daniel 4, where the expression "seven times" occurs in reference to King Nebuchadnezzar and the period of insanity he would undergo. That expression was interpreted to refer to seven prophetic years of 360 days, equalling 2,520 days, which was then transferred back to years and added unto 607 B.C. (the date believed by some to be the destruction of Jerusalem), which was calculated to be 1914.

The eventful year 1914 did offer more to date-setters than most years do, and the Jehovah's Witnesses in the ensuing years have made the most of it. The explanation is given in the Watch Tower's widely distributed book, *The Truth That Leads to Eternal Life:*

Exactly what did Jesus point to as marking his second presence and the "conclusion of the system of things"? He said: "Nation will rise against nation and kingdom against kingdom, and there will be food shortages and earthquakes in one place after another." (Matthew 24:7) Here Jesus tells us to look for a new kind of warfare—total war! The war that began in 1914 fits his description. Not only did armies fight on the battlefields; civilian populations too were organized to give full support to the war. . . . For the first time in history the whole world was at war.[21]

The date had more significance, however, than merely a fulfillment of prophecy for the Jehovah's Witnesses. "What especially distinguishes their teachings from any other denomination is the keystone doctrine centered on 1914," writes Raymond Franz. This is "the date when Christ's active rulership began, his commencing judgment then and, above all, his selecting the Watch Tower organization as his official channel, his assigning full control of all his earthly interests to a 'faithful and discreet slave class' and, factually, giving ultimate authority to its ruling body."[22]

Pyramid gravestone of Charles Taze Russell.

Prophesying Through a Pyramid

That Russell would seek to calculate the end times on the basis of the Book of Daniel was not in itself a peculiar exercise. He was only one of many searching for biblical clues to the time of the Lord's return. But he did not limit his sources to the Bible. In the 1880s, he became intrigued by published accounts speculating that the Great Pyramid of Gizeh was some sort of "miracle in stone." He was convinced that God has purposely designed it as an indicator of the end times. The measurements could be calculated in years rather than inches, he confidently revealed to his readers in *Studies in the Scriptures:*

> Then measuring *down* the "Entrance Passage" from that point, to find the distance to the entrance of the "Pit," representing the great trouble and destruction with which this age is to close, when evil will be overthrown from power, we find it to be 3416 inches, symbolizing 3416 years from the above date, B.C. 1542. This calculation shows A.D. 1874 as marking the beginning of the period of trouble; for 1542 years B.C. plus 1874 was the *chronological* beginning of the time of trouble such as was not since there was a

nation—no, nor ever shall be afterward.[23]

"The significance of the acceptance by Russell and his followers of pyramidology has a sinister overtone to it," write Leonard and Marjorie Chretien. "The Great Pyramid figures prominently in many medieval and Renaissance cults, especially in the Rosicrucian and occult traditions." This "Bible in stone" doctrine was renounced in 1928, by Joseph Rutherford, Russell's successor, but books containing the doctrine were distributed by Jehovah's Witnesses as late as the mid-1940s.[24] Russell died in 1916, and was buried beneath a massive pyramid grave marker. He was eulogized by his followers with a long list of credits to his name in the eyes of his followers: "he traveled a million miles, delivered 30,000 sermons and table talks—many of them 2 1/2 hours long—wrote over 50,000 pages . . . of advanced Biblical exposition, often dictated 1,000 letters per month, managed every department of a world-wide evangelistic campaign employing 700 speakers."[25] But despite the debt Jehovah's Witnesses owe him as their founder, he is rarely mentioned today by a movement that insists it will not honor a mere man.

Joseph Franklin Rutherford

Within months after the death of Russell in 1916, Judge Joseph Rutherford had effectively assumed control of the Watch Tower organization. He had been a faithful defender of Russell—both personally and legally—and was convinced that he was the most qualified to serve as a successor. He had been raised a Baptist in Missouri, but had turned away from organized religion in adulthood. His law profession was undistinguished as was his tenure as a substitute judge. The most eventful episode during his residence in Missouri was his conversion to Russell's new movement. He later reflected on the occasion:

> Long before I knew Pastor Russell he had done much for me. While I was engaged in the law practice in the Middle West, there came into my office one day a lady bearing some books in her arms. She was modest, gentle, and kind. I thought she was poor, and that it was my privilege and duty to help her. I found that she was rich in faith in God. I bought the books and afterwards read them. Up to that time I knew nothing about the Bible; I had never heard of Pastor Russell. I did not even know that he was the author of the books at the time I read them; but I knew that the wonderfully sweet, harmonious explanation of the plan of God thrilled my heart and changed the course of my life from doubt to joy.[26]

Dissension Following Russell's Death

Rutherford's experience as a lawyer was a welcome asset to Russell who was often involved in one form of litigation or another, and it was in that capacity that the Judge, as he was referred to, became intimately acquainted with Russell and the developing Watch Tower organization. At Russell's death, however, he was not named the successor or even viewed as a likely candidate by most insiders. Indeed, "it was inconceivable that anybody should have expected to assume the leadership of the Watch Tower movement in Russell's own fashion, and that was why he had entrusted in his will all his voting rights in the society to a group of women who, by reason of their sex, were disqualified from holding any office."[27]

There was a "fierce struggle for power," according to Alan Rogerson, but in the end, through clever maneuvering, Rutherford managed to seize control and maintain his position despite the intense opposition from individuals and factions. So heated did the conflict become that at one point there was a physical tussle between Rutherford and one of his antagonists during a noon meal at the Bethel headquarters in Brooklyn, New York. In the end, Rutherford prevailed and brought a new style to the movement. As a result, many of Russell's Bible Students deserted the organization and formed groups of their own such as the Dawn Bible Students Association, The Standfast Movement, the Layman's Home Missionary Movement, the Eagle Society, the Elijah Voice Movement, and the Pastoral Bible Institute of Brooklyn. "Thus," writes Rogerson, "modern-day Jehovah's Witnesses are not necessarily direct successors of Pastor Russell."[28]

Joseph Franklin Rutherford. From *Faith on the March* by A. H. Macmillan.

Anti-war Stance

One of the reasons that Rutherford saw success in his efforts to control the organization was a sense of solidarity that developed due to the outside opposition to the anti-war stance. He made vehement public attacks against the war effort, and he "openly criticized Russell for suggesting that Bible Students should pray for the sake of the allied effort in 1916." His bitter criticism of the war effort was reinforced by his outlining distinct policies on conscientious objection and other means to circumvent the draft.[29]

In February of 1918, the Canadian government banned a number of books published by the society, and three months later a district court in New York issued warrants for the arrest of Rutherford and seven of his close associates for "unlawfully, feloniously and wilfully causing insubordination, disloyalty and refusal of duty in the military and naval forces of the United States of America when the United States was at war." In June of 1918, seven of them were sentenced to twenty years in prison and one was sentenced to ten years. Their incarceration in the Atlanta Federal Penitentiary lasted for less than a year, however. In 1919, their convictions were overturned, and the following year the attorney general exonerated them.[30]

Development of "Theocratic Government"

Unlike Russell, who had depended heavily on his own personal charisma, Rutherford used organizational strategy and fear tactics to change the movement from a decentralized Bible student society into a tightly structured order controlled from the top, which he later referred to as a "Theocratic Government." Anyone who opposed the president, was in effect opposing God—or at least the will of God. Many lamented the change that had come about, and there were continual comparisons between the "good old days" of Russell and the misery brought on by Rutherford. One such lament is that of William Schnell, whose widely circulated book, *Thirty Years a Watch Tower Slave*, is a stinging attack on the Watch Tower Society. The author, however, traces the evil within the organization to Rutherford, not to Russell, who at times is depicted as a virtual saint in comparison to his successor.[31]

Scandalous Personal Life

Rutherford's personal life was in many ways more scandalous than his predecessor's had been, but it was not the subject of newspaper vendettas as Russell's was. Like Russell, he was separated from his wife, who was described as "a semi-invalid who could not render the judge his marital dues." There was other apparent strife between them as well—some of which may have been heightened by his alcoholism. "Although Jehovah's Witnesses have done everything possible to hide accounts of the judge's drinking habits," writes Penton, "they are simply too notorious to be denied. Former workers at the Watch Tower's New York headquarters recount tales of his inebriation and drunken stupors. Others tell stories of how difficult it was to get him to the podium to give talks at conventions because of his drunkenness."[32]

Although many of the accounts of Rutherford's behavior may have been exaggerated by his enemies, there was a general perception that he was living a double life, and his drinking was only one indication of that. His vulgar language was known to many insiders, and he "was once publicly accused by one of his closest associates of attending a nude burlesque show with two fellow elders and a young Bible Student woman on a Wednesday evening before the celebration of the Memorial of the Lord's Supper." Another facet of his private life was his opulent living. He had a luxury apartment in New York City, a "palatial residence" on Staten Island, and a San Diego "mansion," named Beth Sarim, located on a two-hundred acre estate.[33]

Despite Rutherford's personal vices and bent for luxurious living, no one could accuse him of not being dedicated to the success of the Watch Tower society. "He proved to be every bit as much a human dynamo as Pastor Russell had been," writes Penton. "Again and again he spoke at Watch Tower conventions, over national and international radio between the mid-1920s and 1937, and on many phonograph recordings." Perhaps even more amazing was that in the midst of this busy schedule, he maintained a heavy writing schedule, averaging a book a year.[34]

New Eschatology

More important than personality and life style differences between Russell and Rutherford were the doctrinal differences. In some instances, Rutherford expanded on his predecessor's positions and in other instances he contradicted them. One of the most significant innovations in practical theology that Rutherford made was to change the custom of keeping the Sabbath. It was in the area of eschatology, however, that Rutherford deviated most from Russell. He downplayed the year 1874, in favor of 1914; he then focused on 1925 for "the completion of all things." Taking his cue from the Book of Revelation, he reinterpreted the Battle of Armageddon, describing it as a universal war during which time all people outside the Watch Tower organization would be destroyed. Only a remnant of 144,000 would then go to heaven, and the remainder would spend eternity on earth.[35]

Rutherford's prediction that the year 1925 would be "the completion of all things" was more than an idle statement that failed to be taken seriously by the rank and file of the society's membership. On the contrary, it was taken very seriously, and in many ways was reminiscent of the Great Disappointment of 1844. "Many gave up their businesses, jobs, and even sold their homes in the expectation that they would soon be living in an earthly paradise. . . . Numerous Bible Student farmers in both Canada and the United States refused to seed their spring crops and mocked their co-religionists who did."[36] In light of this fiasco—and others in Watch Tower history—it is peculiar that the organization would denounce false prophecies, as was the case in a 1968 issue of *Awake!* magazine:

> True, there have been those in times past who predicted an "end to the world," even announcing a specific date. Some have gathered groups of people with them and fled to the hills or withdrawn into their houses waiting for the end. Yet, nothing happened. The "end" did not come. They were guilty of false prophesying. Why? What was missing?
>
> Missing was the full measure of evidence required in fulfillment of Bible prophecy. Missing from such people were God's truths and the evidence that he was guiding and using them.[37]

Evangelistic Outreach

Winning converts became the all-consuming obsession of the movement during the Rutherford years, and door-to-door witnessing with literature and phonographs was re-quired for all members who wished to remain in good standing. As a reflection of this emphasis, and in an effort to break away from the nostalgia of the more laid-back days of Russell, Rutherford, in 1931, began referring to the movement as Jehovah's Witnesses. Despite the intense proselytizing, there was very slow growth during the first two decades of his rule. Nearly as many dissidents left the movement as converts joined. But his methods took hold and during his last years, there was a significant growth factor.[38]

Nathan Homer Knorr

Following the death of Rutherford in 1942, Nathan H. Knorr assumed the presidency of the Watch Tower Society. His ascendancy to power was uneventful and smooth in comparison to that of his predecessor a quarter of a century earlier. Under him, the organization shifted away from being a personality cult as it had been to a large extent under Russell and to a lesser extent under Rutherford. Knorr was by nature a more quiet and shy individual, but his changes reflected more than efforts to accommodate his own personality. He had worked his way up through the ranks, having spent his entire adult life working at the Bethel headquarters in Brooklyn. He avoided public appearances and was content to work behind the scenes whenever possible.[39]

Knorr, in fact, made a very conscious effort to depersonalize the organization. The emphasis was now on numbers and on all the anonymous workers in the field who were witnessing and winning converts. All

Nathan Homer Knorr. From *Faith on the March* by A. H. Macmillan.

literature was, likewise, produced anonymously. This may have been, as some have suggested, to cover his own inability to write as his predecessors had done, but whatever the motives, "he sought to turn Jehovah's Witnesses into a far more sophisticated, moral, and effective band of preachers of Jehovah's Kingdom than they had ever been in the past."[40]

Foreign Missions

One of his innovations to carry out this goal was the establishment of the Watch Tower Bible School of Gilead. It was a missionary training school that provided the necessary leadership for overseas and domestic evangelistic activities, and only the most active and faithful Jehovah's Witnesses were accepted as candidates.

Previously foreign missionary work had been done only haphazardly, but Knorr sought to systematically develop a worldwide expansion program that would cover the globe within his own lifetime. He also instituted the Kingdom Ministry School, which offered training for people on the lay level.[41]

Codified Moral Standards

It was during Knorr's years that the Watch Tower Society also took steps to impose a strict moral code on its membership—a code which became more and more complicated. Timothy White enumerates some of the specifics in his book *A People for His Name:*

> The Witnesses are specifically forbidden to practice gambling, hunt or fish for sport, tell lies among themselves, laugh at dirty jokes, wear mourning clothes for long after the death of a relative, justify themselves, masturbate, become an officer in a union or picket, go out on a date without a chaperon, throw rice at weddings, display affection in public except for momentarily at greetings and partings, become a member of, or frequent a nudist colony, participate in prayer led by one not dedicated to Jehovah, give free rein to unbridled passion whilst having allowed sexual intercourse, use profanity, or do the twist.[42]

Such rules for social behavior were not entirely unique to the Jehovah's Witnesses. Various Holiness and Fundamentalist congregations of the period had lists of "dos and don'ts" that could have easily rivaled theirs. What was unique about the Watch Tower Society, however, was it's "Orwellian" masterplan of organizational

Frederick W. Franz. From *Faith on the March* by
A. H. Macmillan.

was likewise a period of consolidating the worldwide ministry of the movement, which was celebrated through international conventions held periodically in New York City. In a sense, these gatherings constituted a public show of force by a group that was very conscious of being a persecuted minority in much of the world. More than a quarter of a million people attended the convention in 1958 in Yankee Stadium—a setting which allowed them to vent their animosity to the world outside. Their exclusiveness was demonstrated in many ways, among which was a declaration "to the effect that the clergy of Christendom were the most reprehensible class on earth today."[43]

control to insure uniformity among the rank and file of the membership. Informants were designated to keep track of conversation in small group meetings and report back any views that conflicted with the policy line. It was a systematic program of employing fear tactics that has been graphically detailed in two recent books, *The Orwellian World of Jehovah's Witnesses* and *Crisis of Conscience.*

Organizational Growth

Despite the strict controls that were being instituted on a broad scale during the Knorr years, it was a period of unprecedented growth. This factor was meticulously documented in detailed records of outreach activities—the records themselves being an impetus to growth. It

Frederick W. Franz

In 1975, after the death of Knorr, Frederick W. Franz took over the top position at Bethel headquarters, where he had been moving up through the ranks for the previous thirty-five years. He has been referred to as the society's leading idealogue and foremost Bible scholar, and with good reason. He has been one of the few Jehovah's Witnesses who has had a knowledge of both Greek and Hebrew as well as other languages. Although he would earn a reputation as being as ruthless as his predecessors in the area of authoritarian control and purging dissidents (including his own nephew), he was known by many insiders for being warm and likable. Barbara Harrison, who worked under him in the Brooklyn offices, wrote the following:

I remember Franz as an ascetic, kindly man, with an engaging sense of humor and a gift for self-mockery. Much loved by the Witnesses, he is as unworldly as Knorr was businesslike. When I knew him, he was adorably sweet-spirited (though, from my point of view, maddeningly earnest when it came to dogma). A flamboyant orator, he was personally reticent, though not inaccessible. He seemed to have scant regard for his personal appearance; still slim and handsome in his 60s, he was as likely as not to be found shuffling around headquarters in bedroom slippers and mismatched socks. His minor, unselfconscious eccentricities of dress and demeanor, and a nature that was by turns reclusive and gregarious, endeared him to all of the headquarters staff. I have never met a Witness who did not like Franz. He seemed never to have incurred the animosity that Russell, Rutherford, and Knorr, all in their turn, did. It was regarded as an honor to be invited to his spartan room.[44]

Prophecy Debacles and Disfellowshiping

By the end of Knorr's presidency in 1977, there was trouble brewing in the ranks. One of the tension points related to the 1975 prophecy of the end of the world—a designation that was made in 1966 after a six-year slump in baptisms. This date was based on findings that showed there had been a one-hundred-year miscalculation in the original designation of 1874 as the end of the world. As a pragmatic ploy to increase membership, the prophecy worked. A 1968 issue of *Kingdom Ministry* urged Jehovah's Witnesses to abandon their regular employment in exchange for full-time Pioneer service. "In view of the short period of time left," the article entreated, "we want to do this as often as circumstances permit. Just think, brothers, there are only about ninety months left before 6,000 years of man's existence on earth is completed." Many responded, as a later issue of *Kingdom Ministry* indicated: "Reports are heard of brothers selling their homes and property and planning to finish out the rest of their days in this old system in the pioneer service."[45]

With the failed prophecy, the number of full-time publishers dropped nearly forty percent, and rumblings of discontent were on the upsurge. As a result, the organization further tightened its reigns in an effort to banish the "apostates." In that sense, 1978 was a banner year. Nearly thirty thousand were expelled. The 1979 *Yearbook* of the Jehovah's Witnesses acknowledged the magnitude of the problems as a warning to those who themselves might be lured away by Satan.

The Lord Jesus Christ, who knows the spiritual condition of each one who professes to be his follower, does not tolerate lukewarmness. He advises any who are in that state now to rectify their condition if they are to please him. And just as some deviated from the truth in the first century, it is not surprising that the same thing happens today. Jehovah knows those who belong to him. Warning examples of what befell the Israelites as they were about to enter the Promised Land should keep us individually from becoming overconfident. The seriousness of this matter is emphasized in the fact that 29,893 were disfellowshiped last year. There is no question that our faith is being tested today.[46]

The Disfellowshiping of Raymond Franz

For many Jehovah's Witnesses, the ordeal of being "disfellowshiped" is a painful misfortune that can only be understood by one who has experienced it. The most celebrated case of disfellowshiping during this post-1975 purge was that of Raymond Franz, the nephew of Frederick W. Franz, who moved into the leadership position at Bethel headquarters following Knorr's death. Raymond Franz himself was a member of the elite who sat on the Governing Body—a reward bestowed upon him after more than three decades of faithful and diligent service. Referring to his expulsion as a "downfall as dramatic as an excommunication within the College of Cardinals," *Time* magazine reported that the organization used "star-chamber tactics" in its efforts to eradicate dissent. A "secret investigation of heresy rumors" was conducted and "members were allegedly threatened with disfellowshiping to get their testimony about doctrinal discussions." In the end, his downfall came as a result of his having lunch with a "disassociated" Jehovah's Witnesses friend. "By one stroke, they eliminated all my years of service," lamented Franz. "I frankly do not believe there is another organization more insistent on 100% conformity."[47]

The "Remnant" Class

Another area of conflict in the 1970s related to the "remnant" class of 144,000 who could count on spending eternity in heaven rather than on earth with the rest of the "great crowd," spoken of in Revelation 7:14. By 1939, the remnant had reached its capacity, and from then on, only a very few could be added, and those only as "replacements" for ones in the remnant who had become unfaithful. But, contrary to the organization's plans, active witnesses in the early 1970s began claiming that they were part of the remnant—signifying that by participating in communion at the yearly Memorial meeting. Although this had previously been a very private individual decision between the individual and God, it became a point of contention as the numbers continued to increase. "Consequently, if one were much less than sixty-five years of age and began partaking the Lord's supper," writes Penton, "he was under intense social and organizational pressure to stop. Sometimes he would be gossiped about, virtually shunned, and treated with the utmost disrespect. Thus some partakers were bullied into denying their heavenly calling by peer pressure, the elders, or the circuit overseers."[48]

Official Policy on Civil Government and Blood Transfusions

A far more serious problem that created discord in the Watch Tower organization during the 1970s related to policy on civil government. The society, since the days of Rutherford, had taken a strong stance against any certificate or official documentation that would link an individual with a government or political party. The consequences of this action were often severe, as was true in the African country of Malawi in 1972. The charge against the Jehovah's

Witnesses there was that they refused to buy the thirty-four-cent Malawi Congress Party card, indicating they were members of the party—a regulation required of all citizens. Their refusal to cooperate resulted in widespread imprisonment, torture, and even murder. There were reports that they were in some instances "hacked to death, gang-raped and forced to walk with nails through their feet."[49]

Because of the highly publicized harassment that Jehovah's Witnesses were enduring in various countries, Raymond Franz was assigned to write a defense of the organization's policy. In his attempt to do so, he realized that the policy could not be defended biblically. But even worse than that discovery was the realization that the policy was altogether inconsistent, allowing some Witnesses, such as those in Mexico, to comply with government regulations by a systematic program of bribes, while their African counterparts were being hacked to death. The bribing was justified by officials because the money went to private individuals instead of the government itself.[50]

Saluting the Flag

There have been other volatile issues tied to government policy that have plagued the Jehovah's Witnesses over the years, such as saluting the flag. It was Rutherford who condemned the practice in 1935, during a time when pledging the flag was compulsory in most American public schools. The issue had actually arisen some years earlier, when German Witnesses "adamantly refused to participate in Nazi or state

functions where they would be required to perform such activities." When their ardent stance on the issue was visibly observed on the American scene, the matter went all the way to the Supreme Court, where the judges ruled in an eight-to-one decision in the *Gobitis* case against the Jehovah's Witnesses. "As a result, mob action against them increased dramatically. Hundreds of such incidents, generally promoted by the American Legion, the Veterans of Foreign Wars, and certain Catholic writers, occurred throughout the nation until the Supreme court reversed its ruling . . . on 14 June 1943—Flag Day in the United States."[51]

Blood Transfusions

One of the most publicized features of Watch Tower doctrine and practice relates to blood transfusions. During the Russell and Rutherford years, the issue was not raised because the widespread use of blood transfusions did not begin until the end of World War II. At that time, the organization took a hard-line position against blood transfusions in any circumstances, basing their stand on biblical texts that forbid the eating of blood—the most frequently quoted verse being Leviticus 17:10, which states: "As for any man . . . who eats any sort of blood, I shall certainly set my face against the soul that is eating the blood." The New Testament is also used to support this position:

Examine the scriptures carefully and notice that they tell us to "*keep free from blood*" and to "*abstain* from blood." (Acts 15:20, 29) What does that mean? If a doctor were to tell you to abstain from alcohol, would that mean simply that you should not take it through your mouth but that you could transfuse it directly into your veins? Of course not! So, too, "abstaining from blood" means not taking it into our bodies at all.[52]

Not surprisingly, there have been a number of highly publicized and controversial cases relating to this unbending principle. One such case involved Joyce Prudhomme, a twenty-eight-year-old woman suffering from a rare blood disease, who died in a Miami hospital in 1980, after she resolutely refused to have a blood transfusion. "I just can't believe that a religion would let her commit suicide," her husband lamented. "I know that if she had had more time to think about it, she would have never thrown her life away." What was unusual in her situation was that she had only been attending Jehovah's Witnesses meetings for two years and "had not formally become a member." In defending her stance, an elder in her congregation said, "If you save your life by violating God's laws, you have no hope of resurrection."[53]

Fighting in the Courts

Jehovah's Witnesses, more than any other religious movement, have made a mark on American history from a legal standpoint. Numerous cases have set legal precedent and established guidelines for interpreting constitutional law. This has been documented in a journal article published by the American Bar Association, which maintains that religious liberties for all Americans have been reinforced by these court battles.

Seldom, if ever, in the past has one individual or group been able to shape the course, over a period of time, of any phase of our vast body of constitutional law. But it can happen, and it has happened, here. The group is Jehovah's Witnesses. Through almost constant litigation this organization has made possible an ever-increasing list of precedents concerning the application of the Fourteenth Amendment to freedom of speech and religion. . . . The decisions resulting therefrom now set the pattern for state courts in determining how far state legislatures may validly proceed on matters pertaining to freedom of speech and religion. . . . Thus, while the cult though vigorously active, has but negligible influence, its incidental contributions to constitutional law have been tremendously significant.[54]

The first major case related to proselytizing that went to the Supreme Court was in 1938, when Jehovah's Witnesses were prohibited from distributing their literature door-to-door in Griffin, Georgia. The Court struck down the city ordinance, giving the Watch Tower Society a victory that had far-reaching consequences. The following year similar regulations were invalidated in New Jersey. There were other cases involving proselytizing that went to the Supreme Court, but equally significant was the litigation over refusal to salute the flag. Watch Tower lawyers were ready for battle after two young children had been expelled from school in Minersville, Pennsylvania, for declining to participate in a flag salute ceremony at an assembly. They argued that the school board had violated the Fourteenth Amendment. "But in the celebrated *Minersville v. Gobitis* case the Supreme

Bethel Headquarters in Brooklyn, New York.

Court upheld the school board's action." Three years later, however, in *West Virginia State Board of Education v. Barnette* the Court reversed itself and offered the following memorable words:

"If there is any fixed star in our constitutional constellation, it is that no official, high or petty, can prescribe what shall be orthodox in politics, nationalism, religion, or other matters of opinion or force citizens to confess by word or act their faith therein."[55]

Organizational Structure

More than any other alternative religion, the Watch Tower organization itself is supreme, for Jehovah himself designated the organization to be his representative on earth since 1914. Since that time it has become a powerful bureaucracy that is rigidly structured from the top down.

Bethel Headquarters

The only thing most people know about the Watch Tower Bible and Tract Society—if they know anything at all—is that it is the publishing house for the literature distributed by the Jehovah's Witnesses. It is a colossal publishing industry that prints billions of pieces of literature each year. More than ten million copies of *The Watchtower* magazine alone are printed each edition, and this magazine is issued twice each month.[56]

But the significance of the Bethel headquarters in Brooklyn is far greater than simply publishing books and tracts. Unlike the Mormons, who so obviously fall into a "cult" category with their claims to a prophet-founder and extrabiblical scriptures, the Jehovah's Witnesses make no such claims. Indeed, they seek to downplay their association with Russell, recognizing him only as the initiator of the movement that became known as Jehovah's Witnesses, and his successors were mere men who carried on many of his teachings. Likewise, they would shun the idea of extrabiblical scriptures. But it is important to realize that there is only a subtle difference between the extrabiblical authority given to prophet and scriptures by the Mormons and the same type of authority given to the Governing Body at Bethel headquarters. Indeed, in the minds of many, the Bethel power base in Brooklyn is an authority unto itself that is beyond the challenge of scholarly biblical debate. Certainly this was true in the case of Raymond Franz, whose disagreements with the "party line" terminated his lifelong involvement with that organization.

Little has been known about the inside workings of the Bethel headquarters until recent years when "defectors" have told their stories—Raymond Franz being the most prominent member to leave and then write about his experiences. For most Jehovah's Witnesses, the inner sanctums of the Bethel headquarters are utterly remote. Even living and working at the vast Brooklyn complex—comprised of office buildings, publishing warehouses, and residences—offers virtually no opportunity to observe how the system actually operates. Loyal Bethel workers tend to turn their back on rumors of surveillance and spying, dutifully accepting the fact that they have no voice in policy making.[57]

Challenging the authorities is simply not considered to be a matter of concern or interest to Jehovah's Witnesses. "To the average Witness his community is first and foremost his local congregation. For life revolves around the kingdom hall." The kingdom hall is essentially the church building of the Jehovah's Witnesses—a building reserved exclusively for church activities. Yet, according to Penton, "they none the less dominate the lives of those who attend them. True, only congregational meetings, funerals, and weddings are ever held in them. But because so much Witness activity revolves around the five regular meetings and regular rendezvous for preaching, what occurs at the local kingdom hall becomes fundamental to the establishment of social relationships within the congregation."[58]

Kingdom Halls

The local congregations are tied organizationally to Bethel headquarters through the supervision of district and circuit overseers. "These men, frequently accompanied by their wives, visit each congregation twice a year, instructing congregational elders and accompanying Witnesses from door to door to help perfect their proselytizing techniques. They inspect and audit local finances, and they file with headquarters confidential progress reports on each congregation. . . ."[59]

The buildings themselves are basic, simply-designed, modern structures that might appear at first glance to be a clinic or place of business rather than a church. In recent years, it has become the practice to standardize the architectural design and to construct them with volunteer labor—sometimes in the space of one weekend. According to a newspaper article in 1982, "Jehovah's Witnesses believe there are more important things than building a church. That's why they seldom spend more than 48 hours constructing one." They "are constructing an average of four to six similar halls each month across the nation, and the quick-building system is spreading internationally, to Canada, England and South Africa. . . . The halls usually are built by about 300 volunteers who begin work early on Saturday."[60]

Lay Leadership

There are no pastors or full-time ministers who serve as leaders of the local congregations. All Jehovah's Witnesses view themselves as ministers. The leaders of the kingdom halls are laymen, referred to as elders, who are chosen on the basis of their faithfulness to the work and their ability to defend the doctrine. Only baptized men over the age of twenty are eligible. Women are often the most heavily involved in the door-to-door "publishing," but it is left to men—and men only—to oversee the ministry at the kingdom hall. The concept of a paid, trained clergy is anathema to the Jehovah's Witnesses. "The Clergy's God," wrote Russell, "is plainly not Jehovah but the ancient deity, hoary with the iniquity of the ages—Baal, the Devil himself."[61]

Because of the tight controls and intolerance of criticism, there is very little opportunity for innovation and creativity in the several meetings that are held each week. Indeed, this is an area that is disparaged by ex-Jehovah's Witnesses, such as Gordon Duggar, who has little but contempt for the time he consumed at kingdom hall meetings.

A principle meeting is usually held on Sunday and consists of two main parts. The public talk consists of a discourse by one of the male members or by a visiting Witness. He is rarely a skilled speaker, and most of the talks are monotonous, low key and, as a matter of fact, dull. The format sent down from headquarters is strictly followed. One or two songs are sung, perhaps accompanied by a piano or occasionally by tapes supplied by headquarters. Note that there is no music servant, and the singing is often disastrous. . . . After the lecture (sermon would not be a good word), the second meeting, an hour, is a study of the *Watchtower*. . . . Nothing is left to chance. To make sure that everyone understands the message of the *Watchtower* article according to the society, questions are printed at the bottom of the pages and the answers are given in the body of the article. The question is read by the reader; the leader and various audience members answer. If the answer is not the one desired, the subject is continued until the right answer is given or until the leader explains the correct answer.[62]

The Role of Women

The place of women among Jehovah's Witnesses is not unusual for sectarian movements, and is not entirely unlike many evangelical churches. Women are the backbone of the movement, as concerns the actual witnessing. Indeed, without faithful female Witnesses, it is difficult to imagine where the organization would be today. Women, likewise, play an important role at the Bethel headquarters and the local kingdom halls, but they are strictly barred from leadership roles. Even in their informal training sessions, women are not permitted to speak—unless the woman makes her presentation to another woman (often referred to as a "householder"), and the men in the congregation simply listen in. By this means she is able to circumvent the tight regulation that prohibits her from teaching men. The *Watchtower* magazine through the years has reminded women of their place in relation to men. In 1951, they were admonished not to cut their hair, for such would "remove this natural, God-given sign of a woman's subjection to man," and in 1960, they were exhorted to wear hats when they conducted kingdom hall activities, because it "alerts Christian men against succumbing to female influence."[63]

The attitude toward women has a long tradition in the movement. Russell's view of women may have reflected the conflict he had with his own wife. He described women in very unflattering terms:

> Depraved and selfish, disposed not only to rebel against an unreasonable and improper headship, but even to dispute any and every proposition, and to haggle and quarrel over it . . . while not claiming to be the provider for the family, nevertheless directly or indirectly, to usurp the authority of the head of the home, to take and to hold the control of the purse and of the family. . . .

This view was reaffirmed in 1946 in the widely-circulated Watch Tower publication, *Let God Be True*, which stated that "Woman is merely a lowly creature whom God created for man as man's helper."[64]

Distinctive Doctrines

Jehovah's Witnesses, unlike the Mormons, do not claim to offer a new or "restored" gospel for this age. Rather, they insist that they are simply interpreting the Bible as the early Christians did before heresy crept into the church in the third and fourth centuries. To people who are not well versed in Christian doctrine, the Jehovah's Witnesses could easily be mistaken as simply another denomination within the framework of historic Christianity.

Exclusivity

A very significant aspect of Watch Tower belief that sets the movement apart from all other religious denominations is a characteristic that is common among groups referred to as cults. This trait is exclusivity. Exclusivity is pervasive in Watch Tower literature, and is summed up in various books, including *Religion A Snare and Racket* and *What Has Religion Done for Mankind?* Religion—all religious movements apart from the Jehovah's Witnesses—was defined as "a form of worship but which worship is given to a false God and hence given to a creature." This definition in recent years, however, has been forsaken, and the term has been given a positive connotation. But the exclusivist stance remains. The Jehovah's Witnesses regard themselves as "*the religion*, the *only* pure religion."[65]

The Trinity and the Deity of Christ

The doctrinal tenet of the Jehovah's Witnesses that Christians find most objectionable is that which denies the concept of the Trinity and the deity of Christ. The passage of Scripture that has been used most frequently to defend their position is John 1:1, which is translated in the King James Version into the familiar words, "In the beginning was the Word, and the Word was with God, and the Word was God." The Jehovah's Witnesses object to that rendering, insisting the correct translation is that which is found in their New World Translation, which renders the last phrase, "and the Word was a god." Their argument is that in the Greek there is a definite article used for God (*Ton Theon*) with the phrase, "the Word was with God," thus indicating that "God" is referring to Jehovah. In the following phrase, "the Word was God," however, there is no definite article for God (*Theos*), thus showing a difference between the two—the second meaning "a god" or a divine being inferior to Jehovah.[66]

Jesus, then, to the Jehovah's Witnesses is no more than a perfect man, rather than God incarnate. According to Rutherford, in his book *The Harp of God*, "The incarnation is scripturally erroneous. Indeed, if he [Christ] had been an incarnate being, he could never have redeemed mankind."

This viewpoint was given further support in 1952 by the Watch Tower publication, *Let God Be True:* "God's justice would not let Jesus, as a ransom, be more than a perfect man. So he could not be the supreme God almighty in the flesh."[67]

This denial of the Incarnation radically modifies the doctrine of the atonement, as biblical scholars have pointed out:

If it was only a perfect man who died on the cross, the value of that death is clearly limited. This undoubtedly explains why Jehovah's Witnesses place little emphasis on the atoning work of Christ. In reality, they do not conceive of him as a Savior from sin but as a Messiah and King about to free them from the present wicked world and set up a new social order.

And, the denial of the Incarnation affects other doctrines as well, including the historic orthodox view of Christ's resurrection:

Moreover, in consonance with their anthropology, "the man Jesus is dead, dead forever." Thus the bodily resurrection of Christ is denied. His resurrection was spiritual and not corporeal. At his death, Christ again became a spiritual being. How then do Witnesses explain the empty tomb? What happened to his body? Russell conjectured that it might have been dissolved into gasses and Rutherford believed that God removed it miraculously and has it preserved somewhere in the world for exposition during the millennial age.[68]

Eschatology

The denial of the Incarnation also relates very directly to Watch Tower eschatology. The first "presence" of Christ was the three-and-a-half-year period between his baptism and death. As previously mentioned, his "second presence" began in 1914, at which time "Christ has turned his attention toward earth's affairs and is dividing the people and educating the true Christians in preparation for their survival during the great storm of Armageddon."[69]

The most controversial and widely publicized aspect of Watch Tower eschatology has been their date-setting. Russell began referring to specific future dates as early as 1889, at which time he wrote, "The 'battle of the great day of God Almighty' (Rev. 16:14), which will end in A.D. 1914 with the complete overthrow of the earth's present rulership is already commenced." The year 1918 was also marked as a pivotal year in the end-times chronology, but during that very year, Russell's successor pointed to a new date when he wrote, "Therefore we may confidently expect that 1925 will mark the return of Abraham, Isaac, Jacob and the faithful prophets of old," and four years later he confidently asserted that "the date 1925 is more distinctly indicated by the Scriptures than 1914."[70]

Rather than admitting the eschatological errors, the Watch Tower officials have simply reinterpreted the events. The year 1918, for example, became the year when Christ "came to the spiritual temple as Jehovah's Messenger and began to cleanse it . . . the beginning of the period of judgment and inspection of his spirit-begotten followers."[71]

There were, however, some rare reflections that seemed to concede failure. In a 1931 publication, the following admission was made: "There was a measure of disappointment of the part of Jehovah's faithful ones on earth concerning the years 1914, 1918, and 1925, which disappointment lasted for a time . . . and they also learned to quit fixing dates."[72] But within decades, the faithful Witnesses would once again be expected to wait for another pivotal year. In a book written by Frederick Franz in 1966, it was determined that "the seventh period of a thou-

sand years of human history will begin in the fall of 1975."[73]

Watch Tower eschatology, to say the least, is confusing and contradictory. It, nevertheless, remains a popular theme of the society's literature, and has had a powerful effect in both the gaining and losing of members. Living in the light of the end times is the entire thrust of the movement even though only a very limited number (144,000) will be part of the "first resurrection"—a heavenly and spiritual resurrection that began in 1918. The remainder of faithful Witnesses—the sheep separated from the goats—will be resurrected to an earthly life. The goats are those who have not accepted the Witnesses message of Jehovah, and they will be destroyed. "A short time yet remains until the separation will be finished, and then follows the Battle of Armageddon."[74]

The Battle of Armageddon is the "most terrific war of all time"—a war in which Jehovah with the help of Jesus will lead the heavenly armies of righteousness against Satan and the earthly armies. It has been referred to as World War III and by many calculations is long overdue. Many people who were alive in 1914 will still be alive when this battle takes place, according to Watch Tower literature, and people in 1952 were told it would occur in their generation.[75]

In the end, Jehovah will prevail and more than two billion unrighteous people will be dead—paving the way for the "other sheep" of the Jehovah's Witnesses to inhabit the earth during the millennium. "During the thousand-year reign the 144,000 will reign and rule with Christ from heaven. The earth will be cleansed and become a paradise under the direction of Jehovah." There will be one final test or judgment at the end of the millennium, followed by an "endless existence and blessing upon the paradise earth."[76]

Everlasting Conscious Punishment in Hell

What about those who reject the teachings of Jehovah's Witnesses? One thing is certain in Watch Tower theology. They do not suffer everlasting conscious punishment in hell, but are rather annihilated. Such a belief in everlasting punishment, according to Jehovah's Witnesses, is not only unbiblical but satanic:

> Who is responsible for this God-defaming doctrine of a hell of torment? The promulgator of it is Satan himself. His purpose in introducing it has been to frighten the people away from studying the Bible and to make them hate God. Imperfect man does not torture even a mad dog, but kills it. And yet the clergyman attributes to God, who is love, the wicked crime of torturing human creatures merely because they had the misfortune to be born sinners. (1 John 4:16) The hell-fire doctrine was taught by pagans hundreds of years before Christ. It, as well as the doctrine of 'purgatory,' is based on another pagan false doctrine, that of the immortality of the human soul.[77]

Salvation

Salvation is not a simple aspect of Watch Tower belief. For the "elect" 144,000 in the remnant class, salvation is granted by the sovereign will of Jehovah. For the "other sheep," there is less security: "God's will is that to make good his salvation to everlasting life, the believer must be a preacher in this world." The Watch Tower organization, like some Christian denominations, scorns any notion of the doctrine of eternal security. "The popular religious expression, 'Once saved, always saved!' is false and dangerous."[78] However, in the Jehovah's Witness framework, the doctrine bears directly on salvation by works.

Do Jehovah's Witnesses hold to a doctrine of salvation by works? This is the conclusion that some people have drawn from their heavy emphasis on witnessing—witnessing that is not optional as Heather and Gary Botting found in their years of active involvement in that organization. They argue that James 2:26, which states that "faith without works is dead," is to be taken to the extreme. "Consequently, no matter how long a Witness remains an active distributer of literature, the moment he ceases to be active he is regarded by his peers as good as dead in terms of achieving the ultimate goal of life everlasting in an earthly paradise." Although the Jehovah's Witnesses would deny it, "the emphasis on the individual's personal track record results in a situation in which salvation must be bought. But few realize upon entering the movement that the purchase price is open-ended and that the bill can never be paid in full until death or the advent of Armageddon."[79]

The New World Translation

The *New World Translation of the Christian Greek Scriptures* was first published in 1950 by the Watchtower Bible and Tract Society, with an initial printing of nearly a half million copies. As with other publications of the organization, there are no individuals identified with the volume, nor is a list of translators available upon request. The most unique aspect of this translation is the insertion of the Hebrew Tetragrammaton (YHWH, popularly rendered Jehovah) for the Greek words *Kyrios* and *Theos*, which in standard translations are rendered "Lord" and "God." In the forward to the *New World Translation*, the editors emphasize the fact that "In the Hebrew Scriptures the name, represented by this Tetragrammaton, occurs 6,823 times," and that the "sudden disappearance from the Greek text seems inconsistent." The editors proceed to make a defense of their use of "Jehovah," arguing that "the Tetragrammaton persisted in copies of the LXX [Greek Septuagint—the Greek translation of the Hebrew scriptures] for centuries after Christ and his apostles."[80]

While some of the claims of the editors are based on fact, others are based on faulty suppositions, and it is noteworthy that no serious Greek or New Testament scholar supports the Watch Tower conclusions. In his book *The Jehovah's Witnesses' New Testament*, Robert Countess argues that the restoration of the "Divine Name" was very purposeful:

> The translators of the NWT were not merely intending to restore to the pages of the New Testament God's name, which name, it is alleged, was perhaps excised due to anti-semitism or ignorance on the part of the early Christian scribes. NWT has introduced "Jehovah" into the Greek Scriptures for the sole purpose of wiping out any

vestige of Jesus Christ's identity with Jehovah.[81]

But if Jehovah, the "Divine Name," serves to downplay the deity of Christ, its more obvious purpose is to give credibility to the *Jehovah's* Witnesses themselves. The editors quote from Acts 15:14, "how God for the first time turned his attention to the nations to take out of them a people for his name"—his name, of course being *Jehovah*, and the people for his name, being the *Jehovah's* Witnesses. "If Christians are to be a people for God's name," write the editors, "why should his name, represented by the Tetragrammaton, be abolished from the Christian Greek Scriptures?"[82]

Besides inserting the name "Jehovah" where it is not warranted, in an effort to make themselves fit the description of "a people for his name," the translators of this version have also distorted the meaning of other texts to fit their purposes. John 1:1 has previously been mentioned, which is a key text pertaining to the deity of Christ. But even verses that would never be perceived to have doctrinal significance have been translated to support Watch Tower principles and practices. An example is their rendering of Ephesians 6:4. The King James text (which the Jehovah's Witnesses used until they had their own translation in 1950) reads "And, ye fathers, provoke not your children to wrath: but bring them up in the nurture and admonition of the Lord." The first edition of the *New World Translation*, rendered the last half of the verse, "but go on bringing them up in the discipline and authoritative advice of Jehovah." And, the most recent edition of the *New*

Jehovah's Witnesses at the door.

World Translation reads, "but go on bringing them up in the discipline and mental-regulating of Jehovah." This "progression," write Heather and Gary Botting, "reflects the increasingly tight regulation of the membership over the years."[83]

Although the *New World Translation* did not appear until most of a century after the founding of the Watch Tower organization, it plays an important function in sustaining long held doctrines. Thus, while the movement does not have extrabiblical scriptures per se, it does have its own version of the Bible. In fact, the Jehovah's Witnesses "can lay claim to being the first of the cults to produce *en toto* its own translation of the New Testament." In summing up his conclusions about this version, Countess writes that it "thoroughly deserves to be regarded as a unique translation, because it reflects more clearly than any other English translation a particular doctrinal slant."[84]

Door-to-Door Witnessing and Overseas Outreach

The attribute for which Jehovah's Witnesses are most universally associated is their persistent door-to-door evangelism. To maintain an active status in the organization, an individual must engage in a bare minimum of one hour of house-to-house witnessing a month, but ten hours per month is considered the "quota" for anyone who is in good standing. All Jehovah's Witnesses are encouraged to spend part of their lives in full-time "Pioneer" service, which requires a minimum of ninety hours a month. Witnessing begins early in life for many Jehovah's Witnesses as Gary Botting's testimony illustrates. He tells of the confidence he experienced after selling his first *Watchtower* magazine at the age of five:

From that moment on, I became a regular publisher for Jehovah's Witnesses, meeting my quota of ten hours and twelve magazine placements per month, every month. Within a year, the time came for me to give my first talk at the Theocratic Ministry School . . . at the Kingdom Hall. Standing before the makeshift podium, I . . . delivered by rote a six-minute sermon called "Knorr-and-the-Ark," in which I recited Watch Tower Society speculations on the size of the ship and the number of representative specimens . . . that God had gathered together to escape the flood. It was not until several years later that I was able to distinguish between Noah, the patriarch of old and Nathan H. Knorr, the president of the Watch Tower Bible and Tract Society;

to my uncritical, six-year-old mind they were one and the same man.[85]

The overseas missionary outreach of the Jehovah's Witnesses is in style very similar to door-to-door witnessing done every week by "publishers" on the home front. Indeed, there has been little effort to make changes that would serve the purposes of cross-cultural communication. Yet, according to recent editions of the *Yearbook*, growth has continued at a high rate. In 1983, there were missionaries serving in more than two hundred countries, with more than one hundred and fifty thousand baptisms. Each country is listed separately in the *Yearbook*, with the number of baptisms and the number of hours of publishing, as well as other vital statistics. Mexico, for example, was one of the most productive fields, with 13,000 baptisms, with an average of 1,729 hours expended per baptism. Brazil's ratio was even better, with 11,649 baptisms and only 1,584 hours per baptism.[86]

Just four years later in 1987, the number of baptisms in Mexico had more than doubled to 31,703, rivaling the some thirty-nine thousand baptized in the entire United States. Brazil reported a significant increase of nearly seven thousand, bringing the yearly total to 18,467. The most amazing growth in recent years has come in Italy, where reception to the anti-Catholic message of Jehovah's Witnesses would not be expected. Nearly twelve thousand baptisms were reported in 1987.[87]

Building Bridges in Evangelistic Outreach

Building bridges of commonality is a first step in the process of reaching out to people in other faiths, whether those individuals are Buddhists, Muslims, Mormons, or Jehovah's Witnesses. In some cases, it is difficult to find that common ground of belief. In many respects, that is true of Mormons, whose additional scriptures, plurality of gods, and reverence for Joseph Smith are so utterly incompatible with orthodox Christian doctrine. Not so with the Jehovah's Witnesses. As much as they deviate from historical Christian orthodoxy, it is important to remember that there are many beliefs which they share in common with evangelical Christians.

Jehovah's Witnesses claim to hold a high view of holy Scripture, albeit a scripture that is translated and interpreted by the Watch Tower elite, without the benefit of outside challenge. They should be challenged on their view of the Bible as their authority, as opposed to Watch Tower literature—challenged by that very Watch Tower literature itself:

> To let God be found true means to let God have the say as to what is the truth that sets men free. It means to accept his Word, the Bible, as the truth. Hence, in this book, our appeal is to the Bible for truth. [88]

Another point of commonality between Jehovah's Witnesses and evangelical Christians is the shared conviction that it is imperative for believers to share their faith with others. Indeed, most Witnesses put Christians to shame in their zeal for witnessing.

Still another point of similarity is their conviction that an individual must have a personal relationship with God. While this is not an openly shared experience, as it is in most evangelical circles, where testimonies of "accepting Jesus as Savior" are common, Jehovah's Witnesses literature does emphasize the need for a personal dedication of oneself to Jehovah, through Jesus.

When love for God moves you so that you want to do his will, then it is proper that you go to him in prayer through Jesus Christ and express your desire to be one of his servants, walking in the footsteps of his Son. It is appropriate that you tell Jehovah that you want to belong to him and that you want to do his will both now and for all time to come.... In this way you dedicate yourself to God. This is a personal, private matter. No one else can do it for you.

After you have made your dedication to Jehovah to do his will, he will expect you to keep it. It is no light matter. Prove that you are a person of your word by faithfully sticking to this decision or dedication as long as you live....

Deciding personally to serve Jehovah and expressing this determination in prayer is important. But there is something more.... Since Jesus set the pattern, dedicated Christians today should be baptized.... What does Christian baptism signify? It is not a washing away of one's sins, because cleansing from sin comes only through faith in Jesus Christ. (Ephesians 1:7) Rather, it is a public demonstration, testifying that one has made a solemn dedication to Jehovah God and is presenting himself to do his will.[89]

While many of the terms that Jehovah's Witnesses use do not necessarily have the same connotations as they do in an evangelical context, yet such admonitions as the above can be used to challenge Jehovah's Witnesses on a personal level about their relationship with God.

In coming to an understanding of Jehovah's Witnesses, it is essential to overcome the effects of certain myths that have developed over the years about them—myths that are commonly held about Mormons and other unorthodox religious groups as well. In an article entitled "A Jehovah's Witness? Next Time Open the Door," Robert Morey underscores three of these myths.[90] The first myth is that *Jehovah's Witnesses never give up their religion.* The only Jehovah's Witnesses some people meet are the ones who come to their door—people who give the impression of being so zealous and committed that they could never objectively consider viewpoints other than their own. The truth is that there are vast numbers of Jehovah's Witnesses who do not come to your door, who struggle to witness their minimum of one hour a month. And those who are more faithful in witnessing are not necessarily as self-assured about their beliefs as they may appear. That presumption is supported by the fact that thousands leave the movement each year.

A second myth is that *Jehovah's Witnesses know their Bible well.* One of the reasons that they appear to know the Bible so well is that they have been trained in proof-texting, purposely indoctrinated in the "art" of defending key doctrinal positions with particular verses. During their weekly training meetings they learn how to anticipate common questions and to answer them with the proper verse or passage. At kingdom hall meetings and in private, Jehovah's Witnesses always study the scripture with the aid of Watch Tower material, which is prepared by the so-called biblical scholars at Bethel headquarters. But according to Raymond Franz, who was for many years one of these very individuals, "Many Governing Body members admitted that they found themselves so occupied with various matters that there was little time for Bible study."[91]

Another myth is that *Jehovah's Witnesses are antagonistic and argumentative.* The reputation for "an aggressive I-can-talk-you-down approach" was far more true in the past than it is today. In recent years, the organization has been "concerned to upgrade the image of their cause, to make their Bible study appear less shoddy, and their house-to-house campaigns less truculent. This new 'friendliness' makes it much easier to talk to a Witness about Christ, for now some of them will listen. . . . He needs to experience the compassion of Christ. Christian love does far more than harsh rebuking."[92]

Challenges to Watch Tower Dogma

Treating a Jehovah's Witness or any member of an alternative religion with Christian love in no way negates the responsibility that Christians have to challenge false doctrine directly. This should be done with courtesy and respect, and the views and questions of the individual should be accepted as being sincere. Indeed, it is difficult to imagine an individual making the required sacrifices to be a part of the Watch Tower movement without deep personal or family convictions. Ridiculing Watch Tower literature as "nonsense perpetrated on gullible people"

and regarding its challenges to orthodoxy as "childish questions—some of which are painful to record," as one critic does, is a disservice to Jehovah's Witnesses.[93] It is the very treatment that evangelicals so dislike from liberal scholars who deride their "nonsense," "gullibility," and "childish questions."

There are a number of areas where Jehovah's Witnesses should be challenged, including scriptural passages, false date-setting for Christ's return, and Watch Tower authority. For someone who has even the most elementary knowledge of Greek and has access to a Greek New Testament, it is very simple to confront a Jehovah's Witness with the faulty *New World Translation* of John 1:1. Their insistence that the Greek word *theos* must have a definite article when it refers to God the Father (Jehovah), and that without the article, it refers to "a god," is easily countered with other references to this Greek term in the Gospel of John. The *New World Translation* is inconsistent in following its own rule, as is seen in its rendering of John 1:18, which has no definite article in the Greek for *theos* in either of the instances it appears. Yet the Watch Tower editors translate the verse as follows: "No man has seen God at any time; the only-begotten god who is in the bosom position with the Father is the one that has explained him."[94]

Another instance in the Gospel of John where *theos* is not accompanied by a definite article and is translated by the *New World Translation* committee as though it did, is the powerful pronouncement of Jesus' identity by Thomas in John 20:28. To be consistent, the Watch

Tower should have rendered the statement, "My Master and a god" (or "my god"), but right from the pages of the *New World Translation*, we read that glorious declaration of who Jesus is: "My Master and my God!"[95]

The Gospel of John offers many opportunities to present the claims of Christ to a Jehovah's witness—from their own version, the *New World Translation*. In John 5:18, we read that "the Jews began seeking all the more to kill him, because not only was he breaking the Sabbath, but he was also calling God his own Father, making himself equal to God." This is about as explicit as the Bible could be in confirming that Jesus indeed was "making himself equal to God." Then a few verses later in 5:22–23: "For the Father judges no one at all, but he has committed all the judging to the Son, in order that all may honor the Son just as they honor the Father. He that does not honor the Son does not honor the Father who sent him." A simple reading of that passage requires the obvious conclusion, that Christians should "honor the Son just as they honor the Father." Another passage where Jesus identifies Himself is John 10:30, where He emphatically asserts, "I and the Father are one."[96]

There are countless more verses and passages that can effectively be used to counter false teachings of Jehovah's Witnesses, and there are books and pamphlets available that can aid the individual who has opportunity for more in-depth Bible study with a member of that movement. False biblical and doctrinal teachings, however, are not the primary reasons people abandon their belief systems. Rather, the reasons more often pertain to issues that are more personal in nature. That is why there was such a massive defection following the 1975 failed prophecy of the end of the world. Many individuals suffered a personal disappointment and affront that was too deep to simply brush aside. Doubts festered, and bitterness and hurt surfaced, and in the eyes of many of these once faithful Witnesses, the impregnable Watch Tower walls began to crumble.

Challenging Jehovah's Witnesses with their history of false prophecies can be an effective offensive to take when interacting with them, but for many who have already weathered the 1975 debacle, the issue is not critical. But there may be other areas of vulnerability, that can only be detected by developing a close personal friendship—which in itself is a challenge since friendship with outsiders is discouraged. An area of vulnerability may involve personal relationships at the kingdom hall. Congregations are often small and controlled by domineering leaders who have a penchant for alienating people. That very type of situation may be enough to prompt an individual to look objectively at some long-held beliefs that had simply been taken for granted.

Other areas of vulnerability may involve personal pain over a disfellowshiping of a friend or relative, or the news that a child has died of accidental injuries when the life might have been saved through a blood transfusion. Doubts may arise also through reading a book or tract by an ex-Jehovah's Witness. The picture that Heather and Gary Botting paint in the book, *The Orwellian*

World of Jehovah's Witnesses, can be disconcerting to a member who knows all too well that many of the things they say are frighteningly true. And Raymond Franz, in his book *Crisis of Conscience*, has a message that is difficult for a member to ignore, especially when they recall the high position he held at the Bethel headquarters. Such books, of course, are not on the recommended reading list for Jehovah's Witnesses, so friendship and caring concern are prerequsites to opening the door to such literature.

Still another factor that can be used to challenge Jehovah's Witnesses is that of Watch Tower authority. Rather than to challenge the authority directly, a more appropriate approach might be to encourage the individual to read the Bible with an open mind, without the aid of Watch Tower literature. A topical study might be suggested—on a theme that is nonpolemical such as prayer or forgiveness.

The Jehovah's Witnesses, with their emphasis on witnessing and their efforts to win converts from orthodoxy, ought to serve as a challenge to Christians to reevaluate their own faith and to reach with meaningful witness to them and members of other cultic movements.

Chapter 6

Christian Science:
A Denial of
the Material World

Like Mormonism, Christian Science developed initially as a personality cult centered around the personal life and teachings of one individual—Mary Baker Eddy. Her life was intimately entwined with the movement she founded, and it is impossible to understand Christian Science without a knowledge of her character. As with all successful religions, though, the movement moves far beyond the personality of the founder and takes on in a sense a personality of its own. In some instances, this "personality" offers new vitality and growth to the movement, as is true of Mormonism; in other instances the movement begins to wane—often within a few years or decades after the prophet-founder's death. This has been true of Christian Science. Growth continued after Mrs. Eddy's death, but in recent decades, the movement has declined and the vitality is gone. Many Christian Science churches are scarcely filled, and those in attendance are primarily elderly women. Yet, this movement has had a powerful impact on religious life in America and continues to have an influence far beyond what membership statistics would indicate.

Mary Baker Eddy

"Mother Mary," as she was known by thousands of her followers, was possibly the most influential woman in nineteenth-century America. Mark Twain referred to her as "the most daring and masculine and masterful woman that has appeared on earth in centuries."[1] Her life touched men and women in every stratum of society from Maine to Minnesota and beyond. When she died she left behind a powerful religious organization whose influence far exceeded its numerical size.

Yet, for all she accomplished, Mrs. Eddy was not exceptionally bright or creative. She was often deeply troubled and at times almost incapacitated by what she perceived to be negative thoughts of others. And despite her success in building a religious philosophy and movement that denied the reality of physical sickness, she herself was never able to escape debilitating physical problems. She was an enigma to those who knew her well as well as to those who did not. She was loved and she was hated. But ignored she was not. Her followers idolized her, and her detractors ridiculed her every move. Newspaper reporters contradicted each other in their descriptions of her—often in such conflicting terms as to utterly perplex the reader. Following her appearance at Steinway Hall in New York in 1899, she was described by the New York *World* as "a pleasant little woman, with dark hair and dark eyes, [who] does not look more than forty years old." But, according to the New York *Times*, she was a ghastly spectacle with "her keen and sunken black eyes peering weirdly from her colorless face, and her dark hair brushed severely down on her temples."[2]

Who was this uncommon woman? What was the make-up of her character? How did she rise above her own personality flaws? What was there about her that attracted such a large following? Recreating Mary Baker Eddy is a task beyond the ability of any biographer or historian, but the voluminous writings from her own pen and the many biographies from both her supporters and detractors help weave together the story of this remarkable and yet very strange woman.

Mary Ann Morse Baker was born in a small New Hampshire town in 1821, the youngest of six children. Her parents, Mark and Abigail Baker, were in many respects striking opposites.

Her father was a hard-working New England farmer whose leisure time was spent in church or reading the Bible. He was a staunch Calvinist, "hard-faced and tough-minded, delighting to wage dialectical battle . . . over fine points of doctrine." Her mother, who was described by an acquaintance as having "a strong intellect, a sympathizing heart, and a placid spirit," was a sharp contrast to her domineering husband, and yet in "her own subversively simple way" she wielded a strong influence in the home. "She represented the strain of New England womanhood which rebelled against the stark absolutes of Calvinism—not the overt rebellion of an Anne Hutchinson, aflame with the Holy Ghost, but the quiet, almost unnoticed rebellion that life itself makes against the system."[3]

Early Life

Mary's birth brought happiness to the Baker family, and, as the youngest and frailest of the children, she "was clearly the favorite." Her oldest sister may have spoken for the others when she wrote, "I loved Mary best of all my brothers and sisters."[4] Although her birth was not particularly eventful at the time, her mother later related that she had had a strange feeling before Mary was born that the child was consecrated by God to be used in a special way. Later, when Mary was a young woman, her mother wrote, "sometimes I fear I worship Mary instead of the great Jehovah."[5]

From her earliest childhood, Mary was "spoiled, petted, and much valued," She was a sickly child, frequently treated as a helpless invalid. Her physical ailments, including complaints of spinal paralysis and pain, were only part of the problem. "These chronic complaints, writes Julius Silberger, "were as nothing compared to her paroxysmal attacks." She had seizures or "fits," as they were described by observers, that "resembled a convulsion." Sometimes she pitched headlong on the floor, and rolled and kicked, writhing and screaming in apparent agony," while on other occasions "she dropped limp and lay motionless," and still other times "she lay rigid, almost in a state of suspended animation."[6]

The cause of Mary's seizures and physical problems during her youth remains a puzzle. That the seizures were an attention-getting device and that she was severely disturbed emotionally seems unlikely. Her letters during this time, rather, seem to show her to be a contented and compassionate young woman. In a letter to her brother that she wrote just after her fourteenth birthday, she reminisced about the "many hapy [sic] sabbaths" they spent together, and she expressed her gratitude for their close relationship: "There is one thing . . . I have lerned [sic] from experience to prize more perhaps than ever I did before that is Dear brother the friendly advice and council you was ever giving me. . . ."[7]

First Marriage and Family Life

Despite the problems that Mary faced in her youth, she had aspirations of being a great scholar and author. Though poorly educated, she spent hours upon hours reading and writing bits of poetry and prose— mediocre at best—that were occa-

sionally published in local newspapers. She was an attractive young woman, described by a local resident as "the village beauty," and was not without eager suitors. Among them was George Washington Glover, eleven years older than Mary and a friend of her oldest brother. She first met him when she was ten, and twelve years later she married him. Following the wedding, they moved to North Carolina, where George had business endeavors, but six months later he was dead from an apparent attack of yellow fever. Mary returned home to New Hampshire, where she soon gave birth to her first and only child, a son, George. Life was most unpleasant during this period for Mary. She lived "as an impoverished dependent widow," and "her nervousness, chronic ailments, and signs of infantilism returned in acute form."[8]

Because of her condition she relinquished the care of her son to others. She frequently visited him during his early years, when he was in the care of his grandmother and a hired maid, but after his grandmother died he was sent to live with the maid and her new husband; and after they moved west, young George had very little contact with his mother. It was not a normal mother-son relationship—a situation that later proved to be a source of embarrassment to her.

Throughout her youth Mary had been very interested in spiritual matters. She was involved not only in the Congregational church that her family attended, but also in the local Methodist church. Following a Methodist revival in which she apparently had a conversion experience, she wanted to join with the Methodists, but her father intervened and convinced her to return to the Congregational church. She did, and later taught a Sunday school class there.

Though brought up in the religious atmosphere of stern Calvinism, Mary had a mind of her own and vehemently took issue with her father's strong views on predestination and eternal punishment. So exasperated was he with her independent spirit that he reportedly lamented to the local Congregational minister when she was yet a teenager, "If Mary Magdalene had seven devils, our Mary has ten."[9]

Spiritualism and the Occult

After her husband died, Mary seemed to abandon entirely the faith of her childhood. She began dabbling in such things as spiritualism, the occult, clairvoyance, and mesmerism. She had an insatiable curiosity for anything supernatural, not necessarily an unusual trait for a young woman of her day. "It has been said," writes Robert Peel, "that one way of escaping the tedium of conventional American life in the nineteenth century was to go West, the other way was to go 'beyond.'" Mary went "beyond." Like the famous spiritualists Kate and Margaret Fox, who made their claim to fame when they began hearing mysterious rappings, Mary was intrigued by the idea of making contact with the spirit world. It was not an interest, however, that had developed overnight. "From her earliest years, according to her own later account, certain unexplained phenomena had marked her experience. As a small child, she had repeatedly heard a mysterious 'voice' calling her."[10]

Mary's interest in the supernatural was due in part to her physical condition. She was seeking relief not only from her physical problems but also from the anxiety that so plagued her. "Her invalidism," according to a woman who knew her well, "combined with her extreme nervousness, sometimes repelled young people . . . and caused her to be misunderstood."[11] Often she could be calmed only through rocking—at times in a cradle constructed especially for her. Still at other times she was so vexed that she resorted to drugs, though she apologized for it: "My only relief is to take *Morphine* which I so much disapprove."[12] Often morphine was her only source of relief, and her use of this drug apparently continued throughout her life.[13]

Second Marriage

In 1853, nine years after the death of her first husband, Mary entered her second marriage. She was so ill on her wedding day that the bridegroom, Daniel Patterson, had to carry her down from her upstairs bedroom for the ceremony and back up again when it was over. He then returned to his home, leaving her to be cared for by her sister until she was able to join him some months later. Patterson was a less-than-successful traveling dentist with a reputation for being a ladies' man. He "was a handsome, genial man, tall, dark, bearded, a bit of a rural dandy . . . dressed always in broadcloth and fine linen, kid gloves and boots, frock coat and top hat."[14] He had become enamored by the sickly but attractive Mrs.

Glover, and during the early years of their marriage he seemed to almost enjoy catering to her whims.[15]

The marriage, however, did not endure. During the Civil War, Patterson became involved in a smuggling operation for the Union Army and was captured by the Confederates and locked up in prison where he languished for nine months while Mary was undergoing a dramatic change in her life. When he returned, he was amazed to find his wife virtually a different woman than she was when he had left. Mary had been transformed. Phineas Parkhurst Quimby had entered her life, and she would never be the same again.

The Influence of P. P. Quimby

P. P. Quimby was one of many "mental healers" plying his trade during the decades prior to the Civil War. There was tremendous interest in this field, largely as a result of the experiments that the German physician Franz Anton Mesmer was conducting with hypnosis. Mesmer "concluded that a mysterious magnetic fluid was the explanation of the mental power one person could exercise over another." Quimby, along with many other Americans, had become intrigued with his concepts, but like so many others he went beyond Mesmer and "ultimately came to believe that disease could be cured by cultivating "healthy attitudes"— positive rather than negative thoughts—through suggestion, and without the use of hypnotism." He lived and practiced in Portland, Maine, but his reputation as a highly successful healer was not confined to that city. People came from great distances to be cured through his methods.[16]

Mary Baker Eddy. Used by permission of The Christian Science Board of Directors.

It was Mary's husband, Daniel Patterson, who had initially made contact with Quimby in behalf of his wife, explaining that she had been "an invalid for a number of years . . . not able to sit up but a little." Nothing developed out of that contact, however, and Mary made arrangements to receive treatment from a healer closer to her home who specialized in a water cure. Despite such efforts, her health continued to decline, and in the spring of 1862 she took it upon herself to write to Quimby. Her letter was pathetic:

Last Autumn my husband addressed you a letter respecting my case and has always been anxious for me to see you. . . . I was getting well this spring but my dear husband was taken prisoner of war by the Southerns and the shock overcame me and brought on a relapse. I want to see you above all others. I have entire confidence in your philosophy. . . . *Can* you, *Will* you visit me at once? I must die unless you can save me. My disease is "chronic" and I have been unable to turn myself to be moved by any but my husband for one year at a time. . . . Do come and save me.[17]

Quimby was apparently unmoved by Mary's plight, and some months later she wrote to him again, explaining that she was "so excitable" that she was not sure how long she could survive. Finally, in the fall of 1862, a year after her husband's initial letter to Quimby, friends conveyed the ailing woman to his seventh-floor office suite in Portland, Maine. Though Quimby no doubt had treated a number of psychopathic cases, Mary had a uniqueness all of her own. A fellow patient described her as "the most peculiar person" he had "seen of late."[18]

The cure was instantaneous—or so it seemed. In less than a week, Mary could report that she was "improving ad infinitum." Never had she encountered such a man as Dr. Quimby, who, in her words, "heals as never a man healed since Christ." How did he perform such cures? What secret did he possess that was hidden to the other medical practitioners who had treated Mary? His method was as simple (or complicated) as convincing his patients that their illnesses, though physically real, were caused by their beliefs. If such beliefs, then, could be changed, the cause of the illness would be removed and the patient would be cured. "P. P. Quimby rolls away the stone from the Sepulchre of error," Mary extolled, "and health is the resurrection."[19]

What did Quimby think of Mary? Except for Mary's own account, there is little evidence. Years later she recalled a discussion they allegedly had, during which time he shocked her by saying, "I see now what you mean, and I see that I am John, and that you are Jesus." If Quimby made such a statement, he was not implying that Mary was God, for his view of Jesus was hardly orthodox. "As Jesus became clairvoyant," he had written in his notes, "He became the son of God."[20]

Mary remained in Portland three months following her initial visit, and that is where her husband found her after his escape from Confederate prison. The helpless invalid that Patterson had left behind had turned into a much healthier and far more independent woman who had turned her attention from him to another man—her mentor and healer, P. P. Quimby. The fact that she no longer needed him apparently sealed the fate of an already shaky marriage. They continued to live together off and on for three more years, but then they separated permanently, and in 1873 Mary sued for divorce. She later justified the divorce, claiming that Patterson had been unfaithful to her. For a long time it had been rumored that he had been doing more than pulling teeth when he traveled from house to house on his dentistry circuit, and according to one account he deserted Mary and "eloped with the wife of a wealthy citizen who had employed his services professionally."[21]

The "cure" that Mary had experienced at the hands of P. P. Quimby did not have a long term effect. Within weeks after she had returned to her home she was again experiencing physical pains. Yet, she was a different woman. She was convinced she had found the answer to suffering and pain, and she refused to be defeated by her own problems. Though removed by distance from Quimby, she felt his spiritual presence and thanked him for his "angel visit" that removed all her stomach pain. But if sickness was a result of a person's beliefs, why did she continue to suffer? Mary developed a variety of explanations, one related to her new sideline as a health practitioner. She was eager to demonstrate Quimby's methods to others by curing friends and neighbors, but the profession was not without its risks and negative side effects. At times she was convinced that by identifying so closely with her "patients" she was actually taking on their symptoms.[22]

Mary's relationship with Quimby during the months following her first visit to him was to a degree a one-sided psychic dependence on him, reminiscent of relationships she had developed in earlier years. For example, after she moved to the South with her first husband she arranged to meet with her mother "in spirit" at an appointed time each day. Her spirit contacts with Quimby, however, were far more serious business. "I wish you would come to my aid— help me sleep and relieve the confined state of my bowels," she pleaded in a letter. On another occasion when she did not experience relief she resorted to scolding: "I did feel once Why hast thou forsaken me?" But if Quimby was less than faithful in maintaining the spiritual relationship, the same could not be said for Mary. Not only did she sense his spiritual presence, but she saw his apparition: "Last Wed. at 12 M. I saw you in this parlor where I am now writing. You wore a hat and dress coat. . . ."[23]

In addition to her spiritual contacts with Quimby, Mary made return trips to Portland to learn from his methods and to take copious notes from his unpublished manuscripts. It was not a long-term relationship, though, for Quimby died in January of 1866, only a few years after Mary had first made his acquaintance. His death was a devastating blow, coming as it did only two months after the death of her father, but Mary was determined to pick up the Quimby mantle, and refused to allow sorrow to stay the course.

The Birth of Christian Science

The turning point in Mary's life came only two weeks after Quimby's death. She slipped and fell on the ice on February 1, 1866—not a particularly unusual incident for a woman braving the elements of a normal New Hampshire winter. Yet it would later be considered an event of historic significance, "celebrated in Christian Science as its founding moment."[24]

The actual extent of Mary's injuries and her subsequent recovery have been debated for more than a century. Mary's own version that later became shrouded in myth differed significantly from the account of others who knew her at the time. According to Sibyl Wilbur, whose source was Mary herself, she was critically injured but refused treatment from the local doctor, except for a dose of medicine that he administered while she was in a state of semiconsciousness. Then, paralleling the account of the resurrection, "on the third day, which was Sunday, she sent those who were in her room away, and taking her Bible, opened it. Her eyes fell upon the account of the healing of the palsied man by Jesus. . . ." Almost immediately, as the account continues, "Mrs. Patterson arose from her bed, dressed and walked into the parlor where a clergyman and a few friends had gathered, thinking it might be for the last words on earth with the sufferer who, they believed, was dying. They arose in consternation at her appearance, almost believing they beheld an apparition. . . . She stood before them fully restored to health."[25] Not only had Mary been healed, but she had received a revelation directly from God that would eventually launch her into her career as America's most widely acclaimed religious health practitioner.

There were other accounts of Mary's fall on the ice, including that of Doctor Cushing, the physician who treated her. He described her as being "very nervous, partially unconscious, semi-hysterical, complaining by word and action of severe pain in the back of her head and neck," when he first saw her. He administered medicine to calm her, including morphine, which had a remarkable therapeutic effect. He visited her several more times, and on February 13, less than two weeks after the fall, judged her "to have recovered from the disturbance caused by the acci-

dent and to be, practically, in her normal condition." He also maintained that he never believed or stated that there was no hope for her recovery.[26]

Interestingly, a letter from Mary (dated February 14, the day after her doctor's last visit) to a fellow patient of the late Dr. Quimby, indicates exactly the opposite. To Julius Dresser she wrote, "The physician attending said I had taken the last step I ever should." She related how she had gotten out of bed alone two days later but since had found herself "slowly failing." In that letter, she mentioned nothing of the sudden "resurrection" that she later related to Sibyl Wilbur.[27]

The Lynn, Massachusetts, Era

Although the celebrated fall on the ice is viewed as the genesis of Christian Science, Mary had difficulty pulling her life together in the aftermath, and she at times appeared to be more defeated than ever. Her marriage had dissolved, and she was no longer a welcome house guest at her sister's home. For a time she lived with friends, but her presence created so much turmoil that she was forced to move on. "She had to move at least eight times during the year of 1866, driven by dwindling finances and the exhaustion of her hosts' patience." Finally at the age of forty-five, she ended up at a boardinghouse in Lynn, Massachusetts, where she settled down for a time and began to develop her practice of mental healing. She was not alone in her interest in supernatural phenomena. At that same boardinghouse were some who held seances and practiced hypnotism, and Mary was reportedly involved.[28]

In Lynn, Mary represented herself as the successor of P. P. Quimby and quickly recruited a disciple, Hiram Crafts, a shoemaker, who became convinced he could improve his status by becoming a healing practitioner. Mary promised to teach him—and him alone—the Quimby method of healing for a percentage of the profits from his practice. The following year Crafts and his wife and Mary moved to another town in Massachusetts, and the new practice commenced. The arrangement, however, did not work out satisfactorily, and within a matter of months, Crafts was back to making shoes.[29]

Once again, Mary was on the move, making additional acquaintances but not able to settle in one place. In 1870, she returned to Lynn to begin a new partnership with another disciple—this time, the twenty-one-year-old Richard Kennedy, less than half her age. "Doctor" Kennedy served as the practitioner, having agreed to turn over half of his earnings to Mary, while she spent her time writing and assembling a class of new students. As had been the case with Crafts, the business arrangement with Kennedy proved to be far less than satisfactory. Mary permitted virtually no freedom of self-expression for those working under her. For Kennedy, as with others who would follow him, her style was too restrictive and he soon parted company.[30]

Despite her high fee of one hundred dollars (later raised to three hundred) for her series of twelve lectures, many of her students were poor working class people. "Their hands were stained with the leather and tools of the day's occupation," wrote Sibyl Wilbur. "They could not come to Mrs. Glover in the daytime, for their days were full of toil. At night, then, these first classes met, and it was in the heat of August. . . . Insects buzzed at the windows, and from the common over the way the hum of the careless and free . . . invaded the quiet of the room. Yet that quiet was permeated by the voice of a teacher at whose words the hearts of those workmen burned within them."[31]

Malicious Animal Magnetism

With Kennedy gone, Mary was forced once again to fend for herself. To conserve resources she once again began moving from place to place, living with one student after another, staying until personality conflicts forced her to move on. And despite her well-publicized healing profession, she herself continued to suffer from ill health. But she made it clear to her students and to other inquirers that her "attacks" and fainting spells were beyond her own control. As hard as she might try to mentally overcome her own physical afflictions, she could not prevent the malicious thoughts of others from defeating her efforts. It was her disloyal students, she insisted, who were causing her such physical torment through a form of black magic or "Malicious Animal Magnetism," as it was officially termed. Kennedy, she believed, was the main source of this M.A.M. that was plaguing her, and she compelled her loyal students to mobilize all their mental energy to combat him.[32]

Founding the Organization

It took Mary nearly a decade after her fall on the ice and subsequent healing to establish a reputation and following as a healer. Despite continued mental and physical distress, she demonstrated an unusual degree of productivity and business acumen. 1875 was a significant year. She completed her first edition of *Science and Health with Key to the Scriptures*, purchased a piece of property, and christened her movement "Christian Science," a term Quimby himself had used. Mary made it quite plain that her new movement was not just another denomination or sect. Her position was clearly enunciated in *Science and Health:*

> We have no need of creeds and church organizations to sustain or explain a demonstratable platform, that defines itself in healing the sick, and casting out error. . . . The mistake the disciples of Jesus made was to found religious organizations and church rites. . . . No time was lost by our Master in organizations, rites, and ceremonies, or in proselyting for certain forms of belief.[33]

The first actual headquarters for the new Christian Science movement was in the home that Mary had purchased in Lynn, Massachusetts, identified by a large sign that read: MARY B. GLOVER'S CHRISTIAN SCIENTISTS' HOME. In 1875, she "withdrew her membership from the Tilton Congregational Church to which she had belonged since the summer, thirty-seven years before, when she had wrestled spiritually with the Reverend Enoch Corser over the question of predestination." This was not a sudden move. Only "gradually the ties of orthodoxy had loosened,"

writes Peel. "After returning to Lynn in 1870 she had attended for several years the Unitarian Church . . . but had not joined it. Now, as she took the first tentative step toward a church of her own, it was clear that she must sever the ecclesiastical links of the past."[34]

Despite her efforts to gain respectability, Mary was plagued by problems of dissident students, who often became her most bitter enemies and detractors. "Numerous disquieting rumors about Mrs. Glover flew around Lynn in those days," writes Peel. "Many shared the sentiment of Putney Bancroft's uncle, a deacon of the Congregational Church : 'My boy, you will be ruined for life; it is the work of the devil.' "[35]

Third Marriage

One student who did not turn against Mary was Asa Gilbert Eddy, a "self-effacing" sewing machine salesman from East Boston. "He was a short, negative, quiet little man, according to Edwin Dakin, capable of obstinacy but for the most part docile, dull, and utterly uninspired."[36] Unlike the other men who had and would develop a close working relationship with her, he was not threatening. She did not have to be concerned that he would take the limelight away from her. The relationship between Mary and Gilbert Eddy developed quickly and resulted in a hastily planned marriage. When one of her students, Daniel Spofford, was assigned the task of notifying the minister to perform the ceremony, he asked Eddy why the engagement had been kept so secretive, to which Eddy reportedly replied, "Indeed, Dr. Spofford, I didn't know a thing about it myself until last night."[37]

The "Salem Witchcraft Trial" of 1878 and Other Cases

During these years Mary was involved in a number of lawsuits, one of which was brought against Daniel Spofford in Massachusetts' highest court at Salem, and it became known as the "Salem Witchcraft Trial" of 1878. In the words of Dakin, it was "one of the most bizarre court-room sessions ever held in the United States."[38] In it, Mary charged Spofford with inflicting "great suffering of body and mind and severe spinal pains and neuralgia and a temporary suspension of mind" on one of her female students. The Newburyport *Herald* decried the "madness," suggesting the "witchcraft delusion" was still alive. In the end, however, there was no final verdict on the matter because the judge ruled, that it was beyond the power of the court to litigate the alleged malevolence of a person's thoughts, and the case was dismissed.[39]

Despite the judge's ruling, the strange drama of *Eddy vs. Spofford* was not over. Mary worked out a timetable whereby twelve of her loyal students would "concentrate their thoughts against Spofford in relays of two hours each." But, not satisfied with the results of the mental efforts, Mary apparently decided to make a more drastic move. Though not implicated herself, her husband and Edward Arens were arrested on a charge of conspiracy to have Spofford killed. Before the case came to trial, however, more than one witness was allegedly bribed to change his testi-

mony, leaving the judge with no choice but to dismiss the proceedings. The judge's personal view of the matter appeared evident, though, when he ordered Eddy and Arens to pay court costs.[40]

It was but a short time until Mary was back in court again. This time it was to bring suit against Edward J. Arens. As with Kennedy and Spofford, she became convinced that he was seeking to destroy her through M.A.M., and she claimed she could distinguish between his M.A.M. and those currents sent out by others. They each afflicted her in their own unique ways. Arens, for example, attacked her by mental arsenic poisoning, a form of M.A.M. that required special defenses to withstand. In the lawsuit, she charged him with copyright infringement, alleging that he had used portions of *Science and Health* without permission. She won the suit, even though Arens presented convincing evidence that she herself had taken the material from Quimby's writings. The fact the Quimby had not obtained a copyright on his manuscripts, however, made such evidence irrelevant.

The Boston Headquarters and Tightening Authoritarian Control

It was in 1875 that Mary had formed "The Christian Scientists' Association," and not until four years later that "The Church of Christ (Scientist)" was organized. It was located in Boston, and Mary traveled there each Sunday to preach to a small group of faithful followers. In 1881, at the age of sixty, she was officially ordained and installed as the pastor of the church. Shortly thereafter the Eddys moved to Boston permanently. A revolt in the ranks of their following in Lynn "marked the death-knell of her efforts there."[41]

The Move to Boston

The decision to move to Boston was most significant. It was only then that the movement began to flourish. Besides the church, Mary founded a school, the Massachusetts Metaphysical College. In the years that followed, the two organizations together grew to become the powerful Christian Science movement. What is most amazing is that Mary accomplished all this while being tormented by what she perceived as M.A.M. "She was remarkable," writes Silberger, "for the steadfastness of her attachment to purpose, to her desire to become wholly independent by capitalizing on her own resource—what she had made of Quimby's method."[42]

Soon after moving to Boston, Gilbert Eddy's health began to decline. The problem was diagnosed by a local physician to be organic heart disease, but Mary was convinced it was nothing other than the effects of M.A.M. His condition rapidly deteriorated, and in the early summer of 1882 he died in his sleep. Mary immediately charged that he had been killed by mental arsenic poisoning, an explanation that conveniently released her from any accountability in regard to her supposed healing powers.[43]

Within months after her husband's death, Mary found another man to lean on. This time it was Calvin Frye, a grocer whose wife was mentally incapacitated. Unlike her previous associates, Frye would remain her loyal supporter until she died twenty-eight years later. According to Silberger, "He was never to leave her side for as much as a whole day." Indeed, he chose to remain with her rather than attend his mother's funeral, and later the funerals of his father and sister.[44]

With her headquarters in Boston and a loyal associate to stand by her side, Mary was prepared to move ahead with her Christian Science movement. She was eager to move beyond the scandal of the past and to make Christian Science more presentable to a higher echelon in society. She controlled all aspects of the organization and took great care to groom its image. She no longer would tolerate disloyalty. Dissidents were threatened with "expulsion"—disciplinary action that was frequently accompanied by the charge of immorality. Indeed, Mrs. Eddy spoke of immorality and disloyalty as one and the same. On one occasion she accused a leading woman in the Boston church of adultery, and it was only later, after the damage had been done, that the interpretation of the charge was made public: "You have adulterated the Truth; what are you, then but an adulteress?"[45]

Mothering Instincts

Frye was not the only young man that Mary brought under her influence in the years following Gilbert Eddy's death. Ebenezer Foster entered her life in the fall of 1887, and it was then that her maternal instincts were manifested as never before. Her own unpolished son,

George, had maintained little contact with her over the years. He and his family made their home in the Dakota Territory, and his visit back East after a twenty-three-year absence did not prove to be a pleasant homecoming. "His manner was so boisterous and his custom so unusual that . . . he seemed entirely out of keeping with" Boston society life.[46]

Foster, on the other hand, was cultured and well-bred, and was the type of individual she could be proud to call her son. So, in 1888, less than a year after she first met him, she had papers drawn up by a lawyer to legally adopt him. Her new son, known as Foster Eddy, worked closely with her for the next five years, but like so many of the other young men with whom she was associated, they had a parting of the ways. She accused him of having been "governed by hypnotism to work against" her. Shortly thereafter she found another young man to "mother" and was addressing him as "My beloved Son" in her letters to him.[47]

Mary's maternalism was not only manifested toward the young men who worked with her, but to all those with whom she was associated. She viewed herself as divinely chosen to lead her church, and as such she viewed all her followers as her spiritual children. Indeed, she "encouraged her followers to call her Mother Mary, issuing a bylaw to assure that title to herself." When critics began using the term derisively against her, however, she discontinued its use.[48]

Women Associates

While it was the young men in her organization who caused her the most trouble, she also ran into difficulties with her female associates. Women were allowed an equal place with men within the organization, and there were many aggressive young women who found their way into the ranks. In some instances, Mary viewed them as threats to her own leadership and prominence in the movement, especially in the rare instances when they were able to steal the limelight from her.

One such incident involved Josephine Woodbury, a long-time loyal supporter of Mary's. Her active involvement in Christian Science offered her many opportunities for travel, and during the summer her students would follow her to Maine, where they lived communally and studied the science of mental healing. Although Mrs. Woodbury encouraged her followers to abstain from sexual intercourse and claimed that she and her husband were doing the same, she herself became pregnant following one excursion in behalf of Christian Science. How to explain such a phenomenon would have distressed most women, especially during that era when women were expected to model a life of chastity, but Mrs. Woodbury had a ready answer. She announced to her followers that she had undergone a virginal or "immaculate" conception. "Mr. Woodbury and the more bedazzled of her students," writes Peel, "found the explanation acceptable, if startling."[49]

In June of 1890, Woodbury gave birth to a baby boy, whom she named "The Prince of Peace," and shortly thereafter, on July 4, she baptized him before a crowd of loyal disciples at Ocean Point, Maine. When news of the circumstances reached Mary, she was beside herself. Not only did the incident have the potential for great embarrassment to the movement, but it also allowed one of her own followers to upstage her and become the focus of adulation. Mrs. Woodbury was later expelled from the movement, and with her went a large segment of her disciples. The excommunication, however, did not occur until 1896, six years after the scandal broke.[50]

Of all the women to rise to prominence in Christian Science, the most threatening to Mary was Mrs. Augusta Stetson, the founder and presiding officer of New York City's fashionable First Church of Christ, Scientist. Though Mrs. Stetson frequently displayed her loyalty to Mary by showering her with expensive gifts and praise, Mary was distressed by the attention bestowed upon her by her New York City congregation. Like Mary herself, Mrs. Stetson was often the center of controversy. She was accused of practicing M.A.M. against enemies—enemies that allegedly included some of the Directors of the Mother Church in Boston. She was brought to trial before the Board of Directors, found guilty, and expelled from the church.[51]

There were other scandals and dissident movements that created problems for Mrs. Eddy during the foundational stages of Christian Science, and not surprisingly many of these involved women. There was little opportunity for women's leadership in the orthodox churches, nor did Mormonism or the emerging Jehovah's Witness movement allow for women to play decisive leadership roles. But Christian Science and its New Thought cousin offered opportunities for women that gave them an influence comparable to their male counterparts, and for that reason alone, women may have gravitated to the movement.

Competing Christian Science Movements

One of the dissident movements that caused a furor was one centering around Mary H. Plunkett, who had become known as the "High Priestess" of a Christian Science group in New York. She, along with Emma Hopkins, began teaching their own version of Christian Science—a broader and less dogmatic one. They began publishing their own journal, *Truth: A Magazine of Christian Science* and organized schools to promote their teachings in New York and several midwestern cities. Their relationship ended, however, in 1889, when Plunkett began having a romantic affair with one of her male employees and announced that she had taken him as her spiritual husband—this, without bothering to divorce her own husband. When it was discovered that her new "spiritual" husband had been previously charged with being a bigamist and thief, she lost her credibility entirely.[52]

Emma Hopkins went on to become a very successful independent Christian Science leader, whose students included Charles and Myrtle Fillmore (founders of Unity) and Malinda Cramer (Cofounder of Divine Science). Another well-known dissident was Ursula Gestefield, who wrote her own book on her version of Christian Science. Many of these "subversive" splinter groups were located in the Midwest, but Clara Choate and Luther Marston established rival groups right under Mary Baker Eddy's nose in Boston.[53]

Competing "Mind-Cure" Movements

It was at the very time that Mrs. Eddy was beginning to establish credibility for Christian Science that she was being threatened by new "mind-cure" movements springing up under the generic designation of New Thought. She looked upon these groups—though similar in many ways—as her most menacing enemies. Speaking of them, she wrote: "The higher Truth lifts her voice, the louder will error scream, until its inarticulate sound is forever silenced in oblivion." In 1886, she made a lengthy statement, accusing her competitors of dishonesty and willful misrepresentation of the truth.

> Just now, the darkest spot on the horizon of mortal mind that Christian Science can illumine is envy, and the strife for "who shall be greatest." It pushes Christianity aside to elbow in a crowd of robbers, that enter not in by the door, Truth, but would climb up some other way. Obscure, unlettered, unprincipled people are filling the field as mind-healers, who are mind-killers, building their only superstructure on false foundations—the power of evil and substance of matter. They are working out, through mortal mind, the claim of total depravity, in all its forms of animal magnetism. They rise on the merits of the true healer, to at length fall from their own demerits.[54]

Establishing Credibility

Despite all the controversies and problems that Mary faced, she had an amazing capacity to rebound and move forward in her determination to build a powerful organization under her control. During the earliest years of her work, she was viewed as eccentric and of little threat to the religious establishment. Indeed the movement got off to a faltering start that gave no indication of its ability to persevere. In 1879, when she rented Hawthorne Hall in Boston for church services, her congregation did not begin to fill the 250-seat auditorium, and two years later, torn by strife, nearly one-third of her following abandoned the church. Moving her headquarters to Boston, however, paved the way for success, and by 1885, she and her Christian Science movement were regarded a serious threat to orthodoxy.[55]

Opposition from Protestant Pastors

In some respects, the most spirited of Mrs. Eddy's opponents were the very ones who gave her the limelight she needed to establish credibility. In 1885, after being attacked in print by two of Boston's leading Protestant ministers, Joseph Cook and A. J. Gordon, she was invited to present her case. "This was a momentous occasion," writes Stephen Gottschalk." "She was answering the attack of two of Boston's most prestigious ministers, in one of its greatest halls, before a distinguished audience including large numbers of clergymen, business figures, and assorted New England notables. . . . And if the assembled . . . did not like what they knew of Christian Science, at least they knew of it."[56]

By the turn of the century, she had tens of thousands of loyal followers

Boston First Church of Christ Scientist. Used by permission of The Christian Science Board of Directors.

from all over the country. Indeed, "The striking growth of Christian Science led some observers to fear that if it continued, the movement would soon become the dominant Protestant religious congregation in the world."[57] Her detractors were many: those who essentially agreed with her healing philosophy but denounced her authoritarian leadership; disgruntled students and church members, and virtually the whole of the orthodox Christian community. Yet, she had an appeal that few other religious leaders have generated. Characterized as the "petticoat pope," she maintained a powerful hold on a rapidly expanding movement.

Turn-of-the-Century Growth in Membership

In 1882, the church "consisted of one fractious fifty member congregation,"[58] but only two decades later, in her annual address in 1902, Mary was able to say, "with no special effort to achieve this result, our church communicants constantly increase in number, unity, steadfastness." The growth continued, and between 1903 and 1906 "membership in the Mother Church increased from twenty-four thousand to thirty-six thousand, while new branch churches were springing into existence every week."[59]

Personality Cult

From the earliest years after its inception, Christian Science was regarded a cult. The principal arguments for this were theological and biblical, but the place of Mrs. Eddy in the movement was also frequently cited. Indeed, her style of leadership and the near idolization of her in the minds of her followers all contributed very significantly to this public perception of her as the epitome of a cult leader. Much of this adulation may have been brought on by Mrs. Eddy herself. Although she always sought to curb it once it got out of hand, she said and did things that seemed to encourage undue devotion. She viewed herself as God's mouthpiece not only on spiritual matters contained in *Science and Health*, but in organizational and ethical issues. "No greater mistake can be made than to fail to obey or delay in obeying a single command of mine," she penned to a student. "God does speak through me to this age. This I discern more clearly every year of my sojourn with you."[60]

So convinced was she that God was speaking through her that Mrs. Eddy often closed herself off entirely from the ideas and input of those around her and the brightest minds within the movement. In the late 1890s, after her list of topics for Bible lessons had been circulated, members of the committee in charge of carrying out her orders suggested a more systematic and thoughtful alternate list. Her response to the suggestion was blunt: "Tell the committee the original subjects were given of God—they are sufficient, and they will remain forever." Her word was not challenged,

and the "the lessons on the twenty-six original topics are studied by Christian Scientists today.[61]

Mrs. Eddy's actions as well as her words demonstrated the personality of a cult leader. She required that all her followers refer to her as "our Leader," and in the *Manual of the Mother Church* which outlines church practice she spoke of the duty of each member "to God, to his Leader, and to mankind." Several pages of that manual are devoted to a section entitled "Relations and Duties of Members to Pastor Emeritus," referring, of course, to herself. One area of "duty" involved personal labor of members in the service of their Leader—requiring "a Christian Scientist to begin service in Mrs. Eddy's home for three years within ten days of being requested by her to do so, on pain of excommunication from The Mother Church."[62]

There were some followers of Mrs. Eddy who balked at her authoritarian style, and some of those left the movement, but the majority seemed to almost enjoy her godlike status. In an article published in the *Christian Science Journal* in 1900, James Logwood told his readers how a "prayer of gratitude to God and to our dear Leader and Mother" saved him from sure peril during an excursion in the Rocky Mountains.[63]

In another article, "With Sandals on and Staff in Hand," Clara McKee associated miraculous power over nature's storms with her Leader:

One day Mrs. Eddy called her students into her study and pointed to a very black cloud, shaped like a cornucopia, coming toward the house in direct line with her front study window. She asked each one to go to a window and face it, and to realize that there were no destructive elements in God's creation. Although appearing to whirl straight toward Pleasant View, a mile or so away the cyclone changed its course and went around Concord into the mountains, doing very little damage.[64]

Part of the mystical aura surrounding Mrs. Eddy resulted from her seclusion and inaccessibility to the public and to her followers. In this atmosphere, apocryphal stories of supernatural feats and sentimental deeds of kindness abounded. Although she publicly condemned those who would look to her rather than God for their solace, she seemed at times to not-so-subtly encourage this type of adulation, and "after her death, cultish fascination with anything to do with Mrs. Eddy was conspicuous among some Christian Scientists. Those of this disposition delighted in circulating writings purported to have originated with her and in relating stories to her healing prowess."[65]

Accumulation of Wealth

A factor that aided in the mysterious nature of Mrs. Eddy was money—a tool that allowed her to live in luxurious seclusion. As the church grew, so did Mary's wealth. Less than a decade after she had opened her metaphysical college in Boston she had collected some one hundred thousand dollars in tuition. Another source of income was publishing sales. After her third edition of *Science and Health* appeared in 1881, "new editions appeared with dizzying speed, reaching a total of 382 before her death. By 1891 this personally controlled and very profitable

publication had sold 50,000 copies and by 1910, 400,000."[66] During her last years she lived in lavish surroundings, first on Commonwealth Avenue in Boston, then at "Pleasant View" outside Concord, New Hampshire, and finally at a large mansion in Brookline, Massachusetts.

Last Years and Death

Most of the time during the last years of her life, Mary was secluded from the public. Rumors surfaced periodically that she was dead or dying, and during her last years she declined steadily, both mentally and physically. Calvin Frye, who remained close to her to the very end, feared that she had become addicted to the morphine she was taking to relieve her pain, and he restricted the dosage. She was a fearful woman to her dying day, and Frye was asked by her more than once "to testify that if she died, it was because of Malicious Animal Magnetism rather than from natural causes."[67]

The end came in 1910, but even death, many believed, did not break the ties that Mary had with this present world. Her burial was delayed until a suitable tomb could be constructed. During the interim a telephone was in the room near her coffin—"a telephone, whose fame has had a surprising longevity." Even today, writes Silberger, "almost three quarters of a century later, people who know very little about Mrs. Eddy will know about that telephone and wonder whether it is in her tomb, connected and functional, should she awaken and have need of it!"[68]

Surprisingly, her death did not seriously disrupt the Christian Science movement. Some of her followers were deeply distressed by the fact that she would die at all—if death was not real—and others were convinced that she would quickly be resurrected back to life. But such speculation came more in ridicule from critics than from admirers. The outspoken evangelist and temperance champion Billy Sunday expressed his derision through a public wager: "If old Mother Eddy rises from the dead I'll eat polecat for breakfast and wash it down with booze!"[69]

Following her death there were struggles for power and lawsuits that took many years to settle, but the movement, under the control of the Board of Directors, continued to grow without its celebrated founder. Yet, she remained its guiding light, and her memory will ever be revered in Christian Science circles.

Church Reorganization

One of the reasons for the lack of disruption following Mrs. Eddy's death was due to the fact that she had radically reorganized the church more than a decade prior to her death. It was a reorganization that prevented the church from allowing another prominent figure to perpetuate the personality cult she had started. There would be no Brigham Young in Christian Science. "In sociological terms," writes Stephen Gottschalk, "Mrs Eddy presided over the transformation of her church from a charismatic into a bureaucratic institution."[70]

Like other developments that had occurred in Christian Science from its inception, this change came through the authority of Mrs. Eddy,

with the claim of God's clear direction. The reorganization of the church began in the early 1890s, when Mrs. Eddy founded The Mother Church in Boston. This church was not merely a "First" church as many denominations may have to designate a pioneer church in a particular area. The Mother Church was established to serve as the headquarters and governing organization of the entire movement, and all other churches, no matter how large or wealthy they may become were considered branches and would look to this church for leadership and oversight. *The Manual for The Mother Church*, published in 1895, lays out the structure and regulations of the movement. Like *Science and Health*, this writing was viewed as the word of God. "This Church Manual is God's law, as much as the Ten Commandments and the Sermon on the Mount," Mrs. Eddy told a follower. "It is God's law and will be acknowledged as law by law." The actual day-to-day decision making of Christian Science was handled first by a group designated as the First Members and later by the Board of Directors, a body that continues to function to the present.[71]

Although Mrs. Eddy was very much opposed to magnificent church buildings and the ritual and formalism that went with them, she could not prevent some of these characteristics from creeping into Christian Science. Large and ostentatious Christian Science churches were built despite her initial misgivings. Her insistence on simple church services, however, was maintained. She criticized the emphasis on liturgy, creeds, sacraments, public

Christian Science headquarters in Boston. Used by permission of The Christian Science Board of Directors.

prayer and sermons that were characteristic of the mainline denominations, and demanded that Christian Science services be different. This was made clear in *Science and Health:* "To the ritualistic priest and hypocritical Pharisee Jesus said, 'The publicans and the harlots go into the kingdom of God before you.' . . . He knew that men can be baptized, partake of the Eucharist, support the clergy, observe the Sabbath, make long prayers, and yet be sensual and sinful."[72]

She viewed liturgies and creeds as man-made documents, and she referred to communion as a "dead rite" with no meaning for today. "If Christ, Truth, has come to us in demonstration, no other commemoration is requisite, for demonstration is Immanuel, or *God with us;* and if a friend be with us, why need we memorials of that friend?" Her attitude toward water baptism was similar. "Our baptism," she wrote, "is a purification from all error."[73]

But despite her opposition, the memorial of communion was permitted in Christian Science churches— largely in an effort to appease converts, the vast majority of whom came out of Protestant churches. Baptism has never been an approved rite of the church, but because of pressure from a group of parents, she herself on one occasion verbally blessed a group of young children with "the baptism of Christ."[74]

From the very beginning, Christian Science, like the Mormons and Jehovah's Witnesses, has not ordained clergy to serve as full-time ministers. Christian Science, however, does offer members who have been properly trained to serve as practitioners, who pray for the sick. Some of these have served in a full-time capacity, but the vast majority do not treat enough patients to earn an adequate income. In many cases, this is not a serious problem, as a large proportion of practitioners are retired or are married women who do not depend on their fees for their sole source of income. Some of those who do work as full-time professionals operate out of modern offices much as a medical doctor would and, amazing as it may seem, "fees are covered by many group and individual insurance plans."[75]

Sermons were another aspect of the mainline denominations that could not be tolerated in Christian Science. A sermon could potentially elevate the preacher to a position of authority that might conflict with The Mother Church, or it could be a forum for new interpretations of Christian Science belief. To prevent this, the Bible and *Science and Health* were designated as the "impersonal pastor" for all church services. Indeed, the Bible and *Science and Health* were "ordained" to this office, first for The Mother Church and then for all branch churches. Portions of these volumes were edited for the "International Series," and they were then read each Sunday by an individual designated as simply a "reader"—a practice which continues to the present.[76]

Science and Health with Key to the Scriptures

The place of *Science and Health* as the unique scripture of Christian Science and as the "impersonal pastor" makes it one of the most significant documents in the literature of alternative religions. Without this book, Christian Science may have become no more than a short-lived health cult.

The rapid growth of Christian Science was due to a large degree to the frustration people felt with the medical profession. Quimby had taught that disease was a result of wrong thinking, and Mrs. Eddy's adaptation of that line of reasoning combined with her interpretation of the Bible in *Science and Health* had a compelling attraction to many people who had personally found the health profession utterly inept in its treatment of diseases.

Although Mrs. Eddy insisted after it was published that she had based *Science and Health* solely on the Bible, she previously admitted her access to and dependence on Quimby's written notes. After her volume was published, critics charged that she relied heavily on him, and, in fact plagiarized him. This charge was widely publicized in the July 10, 1904 edition of *The New York Times*. Parallel columns were displayed that showed very similar ideas, though not word-for-word reproduction. Quimby's phrase "Disease being made by our belief," was rephrased as "Disease being a belief" in *Science and Health*. In similar instances, "the idea, man is the highest—hence the image of God, or the Principle," was rephrased as "Man was and is God's idea. . . .Man is the idea of Divine Principle." The sentence "God is Principle," was quoted verbatim, and "Error is matter," was reversed to read "Matter is mortal error." There are many other similar parallels, not only from Quimby's writings but also from other sources—none of which are acknowledged.[77]

God's Final Revelation

The source of her authority, she insisted, was the Bible, "my only textbook." Like other leaders of variant religious movements, Mrs. Eddy believed that God had given her his final revelation. "God has been preparing me during many years for the reception of this final revelation of the absolute divine Principle of scientific mental healing." If there was yet any doubt as to where this revelation originated and the specific nature of the revelation, she made it plain that it emanated from a supernatural source and was revealed in a specific book. "No human pen nor tongue taught me the Science contained in this book, SCIENCE AND HEALTH; and neither tongue nor pen can overthrow it."[78]

While using the term "revelation," Mrs. Eddy did not mean revelation in the same sense that it is used in orthodox Christian circles or even in the sense that Joseph Smith used it when he was "translating" the *Book of Mormon*. God does not *give* a revelation because, according to her, God *is* revelation. "She maintains that God is continuously self-revealed and self-revealing to His creation, and could not by His very nature be self-concealed or arbitrary in His self-disclosures." Hence, revelation is "a divine breakthrough occurring when individuals respond to God's continuous revelatory self-action," as Mrs. Eddy testified she did when she "discovered" Christian Science.[79]

Errors in the Bible

Although the Bible is frequently quoted, it is *Science and Health* that is regarded as the most relevant scripture for today. It is this "textbook" rather than the Bible that is seen as absolute and perfect. Mrs. Eddy maintained that she "received it ... by the revelation of Jesus Christ"—that she "was only a scribe echoing the harmonies of heaven." The Bible, on the other hand, was filled with "mistakes in the ancient versions" with "thirty thousand different readings in the Old Testament, and three hundred thousand in the New," indicating "how a mortal and material sense stole into the divine record, with its own hue darkening to some extent the inspired pages."[80]

Although she spoke of the Bible being inspired, she used a very limited application of that term. Some portions were more inspired than others, and some were not inspired at all. Even those passages that were most frequently quoted by Mrs. Eddy were often not interpreted literally. "Indeed, she felt that the genius of Christian Science lay in the fact that it had penetrated behind the literal interpretation of the Bible and grasped its spiritual signification." It was, of course, her own interpretation of the Bible that was determined to be the spiritual meaning of any particular passage.[81]

Biblical Miracles

While Mrs. Eddy was far from being a biblical literalist in any sense of the word, she parted company from liberals of her day who demythologized the Bible and insisted that passages reporting miracles were merely embellished stories told by Jesus' followers. She, to the contrary, upheld the accuracy of the miracle narratives, arguing that the actual works of Jesus formed God's revelation to mankind far more than the written accounts of those works. But while accepting the miracles as being literally true, her analysis of them was far different than traditional biblical scholars, who maintain that a miracle is an interruption of the laws of nature—a *super*natural event—and that the laws of nature themselves are ordained by God. She, on the other hand, argued that the material world was so filled with pain and desolation that it could not be ordained by God. "The miracle introduces no disorder," she maintained, "but unfolds the primal order, establishing the Science of God's unchangeable law." Miracles are thus "natural demonstrations of the divine power."[82]

Unlike the dispensationalists of her day, Mrs. Eddy argued that "the so-called miracles of Jesus did not specially belong to a dispensation now ended, but ... they illustrated an ever-operative divine Principle. The operation of this Principle indicates the eternality of the scientific order and continuity of being."[83]

Doctrinal Distinctives

Christian Science doctrine developed out of Mary Baker Eddy's biblical reflections on what has been termed Mind Science, or the Science of Health. She assimilated this philosophy largely from P. P. Quimby and later published it in updated revisions in the numerous editions of *Science and Health.*

The Science of Health

The most distinctive and widely-publicized doctrine of Christian Science can be summed up in one terse statement made by Mary Baker Eddy: "It is unchristian to believe that pain and sickness are anything *but* illusions." She was not the first to make such claims. Indeed there were many others who insisted that good health was simply a matter of mind over matter. She was quick to disassociate herself with such "heresy," however. When asked why Christian Science theology alone is valid in healing the sick, she responded:

The theology of Christian Science is Truth; opposed to which is the error of sickness, sin, and death, that Truth destroys.

A "mind-cure" is a matter-cure. . . .

The theology of Christian Science is based on the action of the divine Mind over the human mind and body; whereas, "mind-cure" rests on the notion that the human mind can cure its own disease, or that which it causes, and the *sickness of matter*,—which is infidel in the one case, and anomalous in the other. . . .

Our Master understood that Life, Truth, Love are the triune Principle of all pure theology; also, that this divine trinity is one infinite remedy for the opposite triad, sickness, sin, and death.[84]

One of the most enduring criticisms of Christian Science has been not simply that pain and sickness are illusions, but that when healing did not occur through prayer and the aid of a practitioner the individual was often left to die. The reason for this is explained in Christian Science literature: "Bodily conditions" are "effect rather than cause—the outward expression of conscious and unconscious thoughts." That being so, "what needs to be healed is always a false concept of being, not a material condition. The purpose of turning to God for healing is therefore not merely to change the evidence before the physical senses but to heal the deeper alienation of human thought from God."[85]

Whose fault is it if a Christian Scientist is not healed of his illness? This in itself is a very controversial point. The blame—the burden of responsibility—is placed directly on the individual. "The Christian Scientist does not blame the perfect Principle" that Mary Baker Eddy articulated, but rather "he asks himself where he needs to bring his own thinking and living into closer conformity with God's law."[86]

Theology of God and Christ

Unlike Scientology, a pseudoscience of health which would develop most of a century later, Christian Science claimed to be thoroughly Christian and Mrs. Eddy upheld certain orthodox doctrines, while adding her own distinctive bias. Her "insistent rejection of anthropomorphic views of Deity is one of the key points that differentiates her theology from Protestant orthodoxy." God could simply not be described in human terms because God is beyond any human depiction. She denied the personality of God, unless personality was understood as "infinite personality." She likewise denied an orthodox view of the Trinity, arguing that the "theory of three persons in one God (that is, a personal Trinity or tri-Unity) suggests polytheism, rather than

the one ever-present I AM." The only trinity she could subscribe to was the trinity of Life, Truth, and Love.[87]

Because of her very impersonal terms for God, which included "Principle," "Mind," "Spirit," and other remote expressions, Mrs. Eddy's philosophy was sometimes associated with transcendentalism or pantheism. In both instances, however, she rejected the association. In regard to the latter, she wrote, "I am the only anti-pantheist, for I see that God, Spirit, is not in His reflection any more than the sun is in the light that comes to this earth by reflection." Yet, her writing was sometimes mistaken for a form of pantheism: "God is All-in-all. . . . He is all the Life and Mind there is or can be. Within Himself is every embodiment of Life and Mind. . . . If He is omnipresent, there can be nothing outside of Himself."[88]

Despite her unwillingness to characterize God in human terms, Mrs. Eddy did not hesitate to refer to God as "Father-Mother," for it "is the name for Deity which indicates His tender relationship to His spiritual creation." She credited Christian Science with its contribution in pointing to the motherhood of God as particularly revealed in the Holy Spirit, and she wrote that "in divine Science we have not as much authority for considering God masculine, as we have for considering Him feminine, for Love imparts the clearest idea of Deity."[89]

Other churchmen at various times had suggested that the Holy Spirit reflected the feminine nature of God, but her emphasis on a feminine Holy Spirit had a unique slant in that she equated the Holy Spirit with Divine

Science, and Divine Science was the divine essence of what she, as a woman, had offered to the world in human terms. Was she in some way associating her own role to that of the Holy Spirit?

In her rejection of the orthodox view of the Trinity, Mrs. Eddy also rejected an orthodox position of the deity of Christ. "She wholly rejects the belief that Jesus was God," writes Stephen Gottschalk, "and distinguished between Jesus as a man and Christ as one office of God. In Christian Science, Christ is the divine ideal of manhood, the model of perfect spiritual sonship; while Jesus was a human being who through the extraordinary conditions of his birth completely demonstrated this Christ ideal."[90]

Virgin Birth

Although Mrs. Eddy spoke of the extraordinary conditions of Jesus' birth, her description of the Virgin Birth was not in traditional terminology: In *Science and Health*, she wrote that "Jesus was the offspring of Mary's self-conscious communion with God." Jesus was conceived when Mary "perceived" the "spiritual idea" of Christ who had "dwelt forever an idea in the bosom of God." Indeed, the Virgin Birth, like healings and other miracles, was another example of mind (or spirit) over matter. "The illumination of Mary's spiritual sense put to silence material law and its order of generation, and brought forth her child by the revelation of Truth."[91]

Mrs. Eddy testified that through her development of Christian Science she had come to "reverence and adore Christ as never before." She spoke of her gratitude for His atonement that had provided salvation to mankind, but it was not a belief in Christ's finished work of atoning for mankind's sins on the cross. "The atonement requires constant self-immolation on the sinner's part," she wrote. "That God's wrath should be vented upon His beloved Son, is divinely unnatural. Such a theory is man-made."[92] And what type of salvation was provided through the atonement? A salvation that was expanded to include "man's redemption from sickness as well as from sin."[93]

Salvation and the New Birth

She spoke of salvation as "the new birth," but argued that it "is not the work of a moment." Rather, "it begins with moments, and goes on with years; moments of surrender to God, of childlike trust and joyful adoption of good; moments of self-abnegation, self-consecration, heaven-born hope, and spiritual love." While the new birth may have a beginning point, it has no ending, "for progress is the law of infinity."[94]

The Holy Spirit

It is the doctrine of the Holy Spirit that sets Christian Science apart from orthodox Christianity as much as any other. Who was the Comforter that Jesus promised the Father would send in his name? Jesus answered that himself. The Holy Spirit. In *Science and Health*, Mrs. Eddy wrote: "This comforter I understand to be Divine Science." Divine Science and Christian Science are one and the same, except that Christian Science is the Divine Science of God rendered in human terms for human understanding.[95]

Spiritualism and the Occult

Was Christian Science influenced by spiritualism and the occult? It was. So said the well-known Baptist churchman A. J. Gordon and other critics of the movement. Such accusations, however, were vehemently denied by Mrs. Eddy. Indeed, she argued that Christian Science had done more to reverse the upsurge in spiritualism and the occult than any other religious movement. She denied any possibility of the living communicating with the dead, and insisted that "haunted houses, ghostly voices, unusual noises and apparitions brought out in dark seances either involve feats by tricksters, or they are images and sounds evolved involuntarily by mortal mind."[96]

Despite Mrs. Eddy's disavowals, however, there was a closer affinity between Christian Science and the occult than may have appeared obvious on the surface. She herself had been fascinated with spiritualism as a young woman, and she sought to have spiritual contacts with Quimby during her acquaintance with him. And, it was from the ranks of spiritualists that she won some of her first converts. More than anything else, though, it was the emphasis she placed on M.A.M (malicious animal magnetism) that tied Christian Science to the occult.

Although she conceded that M.A.M. was occultic, she insisted it was a product of the mortal mind, not a manifestation of divine power.

Yet, M.A.M. became such a fundamental teaching in Christian Science—especially during the 1880s—that it was virtually turned into an occultic practice on its own merit. This is evident in testimonies given about Mrs. Stetson and her influential Christian Science church in New York. According to one source, "Relays of practitioners were employed to keep up a continuous mental effort directed toward a certain person who was in disfavor."[97]

The Controversy Over Healing

From the earliest days of Christian Science the issue of healing without medicine has been highly controversial, and this matter has become even more problematic in recent decades as medicine has advanced and members of the movement have become better educated. News stories have detailed tragic accounts of young children dying because parents refused to permit doctors to give them necessary medications. One of the most highly publicized accounts in recent years focused on the deaths of two students at Principia College, a Christian Science institution in Illinois. The cause of death? Measles—a disease that can be easily controlled through simple vaccinations. "We believe in healing through prayer," the dean insisted. "But if they choose to seek medical help, they are free to go to an outside hospital. It's a matter between them and their conscience."[98] As a result of widespread negative publicity and greater confidence in the medical profession more and more Christian Scientists are ignoring the admonitions of Mary

A Christian Science reading room. Used by permission of The Christian Science Board of Directors.

Baker Eddy and seeking medical help.

Missionary Outreach

Unlike the Mormons and the Jehovah's Witnesses, Christian Science does not have an extensive missionary program. The church has expanded worldwide over the past century, but it still has fewer than one thousand congregations outside the United States. There are no full-time missionaries per se, but individual church members are expected to share their faith with others, and when they go abroad they are encouraged to initiate study groups that may eventually develop into churches. This concern for foreign growth began with Mrs. Eddy herself. According to Irving Tomlinson, in his *Twelve Years with Mary Baker Eddy*,

"She had a breadth of vision that was worldwide. Her love was broad and expanding, encircling all mankind."[99]

Christian Science does not sponsor conventional missionaries as Protestant missions or independent mission societies do. According to the organization's literature, "The religious periodicals help to fulfill this missionary function; so do the Reading Rooms, and the literature distribution committees of branch churches." There are other means as well. "While the Mother Church does not maintain missionaries, it does maintain a board of about 28 lecturers who travel all over the world wherever Christian Science groups are located." These lecturers "deliver an aggregate of about 4,000 public lectures" annually. "The groups they address cover a tremendous range— from a cultivated audience in a lecture hall at Oxford or Cambridge to a group of barefoot natives clustered around an outdoor platform on an island off southeast Asia."[100]

If there is anything that symbolizes Christian Science "evangelism" it is the Christian Science Reading Room. These are usually small store front libraries, each supported by local congregations, and located in nice shopping or residential areas. The literature is only that published or approved by the organization, and the public is encouraged to spend quiet time reading or discussing issues related to the religion. Any religious solicitation would be very low key.

Despite these efforts to attract new members worldwide and in the United States, recent studies show that the organization is in decline.

Although the church claims that it has no membership lists, some observers believe that membership may have dropped below the 1936 statistics that showed 269,000 members and some two thousand congregations. In just the past two decades, 17 percent of the churches have shut their doors, and the number of practitioners has dropped off sharply. The number of practitioners reached an all-time high in the 1940s, dropping to eight thousand in the 1950s and to less than four thousand today. The decline is due in part to the widely publicized controversies relating to health practices and to "fundamentalist literature labeling Christian Science as a cult" that, according to one observer, has been disseminated in "unprecedented volume over the past several years."[101]

Chapter 7

New Thought and Unity: Health and Happiness

For many people the concepts of mental healing that had been propounded by Phineas Parkhurst Quimby were too innovative and resourceful to be confined to the tight system that Mary Baker Eddy had developed as Christian Science. These individuals wanted to take Quimby's ideas and move beyond to explore new realms in the field of mental healing and mind-altering activity. They were not content with one tight system of thought such as Christian Science offered, and they were eager to erase the effects of Calvinistic Christianity on the American psyche. In his *Handbook of New Thought*, Horatio W. Dresser, a spokesman for the movement, gave an overview of this emerging philosophy:

> It was once the custom so greatly to emphasize the majesty of God, that little was left for the creature save to minimize himself in the presence of the Creator. The result was an essentially negative attitude, lacking in powers of resistance. . . . In relation to life it

meant submissiveness to the divine will, quiescent readiness to take what might come. It implied a weak mode of thought, an inefficient attitude, and a will that struggled to hold itself up to the mark, to the level of unpleasant duty. Then New Thought came as the corrective to this abject submissiveness. It substituted self-realization for self-sacrifice, and development for self-effacement. It is nothing if not an affirmative thought, and this positiveness has come to stay.[1]

In the 1880s, at the very time that Christian Science was in its developmental stages, Julius Dresser and Warren Evans, both former patients of Quimby, organized a movement known as the Church of Divine Unity. Because the movement "was highly individualistic and expressed a wide variety of doctrine within its ranks," however, it was difficult to maintain the cohesiveness that was evident in Christian Science. It soon fragmented and became a loose association of groups known as New Thought.[2]

A necessary component of any

religious movement that grows in numbers and influence is that it meet the basic needs of people—or at least pretend to meet their needs. It is that factor more than anything else that accounts for the growth and influence of New Thought, Unity, and Christian Science in the late nineteenth and early twentieth centuries. The science of medicine was still hardly beyond its infancy, and there truly was a need to be met in the area of health care. Death was an ever-present reality, and it is not surprising then that philosophical religions of healing, reincarnation, and positive thinking moved in to fill up the slack.

New Thought, like New Age today, was a popular religious mindset that attracted people from all segments of society. It was a term, like New Age, that represented a wide variety of religious thinking and encompassed an assortment of religious organizations. In 1915, the International New Thought Alliance was formed to bring together in a loose federation the various New Thought groups. It published a list of "Affirmations" which reflect the basic tenets of the philosophy. Included in these affirmations are the following statements:

> The essence of the New Thought is Truth, and each individual must be loyal to Truth as he sees it. . . .
>
> We affirm the Good. . . . Man is made in the image of the Good, and evil and pain are but the tests and correctives that appear when his thought does not reflect the full glory of this image.
>
> We affirm health. . . .
>
> We affirm the divine supply. . . . Within us are unused resources of energy and power. . . .

> We affirm the teaching of Christ that the Kingdom of Heaven is within us, that we are one with the Father, that we should judge not, that we should love one another. . . .
>
> We affirm the new thought of God as Universal Love, Life, Truth and Joy.[3]

Unlike Christian Science which was viewed as pessimistic and authoritarian, New Thought proponents were avowed optimists. They were convinced that positive thinking in itself would have a positive effect outside the mind. Evil, they insisted was the lack of good; thus any appearance of evil or pessimism should be obliterated. "Mirth is heaven's medicine," wrote one such idealist. "Everyone ought to bathe in it. Grim care, moroseness, anxiety, all the rust of life, ought to be scoured off by the oil of mirth."[4]

New Thought proponents also emphasized the unity of all religions. This is illustrated in the writing of Emma Hopkins, one of the most celebrated of the New Thought champions.

> The remarkable analogies of the Christian Bible, and Hindu Sacred Books, Egyptian Ancient Teachings, Persian Bible, Chinese Great Learning, Oriental Yohar, Saga, and many others, show that the whole world has had life teachings so wonderfully identical as to make them all subjects for respectful attention and investigation by the thoughtful of our age.[5]

One of the New Thought organizations that developed in the late nineteenth century—indeed, the largest of all New Thought religions—has been The Unity School of Christianity. It is in that sense that the two are closely related. In fact, the latter has outgrown and overshadowed the former to the point that the former is hardly known today.[6]

Charles and Myrtle Fillmore

Unity, perhaps more than almost any other of the variant religious groups that sprang up on American soil, was cofounded by a husband-wife team. "Charles and Myrtle Fillmore worked together to build Unity," writes James Freeman. "It was Myrtle Fillmore who first accepted the idea of divine healing; it was Charles Fillmore who edited the first magazine. It was Myrtle Fillmore who first led Silent Unity; it was Charles Fillmore who named the work Unity and developed it into the worldwide organization it is today. It was Myrtle Fillmore who led the people in meditation and prayer; it was Charles Fillmore who made speeches and wrote books." Indeed, it was a true partnership, but it was one that was dominated by the husband. She "supplied the original impetus," while he "supplied the greater part of the energy that carried it forward."[7]

Charles Fillmore, a distant cousin of President Millard Fillmore, was born in a log cabin on an Indian reservation in Minnesota, in 1854. He spent much of his early boyhood hunting and trapping animals with his Indian friends. His early years were relatively uneventful until a skating accident as a youth left him handicapped for the rest of his life. It was then that his mistrust of the medical profession began. "I was bled, leached, cupped, lanced, seasoned, blistered, and roweled," he later wrote. "Physicians of different schools were employed, and the last

one always wondered how I ever pulled through alive under the treatment of the 'quack' that preceded him; and as I look back at it now it's a miracle to me how I ever got away from them all with the little bundle of bones and sinews that I found in my possession after they had finished their experiments."[8]

Charles Fillmore. From *The Household of Faith* by James D. Freeman.

At the age of nineteen, Charles moved to Texas, where he met and later married Myrtle Page. She was nine years his senior and much better educated, having attended Oberlin College before she began her teaching career. She was raised in a Methodist family and continued to attend Methodist meetings, but even before her marriage was beginning to develop beliefs of her own. In a letter to Charles, she wrote, "You question my orthodoxy? Well, if I were called upon to write out my creed it would be rather a strange mixture. I am decidedly eclectic in my theology." She told about an outdoor meeting and the difference between her perception of nature and that of the "simple hearted country folk." "They saw rock and moss, listened decorously to the man of God, while I, in a kind of charmed life, was part of all I saw—and a part of God. What have I said? But you understand me, you know there are times when we go out and seem to become a part of this great Spirit of the universe. . . ."9

Following their marriage in 1879, Charles and Myrtle moved to Colorado, where their two sons were born and where Charles had become involved in mining and speculating in real estate. After some initial setbacks, Charles branched out in his financial dealings and was swept away in spiraling properties investments and sales and quickly "amassed a fortune of $150,000 in real estate, but he lost it all during a depression." It was a difficult time for him and his family now living in Kansas City. Myrtle had contracted tuberculosis and was seriously failing in health. "Penniless and sick, they saw little ahead that was hope-inspiring."10

Confirmation of Beliefs

This was a time of indecision and despondency for the Fillmores—not knowing whether to remain in Kansas City or to return to Colorado where financial prospects appeared to be more promising. It was then that Charles had a life-changing experience:

> I had a strange dream. An unseen voice said, "Follow me." I was led up and down the hill streets of Kansas City and my attention called to localities I was familiar with. The Presence stopped and said: "You will remember having had a dream some years ago in which you were shown this city and told you had a work to do here. Now you are being reminded of that dream and also informed that the invisible power that has located you will continue to be with you and aid you in the appointed work." When I awoke, I remembered that I had had such a dream and forgotten it.11

This was not his first experience with a supernatural "presence." As a youth, Charles had dabbled in spiritualism with a friend, "and the two of them had spent many evenings together in the dark facing each other silently across the table, their fingers pressed lightly against the table top to see if they could not waft it mysteriously into the air." As he grew to adulthood, he began studying Hinduism, Buddhism, Rosicrucianism, and Theosophy. This continued after his marriage to Myrtle to the extent that he could write: "We have taken more than forty courses (in metaphysical subjects), some of them costing as much as $100."12

So it was that following his dream and in a frame of mind that was open to religious beliefs of all sorts, especially those of a metaphysical nature, Charles and Myrtle were persuaded to attend a series of lectures in 1886 by a Dr. Weeks who represented New Thought ideology. "Charles Fillmore came away from that lecture . . . feeling no different than when he had

Myrtle Fillmore. From *The Household of Faith* by James D. Freeman.

gone in, but the woman who walked out of the hall on his arm was not the same woman who had entered. A new, a different, a liberating, a transforming conviction was blazing in her heart and mind." This change was inspired by one phrase that she heard—a phrase that echoed again and again in her mind: "I am a child of God and therefore I do not inherit sickness."[13]

Some years later, Myrtle Fillmore reflected on what had happened to her during this time in her life and how she gave a personal flavor to what was termed "the science of mental healing."

I have made what seems to me a discovery. I was fearfully sick; I had all the ills of mind and body that I could bear. Medicine and doctors ceased to give me relief, and I was in despair when I found practical Christianity. I took it up and I was healed. . . .

I was thinking about life. . . . Life is simply a form of energy, and has to be guided and directed in man's body by his intelligence. How do we communicate intelligence? By thinking and talking, of course. Then it flashed upon me that I might talk to the life in every part of my body and have it do just what I wanted. I began to teach my body and got marvelous results.

I told the life in my liver that it was not torpid or inert, but full of vigor and energy. I told the life in my stomach that it was not weak or inefficient, but energetic, strong, and intelligent. I told the life in my abdomen that it was no longer infested with ignorant thoughts or disease, put there by myself and by doctors, but that it was athrill with the sweet, pure, wholesome energy of God. I told my limbs that they were active and strong. I told my eyes that they did not see of themselves but that they were drawing on an unlimited source. . . .

I went to all the life centers in my body and spoke words of Truth to them—words of strength and power. I asked their forgiveness for the foolish, ignorant course that I had pursued in the past, when I had condemned them and called them weak, inefficient and diseased. I did not become discouraged at their being slow to wake up, but kept right on, both silently and aloud, declaring the words of Truth, until the organs responded. . . .[14]

The Unity School of Christianity, which developed out of Myrtle Fillmore's search for healing, unfolded naturally as an answer to her own personal problems and as the logical interpretation of Charles Fillmore's dream. But more than that, it was the fruition of a long religious pilgrimage that had begun for both of them in their earliest years. They were sincere in their own search for God, and genuinely wanted others to share what they had found. Myrtle was convinced that she had discovered an untapped source of energy for healing, and she and her husband were both determined that they should not keep this secret to themselves. Myrtle began practicing her healing "art" on others, and Charles, though initially with great reluctance, began disseminating the message— taking full advantage of his own writing skills and printing experience.

Organizational Beginnings

In 1889, three years after his wife's "discovery," Charles began publishing a magazine initially titled Modern Thought, then retitled Christian Science Truth, and finally became known as Unity—a word that came to Charles after he "heard a voice." In 1892, the Fillmores signed a covenant that reflected their philosophy of a covenant religion—one that held God, the "Spirit of Truth," responsible for their welfare.

Dedication and Covenant

We, Charles Fillmore and Myrtle Fillmore, husband and wife, hereby dedicate ourselves, our time, our money, all we have and all we expect to have, to the Spirit of Truth, and through it, to the Society of Silent Unity.

It being understood and agreed that the said Spirit of Truth shall render unto us an equivalent for this dedication, in peace of mind, health of body, wisdom, understanding, love, life and an abundant supply of all things necessary to meet every want without our making any of these things the object of our existence.

In the presence of the Conscious Mind of Christ Jesus, this 7th day of December, A.D. 1892.

Charles Fillmore
Myrtle Fillmore[15]

With that publishing venture and a covenant signed in 1892, the Fillmores launched their effort to reach out to others in earnest.

Publishing and Direct Mail Enterprises

The eventual result was a vast publishing and direct mail venture that brought the Unity message into millions of homes. That "Unity supplies salvation as Sears Roebuck supplies overalls, cut to size and delivered parcel post," as one cult authority has cynically claimed may be an unfair assessment.[16] In comparison with other religious movements, Unity has not excessively commercialized its message. Nor has the message been packaged to fit particular clusters of people. It is a religious ideology that has broad appeal because of the hope, health, and prosperity it offers to people of all walks of life, and it is broad enough to accept virtually any belief system, including spiritism and eastern mysticism.

Opposition to Christian Science

While Unity was still in its developmental stages, Charles Fillmore sought to differentiate it from Christian Science and New Thought in general. He strongly opposed the exclusivity of Christian Science and wanted to rise above those who claimed their movements had a corner on the truth. Yet, Unity was

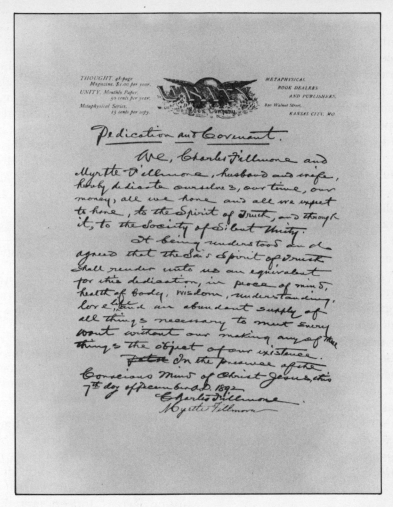

Letter of Dedication and Covenant. From *The Household of Faith* by James D. Freeman.

quickly classified by many as a cult. Years later, in an effort to counter this impression, he gave the following defense of Unity:

We have studied many isms, many cults. People of every religion under the sun claim that we either belong to them or have borrowed the best part of our teaching from them. We have borrowed the best from all religions, that is the reason we are called Unity. . . . Unity is not a sect, not a separation of people into an exclusive group of know-it-alls. Unity is the Truth that is taught in all religions, simplified and systemized so that anyone can understand and apply it. Students of Unity do not find it necessary to sever their church affiliations. . . .[17]

Lack of Church Organization

It was this lack of church organization that most appealed to many people as well as the concept of a religion that "borrowed the best" from other religions and cultures. An example of this is the Unity tenet on reincarnation. When Fillmore was accused of being "a bit of a heathen" in his acceptance of this Hindu belief, he responded, "Through the light of the indwelling Christ the so-called heathen have discerned many truths to which the more material-minded people of the newer countries have been blind. Whenever there has been a nation of thinkers who were not bound in materialism, those thinkers have accepted reincarnation as a fact."[18]

Despite the initial intent of avoiding organization as a church, Unity became more and more churchlike as the decades passed. In 1903, the Unity Society of Practical Christianity was incorporated in Kansas City, and in 1914, the Unity School of Christianity was formed in Lee's Summit, Missouri.[19] By the middle of the century Unity had succumbed to the temptation and begun establishing churches.[20]

Underlying Tenets of the Faith

Although he was uncomfortable formulating a Statement of Faith, Charles Fillmore's followers urged him to do so. But even that statement was qualified to reject dogmatic articles of belief: "We are hereby giving warning that we shall not be bound to this tentative statement of what Unity believes. We may change our mind tomorrow on some of the points, and if we do, we shall feel free to make a new statement."[21]

A God of Contradictions

Fillmore's view of God was at times contradictory. In one sense he was pantheistic or monistic, believing God was everything and that every individual was a part of God. At other times he viewed God as though He were a friend or benefactor, who responded personally to individual needs. The Statement of Faith is framed in orthodox terms, but it purposely describes God in impersonal and vague terms:

> We believe in God, the one and only omnipotent, omniscient, and omnipresent spirit-mind. . . . We believe that creative Mind, God, is masculine and feminine, and that these attributes of Being are fundamental in both natural and spiritual man. . . . We believe that we live, move and have our being in God-Mind; also that God-Mind lives, moves, and has being in us to the extent of our consciousness.[22]

The pantheistic theme is the most prominent of Unity writings. Man is part of God as a drop of water is part of the sea, and every individual "is God come forth . . . in different quantity or degree." Indeed, everything is part of Divine essence. "Each rock, tree, animal, everything visible, is a manifestation of the one spirit—god—differing only in degree of manifestation, or individualities, however insignificant, contains the whole."[23]

Miracles

Individuals, in the Unity framework, are not only part of the Divine essence, but they duplicate God in action. "God never performs miracles, if by this is meant a departure from universal law," wrote Fillmore. "Whatever the prophets did, was done by the operation of laws inherent in Being, and open to the discovery of every man. Whatever Jesus of Nazareth did, it is likewise the privilege of every man to do." Fillmore went on to argue that every human being has the obligation to become "the word of God incarnate," even as Jesus did. "He became the word of God incarnate, because he fulfilled all the requirements of the law. This is the privilege of every man."[24]

The subject of miracles is a common topic in Unity. Unlike modern skeptics who discredit the reality of miracles, Fillmore and his followers went to the opposite extreme of turning them into natural phenomena that could be performed by anyone. In an article entitled "The Atomic Prayer," Fillmore made his position clear:

> Our modern scientists say that a single drop of water contains enough latent energy to blow up a ten-story building. This energy, existence of which has been discovered by modern scientists, is the same kind of spiritual energy that was known to Elijah, Elisha, and Jesus, and used by them to perform miracles.
>
> By the power of his thought Elijah penetrated the atoms of hydrogen and oxygen and precipitated an abundance of rain. By the same law he increased the widow's oil and meal. This was not a miracle—that is, it was not a divine intervention supplanting natural law—but the exploitation of a law not ordinarily understood. Jesus used the same dynamic power of thought to break the bonds of the atoms composing the few loaves and fishes of a little lad's lunch—and five thousand people were fed.[25]

Humanizing God

But in deifying man, Fillmore at the same time humanized God in such a way as to *use* God to do his bidding. This is nowhere more evident than in his attitude toward prayer: "Never be formal with God. He cares no more for forms and ceremonies than do the principles of mathematics for fine figures or elaborate blackboards. You cannot use God too often. He loves to be used, and the more you use Him the more easily you use Him and the more pleasant His help becomes."[26]

Jesus, according to Unity terminology, is an "inner Christ" who resides in every individual. "The difference between Him and us is not one of inherent spiritual capacity but a difference in demonstration of it. Jesus was potentially perfect and He expressed that perfection; we are potentially perfect, but we have not expressed it. . . . Jesus attained a divine awareness and unfoldment without parallel in this period of the world's history."[27]

The resurrection of Jesus, according to Fillmore, was not a unique event that would be above the power of any individual who through years of training learned to control the energy forces around and within. He explained this in his book *Mysteries of John:*

> It is not at all surprising that the very near friends of Jesus were filled with astonishment and fear when they found that He was not in the tomb where they had laid Him. They could not understand that for years He had been training His soul to accomplish

this very thing. He had spent whole nights in prayer, and through the intensity of His devotions had made union with Divine Mind. This union was so full and so complete that His whole being was flooded with spiritual life, power, and substance and the wisdom to use them in divine order. In this manner He projected the divine-body idea, and through it His mortal body was transformed into an immortal body. This was accomplished before the Crucifixion, and Jesus knew that He had so strengthened His soul that it would restore His body, no matter how harshly the body might be used by destructive man.

Jesus had obtained power on the three planes of consciousness: the spiritual, the psychical, and the material. After His resurrection He held His body on the psychical and the astral planes for forty days, and then translated it to the spiritual, where it exists to this day as a body of ethereal substance directed and controlled by His thought and mind force. . . .[28]

Reincarnation

Reincarnation was viewed by Charles Fillmore as a positive answer to the negative notion of death. The Unity Statement of Faith sets forth this conviction: "We believe that dissolution of spirit, soul and body, caused by death, is annulled by rebirth of the same spirit and soul in another body here on earth. We believe the repeated incarnations of man to be a merciful provision of our loving father to the end that all may have opportunity to attain immortality through regeneration, as did Jesus."[29]

Most adherents of Unity would seek to differentiate their view of reincarnation from that of standard Hindu or Buddhist belief. According to Marcus Bach, "Unity never believed . . . in transmigration of souls, by which is meant the retrogression of spirits in a strictly Eastern sense. To Eastern, non-Christian groups, reincarnation is an evolutionary process, a chain of cause and effect. To Unity, it is a 'unifying force' through which God seeks to restore man to his original deathless state." Restoring this "deathless" state is a key tenet of Unity. "Death came into the world through the Adamic man and this resulted in body dissolution. But in the demonstration of the overcoming of death, as shown in the resurrection of Jesus Christ, the restoration of the 'lost Eden' is already begun."[30]

Unity, likewise, rejects the Hindu law of karma, which is an integral part of the doctrine of transmigration. For the Hindu his station in life is a direct result of his good and bad actions in the previous life. Fillmore spoke of the Hindu who was in this type of reincarnation cycle as "a weary treadmill traveler from birth to death and from death to birth." He argued "that the regenerative work of Christ released man from the karmic wheel and prepared him for new life, a series of new lives, in fact, which might be looked upon as vehicles for the attainment of the perfect, deathless body." Thus reincarnation was a merciful provision of God, which allowed individuals to have further opportunities for fulfillment and happiness. Otherwise, how could a death of a child be rectified? "A single span of life," he argued, "does not constitute man's entire opportunity for life."[31]

Heaven

According to Marcus Bach, "there is no room in the Unity eschatological system for a heaven filled with busybody souls living a 'spiritually suburban' kind of life." Fillmore believed that the traditional concept of heaven, which portrayed "all the old family relationships ... as man knows them in his present life," was a creation of the mortal mind. In his view, "The great family of Christ, the whole redeemed Adam race is all *one*, and the little selfish relationships of the Adam man have no place in the new order."[32]

Fillmore rejected the idea that the only way to get to heaven was to die. He argued that the only so-called kingdom of heaven was in the here and now. He also repudiated the concept of hell, arguing that a loving God would never consign anyone to eternal damnation.[33]

The Bible

Although the Bible is regarded as an important source of revelation, Charles Fillmore believed that "Beginning with the very first chapter of Genesis, the Bible is an allegory." From his perspective, nothing in Scripture ought to necessarily be taken literally. That can be seen in his interpretation of some of the most straightforward narratives: "The 'upper room' is the very top of the head. Jesus was in this 'upper room' of his mind when Nicodemus came to see him 'by night'—meaning the ignorance of sense consciousness."[34]

Health and Prosperity

At the core of Unity teaching is that the mind has power over the body—particularly in regard to maintaining health and vigor. Even as Myrtle Fillmore had claimed she had conquered disease, Unity believers are instructed to make the same claims: "Pain, sickness, poverty, old age, death, cannot master me, for they are not real."[35] Death was real for Myrtle, who "passed to the invisible side of life" in 1931, but her attitude toward health may have prolonged her life. She lived beyond the age of eighty-six, and continued teaching classes on Unity principles to the very end—quite remarkable considering her extensive medical problems in her early adult years.[36]

In his book *Atom-Smashing Power of the Mind,* published in 1949, a year after his death, Fillmore wrote, "People the world over were amazed and terrified when they read of the destruction wrought on the cities and people of Japan by two atomic bombs. But do we realize that millions of people are killed every year by atomic force? Doctors tell us that it is the toxin generated in our own bodies that kills us."[37]

How could an individual avoid death and disease from this toxin? Fillmore maintained that the germs that caused sickness were "the manifested results of anger, revenge, jealousy, fear, impurity, and many other mind activities." But if an individual allows "God-love" to control the thoughts, physical health would vastly improve: "When the white heat of God-love comes upon man there is exaltation and transfusion of elements. The result of soul exaltation is a finer soul essence forming the base of a new body substance."[38]

Overcoming Old Age

Charles Fillmore was convinced that he would triumph over old age and death. He later told how as he was approaching fifty, "the belief in old age began to take hold" of him, and that he "began to get wrinkled and gray . . . and great weakness came over" him. Then he realized that his problem was caused by his "associating with old people," so to reverse the process, he "associated with the young, danced with the boys, sang songs with them, and for a time took on the frivolity of the thoughtless kid." By doing this he "switched the old age current of thought" and vowed to "never submit to the old age devil." Within months, as his testimony continues, he was a changed man: "Gradually I felt a new life current coming up from the life center. It was a faint little stream at first, and months went by before I got it to the surface. Now it is growing strong by leaps and bounds. My cheeks have filled out, the wrinkles and crow's feet are gone, and I actually feel like the boy that I am."[39]

Overcoming Death

If old age could be overcome, reasoned Fillmore, so could death. In response to the question, "Do you expect to live forever?" he wrote:

> This question is often asked by *Unity* readers. Some of them seem to think that I am either a fanatic or a joker if I take myself seriously in the hope that I shall with Jesus attain eternal life in the body. But the fact is that I am very serious. . . .
>
> It seems to me that someone should have initiative enough to make at least an attempt to raise his body to the

Jesus Christ consciousness. Because none of the followers of Jesus has attained the victory over this terror of humanity does not prove that it cannot be done. . . .[40]

Unity Tower in Lee's Summit, Missouri.

Health and the Sex Life

In his emphasis on health, Fillmore took a controversial position on sex and its effect on an individual's physical constitution. His conclusion was that only by renouncing sex could an individual avoid death. "Through the sins of the sex-life the body is robbed of its essential fluids and disintegrates," he wrote. "The result is called death, which is the last great enemy to be overcome by man. Immortality in the body is possible to man only when he has overcome the weakness of sensation and conserves his life substance." In this conviction, he was uncharacteristically dogmatic: "So long as your eyes see sex and the indulgence thereof on any of its planes, you are not pure. You must become mentally so translucent that you see men and women as sexless beings—which they are in the spiritual consciousness."[41]

Pennies from Heaven

If Fillmore's prescription for health and endless life was controversial, so was his prescription for prosperity. In a book entitled *Prosperity*, he offers his own rendition of the Twenty-third Psalm that some would feel borders on blasphemy.

> The Lord is my banker; my credit is good
>
> He maketh me to lie down in the consciousness of omnipotent abundance;
>
> He giveth me the key to His strong-box.
>
> He restoreth my faith in His riches,
>
> He guideth me in the paths of prosperity for His name's sake.
>
> Yea, though I walk through the very shadow of debt, I shall fear no evil, For Thou art with me; Thy silver and gold, they secure me.
>
> Thou preparest a way for me in the presence of the collector;
>
> Thou fillest my wallet with plenty; my measure runneth over.
>
> Surely, goodness and plenty will follow me all the days of my life;
>
> And I shall do business in the name of the Lord forever.[42]

Prosperity, like health, could be secured through the power of the mind, and negative thinking was a sure way to guarantee poverty. "Do not say money is scarce," wrote Fillmore; "the very statement will drive money away from you. Do not say that times are hard with you; the very words will tighten your purse strings until Omnipotence itself cannot slim a dime into it. Begin now to talk plenty, think plenty, and give thanks for plenty. . . . It actually works."[43]

Positive Thinking

It is appropriate to view Unity as one of the "positive thinking" philosophies that has emerged in the past century and more in America. Like Christian Science and the broad spectrum of New Thought groups, it seeks to maintain a Christian base. Its perspective, however, goes far beyond a biblical view of positive thinking. "The Unity School of Christianity is the result of positive thinking in its most dangerous extreme," writes Harold Berry. "This movement is so intent on looking for the good that it has become blind to the reality of sin and the resultant need to accept Christ as the One who has paid the penalty for sin. Unity is a system of human merit and salvation by enlightenment."[44]

Unity's acceptance of non-Christian tenets such as reincarnation and its rejection of various biblical tenets have placed the movement outside traditional Christian orthodoxy, but there have been other movements and individuals regarded by some to be within the framework of orthodoxy that have been deeply influenced by the same philosophy of positive thinking. The Modern Faith movement that focuses on health and wealth—as proclaimed by such preachers as Charles Capps, Kenneth Hagin, and Kenneth Copeland—is an example of this, as is the theme of positive thinking which is preached by such mainline celebrity preachers as Norman Vincent Peale and Robert Schuller.

Evangelistic and Missionary Outreach

Unity relies primarily on literature to reach out with its message to people in North America and around the world. The movement offers both adult and children's magazines that present a positive message of hope and optimism. In recent years, an assortment of New Age material has become available through local Unity churches, adding to the popularity of the movement.

Unity places very little emphasis on evangelism and missions through a direct or personal approach. The underlying philosophy of the movement is one of acceptance of others and thus proselytizing is viewed negatively. Indeed, many individuals who attend Unity meetings and regularly read Unity literature are members of mainline churches. Since the movement considers itself more of a "school" than a "church," it sees its primary purpose as one of education. This philosophy is made clear in its literature welcoming people from all walks of life:

> Unity students are invited to study according to their own needs and desires, to participate as they wish in organized activities in Unity ministries. The Unity ministry is conducted on the free-will offering plan. No pledges are required. There is a freedom in Unity that allows the individual to advance spiritually according to his or her own level of understanding. Respect for and faith in the spirit of God in every person makes it unnecessary to set down fixed creeds or impose limiting beliefs. Each individual is encouraged to follow the Unity teachings in determining personal response to political, medical, and economic issues.[45]

More than any other established alternative religion, Unity has embraced the New Age Movement. The religious philosophy of Unity is entirely compatible with New Age concepts, and Unity has become a church home for many New Age people who seek a more established and traditional religious community than is offered by most New Age organizations.

Chapter 8

The Worldwide Church of God: Reinterpreting Israel and the Law

Most of the prominent nontraditional religious movements that sprang up in America during the nineteenth century were quickly identified as being outside the boundaries of orthodoxy. The Mormons proudly exhibited their new scripture and were unable to conceal for long their practice of polygamy. The Jehovah's Witnesses, aside from making their presence known through public protests, had their proclivity for date setting and denial of the Trinity quickly associated with them. And Christian Science, which gained attention through its often eccentric female founder, was readily acknowledged to be unorthodox. In other instances, however, there has been an overt attempt to disguise heretical teachings, and this has been particularly true of religious movements that have arisen in the twentieth century.

For many unwary Christians, the Worldwide Church of God, known mainly through its radio and television programming and its widely circulated magazine *The Plain Truth*, is perceived to be a fundamentalist Christian organization that opposes such avowed evils as liberalism, communism, and evolution. They hear and read messages they can heartily embrace, without realizing that the movement denies cardinal teachings of the Christian faith, such as the doctrine of the Trinity, upholds the tenets of British-Israelism, maintains the Sabbath and other Jewish laws, and regards itself as the only true church. Its belief system and practices bear the imprint of its founder Herbert W. Armstrong, who a century after Joseph Smith went into the woods to inquire of God as to which of all the churches was the right one, was "haunted" by the question "Where *is* the one true Church today?"[1] That question led him, as it did Smith, to found his own movement outside the confines of orthodox Christianity.

Although Armstrong's Worldwide Church of God is very small (fewer than one hundred thousand members) in comparison to other nonorthodox religious movements such as the Mormons and Jehovah's Witnesses, it has a broad influence that extends far beyond its own membership. Radio, television, literature, and a very effective public relations campaign have given Armstrong an image of statesmanship, and his organization an aura of respectability, that few cults have achieved in so few decades.

Although church members revere the memory of their founder, there does appear to be a shift away from some of his doctrinaire views—some of which had begun to change in his later years.

Herbert W. Armstrong

Herbert W. Armstrong was born into a Quaker family in Des Moines, Iowa, in 1892. His childhood days were uneventful and he was "just an average student in school"—except for his claim that he spent his after-school hours at the library studying "Plato, Socrates, Aristotle and Epictetus." By age sixteen, by his own account, he "was *burning* with desire to go somewhere in life—to become a success." The avenue that appeared most promising for success was the field of advertising. "In those days," he later wrote, "I had developed a very excessive case of swelled head. . . . I soon became known as a 'hustler.' On the street I hurried—walked rapidly. I was a dynamo of energy."[2]

Financial Successes and Failures

As he became more confident in his advertising work, Armstrong moved from Iowa to Chicago and began dreaming of the financial fortune he hoped to earn. He was inspired by his new job which, as he later recalled "now brought me into contact with many of the nation's leading bankers." It was during this time that he returned to Iowa to visit relatives and met and fell in love with Loma Dillon, his third cousin. They were married in a Baptist church on Armstrong's twenty-fifth birthday. During the next three years they had two children and lived at ten different addresses. For a time he returned to Iowa with his family to work on his father-in-law's farm.[3]

The success that Armstrong had so zealously strived for somehow eluded him. He enjoyed short-term periods of prosperity, but he was not able to avoid severe financial setbacks. His flourishing job as a publishing sales representative in Chicago showed every indication of financial success, but "the flash depression of 1920," he later wrote, "swept it away." At age thirty, he was "broken in spirit," but determined to turn his fortunes around. He moved to Oregon with his young family and began advertising for laundries. By 1926, he was grossing a thousand dollars a month—a modest sum, but enough to inspire dreams of grandeur that were once again quickly squelched. "I saw visions of a personal net income mounting to from $300,000 to a half million a year with expansion to national proportions. Then an action by the Laundryowners National Association [to utilize the services of a single nationally-known advertising agency] swept the laundry advertising business out from under my feet."[4]

Wife's Religious Awakening

It was during this period of financial reverses in 1926, when the family was "behind on the rent, completely out of groceries except for some macaroni," and with the gas and electricity shut off, that Armstrong began to study the Bible. This new interest was "goaded" by his wife's "religious fanaticism" that came through her association with a Seventh-day Adventist woman who had convinced her it was a sin against God to worship on Sunday rather than Saturday. "I thought I could not tolerate such humiliation," Armstrong later wrote. "Nothing had ever hit me where it hurt so much—right smack in the heart of my pride and conceit and vanity. And *this* mortifying blow had to fall on top of confidence-crushing financial reverses. Why, *what would my friends say? What would former business acquaintances think!*"5

Armstrong's recollection of his response to his wife is a significant moment for the genesis of the Worldwide Church of God:

> "I will give you just one more chance, before we separate and get a divorce," I said. "I don't know just *where* it is, but I know all these Churches can't be wrong! I know it's in the Bible that we are to keep Sunday! I'll give you this one more chance, before you break up our home. I won't tolerate fanaticism! I'll make you this proposition: I have an analytical mind. I've been trained in research into business problems, getting the facts and analyzing them. Now I'll make a complete and thorough research into the Bible. I'll *find* where the Bible commands us to observe Sunday. I'll prove

it to you out of the Bible! Will you give up this fanaticism when I *prove* it?"6

Intensive Bible Study

With his wife in agreement that she would abandon her "fanaticism" if he could prove to her that the Bible taught Sunday worship, he plunged into an intensive self-study. At the same time, his sister-in-law began to plant doubts in his mind regarding the validity of the Bible, based on the theory of evolution. In response to her challenge, he began reading the works of Darwin, Spencer, Huxley, and other proponents of evolutionary theory—becoming convinced that a belief in God was contrary to a strict view of evolution. "And so it came about," he later wrote, "that, very early in this study of evolution and of the Bible, actual *doubts* came into my mind as to the existence of God!"7

The more he studied the theory of evolution, however, the more Armstrong was convinced it was an untenable ideology. He became convinced that the method of dating the fossils was based on supposition rather than actual scientific data. After writing a "short paper" confirming his "discovery," he presented it to a librarian who agreed he had "chopped down the trunk of the tree" of the evolutionary theory. With that concession, he confidently disclaimed the scientific books he had been reading and affirmed the truth of Scripture: "I had *disproved* the theory of evolution. I had found proof of creation—proof of the existence of God—proof of the divine inspiration of the Bible."8

Propelled by his rebounding self-confidence, Armstrong tackled the issue of the Sabbath, and became convinced that the six-day creation with a seventh day of rest was the key to understanding worship for the church. He was initially reluctant to admit his change of heart, but later insisted it was the turning point in his life.

I saw plainly what a decision was before me. To accept this truth meant to throw in my lot for life with a class of people I had always looked on as inferior. . . . It meant being cut off completely and forever from all to which I had aspired. It meant a total crushing of vanity. It meant a total *change of life!*. . .

Finally, in desperation, I threw myself on God's mercy. I said to God that I knew, now, that I was nothing but a failure, a burned-out hunk of junk. My life was worth nothing more to me. I said to God that I knew now I had nothing to offer Him—but if He would forgive me—if He could have any use whatsoever for such a worthless dreg of humanity who had fallen all the way down in failure and disillusionment, that He could have my life; I knew it was worthless, but if He could do anything with it, He could have it—I was willing to give this worthless self to Him—I wanted to accept Jesus Christ as personal Saviour![9]

"Call of God"

Several years after this period of intense Bible study, Armstrong received what he later termed "the unrecognized call" of God. It came through his wife's dream—"a dream so vivid and impressive it overwhelmed and shook her tremendously." Indeed, "it was so realistic it seemed more like a vision. . . . It was a dazzling spectacle—the sky was filled with a gigantic solid mass of brilliant stars." As one set of stars and then another began "quivering, separating, and vanishing . . . three white birds suddenly appeared. . . . As they descended nearer, she perceived that they were angels." Then, "Christ descended from among them and stood directly in front of us. . . . He put His arms around both of us, and we were so happy!" After that brief appearance, Christ turned into an angel, and told her that "Christ was really coming in a very short time." She then asked the angel about moviegoing. "He replied Christ had important work for us to do, preparing for His coming—there would be no time for movies. . . . Then the angel and the whole spectacle seemed to vanish, and she awakened, shaken and wondering!"[10]

When his wife Loma shared her dream with her husband the following morning, he "was embarrassed" but "afraid to totally dismiss it." It was not until some years later that he had "come to believe that this dream was a bona fide call from God." He was not, however, willing to concede that others might also receive such personal calls from God. "In about 99,999 times out of 100,000 when people think God is speaking to them in a dream or vision in this day and age, it is pure imagination, or some form of self-hypnotism or self-deception."[11]

Baptism and Beginning of Itinerant Ministry

In 1927, the year after his religious conversion, Armstrong was baptized by a Baptist preacher, rather than by a minister associated with the Sev-

Herbert W. Armstrong. Courtesy of the Worldwide Church of God.

enth-day Adventists, whose views would have more closely paralleled his own. The Baptist preacher, he later recalled, "had the best and clearest explanation, and was warm and friendly. . . . I asked him to baptize me, not into his church, but into Christ. . . . On being baptized I *knew* God then and there gave me His Holy Spirit."[12]

Following his baptism, he began searching for the "true" church—convinced that only congregations worshiping on the seventh day qualified. After eliminating the Seventh-day Adventists and Seventh-Day Baptists, he became associated with the Church of God (Seventh-Day), with publishing headquarters at Stanberry, Missouri. In 1928, he began preaching, and in 1931 he was ordained. Within two years, Armstrong broke from that tiny denomination and began an independent ministry, which he expanded into "The Radio Church of God" in 1934. Besides radio programming, he was also disseminating his message through *The Plain Truth*, a mimeographed bulletin he initiated some years earlier. The movement grew slowly until 1946, when Armstrong launched "an organized national and worldwide work." He significantly increased his radio broadcasting and circulation of *The Plain Truth*, and "undertook his first baptizing tour," in an effort to bring new converts into the movement who initially were introduced through radio and literature.[13]

Individualist Standing Alone

Armstrong's rejection of all other churches and his creation of an independent church was consistent with his character. He was an extreme individualist who was often perceived by others to be stubborn and arrogant. Soon after he became affiliated with the Church of God at Stanberry, Missouri, he put the church to the test by writing a sixteen-page treatise "proving clearly, plainly, and beyond contradiction that a certain minor point of doctrine proclaimed by this church, based on an erroneous interpretation of a certain verse of Scripture, was in error." He sent the document to the president of the General Conference, who, according to Armstrong "was forced to admit, in plain words, that their teaching on this point was false and in error," but nevertheless refused to change the church's position to agree with Armstrong's. He put the church to a second test when he submitted a three-hundred-page manuscript which "proved that the so-called 'lost Ten Tribes' of Israel had migrated to northwestern Europe, the British Isles, and later the United States." These and other matters led to a rift between Armstrong and church officials, which culminated in his disassociation with the movement.[14]

More than doctrinal issues were at stake in Armstrong's assurance that he alone was carrying out the will of God, and that others—even those in his own denomination—only thwarted his efforts. "Never once, when I was working *with* any of these other ministers, were any results apparent," he wrote. "Yet *never* did God fail to grant good results, with people converted and baptized, when I was working alone."[15]

God's Messenger for This Age

From the beginning Armstrong perceived his movement as uniquely "true" among all the churches, and he regarded himself as specially cho-sen to proclaim God's message. Indeed, he cited himself along with only two others in all of church history who were thus chosen: "Jesus chose Paul, who was highly educated, for spreading the gospel to the Gentiles. He later raised up Peter Waldo, a successful businessman, to keep His truth alive during the Middle Ages. In these last days . . . Jesus chose a man amply trained in the advertising and business fields to shoulder the mission—HERBERT W. ARMSTRONG.[16]

Armstrong's sense of his own personal significance to God's divine plan for the ages is also illustrated in his later reflection on the "series of almost incredible facts" relating to the time and circumstances of his own ministry as compared to that of Jesus:

> First, Jesus Christ began His earthly ministry at about age 30. God took away my business, moved me from Chicago, started bringing me to repentance and conversion preparatory to inducting me into His ministry, *when I was 30!*
>
> Second, Jesus began the actual *teaching and training* of His original disciples for carrying His Gospel to the world in the year 27 A.D. *Precisely 100 time-cycles later*, in 1927 A.D., He began my intensive study and training for carrying His same Gospel to all nations of today's world. . . .
>
> The actual ordination, or completing of the ordination and inducement of power for sending out the original disciples into the ministry occurred after 3½ years of intensive instruction and experience. It was on the Day of Pentecost. And the year was 31 A.D. *Exactly 100 time-cycles later*, after 3 1/2 years of intensive study and training, Christ ordained me to preach. . . . *This*

ordination took place at, or very near, the Day of Pentecost, 1931.[17]

In reflecting on his place in history and claiming to be in a very select company composed only of the apostle Paul and Peter Waldo (a thirteenth-century religious nonconformist who emphasized Bible study and who opposed corruption in the Roman Catholic Church), Armstrong seemed to be equally disavowing any association with either Roman Catholics or Protestants. Indeed, his contempt for both traditions is woven into the very fabric of his thought. "Most Protestants assume . . . that the Protestant reformers purged out all the false doctrines and evil practices, and restored the pure faith once delivered," he wrote. "But my shocking, disappointing, eye-opening discovery . . . revealed in stark plainness that both Catholic and Protestant teachings were in most basic points, the *very opposite* of the teachings of Christ, of Paul, and of the original true Church!"[18]

Family and Organizational Developments

Armstrong's perception that he was singled out by God as the mouthpiece for the modern age is a common trait among prophet-founders of alternative religions, and it was a key factor in his powerful leadership of the movement.

Authoritarian Control

From the very beginning, Armstrong's religious organization was entirely dominated by himself. However, that dominance was not as evident in the early years as it was when the movement began to rapidly expand. His personal control was seen in every facet of the movement, but it was at his Ambassador College where this was most pronounced. His initial dependence on others to fill administrative and faculty positions threatened his control and his perception of himself as the apostle for this age. Matters were brought to a head when he realized that his own course in theology had been relegated to the category "two-hour minor subject." He vowed to recoup his authority:

I immediately decreed that faculty members, as well as students, must attend all my classes. I taught entirely by the lecture method. I did this, not so much as a retaliatory measure, but as a means of getting the new college off to a start as the very *kind* of college God was building. . . . I took great pains to make my lectures so rational and factual as to leave no room for refutation.[19]

Garner Ted Armstrong

As Armstrong's organization grew, increasing numbers of individuals were required to maintain the various educational and media developments. The most prominent of these individuals to emerge as a leader and anticipated successor to Armstrong was his son, Garner Ted, a handsome and articulate radio preacher whose charismatic charm attracted a wide following. He was the youngest of the Armstrong children, and had dreamed as a youth of being a night club performer. He rebelled against his religious upbringing and joined the Navy after high school, but in

1923, following his stint in the military, he enrolled at Ambassador College and became convinced that "'Dad's religion' was not . . . some sect or cult, but the religion of Jesus Christ."[20]

Father/Son Conflict

At age twenty-seven, only four years after he enrolled at Ambassador, Garner Ted was being heard regularly on radio broadcasts, and by the time he was in his early thirties he served as the executive vice-president of the church, the executive editor of both *The Plain Truth* and *Tomorrow's World,* and the president of Ambassador College. He was in a position to step in and take over the leadership at such time his father could no longer continue, but that plan was eventually frustrated by Garner Ted's own undoing. "From 1966 through 1970," writes Stanley Rader, "rumors concerning misconduct on the part of Garner Ted, coupled with his failure to tend to his duties as a minister and a broadcaster, grew in number and volume." His father, in an effort "to shield his son, was giving him the benefit of every doubt. Three times he banished his son for transgressions, only to forgive him when Ted pleaded to be allowed to return."[21]

In 1971, Armstrong took even stronger action against his son and "privately put him out of the Church," ordering him "to leave Pasadena," but he was allowed to return not long afterwards when he professed "complete repentance." According to Rader, however, "the misconduct did not cease." Finally, "in February 1972, Mr. Armstrong was forced to disfellowship Ted a third time, but this time with the knowledge of all evangelist-rank ministers at Pasadena." Within months, however, Garner Ted had once again "truly repented," and "he was permitted to resume his Church activities."[22]

What were the specific sins that caused such upheaval in the Worldwide Church of God? According to one report, he had had a struggle with adultery that lasted "over a nineteen year period," a sin he accepted, claiming to have been "prophesied in Malachi 2:14 to be an adulterer." He was also accused of being involved in excessive gambling, spending time in Las Vegas casinos and sometimes "rolling dice for five hundred dollars a throw."[23]

As much as his conduct distressed his father, his appealing manner and speaking ability made him an asset to the movement that his father feared would be devastating if lost. In 1973, Armstrong named him as his successor, a move that was very controversial among some church leaders, though Armstrong himself compared it with King David's appointment of Solomon to the throne before he died. "Though no other minister in the history of the organization had been reinstated after dismissal for sexual violation," writes William Martin, "Ted was back on the air in a matter of months. . . . Armstrong rationalized that 'Ted is divinely called' and 'above the scripture.' "[24]

The fourth disfellowshiping and final break between father and son came in 1978, after Garner Ted had "attempted to seize control" of the organization while his father was ill. This final rift between them appeared to be focused more on power and authority rather than moral issues. "My son assumed authority beyond that delegated to him," the elder Armstrong charged. Under him, God's Church, the World and the College had been turned around until it was actually scarcely God's Church any more. Everything was run as a strictly secular and worldly organization. To his son, he wrote, "You are defying and fighting against Jesus Christ, whose chosen servant I am."[25]

The Church of God International

The final removal of Garner Ted Armstrong from the organization not only created public scandal and embarrassment for the elder Armstrong and the movement as a whole, but it also left a gaping hole in the ministry. Gone was the visibility that 4,500 radio programs, 720 television broadcasts, hundreds of magazine articles, and thousands of sermons and Bible studies had given him. Yet, according to a reporter in 1981, three years after his banishment, Garner Ted was "as handsome and dashing as ever, his silver hair and silver tongue intact." Though ousted from his father's organization, he was determined to continue his work independently under a newly formed religious organization called the Church of God International, with headquarters in East Texas. In response to questions about his new independent religious venture, he insisted he had not deviated from the faith:

Here I'm preaching the same thing. It's the same person, the same personality, the same voice, the same Bible, the same marks in my Bible, the same old notes sometimes.

It is the same message that brought about 85 percent of the Worldwide Church of God membership into that church in the first place. Yet, those members have been told they will be excommunicated if they listen to me or even talk to someone who has. That's ironic beyond belief.[26]

Dissension in the Ranks

Even before Garner Ted left the organization, there were resignations and disfellowshipings of ministers and regional leaders due to disagreements over policy. No longer was the elder Armstrong able to contain controversies as he had in the past. The movement had grown too large to maintain the personalized style of authority he rendered in the early years. There were other changes as well. As the Worldwide Church of God grew in size and influence, the style of Armstrong's ministry was significantly modified. Gone were the days when he would travel by car crisscrossing the country on preaching tours, baptizing converts. His travel soon began to reflect his interest in international affairs, and his mode of transportation became a private jet as he visited capitol cities throughout the world, always seeking interviews with government officials and heads of state.

It was this style of ministry that came under fire in 1979, when a California judge placed the church under temporary receivership. Both Armstrong and his close associate Stanley R. Rader were charged with "pilfering" assets and diverting millions of dollars of church funds "to their own use and benefit." The lawsuit, brought by dissident church members, also charged that Armstrong and Rader had sold some fifty parcels of land without proper authority and had "shredded and destroyed" church records.[27] "The case was dropped in 1980 after a new state law, prompted by the Armstrong case, prohibited the attorney general from investigating the finances of religious groups for fraud and mismanagement."[28]

Personal Scandals

There were other scandals which plagued the Armstrong organization as well—not the least of which was his 1977 remarriage (after Loma's death) to a divorcee some forty-five years younger than he. Although it was claimed that her first marriage had been annulled, the situation was particularly controversial in light of Armstrong's adamant position on divorce and insistence that "new members ... dissolve second marriages and remarry their original spouses." Further scandal erupted in 1982, when it was reported that Armstrong was divorcing his second wife and that she was contesting his action. The divorce was finalized in 1984, and less than two years later in 1986, Armstrong died at the age of ninety-three.[29]

Church Organization, Membership, and Practices

Like many other nontraditional religious movements founded by an individual with a strong and domineering personality, the Worldwide Church of God has operated from the top down. Armstrong insisted that the human institution that most closely parallels the "Government of God" is the military, which operates on a chain of command.

Church members are told that disrespect for a minister is disrespect for God, that doubting is of the devil ("If you doubt, you're damned"), and that any questioning of "the Work" will be punished by God as blasphemy. Dissenters and other rule-breakers are "disfellowshiped and marked," an excommunication process that involves explicit naming of the sin and total shunning of the sinner. The result, in one ex-member's words, is "a spiritual concentration camp" in which total submission is demanded and given.[30]

What is the rationale for such strict control and discipline? Armstrong was convinced he represented God's government on earth, and that God's government was one of absolute theocratic rule.

The Hidden Church

Since Armstrong had a business background in advertising, one might think he would have sought to use all his acquired skills to advertise his church. It thus seems curious that his churches are so difficult to find. Indeed, it virtually requires the expertise of a private detective even to locate the meeting place of one of his congregations. In many respects, however, this very feature of his religious work closely resembled his advertising methodology of earlier years. People are brought under Armstrong's influence before they realize that the church is unorthodox in its doctrinal stance. This is precisely how he initially became so successful in his door-to-door advertising work.

An example is when he solicited a landlady for advertising the rental of a room. He did not represent himself as an ad man, but rather as a person looking for a room to rent. Once he was inside, the advantage was his.

But she could not slam the front door in my face now—nor did she appear big enough to attempt throwing me out bodily.

"Now look," I said calmly. "This is a lovely room. Do you know why your want ads have not rented it for you? . . . *You are not a professional advertising writer!"*

By this time I had the want ad written—at least two or three times longer (and costlier) than the average. . . .

I read the ad, which certainly made the room sound very desirable. In fact, its glowing terms probably flattered her. She just *couldn't* resist seeing that flowery description of her room in print in the paper.

"Why, I'd certainly want to rent *that* room, instead of those ordinarily described in the want ads," she replied. "That *does* make it sound good." She bought the ad—as large as three ordinary ads.

And the ad did rent her room![31]

In virtually the same manner, Armstrong enticed individuals into his church. Unlike other churches that have listings in the telephone directory and signs posted outside the meeting place, the congregations of the Worldwide Church of God are closed to the public. Advertising, however, is a key element of church growth—advertising that consists of literature and media programming focusing on issues not central to the doctrinal position of the church. Thus, individuals are enticed into the

movement through Armstrong's concern for social problems and his stand against blights on traditional values such as crime, pollution, feminism, abortion, and evolution, without even being aware of his denial of cardinal doctrines of historic Christianity.

If an individual indicates interest in the movement after reading literature or seeing a television program, an application is sent by mail. After the application has been returned, a representative makes a visit. It is only after a satisfactory interview that the individual is permitted to attend one Saturday church service. Whether or not return visits are allowed depends on the individual's willingness to conform to the beliefs and practices of the movement. In the final analysis, "the key requirement for joining the Worldwide Church of God is willingness to submit to Herbert W. Armstrong as the last-days apostle of God."[32]

Tithes and Offerings

One of the most attractive aspects of the Armstrong ministry to an unwary outsider is the absence of appeals for money. Unlike most radio and television preachers who plead for funds to keep them on the air, Armstrong resisted the temptation even when times were hard. According to Joseph Hopkins, "Since its inception the Armstrong operation has relied entirely on voluntary, completely unsolicited offerings for its support."[33]

But voluntary offerings only apply to nonchurch members. For those who become members, or "coworkers" in the cause, financial tithes and offerings are compulsory. The "First Tithe," which constitutes one tenth of an individual's net earnings, is given directly to the church headquarters and is used to finance the church administration, publishing, and educational concerns. The "Second Tithe" is for maintaining personal and family spiritual growth— especially for costs incurred in attending the annual Feast of Tabernacles, a conference church families are expected to attend. Anything left over is to be given for the general expenses of the Feast. A "Third Tithe" is collected twice every seven years and is specified for charity, though it is alleged that much of this goes for such things as travel expenses for church executives. In addition to the tithes, there are Holy Day offerings collected at each of the seven holy days, building fund offerings, freewill offerings, and collections taken for the Emergency Fund.[34]

Personal Lifestyle

The tight regulations imposed on members of the Worldwide Church of God have not been limited to matters relating to leadership loyalty and financial support. Strict controls have likewise been imposed on members' personal lives. "From the beginning," writes William Martin, "Armstrong laid a heavy yoke on his followers. If they became ill, they could pray, but could not take medicine or seek relief from a doctor. If they had been divorced prior to joining the church, they could never remarry; if they had already remarried, they were forced to separate and urged to move at least one state away from each other to minimize

the temptation to reunite." Even in church-sanctioned marriages, however, there were restrictions. While married couples were permitted "the ecstasy of occasional coitus," they were restricted to "the most natural and commonly used positions."[35]

Some of these strict rules have in recent years been relaxed, due in part to discontent within the ranks. When ordinary church members became aware that their leaders were in many instances not abiding by the regulations themselves, there was widespread indignation. Both ministers and members began leaving the church. "In the face of this revolt, Herbert Armstrong began to lighten the burden his people bore," writes Martin. "Prior marital mistakes were forgiven at baptism, tithing obligations were relaxed somewhat, and the use of physicians and scientific medicine was approved." These concessions were made prior to the banishment of Garner Ted Armstrong, whose "harshest critics concede he pushed his father to make these more humane decisions."[36]

Political Involvement

Like the Jehovah's Witnesses, the Worldwide Church of God eschews political involvement. It was reasoned that since this world is controlled by Satan, true Christians should have no active involvement in it. They should obey the law only to avoid court cases. "The Christian is in no way to attempt to improve Satan's world. He cannot vote. He cannot serve in the armed forces. He must not belong to the P.T.A. and promote a pagan system of education."[37]

Ambassador International Cultural Foundation

In many respects, the Worldwide Church of God resembles the Jehovah's Witnesses. Not only are many of the doctrines similar, such as the denial of the Trinity and the emphasis on date-setting eschatology, but the religious practices also bear a resemblance—refusing to celebrate Christian holidays and the disfellowshiping of dissenters being prime examples. What makes this movement unique, however, is the shift in emphasis that took place in the 1970s allowing Armstrong the opportunity to feign a role as counselor to world leaders, a role befitting God's chosen servant for this age. Like the Jehovah's Witnesses, he saw his organization as the one through which God would work in establishing His kingdom on earth, but unlike the Jehovah's Witnesses, he chose to maintain a high profile and actively consort with the present government leaders controlled by Satan.

Stanley Rader

Thus what began as an obscure fundamentalist cult was transformed into a cultural/political organization seeking status and respectability. The individual most responsible for engineering this transformation was Stanley Rader, a prestigious Jewish lawyer who began working for Armstrong in 1958. Their relationship gradually developed into a personal friendship, and "after Rader's baptism in 1975, in a bathtub in Hong Kong's Mandarin Hotel, Herbert Armstrong began to speak of him as 'my beloved son, in whom I am well pleased.' "[38]

Celebrity Concerts and World Travel

It was Rader who convinced Armstrong that "the best way to gain respectability and facilitate his mission to world leaders would be to establish a foundation that could sponsor a wide range of educational, cultural, and humanitarian projects." This seemed an unlikely venture for an uneducated, prophet-of-doom preacher, but Armstrong, "who admitted he had often been embarrassed at having to identify himself as a representative of a little-known church or college, embraced the plan with enthusiasm." It was not long before the Ambassador International Cultural Foundation (AICF) became the most visible focus of the church. Celebrity concerts were hosted at Ambassador Auditorium, including some of the nation's top performers such as Arthur Rubinstein, Marilyn Horne, Luciano Pavarotti, and Vladimir Horowitz. Armstrong quickly became known as more than a radio preacher, and his focus and lifestyle began to change.[39]

Such musical extravaganzas, in addition to world travel and first class accommodations for Armstrong and his entourage, drained heavily on church funds. By 1978, the AICF was millions of dollars in debt to the church, and the church, according to Martin, "developed fiscal hyperextension." Even the sale of valuable church property did not resolve the deficit problems. It was primarily the use of church money for foundation matters and Armstrong's dependence on Stanley Rader that prompted dissident church members to take action in the courts, resulting in the

Herbert W. Armstrong with children in Jerusalem. Courtesy of the Worldwide Church of God.

State of California placing the church into receivership in 1979.[40]

In the end, had Armstrong accomplished his purposes by placing so much confidence in Stanley Rader and so much emphasis on gaining respectability on the world scene? This shift in focus, though defended by Armstrong as part of his role as a church leader preparing the way for God to bring in His kingdom, perhaps more than anything else brought division and disarray to the once tightly unified cult. Millions of dollars were spent on "expensive meals and lavish gifts for foreign dignitaries," and in return Armstrong was able to embellish *The Plain Truth* with photos of himself and such world leaders as Golda Meir, King Hussein, Anwar

Sadat, and Menachem Begin. According to his son, "those trips are just glorified autograph-hunting tours—window dressing." He even maintained that his father "boasted about how he does not mention the name of Jesus Christ on these visits."[41]

Dishonest Publicity

In some instances, highly touted meetings never took place. In 1978, Armstrong sent out a letter to supporters informing them that he was scheduled to "co-host an important premier of a charity motion picture to raise funds for the handicapped children in Britain." Indeed, so important was this charity benefit that "Queen Elizabeth II has promised to co-host . . . and in the event she is unable to be present, either Prince Charles or Prince Philip will be there." What Armstrong's supporters were not told was the Buckingham Palace version of this alleged upcoming event: "There is no truth whatever in Mr. Armstrong's claims to be associated with the Queen, Prince Philip, or indeed any other member of the Royal family in sponsoring a project in this country."[42]

In the eyes of many of his followers, who never learned that the benefit with British Royalty never took place, Armstrong was truly a larger-than-life figure who was carrying out the will of God. But, despite all his efforts, Armstrong was never truly able to *buy* the respectability that he was unable to *earn* in the eyes of world leaders. In the end, he was not able to earn this even in the eyes of many of his once loyal followers. His methodology has paralleled that of the Unification Church, which has sought to gain respectability by inviting church and professional leaders to lavish retreats and conferences.

Doctrinal Distinctives

Like the Mormons and the Jehovah's Witnesses, Armstrong maintains that his theology is the theology of the early church that was lost for many centuries. The "counterfeit Christianity spawned by Simon the Sorcerer" was further enhanced by Emperor Constantine. Despite the faithful efforts of "Dr. Arius and God's people" to keep the church free from heresy, the forces of evil won. But the problem had actually begun long before Arius in the fourth century,

according to Armstrong: "The gospel of Jesus Christ was not proclaimed *to the world* from about A.D. 50 until the year 1953." How can such an extended period of spiritual darkness be explained? Armstrong refers to 2 Corinthians 4:4: "The god of this world hath blinded the minds of them which believe not."[43]

Seventh-day Worship

One of the doctrines Armstrong most vehemently insisted was lost since the time of the early church was the seventh-day Sabbath. This was the first issue that set him at variance with orthodoxy. His emphasis on Sabbath keeping prompted the allegation that he was initially associated with Seventh-day Adventists, but he strongly denied the accusation, insisting that he had never even attended a Sabbath-day service of that denomination. His study of Seventh-day Adventist teachings convinced him that the church was wrong. He maintained that a church must live solely in accordance with the Bible, "the testimony of Jesus," which "ruled out the denomination that had 'the testimony of Mrs. White.' "[44]

For Armstrong, the issue of Sabbath keeping became the ultimate test of faith. Indeed, he far surpassed the Seventh-day Adventists in his insistence that true faith could not be demonstrated unless the Sabbath was maintained. This is illustrated in an incident involving prayer for physical healing. His wife's healing as a result of prayer prompted him to study the matter, and as a part of his inquiry he attended an evangelistic campaign featuring Aimee Semple

McPherson, who was at that time the nation's most celebrated healing evangelist. At this meeting he encountered "a terribly crippled elderly man" who had come for healing only to be turned away due to the crowds. Armstrong offered to come to his home and pray for his healing. During that visit, Armstrong explained that healing was dependent on two factors: keeping God's commandments and believing. In regard to the former, he explained to them "particularly about God's Sabbath" and enquired "whether this cripple and his wife had a spirit of willingness to obey God." When he discovered they did not he was convinced the man could not be healed: "I told them that, since they were unwilling to obey God and comply with God's written conditions for healing, I could not pray for him."[45]

Armstrong's theology of healing was in some ways similar to that of orthodox theologians who have maintained that physical healing was provided by Christ in the atonement—"With His stripes, we are healed." Armstrong argued in a similar vein, but then went on to carry his argument a step further:

> Healing is actually the *forgiveness* of the transgressed *physical* laws just as salvation comes through forgiveness of transgressed *spiritual* laws. It is the forgiveness of physical sin. God forgives the physical sin because Jesus paid the penalty we are suffering in our stead. He was beaten with stripes *before* He was nailed to the cross.[46]

It is important to understand that Armstrong did not limit the effects of Sabbath-breaking to lack of physical healing. Indeed, a crucial test of the "true" church was based on the seventh-day worship commandment.

Armstrong's dogmatic stance on Sabbath-keeping was closely linked with his doctrine of salvation and sin. Indeed, "Satan's first effort was to persuade Adam and Eve to switch from the seventh-day sabbath to the first day of the week." So serious is the sin of Sunday worship that those who continue to practice it during the Tribulation will receive the mark of the beast and be condemned to the lake of fire.[47]

Tied very closely to his insistence on keeping the Sabbath was Armstrong's dogmatic assertion that Jesus rose from the dead on Saturday rather than on Sunday. As with his other "discoveries," this came very early in his personal Bible study. He argued that Jesus was not crucified on Friday, as had been generally assumed, but on Wednesday, and that he was for three full days and nights in the tomb. This was certainly not an original proposition made by Armstrong, but he, more than others, sought to correlate the claim with his views on seventh-day worship.

In practical terms, keeping the Saturday Sabbath means renouncing pleasure and devoting extra time to Bible study, prayer, and meditation. Things to be avoided are leisure-time activities, with the list being very specific: "hunting, fishing, golfing, swimming, cards, movies, boating," and "hobbies such as the 'ham' radio operator, wood-working shop, stamp collecting, etc. . . . Whatever *your* pleasure or leisure-time activity is, you should not engage in it on the Sabbath."[48]

British-Israelism

Another teaching Armstrong adopted that was not original with him was a form of British-Israelism. Although he did not originate the theory, it is this feature of his doctrine that is most distinctive and brings to his message a unique flavor that finds appeal among a certain segment of people—especially those who have a personal interest in seeing God's purposes fulfilled in the white Anglo-Saxon peoples.

The issue of British-Israelism is crucial to Armstrong's message, as it has been since the very beginning of his ministry when he was still part of the Church of God in Stanberry, Missouri. Indeed, he regarded the teaching so significant that he made it part of a test "to help settle the question of whether this [denomination] was, in actual fact, the true Church of God." He claims in his autobiography to have "proved" this theory only "after exhaustive study and research." Through his study he concluded not only that the "lost Ten Tribes" had migrated into Europe and Britain, and later North America, but that "the British were the descendants of Ephraim, younger son of Joseph, and the United States modern-day Manasseh, elder son of Joseph—and that we possessed the national wealth and resources of the Birthright which God had promised to Abraham through Isaac, Jacob and Joseph."[49]

Long before Armstrong made his "discovery," others made many of the same claims about the "lost ten tribes." Although he maintained that God has specially revealed this truth to him, there were many people—

estimates of some two million—who believed some version of British-Israelism decades before he even came on the scene, during the "heyday of British-Israelism" in nineteenth-century England. Centuries earlier in 1649, however, John Sadler had written a book suggesting that Englishmen could find their ancestry in ancient Israel. Armstrong's source for his study and teaching was probably a much later author, J. H. Allen, who wrote *Judah's Sceptre and Joseph's Birthright*, published in 1902 and later revised. According to Joseph Hopkins, "There is a close correspondence between Armstrong and Allen. Some material has been rearranged, abbreviated, or expanded; but the basic outline is followed to such a degree as to make it unlikely in the extreme that the latter source was written independently of the former."[50]

Today, the concept of British-Israelism is viewed as an archaic curiosity by scholars. No serious biblical scholar or anthropologist would give credence to it. Its promoters are largely within the ranks of the Worldwide Church of God, who have depended on the naive and faulty "research" of Armstrong. Joseph Hopkins, in his book *The Armstrong Empire*, assesses Armstrong's writing on this subject.

The United States and British Commonwealth in Prophecy, Armstrong's exposition of his "master key," indulges in unwarranted assumptions, exaggerations, misstatements, dubious interpretations of Scripture, and imaginative speculations. Its racist tone is never far beneath the surface, as in Armstrong's remark early in the book that "our white, English-speaking peoples—*not* the Jews—have inherited the national and physical phases of [God's covenant] promises[51]

The race issue is an important aspect of Armstrong's focus on the white Anglo-Saxons of the United States and Britain—not only in this present age but in the world to come, where there will be an absolute termination of "man's efforts toward integration and amalgamation of races," efforts which Armstrong felt to be contrary to God's laws. In that "World Tomorrow," the resurrected Noah "will be given the power to enforce God's way in regard to race." He "will head a vast project of the relocation of the races and nations, within the boundaries God has set. . . . Peoples and nations will move where God has planned for them, and no defiance will be tolerated."[52]

Very closely tied to Armstrong's notions of British-Israelism are both his reflection on God's working through history and his plan for the end times. In this realm, his views are very similar to those of other non-traditional religious movements that grew out of nineteenth-century millennial speculations.

The Historical Timetable and Eschatology

Like many other millenarians before him, Armstrong advanced the notion of a very brief and neatly packaged span of history. The history of the world, by his calculation, will extend six thousand years (to correspond with the six days of creation), followed by a one-thousand-year period, the Millennium (to correspond with the seventh day of rest).

His view that God created the world in 4025 B.C. led him to conclude that the end of this age would occur around 1975. So convinced was he of the timing that in 1966 he predicted that this "Wonderful World Tomorrow" would come about "in just ten or fifteen short years."[53]

In his reflection on church history and in his anticipation of the Lord's return, Armstrong's views closely paralleled those of other cult leaders. Like Joseph Smith, he believed that he was commissioned by God to bring light to a world which had been in spiritual darkness since the time of the apostles. "For nearly 19 centuries," he wrote, "the world has been rendered spiritually drunk on the wine of *this counterfeit gospel*!" His own appearance on the scene, however, reversed the trend and set the stage for the Lord's return.[54]

Armstrong even more forcefully presents his own version of church history in *The Incredible Human Potential*, which begins with the following paragraph:

> Prepare yourself for the most shocking revelation of your life. Does it come as an astonishing shock to learn that the most important dimension in all knowledge was sent from God to this earth by Jesus Christ—but that message was suppressed in the very first century? That Jesus Himself was put to death for revealing it? That His apostles with one possible exception, were also martyred for proclaiming it?[55]

He goes on to reveal the specific details of this suppression. Simon the Sorcerer (referred to in Acts 8) "appropriated the name of Christ, calling his Babylonian mystery religion 'Christianity.' Satan moved this man and used him as his instrument to persecute and all but destroy the true Church of God," and within a matter of a few short decades, "he managed to suppress the message Christ had brought from God." This was "a well-organized conspiracy to blot out all record of Church history during that period," and the religion that became known as Christianity was simply a Babylonian mystery religion.[56]

In the tradition of Seventh-day Adventists and Jehovah's Witnesses, Armstrong looked to the Old Testament for specific prophecies and events that would shed light on future generations—particularly nineteenth- and twentieth-century Britons and Americans. His book *The United States and Britain in Prophecy* offers a prophetic scheme that in many ways parallels earlier prophetic schemes, but also has a uniqueness all its own. Beginning with the "pivotal prophecy" of Leviticus 26, which states, "then I will punish you seven times more for your sins," Armstrong plots out the timetable of God's intended punishment. He dates that prophecy at 717 B.C., and then works forward with his "seven times," which are actually seven years of 360 days which he converts back into years for a total of 2,520 years—the length of time that God withheld His birthright from His people. His mathematical calculations bring him to the beginning of the nineteenth century:

> So—beginning A.D. 1800–1803, after 2520 years—God did cause the birthright nations—and them *only*—to become *suddenly* the recipients of such national wealth, greatness and power as no nation or empire ever before had acquired! Together they—the British

and Americans, descendants of only *one* original tribe, Joseph—came into possession of more than two-thirds—almost three-fourths—of all the cultivated resources and wealth of the whole world![57]

One might expect that after going through such a series of eschatological gymnastics, the date arrived at would be truly significant. Or, if not really that significant, the date could at least be turned into something important—such as a heavenly sanctuary milestone or an invisible return of Christ to earth. But in the case of Armstrong's prophetic calculations, the period of time had already come and gone, and the events seem to the casual observer to be less than extraordinary. What happened during the first years of the nineteenth century to signify the restoration of the birthright to God's people? "*How significant*, then," writes Armstrong, "that Robert Fulton operated the first steamboat in 1803—precisely when Britain and America suddenly began to multiply in national wealth!"[58]

For Armstrong, the approximate year 1800 was significant for more than a steamboat, however. This period was also the dawn of the age of railroads, and "more than half of all tillable, cultivatable, temperate-zone lands of this earth came after A.D. 1800 into the possession of our two great powers alone!" Right on target for this prophetic timetable for geographical expansion, according to Armstrong, was the Louisiana Purchase in 1803.[59]

One of the unique aspects of Armstrong's interpretation of biblical prophecy is that he applies it to modern life, dogmatically asserting that "prophecies of world conditions

... fill a third of the entire Bible" and "some 90 percent of all those prophecies pertain to national and international world happenings of *our time, now*."

> On the world scene nothing is so important right now as to know where the white, English-speaking peoples are identified in scores and hundreds of prophecies—prophecies which describe vividly our sudden rise to national power and reveal the causes of that greatness; prophecies that paint a crystal-clear picture of our present international dilemma; prophecies that open our eyes wide to see what now lies immediately ahead for our nations—and what our ultimate and final status shall be.[60]

One of the prophecies that Armstrong maintains has great significance for today is in Micah 5, where the "remnant of Jacob," which he identifies as America and Britain, receives great blessings from God. But then, the remnant is cut off from God's blessings and is militarily stripped of power. This, according to Armstrong, has been the fate of America and Britain since 1950. "God's birthright blessing," manifested through the First World War, the Second World War, and the Korean War, is no longer in evidence. "Since that time [1950]. . . these blessings are surely being *taken away*—and neither America nor Britain has come out on top in any major skirmish since that time!"[61]

This military impotence resulting from God's indignation, however, could be overcome. "God will punish and *destroy us*—*unless we repent*—just before and leading up to the utter destruction to come '*upon the heathen*' . . . which will take place at the very end of this age and at the second return of Jesus Christ as King of kings!" This Great Tribulation will be the cause of many turning to the truth. When people around the world "are cruelly treated, beaten unmercifully, even martyred and put to death—then millions of those who remain alive will cry out to God—will repent—will turn to live God's way." How will they know they must turn to God? Millions then will remember they heard Christ's true message over *The World Tomorrow* or read it in *The Plain Truth*.[62]

Armstrong's personal part in ushering in Christ's Second Coming, according to his scheme, was more than his simply being used as God's instrument through media ministry. Indeed, he was convinced that God confirmed him as his anointed agent through dates and numbers that were far more significant than mere coincidence might suggest. Although he insisted that "We do not set dates," Armstrong was not averse to "suggesting" appropriate dates that might be significant in God's timetable. Like date-setters before him, he combed the Bible looking for incidents and dates from which to formulate his end-time interpretations. His fascination with the number 19 became the basis of prophecies for biblical times as well as prophecies that related to him personally. The significance of that number is based on the fact that "the earth, the sun, and the moon come into almost exact conjunction only *once in 19 years*. Thus 19 years mark off one complete time-cycle!" This nineteen-year period, according to Armstrong, was precisely the amount of time expended by the apostles in their effort to reach Asia (A.D. 31–50). Then, "after *precisely one 19-year time-cycle*, 50 A.D., Christ *opened a door* for the Apostle Paul to carry the same Gospel to Europe. . . . *Exactly one time-cycle later*, 69 A.D., the disciples . . . fled from Judea northward to Pella. The following year, 70 A.D., Roman armies besieged Jerusalem."[63]

The significance of these "time-cycles" might be entirely lost were it not for the fact that Armstrong maintained that he himself reached out with his message to his homeland for nineteen years (1934–1953), and then began preaching worldwide. So, even as God used two "time-cycles" to inaugurate his message, "so now," wrote Armstrong in 1959, "God has marked off *two 19-year time-cycles* just before Christ returns for the restoring of the knowledge of the same Gospel." Such a conclusion was not viewed with casual interest. "Think what terrifying significance! Think what this means!," wrote Armstrong as he contemplated ahead to 1972, when that second "time-cycle" would be completed.[64]

Like others before him who pinpointed significant prophetic dates, Armstrong did not despair when the year 1972 passed without major consequences. He was prepared to fall back on his more general timetable, that of some six thousand years of human history prior to the Lord's return. Six years later, in 1978, he wrote, "Happily, the 6,000-year sentence on Adam's world—being *cut off* from God, is due to end in our present living generation." It is then that "Satan will be banished," and everyone who has ever lived will be given an opportunity to repent. "God will call all living to His salvation. After the Millennium shall come the Great White Throne Judgment (Rev. 20:11–12) when all who had been cut off from God for 6,000 years shall be resurrected mortal—and all called to God's salvation and eternal life!"[65]

The Plurality of Gods and the Doctrine of the Trinity

Armstrong's concept of eternity after the Millennium is similar in many respects to Mormon speculation, and bears very significantly on his view of the nature of God. He contends that "all saints" will be busy "renewing the face of all decayed planets, finishing the glorious beautiful creation throughout the whole endless universe." Indeed, his portrayal of eternity, like that of the Mormons, seems to depict the "saints" as gods themselves.

> Our potential is to be born into the God Family, receiving total power! We are to be given jurisdiction over the entire universe!
>
> What are we going to do then? . . . We shall impart life to billions and billions of dead planets, as life has been imparted to this earth. We shall create, as God directs and instructs. We shall rule through all eternity! . . . It will be an eternal life of accomplishment, constantly looking forward in super-joyous anticipation to new creative projects. . . .[66]

Publications from the Worldwide Church of God have been even more blatant in advancing the belief that humans can become gods. According to David Hill, in an article published in *Tomorrow's World*, "we grow spiritually more and more like God, until, at the time of the resurrection we shall be instantaneously changed from mortal into immortal—we shall then be born of God—WE SHALL THEN BE GOD!"[67]

This concept of humans becoming members of the god family was reiterated in 1978, when the Armstrong organization gave the following response to a question concerning the deity of Christ and the Trinity:

> "God" is a "family name," referring to a family composed of two separate personalities—the Father and the Son. . . . Man's goal is to become a member of the God-family. God is spiritually reproducing himself through man. Once man has developed the necessary character, he will be born into God's own family as a "Son of God" and therefore a "God" (family name) himself. Of course, the Father and Son will always be superior in authority and rank. God is literally making man in his image (Gen. 1:26).[68]

It is in light of his belief that all humans can potentially become gods that Armstrong must be understood in his affirmation that Jesus is God. On the surface his position sounds orthodox: "It is vital that we understand . . . that Jesus, during his human life, was both God and man. . . . In other words, Jesus was God as well as human man. He had no human father. God Almighty was his father who begat him by means of the Holy Spirit." Despite such statements, however, a closer look at his teaching indicates that he does not mean to convey what his words imply. Yes, Jesus is God, but not eternally so, as orthodox Christianity teaches. According to Armstrong, "Jesus Christ, by his resurrection, was BORN a divine son of God . . . the first so born into the God family."[69]

Armstrong's view of the Godhead is different from that of the Mormons and Jehovah's Witnesses. "There is not one God, but two: God the Father, the Possessor of heaven and earth, the Father of Jesus Christ; and the God of Abraham, Isaac, and Jacob, the active Creator of heaven and earth—the One who became Jesus Christ."[70]

Armstrong vehemently opposed the doctrine of the Trinity, insisting that it was a notion perpetrated by Satan. "The Trinity doctrine completely does away with the gospel of Jesus Christ," he wrote. "His gospel is the MESSAGE he brought mankind from God the Father, the good news of the coming KINGDOM of God! That is the one thing above all Satan wants to defeat."[71]

He was particularly perturbed by the teaching that the Holy Spirit is God and a full personality in the Trinity. "The Holy Spirit is the one harmonious, perfect holy attitude of mind which is shared by both Father and Son," he wrote. "The Holy Spirit is the very power of God! It expresses the unified creative will of the God family. . . . How clear it is that the Holy Spirit is not a third person of the Godhead as taught by the pagan 'trinity' idea!"[72]

In his depiction of God the Father, Armstrong, like the Mormons, emphasizes His physical characteristics—though he insists that "he is composed of spirit, not of matter as is man." In response to the question, "What is God's form and shape?," Armstrong writes:

> In various parts of the Bible, it is revealed that God has a face, eyes, a nose, mouth and ears. He has hair on his head. It is revealed God has arms

and legs. And God has hands and fingers. . . .

If you know what a man looks like, you know what is the form and shape of God, for he made man in his image, after his very likeness![73]

Salvation and the Law

Armstrong has been very disparaging of Protestant Christianity over the years because of its frequent emphasis on salvation by faith alone. He maintains that there is no salvation apart from obedience to God's Law. Faith is of no effect unless it involves obeying the law. As with other religious thinkers who have sought to uphold the teachings of the Apostle Paul, while at the same time retaining Old Testament law, Armstrong has been faced with a multiplicity of contradictions. His effort to maintain the Old Testament legal code is not compatible with New Testament teachings—especially as found in such writings as Paul's Epistle to the Galatians. Precisely what laws are to be retained and what laws are not applicable for today is another area of inconsistency and contradiction in Armstrong's message, as Joseph Hopkins points out:

> Much of the Old Testament law has been brought by Armstrong into the new dispensation almost intact. Jewish feast days and holy days (except the new moons), the Hebrew Sabbath, the practice of tithing, dietary laws, and the Decalogue, all have been retained. Most of the Israelite civil statutes and the intricate regulations governing priestly garb and duties, as well as animal sacrifice and outmoded Temple rituals, have been dropped.[74]

Unlike the Seventh-day Adventists, who make a distinction between the ceremonial and the moral law and include seventh-day worship in the moral law, Armstrong makes no such distinction and maintains that "the *whole* of the ceremonial law must be kept to the very letter." On the other hand, Christian traditions that have emerged since the apostolic era are prohibited. As is true with Jehovah's Witnesses, members of the Worldwide Church of God are forbidden to participate in the Christian holidays of Christmas and Easter, which are viewed as pagan.[75]

Dietary regulations maintained by the Armstrong organization correspond with those outlined in the Books of Leviticus and Deuteronomy. Armstrong argues that God's restriction of certain "unclean" foods was a decree for all times for mankind's protection. In a paper entitled "Is all Animal Flesh Good Food?" he wrote, "Swine flesh—pork, ham, bacon, sausage, etc.—is simply not fit for human consumption. The same is true with oysters, lobsters, clams, crabs, shrimp, crawfish, dogs, snakes, rats, and skunks."[76]

Evangelism and Missions

Unlike the Mormons and Jehovah's Witnesses and most other nontraditional religious movements that have arisen over the past century, the Worldwide Church of God does not have a high-powered evangelistic or missionary program. The underlying rationale behind this lack of evangelism is theological in nature. According to Armstrong, "the purpose and function of the Church has been grossly misunderstood," and this misunderstanding has been the primary motivation for traditional evangelism and missionary outreach. "So let us clarify once for all time," he writes, "that the purpose of the Church is definitely not to preach or persuade the whole world into a spiritual salvation, now—before Christ's second coming!"

> Jesus had not come on a "soul-saving crusade." The most widespread false assumption of all is that Christ is contesting against Satan to "get everybody saved now!" And with it, the supposition that all not saved are "lost"—condemned! They are neither. They are not yet judged![77]

Armstrong's position on missionary endeavors is not entirely unlike that of churchmen who disputed with William Carey in the late eighteenth century when he challenged his contemporaries to accept their responsibility in carrying out the Great Commission. They argued that the Great Commission was given to the Apostles who had opportunity to fulfill its directive in the first century. According to Armstrong, the "Great Commission to be sent forth with Christ's Gospel Message was given only to those who were apostles. . . . not the lay members of the Church," and not surprisingly, he viewed himself "God's apostle for our day."[78] The fulfilling of the Great Commission, then, is spreading the message of Herbert W. Armstrong through radio, television, and the printed word.

Armstrong began his worldwide outreach in the 1950s with a lecture tour to various cities in the British Isles. His following grew rapidly as his radio ministry expanded. By the end of that decade his radio messages penetrated every continent, with more than four million listeners worldwide.[79]

The message of Herbert W. Armstrong that reaches some one hundred and fifty million people through the printed page and the air waves is certainly not a typical missionary message of evangelism or even doctrine. It is a message to a world blinded by Satan, with the focus on moral and family values or international affairs. "Millions have experienced changes in their marital lives through our broadcasts and through reading the instructional booklets and magazine articles," exudes a church publication. "From New Zealand to Africa, and from the Swiss Alps to Puget Sound, tens of thousands write of the deep and far reaching changes effected in their homes and families through a better understanding of God-revealed ways of right, clean, wholesome living."[80]

Another aspect of the Armstrong "missionary" outreach is that of recruiting students from abroad. One example is Isaiah Issong, a young Nigerian who has testified how he was tempted and nearly enticed by the offer of a free American education: "Ambassador College has been an arm of Armstrong's dragnet. . . . Most of our Nigerian students who obtain their scholarships into the Ambassador College do not . . . realize that the Worldwide Church of God is never a true church of God. I would have been personally entrapped sometime in 1969 when there was a recruitment drive or a cry for willing young men to take the offer."[81]

Contemporary Perspective

Since the death of Herbert W. Armstrong in January of 1986, significant changes have occurred in the Worldwide Church of God. The era of Armstrong had passed, and younger and less doctrinaire men were already established in leading positions to carry on with the work. Heading the movement is Pastor General Joseph W. Tkach, Armstrong's designated successor–a man who worked his way up through the ranks since his baptism in 1957.[82]

While some observers predicted the movement would decline with the death of its founder, the opposite has been true. According to Michael A. Snyder, the Assistant Director of Public Affairs, the circulation of *Plain Truth* has increased as has the viewing audience of "The World Tomorrow," which was "the second most popular religious television program in the United States as rated by Arbitron (as evidenced by the July and November, 1988 surveys)."[83]

Besides growth in the movement, there appears to be a new openness that was not evident to outsiders in the past and a willingness to reassess doctrine and practices. "In March of 1988," according to Snyder, "Mr. Tkach wrote . . . to the entire membership of the Worldwide Church of God: 'None of us is infallible, and I am the first to know that I surely am not.' He went on to say that he would not shrink from his responsibility to correct any doctrine proven to be in error, stating that God's judgment is on me if I don't take action to correct that wrong.' "[84]

Some of the wrongs that will apparently be corrected pertain to

Joseph W. Tkach, Pastor General of Worldwide Church of God. Courtesy of the Worldwide Church of God.

the writings and beliefs of Armstrong–many of which are contained in his 1985 volume, *Mystery of the Ages*. When the book was issued, Armstrong offered it to his followers: "It puts the many different parts of the 'jigsaw puzzle' together. It is, in fact, a synopsis of the entire Bible. It is my prayer that you will read it along with your Bible–that it will make your Bible come alive and understandable. . . . I am now in my 94th year and I feel that this book is the most valuable gift I could possibly give you." When he announced the death of Armstrong, Joseph Tkach referred to the *Mystery of the Ages* as "his most powerful and effective book."[85] Since that time, however, this "most valuable gift" of Armstrong "has been pulled from circulation pending a doctrinal review."[86]

Mystery of the Ages is a major statement on doctrine, containing chapters on such theological issues as God, man, and the church. Here Armstrong argued that Satan has deceived people to the point that "They even worship Christ. . . . Deceived millions do not realize that they are worshipping Christ in vain." He also repeated his dogmatic belief that the "one *true* church is the Church of God!"[87] This is not the only book of Armstrong's that has come into question by the leadership. Other books, such as *The Plain Truth About Healing* and *The United States and Britain in Prophecy* have been reissued in entirely different editions, eliminating or reinterpreting significant portions of Armstrong's message.[88]

At the time of this writing, the Worldwide Church of God is revising its doctrinal statement, so it is impossible to assess how significant any changes in church doctrine will be. Will they, in fact, be more cosmetic than real? In a letter written in 1989, Michael Snyder insisted that "The Worldwide Church of God makes no claim to being the exclusive assembly of all members of the body of Christ."[89] This statement, however, is not entirely compatible with a statement made by Joseph Tkach, in May of 1986, soon after he assumed the leadership: "Jesus Christ, the living Head of the Church (Ephesians 1:22-23), is at the right hand of God the Father in heaven. He continues to actively lead and govern the church through Mr. Armstrong's designated successor, Joseph W. Tkach."[90] If indeed the Worldwide Church of God

is "the Church" of which Jesus Christ is the head, the charge of exclusivity still seems to be in order.

While the Worldwide Church of God continues to reject the orthodox view of the Trinity, Snyder maintains that it is "a Christian church, believing that the sacrifice and resurrection of Jesus is the only means by which a person may be redeemed and ultimately saved" and that salvation is "by grace–the free, unmerited pardon by God through the sacrifice of Jesus" and that "Jesus is the Son of God and must be the personal Savior for every Christian who is to be saved."[9 + sl] Here the implication seems to be, as Armstrong taught, that salvation is something to be anticipated in the future–not an assurance for the here and now.

In areas regarding practical matters, Snyder insists that "Church members are *encouraged*" to seek "medical attention as appropriate," that the Church "positively teaches racial equality," that "financial accountability is important," that the church "does not set dates for prophetic events," and that "British-Israelism" should not be equated with the Church's stance on the United States and Britain in prophecy.[92]

The leadership of the Worldwide Church of God must be commended for its commitment to reassess previously held doctrines and practices. This is a positive step, but as yet there is no indication that the movement will reject its long standing denial of the Trinity and the deity of Christ.

Chapter 9

The Way International:
Denying the Deity
of Christ

"One group you mentioned, The Way International, did not seem to fit into your cult definition. I've read their magazine, and frankly it seems to promote the teaching of Jesus Christ much more than your own magazine." This is an excerpt from a letter to the editor, following a 1977 article on cults in *Moody Monthly*. The letter went on to say: "I am outraged by . . . your lumping The Way International among other sects. . . . I don't know about what the other groups believe or teach, but I am familiar with The Way International and am angered that you would attack this ministry as heresy and a cult."

Many other people, besides this angry letter writer, have been mislead by The Way International, which closely parallels evangelical Christianity in many ways and is considered by some observers to be one of the most dangerous counterfeits of Christianity to appear in recent decades. It certainly requires the discernment of a perceptive Bible stu-

dent to recognize the unorthodox teachings in the movement's doctrinal statement. (See Appendix B.)

Victor Paul Wierwille

Victor Paul Wierwille, the late founder and long-time president of The Way International, was born into an Ohio farm family in 1916. He was reared "in the fundamental atmosphere of the Evangelical and Reformed Church" and "from his youth he wanted to be a minister." In high school, he excelled in basketball and was offered an athletic scholarship to Ohio State University, but he turned it down to attend Mission House College instead. After graduating from Mission House, he enrolled at Princeton Seminary in 1940. He also took some correspondence courses on the Bible from Moody Bible Institute, and even taught homiletics for a brief time at Gordon Divinity School.[1]

Wierwille's education has been a matter of controversy over the years. Although he maintained that he took all the courses that were available through correspondence at Moody Bible Institute, that school has no record of his completing any courses whatsoever. His degree from Princeton was valid, but his transcripts indicate that he did not take intense training in biblical studies, as he later implied he had. Rather, according to the registrar, his "degree represented advanced study in the field of preaching, and contained no work in the Greek language." The most controversial aspect of his education, however, is his "doctor's" degree—a degree that has prompted his followers to refer to him simply as "the doctor." This degree, a Doctor of Theology (Th.D.), was granted by Pikes Peak Seminary, a school cynically referred to as a "degree mill" because it had "no resident instruction, no published list of faculty, and no accreditation."[2]

Power For Abundant Living

Following his ordination in 1941, Wierwille served in the pastorate at a number of small churches. He later reflected on these pastorates as years of "plodding ahead with the things of God." What was wrong? "We lacked the abundant life. . . . As I looked about me at communities where I had served and among the ministers with whom I had worked, the abundant life was frequently not evident. In contrast to these Christian people, I could see that the secular world of non-Christians were manifesting a more abundant life than were members of the Church." This, he maintains, prompted him to search out how a person could have abundant life as is spoken of in John 10:10.[3]

Wierwille touted his "discovery" of the "power for abundant living" as a breakthrough in practical Christianity, and the "abundant life" became the predominant theme in his ministry. In 1953, he taught his first PFAL (Power For Abundant Living) course—a course that was later required for all those who wished to become a part of the movement. Why had Wierwille not realized the truth of abundant living prior to this time while he was a preacher? "For years I did nothing but read around the Word of God," he writes. "I used to read two or three theological works weekly. . . . I know what Professor so-and-so said . . . but I could not quote you The Word. I had not read it. One day I finally became so disgusted and tired of reading around The Word that I hauled over 3,000 volumes of theological works to the city dump."[4]

Founding of the Movement

In 1955, Wierwille officially incorporated The Way International, and in 1957, two decades before he would make his public protest against the teaching of the Trinity, he resigned from his parish and began devoting all his energies to the movement. Initially the organization appeared to be just another church-related ministry that grew slowly through Wierwille's radio ministry and Biblical Research Center. "But in 1968, he took to the road, riding a raspberry-colored Harley-Davidson motorcycle and preaching his anti-Trinitarian notions and antichurch views to the turned-off generation. For young people who didn't want to stray too far afield from conventional Christianity, The Way seemed just a step outside

Victor Paul Wierwille.

the churches that they had reject-ed."[5]

Capitalizing on the Jesus Movement

Wierwille's change in style and his effort to reach out to hippies disillusioned with drugs and sex allowed him to capitalize on the Jesus Movement that was already spreading across the country. This paved the way for an expanded ministry that would bring thousands of youth under his influence. His activities involved street work in the Haight-Ashbury district of San Francisco and organizing rock music concerts to draw his followers to Ohio for indoctrination. These annual "Rock of Ages" festivals served to attract many young people who would never otherwise attend church.[6]

During the developmental years of The Way International, Wierwille was accessible to his followers. They revered him and he responded with the affection of a kindly father.

"You're my kids. . . . You're beautiful. . . . You're just the greatest. . . . You're God's best!" he extolled. "The greatest young people in the world came up out of the Way Ministry! The finest students in America today are Way students! You are the most beautiful men and women of God the world has ever seen. Let them see you—they haven't seen any in centuries."[7]

God's Spokesman for This Age

In many respects, Wierwille viewed himself as God's spokesman for this age, even as Joseph Smith and Herbert W. Armstrong had. He did not equate his writings with Scripture, as Smith did, but he did challenge his followers to treat his writing and speaking as though it were coming directly from God. "If you will be as honest with God as that Word of God says," he wrote, "you too can walk into the greatness of the manifestation of the power of God. But if you think this is just Victor Paul Wierwille writing or speaking to you, you will never receive it. If you know that what I am saying to you are the words which the Holy Ghost has spoken . . . then you too will manifest forth the greatness of the power of God."[8]

Organizational Development

As the founder and president of The Way International, Wierwille was clearly in command of the movement from the beginning. He could not manage a mushrooming organization by himself; however, so he developed an efficient structure that served his purposes well. Each level of organiza-

Rock of Ages festival.

tion was designated by a component of a tree. The *roots* are the various executive office locations. The *trunks* are the various countries in which the movement is located. The *limbs* are the state headquarters. The *branches* are the city and county associations, and the *twigs* are the local community fellowships—often located on campuses. As the movement grew, more full-time staff members were added, and eventually coordinators were named for each Twig, Branch, Limb and Trunk. Although Wierwille did not claim that this organizational structure was inspired per se, it is seen as a pattern taken from the early church, as the final item in the "Statement of Beliefs" indicates: "We believe the early Church flourished rapidly because they operated within a Root, Trunk, Limb, Branch and Twig setup, decently and in order."[9]

According to literature distributed by The Way International, the organization does not have an official membership. By 1983, some one hundred thousand individuals had "participated" in the Power For Abundant Living class, but that figure is not meaningful since participation could include those who might visit for only a session or two. Way membership is very difficult to ascertain because, "Technically, followers of the Way aren't members because there is no membership as such. To be a follower requires only a desire to learn more about God and the Bible. This is engendered by attending Twig fellowships, taking classes or participating in correspondence courses." There are no church buildings. Rather, followers meet in private homes or dormitories for fellowship meetings which, according to organization literature, "include a short, positive teaching from the Bible, prayer, singing, and the manifestation of the spirit of God."[10]

Religious Practices and Lifestyle

The Way International would not correctly be characterized as a puritanical religious movement, as would such groups as the Jehovah's Witnesses, the Worldwide Church of God, and the Hare Krishnas—all groups that would shun worldly activities. To the contrary, Way followers—except for their frequent Bible studies—exhibit a lifestyle not unlike the typical college student. Drinking and smoking are familiar sights at Rock of Ages festivals, and the music is often difficult to distinguish from secular rock music.

Indeed, there is the appearance of an easy-going, laid-back lifestyle—an appearance unreflective of the actual situation. Like Jehovah's Witnesses and members of the Worldwide Church of God, Way followers who leave the fellowship are shunned. The organization is tight, and those who would challenge the authority of the leadership are viewed as dissidents and are not welcome in the fellowship. In recent years, Wierwille's PFAL course has been offered through a thirty-three-hour videotaped series, during which time no questions are permitted. This has given rise to "charges of brainwashing by parents who complain that their children, since converting to The Way, have evidenced radical personality changes."[11]

Doctrinal Distinctions

Although The Way International appears to be similar to evangelical Christianity in many respects, there are some notable differences that prospective members discover as they participate in the introductory courses. These differences involve major doctrines as well as seemingly minor variations in biblical interpretation.

Biblical Literalism

One of the close parallels between The Way International and evangelical Christianity is the emphasis on biblical authority. Statements by Wierwille on this subject sound no different in many cases than statements made by leading evangelicals:

Many times a critic of the Bible comes along and says, "Well, the Bible is not true. I feel that there are too many contradictions; the Bible really is just another book among the rest of them." This is not the testimony of the Word of God. The testimony of the Word of God is that all Scripture is God-breathed and is profitable for doctrine, which is to teach us how to believe rightly, how to believe positively. If we are going to tap the resources for the more abundant life we must know how to believe rightly. To people who say that the Bible has lots of error in it, I would like to state that the true Word of God is accurate from Genesis to Revelation. The errors have come in by man propounding those errors. Men have brought their opinions and desires into the Word. When men come and say that they do not believe the Bible, we must remember that the Bible was never written for the unbeliever, the agnostic, or the infidel; the Bible was not written for the God-rejectors and the God-deniers. The Bible was written for men and women who want to find answers. . . .[12]

Despite his emphasis on the sufficiency of Scripture, however, Wierwille, like other leaders of variant religious groups, insists that he has special insight into God's Word. That position is based in part on his insistence that he, unlike the vast majority of Christians, uses the most authentic and authoritative texts—to be precise, the Syriac Peshitta, the text used by the Syrian Orthodox Church. According to Walter Martin, Wierwille disregards the consensus of textual critics and maintains that the New Testament was originally written in Aramaic—even though "that form of Aramaic was not known at the time of Christ and in fact did not develop until the beginning of the third century."[13]

Wierwille places other qualifiers on the Bible's authority—the most significant of which would be his strong dispensational position. "Most people believe that the entire Bible—from Genesis to Revelation—is written to them," he writes. "This is not true. . . . Those things written before the day of Pentecost are not addressed *to* us but are *for* our learning. . . . One of the greatest errors in the translation of the Bible was placing the four Gospels in the New Testament. The Gospels logically belong in the Old Testament."[14]

The Trinity and the Deity of Christ

Wierwille's opposition to the historic doctrine of the Trinity has been characterized by sarcasm and ridicule and was never something he sought to conceal. In an interview on the subject, he cynically asserted that "Christianity never had three gods," and went on to argue that "If Jesus Christ was God, and God died on the cross, the teaching that God is dead is right." His often clever scorn of orthodox teaching had an appeal with his youthful following. "Then who raised God from the dead if God died on the cross? You see, man's mind is so tricky. His logic blows my mind! They cannot add two plus two spiritually. They can do it in math; when it comes to God's Word, they can't track!"[15]

Wierwille publicized his position in a widely distributed book—the title of which left no doubt about his adamant declaration: *Jesus Christ Is Not God*. It was this claim—this denial of the deity of Christ—that Wierwille regarded as his most notable contribution to modern Christianity. He publicly proclaimed his stance in New Knoxville, Ohio in 1977. There on Reformation Sunday, in the tradition of Martin Luther, he posted a statement on the door of the First United Church of Christ. The title read: "Jesus Christ is not God—never was and never will be." Beneath he listed dozens of Bible verses that refer to Jesus as the Son of God. Following this demonstration of protest, according to an editorial in *Way Magazine*, "Dr. Wierwille strode back to the custom coach after placing an autographed copy of *Jesus Christ Is Not God* at the foot of the church door for all to see." He later made the following analysis of his declaration:

When my life is over I think my greatest contribution may prove to be the knowledge and teaching that Jesus Christ is not God. Before I finish, my life may stir up the biggest beehive in Roman Catholicism and Protestantism since the religious leaders took a shot at Martin Luther. May there be a true reformation in our day and time.[16]

Wierwille considered Martin Luther to be a great Christian dissenter, who would have joined in his own protest. "If Martin Luther'd had more time, and lived in our culture," he insisted, "I'm confident he would have come up with a far better work on *Jesus Christ Is Not God* than I did, 'cause he knew it. But he just didn't have time."[17] Such a statement, considering Luther's strong Trinitarian views, only indicates the extent to which Wierwille was willing to embellish the truth in an effort to gain credibility.

The book Wierwille predicted would start another Reformation.

Although Wierwille staged a public demonstration to proclaim his opposition to Trinitarianism—and perhaps to promote his book—he insisted that he had not initially intended to challenge orthodoxy. "I didn't begin research of this topic from a negative framework," he wrote. "It was never part of my motivation to disprove the trinity. If the Bible had taught that there is a Christian trinity, I would have happily accepted it. . . . I have checked God's Word hundreds of times over, and thus I am convinced beyond a shadow of a doubt that Jesus Christ is not God but the son of God." As the Son of God, Wierwille maintains that Jesus and the Father are not "co-eternal, without beginning or end, and co-equal"—that "Jesus Christ was not literally with God in the beginning; neither does he have all the assets of God."[18]

Like the Jehovah's Witnesses, Wierwille defends his position by offering a new interpretation of the key passage on the deity of Christ, John 1:1: "In the beginning was the Word, and the Word was with God, and the Word was God." He does not claim, however, as do the Jehovah's Witnesses, that the third phrase in that verse ought to be rendered "and the word was a god." Rather, he redefines the Greek word *logos*, which is typically rendered *word*. "In John 1:1 the *logos*, which is God, has reference to the thoughts and ideas conveyed by the spoken Words, the written Words and the incarnate Word. All the spoken, written and incarnate Words were with God in His foreknowledge. They did not come into existence in the sense world until God had someone with whom to communicate."[19]

Many of the claims that Wierwille makes concerning the first chapter of John are undocumented, and are best categorized as pure speculation. He conjectures, for example, that scribes inserted words into the original manuscripts to make the text appear to teach the deity of Christ. He makes this case for the biblical claim that Jesus is the "only-begotten God," in John 1:18.

> In some of the ancient uncial manuscripts, the word "son" in the phrase "only-begotten Son" was changed to "God," thus reading "only-begotten God." . . . A scribe just having copied verse 14 which reads "the only begotten of the Father" could easily have carried the same thinking into verse 18 and transcribed the verse to read "the only begotten God." This kind of error in which one passage is assimilated to the wording of a similar passage is not uncommon. On the other hand, the error in John 1:18 could have been an intentional change due to the doctrinal error propounded as early as the second century.[20]

The Virgin Birth

Wierwille takes strong issue with the notion of the virgin *birth* of Jesus and emphasizes instead the virgin *conception*. Even here, however, he offers his own interpretation that is at variance with most traditional teaching on the subject in that he implies there was literal physical sexual intercourse between Mary and the Holy Spirit. "Conception by the Holy Spirit was the only way Jesus Christ could be conceived," he writes. "The Holy Spirit contributed the soul-life in the blood of Jesus by way of the sperm. In His arteries and veins there was sinless soul-life." How could the Holy Spirit implant sperm in Mary? "The word 'overshadow' means 'cover,' according to Wierwille. "In the animal kingdom we speak of a bull covering a cow, meaning the sexual position for conception. The same meaning is evident in human beings."[21]

In his attempt to discredit traditional teachings about the Virgin Birth, Wierwille insists that Mary had sexual relations with Joseph before Jesus was born. "Joseph was explicitly told not to fear to have intercourse with his wife," he writes. "Joseph now carried out exactly the angel's commands. He 'took unto him' simply means he had intercourse with Mary. From this point on, Joseph and Mary live in a normal marital relationship." To make such an assertion requires that Wierwille reinterpret key verses such as Matthew 1:25, which states in the King James Version, the translation he refers to, that Joseph "knew her not till she had brought forth her firstborn son." Here Wierwille seeks to explain what otherwise appears obvious by claiming that "Mary had intercourse with Joseph but did not conceive by Joseph until after the birth of Jesus."[22]

The Holy Spirit

In his opposition to the doctrine of the Trinity, Wierwille maintains that the true biblical teaching on the Holy Spirit has been grossly distorted by historic Christian orthodoxy. His teaching on this point can be very confusing to an untrained Bible student. He does not concur with other nontraditional religious proponents who would simply argue that the Holy Spirit is not God—only the spirit of God—and therefore render all biblical citations to the Holy Spirit as a thing, holy spirit, with no capital letters. He rather differentiates between the *Giver* and the *gift*:

> The *Giver* is God, the Spirit. His *gift* is spirit. Failure to recognize the difference between the *Giver* and His *gift* has

caused no end of confusion in the Holy Spirit field of study as well as in the understanding of the new birth.

The *gift* from The Holy Spirit, the *Giver*, is *pneuma hagion*, holy spirit, power from on high, spiritual abilities, enablements. This power is spirit in contrast to the senses. Spirit is holy as opposed to the flesh, which is called by God unholy. God is Holy Spirit and *God can only give that which He is;* therefore, the *gift* from the *Giver* is of necessity *holy* and *spirit.*[23]

Wierwille's theology relating to the Holy Spirit and to Christ is certainly not novel. Indeed, as is true of many other non-Trinitarian theologies, it is a version of third-century Sabellianism or Modalism—the teaching of the primacy of God the Father with the Son and the Holy Spirit being merely modes of the Father's self-revelation and self-expression.

Speaking in Tongues

Wierwille's emphasis on the *gift* of the holy spirit is one that is derived in part from his own personal experience. "For six years I prayed, asked, pleaded and begged God for this spiritual power," he writes. "I literally traveled thousands of miles just to ask people about the Holy Spirit and the gift. I always returned spiritually lacerated and bleeding because those Christians who had received it were in such confusion that they had no ability to communicate the blessing to me." He "almost gave up in despair" until he was "made to realize that receiving the holy spirit did not depend upon good works, agonizing in prayer, nor in personal merit, but rather upon believing." It was only then that he "received into manifes-

tation the fullness of the power from on high"—that manifestation being speaking in tongues.[24]

The Way International is often viewed as a fringe segment of the Charismatic renewal that swept the country in the 1960s and 1970s. The emphasis on signs and revelations is the basis for this association, as well as the emphasis on the "gift of the holy spirit" which "has nine parts or manifestations." These nine manifestations, according to Wierwille, must be reflected in the Christian's life today. They were not simply signs for the New Testament believers. The manifestations are (1) word of wisdom, (2) word of knowledge, (3) faith, (4) gifts of healing, (5) miracles, (6) prophecy, (7) discerning of spirits, (8) tongues, and (9) interpretation of tongues.[25]

Of these manifestations, speaking in tongues (which is referred to as SIT) is the most emphasized. It is viewed as an utterly essential aspect of Christian life. "Speaking in a tongue," according to Wierwille, "is the believer's external manifestation in the senses, world of the internal reality and presence of the power of the holy spirit. Speaking in tongues is a constant reminder even in the hours of bereavement and sorrow, temptation and trouble, that Christ by way of God's power is in you. Therefore you have victory over the enemy in every situation. . . ."[26]

Unlike some Pentecostals and charismatics, Wierwille takes a very pragmatic approach to speaking in tongues. "*What* you say when you speak in tongues is God's business, but *that* you do speak is your responsibility." Insisting that speaking in tongues is each Christian's individual responsibility removes any sort of miraculous element from the process that was so frequently claimed by the Pentecostals and charismatics of recent generations. Wierwille emphasized this distinction. In his mind, there was nothing supernatural about speaking in tongues. It was simply a mechanical process that anyone could duplicate and in which anyone could participate. The instructions were easy to follow:

> While you are sitting, follow this instruction. Open your mouth wide and breathe in. . . . Just breathe in. Open your mouth wide. While you are breathing in, thank God for having filled you with the fullness of the power of His holy spirit. Don't beg Him; thank Him for it.
>
> When you begin to speak in tongues, move your lips, your throat, your tongue. Speak forth. When you have finished one sound, speak another. Do not pay any attention to what you are thinking. You formulate the words; you move your lips, your throat, your tongue; you say it. You are magnifying God no matter what the words sound like to your ears. It is your part to speak in tongues; it is God's part to give the utterance.[27]

When asked if it were possible for a Christian to receive false tongues, or a false spirit instead of the holy spirit, Wierwille responded, "The answer is a loud and clear no. As a matter of fact, speaking in tongues is the only manifestation which basically Satan cannot counterfeit." Such a suggestion, he asserts, is a "wicked thought" that "sinfully dishonors God."[28]

Extrabiblical Revelation

Like Joseph Smith, Charles Taze Russell, and Herbert W. Armstrong,

Wierwille believed he had God's true message which was not preached since the early church fell into apostasy. How did he know this? God spoke to him directly and told him so:

> I was praying. And I told Father outright that He could have the whole thing, unless there were real genuine answers that I wouldn't ever have to back up on.
>
> And that's when He spoke to me audibly, just like I'm talking to you now. He said He would teach me the Word as it had not been known since the first century if I would teach it to others.
>
> Well, I nearly flew off my chair. I couldn't believe that God would talk to me. . . . But He spoke to me just as plainly as I'm talking now to you.[29]

Wierwille later claimed that God's audible speech was not enough to convince him. He thus decided to put God to the test. He prayed that God would give him a sign—a sign that Wierwille specified himself, similar to Gideon's fleece:

> The sky was crystal blue and clear. Not a cloud in sight. It was a beautiful early autumn day. I said, "If that was really you, and you meant what you said, give me a sign. Let me see it snow." My eyes were tightly shut as I prayed. And then I opened them.
>
> The sky was so white and thick with snow, I couldn't see the tanks at the filling station on the corner not 75 feet away.[30]

For Wierwille, having an audible two-way conversation was a normal and natural aspect of life for a true believer—a child of God.

> Man, if God isn't talking to people today, you better get on talkin' terms

with God. Why shouldn't He speak to us? You see, it seems like you're a freak if God talks to you. Maybe the freaks are on the other side if He doesn't talk to you! . . . If my father didn't talk to me, I'd get me a new father. If He can't talk to me, but my earthly father can, then my heavenly Father is less than my earthly father, and that, to me is almost blasphemy.[31]

Law and Grace

Wierwille's concept of the Law and its application to present day Christianity is diametrically opposite the position held by Armstrong's Worldwide Church of God. In a chapter entitled "The Bondage of the Sabbath Day," he writes, "It is folly for a Christian to try to live under a law or laws which no longer exist." Sabbath keeping or Sunday worship is an example of this. "The laws of the Sabbath were given *to* Israel," he writes, "and, therefore apply *to* Israel. Since these laws were never given *to* the Church, their interpretation cannot be *for* it. . . . We are not believers tied to one legalistic day of worship. We worship God daily in spirit and in truth. Tradition dare not blind us to the truth of the light of God's word."[32]

Water baptism is another aspect of the law that holds Christians in bondage, according to Wierwille. "Since Pentecost, we are indeed free from the law; and part of that law was water baptism." He maintains that "water baptism was indeed instituted by God, but only for Israel and the kingdom, and then for only a limited period of time." After Pentecost, anyone who believed in Christ was "given something far greater than the benefits of water baptism. . . . To be

born again is to have Christ within; He is the hope of glory; He cleanses us from all sin. It's a spiritual baptism. . . . There is nothing that can add to our completeness in Him."[33]

Unique Biblical Interpretations

It is normal for biblical scholars to disagree on interpretations of various passages, and from that perspective, Wierwille might be seen as simply another student of the Bible with a "revisionist" interpretation of a particular passage. But his "new" interpretations—most of which are not new at all—are more than mere challenges to traditional scholarship. They are designed to generate doubts about historic orthodoxy in general. An example is Wierwille's insistence that four criminals, rather than two, were crucified with Jesus. To many this may seem like a relatively minor matter and certainly no tenet of faith, but Wierwille devotes a chapter to the subject, arguing that "the major reason for so much confusion regarding the 'others' crucified with Jesus is that men have divided the Word of God to suit themselves and according to tradition."[34]

In making his case, Wierwille points out that "the two thieves and the two malefactors have by tradition been made the same." But, "if this were true," he argues, "we would have a major discrepancy in the Word of God. Matthew 27:38 and Mark 15:27 distinctly state that there were 'two thieves,' while Luke 23:32 says 'two malefactors.' " Wierwille uses this example, not simply to correct what he deems to be an incorrect interpretation, but to spurn traditional teachings in general. "We have failed to give sufficient heed to The Word and to rightly dividing it," he writes. "We must change our theology and beliefs to agree with The Word. . . . Instead of being conditioned by the pictures we have seen, we must believe what The Word says. . . . So the answer to this subject is simple. Four were crucified with Jesus."[35]

The day of the Crucifixion and Resurrection is another point of biblical interpretation that Wierwille uses to cast doubt on historical orthodoxy. Again, it is an issue raised by various scholars long before he "blew the whistle" on those who fail to rightly divide the Word of God. "For people to say that Jesus died on Good Friday and arose on Easter Sunday morning," he writes, does "great damage to the integrity of God's Word." He insists, as have others, that "Jesus Christ literally fulfilled the law; He carried out the Word of God by being buried on Wednesday afternoon and being raised seventy-two hours later on Saturday afternoon."[36]

Missionary Outreach

The Way International does not sponsor missionaries in the traditional sense of sending out trained professionals for lifetime ministries. Indeed, the organization has purposely avoided that method of evangelism for philosophical reasons. Correspondence from The Way College of Biblical Research in Rome City, Indiana, outlines the movement's concept of foreign missions:

> We do not believe in missionary programs. We feel that the Word clearly states that every believer is responsible to speak God's Word and bring people to Christ. We are an international ministry, not because we have a mission program, but because our people so love God that they speak of Him wherever they go.
>
> Most of the outreach in our sister countries has come in one of three ways. First, it comes from winning a foreign student in college in this country who goes home and takes the Word with him. Secondly, it comes from U. S. servicemen stationed overseas, speaking the Word in the course of their daily activities. Lastly, it comes from students who go and study abroad.[37]

But despite this disavowal of missionary activity, the movement sponsors WOW (Word Over the World) Ambassadors who conduct intensive evangelistic outreaches much like Mormon missionaries do. They volunteer for one year of service, during which time they are required to meet their own expenses and return a tenth of their earnings back to the headquarters. In 1974, more than a thousand Ambassadors were commissioned to various regions of the United States, and in 1975, the number more than doubled. The projected goal was to commission more than two hundred thousand by 1985, and more than three million by 1990, goals that have had no bearing on reality.[38]

Some of the most successful evangelistic outreach in recent years has been realized overseas, where, according to the movement's own *Way Magazine*, the missionary activity has expanded greatly since the 1960s. As in the United States, this has been largely through the WOW arm of the movement. "The WOW Ambassador outreach worldwide has proven to be a great catalyst in reaching the world with God's Word and in raising up leadership among the believers."[39]

The vastness of this worldwide outreach is significant for such a relatively young organization. "From the southern port of Punta Arenas, Chile, to the northern gold fields of Fairbanks, Alaska—from the industrial city of Tokyo, Japan, to the small villages of Zaire, Africa—from the sprawling suburbs of Sydney, Australia, to the streets of Amsterdam—World Over the World Ambassadors are living up to their name." The article goes on to say that "WOW Ambassadors are speaking God's Word on every continent of the world. These lay missionaries are natives not only of North America but of Third World countries as well." In 1985, many South American Ambassadors were commissioned in Colombia, Peru, Chile, and Argentina, and in Africa, WOW Ambassadors are now serving in the countries of Zaire, Angola, and the Congo. In September of 1985, "Zaire commissioned over one thousand WOWs, to begin the fifth year of the program there."[40]

This worldwide outreach is based on Wierwille's strong emphasis on personal evangelism by every believer—an emphasis patterned after that of the early church and one that he maintains totally contradicts the missionary methodology of most denominations and mission organizations.

In two years and three months all Asia Minor heard the Word of God. In our day and time, with our multi-million dollars spent for foreign missions, publications, newspapers, radios, televisions and all other media, this event has never been repeated. We have never reached all Asia Minor with the Word of God in one generation. But the Apostle Paul and a handful of believers accomplished the feat in two years and three months. Either God has changed or Paul and those men who studied at the school of Tyrannus tapped into something which they utilized to its capacity.[41]

Recent Controversies

Since the death of Victor Paul Wierwille in 1985, controversy and internal dissension have plagued the movement. Even before Wierwille's death, however, there were suggestions that the movement was a paramilitary organization with a large stockpile of weapons and ammunition—munitions a spokesman later claimed were needed for a hunters' safety course that was being taught at The Way College of Emporia, Kansas. Another controversial issue centered on two books released by the publishing arm of the movement: *The Hoax of the Twentieth Century* and *The Myth of the Six Million*, both drawing charges of anti-Semitism because of their claim that Hitler's genocide of the Jews has been grossly exaggerated.[42]

In the early 1980s, the Internal Revenue Service initiated an investigation of the organization, and in 1985, as a result of its findings indicating funds had been diverted for political causes, the tax-exempt status of the group was revoked. However, the organization challenged the IRS decision and in October of 1987, its tax-exempt status was reinstated.[43]

The IRS matter was viewed by Way followers as a blatant instance of

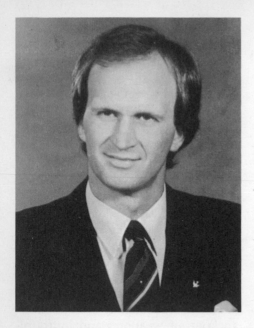

Craig Martindale, Director of The Way International.

religious persecution and it served as a symbol of solidarity in the ranks. A far more serious matter for the organization has been the internal feuding. In 1982, three years before he died, Wierwille announced that he was resigning his leadership of the movement and that Craig Martindale, the director of The Way Corp, would be his successor. Martindale converted to the movement from active involvement in evangelical causes—having been a former president of the Fellowship for Christian Athletes and the Baptist Student Union. After Wierwille's death, however, leading Way officials challenged Martindale's leadership and the morality of the late founder. After pressuring Martin-

dale to resign, John Lynn, one of the dissidents, "openly accused the leadership of endorsing adultery and forced tithing, and negating the divinity of Christ."[44]

By early 1988, three separate breakaway movements had organized: The American Fellowship Services, The Pacific West Fellowship, and the Great Lakes Fellowship. When questioned about any differences between his fellowship and The Way International, Paul Rawlins, cofounder of the Great Lakes Fellowship responded, "People are free here. We don't have a hundred different things to tell the people to do. And we believe that Victor Paul Wierwille made mistakes with adultery and plagiarism. They still don't want to believe that."[45]

These splinter groups, in the minds of some observers, would signal the downfall of The Way International, but that has not occurred. The 1988 Rock of Ages Festival in New Knoxville, Ohio, attracted thousands of people from around the country just as in previous years, and there was no sign whatever of the movement's demise. The most apparent outward difference in this festival, compared with the ones sponsored in the 1970s, was that of age. College students were still highly visible, but the atmosphere was more of a family conference than a rock concert. Young couples with strollers were more prominent than teenagers with guitars. Like many of the other cults of the 1960s, The Way International has come of age.

Chapter 10

The Children of God:
Evangelism and Sex Perversion

The Children of God (also known as the Family of Love) is a cult whose roots are in evangelical Christianity. It is a graphic illustration of how a religious movement can move from orthodoxy to aberrant beliefs and practices—beliefs and practices that sometimes defy the imagination. Perhaps more than any other religious group in American history, it has distorted basic scriptural teaching in an effort to promote sexual promiscuity. The group had its heyday in the 1970s during the height of the hippie movement, when many disillusioned young people were brought under its authoritative structure, unaware of the exact nature of the movement in which they were becoming involved. The founder and leader, "Moses" David Berg, became a messiah of sorts to the thousands of college-age youths who accepted his messages as coming directly from God. By the 1980s the movement had begun to decline, and today its numbers have dwindled considerably. Yet, its influence is still felt by those who were once caught in its clutches.

David "Moses" Berg

David Brandt Berg was born in California in 1919, and raised in an intense Christian atmosphere. His father was a pastor and teacher at a Christian college, while his mother was a radio evangelist who became well known in Southern California. Berg was deeply influenced by his mother, and followed her footsteps into evangelistic ministry with the Christian and Missionary Alliance Church. After more than a quarter century of independent as well as church-related evangelistic ministries in various localities, he returned to Huntington Beach, California, with his wife and children to work with his mother in a Teen Challenge Coffee House ministry. Here he felt at home in the free style of evangelism that allowed him to almost become one with the hippies he was seeking

David Berg and family in early years.
From *The Children of God* by Deborah Davis.

to reach on the beaches and on the streets.[1]

Fiercely independent, Berg soon disassociated himself with Teen Challenge, and turned the ministry into one that was centered on his own personal leadership. His preaching became more and more exclusivistic as he loudly condemned other Christian ministries. At the same time he began preaching a radical evangelistic style, encouraging his youthful followers to interfere with school activities if need be to get their message across. He also sought to disrupt local church services:

> Berg and thirty or forty of his followers would arrive at respectable middle-class churches attired in hippie garb, troop down to the front of the church, and sit on the floor in front of the pews. Berg was to refer to these later as "goodwill visitations to local churches to help them get better acquainted

with us," but this description is perhaps more than a little self-serving. The hostility felt by the group toward organized religion led its members on occasion to challenge the minister or shout abuse at worshipers. Their radical enthusiasms led them to loud praising and prayer to which the church members were unaccustomed.[2]

Within a year Berg had so alienated himself to local law officials and residents that he was forced to leave the area.

This alienation in many ways reflected Berg's "call" to ministry, a call he claimed came as a direct revelation from God. He wrote, "One of the first prophecies we ever received regarding my personal ministry was 'I have made thee a sharp-toothed threshing instrument which shall beat the mountains as chaff and rip with violence the pillows from under the arms of them which sit at ease in Zion.' "[3]

Berg's decision to leave California corresponded with a prophetic message he claimed came from God—a message portending doom for California, which would soon be so shaken by an earthquake that the whole state would be buried by the ocean waves. With him he took some fifty loyal followers who were committed to his apocalyptic message and his antimaterialistic philosophy. They traveled across the United States and Canada, "witnessing and demonstrating as they wandered" and picking up new converts as they went. They settled temporarily at various locations until they wore out their welcome.[4]

Charismatic Experiences and the Occult

One of the places where Berg and his followers settled down for a time was at the Texas Soul Clinic, a ranch owned by an evangelist. Here the converts were trained how to witness, and then they were sent out to win new converts—an activity that sometimes kept them busy up to twelve hours a day. There were specific instructions for witnessing, recalls Deborah Davis, Berg's daughter: "First get'm to ask Jesus into their heart. Then get'm filled with the Holy Spirit. Then ask'm if they want to forsake all and follow Jesus." But, at the very time this intensive witnessing was being conducted by Berg's followers, he himself was veering off into sexual immorality and the occult. In 1970, he began living with Maria, one of his followers, though not entirely abandoning his wife Jane. Soon after that he was joined by "a girl named Martha, whom he had taken as another wife." It was then also that his occultic involvement came to the fore—he began speaking in tongues with the help of Abrahim, a "spirit guide" (Berg's own description), whom he acquired at a Gypsy camp several months before. He later described his tongues experience:

I was lying there between Martha and Maria praying like a house afire, and all of a sudden before I even knew what happened I was praying in tongues. . . . it was probably Abrahim. I was finally desperate enough to really let the Lord take over and take control. Abrahim was praying through me in the Spirit.

Three days I couldn't speak any English. . . .

I went for years and years and years and years wanting the gift of tongues because that was such a marvelous manifestation to me, to think you could speak another language you had never learned. That was obviously a miracle, obviously a proof of the miraculous. But the Lord never gave it to me for years!

I begged Him! I besought Him! I fell on my face before Him! I did everything! . . .

He finally started giving me those audibly manifested gifts when I least expected it. I was lying naked between two naked women in the same bed in the back end of our camper when I first received the gift of tongues.[5]

In addition to his spirit contacts with Abrahim, Berg claimed that the entire movement had a guardian angel of sorts—Abner, a faithful member who had died. Abner served Berg as Chief of Security while living, but since his death he was promoted "to an even higher position amongst God's Heavenly Security Forces to watch over us from an even better vantage point. . . . He is now the Personal Representative of the Children of God in the Counsels and Courts of Heaven! He Stands in the Gap."[6]

Berg openly boasted about his spiritual contacts with the dead, claiming that they included such individuals as his parents, William Jennings Bryan, Martin Luther, Peter the Hermit, the Pied Piper, Ivan the Terrible, Anne Boleyn, and many other historical figures. He compared himself with William Branham, who once claimed to be guided by an angel appearing in a ball of light, and with Joseph Smith, who was also guided by an angel. "Maybe some of the spiritualistic churches are not so bad after all!" he wrote. "They sing hymns and talk about Jesus and preach the Gospel."[7]

Berg was a shadowy figure, who often went for long periods of time without any personal contact with his followers. This gave him a sense of mystery and awe. "A man perceived on paper is always more impressive than one known in the flesh." At the same time, he seemed to get a perverse pleasure out of exposing his personal life. His primary method of communication was through "Mo Letters," which often gave explicit details about sexual and occultic experiences. In one, he wrote about an out-of-the-body experience he had after dying. He was then "visited by the departed spirit of an old friend of his mother" who told him to return to his body and life. In another Mo Letter entitled "the Goddesses," he wrote: "I've not understood until now . . . those other goddesses I've made love to in the Spirit. . . . In each case, the one I was making love to would suddenly turn into one of these strange and beautiful goddesses, and I would immediately explode in an orgasm of tremendous spiritual power while at the same time prophesying violently in some foreign language."[8]

Domestic Troubles and Foreign Expansion

For more than a year in 1970 and 1971, Berg and his Children of God were heavily supported by radio evangelist Fred Jordan, who apparently was unaware of many of the beliefs and practices developing in the movement. From his ranch in Texas, members were sent to California and elsewhere to start new colonies, but wherever they went there was conflict and controversy. Charges of kidnapping, holding members against their will, brainwashing, and fraud were lodged against the Children of God. Groups of concerned parents formed. With public scandal mounting, Jordan expelled the movement from his property, but the growth continued. "The 2,100 members scattered to the 40 other colonies, which were by then in strong operation."[9]

At the very time of the expulsion from the Texas camp, Berg maneuvered himself into control of the Jesus People Army, a youth-oriented religious movement located in the Pacific Northwest. This resulted in a sudden influx of new members and an increase in sexual promiscuity due to communal living and mixed signals coming from "Moses." With outbreaks of social disease and reports of converts being raped, the movement suddenly became the focus of news media exposés and of government investigations. Berg reacted by lashing out at the colony leaders with a letter entitled "Sin in the Camp," blaming them for the problems. "They were reprimanded, not because they had committed immorality, but because through their lack of control they had neglected the sheep and gotten the work into trouble through bad publicity."[10]

Because of these problems and other concerns, Berg left the United States for England in 1972. He was never to set foot on American soil again. From England he began making dire predictions on the fate of America: "The storm of God's judgments upon the ease and luxury of these nations, particularly America, is fast approaching, and the sea and waves of the uprisings of people are about to rage." Soon after issuing this prophecy, "he warned his disciples to run for their lives while there was still a chance."[11]

By 1975, there were Children of God (COG) colonies in most of the countries of Western Europe, and by the late 1970s more than seventy countries had been penetrated by the Children of God, including such faraway places as Fiji, Thailand, and Singapore. The total number of colonies was estimated at four hundred, with some five thousand members. Only the most dedicated members lived in the colonies—members who spent most of the hours of each day seeking to win converts. Exaggerated claims were spread that converts numbered a quarter of a million, but those claims have been impossible to substantiate.[12]

Literature and Fund-raising

Along with personal witnessing, the movement was involved in a massive program of literature distribution. The literature was produced by the organization and was targeted for various levels of understanding—from an unsuspecting potential convert to Berg's inner circle, who alone received his most secretive messages. Between 1972 and 1976, publications grew from three million to nearly seventy million units.[13]

Literature distribution was referred to as "litnessing" (literature witnessing), and this was a profitable source of revenue for the Children of God. Each member was expected to sell two thousand pieces each week, charging approximately ten cents each. According to a *New York Times* report in 1974, "The Staten Island colony, one of the most profitable for litnessing, gets out up to 40,000 Mo letters a week, taking in about $4,000. That adds up to $200,000 a year."[14]

Berg gave specific instructions to his followers for litnessing, always emphasizing the importance of the financial donations: "When at a concert or a high school and kids are moving fast, it often helps to shorten your speech to 'Can you help with change for kids?' or 'Any change for kids?'" He likewise admonished his followers not to "get hung up on people who want lengthy explanations before they feel led to give a donation. Keep moving! And remember, the guy behind him is probably willing to give a dollar for a good cause."[15]

In addition to witnessing, members are admonished to approach businessmen and request tax-deductible donations of such things as food, clothing, and free rent. A worthy cause is the motivating factor—helping a young person kick the drug habit or supporting a Bible college student. Members are also advised to obtain as much money and supplies as possible from their parents.[16] In one "Mo Letter," Berg insisted colony leaders "make everybody sit down for at least 1–2 hours and write letters home.—One letter to the parents, one letter to their . . . relatives they know could help them. Tell them we are in desperate need and having a hard time meeting our needs, could you please help us?"[17]

Authoritarian Leadership

The personality of Berg—though he himself has been secluded from the membership at large—has dominated the Children of God from the very beginning. His claims that he speaks for God as "Moses" and that he rules a theocracy as "King David" place him in unquestioned control of every aspect of the worldwide network. Some of those who hold the highest levels of authority beneath him have been his own "wives" and children. The organizational structure beneath him consists of a Prime Minister, a Council of Ministers, and Bishops, each of whom supervises one of the twelve regions of the world. Beneath them are Regional, District, and Colony Shepherds.[18]

In his effort to maintain absolute control over his followers, Berg has frequently resorted to scare tactics, threatening his followers with divine judgment if they doubt him, and proclaiming "divine curses on those who disobey him." To members at large he wrote, "Now I'll tell you one thing right now, that God won't bless if they have had doubts about me or the Letters and some troublemaker has instilled some of his doubts into them. I know God wouldn't bless that. . . . There is no such thing as half-way obedience." When his daughter Deborah and her husband began having doubts, Berg ordered a woman to be "the executioner" and "to obey the Word of God and the King [Berg] and sock it to them, and it's either going to kill them or drive them stark raving mad or insane, or it's going to deliver them, one or the other!"[19]

But merely prophesying doom was not enough for Berg. He went far beyond that in response to his daughter's alleged "heresy." In an outburst of violence, he wrote, "Get busy and kill them! Kill them! The quicker the better! I mean if they can't stand the truth they ought to die and be dead! Let's hope maybe they'll go to Heaven and not to Hell."[20]

Revolution Against the Establishment

From the earliest days of his hippie, antiestablishment audacity, Berg viewed himself as the revolutionary leader of a movement that would overturn traditional values and challenge governmental controls. His bitter resentment of authority was reflected in his own dictatorial treatment of his followers and in his insistence that they likewise renounce all outside influences that represented authority figures or the establishment. In instructing his followers how to deal with "the system" and all it represented, Berg wrote:

You, my dear parents, are the greatest rebels against God and his ways—not us, and unto you will be the greater condemnation; for how can we rebel against a God whom we know not, whose ways you never showed us, and you denied him. . . .

To hell with your devilish system. May God damn your unbelieving hearts. It were better that a millstone be hung around your neck and you be cast into the midst of the sea than to have caused one of these little ones to stumble. You were the real rebels, my dear parents, and the worst of all time. God is going to destroy you and save us, as we rebel against your wickedness, deny your ungodliness, break your unscriptural traditions and destroy your idolatrous System in the name of God almighty.[21]

In his frequent outbursts of verbal violence, Berg condemned anyone he perceived to be standing in his way to power or to be the cause of oppression in society. Often those whom he viewed as deterrents were more imaginary than real, and his rantings appeared to be little more than bizarre neurotic expressions of a sick mind. This was evident in his diabolical sentiment toward Jews. "May God damn the god-damned Jews!" he wrote. "My God, I think if I could get over there and had a gun I think I'd shoot 'em myself! . . . God damn those rich U.S. Jews, those anti-Christ God-hating Jews who hate us. . . . There's nothing but those God-damned anti-Christ horrible hateful awful Jews, the devils incarnate, the devils themselves!"[22]

Sex and Evangelism

The most scandalous activity— and the evangelistic method that has given the movement the most notoriety—is known as "flirty fishing." "It began in London," writes Berg's daughter. "Mo and Maria enrolled in an evening dance school. Dad's ploy was to send Maria out on the dance floor as 'bait' to lure unsuspecting men into their lair. The very first person caught through Flirty Fishing was an Englishman named Arthur. . . . My father boasted that he had found a new method of ministry." Fearing opposition from law authorities in England, Berg took Maria and some women disciples to Tenerife, an island off the northwest coast of Africa, where the tourist lifestyle was free and where "the technique of 'FFing,' as Mo calls it, was developed and refined practically into an artform."[23]

At Tenerife, Berg changed the focus of the Children of God, renaming the group the Family of Love. His followers were engaged mainly in Flirty Fishing and in conducting "Love Church" services, for potential wealthy supporters who were lured into the movement by attractive young women. "This marked a significant change in the movement," writes Deborah Davis. "No longer was every proselyte to the movement expected to become a Forsake All Follower. There were now 'closet' followers who indulged in the Children of God as their religion, but kept their established way of life."[24]

Berg's guidelines for the group's religious prostitution were published in a pamphlet entitled "The Flirty Little Fishy," enumerating one-hundred-and-one admonitions for disciples engaged in this work. It was illustrated with graphic pencil drawings depicting FFing in an underwater marine life setting. The following are a sampling of points emphasized in the pamphlet:

10. IF THEY HAVE TO FALL IN LOVE WITH YOU FIRST before they find it's the Lord, it's just God's bait to hook them! You have to love them, Honey. You have to love them with all your heart and with all your soul and thy neighbor as thyself.

11. DID YOU LOVE HIM TONIGHT as much as you love yourself? Did you hang onto him and try to keep him and try to catch him, or did you let him get

Flirty Fishy illustrations from Mo Letters. From *The Children of God* by Deborah Davis.

away? Lord, have mercy and bring him back!

19. HELP HER, O JESUS, TO BE WILLING TO BE THE BAIT, impaled on Thy hook, torn by Thy spirit, O Lord, crucified on Thy cross, Jesus! Tis a cross, Lord, a hooked cross, a pronged cross—O Jesus, in Jesus' Name!—from which she cannot escape nor those that feed of her flesh, O God, neither can they escape!

84. YOU'RE SUCH A CUTE LITTLE FISHY, SO PRETTY! You roll those big eyes at them and you peck them with that pretty little mouth and you flirt all around them!—You wrap your pretty fins around them and you wiggle your little tail between their legs!

100. MAY GOD HELP US ALL TO BE FLIRTY LITTLE FISHIES FOR JESUS to save lost souls for his creel!—Amen? God bless and make you a flirty little Fishy for Jesus!

101. —And don't forget: There are different kinds of bait!—Some fish like flesh, some like brains, some like beauty, some like spirit and some like 'em all!—Be sure you use the right bait for the right fish![25]

Not surprisingly, Berg's methods were discovered by law enforcement officials, and he was summoned to appear before a judge in Tenerife. He fled the island, however, before the trial date, leaving his female disciples to face the consequences. It would not be the end of his religious prostitution, though, as his 1979 annual report indicates: "Our dear FF'ers are still going strong, God bless'm, having now witnessed to over a quarter-of-a-million souls, loved over 25,000 of them and won nearly 19,000 to the Lord, along with about 35,000 new friends."[26]

David "Moses" Berg and some of his Flirty Fishers. From *The Children of God* by Deborah Davis.

In defending his program of prostitution, Berg spared no words to justify his evil. In an obvious effort to destroy whatever reverence his followers may have had for God, he wrote, "God is a Pimp! How about that!—Boom! He's the biggest one there is—He uses His Church all the time to win souls and win hearts to Him to attract them to Him."[27]

Berg's perverted views of sex went beyond religious prostitution to the point of recommending the sexual abuse of children. In his book *Revolutionary*, he detailed his own life of sexual promiscuity, which began at the age of seven, and he sanctioned lesbianism and polygamy. He likewise advocated the practice of parents sleeping naked with their children and exploring each others bodies.[28]

Doctrinal Distinctives

It is difficult summarizing Berg's theology, for his theological positions have been exposed only through his various letters—and his opinions on different matters have changed significantly over the years from one letter to another. But certainly at the core of his religious belief is the notion that God has chosen him as the prophet for this age. "The King James Version of the Bible, long revered among COG members, is now called the Word of God for yesterday. The 'Mo' letters are the Word of God for today." He also adds heretical stories to the biblical account: "According to Berg, just as God the Father had intercourse with the Virgin Mary in order to have Jesus, so

Jesus enjoyed sexual relations with his female followers, including Mary and Martha. His proof? 'I saw Mary making love to Him in a vision I once had.' "[29]

Berg's confused theological opinions are found throughout his writings, but his work entitled *Islam* includes one of his most comprehensive statements on the nature of God. His style, as usual, is informal and disparaging of orthodoxy:

> Well, if they believe in the virgin birth then they have got to believe in the divinity of Jesus, that He was partly God, even though according to some of their advocates they claim they don't. See they're contradicting their own Bible, because if He was virgin-born then He was the Son of God!
>
> Even so God createth what He willeth—In other words He, Jesus, was a creation of God. Oh, this is exactly according to the Scriptures! . . .
>
> Now you know the Catholics and some are so strong on the so-called Trinity, but I don't even believe in the Trinity. You can't find that word in the Bible, so why should I believe it? But I believe in the Father and I believe in the Son, Jesus, and I believe in the Holy Ghost.
>
> If you want to call it Trinity, all right, but I don't believe it in some ways, the way some overemphasize and stress it, you know. You would think that Jesus just always was, just like God, but in a sense He was not until He was made man, although He was in the beginning and He was a part of God.[30]

When Berg claims to "believe in the Holy Ghost," one must remember that this is a belief in a spirit that is not compatible with historic orthodoxy. Who is the Holy Spirit according to Berg?: the "Goddess of Love," or "God the Mother," who is fre-

quently portrayed as a enticing and sensual young woman.[31]

The End Times

"Probably the most important COG teaching is 'End Time Prophecy,' " writes Jack Sparks. "This concept is their key to understanding every part of the Christian life. If you don't understand this, you can't really follow Christ in these last times." Berg claims that the end times are fast approaching, as evidenced by the wickedness of society, especially that of the Western world. The final collapse will come when communism takes over the western nations, and paves the way for the anti-Christ. Under his rule, professing Christians will show their true colors and will receive the "mark of the beast," spoken of in the Book of Revelation. The Children of God, however, will stand firm as God's faithful remnant of 144,000.[32]

In some ways, Berg's eschatology resembles a dispensational premillennialism, with great emphasis placed on the coming Great Tribulation and the "rapture of the saints." Unlike traditional biblical dispensationalists, however, his eschatology is characterized by date-setting and exclusivism—not entirely unlike the Jehovah's Witnesses and Worldwide Church of God. In 1968, Berg announced that the "End of Time of the Gentiles" and the dawning of the "Restoration of the Remnant of Israel in the Children of God" had occurred. From that time forward, his followers were to spread the message and disassociate with the world—the "Whore of Babylon." Following the "Time of the Great Confusion" during the 1970s, the Anti-Christ would assume power, and the preparation for the Battle of Armageddon would begin. Then would come the Great Tribulation, a time of bitter persecution for all those who would not worship the Anti-Christ, and finally "Around 1993 'The Rapture of the Saints' will occur. The returning Christ and his defenders will do battle with the followers of Anti-Christ, achieve victory, and establish a throne in Jerusalem with COG members serving as important rulers and officials during Christ's 1000-year reign."[33]

Escaping the Clutches

How could young men and women who have given their lives to serve God be caught up in the kind of immorality and blasphemy espoused by David Berg? David Jacks, who served for some time as an archbishop in the movement and who later left the Children of God, told how he was brought into the movement unsuspecting of Berg's perverse doctrine and how the movement changed over the years: "I am convinced that in the early days most members really received Jesus as their personal saviour when they entered the group. . . . But now the Children of God is degenerating. David Berg is getting more and more into pornography, spiritism, astrology and other far-out things—substituting this garbage for the fundamental Christian faith."[34]

For Deborah Davis, Berg's daughter, escaping the clutches of the Children of God was far more difficult than it was for most members. Like Berg's other children, she was a faithful follower of her father, and had risen high in the organization—indeed, so high that in 1972 she was crowned "Queen of God's New Nation." But the lavish banquet and ceremony for her royal coronation could not erase the pain inside her: "By the time of my Coronation, my life was at the very least an atrocity. My marriage had been virtually destroyed, traditional Christian principles obliterated, and all ties with outside relatives severed. Only one thing mattered: The Cause. . . . Normal friendships and relationships were rendered useless."[35]

Very soon after her coronation, Deborah faced the ultimate nightmare in her relationship with her father. He entered her room one night, and as soon as she awoke she realized what was happening: "Memories came to life of the times when Dad had made similar advances—once when I was seven, once when I was twelve. Now I was twenty-six, and Dad was attempting it again under the banner of prophetic revelation: Incest." She was able to stop his advances, but six weeks later she was "demoted, removed from all power and authority, ordered to be subservient to all present [Berg's family], and stripped of my right to the throne." Had she been more mentally stable, Deborah would have been relieved at the news. Instead, she was bitter: "I hated my father. He had ruined everything I held dear in my life." That night while everyone was sleeping, she escaped from the compound, planning to take revenge on her father by committing suicide.[36]

After four days in a cheap hotel room, Deborah relented and returned to her family—realizing that

241

she had no other choice if she wanted to be with her children. She reentered the work, but her life was miserable. Adding to her despondency was the death of her younger brother Aaron, who had been experiencing doubts and suffering mental problems of his own. He fell to his death while mountain climbing in Switzerland, an apparent suicide—at least in Deborah's mind. During this same period of time Deborah's marriage began to unravel. In 1974, she was living with Bill Davis, and they worked together in Europe and Latin America until 1978, when Berg accused Bill of being an "evil magician" and of tampering with his "Mo Letters." As a result he was exiled to a Caribbean island, where he remained faithful to Berg until "Mo Letters" arrived threatening death to Deborah and to the Jews. That was the final straw.[37]

Once they made the decision to leave, they quickly discovered they were not free from the years of turmoil and abuse. "Our real deliverance came three years after we left the Children of God," writes Deborah. "For those three years we wandered on the edges of reality, drifting about in a fog of spiritual darkness. Those were dark years, void of peace and clarity of mind." In 1981, after attending a Christian seminar sponsored by the Institute of Youth Conflicts, they were able to start putting the past behind them and to see a bright future.[38]

Recent Developments

While Deborah and Bill were finding deliverance, Berg continued to be tormented. In 1980, he wrote:

. . . The Devil terrifies me sometimes at night! And I'm getting worse, not better. Sometimes I'm so terrified I could get up and scream.

. . . Sometimes I almost go crazy in the night, I get so terrified and so paranoid! It doesn't really seem to matter how much I pray and cry to the Lord and agonize and fight and battle, or even try to drink to drown my fears. . . .

My God what horrors and nightmares I have![39]

The cause of Berg's nightmares was no doubt multifaceted. Surely the fact that he grew up in a Bible-believing home and yet strayed so very far away from the Lord was a significant factor. Alienation from his family also caused him stress, as did alienation from members of the organization, some of whom later filed lawsuits against him. One of the most celebrated of these cases was brought by his one-time loyal follower Una McManus. She left the movement, repulsed by the flirty-fishing requirement of all young women, but was unable to take her children with her. In court, she not only won custody of her children, but also was awarded one and a half million dollars—an award that will probably never be paid by the movement that has long since gone underground.[40]

There have been others besides Deborah Berg Davis and her husband who have escaped the clutches of the Children of God in recent years, but never without deep personal trauma. In her book, *Children of Darkness*, Ruth Gordon tells how difficult it was for her husband and herself to leave the movement and separate themselves from the man they were convinced was a true prophet of God.

They were fortunate they had each other and could talk out their doubts and fears. "There are no 'coming out' programs for COG members, and the vast majority aren't as fortunate as Mark and I were in readjusting to society," she writes. "When the average COG member leaves the group, he's usually in a rebellious state. . . . He has lived without luxuries of any kind for a long period of time, so his natural tendency is to do exactly what the COG had told him not to do: to gain material possessions, or, for many COG members, to return to their former bondage of drugs or alcohol."[41]

The number of active members who still remain loyal to the Children of God is very difficult to determine, since many of them live abroad and the organization operates under various names, including Family of Love, Heavenly Magic, and Music with Meaning. Most observers believe that membership has dropped since 1980, with current estimates as high as ten thousand.[42]

Chapter 11

The Unification Church: Proclaiming a New Messiah

The Unification Church, commonly referred to as the Moonies, was one of the most publicized and feared religious groups of the 1960s and following. Television and newsprint reporters sensationalized the mass weddings and church deep-sea fishing ventures, and stories of kidnapping and brainwashing abounded. College students of the hippie era were easy prey of aggressive and enthusiastic recruiting efforts, and middle-class parents despaired when they learned their sons and daughters had dropped out of school to sell flowers on the streets of New York— all because they had discovered the message for this age, conveyed by a religious guru who had emigrated to America from Korea. Who was he and what was his mission? His own literature answers this question in unequivocal terms:

With the fullness of time, God has sent His messenger to resolve the fundamental questions of life and the universe. His name is Sun Myung Moon. For many decades, he wandered in a vast spiritual world in search of the ultimate truth. On this path, he endured suffering unimagined by anyone in human history. God alone will remember it. Knowing that no one can find the ultimate truth to save mankind without going through the bitterest of trials, he fought alone against myriads of Satanic forces, both in the spiritual and physical worlds, and finally triumphed over them all. In this way, he came in contact with many saints in Paradise and with Jesus, and thus brought into light all the heavenly secrets through his communion with God.[1]

In many ways, Moon was the embodiment of the Unification Movement, and without his awe-inspiring and winsome personality to inspire enthusiasm within the ranks and attract interest from outsiders, the movement would have quickly faltered. Indeed he had all the characteristics of Max Weber's charismatic leader—one "endowed with supernatural, superhuman, or at least specifically exceptional powers or qualities."[2]

As a superhuman religious figure, Moon has been enveloped in fantasy and myth. Stories are told of how he wept so uncontrollably and profusely when he contemplated the suffering of Jesus that his tears soaked through the floor on his room, making a puddle in the apartment below. One disciple testified that "Moon had a certain magnificence about him. When he walked into the room, you felt blown against the wall. He had an invisible force around him. You felt that if someone were to shoot him, the bullet would swerve." There was also a story that circulated among followers that "whenever he went to the zoo, all the animals would run over to that part of the zoo. When he visited a fish pond, all the fish would swim over to him."[3]

Sun Myung Moon

Who is this man surrounded by mystique who has made such a profound influence on his thousands of followers? Sun Myung Moon is the founder and leader of the Unification Church, officially named the Holy Spirit Association for the Unification of World Christianity. Because this movement reflects to such a very significant degree the personality and the philosophy of Moon himself, the details of his life are crucial. He was born in a village in North Korea in 1920, into a farm family of eight children. As a youth of ten, his parents became Christians and joined with the Presbyterians, an event that changed the course of his life. He was determined at that young age to pursue an education and make an impact beyond his rural village.[4]

The Call of God

During his high school years in Seoul, he became associated with a Pentecostal group which may have helped to satisfy his yearning for mystical and visionary experiences. He later related that on Easter Sunday of 1936, at the age of sixteen, while praying alone on a mountain in North Korea, he experienced an electrifying vision that had a powerful influence on him. Jesus, he testified, appeared to him and audibly instructed him to fulfill the mission that he had failed to complete. "The mission for the accomplishment of God's will on earth has been unfulfilled. You, now, must be responsible for the accomplishment of that mission."[5]

It was this vision that set the stage for Moon to assume the messianic role that he would later fill. According to a short biographical sketch of Moon prepared by the Unification Church, Jesus told Moon that "he was the only one who could do it, and asked him again and again." It was, according to Moon, a difficult decision for him, and the years that followed bore this out. He tells that he wept uncontrollably at times and endured severe testing: "If anyone knew what I passed through during those years, his heart would stop in shock and sorrow. No one is capable of bearing this story."[6]

Part of what Moon "passed through" in the years immediately preceding his full-time vocation in religion was an electrical engineering program at Waseda University in Tokyo. While there, he allegedly joined an underground movement that was working to free his homeland from Japanese domination. For this he was arrested, and when he refused to cooperate with the police investigation "he was beaten and tortured." Following the defeat of the Japanese by the Americans in 1945, he returned to Korea to make further preparations for his ministry. "He married and began making his family into the God-centered ideal of husband and wife in service to God and humanity."[7]

During these years he also began preaching—an endeavor which was bolstered by God's special anointing, according to Unification literature:

> After nine years of search and struggle, the truth of God was sealed into his [Moon's] hands. At that moment, he became the absolute victor of heaven and earth. The whole spirit world bowed down to him on that day of victory, for not only had he freed himself completely from the accusation of Satan, but he was now able to accuse Satan before God. Satan totally surrendered to him on that day, for he had elevated himself to the position of God's true son. The weapon to subjugate Satan then became available to all mankind.[8]

Early Ministry

In 1946, according to J. Isamu Yamamoto, Moon went to South Korea where he spent time with Paik Moon Kim, who was "familiar with the prophecy of a Korean messiah, considered himself a savior and declared it publicly." Kim was six years older than Moon, and had already established a reputation for messianic teaching. "In Paju, a town north

of Seoul and near the 38th parallel, Kim established a community called Israel Soodo Won (Israel Monastery), where Moon spent six months. There he learned what was to become the basis of his own theology as set forth in the *Divine Principle*."[9]

Sun Myung Moon. Courtesy of the Unification Church.

The early years of Moon's ministry were filled with conflict and setbacks. Although there is confusion over various details, he was apparently arrested by communist authorities and imprisoned. According to Unification literature, "the police came and an innocent man [Moon] received a terrible beating, pints of blood flowed from an internal injury. He lost consciousness. His broken body was thrown outside the Daedong Police Station onto the frozen ground. Other disciples carried it away for a Christian burial. The catacomb existence of the underground saint began."[10]

In 1948, Moon was expelled from the Korean Presbyterian Church, and in that same year was again arrested and this time sent to a labor camp, where he remained until released by U.N. forces in 1950. He resumed public preaching with two of his followers and relocated to Pusan a few months later. "He began to preach the Principle there," according to Frederick Sontag, "and members who joined the movement at that time tell of the struggle to survive in a crowded refugee town. Each follower worked to support himself, Reverend Moon as a laborer on the docks. They lived together under primitive conditions in a shack they built themselves."[11]

Much of Moon's time in Pusan was spent transcribing revelations that he claimed came to him directly from God and which became the basis for the *Divine Principle*. Indeed, it is said that he wrote the messages so fast that his aide who sharpened his pencils could not keep up with him. His scribe gave the following account of one such incident:

> Once, very early in the morning, Father woke me up and told me to light the lamp and prepare paper and pencils. Except for that one lamp, everything was dark. Father instructed me to write down what he was going to say, and then he dictated the chapter about the second coming. . . . Father dictated without pause and finished the whole chapter in one sitting. It seemed to me as if Father were reading aloud from a book, since he spoke without stopping, from beginning to end.[12]

Moon moved to Seoul in 1954, and there the Unification Church was officially founded. Growth was slow in the early months with only some fifty followers, "but after August 1954 a major breakthrough occurred. This was due to several events, among them to the activity of Professor Yang who successfully taught *The Principle* at the highly respected Ewha Women's University in Seoul." The students responded positively to her teaching, much to the chagrin of the school officials. Soon two other single women professors joined the movement and began propagating its teachings. All three were dismissed from the school shortly after, and one of them—Young Oon Kim—went on to become the movement's chief theologian.[13]

Korean Religious and Sociological Influences

It is important to keep in mind that Moon's Unification Movement was only one of many such religious groups arising in Korea during this period in history. The religious restrictions imposed on the Koreans during Japanese occupation were lifted after Japan's defeat in World War II. According to David Bromley and Anson Shupe, "The combination of postwar chaos and the removal of these restrictions provided the context for a sudden spurt of religious innovation in terms of doctrines and organizations." Consequently, "Korean society saw the rapid emergence of a number of groups that featured charismatic founders with messianic or prophetic claims and syncretic blends of Confucian, folk, and Christian traditions."[14]

The Unification Church, like many of the other new religious movements springing up, met a need in society at a time when the country was in the grips of a serious economic depression, and when the forces of communism and anticommunism were beginning to polarize the masses. These new religions "struck a responsive chord at the popular level" by offering belief systems that "stressed a distinctly this-worldly orientation in their doctrines, emphasizing not only the hope of human perfectability and salvation but also of achievable prosperity."[15]

Accusations of Immorality

From the very beginning the movement was shrouded in controversy. Soon after he began his preaching, his wife of ten years left him because, according to Moon, "she could not understand my mission." The break-up of this marriage has been a source of embarrassment to the Unification Church, but it is explained by Mose Durst, Moon's authorized biographer, as a natural consequence brought on by an unbelieving wife: "This first wife would divorce him after seeking to destroy the work of his church. She was wildly jealous of the time that Reverend Moon would spend with church members and church activities rather than with her."[16]

Moon's critics argue that Moon's church activities involved more than developing new doctrine—that according to a newspaper account, "A third jailing in 1955 reportedly was for 'causing social disorder' and having bad morals stemming from ritual sex with women in his church." Followers of Moon strongly deny

such allegations, claiming that Moon was arrested for draft evasion and later acquitted of the charges.[17]

The accusation of practicing the ritual of *pikarume* ("cleansing of the blood") was specifically the charge that "Moon purportedly performed intercourse with each female initiate to purify her of the pollution she had inherited from Eve." So widely believed was the charge that "the Korean National Council of Churches, representing various mainline Christian denominations, condemned the movement and refused it membership."[18]

The accusations of practicing ritual sex rites are the most devastating charges lodged against Moon during his early ministry. Are they warranted, or were they simply fabricated by enemies? Sontag rightly points out that "Every strong religious leader has been charged with sexual irregularities. Such stories surround Jesus too and survive in the early literature."[19] Yet, the accusations against Moon were made in many cases by reputable individuals. A Presbyterian minister in Seoul gave the following testimony: "If we believe those who have gone into the group and come out, they say that one has to receive Sun Myung Moon's blood to receive salvation. That blood is ordinarily received by three periods of sexual intercourse. But this fact they themselves keep absolutely secret."[20]

While such stories may be scurrilous lies, critics argue that they are made more believable within the context of Unification theology. A one-time supporter of Moon made the following observations of the sex allegations:

Sun Myung Moon with his wife, Hak Ja Han. Courtesy of the Unification Church.

It is entirely possible that those sexual rituals were a part of the early church in Korea. Since original sin came through the woman's [Eve's] intercourse with Lucifer through which she received his evil characteristics, it is perfectly logical that the reversal of this, woman's intercourse with the perfect man through which she could receive his perfect characteristics, would liquidate original sin. Then, as Adam received Satan's evil characteristics from Eve through intercourse, so man would receive perfect characteristics through intercourse with the woman.[21]

In 1960 Moon married again—some say for the fourth time. His new bride was Hak Ja Han, an eighteen-year-old follower who was less than half his age. That marriage is referred to as "the Marriage of the Lamb," and through it, the couple became the Father and the Mother "of the universe."[22] Han, according to Moon, had been preparing for this role since the age of four, at which time she was blessed by a Korean mystic. "Being so young at the time, she did not remember the experience. But Moon was aware of it from the moment he met her." Moon's own marriage would reverse the sin of Adam and Eve that had infected all mankind. According to Robert Boettcher:

Once the vows of matrimony were exchanged, Moon as Perfect Adam could not let himself fall into the same trap as the first Adam. He "snatched her out of the Satanic world" and taught her to obey. Since Adam fell by being dominated by Eve, he had to reverse the precedent by achieving complete domination over his wife. Obedience training went from formation to growth and perfection, to the point where, after three years, he says, she would sacrifice her life if he so ordered.[23]

Doctrinal Distinctives

Of all the new religious movements that have arisen over the past several decades, the Unification Church is distinct in having not only a "new" theology but a liberal theology. Unlike many cult theologies which, while denying the Trinity and presenting a new eschatology, tend to parallel orthodox Christian theology, the Unification Church seeks to construct an entirely new theology that is heavily indebted to nineteenth- and twentieth-century liberal theologians. This is seen most notably in the writing of Young Oon Kim, whose work *Unification Theology* is a standard textbook of the movement.

Christology

Kim's Christology is a prime example of liberal theology. She is very critical of "the old theology" which maintains that "Jesus' death was an essential part of his messianic mission" and that "by dying on the cross, Jesus has freed men from the law of sin and death." In response, she writes: "The Biblical proof-text interpretation of the life of Jesus described above collapsed like a house of cards as soon as 19th-century scholars began to examine the Scriptures historically." She goes on to say that "Unification thought diametrically contradicts the Fundamentalist view that Jesus' sole mission was to atone for the sins of mankind by dying on the cross."[24]

In her development of Unification Christology, Kim relies heavily on Emil Brunner, a twentieth-century Swiss theologian. This identification not only offers potential intellectual credibility to her and her theological framework but diminishes the role of Christ in the redemption of mankind. "Brunner," she writes, "denies the physical resurrection and bodily ascension of Jesus. These dogmas are not an essential part of the Easter faith in Jesus as the risen Lord."[25]

By diminishing the role of Jesus, Kim paves the way for the exaltation of Sun Myung Moon. This is done not only in denying the orthodox view of his atonement and bodily resurrection, but also of his virgin birth. Citing the work of Leslie Weatherhead, she suggests that Zacharias was most likely the father of Jesus:

Now Zacharias was the priest on duty in the temple when Mary had a mystical experience in which she agreed to be a "slavegirl of the Lord." Though an elderly man, Zacharias was not impotent, for he had just made his wife Elizabeth pregnant in spite of the fact that she was past the normal time of childbearing.

When the angel Gabriel announced to Mary that she would give birth to the Messiah, she replied, "How can this thing be, seeing that I know not a man?" The angel then told her that the Holy Spirit would come upon her and the power of the Most High would overshadow her (Lk. 1:35).

As soon as the young girl heard that she had been chosen to give birth to the Son of God, she "went with haste and entered the house of Zacharias" (Lk. 1:39). By giving herself to the aged priest, Mary would prove that she was truly a handmaiden of the Lord. Such an act of total surrender, far from being considered immoral in the ancient world, revealed the highest degree of spiritual dedication. By uniting with the priest, Mary "found favor with God" (Lk. 1:30).[26]

Despite her heavy reliance on liberal theology, Kim insists that "Liberalism is inadequate because it thinks of Jesus as merely a great teacher or religious genius." She argues that "This notion ignores the basic New Testament claim that Jesus is the Christ, a unique person and not simply one of a number of outstanding religious personalities in history." Yet, while attempting to support her claim that "Jesus is the Christ" on the basis of the New Testament, she criticizes religious fundamentalists because "they derive their faith in Christ from the authority of the Bible. This means that they implicitly substitute faith in Scripture for personal faith in Jesus. In effect, theirs is a religion of the Book rather than trust in Christ."[27]

In claiming that Jesus was the Christ, the messiah, Kim argues that he was "a human being and not a supernatural person" who "came to establish the kingdom of heaven on earth." Why then did he fail? "A distinctive contribution of Unification theology is its radical interpretation of the role of the Baptist. Traditionally, Christians have praised him as the faithful precursor and called him a saint. For the first time it becomes clear that John proved to be 'an offense' to Jesus, a stumbling block in the way of realizing the kingdom."[28]

The Divine Principle

Although much of Kim's theology goes beyond what is specifically stated in the *Divine Principle*, it is certainly compatible with that work, and with the general teachings of Sun Myung Moon. The *Divine Principle* is the basis for all Unification theology, but it has been left to Kim to offer the broader theological ramifications of what was presented in a more straightforward manner in that volume—which is itself an interpretative commentary on the Bible. "Unless you truly know the meaning behind it, the Bible can reveal very little," writes Moon. "The Divine Principle gives the true meaning of the secret behind the verse."[29] This is seen in the section on John the Baptist:

> John the Baptist later became gradually more skeptical about Jesus and at last betrayed him. Naturally, the Jewish people, who believed and followed John the Baptist as the Messiah (Luke 3:15) were forced to stand in the posi-

tion of disbelieving Jesus. . . . Accordingly the foundation of faith that John the Baptist had set up for the first worldwide course for the restoration of Canaan was, in the end, invaded by Satan.[30]

If the *Divine Principle* is in part a commentary on the Bible, is it viewed as scripture itself? This is a difficult question to answer, because the volume is perceived in different ways by church members. Although the *Divine Principle* is based largely on the Bible, the Bible itself is not seen as God's final, infallible revelation of truth. Nor is the *Divine Principle* viewed in this light, though it is, however, clearly regarded as the message from God for this age. It is in that sense considered to be a higher revelation than the Bible. This is indicated in the General Introduction to the book:

> It may be displeasing to religious believers, especially to Christians, to learn that a new expression of truth must appear. They believe that the Bible, which they now have, is perfect and absolute in itself. Truth, of course, is unique, eternal, unchangeable, and absolute. The Bible, however, is not the truth itself, but a textbook teaching the truth. . . . Therefore, we must not regard the textbook as absolute in every detail. . . . Scripture can be likened to a lamp which illuminates the truth. Its mission is to shed the light of truth. When a brighter light appears, the mission of the old one fades.[31]

Indemnity

One of the most persistent and difficult-to-understand doctrines that appears in the *Divine Principle* is that of indemnity. It is a tenet that is at the very core of the Unification teaching that John the Baptist betrayed Jesus. The immediate consequence of John's betrayal was that Jesus himself was compelled to restore through indemnity that foundation of faith set up by John the Baptist. What constituted the indemnity? "Jesus separated himself from Satan by fasting 40 days in the wilderness."[32] Indemnity, according to Kim, goes beyond the secular meaning of payment for a debt. It is a Christian concept—"we atone for our sins through specific acts of penance."[33]

In simple language, indemnity is salvation by works. This is taught very explicitly by Kim: "Because man failed to carry out his original portion of responsibility and fell under Satan's domination, man must restore himself in God's sight by fulfilling the obligations implicit in his status. There is no way but for you to 'work out your own salvation.'" Although she insists indemnity is a Christian concept, she compares it with the Hindu concept of karma. "If one does evil, there is no way to escape its consequences. Somehow and sometime one has to pay the heavy price and restore his proper state through the compensation of numerous good deeds."[34]

Salvation and Perfection

It is difficult to separate the concepts of salvation and perfection in Unification thought. The whole course of human history has progressed for one purpose—to restore the original perfection that God created in the Garden of Eden. "Salvation is the restoration of God's original purpose of creation," writes Mose Durst. "Unlike many religions, which believe that salvation is merely personal, or perhaps primarily mystical, the Unification view is that salvation is the restoration of this world to the fulfillment of God's original ideal of the Kingdom of Heaven on earth."[35]

The Creation and the Fall and Subsequent History

The interpretation of the biblical accounts of Creation and the Fall constitutes a significant portion of Unification doctrine. Indeed, so significant are the theological implications of these that Kim devotes more than one fourth of her book to Creation and the Fall and related issues. In defining God, the creator, Kim begins by challenging "the traditional Christian view that God is masculine or the fairly common notion today that God transcends masculinity and femininity." On the contrary, "Unification theology asserts that God has both masculine and feminine qualities based on the universal fact of polarity and the Biblical record." The marriage union, and integral aspect of attaining perfection once enjoyed by Adam and Eve, reflects this dual nature of God. "Unification theology explains that since God exists in polarity, a husband and wife can reflect more fully God's dual essentialities."[36]

Attaining the state of perfection that characterized Adam and Eve in the Garden of Eden is only possible if one understands the ramifications of their fall into sin and how the effects of that fall can be reversed. Unification theology teaches that there were actually two falls—the spiritual fall and the physical fall. The spiritual fall occurred when Eve had sexual relations with Lucifer in the Garden. "It was not merely adultery in Eve's heart but actual sexual intercourse which affected her in both spirit and body. Their union is called a spiritual fall because the male partner was a spirit rather than a human being." The spiritual fall was followed by a physical fall. "Once Eve realized that she had sinned with Lucifer, she longed to recover God's favor. Since she now realized that Adam was her true partner, she tempted him to unite with her. . . . As Satan had polluted Eve, Eve polluted Adam and both at that moment lost their status as God's children and became servants of Satan, the fallen Lucifer."[37]

The spiritual and physical fall are also referred to as the *vertical* and *horizontal* fall. The *vertical* fall resulted in Satan supplanting God as the spiritual progenitor of mankind. The *horizontal* fall resulted in the fragmentation of human beings among themselves. Eve gave birth to Cain through her sexual relationship with Lucifer; she gave birth to Abel through her sexual relationship with Adam. The breach between these two sons symbolized the *horizontal* fall, placing all humankind into two opposing camps—the communist nations and the democratic nations.[38]

The physical fall was not an inevitable result of the spiritual fall. "If Adam had resisted Eve's temptation, the entire picture would have changed. God would still have been able to work through Adam to restore Eve or create another woman to take her place." But as a result of the physical fall, "original sin is transmitted to all of Adam's descendants and can only be removed when the Mes-

siah comes to restore man's original lineage as a child of God."[39]

God's Need for a Messiah

Theologians have generally evaluated the Fall according to its effects on mankind and Creation in general. But Kim argues the "the worst result of the Fall is its effect upon God. His purpose for creation became frustrated. As a consequence of the Fall, God was virtually deprived of His sovereignty over creation. He lost His hold over the human heart." Thus, it is in alleviating "God's overwhelming grief" that the work of the messiah—Sun Myung Moon—is most crucial:

> What then is the Messiah's ultimate goal? To remove the intolerable burden now pressing down on the divine heart. To liberate not only a suffering humanity but an anguished God as well. Once God is free to exercise His loving sovereignty over creation, His great joy will bring about a cosmic springtime. When the heart of God is filled with gladness, the entire universe will radiate with happiness and harmony.[40]

According to Unification teaching, God has long waited for a messiah to reverse the effects of the physical fall. A large portion of the *Divine Principle* is devoted to the accounts of how Noah failed to do this, as did Abraham, Moses, *and* Jesus. Indeed, "Jesus could not accomplish the purpose of the providence of physical salvation because his body was invaded by Satan. However, he could establish the basis for spiritual salvation . . . through the redemption by the blood of the cross."[41]

Eschatology

Like most of the new religious movements that have appeared on the American scene in the past several generations, the Unification Church places great significance on doctrines of the end times. But unlike most of the other groups, it offers a version of postmillennialism rather than premillennialism. Mose Durst, the president of the Unification Church in America, summarizes this position:

> The concept of the Last Days, from the Unification point of view, is not one of mystery in which God will magically lift up those who are to be saved and turn away from those who are damned. Rather, it is a time when human beings will exercise their full responsibility in turning away from the selfishness of the past to the God-centeredness of the future.[42]

When will the Millennium be ushered in? Moon and his close associates, like so many other leaders of new religions, have not been averse to setting dates. Young Oon Kim initially declared that 1967 would be when the Millennium would begin, but

> in the early seventies Moon expanded the 1967 date into three seven-year "courses": 1960–67 was the course devoted to "restoring" the ideal family institution and consolidating the Korean Church; 1968–1974 was the "national" course during which spiritual and physical foundations were to be established in the "archangel" nation (i.e., the United States); and 1975–1981 was the "international" course in which the UN would take on its global mission.[43]

This prophetic timetable was used in some instances to frighten members into more active recruiting before it was too late. "Father's mission will finish in seven years," warned a training instructor. "If you join Father's seven-year course, this means that this is the most glorious time in your life. At the end of the course, people will go to Father, but he will say that he has finished . . . afterwards even the President or Rockefeller may come but Father will say, My mission is finished."[44]

When the end did not come in 1981, the prophetic timetable was altered. "The current postponement extends to the year 2001, after which time Moon will presumably no longer be around to make further postponements."[45]

Moon's Messiahship

Is the Reverend Sun Myung Moon the Messiah? This is a question that "Moonies" are frequently asked, and the responses vary. The most typical response is somewhat vague, but leaves little doubt that the messiah—the Lord of the Second Advent—could be no other individual than Moon himself. "The Messiah," writes Mose Durst, "will be one who appears in this age as a mode of God's love to a world that knows little about God and even less about His love. He will be one who seeks to bring unity of religion, race, and culture centered upon God's ideal."[46]

However, it is important to understand that the "Messiah," according to Unification doctrine, is more than just a mere man who brings unity and God's love to this age. The final chapter of the Divine Principle deals with the subject of the "Second Advent," and Section III is entitled "Where Will Christ Come Again?" That country is specifically named, and its people are recognized as God's chosen people.

> Now we know . . . that Christ would not come again among the lineal descendants of Abraham, but to the nation that would take their heritage and produce the fruits of it; that the nation which would produce the fruits should be one of the Eastern nations. . . .

> Therefore, the nation of the East where Christ will come again would be none other than Korea. Now, let us prove, from several viewpoints based on the Principle, that Korea should be the nation that can receive the Lord of the Second Advent. . . . The Korean people will become the "Third Israel," God's elect.

The *Divine Principle* goes on to explain that "Abraham's lineal descendants . . . were the First Israel," while the Christians who were "branded as heretics by the First Israel . . . were the Second Israel." Even as the first persecuted the second, so it is not unlikely that the second will persecute the third. "If so, God will have to abandon the Christians when they persecute the Lord of the Second Advent, just as He abandoned the Jewish people who refused Jesus."[47]

Perfection and the Sacred Wedding

The Unification mass wedding ceremony has become one of the more controversial aspects of the church, largely because it is viewed by outsiders as an extravaganza staged for publicity purposes. In reality, it is a fundamental feature of the religion based on the concept of perfection. The seemingly random pairing of couples by Moon is not as peculiar to the Asian observer, who may be used to arranged marriages, as to the Westerner who is often dismayed by the practice. The first of these highly publicized weddings was in 1969, when 777 couples exchanged vows in Seoul, Korea. In 1975 a similar wedding was performed in Seoul for 1,800 couples. Then in the summer of 1982, more than two thousand couples were married in Madison Square Garden, and a few months later an even larger ceremony involving 5,837 was performed by Moon in Seoul. The vows were worded in accordance with the Unification emphasis on the ideal family. One of the questions Moon asked the thousands of couples standing before him was, "Do you pledge, centering upon the ideal family, to become a center of love before the society, nation, world and cosmos?"[48]

The weddings increase in size each time—with each number having a symbolic meaning. Due to the slowed growth of the movement, however, they have not occurred as frequently since the early 1980s. Following the two massive weddings in 1982, Unification Church members had to wait six years until the fall of 1988 for the next wedding, which took place in Korea. Of the 6,516 couples married, the vast majority were pairs made up of individuals with different national origins, including two thousand Korean matched with Japanese. "You will overcome international barriers to create one world of the heart and a blessed race for the future," admonished Moon, who was convinced that such Korean/Japanese marriages would "heal and spiritually cleanse bad feelings."[49]

Church Expansion

During the decade following his second marriage while his wife bore him children, Moon solidified his new movement in Korea and extended out to Japan and the United States, where the first missionary had been sent in 1958 and 1959 respectively. Then, in 1973, after two speaking tours, he and his family moved to the United States where they have maintained an estate in Irvington, New York.[50]

Theologically Oriented Recruitment

As the Unification Church took root in the United States, it was so influenced by sociological and geographical factors that two quite different styles of religion developed— one on the East Coast and the other on the West. According to Bromley and Shupe, "The mainstream East Coast tradition closely followed the theological orthodoxy of *The Divine Principle;* what eventually became the West Coast's 'Oakland Family' was much more humanistic and less theological in its orientation." The earliest efforts at recruitment stressed the theological/intellectual approach, but certain aspects of the message were withheld from the public because it was considered too controversial. "The insider portions of the theology included revelations that Moon was himself either the Messiah or a prophet who immediately foreshadowed his coming, that Korea was the New Israel, and a relatively precise timetable by which

the restoration of man to God could proceed if mankind seized the opportunity."[51]

Psychologically Oriented Recruitment

This method of recruitment and church expansion began to change by the 1970s. During the 1960s when Unification theology was stressed, the conversion rate was slow. Few people were attracted to the new faith, and those who were required a period of weeks and often months before joining the movement. Those who made the commitment, however, were prone to stay with the movement. On the contrary, "the 1970s saw rapid 'conversions' but high rates of defection after a year or two of involvement." This change was due largely to a strategy that focused on the individual rather than on theology. This type of recruitment constituted "little more than fraternity 'rush' promotion tactics—insincere flattery and personal interest, exaggerated friendliness and outgoingness, and inappropriate warmth."[52]

The recruitment strategy of the Unification Church was widely criticized for utilizing tactics that were sometimes compared to brainwashing techniques. After an initial friendly contact was made with an individual—generally a young adult experiencing a time of uncertainty—an invitation was extended first to attend an evening of entertainment and food and then to participate in a weekend retreat. The style and agenda of these retreats were designed to lure the unsuspecting and often very impressionable youths into commitment to the movement without explaining the ramifications of their decision. "There they found a rigorous, fast-paced schedule of group activities with lectures and discussions on humanistic topics interspersed among recreational activities such as swimming and volleyball." A "buddy system" insured that the guests would never be alone or in unsupervised situations with other guests. "Individuals were encouraged to drop inhibitions and participate fully in expressive activities such as introducing oneself to as many persons as possible in thirty seconds, engaging in pantomime games and exercises that otherwise might have seemed 'silly,' 'group hugs,' and frequent, vociferous cheers." Although this style of recruitment did not bring in theologically committed members and defections were common, the overall effect was to dramatically increase the size of the movement nationwide from hundreds in the early 1970s to thousands by the end of the decade.[53]

The West coast wing of the Unification Movement—the Oakland Family—was directed in the 1970s by Mose Durst, who would later become the president of the American branch of the Unification Church. He continued in the style of his predecessor by downplaying Moon's conservative anticommunist stance. "This is not to say that the Oakland Family members were unfamiliar with either Rev. Moon or *The Divine Principle*," wrote Bromley and Shupe. "But the overarching emphasis on Moon's messianic purpose, his legitimation as a charismatic authority, the pervasive threat of communism, and America's unique archangelic role in helping to

usher in the millennium were seriously underplayed. . . ."[54]

Political Connections

One of the most significant developments to occur during the early decades of the Unification Movement was the arrival of Sun Myung Moon in America in 1971. Before this, the United States was not a vital factor in Moon's theology of the kingdom of God on Earth. With his change of residence and his realization that America offered great potential for the movement's numerical and financial growth, however, this nation became a key element in his prophetic timetable.[55]

How could the new focus on America correlate with the emphasis on Korea as the "Third Israel" in the *Divine Principle*? Amazingly, the shift was made quite smoothly. The Unification Church sees itself as having a vital role in the world political order of the twentieth century and beyond, and fighting communism has been from the earliest days a top priority. This anticommunist stance is rooted deeply in Unification theology. Indeed, to an outside observer it would appear as though the Bible has been interpreted in light of the South Korean fear of communism. The seeds of communism germinated in the Garden of Eden, and they took root in the soil cultivated by Cain. According to the *Divine Principle*, "the Cain-type view of life matured to form the communist world of today," and "the Abel-type view of life has matured to form the democratic world today."[56]

It is crucial that Korea reflect more of the Abel-type democracy because

Korea is the Third Israel, the birth-place for the messiah, the Lord of the Second Advent, namely Moon himself. Yet, it is in America where Moon has concentrated his efforts. The reason for this is that the United States is the world's leading democracy, and thus "America must be God's champion."[57]

But while Moon would champion democracy over communism (treating them almost as though they were opposite philosophies), he believes that neither has the potential to solve the world's problems. "What is needed, then, is a third alternative, a movement based upon a new understanding of truth, one which gives hope by presenting a new vision of world society. This is, in fact, the Unification Movement, with the Unification theology—a complete, systematic world view grounded in truth and absolute values."[58]

Moon not only sought to mix theology and politics in theory, but also to mix them on a very practical and personal level and to tie the political aspect of his ministry with his effort to gain credibility and new members. From the very beginning of his residence in America, his followers sought to promote both Moon and the movement through mass rallies. Since Moon himself did not have the fame needed to draw thousands of people, political figures were often solicited to lend their support. The return for them was free advertising and publicity with the hope of attracting young activists into their political camp. Support was bipartisan, ranging from Senator Edward Kennedy to William F. Buckley, Jr.[59]

In most instances, the political figures who lent their support to Moon were not seen as being connected to his theological framework. Such was not the case with President Nixon, however. Nixon, like other politicians, had posed for pictures with Moon, and Moon became a strong supporter—particularly during the Watergate crisis. Indeed, Moon testified that while he was in Korea in 1973, he had a vision from God enjoining him to forgive Nixon, and he insisted that "at this moment in history God has chosen Richard Nixon to be President of the United States." Full page advertisements in support for the President, and paid for by the Unification Church, soon appeared in newspapers all over the country—all in an effort to preserve the world's largest "Abel-type" democracy.[60]

Religious Practices and Lifestyle

That the "Moonies" would have their own "bible," revere their leader as the "messiah," and participate in mass weddings, among other things, is viewed by most Americans as merely the peculiarities of just one more "cult." But what roused media interest and fear and outrage among vast segments of the population were the movement's practices—especially those involving proselytizing and solicitation of funds.

All full-time members of the Unification Church—at least in the early years—were expected to be very actively involved in winning converts and fund-raising, with the exception of those who were studying at the Unification Seminary, and even they were expected to forfeit weekends and vacations to go into New York City to help out in the work. For most "Moonies" this has meant forsaking their previous way of life and committing themselves entirely to the movement. Personal possessions, including automobiles and homes, were expected to be relinquished to the church. "Careers and career aspirations as well, not at little personal sacrifice, were also jettisoned." One young woman from New Zealand—the first woman from that country to become a civil engineer—testified that she had painfully and reluctantly given up that career for the cause. And another young woman gave up her opportunity to represent Iceland in its international volleyball competition.[61]

Deprograming

How could any intelligent, respectable, middle-class young adult give up family and future, unless that individual had been brainwashed—or worse yet, kidnapped and then brainwashed? Such charges were made by many despairing parents, anticultists of varying stripes, and reporters who were sometimes seeking to sensationalize their stories. Sometimes the response to the alleged kidnapping and brainwashing was kidnapping and brainwashing. Under the guise of professionalism, deprograming became a widely-used method of last resort in bringing young adults out of cults in the 1960s. Members of the Unification Church were certainly not the only ones targeted, but because of the movement's highly questionable and misleading proselytizing tactics, they were likely victims.

Deprograming was also used in many situations involving members of The Way International, the Children of God, and the Hare Krishnas. But the technique was not always limited to groups that could be classified as cults. Indeed, the issue at times had virtually nothing to do with whether an individual had originally come into the particular group through kidnapping or brainwashing, nor even what the actual teaching of the group was. Ted Patrick, the nation's most publicized and notorious deprogramer, often failed to distinguish between those who joined a group willingly and those who might have been wrongfully duped. In an interview with a reporter, he revealed this lack of discernment:

> Hell, Jimmy Carter's sister is one of the biggest cult leaders in the nation. Ruth Stapleton uses all the same techniques they do. She's nothing but a cult leader. . . . she programs people. I've seen members do it in meetings, and she's got a mailing list like you wouldn't believe. I also have reason to think she's using the same techniques on members of the government. I saw one Cabinet member on TV talking about how he was born again through Ruth Carter Stapleton. He looked just like a Moonie, glazed eyes, the works. . . .[62]

In his book *Let Our Children Go!* Patrick defends the philosophy and methods of deprograming. Indeed, he boastfully described instances of abuse that are more characteristic of torture than what might be described as "exit counseling." This was true in the case of Wes, who became involved with the New Testament Missionary Fellowship while he was studying at Yale University, which, according to Patrick, "gradually isolated [him] from the rest of the university as a result of frequent Bible study sessions and prayer meetings." With the help of the youth's father and uncle, Patrick "rescued" him in a brutal fashion. Wes screamed for assistance—"Help! Help! They're kidnapping me. Call the police! Help me!"—but to no avail. The three men then forced him into their car.

> Wes had taken up a position facing the car, with his hands on the roof and his legs spread-eagled. There was no way to get him inside while he was braced like that. I had to make a quick decision. I reached down between Wes's legs, grabbed him by the crotch and squeezed—hard. He let out a howl, and doubled up, grabbing his groin with both hands. Then I hit, shoving him headfirst into the back seat of the car and piling in on top of him.[63]

"Moonies" were also treated in this fashion by Patrick and other deprogramers. Many of the deprogramers were involved not for philosophical reasons but entirely for the money and excitement the "profession" offered. Distressing testimonies are given by "Moonies" about deprogramings they have endured, many of which have made these individuals only more committed to the Unification Movement.

Mysticism, Spiritism, and the Occult

Themes relating to psychic phenomena and the supernatural are a significant aspect of Unification thought. Here again Young Oon Kim challenges what she maintains is the conservative Protestant position: "According to Fundamentalists, to explore the evidence for psychic phenomena is to dabble in a forbidden region labeled the occult. This attitude is rather peculiar since the Bible is saturated with parapsychological experiences." In her defense of psychic spiritual experiences, she not only cites such scholars as William James, known for his classic work *The Varieties of Religious Experience*, but also the well-known seventeenth-century religious mystic and psychic Emanuel Swedenborg, who founded the Church of New Jerusalem. According to Kim, the spirit world corresponds with the natural world and cooperates with it. "Beneficial spirits aid people to accelerate their work for God and in turn they can advance to a higher level through the persons they have helped. . . . Low spirits possess people to do destructive acts and give vent to their deep-seated frustration and bitterness."[64]

These beneficial spirits are utilized in the missionary outreach of the church. Church members are expected to sacrifice in various ways in order to "indemnify" their work. Fasting is one such typical sacrifice. "Setting a condition" is another. This involves "a process in which members attempted to make contact with the spirit world and mobilize its forces in achieving some restoration-related goals. If members were able to set up the proper spiritual conditions, these would act as a magnet to draw spiritual forces and influence human events."[65]

It is clear that the Unification Church, like many of the unorthodox cults that have arisen in recent generations, borrows from the occult. This aspect of the movement turned into a well-publicized sensation in 1988, when it was reported that Moon's son, Heung Jin Nim, who was killed in an automobile accident in 1984, had come back to life in the body of one of Moon's devotees from Zimbabwe. Dick Richards, a former member of the Moon organization, reported that "in mid-November [1987], I was told that a black brother from Africa . . . had been prepared by Jesus . . . and that Heung Jin Nim had assumed his body. . . . It obviously scared a lot of people there . . . but they went along with the whole thing because it came from Reverend Moon, the Messiah." When asked about the phenomenon, the public relations director at the Unification Seminary insisted that Moon does not believe in reincarnation. "She explained that Moon's dead son is in a place of authority in the spirit world and is sending messages back to the world of the living by channeling through the Zimbabwean."[66]

This channeling involved the transmission of messages from the spirit world to the physical world, and as such the Zimbabwean became a celebrity of sorts, traveling throughout the world offering insights from the "spirit world." Although he reportedly held "confessionals," during which time he physically meted out punishments to church members, a church official defended him as "a brother with his own personality" who "has had his own spiritual connection of oneness with Rev. Moon's son, and so he receives teaching and spiritual inspiration and guidance, and passes it on to the members."[67]

Missionary Outreach

Since the first missionary was sent abroad in 1958, the Unification Church has viewed missionary work as a top priority. Uniting people of all world religions is a central theme of the movement, and missionaries are the vehicle to bring about this one world religion under the leadership of Moon. In 1975, with missionaries already in more than thirty countries, Moon launched a worldwide blitz. It was a strange, if not utterly bizarre, foreign missionary program. Two hundred and sixty-three missionaries were commissioned to go to some one hundred countries to begin pioneer work. In most instances, the missionaries were sent in teams of three—an American, a Japanese, and a German—without any groundwork having been laid in the country to which they were assigned.[68]

Not surprisingly, there were many problems—particularly communication barriers between the missionaries themselves and between the missionaries and their target groups. The church has seen growth in some areas of the world such as Brazil and the Philippines, but the ideal of unifying all religions appeared to be doomed from the beginning.

In addition to its regular missionary outreach endeavors, the Unification Church has a number of "mission" organizations that are not officially under the direct control of the church. The International Relief Friendship Foundation (IRFF) is an example. It was founded by church members for the purpose of church outreach, but it has remained a separate relief organization, which allows it to benefit from government funding for many of its projects. These projects have been conducted in some forty countries throughout the world and include providing such community needs as irrigation systems and elementary schools.[69]

Obtaining charitable donations and endorsements for these organizations has frequently been done without any indication that either the Unification Church or Sun Myung Moon are involved. Indeed, the association has been so elusive that well-known figures have lent their support without discovering the Moon connection until some time later. Bob Jones, III, the president of Bob Jones University, was one such individual to get caught in the Moon web. The following letter from him was printed in *Christianity Today* in 1974:

In the May 10 issue of *Christianity Today* it is stated in "Personalia" that I am on the Advisory Board of the Korean Cultural and Freedom Foundation, Inc., "a front group for the Unification Church." It is true that for a period of three or four months I was a member of their Advisory Board, having been asked to join in the interest of compassion and concern for Korean children. I can certainly be for that and was glad to have my name used accordingly. However, in March it was called to my attention that this organization was affiliated with Mr. Sun Myung Moon and his World Unification Movement. . . .[70]

Contemporary Perspective

One of the most striking aspects of the growth and decline of the Unification Movement in the United States pertains to the prophecies of doom and destiny that never materialized. The Unification Church, more than any other cult of the 1970s, generated terror in the minds of many people. The news media fanned the flames of fear by calling attention to political conspiracies, hidden wealth, and a burgeoning membership. But in comparison to other nontraditional religious movements and other philosophies that have been on the increase in recent decades, the Unification Church has had very little impact. Neither the prophecies of doom or destiny have come to fruition. The Millennium has not been ushered in by a messiah from Korea and there has been no unification of the world religions. Far from uniting the religions, the Unification Church has only created another faction among the religions.

What went wrong? Why did Moon fail to fulfill his own expectations and the fears of his adversaries? David Bromley and Anson Shupe offer a simple explanation that sums up Moon's theological and personal difficulties in creating a new religion in America—a religion based on the Bible but radically different than orthodox Christianity. "One does not rewrite the basic meaning of both the Old and New Testaments," they write, "and then, in lecture format, easily persuade an entire culture (including powerfully entrenched religious institutions and millions of adherents) that this new interpretation is superior." An even greater problem for Moon was the language barrier: "the incongruity of a prophet who claimed to understand the Bible better than all the Western theologians and scholars taken together but yet who could not express that truth without the aid of an English-speaking interpreter remained a persistent stumbling block."[71]

Coalitions and Conferences

But despite its failure to attract masses of American young people into its ranks as willing subjects, the Unification Movement has seen success in its more hidden agenda of infiltrating and gaining influence in various religious and secular organizations. One such organization is the American Freedom Coalition, a political action lobby representing conservative Christians on such issues as antiabortion and anticommunism. The organization, however, has come under fire by some critics since it was revealed that dozens of employees and officials are members of the Unification Church.[72]

Joining existing organizations is only one method the Unification Church uses to "infiltrate" American religion and politics. "In what could be called a legitimacy blitzkrieg," writes a reporter in *Christianity Today*, "the Moonies are launching a multi-pronged, sophisticated campaign to become accepted in America. Biblical Christianity, already arrayed against dozens of cults and competing philosophies, faces a newly formidable foe. The Moonies are vying for their place in the sun." This campaign focuses on professional conferences that attract scholars and leaders in religion and education throughout the country.

The most-publicized legitimation tactic is probably the Moonie professional conferences. Most are organized under the auspices of the church's New Ecumenical Research Association (New ERA). The Moonies have convened with evangelicals, scientists, lawyers, and journalists.

Moon's theology foresees a day when science and religion will be unified, and so there have been 10 annual conferences on the "unity of the sciences." Scientists from such institutions as the Sorbonne, Oxford, Southern Methodist University, Harvard, and Yale have attended the conferences. The conferences are often held in such exotic locations as the Bahamas, and participants' transportation is paid.[73]

Other programs sponsored by the Unification Church come under more patriotic rubrics such as the American Constitution Committee or vague titles such as the Collegiate Association for the Research of Principles, but all of them have the same underlying purpose of promoting Moon's movement. Christians should be aware of these organizations, warns Robert Dugan, the director of the National Association of Evangelicals' Washington Office on Public Affairs. "To join a coalition of which they are a major partner, for a future agenda of political input which is unspecified, I think is extremely dangerous and plays into their hands."[74]

Professional Publications

More than any other alternative religion on the American scene today, the Unification Church has been committed to scholarly research in the field of new religions—with a slant, not unexpectedly, that is favorable to its own interests. Volumes such as *Lifestyle: Conversations with Members of the Unification Church* and *Evangelical-Unification Dialogue* have been published by the church itself, but other works have been published through reputable non-Unification publishers. John T Biermans', *The Odyssey of New Religions Today* is an example. Here Biermans seeks to compare the Unification Church with persecuted movements of the past such as Jews, Catholics, Quakers, Mormons, and Baptists. He rightly points out that the Unification Church has been falsely identified with scandal and sensational news stories that involved other religious movements:

> Uc members. . .are accused of a myriad of practices which have absolutely no basis of fact in the Unification Church. Accusations range from shaving of heads to suicide pacts and promiscuous sexual practices. These particular practices can be traced to the following groups: shaving of heads is done by the Hare Krishna Movement; members of the People's Temple took part in a suicide pact in 1979; and the accusation of promiscuous sexual practices apparently derived from activities of the Children of God and the Rajneesh organization.[75]

In its effort to present itself as just another persecuted minority religion, the Unification Church has succeeded in gaining the sympathy of many prominent intellectuals. Most evangelicals, however, are less inclined to forget the excesses of the past and to ignore the doctrinal heresy of the movement.

Court Cases

In recent years, it has been court litigation, more than anything else, that has focused media attention on the Unification Church. The most highly publicized case was one involving the alleged income tax evasion of Sun Myung Moon. The case was initiated after Senator Robert Dole prodded the Internal Revenue Service to audit the Unification Church. Following a five-year investigation, the IRS found that Moon, like certain Catholic bishops and other religious leaders, had placed donations to the church in accounts under his own name. Religious leaders and organizations rallied to the legal support of Moon, fearing that their own tax-exempt status might be in jeopardy were he to lose the case. The outcome, according to John Biermans, was a mixed blessing for the movement.

> The final upshot of the case was that the Supreme Court refused to hear the case and Rev. Moon served thirteen months in a federal correctional institution, from July 20, 1984 to August 20, 1985. This was an extremely painful period for Rev. Moon, his family, and for the entire movement. Nevertheless, it is believed by many people that Rev. Moon may have gained far more than he lost from this difficult experience. In the eyes of many individuals, particularly clergymen, Rev. Moon is a victim of religious persecution. Because of his willingness to go this course voluntarily, without complaint, he is now seen as a leading champion and spokesman for religious freedom.[76]

Another widely publicized court case has been *Molko and Leal v. Holy Spirit Association*. The suit was brought by David Molko and Tracy Leal, two former members of the Unification Church. In it they charged that the identity of the movement had not been disclosed to them in 1979 when they first became involved and they claimed that they were "hooked" as a result of "brainwashing" or "coercive persuasion." The case was dismissed by lower courts in California. Indeed, the California Court of appeals ruled unanimously "that courts could not analyze church recruiting techniques without conducting a constitutionally forbidden inquiry into the authenticity of church doctrine." Despite that ruling, on October 17, 1988, the California Supreme Court ruled that the Unification Church could be brought to trial by these two former members.[77]

Like the case relating to taxes, this decision could have ramifications for other religious groups—including various evangelical movements and individuals who could be charged with failure to properly disclose their identity in evangelistic efforts.

Through its various religious conferences, coalitions, publications, and court cases, the Unification Church has taken amazing strides in its ambition to move into the mainstream of religion, but the doctrines of the movement remain as far removed from orthodoxy as they were when they were formulated decades ago in Korea.

Chapter 12

The Hare Krishnas:
Transplanted Hinduism

There has always been a certain fascination in the Western world with Eastern religion—a fascination that has been demonstrated by the popularity of New Thought and Theosophy in past generations and by contemporary Hindu sects such as the International Society of Krishna Consciousness (ISKCON or the Hare Krishnas), Transcendental Meditation, and Rajneesh. Besides these highly-publicized Hindu sects, there are literally hundreds of other lesser known Eastern-oriented groups led by gurus of all types. This heightened interest in Eastern religion is also evidenced by the enormous preoccupation on the part of Americans with the New Age Movement, many aspects of which are deeply influenced by the Hindu concept of God and man, as well as by Hindu meditative and mystical practices.

The invasion of Hinduism into the United States in recent decades has been prompted in part by developing trends in India. One of the oldest and most prominent features of Hinduism is the guru, those spiritual masters who withdrew from society and escaped to remote areas in an effort to renounce pleasure and material gain and to seek truth through meditation. They were usually surrounded by a band of devoted disciples, and their lifestyle was characterized by privation and solemnity. In more recent times, however, this picture of the guru has changed.

. . . . The ashram in its earlier form has all but disappeared, and the guru has carried on his work in an urban setting, either in the homes of his disciples or in retreat centers in towns or cities such as Varanasi, Vrindaban, Hardwar, and Rishikesh. Although some gurus have small followings, a few have large numbers of devotees, called chelas. These charismatic gurus have become founders of personality cults. In contrast to the simplicity of life in the earlier ashrams, some of the present cult centers are "big business," with impressive buildings, extensive institutions, and active publishing houses.[1]

Another characteristic of this new style guru is zeal for overseas expansion. The West has proven to be a lucrative market for Eastern philosophy, and the gurus have offered a wide variety of lifestyles and religious practices to satisfy almost every taste. The most visible and controversial of the Hindu religious sects which have come to America has been the Hare Krishnas. It is often viewed by the uninitiated as a counterfeit of true Hinduism; yet this movement, perhaps more than others imported from India, is authentically Hindu. In researching the movement, Larry Shinn found it to be "an American Krishna tradition that was authentically Indian and self-consciously so. To step into the Krishna temple in Berkeley or Dallas is to enter a world of images, cuisine, and activities that can be found throughout northern India in homes and communities devoted to Krishna."[2]

Sri Krishna Caitanya

The Hare Krishna movement actually dates back to early sixteenth-century India, when the Hindu saint Sri Krishna Caitanya called his followers to renewed spiritual devotion to Krishna through meditative absorption or constant chanting of Krishna's name. His devotees expressed this devotion by chanting and dancing in the temples and in the homes, but "before long, these devotees became so overwhelmed and intoxicated by the chanting of the holy names of God that they burst out of their homes into the streets." With their drums and cymbals they danced and sang praise to Krishna. Caitanya often led his ecstatic followers, while crowds of thousands gathered to watch and join in. His renewal of ecstatic devotion soon spread throughout the province of Bengal, and Caitanya was widely recognized as a noted Hindu reformer. "Thus Sri Caitanya," writes Garuda Dasa, "who is accepted by devotees as an incarnation of Godhead and by historians as one of the greatest devotional mystics in the history of the world's religions, introduced this most dramatic expression of devotion, known as *sankirtana*. . . . Nearly five centuries later, in 1966, *sankirtana* was introduced to the West. . . ."[3]

A. C. Bhaktivedanta Swami Prabhupada

Like most of the Hindu sects that have appeared on the American scene in recent years, the Hare Krishna movement was introduced by an Indian guru convinced he had something to offer the West that could potentially change the entire world. The founder of this movement, A. C. Bhaktivedanta Swami Prabhupada, arrived in the United States in 1965, at the age of seventy, to begin his mission—a mission motivated by love for Lord Krishna, according to his devoted biographer:

He was now in America. He was in a major American city, rich with billions, populated with millions, and determined to stay the way it was. Prabhupada saw Boston from the viewpoint of a pure devotee of Krsna. He saw the hellish city life, people dedicated to the illusion of material happiness. All his dedication and training moved him to give these people the transcendental knowledge and saving grace of Krsna consciousness, yet he was feeling weak, lowly, and unable to help them on his own. He was but "an insignificant beggar" with no money. He had barely survived the two heart attacks at sea, he spoke a different language, he dressed strangely—yet he had come to tell people to give up meat-eating, illicit sex, intoxication, and gambling, and to teach them to worship Lord Krsna, who to them was a mythical Hindu god.[4]

Early Life

Prabhupada was born into a prosperous family in Calcutta in 1896. His father was a very devout follower of Krishna who frequently entertained Hindu teachers and gurus in his home and made certain his son was immersed in the enlightenment they had to offer. He also provided his son an excellent formal education at private schools and colleges. Indeed, Prabhupada enrolled at Scottish Churches' College, "a prestigious Christian school in Calcutta, where. . . the study of the Bible and Christian doctrine was compulsory."[5]

At the age of twenty-four, he graduated from the University of Calcutta, where he studied English, philosophy, and economics. He married, became successful in a pharmaceutical company, and actively supported Gandhi in his pacifist movement for independence. But he was not satisfied with his life—not until he met a guru who won his allegiance and brought him into the Goudiya Vaishnava Society, a Hindu sect founded by Caitanya hundreds of years earlier. Initially, Prabhupada divided his commitments between his family, his work, and his religious calling. But "at the age of fifty-eight, he renounced his wife and five children,

according to a Hindu custom. And four years later he likewise abandoned all connection with society, economics, and his large chemical concern, and assumed the saffron robes of a Hindu monk."[6]

A. C. Bhaktivedanta Swami Prabhupada.
Photo taken from ISKCON Publicity brochure.

Prabhupada's renunciation of his wife and family came only after a lengthy period of alienation. His marriage to her had been arranged when he was in his early twenties and she was eleven. She had been raised in a wealthy family, and was very unhappy when he began devoting more of his time and money to his religious activities than to his family and business. After he suffered business losses, she moved back with her family. He accepted the turn of events as an inevitable result of being a true devotee of Krishna. Krishna had prophesied this in the *Srimad Bhagavatam:* "When I feel especially merciful toward someone, I gradually take away all his material possessions. His friends and relatives then reject this poverty-stricken and most wretched fellow." The final break in the marriage came in 1954 when his wife traded a Krishna scripture for some sweets to eat with a cup of tea. He regarded her action as unconscionable, especially since he considered tea an "intoxicant" and had previously warned her that if she persisted in drinking tea he would forsake her.[7]

Years later, when Prabhupada was asked about his desertion of his wife, he responded: "Woman is not given up. She is always dependent—on her father as a young girl and then on her husband, then on her children, older sons. I was in India recently and my son saw me, but my wife could not see me. . . . There is no divorce. She's a devotee of another swami."[8]

Planting the Seed in America

Prabhupada remained in India during his early years as a monk, but he could not forget the order he received from his guru before the teacher died: to carry Krishna consciousness to the West. He waited for thirty years to carry out that commission, and when he did sail to the United States it was with the intention of remaining only a few months. Nothing that occurred during his first months in America offered any promise of success. Indeed, his initial presence in New York City went virtually unnoticed. He worked out of a dingy storefront near the Bowery, where, dressed in his saffron robes, he offered lectures on the *Bhagavadgita* in broken English. His message was one of austerity. He had been warned that the only way to attract a following in America would be to Westernize both his clothing and eating habits, and to "stress the tolerant all-paths-lead-to-truth interpretation of Hinduism," but he was determined to organize a movement that would practice strict asceticism.[9]

Within months, Prabhupada attracted several disciples, who sat around him on the floor under the glare of a bare light bulb and listened to his lectures. From that tiny nucleus he launched his public appeal—a colorful demonstration of dancing and chanting that immediately caught the attention of the media. It also caught the attention of hippies and others who were eager to become involved in activities that represented a defiance of the establishment. Among his early followers were poet Allen Ginsberg and other free thinkers who had found success in the world of Greenwich Village art and music. For some, the austere teachings of the sandal-clad monk was a fascinating alternative that at least deserved debate, if nothing else.

Sex was frequently a topic of discussion, prompted by Prabhupada's conviction that sex offered only an illusion of pleasure. When challenged on the subject, he minced no words. "Sex pleasure binds us to this material world birth after birth," he emphasized, supporting it with a testimony of a Hindu Krishna devotee: "Since I have become Krsna conscious, whenever I think of sex life with a woman my face at once turns from it, and I spit at the thought." On another occasion, the debate was carried further.

Statue of A. C. Bhaktivedanta Swami Prabhupada at St. Louis, Missouri Temple.

"What about sex?" asked the ISKCON attorney, Steve Goldsmith, one evening, speaking out from the rear of the crowded temple.

"Sex should only be with one's wife," Prabhupada said, "and that is also restricted. Sex is for the propagation of Krsna conscious children. My spiritual master used to say that to beget Krsna conscious children he was prepared to have sex a hundred times. Of course, that is most difficult in this age. . . ."

"But sex is a very strong force," Mr. Goldsmith challenged. "What a man feels for a woman is undeniable."

"Therefore in every culture there is the institution of marriage," Prabhupada replied. "You can get yourself married and live peacefully with one woman, but the wife should not be used as a machine for sense gratification. Sex should be restricted to once a month and only for the propagation of children."

Hayagriva, who was seated just to the Swamiji's left, beside the large dangling cymbal, spoke out suddenly.

"Only once a month?" And with a touch of facetious humor he added loudly, "Better to forget the whole thing!"

"Yes! That's it! Very good boy." Swamiji laughed, and others joined him. "It is best not to think of it. Best just to chant Hare Krsna. . . . That way we will be saved from so much botheration. Sex is like the itching sensation, that's all. And as when we scratch, it gets worse, so we should tolerate the itching and ask Krsna to help us. It is not easy. Sex is the highest pleasure in the material world, and it is also the greatest bondage."[10]

For Krishna devotees, commitment to the cause meant a total surrender to an entirely new way of life that involved not only sexual abstinence but also communal living, Hindu dress, a vegetarian diet, and endless hours chanting and dancing and working on the streets to earn money for the movement. This public activity (dancing, chanting, begging, and selling on the streets) is called *sankir-tana*, and was introduced by Lord Caitanya in the sixteenth century. It is considered by many to be "the heart and soul of the movement," and has become the most controversial aspect of the organization. Initially the devotees wore only traditional Hindu attire, but that changed and soon they were discovered dressing as Santa Claus and claiming to be collecting money for humanitarian causes. Hundreds of millions of dollars were brought into the coffers by this means of deception during the 1970s.[11]

Worship and Temple Rituals

The Hare Krishnas, more than any other of the highly publicized religious cults in America, require a strict regimen of religious ritual and worship. Each convert is bonded to a guru through an elaborate initiation ceremony, during which time the initiate takes four vows (to abstain from meat, sex, intoxicants, and gambling), receives a new spiritual name and a set of rosary beads (to be recited 108 times each day), and a sacred necklace. There is a second initiation ceremony, during which time male initiates receive a sacred thread to wear, along with a *gayatri mantra*—a Vedic prayer—the latter given to females as well as males. The daily temple schedule is strenuous, though it is not strictly followed by devotees who have employment outside the commune or who have farm work or other duties that keep them away for long hours.

A.M. 3:30 Rise and shower

4:15 Morning deity worship (*Mangala-aratrika*)
5:00 Chant *japa* (Krishna mantra)
7:30 Scripture reading and lecture
8:30 Breakfast—End of morning devotions
9:00 Work assignment
12:00 Noon meal (*Prasadam*)
1:00 Work assignment
4:15 Afternoon deity worship
5:00 Shower, dinner, and free time
7:00 Evening class at temple
8:30 Retire for the night[12]

Becoming a devotee means total commitment to Krishna and thus often entails quitting college or leaving a position of employment. Prabhupada defends this commitment by quoting Hindu scriptures: "One who has fully surrendered to Krsna no longer has any responsibility to demigods, great sages, relatives, society—anyone." When asked by a devotee whether Krishna conscious parents have a responsibility to care for their children, Prabhupada responded: "Yes. But *why* are we taking care of the children? Just to make them Krsna conscious. This is our responsibility in Krsna consciousness. . . . This is why we are taking so much care to train our children in the *gurukulas* [ISKCON schools]."[13]

Fund-raising

The allotted time for daily communal worship and private rosary chanting is in many instances more an ideal than a reality. One reason for this is the pressure placed on devotees in their fund-raising obligations.

Hare Krishnas have become infamous for their street and airport selling—sometimes pretending to represent a reputable charity to dupe an unwary donor. It is a difficult life, and one that seems to run counter to the Krishna *consciousness* each initiate is expected to develop. "It can be hard sometimes to keep one's mind on Krishna," lamented one devotee, "when there is a quota to meet or an angry person to deal with."[14]

Doctrinal Distinctives

In many ways, the Hare Krishnas are unique among the Hindu sects having an impact in America since the 1960s—their extreme asceticism and their public demonstrations of noisy ecstatic worship are most obvious. But equally unique is their view of God. Hinduism is not a religion revealing a supreme personal God. Indeed, such a doctrine would seem to go against the very fabric of Hinduism with its multiplicity of gods and its concept that All is One. But Hindu tradition is multifaceted, and part of that tradition encourages the worship of a single god.

The Nature of God, Krishna, and Jesus

At the encouragement of Prabhupada, Hare Krishnas address their worship to Krishna, who is revered as the personal creator, the author of the *Bhagavad-gita*, and the "Supreme Personality of the Godhead." In claiming the supremacy of Krishna, Prabhupada teaches that the "so-called Hindu trinity (Brahma, Vishnu, and Siva) are simply incarnations of Krishna. . . . Each of them had a particular role in creation and the ruling of the world. Lord Krishna is held to be supreme, unborn, and unlike the material world."[15]

In an article in *Back to Godhead* (the principal publication of ISKCON), entitled "Brahma, Vishnu, Siva: Clearing up some Misconceptions about the Hindu trinity," the author makes comparisons between the Christian Trinity and the Krishna trinity. "Like the persons of the trinity in Christian doctrine, the *visnu-tattva* expansions are one, but because Krsna is unlimited, His personal expansions are not merely three but unlimited divine persons, all manifested to perform unlimited divine pastimes." What are these pastimes? "One of Krsna's pastimes is to emanate, sustain, and reabsorb the material creation in periodic cycles, and this Krsna does in the persons of Brahma, Vishnu, and Siva."[16]

What are the attributes of this "Supreme Personality of the Godhead"? According to the "Basic Beliefs" of ISKCON (See Appendix B), "God, or Krsna, is eternal, all-knowing, omnipresent, all-powerful and all-attractive, the seed-giving father of man and all living entities. He is the sustaining energy of all life, nature and the cosmic situation."[17]

Although Prabhupada refused to compromise on many issues when he brought his version of Hinduism to the West, there was one significant concession that he made in deference to Christianity. He insisted that Lord Krishna and Christ were one and the same. " 'God' is the general name of the Supreme Personality of Godhead, whose specific name is Krsna. Therefore whether you call God 'Christ,' 'Krsta,' or 'Krsna,' ultimately you are addressing the same Supreme Personality of Godhead. . . . *Krsna* or *Christ*—the name is the same." When asked, "What is your idea of Jesus Christ?" Prabhupada responded, "He is our *guru*. He is preaching god consciousness, so he is our spiritual master."[18]

Such a concession, however, did not constitute a move away from Hinduism toward Christianity. Prabhupada went on to argue that while the names are one and the same, "the main point is to follow the injunctions of the Vedic scriptures that recommend chanting the name of God in this age. The easiest way is to chant the *maha-mantra*: Hare Krsna, Hare Krsna, Krsna, Krsna, Hare Hare/Hare Rama, Hare Rama, Rama Rama, Hare Hare. *Rama* and *Krsna* are names of God, and *Hare* is the energy of God." Prabhupada was likewise very critical of Christianity and how Christians have perceived Christ.

> A Vaisnava [a devotee of Krishna] is unhappy to see the suffering of others. Therefore, Lord Jesus Christ agreed to be crucified—to free others from their suffering. But his followers are so unfaithful that they have decided, "Let Christ suffer for us, and we'll go on committing sin." They love Christ so much that they think, "My dear Christ, we are very weak. We cannot give up our sinful activities. So you please suffer for us."

> Jesus Christ taught, "Thou shalt not kill." But his followers have now decided, "Let us kill anyway," and they open big, modern, scientific slaughterhouses. "If there is any sin, Christ will suffer for us." This is a most abominable conclusion.[19]

Although Prabhupada insisted that Christ is another name for Krishna, his reference to Jesus as a guru and a devotee of Krishna would seem to clearly place him on a lower level. The irony of this comparison is most obvious in the Hindu portrayal of Krishna. He is a "fun-loving god who frolics with his friends. One story tells of his having 16,108 wives, each provided with a beautiful palace. Each wife had ten children, and each of these children had many other children. . . . He is pictured as eternally youthful, perfect, and beautiful" and "somewhat mischievous and frivolous."[20]

Guru and Image Worship

Despite the efforts to fashion the image of God in a more palatable way for people from a Christian framework, the movement remains very Hindu in its basic philosophies and concepts of God. While Krishna alone is presented as the supreme god, the disciples of Prabhupada "were shocked to learn that they would 'have to worship him as God,' until he clarified for them the relationship of the spiritual master to Krishna. That is, the spiritual master is to be treated as God's representative." Indeed, the devotees were given a contradictory message, and as a result many of them seemed to worship Prabhupada almost as much as Lord Krishna.[21]

What is even more shocking to many Western initiates to the Hare Krishna movement is the blatant worship of images. A basic belief in Hinduism is that deity can assume various animate and inanimate forms. Idols are constructed out of a variety of materials, including metal, wood, and stone, and are decorated in vivid colors. "The color of the Krishna image may be white, blue, black, or green. The form may be of a young cowherd boy playing a flute, of Krishna dancing on the hoods of a many-headed serpent, or of a nondescript, squatty, round-eyed black form." The devotees care for these idols as though they were actual living human beings. Part of the worship involves waking Lord Krishna each morning and properly retiring him each night, and in between he is bathed, dressed, and fed.[22]

Reincarnation

As an authentic Hindu sect, ISKCON upholds the doctrine of reincarnation. To conform to contemporary culture, however, the dogma has been stripped of its mythological qualities and has reemerged in more scientific language. In an article in *ATMA*, a publication of *ISKCON*, reincarnation is explained in Darwinian terms:

> Darwin, in his efforts to comprehend and explain the diversion and progressive development of plant and animal life, hypothesized that different species physically evolve into higher ones, primarily through natural selection. But fifty centuries before Darwin, Lord Krsna fully explained the actual principles of evolution. All species are manifested in the early stages of cosmic creation, when the living entities (souls) are impregnated within material nature. These indestructible and eternal souls gradually evolve through the different species of types of material bodies, beginning with microbes and amoebas, rising through the fish, plants, insects, reptiles, birds and ani-

mals to the human and superhuman (demigod) species. So the evolutionary process is really an evolution of consciousness.[23]

The evolutionary theory of reincarnation is far removed from any notion of Darwinian evolution when the regressive aspects of it are taken into account. The reincarnation doctrine of the Hare Krishnas is nothing other than ancient Hinduism: "According to the law of *karma* our next birth may or may not be human. We may come back as human beings, but we also may reincarnate as dogs, hogs, birds, cats, or even lower species. For example, if one acquires the characteristics of an animal such as a hog, one may receive such a body in one's next life."[24]

The Theology of Chanting

The most important activity for any human being during their physical lifetime, according to Prabhupada, is that of chanting. "The logic of the Krishna theology is clear," writes Larry Shinn. "(1) The human soul lies slumbering in a material body and is overshadowed by an everyday material consciousness that is enamored with the sensual world of *maya*, (2) and thus, to awaken the soul and to supplant the material consciousness with god consciousness, (3) one need only prayerfully and frequently chant the names of Krishna."[25]

The Bhagavad-gita

The *Bhagavad-gita* is the bible of the Hare Krishna movement and is considered by Prabhupada to be "the paramount scripture of the Vedic tradition." In his introduction to the

English translation, he writes: "*Bhagavad-gita* is complete. The Vedic knowledge is infallible.... Vedic knowledge is complete, for it is above all doubts or errors. And *Bhagavad-gita* is the essence of all Vedic knowledge.... We should accept it as perfect knowledge, spoken by the Lord himself."[26]

The *Bhagavad-gita* is a "wondrous and holy dialogue between Krsna and Arjuna," a soldier and a devotee-friend who sought enlightenment to find out "what life was all about" in order to be perfected. In the end, Arjuna apparently reaches this state of perfection. The purpose of the book is to instruct the reader how to obtain this same "state of pure consciousness"—a consciousness that is purged from the contamination of the material world. How is this accomplished? By purifying one's activities. "This purification of activity is called *bhakti*, or devotional service," and it is this activity in which Arjuna is engaged.[27]

At the end of the last chapter of the *Bhagavad-gita*, there is a final plea made by Lord Krishna for worship from his devotee: "Always think of Me, become My devotee, worship Me, and offer your homage unto Me. Thus you will come to Me without fail. I promise you this because you are My very dear friend." For those who fulfill these requirements, Lord Krishna expresses his own personal devotion: "There is no servant in this world more dear to Me than he, nor will there ever be one more dear."[28]

Lifestyle, Family, and the Woman's Role

Singleness and celibacy is encouraged in the Hare Krishna communi-

One of many depictions of Lord Krishna. Photo taken from ISKCON publicity brochure.

ties, and austerity is viewed as a mark of spirituality. Indeed, the lifestyle of Prabhupada and his followers, at least during the early years of the movement, was opposite the opulent living style of gurus and devotees of many of the other imported Indian sects. The testimony of one devotee illustrates this: "When I arrived at my parents' home in Washington they were delighted to see me but shocked beyond belief at my long matted hair (highly prized in India but seen as 'filthy' in America). My habits simply blew their minds. I would sleep on the concrete patio outside the house. I sat on the floor to eat my meals and wouldn't take part in their television. . . ."[29]

The role of women is another aspect of the Hare Krishna movement that has been retained from the Hinduism of India. Included with the chapters and verses of the *Bhagavad-gita* is the "Purport" or commentary by Prabhupada, which in many instances gives more insight into the religion than does the actual text. For example, when Arjuna addresses the subject of womanhood, Prabhupada expands on it in his purport:

> Good population . . . in society depends on the chastity and faithfulness of its womanhood. As children are very prone to being misled, women are also very prone to degradation. Therefore, both children and women require protection by elder members of the family. . . . According to the sage Canakya Pandita, women are generally not very intelligent and therefore not trustworthy. So the different family traditions of religious activities should always engage them, and thus their chastity and devotion will give birth to good population.[30]

Family life in a guru commune-temple is virtually nonexistent. Sex within marriage is for procreation only, and husbands and wives frequently have little contact with each other. Children are schooled and cared for by devotees assigned to that area of responsibility. During the daily scheduled worship times of frenzied dancing, the small children are generally with their mothers. At times, when they are in the arms of their mothers, they are shaken wildly to the rhythm of the drum beat. Husband-wife relationships are often strained due to the separations and to the subservient attitude the wife is expected to maintain toward her husband. Many Western women find this to be a difficult role to fulfill, and the structure of the organization sometimes fosters division in the marriage. "If both spouses are initiated by the same guru, there is harmony, a clear line of authority. The guru tells the husband what to do, and he tells his wife. But if the husband and wife have been initiated by different gurus, conflict is inherent. Inevitably the two will give contrary advice."[31]

Because of the absolute subservience and obedience expected of wives, there are not surprisingly many stories of abuse. This was true of Steve Bryant, a devotee who was allegedly murdered by other members of the cult in 1986, for exposing scandal and fraud. "Bryant was an imperious husband who rode his wife unmercifully," write John Hubner and Lindsey Gruson. "He thought nothing of loading Jane, his stepson and his two baby boys into a van on the spur of the moment and moving cross-country. The thing Bryant liked best about Jane was that he could dominate her. She says he beat her. He kept the pressure on, reminding his wife again and again she was his devotee. Therefore she had to do whatever he said."[32]

During the early years of the movement, as is common in sectarian religions, women had freer access to leadership roles in the temples, but as the movement became more institutionalized, these roles gradually disappeared. One woman devotee testified that "in the early days of the movement, she had served as a *pajari*, or ritual priest, and had also given morning classes on the scriptures," but as time went on these opportunities became more and more limited and "she felt offended that her spiritual worth had been lowered, while less worthy men could assume her previous positions."[33]

Conversion and Deprograming

Among the most common criticisms of the Hare Krishnas are their method of proselytizing and their alleged mind control over individuals once they have entered the movement. The devotees are accused of preying on vulnerable young people who are not fully informed about the beliefs, lifestyle, and practices of the movement until they are already too "brainwashed" to leave on their own free volition.

This appraisal has been challenged by Larry Shinn in his book *The Dark Lord.* Shinn interviewed many Hare Krishnas about their conversion experiences and other aspects of their faith, and found that a high percentage claimed they converted to the movement because of the appeal of the philosophical beliefs. His interviews indicated that rather than undergoing sudden conversion experiences, "the far more common pattern was for a convert to experience at least a year of occasional and unpressured contact with ISKCON, coupled with some significant study of ISKCON's teachings prior to his or her decision to become a devotee and move into a temple." He also discovered that, like the born-again experience of Christians, the enthusiasm of the conversion experience tended to diminish in time.

Some Krishna devotees laughed during their interviews at the immaturity of their early faith and at their insensitivity to the way those attitudes and behaviors could be perceived by their parents and critics. One such devotee reported that he tried to convert his parents over the phone on the day he called to inform them of his own conversion! Another devotee said, "I must have looked like a flaming radical to my parents, who did not realize how far I had grown away from their conservative Christian faith." Yet another remarked, "I spoke confidently of Krishna to everyone, but in my heart was not sure at all." In every such description of their early Krishna faith, the devotee remarked how much more congenial or improved relations were with his or her family when the early period of enthusiasm gave way to a more mature and reflective faith.[34]

While it is true that some devotees speak of a "reflective" faith, none are encouraged to reflect too much. When a student asked Prabhupada if it were not wise to "experiment with different mental perspectives ... to understand the world," he responded: "Actually, mental speculators have been condemned [in Krishna scriptures] because they are simply carried away by the chariot of the mind. The mind is flickering, always changing. ... Somebody's putting forward some theory, and after a few years he will himself reject it. All these mental speculators are doing just that." Shinn defends the Hare Krishnas on this point by arguing that "While it is true that new devotees are encouraged to surrender themselves and their 'mundane' thinking to their guru, it is not the case that this means one should stop thinking and reasoning altogether."[35]

It is, however, this lack of rational thinking, on the analogy of operating like a robot, that has most distressed the families of converts to ISKCON. This was true in the case of Rebecca Foster, who forfeited a college scholarship in order to join the Hare Krishnas. So distressed were her family members that they hired the well-known Ted Patrick to perform his deprograming services. Rebecca was unsuccessfully deprogramed, pretending to renounce her new-found faith but rejoining the movement as soon as she had opportunity to escape from her family. In 1981, soon after the incident, she filed a lawsuit against her family on the grounds that they kidnapped and falsely imprisoned her. The family defended their actions by contending that Rebecca "wasn't thinking," was not "capable of making decisions," and had become a "mindless robot."[36]

Had Rebecca truly turned into a "mindless robot" through brainwashing? Was her kidnapping and deprograming warranted? The family was acquitted of the charges brought against them, but they did not celebrate a victory. Rebecca's return to the movement indicated that she was capable of thinking and making decisions. The family was forced to accept the fact that no matter how objectionable her religion may be to them, she was exercising her freedom of choice.

A common justification for deprograming is the argument that inquirers are held against their will, and that once they enter a temple commune and go through the initiation ceremony it is virtually impossible to leave. Statistics disprove that assumption. Indeed, by the late 1980s, fewer than two thousand of the original nine thousand devotees

initiated by Prabhupada remained active in the movement. This high dropout rate calls into serious question the justification for deprograming. Furthermore, the harmful effects of deprograming in many cases can never be undone, as the testimony of one devotee illustrates: "I think the thing that really upset my parents was when I told them, 'You didn't have to do this, I was walking out the door anyway.' ... I've been back home a couple of times since my deprograming, but I can't trust my parents any longer."[37]

The charge that devotees are incapable of thinking clearly and are in a state of delusion has been analyzed by Dr. Michael Ross, a researcher who gave all forty-two members of the Melbourne, Australia, temple commune a battery of psychological tests. From his study he concluded, among other things, that there is "no evidence for claiming that membership in the movement leads to psychopathology and that "the argument that joining the Hare Krishna movement is an attempt to stabilize an unstable personality does not appear to have a strong basis." Indeed, his research indicated that devotees of longer duration "appeared happier and less anxious."[38]

Crime and Contraband

Behind the scenes of the temple communes, the daily routine sometimes involves more than chanting and manual labor. Some of the same Krishna-conscious devotees who outwardly object to any form of violence have been the focus of investigations involving stock piles of arms and ammunition—and conspiracies and murders. "Suspicions about the sect have circulated since 1979," according to a *Time* magazine article, "when California Temple Leader Alexander Kulik was convicted of distributing heroin. He was also accused, with others, of laundering drug money through an investment company, Prasadam Distributors, controlled by sect members." This conviction further compounded the problems of the movement, which had already divided into bitterly opposing factions since the death of Prabhupada in 1977. The leader of the West Virginia faction, Kirtanananda Swami Bhaktipada, was brutally assaulted by an adversary in the movement in 1985, which only aggravated the tensions.[39]

The once centralized power of ISKCON under the leadership of Prabhupada rapidly deteriorated after his death in 1977. Scandals have been only one factor in this decline. The more direct influence has been "an internecine war that has all but destroyed his legacy." Prabhupada failed to prepare for the future. "He left few, if any, instructions on who should succeed him or how the Krishna church should be run. As a result, eleven gurus divided up the world like Mafia chieftains. Each became the godfather in his territory." According to Atreya Rishi, the former president of the Berkeley Hare Krishna temple and a member of the board of directors of ISKCON, "The eleven members of the guru club started building their own empires. . . . They used their power to strengthen themselves instead of the Movement. What was once a religion degenerated into a bunch of cults."[40]

The warring gurus established themselves in the various temples, and competed for members and money. As a result, "membership began to decline as devotees, disenchanted by the factionalism, left the organized Krishna church." The movement still claims that it has some three million members worldwide, with a third of those in the United States, but outside observers maintain that the membership has dropped to ten thousand or fewer. "Many of the disillusioned remain devout. The religion is pure, they insist. It is the gurus who are corrupt." The story of the corruption of Hare Krishna gurus is described in detail in a lengthy 1987 article in *Rolling Stone:*

> Even the Governing Body Commission, which is dominated by the gurus and works hard to protect them, has come to that conclusion. In the last six years, it has excommunicated six of the eleven gurus. Bhavananda (Charles Baces), the Australian guru, was drummed out last year after being accused of homosexuality. Ramesvar (Robert Grant), the L.A. guru, was also kicked out last year because he seduced a teenage girl. Bhagavan (William Ehrlichman), the European guru, left his temple after he was discovered to be conducting a relationship with a woman despite a vow of chastity. . . .
>
> The Berkeley guru, Hansadutta, . . . was booted out in 1983 because of his involvement with guns and drugs. One night, in a very black mood, Hansadutta shot up a liquor store and a Cadillac dealership in Berkeley. . . .
>
> But the most bizarre guru was in London. In 1982 Jayatirtha (James Immel) was the first guru to be thrown out of ISKCON. Until then, Jayatirtha was considered unusually pure. His devotees worshipped him for his spe-

Hare Krishna "Palace of Gold" at New Vrindaban, West Virginia.

cial relationship with Krishna. Often they sat at his feet, watching what they thought were spiritual journeys highlighted by direct conversations with Krishna. But these spiritual journeys were chemically fueled. The guru was an acid freak. While most of his followers lived in squalor, Jayatirtha and a select inner circle lived high in both senses of the word.[41]

The guru legacy that Prabhupada left behind is noteworthy in light of his own personal claim to have separated himself from the "rascal swamis" who were exploiting unwary individuals. "I am not a swami of this rascal group," he insisted.[42] In many ways, Prabhupada, who spent most of his last years teaching and writing in meager or modest surroundings, was different than the "rascal swamis," but he was unable to instill his own standard of discipline among his closest devotees, who sought to succeed him.

Wealth and Opulence

Although Prabhupada maintained that the purpose of ISKCON and the *Bhagavad-gita* was to help people purify themselves from the contamination of the material world—especially the materialistic world of the West, his followers have had difficulty maintaining any such purity, and that is one of the major reasons for the fragmentation of the movement since his death. The most blatant display of lavish opulence is the "Palace of Gold," which Swami Bhaktipada refers to as a "spiritual Disneyland." Located in a remote hilly region in the panhandle of West Virginia, the Palace of Gold is the work of sixty Hare Krishnas "who taught themselves to be artisans by trial and error." The construction which began in 1973, required more than sixty tons of marble, and tons more of wrought iron and teakwood. The final touches included thousands of square feet of gold leaf and more than forty crystal chandeliers.[43]

Evangelistic and Missionary Outreach

One of the central doctrines of ISKCON is that devotees spread the faith. That was the entire rationale behind Prabhupada's pilgrimage to America, and he instilled that objective into the minds of his followers. According to the movement's literature, "It is not recommended that a Krsna conscious devotee go into seclusion to chant by himself and thereby gain salvation for himself alone. Our duty and religious obligation is to go out into the streets where the people in general can hear the chanting and see the dancing. . . ."[44]

The primary method of evangelism has been chanting and street dancing. In the years since Prabhupada took up residence in New York, missionaries have been sent to cities across America and also to the major European cities. Today there are ISKCON centers all over the world, and in recent years there has been a strong emphasis on Latin America. In 1982, "His divine Grace Pancadravida Swami" was named spiritual master and was assigned to oversee the affairs of the Hare Krishna movement in Mexico, Central and South America. His previous experience had included missionary work in Argentina, Thailand, and India.[45] A prayer and devotional volume entitled *Teachings of Queen Kunti*, translated into Spanish, reportedly "won such a following among people in Central and South America that the first printing of 65,000 quickly sold out" and another

printing was ordered to fill the demand.[46]

Hare Krishnas have penetrated harsh environments in their effort to spread their message. Since 1977 they have been active in Iran, first with only a vegetarian restaurant in downtown Teheran, and later expanding the ministry to include a five-acre farm outside the city. After that they opened a temple and a publishing branch in the city. How do they manage to remain in such a hostile Islamic environment? "Through the months of political turmoil, the devotees continued their distribution of sanctified food (prasadam) and their work of propagating love of God according to the teachings of the *Bhagavad-gita*."[47]

Operating restaurants and offering food to temple visitors or to people on the streets is viewed as a form of missionary activity to ISKCON devotees. "As chanting God's name in glorification pleases God," writes Garuda Dasa, "so also does offering food to God. . . . When devotees offer food to the Supreme in worship, the food is spiritually transformed, and devotees gladly distribute it to all, for just by tasting such sanctified food one is purified and begins pleasing God."[48]

Hong Kong, like Teheran, has a branch of the Bhaktivedanta Book Trust. In 1981, that branch announced the completion of a significant project—the publication of Prabhupada's *Bhagavad-gita As It Is* in Chinese. It was a five-year translation project by a Krishna devotee based in Hong Kong. It was of great significance, according to the translator. "Although China and India are neighbors, very little of the rich spiritual tradition of India has penetrated

China, largely because of the language barrier. Now that impediment has been removed—and the significance for the spiritual development of China cannot be overestimated."[49]

Hare Krishnas distributing prasadam (sanctified food). Photo taken from ISKCON publicity brochure.

The sale of literature was from the beginning Prabhupada's primary avenue of missionary outreach. He himself worked tirelessly as a translator, and he commissioned his followers to pass out pamphlets and sell books, along with his magazine *Back to Godhead*, in conjunction with their dancing and chanting in the streets.[50]

The message of Hare Krishna is spread primarily through the street dancing and chanting, publishing, vegetarian restaurants, and the temples, but there have been some unique individual efforts to foster missions as well. One such endeavor was initiated in Hawaii by Narahari, the president of the Krishna temple in Honolulu. He placed an advertisement in a sailing magazine that read, "ISKCON, a non-profit, charitable organization, needs a boat to reach needy people in remote parts of the world." The advertisement was answered by a man who had never heard of the organization, but he had "a beautiful 53-foot teakwood ketch that he wanted to donate to a worthy charitable organization." After two meetings and lengthy explanations of what the movement was all about, the man agreed to transfer the title to ISKCON.[51]

The boat, according to Narahari, was ideal for Hawaiian missions. "The founders of this movement wanted to distribute love of God to every town and village in the world. In other areas our members go by foot, car, train, bus, and in India by bullock cart. But in the Hawaiian Islands the most practical way to travel is by boat. Not by motor boat, since fuel is short, but by sail boat." Indeed, Narahari insists that this mode of transportation served the style of ministry of the Hare Krishnas very effectively. "We can dock in remote ports, conduct seminars, hold festivals, present educational programs, and in that way introduce this very ancient science of God consciousness to people who would otherwise never hear of it."[52]

The Hare Krishna Hawaiian work began in 1970, and it grew steadily after that. After the sailboat project was underway, the movement purchased a one-hundred-acre farm for communal living and outreach programs. Speaking of this work, one devotee wrote: "These three dynamic preaching programs—the boat, the temple, and the new farm—make us confident that Krishna consciousness will continue to blossom in Hawaii."[53]

Despite Prabhupada's intense efforts to firmly plant his Krishna consciousness in America, and despite the commitment and loyalty of many of his devotees, the movement has not found fertile soil. After nearly a quarter of a century of missionary outreach, the number of devotees remaining faithful number fewer than three thousand, and even among that number there has been very little sense of solidarity since the death of Prabhupada in 1977. Yet, there is no sign of the movement simply disappearing from the scene. Children are being schooled in the faith from the time of infancy, and it can be assumed that many of them will go on to carry the mantel into the next generation.

Chapter 13

Baha'i: A Peace and Unity Movement Out of Islam

Unlike its militant noninclusivist parent Islam, the Baha'i faith is a movement of peace and unity. It is an unwanted and despised stepchild of Islam that in recent years has endured bloody persecution. "Since the Ayatollah Ruhollah Khomeini came to power in 1979," according to a *Time* magazine report, "Iran's 300,000 Baha'is have suffered a reign of terror in the land where their faith was born." By 1984 scores of Baha'is had been executed, hundreds imprisoned, and "thousands more have lost their homes and possessions, and mobs have desecrated Baha'i assembly halls, cemeteries and the faith's holiest shrine in Iran, the House of the Bab in Shiraz."[1]

Although Iran's constitution offers freedom for Jews and Christians to practice their faith, the Baha'is are granted no such liberty. This is because the Baha'is are regarded as apostates within Islam—a crime itself punishable by death. Unlike Muslims, Baha'is do not believe that Muhammad was the "Seal of the Prophets," or the last of the true prophets. They believe that two prophets succeeded Muhammad, namely Mirza Ali Muhammad, or the "Bab," and Baha'u'llah, who declared himself to be the Messiah in 1863 and who replaced the militancy of his predecessors with a strong stand against violence.[2]

Today the Baha'i faith has spread around the world and has made a particular appeal in the West where, since the 1960s, the themes of unity and nonviolence have attracted certain segments of the population— particularly those who are well educated and disillusioned with Christianity. But while clearly differentiating itself from Christianity, it is a religion that seeks to build on Christianity, with repeated references to Jesus and the ethical and moral teachings of the Christian faith. Another appealing characteristic of the Baha'i faith is its optimism—an optimism that is often based on an utterly unrealistic view of the world and world historical trends. It is an

285

optimism that in some ways parallels the optimism of the New Age Movement, which sees the dawning of an era of peace and unity. In his book *Baha'u'llah and the New Era*, J. E. Esslemont writes of this new age:

> That the world, during the nineteenth and the early part of the twentieth centuries, has been passing through the death pangs of an old era and the birth pangs of a new, is evident to all. The old principles of materialism and self-interest, the old sectarian and patriotic prejudices and animosities, are perishing, discredited, amidst the ruins they have wrought, and in all lands we see signs of a new spirit of faith, of brotherhood, of internationalism, that is bursting the old bonds and overrunning the old boundaries. Revolutionary changes of unprecedented magnitude have been occurring in every department of human life. The old era is not yet dead. It is engaged in a life and death struggle with the new. Evils there are in plenty, gigantic and formidable, but they are being exposed, investigated, challenged and attacked with new vigor and hope. Clouds there are in plenty, vast and threatening, but the light is breaking through, and is illumining the path of progress and revealing the obstacles and pitfalls that obstruct the onward way.[3]

"What is the cause of this sudden awakening throughout the world?" asks Esslemont, an outspoken proponent of the Baha'i faith. "Baha'is believe that it is due to a great outpouring of the Holy Spirit through the Prophet Baha'u'llah."[4]

Historical Development

It was Baha'u'llah himself who taught his followers that through him the Holy Spirit had been poured out "even in places and among peoples where the name of the Prophet is quite unknown." He, as the "Divine Manifestation, the Sun of Truth shines upon the world of heart and soul, and educates the thoughts, morals and characters of men." Baha'u'llah—whatever else he was—was not modest. He "declared, plainly and repeatedly, that He was the long-expected educator and teacher of all peoples, the channel of a wondrous Grace that would transcend all previous outpourings, in which all previous forms of religion would become merged, as rivers merge in the ocean."[5]

The Long-expected Messiah

This belief in the return of a long expected messiah emerged out of the Shi'ite sect of Islam, which from the time of Muhammad's death was led by Imams—twelve successive descendants of Muhammad's son-in-law, Ali, "believed to be endowed with unqualified infallibility in the discharge of their related responsibilities." Because they were a threat to the larger sect of Islam, the Sunnis, who recognized no successors to Muhammad, "one Imam after another was put to death" until 873, when "the twelfth and last appointed," or Hidden, Imam—only a child at the time—"withdrew into 'concealment' in order to escape the fate of his predecessors." After the disappearance of the twelfth Imam, an eschatological tradition developed among the Shi'ites that he would return again "at the time of the end" to usher in a period of world peace and justice. It was in light of this tradition that the Baha'i faith emerged—much to the vexation of the Shi'ites who were determined to annihilate the Baha'is even as the Sunnis had sought to annihilate them.[6]

Like John the Baptist who came before Jesus, Mirza Ali Muhammad, who assumed the title of the Bab, has been called the forerunner of Baha'u'llah, and the latter's role cannot be fully understood without a knowledge of the former—an individual whose life and ministry has often been enmeshed in controversy. He was born in Iran around 1820, the son of a cloth merchant. As a young man he became interested in spiritual matters and especially the tradition of the Hidden Imam. In 1844, at the age of twenty-four and after a long period of prayer and meditation, he became convinced that God had uniquely called him to perform a special ministry. Thus began the Baha'i movement. What this mission entailed and what specific role the Bab was to play has over the generations been much debated.[7]

The Mission of the Bab

Some scholars insist that the Bab, from the beginning to the end of his ministry, perceived himself as simply paving the way for one who was far greater than he. Others maintain that he initially perceived himself as a forerunner of the Hidden Imam, but gradually became convinced that he himself was the Hidden Imam. Still others claim that the Bab considered himself to be the Hidden Imam from the time he made his declaration in 1844—a view held by J. E. Esslemont, who presumes to represent the official Baha'i position.

According to Esslemont, the Bab's declaration in 1844 was that "God the Exalted had elected Him to the station of Babhood," meaning that "he was the channel of grace from some great Person still behind the veil of glory, who was the possessor of countless and boundless perfections, by whose will he moved, and to the bond of whose love he clung." One by one disciples joined him, and "soon the fame of the young Prophet began to spread like wildfire throughout the land.... The fire of His eloquence, the wonder of His rapid and inspired writings, His extraordinary wisdom and knowledge, His courage and zeal as a reformer, aroused the greatest enthusiasm among His followers...." Who was this man? "The Bab has been compared to John the Baptist, but the station of the Bab is not merely that of the herald or forerunner. In Himself," writes Esslemont, "the Bab was a Manifestation of God, the Founder of an independent religion.... The Baha'is believe that the Bab and Baha'u'llah were Co-Founders of their Faith."[8]

A Second Calvary

In his portrayal of the Bab as the Manifestation of God, Esslemont makes several comparisons between him and Jesus. He trained disciples whom he sent out "to spread the news of His advent." The religious establishment misunderstood his mission and expected him to reign over an earthly kingdom, "just as the Jews in the time of Christ interpreted similar prophecies regarding the Messiah.... As these signs did not appear, the shi'ihs rejected the Bab with the same fierce scorn which the

Jews displayed towards Jesus." Throughout his short ministry of less than six years, the Bab endured "a long series of imprisonments, deportations, examinations before tribunals, scourgings and indignities, which ended only with His martyrdom in 1850." Not surprisingly, Esslemont describes the martyrdom as "a second Calvary."[9]

The Bab's execution took place during an extended period of persecution against the adherents of the new religion, and many of them, like their leader, were put to death. The most prominent adherent of the faith who survived the terrors of persecution was Mirza Husayn Ali. In 1863, thirteen years after the Bab's death, "he announced to several of His followers the glad tidings that He was the One Whose coming had been foretold by the Bab—the Chosen of God, the Promised One of all the Prophets." He had already taken the title of Baha'u'llah, meaning Glory of God.[10]

Baha'u'llah

In the years that followed, Baha'u'llah traveled and taught his growing number of followers. He viewed himself as far more than a local sectarian leader, as is indicated in a letter he wrote in 1868, copies of which were sent to prominent world leaders, including European heads of state, the President of the United States, and the Pope. In it, he explained his mission and asked for assistance in establishing the true religion of peace and justice. "I have seen in the way of God what no eye hath seen and no ear hath heard," he wrote. Fully aware of the crux of the

Christian message, he went on to say, "My eyes rain down tears until my bed is drenched; but my sorrow is not for myself. By God, my head longeth for the spears for the love of its Lord, and I never pass by a tree but my heart addresseth it, 'O would that thou wert cut down in my name and my body were crucified upon thee in the way of my Lord.'"[11]

What effect Baha'u'llah's letter had on world leaders is uncertain, but in the years that followed he spent much of his time in prison—a condition that only served to strengthen the loyalty of his following. After he was released, he lived like royalty, supported by the offerings of his many thousands of followers until he died in 1892. He left behind his writings which made it plain to his followers that he himself was a Divine Manifestation of God: "Were any of the all-embracing Manifestations of God to declare: 'I am God!' He verily speaketh the truth. . . . for it hath been repeatedly demonstrated that through their Revelation, their attributes and names, the Revelation of God, His name and His attributes, are made manifest in the world."[12]

Although Baha'u'llah had been a loyal follower of the Bab, he came to view himself as the far greater Manifestation of God. Even as Mary Baker Eddy later denigrated the importance of P. P. Quimby, Baha'u'llah "sought to lessen the status of the Bab by frequently referring to him as 'my forerunner,' and he made it to appear that the chief function of the Bab was to prepare the way for him, a much greater Manifestation." At times, Baha'u'llah referred to himself as the Hidden Imam of the Shi'ites, and even "claimed to be the 'return' of

Jesus Christ, and the Comforter promised by Christ . . . as well as the Manifestation of God the Father." Indeed, "the position which Baha'u'llah claimed for himself was not merely that of a teacher or prophet, but was that of God."[13]

In one of his prayers, he spoke of his divinity, while at the same time conceding his humanity: "When I contemplate, O my God, the relationship that bindeth me to Thee, I am moved to proclaim to all created things 'verily I am God!'; and when I consider my own self, lo, I find it coarser than clay!"[14]

Baha'u'llah wanted his followers to understand that he was not merely a prophet to herald a new age. He was vastly different from Zoroaster, who prophesied three thousand years of strife before a savior, Shah Bahram, would usher in an era of peace. Nor was he like Moses, who warned of oppression "before the Lord of Hosts would appear to gather them from all nations . . . and establish his Kingdom upon earth." Nor was he like Jesus, who "predicted a period of wars and rumors of wars, of tribulations and afflictions that would continue till the coming of the Son of Man." Even Muhammad "declared that . . . Allah had put enmity and hatred among both Jews and Christians that would last until the Day of Resurrection, when He would appear to judge them all." But Baha'u'llah alone "announces that He is the Promised One of all these Prophets — the Divine Manifestation in Whose era the reign of peace will actually be established."[15]

The Baha'i scriptures confirm that Baha'u'llah is omnipotent and infallible and ought to be praised as God:

If He declares water to be wine, or heaven to be earth, or light to be fire, it is true and there is no doubt therein; and no one has the right to oppose Him, or to say "why" or "wherefore". . . . Verily no account shall be demanded of Him for what He shall do. . . . Verily if He declares the right to be left, or the south to be north, it is true and there is no doubt therein. Verily He is to be praised in His deeds and to be obeyed in His command. He hath no associate in His behest and no helper in His power; He doeth whatsoever He willeth, and commandeth whatever He desireth.[16]

Organizational Development and Religious Life

In Baha'i, as is the case with most new religions and sectarian movements, there is a progression from personality cult to established religion. Baha'u'llah followed the Bab, and he was succeeded by his son — though clearly not outshined by his son.

Line of Succession

With the death of Baha'u'llah, the living-prophet stage of the Baha'i faith passed and the institutionalization of the movement began. According to a covenant that Baha'u'llah established with his followers, his son Abdu'l-Baha was named "the sole authoritative interpreter of his teachings and the source of authority in all affairs of the faith." The Covenant was very specific in clarifying that Abdu'l-Baha "was to be regarded not as a prophet or divine messenger, but rather as the perfect human example of Baha'u'llah's teachings." But if his prestige and preeminence was less than that of his father's, his authority was explicitly confirmed, by the decree of his father:

> Whosoever turns to Him hath surely turned unto God, and whosoever turneth away from Him hath turned away from My beauty, denied My proof and is of those who transgress. Verily, He is the remembrance of God amongst you and His trust within you, and His manifestation unto you and His appearance among the servants who are nigh.[17]

Abdu'l-Baha determined to spread the faith worldwide, and his particular interest was to reach Europe and America. In America, the faith was energized by the efforts of two women: Louisa Getsinger, who traveled and lectured, and Phoebe Hearst, a millionaire philanthropist who was one of Getsinger's converts. They traveled to the Middle East to visit with Abdu'l-Baha, and "in him they believed they saw the spirit of Jesus Christ again moving among humanity." Indeed, "Mrs. Hearst believed that Abdu'l-Baha was himself 'The Messiah,' the return of Jesus Christ." Other pilgrims began traveling to the Middle East, and the enthusiasm for the exotic faith increased. Soon several Baha'i communities were established in the United States and Canada.[18]

In 1908, more than a decade before he died, Abdu'l-Baha formulated a *Will and Testament* which set forth his plan for institutionalized authority and a successor. The Universal House of Justice was designed to serve a governing body administering the affairs of the movement. Abdu'l-Baha's grandson was named as his successor—the interpreter and Guardian of the faith, who would be assisted by an elite corp of individuals known as the "Hands of the Cause of God." At the time of Abdu'l-Baha's death there were some one hundred Baha'is living primarily in Persia, with smaller communities in India and North America.[19]

Lay and Professional Leadership

The Baha'is have no professional clergy per se. Some lay leaders become full-time teachers and are supported by voluntary gifts, but these individuals are not ordained and have no special status giving them recognition within the movement. A professional clergy is considered unnecessary because people are no longer illiterate, as they were in the past when they "were dependent on priests for their religious instruction, for the conduct of religious rites and ceremonies, for the administration of justice. . . . Elaborate rites and ceremonies, requiring the services of a special profession or caste, have no place in the Baha'i system."[20]

Worship Services

The house of worship is an important part of Baha'i religious life, but it is not used primarily for meetings of the membership as is typical in most religious houses of worship. Rather, it is opened to the public to encourage people of various religious backgrounds to attend. "Services are nondenominational and consist of readings and prayers from the scriptures of the world's faiths, with no sermons or other attempts to cast these teachings in a mold of specifically Baha'i interpretation. Selections are often set to music and sung by trained a cappella choirs." The structures are of various sizes and architectural design, but all have the common features of being domed and nine-sided, "symbolic of Baha'i acceptance of all religious traditions and representative of the fact that, although the participants may enter by different doors, they assemble together in recognition of one Creator." They are likewise designed with open space and natural light.[21]

Prayer and Fasting

Unlike Muslims, Baha'is place little emphasis on congregational prayer. Rather, private prayer is the norm. "Only in the case of Prayer for the Dead has Baha'u'llah commanded congregational prayer, and the only requirement is that the believer who reads it aloud, and all others present, should stand."[22] Baha'i believers are encouraged to pray and meditate as often and long as they choose, but they are obliged to repeat at least one prayer each day. There are three versions of the prayer, one of which is to be repeated each day between noon and sunset. The shortest of these is referred to as the "Short Obligatory Prayer": "I bear witness, O my God that thou has created me to know Thee and to worship Thee. I testify, at this moment, to my powerlessness and to Thy might, to my poverty and to Thy wealth. There is none other God but Thee, the Help in Peril, the Self-Subsisting."[23]

Like Muslims, Baha'i believers place great emphasis on fasting. For a nineteen-day period each year during the month of March, Baha'is fast from sunrise until sunset, an exercise

Baha'i Temple and World headquarters and Temple, Wilmette, Illinois.

which is deemed good for the soul and in preparation for the Baha'i New Year. Baha'is are prohibited from indulging in alcoholic beverages or narcotics at any time.[24]

Doctrinal Distinctives

Although the Baha'i faith developed out of Islam, it is now very different doctrinally from that religion, and it has even incorporated some Christian concepts and terminology in order to appeal more effectively to the West. The most significant distinction between Baha'i and Islam is that Baha'i refuses to revere Muhammad exclusively as the most preeminent of the prophets. To honor Muhammad, but not to bestow on him the highest honor, is in the eyes of Islam the gravest transgression.

Incomprehensible God

Although Baha'u'llah has often been referred to by his followers as being God himself, sometimes actually being referred to as the "Father," he himself taught that God was far beyond any human comprehension. "God comprehends all; He cannot be comprehended." In seeking to understand God, he wrote, "the way is barred and the road is impassable." Yet, according to the Baha'i faith, God reveals himself through nature: "the whole universe is eloquent of God. In each drop of water are hidden oceans of meaning and in each mote is concealed a whole universe of significances, reaching far beyond the ken of the most learned scientist," but no matter how far the scientist goes in his discoveries, there comes a time when "the most profound intellect can penetrate no farther, and can but bow in silent awe before the unknown Infinite which remains ever shrouded in inscrutable mystery."[25]

Manifestations of God

God is known through his Manifestations—Baha'u'llah being the chief and most recent Manifestation and equated with God himself. The others, according to the Baha'u'llah, were Adam, Noah, Abraham, Moses, Jesus—"each Manifestation being more perfect than the one which preceded it." But though these Manifestations were different, they were also one, "as the sun of today is the same as the sun of yesterday." This ascending line of Manifestations was not so difficult to comprehend until the Baha'i concept of religious unity expanded, eventually including Zoroaster, Buddha, Confucius, and Krishna among its Manifestations. But if they also are Manifestations, writes William M. Miller, "then there would have been two or more suns in the sky at once, and it would seem that God had become twins or triplets. Hence the message of the modern Baha'i faith about God is far from clear. . . ."[26]

Manifestations of God are also referred to as Prophets. How can a true Prophet be identified? "The greatest proof of a Manifestation of God," writes Esslemont, "is the creative power of His word—its effectiveness to change and transform all human affairs and to triumph over all human opposition. Through the word of the Prophets God announces His will, and the immediate or subsequent fulfillment of that word is the clearest proof of the Prophet's claim and of the genuineness of His inspiration." It is according to this test that Baha'u'llah's "genuineness" has been affirmed by his followers—a test that he would not pass by most objective standards:

> Let us now see what evidence there is to show whether the words of Baha'u'llah have this creative power which is distinctive of the word of God.
>
> Baha'u'llah commanded the rulers to establish universal peace. . . .
>
> Baha'u'llah bade the rulers likewise to act as trustees of those under their control, making political authority a means to true general welfare. . . .
>
> He commanded limitation of the extremes of wealth and poverty. . . .
>
> Baha'u'llah declared the equality of men and women, expressed through

equal responsibilities and equal rights and privileges. . . .

He declared the fundamental oneness of religions. . . .

He commanded universal education, and made the independent investigation of truth a proof of spiritual vitality. . . .

Baha'u'llah commanded the adoption of a universal auxiliary language. . . .[27]

The Manifestations of God, particularly Baha'u'llah, represent "progressive revelation"—the idea that God manifests himself in greater and greater ways throughout human history in his prophets, the last and greatest being Baha'u'llah. These manifestations are considered to be relevant for the contemporary age. "We are compelled to ask," writes, William M. Miller, "Is Baha'u'llah really contemporary? He died in 1892, eleven years before the Wright brothers made their first flight, before automobiles were seen on our roads . . . and before anyone dreamed that bombs would be made that could blow up the world. . . But, according to Baha'u'llah, no new Manifestation will come before 2866 A.D."[28]

Man and Sin

In Baha'i thought, human beings are not viewed as children or sons and daughters in relation to God, but rather as slaves or servants. But this does not denote lowliness or baseness, because Baha'u'llah taught that humankind is basically good so long as the proper education and ethical teachings are available. "The evil that resides in man's heart," writes Miller, "is largely ignored. Neither in the writings of the Bab nor in those of Baha'u'llah and the later leaders, except when they are denouncing their enemies, is there any adequate consideration of man's deadly disease which is sin."[29]

Baha'is clearly do not accept the doctrine of original sin. Abdu'l-Baha argued that there was no such thing as sin in itself, but only the wrong *use* of actually good human qualities:

In creation there is no evil, all is good. Certain qualities and natures innate in some men and apparently blameworthy are not so in reality. For example, from the beginning of his life you can see in a nursing child the signs of greed, of anger, and of temper. Then, it may be said, good and evil are innate in the reality of man, and this is contrary to the pure goodness of nature and creation. The answer to this is that greed, which is to ask for something more, is a praiseworthy quality provided that it is used suitably. So, if a man is greedy to acquire science and knowledge, or to become compassionate, generous, and just, it is more praiseworthy. If he exercises his anger and wrath against the bloodthirsty tyrants who are like ferocious beasts, it is very praiseworthy.[30]

Unity of all Religions

Unlike its parent Islam, which according to the Koran regards not only itself but both Jews and Christians as People of the Book, the Baha'i faith reveres all religions as components of God's design. This emphasis was made clear in the writings of Baha'u'llah:

There can be no doubt whatever that the peoples of the world, of whatever race or religion, derive their inspiration from one heavenly source, and are the subjects of one God. The difference between the ordinances under which they abide should be attributed to the varying requirements and exigencies of the age in which they were revealed. All of them, except a few which are the outcome of human perversity, were ordained of God, and are a reflection of His Will and Purpose.[31]

Ethical Teachings

Ethical principles are the foundation of the Baha'i religion. Claims about God and his Manifestations are certainly very important, but the main emphasis of the Baha'i religion for today's world is almost exclusively focused on ethical and societal issues. Baha'u'llah himself laid out principles "to help bind people together in a united world," and they are summarized in seven short statements:

Men must seek for truth in spite of custom, prejudice, and tradition.

Men and women must have equal opportunities, rights, and privileges.

The nations must choose an international language to be used along with the mother tongue.

All children must receive a basic education.

Men must make a systematic effort to wipe out all those prejudices which divide people.

Men must recognize that religion goes hand in hand with science.

Men must work to abolish extreme wealth and extreme poverty.[32]

Humanitarianism

The Baha'i faith prides itself in being a humanitarian religion. As in the support of other tenets of the faith, biblical passages are frequently employed to support the ethical principles Baha'i propounds. Service to fellow human beings is viewed as a primary function of ethical living, and the foundation for this teaching is found in Christ, who said "Inasmuch as ye did it not to one of the least of these, ye did it not to Me," and in Baha'u'llah, who said "O son of man! If thine eyes be turned towards mercy, forsake the things that profit thee, and cleave unto that which will profit mankind. And if thine eyes be turned towards justice, choose thou for thy neighbor that which thou choosest for thyself."[33]

Shunning Evil Speaking

Another ethical principle supported with the Christian Bible is that which warns against speaking evil of others. "On no subject are the Baha'i teachings more imperative and uncompromising than on the requirement to abstain from faultfinding," writes Esslemont. This is based on Christ's teaching in the Sermon on the Mount, and on the *Hidden Words* of Baha'u'llah and the writings of Abdu'l-Baha. Such admonitions, he maintains, are viewed by Christians as "Counsels of Perfection" beyond their ability to carry out. But Baha'is take these teachings seriously. On this subject Abdu'l-Baha gives his followers these commands:

To be silent concerning the faults of others, to pray for them, and to help them, through kindness, to correct their faults.

To look always at the good and not at the bad. If a man has ten good qualities and one bad one, to look at the ten and forget the one; and if a man has ten bad qualities and one good one, to look at the one and forget the ten.

Never to allow ourselves to speak one unkind word about another, even though that other be our enemy.[34]

Humility and Honesty

Humility and honesty are also essential attributes for Baha'is. "O people of Baha!," wrote Baha'u'llah, "Honesty is the best garment for your temples and the most splendid crown for your heads." And Abdu'l-Baha wrote:

Truthfulness is the foundation of all the virtues of mankind. Without truthfulness, progress and success in all the worlds are impossible for a soul. When this holy attribute is established in man, all the other divine qualities will also become realized.[35]

Self-realization

Self-realization is yet another principle taught in Baha'i, and one that is particularly appealing during an era of New Age mentality when self-actualization is championed as the principal rule of living. In *Hidden Words,* Baha'u'llah wrote:

O Son of Spirit!

I created thee rich, why dost thou bring thyself down to poverty? Noble I made thee, wherewith dost thou abase thyself? Out of the essence of knowledge I gave thee being, why seekest thou enlightenment from anyone beside Me? Out of the clay of love I molded thee, how dost thou busy thyself with another? Turn thy sight unto thyself, that thou mayest find Me standing within thee, mighty, powerful and self-subsisting.

O My Servant!

Thou art even as a finely tempered sword concealed in the darkness of its sheath and its value hidden from the artificer's knowledge. Wherefore come forth from the sheath of self and desire that thy worth may be made resplendent and manifest unto all the world.[36]

The Harmony of Science and Religion

Just as no one religion contradicts another in the Baha'i view, so it is true that scientific or scholarly knowledge will not create disharmony with religion. "No one truth can contradict another truth," wrote Abdu'l-Baha. "Light is good in whatsoever lamp it is burning! . . . You will realize that if the Divine Light of Truth shone in Jesus Christ, it also shone in Moses and Buddha. That is what is meant by the search after truth."[37]

During his visit to the United States and Canada in 1912, Abdu'l-Baha strongly emphasized his position that true science and true religion could not contradict each other:

If religious beliefs and opinions are found contrary to the standards of science, they are mere superstitions and imaginations; for the antithesis of knowledge is ignorance, and the child of ignorance is superstition. Unquestionably there must be agreement between true religion and science. If a question be found contrary to reason, faith and belief in it are impossible, and there is no outcome but wavering and vacillation.[38]

Repudiating Race Prejudice and Nationalism

Baha'is pride themselves in being free from race prejudice. It is probably this attribute as much as any other that has appealed to middle-class intellectuals in the West. On this issue, Abdu'l-Baha wrote that race prejudice was "an illusion, a superstition pure and simple, for God created us all of one race." He went on to admonish his followers that "the only real difference lies in the degree of faithfulness, of obedience to the laws of God. . . . The lovers of mankind, these are the superior men, of whatever nation, creed or color they may be."[39]

Nationalism and patriotism are seen as closely related to racism and are likewise repudiated by Baha'is. In *Tablet of the World*, Baha'u'llah wrote:

> Of old it hath been revealed: "Love of one's country is an element of the Faith of God." The tongue of Grandeur hath . . . in the day of His manifestation proclaimed: "It is not his to boast who loveth his country, but it is his who loveth the world." Through the power released by these exalted words He hath lent a fresh impulse, and set a new direction, to the birds of men's hearts, and hath obliterated every trace of restriction and limitation from God's Holy Book.[40]

Equality of the Sexes

The Baha'i Faith has been unique in its practice of sexual equality. During the nineteenth century, at a time when it was rare for Christian leaders to appeal for equality of the sexes, the founding fathers of the Baha'i movement were making that very appeal. They conceded that there were sexual differences, but insisted that one of the characteristics of the new age would be sexual equality. Abdu'l-Baha wrote that "the world in the past has been ruled by force and man has dominated over woman by reason of his more forceful and aggressive qualities both of body and mind." This was the reality of the old era; the ideal of the new era was beginning to emerge. "The scales are already shifting, force is losing its weight, and mental alertness, intuition, and the spiritual qualities of love and service, in which woman is strong, are gaining ascendancy. Hence the new age will be an age less masculine and more permeated with the feminine ideals."[41]

Missionary Outreach

North America became the most important mission field for Baha'is in the late nineteenth century. The first missionary sent to America was Dr. Ibrahim George Kheiralla, a graduate of the American College in Beirut—a school founded by Protestant missionaries. He was reportedly an individual of "great mental acumen" who was recognized by some as "a healer of nervous diseases." Due to "irregular conduct," however, he was rebuffed by the Christian community, and in 1890 at the age of forty-one was converted to the Baha'i faith. In the years that followed, he traveled to the United States, where he proclaimed the tidings of "the Appearance of the Father and the establishment of His Kingdom on earth." After lecturing in various cities, he settled in the Chicago area and concentrated his efforts there.[42]

Kheiralla's missionary message did not immediately introduce the teachings of the Baha'i faith to his listeners. He offered a series of lectures which were neither truthful or representative of the faith but, according to one observer, served to rouse interest and bring in new converts: "From her reports," writes Miller, "it is evident that the first ten lectures had little to do with the Baha'i faith, and dealt with metaphysics, dreams, numbers, allegorical interpretations of the Bible, prayer, etc. But the intense curiosity of the hearers was aroused by the promise of the revelation of some mystery of the eleventh lesson." In that lesson, Kheiralla summarized the core teachings of the Baha'i faith:

"The Bab had announced that the Father had come, and the Father was Baha'u'llah. Abdu'l-Baha was Jesus Christ, the son of God." He prophesied the millennium would be ushered in the year 1917, at which time one third of the world's population, he predicted, would be converted to the Baha'i faith, claiming that there were already more than fifty million Baha'i believers worldwide. Throughout his lecture, he took great pains not to offend his listeners by claiming to be introducing an entirely new religion. Indeed, "he interpreted all the prophecies in the book of Daniel and the Revelation as applying to Baha'u'llah, in order to convince Christians that his coming had been foretold in their Bible."[43]

What is most interesting about Kheiralla's efforts to derive prophecy relating to Baha'u'llah from the Bible was his virtual duplication of William Miller's study of Bible prophecies. Using the reference of 2,300 evenings and mornings from Daniel 8, he, like Miller, converted the days into years and then added the total to 456 B.C. (When Artaxerxes supposedly gave the edict to rebuild Jerusalem), and

came up with 1844, exactly as Miller had, the only real difference being the fulfillment of that prophecy. For Miller it was unfulfilled (though later accepted as fulfilled by Seventh-day Adventists); for Kheiralla the prophecy had been fulfilled through the Baha'i faith: "The fulfillment of the vision of Daniel took place in the year 1844 A.D., and this is the year of the Bab's manifestation according to the actual text of the Book of Daniel."[44]

Kheiralla was instrumental in arousing considerable interest in the Baha'i faith in America, but his teachings gradually became more and more contradictory of traditional Baha'i beliefs. Because there was so little actual literature available for him to study, he combined his knowledge with ideas from other sources. According to a recent Baha'i study on the faith in America, "he did not use works authored by the great 'metaphysical' thinkers popular in the nineteenth-century America, such as Madame Helena Blavatsky, Mary Baker Eddy ... or religious thinkers as Ralph Waldo Emerson and William James. Rather, most of Kheiralla's reading focused on the Bible and, often, on evangelical interpretations of it."[45] Kheiralla moved further and further away from the teaching of Baha'u'llah and publicly expressed doubts about Abdu'l-Baha's authority. In 1900, after being discredited by the movement in America, he returned to the Middle East, and a schism was avoided.

In the generations since Baha'i was first brought to America, the religion has grown considerably, and not only in the West. In 1974, the movement launched a five-year plan that was largely responsible for a forty percent increase in believers. The regions that witnessed the most rapid growth were in Asia and the Pacific Islands. A previous nine-year plan had spurred growth in Africa and Latin America. A seven-year plan, completed in 1986, was also successful in swelling the numbers of Baha'is.[46]

What accounts for the success of Baha'i missionary outreach and expansion? This question was raised by E. G. Browne in the late nineteenth century. "I have often heard wonder expressed by Christian ministers at the extraordinary success of Baha'i missionaries as contrasted with the almost complete failure of their own." What was his explanation? "To the Western observer, however, it is the complete sincerity of the Babis, their fearless disregard of death and torture undergone for the sake of their religion, their certain conviction as to the truth of their faith, their generally admirable conduct towards mankind, and especially toward their fellow-believers. . . ."[47]

Chapter 14

Scientology: Mind-Altering Pseudo-Psychology

Many of the cults that have developed since the 1960s have veered away entirely from any resemblance to Christianity and have no biblical base whatsoever. The main ingredients for some of these new "religions" are pop psychology, Eastern mysticism, psychic sentiments, positive thinking, and an authoritarian leader. In lieu of church services, there are seminars and retreats. These groups are sometimes referred to as "pseudo-scientific religious cults." One of the largest and most publicized of these groups is the Church of Scientology, organized as a church only after the "psychology" seminars of its founder began growing in popularity.

Scientology, having been the focus of controversy and government investigations throughout its short history, has had many loyal supporters along with many fierce critics. As with other alternative religious movements that have appeared on the scene in recent decades, the controversy has been heightened by the

secretive nature of the group—not the least of which has centered on the organization's elusive founder and leader.

L. Ron Hubbard

One of the most controversial religious leaders to emerge in recent decades has been the mysterious and obscure Lafayette Ronald Hubbard, a one-time science fiction writer and the founder of Scientology. His own publicity brochures acclaimed him as "one of the most popular men of our time," as evidenced by the more than eight million copies of *Dianetics* that have been sold as well as the "millions of people across the world" who are "using his valuable discoveries in some aspect of their everyday lives, with very beneficial results."[1]

It was the popularity of *Dianetics: The Modern Science of Mental Health* that launched Hubbard into his profession as a cult leader. Although his ideas were not perceived as religious per se, the book suddenly turned him into a guru with followers all over the world and he was quick to exploit the opportunity for his own benefit. In 1954, four years after he wrote the book, he founded the Church of Scientology. But that, according to Scientology publicity, was only the culmination of a creative and philanthropic enterprise.

> L. Ron Hubbard . . . a man whose tremendous contributions to virtually all walks of life have made him the greatest humanitarian in history.
>
> Indeed, few men have achieved so much in so many different fields. Author, philosopher, educator, research pioneer, musician, photographer, cinematographer, horticulturalist, navigator, explorer and humanitarian—Mr. Hubbard has been widely recognized for his contributions in all those fields. . . .[2]

The significance of Hubbard's contributions are by no means universally acknowledged. Indeed, some of his critics have suggested that he is little more than an ingenious charlatan who has duped his unwary followers into dedicating themselves to his grand hoax.

Early Years

According to Scientology sources, Hubbard was born in Nebraska in 1911, the son of a Navy commander. Because of his family's frequent moves, young Hubbard was sent to live with his grandparents on a cattle ranch in Montana, where it is claimed that he quickly became a child prodigy of sorts who rode a horse before he walked and began reading and writing by the time he was four years old. His childhood accomplishments continued when

he became the youngest Eagle Scout in the country and a bona fide blood brother of the Blackfoot Indians. He enjoyed his life as a young rancher. "Long days were spent riding, breaking broncos, hunting coyote and taking his first steps as an explorer."[3]

Religious Seeker and War Hero?

At the age of ten, Hubbard began living with his parents, who sought to redirect his interests. By the time he was twelve, according to a Scientology source, he "had already read a goodly number of the world's greatest classics—and his interest in philosophy and religion was born." He also, according to this same source, became a close friend of President Coolidge's son, Calvin, Jr., whose early death accelerated his precocious interest in the mind and spirit of man. During high school years Hubbard traveled in Asia with his father, studying Eastern religions. "It was in Northern China and India, while studying with holy men, that he became vitally engrossed in the subject of the spiritual destiny of Mankind." He then returned to the States, we are told, to earn doctorates in both philosophy and religion.[4]

In 1941, Hubbard was "ordered to the Philippines . . . at the outbreak of World War II." The Scientology account states that "He survived the early war in the South Pacific and was relieved by fifteen officers of rank and was rushed home to take part in the 1942 battle against German submarines as Commanding Officer of a Corvette serving in the North Atlantic." Then "after continual service in the various theaters of war, 1944 found him crippled and blinded in

Oak Knoll Naval Hospital." But after encountering a man who was "a personal student of Sigmund Freud . . . he developed techniques that would help him overcome his injuries and regain his abilities," and he soon "recovered so fully that he was reclassified for full combat duty."5

Not so, say his critics. A former archivist for the movement, Gerry Armstrong, who was assigned to write an authorized biography of Hubbard, unearthed information that proved otherwise, according to a report in *Time* magazine:

Armstrong discovered that even Hubbard's personal background was a sham. Public records show that when Hubbard had claimed to be traveling through Asia and the South Pacific from 1925 to 1929, learning what he called "the secrets of life" from magicians, lamas, priests and wise men, he was actually a mediocre high school student. Although Hubbard presented himself as a highly educated man, he flunked out of George Washington University's engineering school after two years.

Nor was Hubbard a World War II hero who miraculously cured himself of nearly fatal combat wounds, as he claimed. Hubbard never saw combat. After his discharge from the Navy in 1946, he was granted 40% disability pay for arthritis, bursitis and conjunctivitis. He continued to collect this pay long after he claimed to have discovered the secret of how to cure such ailments.6

Dianetics

Before and after his military duty, Hubbard was a busy free-lance writer. That "several million words poured from his pen and into print," as he claimed, is highly doubtful, but

he actually did publish science fiction and adventure stories in many magazines. Initially these stories had little to do with psychological or mind-altering themes, but by the late 1930s, he became known for writing "psychological thrillers" that were propelled by scenes of violence. In his story "Fear," a demon-possessed demonologist murders his wife and best friend. In "Death's Deputy," an incapacitated flying ace becomes a jinx after making a pact with "death" that leads to upheaval and tragedy among those closest to him. Themes of magic and demonology were frequent in Hubbard's writings, as were themes foreshadowing things to come in Hubbard's own journey to becoming a religious guru: "the vision of a dedicated elite with its charismatic leader; absorption with hidden realities that may be partly tricks of the mind; a still guarded but rather more intense interest in the darker side of human nature."7

Hubbard's "major breakthrough" did not come until 1948, when he released *Dianetics*. "The original thesis, his first formal report back from the frontiers of the mind and life, which he had been scouting for years, was a 30,000 word revelation." Whether or not that "revelation" was perceived to be supernatural, the manuscript was hastily expanded six times the original length and released in 1950 as a book, entitled *Dianetics: The Modern Science of Mental Health.* The book drew considerable interest and remained for several weeks on the New York *Times* best-seller list.8

Popularity of the Technique

By 1986, there were some eight million copies of *Dianetics* in print.

Although the contents of the book do not resemble religious scriptures of any sort, the 1986 commemorative edition has the appearance of a Bible with its imitation leather binding, gold leaf, and ribbon marker. For most of its readers, *Dianetics* has simply been another "advice/how-to" book which preceded the onslaught of the "me generation." The popularity of the book was largely due to the timing of its publication. "Were it to appear today," writes Harriet Whitehead, "Dianetics might pass scarcely noticed in the dense growth of popular psychotherapies on the American cultural landscape; but, appearing in 1950, it ranked among the earlier heralds of the popularizing trend that was to flourish so spectacularly in the decade of the 1960s."[9]

The popularity of the book was also due in part to the fact that it was self-contained, and its techniques were so easy to employ. Casual readers "would sit down and blithely audit their friends and relatives through war injuries, birth traumas, and back into the hubbub of the uterus where introduced objects, pressures of constipation, ill-advised medication, and the blows of angry or passionate mates" were found to be the source of misery.[10]

Mental and Physical Cures

Even though the book had no obvious religious focus, it became a bible to some of Hubbard's faithful followers. Indeed, to Hubbard himself the book was a bible of sorts. The book's claims were far more grandiose than even the most bombastic of the self-help diet and money-making books. The first chapter declares that the book "contains a therapeutic technique with which can be treated all inorganic mental ills and all organic psychosomatic ills, with assurance of complete cure in unselected cases." It also "brings forth the non-germ theory of disease, complementing biochemistry and Pasteur's work on the germ theory." These claims are further magnified in later chapters. For example, "by Dianetic technique such illness [psychosomatic] has been eradicated entirely in every case;" and, "the field of bacteriology has been without dynamic principles until now," with the advent of Dianetics. Again, Hubbard claims that Dianetic therapy "increases IQ to an enormous extent."[11]

While Hubbard insists that Dianetics can cure physical ills brought on by germs and other causes, his greatest emphasis is on mental illness. "Aberrations are contagious," he writes. "Like germs they respect none and carry forward from individual to individual, from parents to child, respecting none until they are stopped by Dianetics."[12] Because of his grandiose claims and because his Dianetic therapy resembles in some respects types of genuine mental health therapy, Hubbard has been the target of intense criticism. According to Omar V. Garrison, an ardent disciple of Hubbard, "the psychiatric fraternity was especially active in the attack on Hubbard and his movement, owing to the fact that he was articulate in opposing some of the more brutalizing practices of that discipline."[13]

The clash between Hubbard and the psychiatric community began with the publication of *Dianetics* and has continued in the decades since.

This becomes evident when reading Scientology literature, especially such publications as *Freedom*, a monthly antigovernment and antiestablishment organ issued by the church. Articles such as "Winking at Psychiatric Terror" and "Two Views Opposing Psychiatry's 'Final Solution'" malign the field of psychiatry and those who would seek treatment from it.[14]

Engrams

As popular as the book has been, *Dianetics* is not a book that is easily read. Hubbard has developed his own vocabulary that is defined by footnotes and a glossary in the back of the book, but even with these aids, the reading can be slow and the concepts difficult to grasp. The most fundamental concept in the book—the concept upon which virtually everything else is based—is that of "engrams," a term Hubbard borrowed from scientific disciplines. What is a Scientology engram?

The reactive bank [the portion of the mind that stores the periods of unconsciousness] does not store memories as we think of them. It stores *engrams*. These engrams are a complete recording, down to the last accurate detail, of every perception present in a moment of partial or full "unconsciousness." They are just as accurate as any other recording in the body. But they have their own *force*. They are like phonograph records or motion pictures, if these contained all perceptions of sight, sound, smell, taste, organic sensation, etc.

The difference between an engram and a memory, however, is quite distinct. An engram can be permanently fused into any and all body circuits and behaves like an entity.

In all laboratory tests on these engrams they were found to possess "inexhaustible" sources of power to command the body. No matter how many times one was reactivated in an individual, it was still powerful. . . .

The only thing which could even begin to shake these engrams was the technique which developed in Dianetic therapy. . . .[15]

One might surmise that if there were such things as engrams, they would be both beneficial and harmful. Not so. "Perhaps before man had a large vocabulary, these engrams were of some use to him. . . . But when man acquired . . . language . . . these engrams were much more a liability than a help. And now, with man well evolved, these engrams do not protect him at all but make him mad, inefficient and ill." The solution is to clear the mind of these engrams through Dianetic therapy. "As has been proven by clinical research, clearing of engrams does more than remove psychosomatic illness, potential, acute or chronic. The clearing also tends to proof the individual against the receipt of pathology."[16]

The entire discussion of engrams and the process of "clearing" them, which runs throughout the book, is too lengthy to recount. It should be pointed out, though, that the findings are not considered scientific, nor are the "laboratory tests" and "clinical research" regarded as reputable by the medical community.

Only Positive Results

The aspect of *Dianetics* that is most controversial is the claim that its method of therapy represents the solution to all ills, and that it can never have harmful effects—despite the fact that the counselors ('auditors') frequently have very little training. *"In Dianetics, any case, no matter how serious, no matter how unskilled the auditor,"* writes Hubbard, *"is better opened than left closed.* It is better to start therapy if it is to be interrupted after two hours of work than not to start therapy at all. It is better to contact an engram than to leave an engram uncontacted even if the result is physical discomfort for the patient." It is assumed, however, that the patient will continue with the therapy until the process is completed. "The purpose of therapy and its sole target is the removal of the content of the reactive engram bank. In a *release*, the majority of emotional stress is deleted from this bank. In a *clear* [one who has successfully gone through the process of therapy], the entire content is removed."[17]

Dianetic Therapy

Designed to involve large numbers of people, the simplicity of Dianetic or Scientology therapy was proclaimed to be its primary attraction. Indeed, Hubbard often insisted that "Dianetics is extremely simple." The therapy is a one-on-one interaction between patient and auditor.

The patient sits in a comfortable chair, with arms, or lies on a couch in a quiet room where perceptic distractions are minimal. The auditor tells him to look at the ceiling. The auditor says: "When I count from one to seven your eyes will close." The auditor then counts from one to seven and keeps counting quietly and pleasantly until the patient closes his eyes. A tremble of the lashes will be noticed in optimum *reverie.*

This is the entire routine. Consider it more a signal that proceedings are to begin and a means of concentrating the patient on his own concerns and the auditor than anything else. *This is not hypnotism.* It is vastly different. In the first place, the patient knows everything which is going on around him. He is not "asleep," and can bring himself out of it any time he likes. . . .[18]

Once the condition of "reverie" is established with the patient, the auditor encourages the patient to recount unconscious experiences of the past that have been painful. "Ideally, all the forgotten details of the incident should come to light, the emotion experienced in the past should be reexperienced in the auditing session, and its force fully discharged. Once this has occurred, the incident is 'erased' from the Reactive Mind and can no longer effect the pre-clear's life." These may be experiences that occurred on a fifth birthday, or they may be prenatal experiences of pain inflicted when the patient's mother was douching or engaged in sexual intercourse. Once these unconscious experiences are visualized and then renounced, the engram can be released. This procedure is repeated time and again in repeated therapy sessions until the patient is "cleared" of all engrams.[19]

Dabbling in psychotherapy and toying with a patient's unconscious mind is obviously a risky venture, and is generally considered outside the capability of a hastily trained counselor. To protect his counselors from liability, Hubbard provided a shield in the form of a "canceler." What is a canceler?

It is a contract with the patient that whatever the auditor says will not become literally interpreted by the patient or used by him in any way. It is installed immediately after the condition of reverie is established. A *canceler* is worded more or less as follows: "In the future, when I utter the word *canceled,* everything which I have said to you while you are in a therapy session will be canceled and will have no force with you. Any suggestion I have made to you will be without force when I say the word *canceled.* Do you understand?"

The word *canceled* is then said to the patient immediately before he is permitted to open his eyes at the end of the session. . . .[20]

Dianetics was only the first installment of Hubbard's "modern science of mental health." He went on to write more books, to develop E-meter "technology," and to organize a church that would aid in promoting and conducting his Dianetic therapy.

Church Organization

The popularity of *Dianetics* and the desire expressed by many of the book enthusiasts to learn more about his methodology led Hubbard to organize Scientology as a church in 1954. "This was in keeping with the religious nature of the tenets dating from the earliest of research," according to Scientology literature. "It was obvious that he had been exploring religious territory right along. And . . . it was apparent to those with a sense of history and Man's ages-old spiritual quest that this was indeed the realm of the soul and its havens."[21]

To outsiders it was not so obvious that Hubbard's discoveries were of a religious nature, and a controversy quickly arose as to whether Scientology ought to be given the benefits enjoyed by a valid religion. Was this science fiction writer really serious about religion, or was religion a front to salvage a faltering secular organization? It is not difficult to be cynical about Hubbard's motives since he himself had boasted to friends, "If a man really wanted to make a million dollars, the best way would be to start his own religion." In addition to financial motives, there were, no doubt, organizational motives that prompted Hubbard to create a church out of his secular enterprise. Many of his early followers were independent and only very loosely united—if united at all. They were not committed to a *cause,* and Hubbard realized that religion was the missing element to establish that cause. Although he realized he would lose some adherents, he recognized the value of a hard core following whose financial resources would sustain him and the movement indefinitely.[22]

Black Dianetics

Those who had utilized Dianetics but resisted any type of authoritarian religious connections were condemned by Hubbard. Their variation on his "science" was termed "Black Dianetics," the dangers of which were exposed to the true Scientologists. In many respects, this early division between secularists and religionists resembles the earliest years of Christian Science when Mary Baker Eddy was transforming the healing arts of P. P. Quimby into a self-styled authoritarian religion. She condemned those who went their separate ways and accused them of practicing not Black Dianetics but Malicious Animal Magnetism.[23]

Eclectic Religion

Hubbard himself denied that there was any inherent change in the nature of Dianetics, insisting that the religious nature of his work was evident long before he officially organized the church. He cited both Buddha and Confucius as religious founders to whom he was indebted, but insisted that his spirituality was derived even more from observations he made throughout his lifetime on folk religion and the occult.

In a lifetime of wandering around many strange things had been observed. The medicine man of the Goldi people of Manchuria, the shamans of North Borneo, Sioux medicine men, the cults of Los Angeles, and modern psychology. Amongst the people questioned about existence were a magician whose ancestors served in the court of Kublai Khan and a Hindu who could hypnotize cats. Dabbles had been made in mysticism, data had been studied from mythology to spiritualism. Odds and ends like these, countless odds and ends.[24]

In an effort to present the organization as a religion, the language of *Dianetics* was sometimes reformulated in religious parlance, as was the "E-meter" technology developed to aid in auditing. In defending his "church" against a raid made by agents from the Food and Drug Administration, Omar Garrison accused the agents of confiscating *confessional artifacts* (E-meters), used by the *church* in *pastoral counseling*. In his explanation of Dianetic therapy, Garrison referred to the patient as a *parishioner,* to the auditor as a *minister,* and to engrams as *areas of spiritual travail*—terms never used by Hubbard in his book *Dianetics.* [25]

Church Franchises

Disseminating pop psychology as a religion was not new with Hubbard. What was innovative, however, was the means by which he marketed his merchandise. From the very beginning, he "granted franchise rights to various people, enabling them to set up shop as a franchise of the Church of Scientology. The franchise holder would pay 10 percent of the franchise's income to the Church. . . . Scientology franchises were a sort of religious non-profit McDonald's." The franchise holder was expected to bring in "raw meat" (new converts), but after that was strictly limited to only lower level "auditing." The higher—and much more costly—levels of auditing were reserved for the top echelon of the organization.[26]

Religious Beliefs and Practices

Is Scientology a real religion, or is it, as critics have suggested, "behavior therapy masquerading as a church and making a mockery of honest religious practices"? There is no doubt that Scientology began as a "behavior therapy," but the question remains whether the beliefs and practices later developed are consistent with that of a bona fide religion. Christian Science, for example, though not a religion consistent with orthodox Christianity, is nonetheless rightly regarded as a religion. But the Church of Scientology, despite its

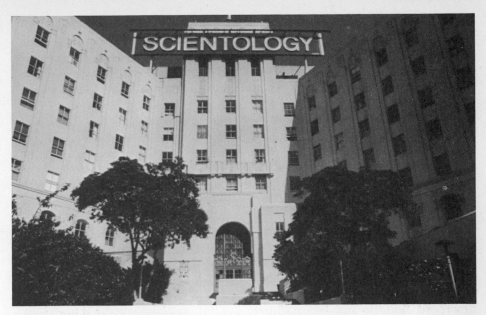

Church of Scientology Headquarters in Los Angeles.

effort to utilize religious language, is in many ways outside the scope of traditional religion. Yet it must be studied as a religion both because of the organization's claim to be such, and because of the religious perception of the organization in the minds of the devotees.

Scientology Theology

Scientology, as it evolved from the initial Dianetics stage, developed a theology of sorts that forms the central core of beliefs. These can be summed up in three tenets: (1) every human being is a thetan, "an immortal spirit with potentially limitless powers;" (2) every individual has a Reactive Mind Bank containing engrams, which suppresses these limitless powers over MEST (Matter, Energy, Space, and Time); (3) through auditing the engrams are erased and the Bank emptied, and then thetans can be restored "to their original powerful state."[27]

Roy Wallis, a sociologist who has studied the movement, has expanded on this theology of the thetans: "The Thetan is immortal, 'omniscient and omnipotent,' the true self of each individual, which has existed since before the beginning of matter, energy, space, and time. These latter are merely the creations of thetans bored with their existence." According to Hubbard, "life is a game" that thetans play. After creating MEST, thetans "became absorbed into the games they were playing, permitting further limitations of their abilities, imposing limitations upon other thetans, forgetting their spiritual nature. . . . The thetans became so enmeshed in their creation they forgot their origins and true states, lost the ability to mobilize their spiritual capacities, and came to believe that they were no more than the bodies they inhabited."[28]

Operating Thetans

Reminiscent of the soul in the Hindu religion, a thetan transmigrates from one life to another, taking on "many millions of MEST bodies during the trillions of years of its existence." The purpose of Scientology is for "the discovery and refinement of methods whereby the Thetan can be persuaded to relinquish his self-imposed limitations." Once they are entirely relinquished, the individual becomes an OT (operating thetan). Since the discoveries of Scientology have never before been available in human history, it should not be surprising to learn that "Neither Lord Buddha nor Jesus Christ were OTs according to the evidence. They were just a shade above Clear."[29]

An OT, it should be pointed out, is entirely independent of physical laws, while a Clear is merely an individual who has, through auditing, erased the engrams from the Reactive Mind Bank. An OT, likewise, is not necessarily encased in a human body at all.[30]

E-Meter Technology

The Church of Scientology, according to its own publicity, is a combination of "Dianetics spiritual healing technology" and "Scientology applied religious philosophy." Some, of course, would suggest that the religious philosophy was "applied" only after the "healing technology" of *Dianetics* became popular, allowing Hubbard to use religion to capitalize on his loyal following. The "technology" Hubbard invented to aid in Dianetic therapy for "spiritual healing" consists primarily of a device called the E-meter (electrogalvanometer). "To use the E-meter, a person holds a tin can in each hand while a galvanometer wired to the cans ostensibly indicates emotional stress. While the subject is 'on the cans,' a Scientologist 'auditor' quizzes him to uncover any embarrassing or painful experiences in his past."[31]

During the auditing session, a low current is transmitted "through the pre-clear from one terminal to another, the resistance being measured on a dial." The needle on this dial is supposed to indicate such emotional responses as would be evidenced by sweating or tightening of the muscles. By observing the dial the auditor can make "body-reads" that show changes that are occurring in the person being audited. "The E-meter is held to be infallible," writes Roy Wallis. "It 'sees all, knows all. It is never wrong.' "[32]

Reincarnation

While the religious nature of this auditing was not initially obvious when Hubbard wrote *Dianetics*, his ideas developed. Reincarnation and other Eastern religious concepts became a significant aspect of the therapy. The desired end result of this process is to remove the distressing thoughts and images (engrams) that every individual carries. These engrams are often inherited from previous lives and stored in the Reactive Mind. It is only by erasing these engrams that a person can come to full potential as a god, or thetan. Human beings are actually gods, but because they are unaware of this fact, they do not act the part. Through the process of auditing with the E-meter, a person can become an operating thetan, free from all the physical and mental ills that plague the rest of humanity.[33]

As an operating thetan, an individual can also enjoy soul travel and explore previous lives. Hubbard himself claimed to have explored past lives that took him back some seventy-four trillion years. Indeed, exploring past lives became an important aspect of his "research" and was the subject matter of his book *Mission into Time*. He scorned people who "fool around with this subject," without scientific objectivity. "In any spin-bin you can find 'Cleopatra,' 'Napoleon' and 'Julius Caesar.' You have people around who are always telling you who they've been. It seems that the only lives they've led are ones you'll find in the Encyclopedia Britannica."[34]

To research "whole track recall" (a moment to moment record of past lives), Hubbard plotted missions in connection with his Sea Org—a select group of Hubbard's followers who did their work on board sailing vessels, which is "likened to a religious order, its members making a symbolic commitment to remain in the Sea Organization for a billion years." On one such mission he sailed to various ports in the Mediterranean, and before each stop gave various members of his crew a map of what they could expect to find—a map based on his "whole track recall" of his previous life in that particular port city. He not only provided a map but also a detailed description of his past life. The following account is an example of his life "in Carthage about the second or third century

B.C., operating there with the Carthaginian Fleet":

I used to have a pretty good time around Carthage—nice sailing water and so on. Around 200 B.C., I knew a girl over in Nora (it wasn't called Nora then) who was the current Goddess of Tanit and a good-looking girl. We had a lot of good-looking girls in Carthage but they didn't come up to her.

And so, I used to sail across to Sardinia. . . . When we were going along the African Coast, it was always easier to go via Nora. Officers used to kid me about this. They seemed to think that all navigational patterns ran through the town of Nora.

It was usually a good thing that I called into Nora with a war vessel because it was almost a matter of war. . . . I probably could have had more duels than sunrises because this was quite a girl. . . .[35]

The real test of Hubbard's ability to recall this past life was to verify it against archaeological research. "There had been a secret entrance into the Temple of Tanit and, from my recall, I drew up the plans of both it and the Temple. . . . Missions were sent ashore to survey and map the area to see if they couldn't discover this old secret entrance. . . ." What did they find? For the sake of objectivity, Hubbard leaves the account of the search to be told by one of his assistants. After discovering the temple itself, they found a "ditch" that led "right up next to the foundation of the temple." Then, she writes, "we kept on digging there until we were quite convinced that this was the ditch that led into the basement of the temple." What was her conclusion regarding this particular past life of Hubbard's? "So, that was totally proven and accurate."[36]

Clerical and Technical Levels of Proficiency

There are various levels of competency within the Church of Scientology and various forms of credentials, including ordination credentials similar to that received by a minister in a traditional religious denomination. The Reverend Arthur J. Maren, who joined the church in 1963, is an example of one such ordained minister. His testimony offers a glowing account of the organization, but it also offers insight into the expectations of full-time ministers: "I joined the church after a two-year ordeal of drug usage and degradation. Within months of joining the Church of Scientology and following its precepts, I had discarded my former life. Quite simply, scientology saved my life." He trained for six years before he was ordained, attaining "the highest technical level of proficiency available." During and after that time, he maintains that he worked "16 to 18 hours a day, six to seven days a week" for a salary that "has never been more than $85 per week."[37]

Like Unity, the Church of Scientology does not require new members to abandon previous church involvement. Ken Hoden, who has served as an ordained Scientology minister in Los Angeles, insists that his religion is nondenominational. Although he wears a clerical collar and conducts Sunday services, funerals, and weddings, he emphasizes that church membership does not exclude other religious affiliations.[38]

Attending church services in not a high priority, and that is one reason why the religious nature of the organization is often held in question. The emphasis, as with many New-Age-oriented groups, is on self-improvement or self-actualization, not on worship. The church buildings are made up of classrooms and offices, and auditing and training is offered during the day and at night. For higher levels of training, Scientologists go to one of the few Advanced Orgs either in the United States or Europe or cruise on the high seas in a Sea Org. In recent years, much of the high level mission work conducted on the ocean crafts has been transferred to a large hotel and office complex in Clearwater, Florida, known as "Flag Land Base."[39]

Attaining Godhood and Perfection

For Scientologists the ultimate goal of religion is specifically to become an OT (operating thetan), which is a complex procedure having many levels preceding that state of consciousness and even higher levels to achieve once that state is attained. The beginner starts on the introductory level and may proceed to New OT I, OT II, OT III (The Wall of Fire), New OT IV (OT Drug Rundown), and all the way up to New OT VII. This "final step through the Second Wall of Fire is a very lengthy but rewarding and exciting journey. . . . Here the final shadowy barriers fall away and the answers to the secrets of life shine clear—with spectacular theta perceptions, abilities and awareness beyond your wildest dreams![40]

On a practical level, how does an OT function differently in life than someone who has not discovered the full potential of being a god? In an article entitled "Cause and Effect," Hubbard offers an illustration that would seem to reflect not so much higher levels of godhood but simply superficial pop psychology. "A man is late for work: full of regret, he walks into the office, blaming others—'The car broke down. . . . My wife didn't get me up on time.'. . . Or blames self: 'It's all my fault. I never get around in time for anything.'" His problem, according to Hubbard, is that he is ascribing "cause" to things or others, unable to be "cause" himself. "Contrast the difference in the person willing to accept full responsibility for his tardiness," writes Hubbard. "Entering the office buoyantly and seeing questioning eyes, some such comment as 'Well, I'm late' suffices, and he plunges into work without negating to the bottom of the tone scale. This man controls environment and his own theta facsimiles."[41]

Becoming first a Clear and finally an OT has its problems. Claiming to have arrived at a state of perfection requires living a life befitting this higher plane of existence. Scientology therefore has constructed a "hierarchy of sanctification" that is complex and most difficult to demonstrate, considering the depravity of human nature.

During the early years of Dianetic teaching, some individuals testified that they became disillusioned because they "weren't clears after one hundred hours of processing," and this disillusionment "was heightened by the apparent failure of those declared 'clear' to perform in a manner regarded as appropriate; . . . and the failure of the two hundred or so individuals Hubbard maintained that he had cleared, before the publication of his book, to manifest themselves in any way." Indeed, "Hubbard's own behaviour between 1950 and 1952 had given some cause to doubt the efficacy of his 'science.'"[42] As with most perfectionist ideologies, there is a failure to work on the practical level, and that has been a persistent complaint against Scientology over the years.

Membership and Financial Data

In 1986, the Church of Scientology claimed that it had more than three million members in the United States alone, and some six million worldwide. While it is true that some eight million copies of *Dianetics* have been printed, that figure would no more reflect Scientology membership than Bible sales would reflect membership in Christian churches. Nor would the numbers of people who have tried Dianetic therapy represent church membership. Indeed, according to religion experts, the membership figures have been vastly overstated.[43]

The recruiting of new members comes in part by street work—passing out literature and inviting passers-by to introductory seminars. In the Los Angeles area, store front centers have specialized in offering free IQ testing, specially-priced copies of *Dianetics*, and a brief sales pitch for the therapy program. Most of the new recruits, however, have been personal friends and acquaintances of people already involved in Scientology who help initiate the novice through the beginning stages of the program.[44]

Only a tiny minority of those who begin the process of Dianetic therapy successfully complete it to become

"Clears" or "optimum individuals." These would be the elite of the church as a whole, but even among this group, there is indication that a large percentage have never had any active church participation. Yet, it is this core of believers who represent by their lives the highest teachings of the church:

Today, documented by their shining success stories, Clears number in the tens of thousands. Their influence is felt in business, law, economics, the arts, childcare, the health professions—indeed, every aspect of society. Every day of their lives, Clears find themselves able to experience a state of spiritual well-being, happiness and self-confidence to which man has aspired for centuries.

Indeed, the figure of "tens of thousands" refers only to those Clears who are actually "certified," i.e., who have reported in to a Hubbard Guidance Center (an auditing center) and who now exist on record. There are probably many thousands more who have achieved this state through auditing with the *Dianetics* book, but who have not yet been officially validated.[45]

The Church of Scientology is not financed by voluntary contributions as most churches are. The major portion of revenues is derived from fees for auditing and training, that is, fees for counseling and seminar sessions. Both types of sessions are graded from lower to higher levels and can consume years of time. The one-on-one auditing fee averaged some thirty-five dollars per hour in the 1970s, and the seminar sessions were between five and ten dollars per hour.[46]

The sale of books also provides a large source of revenue—new books that offer the latest data and techniques, and revisions of older books. Another lucrative aspect of merchandising for Scientology has involved its "technology." The E-meter and other necessary paraphernalia are advertised in organizational literature and are available at Scientology headquarters in Tampa, Florida—but only for those who can afford such a luxury. A 1983 price list showed the Brown Leather Executive Model Mark VI E-meter selling for $4,100. A course lecture cassette set was listed for $1,875. A set of eight organization executive course books was listed for $840.[47]

Authoritarian Leadership and Deviant Lifestyle

After he founded the Church of Scientology, Hubbard continued to write and lecture, spreading his message of mental health wherever he went. His personal life, however, was a mystery. His son later revealed that his father's writings had not been the product of decades of research as had been claimed, but rather were "written off the top of his head"—often while in a state of virtual incoherence due to his drug dependency. In other instances, according to his son, his writings were taken directly from the teachings of others—most notably Aleister Crowley on the subject of black magic and Satanism. There were other problems as well. Hubbard "had a long history of venereal disease, sexual perversion, and mental illness," as well as involvement in "bizarre occult practices." "His delusions . . . led him to believe that he was the Beast of Revelation and that he had the power to control all of mankind."[48]

Despite his alleged mental and physical problems, Hubbard managed to create a personality cult that seemed to thrive on his eccentricities. In this respect, he was similar to Mary Baker Eddy and more recent personality cult leaders like David "Moses" Berg, whose ailments, obsessions, and unconventional behavior was overlooked by devoted followers. Hubbard, like Eddy and Berg, was a powerful authority figure and he forcefully wielded absolute control over his vast organization.

Shunning

Maintaining control over Scientology was not an easy matter. Many of the "converts" were well-educated people who prided themselves in independent thinking. They struggled with the idea of allowing any other individual to completely dominate their opinions. Some of these individuals went on to establish franchises, only to be confronted with serious opposition when it was discovered that their ideas often conflicted with those of Hubbard. The problem of discontented members escalated in the 1960s, as the membership grew and as authoritarian control increased. A form of shunning—similar to what has been employed by such groups as the Jehovah's Witnesses, the Worldwide Church of God, and The Way International—was exercised in order to prevent defections. Any member who was determined to be disloyal to Scientology was deemed an *Enemy* and categorized as a "Suppressive Person." S.P.s were threatened verbal-ly and sometimes physically, and were typically accused of being "criminals, communists or sexual deviants."[49]

Anyone who associated with an S.P. was specified as a Potential Trouble Source (PTS) and was required to "handle" the S.P. by "showing him the error of his ways, or to disconnect from him." Disconnection involved "cutting off all communication with the S.P. and declaring one's intention to do so publicly." Disconnections were accomplished by writing a memo to the S.P. and having that published in Scientology literature. "An individual could be required to disconnect from a relative, friend or a total stranger. Some . . . who had been declared S.P. received as many as 200 disconnecting letters."[50]

Physical Abuse

Shunning is a common cult practice, and it is often perceived as necessary for maintaining control over a developing religion. According to some accounts, however, Hubbard's style could more accurately be compared to that of Jim Jones than of more traditional cult leaders. By 1974, the "blatant breaking of another person's will—'break 'em down, build 'em back up'—became full blown and implemented as official dogma: The Rehabilitation Project Force" (RPF). Under this policy, Scientologists who were falling short of expectations were sometimes locked in cellars, physically beaten, or forced to perform hard labor. A report of such conditions at the Scientology center in Clearwater, Florida, gives a chilling description of the tyranny involved.

313

Scientology members protesting court judgement in Portland, Oregon.
From Religious News Service.

Those under discipline testified to "being locked in the lower boiler rooms to live among the piping, to have to clean the filthiest areas of the property, and to being guarded against "blowing" (trying to escape). The objective was to break the offender's will. "After a few days, one looked like an animal, depraved and degraded. Soot, dirt, grease and grime were everywhere. Inmates were instilled with a deep fear of violating a senior's orders."[51]

Tonja, a girl who was ensnared in Scientology between the age of thirteen and eighteen, was assigned to hard labor and paid some ten dollars per week. She was later sent a bill for $58,000 for auditing fees. She subsequently described her work while she was on board a ship.

I scrubbed clothes from six A.M. until noon without breakfast or any breaks. The clothes were scrubbed by hand in a bucket. . . .

After a half-hour lunch, I was assigned to clean six cabins. These had to meet white-glove inspection. . . . My day ended about midnight.

On rainy days I ironed the clothes dry. This required ironing during the evening hours and into the morning hours. On many occasions I ironed through the night and finished at six A.M. . . . On occasion, I worked three or four days without sleep. . . .

Another young woman testified that while she was assigned to a ship, she was forced on one occasion to have sex with Hubbard.[52]

Law and Violence

More than any of the other religious or pseudo religious cults in modern times, Scientology has been the target of police investigations and litigation. Former members have even accused it of blackmail and mob-style violence. By 1986 there were more than fifteen legal cases pending against the organization from former members who believed they had been defrauded. The most publicized of these law cases was a thirty-nine-million-dollar suit brought before a circuit court judge in Portland, Oregon. The plaintiff was a young woman who alleged that, beginning at the age of seventeen, she had spent more than three thousand dollars on Scientology courses that were guaranteed to increase her eyesight, creativity, and intelligence. It was only after being deprogramed that she realized she had been duped. Although the jury recommended that her claim be assessed against the church, the judge declared a mistrial because the plaintiff's attorney had made prejudicial statements against Scientology.[53]

Government Raids

Not unlike the case against Sun Myung Moon and the Unification Church, the National Council of Churches and the Coalition for Religious Freedom both supported the Church of Scientology in its legal battles. While insisting they did not endorse the beliefs of Scientology, representatives for these groups insisted that they opposed the courts' infringement on the freedom of religion. According to Scientologists themselves, far more than the freedom of religion was at stake in their battles against the courts and law enforcement agencies. After ten years of harassment by various local and federal government officials, "U.S. Attorney General Oliver Gasch and his allies in the FDA and Washington's Metropolitan Police Department were ready for their more drastic course of action," according to Omar Garrison.

On January 4, 1963, under the guise of executing a warrant authorizing the seizure of E-meters, a raiding party of U.S. Marshals, joined by FDA agents and three narcotics officers from the D.C. Police Department, swooped down on the church. In Gestapo fashion, they ransacked desks and filing cabinets and, in addition to E-meters, carted away a truckload of creedal literature. Hoping to find some evidence of drugs (for which they had not the slightest authority to search) the officers invaded residential quarters occupied by the church staff. There they rifled closets, bureau drawers, and even lifted bedcovers. An attorney representing the church later testified before a Senate hearing, claiming that in his forty-five years of practice he had "never seen anything so violative of the Constitution of the United States."

He [the assistant chief marshal] produced what he called a warrant or libel, which contained a complaint by the Food & Drug Administration and said that the seizure was being made under that warrant or libel.

I examined the warrant or libel, and I found that it hadn't been sworn to, it had no affidavit, no oath. It was merely the statement of the U.S. attorney and two of his assistants, and contained nothing—nothing that really verified the charges in the warrant. It contained no evidence.

I found that it did not even name the church in the warrant. . . . Furthermore, the warrant authorized a search of premises not even occupied or rented by the church.

The marshals tramped through the building beating on doors, grabbing books out of the arms and hands of students. They pounded on doors where religious confessionals were being conducted.[54]

In 1969, after six years of litigation, an appeals court ruled that the Church of Scientology "had made a prima facie showing that it was indeed a bona fide religion, protected by the First Amendment." Some of the E-meters and three tons of Scientology documents were returned, but not until four years later. The church was then assessed costs for the ten

years of storing the material confiscated in the raid.[55]

The most sweeping government investigation of Scientology occurred in 1977 after a three-pronged raid on the organization. "There hadn't really been anything like it since the days of Al Capone and the other Chicago gangsters," write Trevor Meldal-Johnsen and Patrick Lusey. "Early on the morning of July 8, 1977, before most people were awake, more than 130 FBI agents in Washington, D.C., Los Angeles and Hollywood gathered for the Raid. . . . Armed with crowbars, battering rams, sledgehammers and power saws, they tore their way into the buildings." Syndicated columnist James J. Kilpatrick described the raid as "gangbusters all over again" and warned of impending danger: "The main point is the monstrous power of the state, whose legal and financial resources are inexhaustible. When that power is fueled by animus—by spite and malice—the machinery of tyranny begins to roll. Last month, the Scientologists. Next month, who?"[56]

The Practice of "Fair Game"

There may have indeed been instances of unwarranted harassment by government agencies, as Scientologists allege, but the confrontation between this "religion" and the government is in many ways understandable. And that the Food and Drug Administration would be involved in investigating an organization claiming to cure all types of illnesses would seem appropriate. There were other reasons for government agencies to suspect that unscrupulous and illegal activity was being conducted in the highest levels of the organization. An IRS investigation and subsequent trial revealed that the church exercised a policy known as "Fair Game" against defectors. This policy has since been admitted and justified by Scientologists:

> The practice of Fair Game, which the church maintains, was never understood by the general public, was formulated in response to heavy attacks by Scientology's enemies in the early 60's. It stated that a Suppressive Person or group (i.e., those seeking to destroy the church) "may be deprived of property or injured by any means by any Scientologist without any discipline of the Scientologists. May be tricked, sued, lied to or destroyed."

While such extreme tactics against a mortal enemy are perfectly acceptable in wartime and, indeed, have been used by warring nations throughout history, they are viewed with abhorrence when practiced openly in peacetime—at least in Western societies, where appearances of good sportsmanship must be maintained.

Perhaps L. Ron Hubbard took the measure of the enemies who surrounded him on all sides, their daggers drawn—so to speak—for the kill. The Scientologists had been tricked, sued, lied to, and made an avowed target for annihilation. Would not turnabout be fair play (or fair game) under such circumstances?[57]

Death of Hubbard

Because he believed that his enemies were real and that his very life was threatened, Hubbard went into seclusion during his later years. Other factors contributing to his reclusiveness may have been mental derangement and a chemical dependency. There are many conflicting accounts of the last years of this man; he was not seen in public for six years before he died in 1986 at the age of seventy-four. The first announcement of his death was made to a large crowd of Scientologists at the Hollywood Palladium by a high-ranking church member. It was not a somber occasion, as his address indicates:

> I'm very happy that you could all make it to this important briefing this evening.
>
> In 1980 LRH moved off the lines so that he could continue his writings and research without any distractions. . . .
>
> Over the past six years LRH has been intensively researching the upper bands of OT. . . .
>
> Approximately two weeks ago, he completed all of his researches he set out to do.
>
> He has now moved on to the next level of OT research. It's a level beyond anything any of us ever imagined.
>
> This level is in fact done in an exterior state. Meaning that it is done completely exterior from the body. At this level of OT, the body is nothing more than an impediment and encumbrance to any further gain as an OT.
>
> Thus at 2000 hours, the 24th of January, AD36 [After Dianetics], L. Ron Hubbard discarded the body he had used in this life time for 74 years 10 months and 11 days. . . .

Following the announcement, the audience broke into applause and cheers that lasted for some twenty minutes. Other high-ranking officials were then introduced, and the crowd was admonished to remain loyal to the church and its leaders.[58]

Missionary Outreach

Scientology is a worldwide organization with "missionaires" reaching into countries on virtually every continent. The original term "missionaire" has been substituted with the term "missionary" by some in more recent years, in an effort to give the organization an appearance of a more conventional religion. But the effect is the same—spreading the message of Hubbard to anyone anywhere who will listen and invest in auditing or training. By 1975, there were 193 Scientology missions around the world. These missions (or centers) are generally located in metropolitan areas and may be operated by one person or an entire staff of a dozen or more people serving both as volunteers and salaried workers.[59]

Like Christian missionaries, Hubbard's missionaries sometimes face adversity and persecution. In 1980, according to Omar Garrison, "two Scientology missionaries" were accused of drug trafficking "in the Barajas airport in Madrid. . . . An American agent led the interrogation, in the foul-mouthed, third-degree style of a Chicago precinct backroom."[60]

Despite the opposition and the law enforcement officials following Scientologists around the world, the movement has effectively established centers in most of the major European cities (including ten cities in Italy alone), and in Japan, Australia, and New Zealand, as well as several cities in Africa and in cities throughout South and Central America.[61]

Although there are some Scientology missions in the poorer third world countries, the vast majority of the converts come from the middle classes (78.5 percent). Most of these were under thirty years of age and had abandoned a Protestant or Roman Catholic heritage. Nearly forty percent of the converts who were surveyed had a university education, a factor which would not tend to support the accusation of brainwashing. Scientology presents itself as a religion that views mankind as inherently good and with a vast potential—a religion for educated and intelligent people. Their publicity has been very successful, so much so that some researchers have called the organization "the fastest-growing religion in the world."[62]

Chapter 15

The New Age Movement: The Occult Made Respectable

The most popular and widely publicized new religion in recent years has been the New Age Movement, a difficult-to-define variety of mystical, spiritualistic, and occultic groups that above all else are not *new*. From channeling to crystals to harmonic convergences, celebrities and ordinary citizens have been captivated by this increasingly popular religious trend. Its supporters are lavish in their praise of its potential for world harmony, societal betterment, human happiness, self-actualization, and inner peace; its critics condemn its religious heresy, its subjectivity, and its blatant materialism. Indeed, the response to the New Age is as varied as the movement itself. It is the butt of jokes by comedians, the great whore of Babylon in the view of many fundamentalists, the answer to humanity's problems according to true New Age believers, and a means to financial success in the eyes of profiteers.

The New Age Movement, by its very name, heralds a new age that is dawning in the universe. This mythical Age of Aquarius (popularized in the musical *Hair*) is an astrological "star age" that has a powerful influence on humanity—especially in the area of religious beliefs. "For the past 2,000 years the Earth has been influenced by the sign of Pices, the fish," so the theory goes. "This sign is identified with Christianity because the symbol of the fish was one of the marks of identification adopted by the early church. Astrologers say that the Piscean Age was a 'watery' one in which occult knowledge was undervalued and occult powers were in decline."

That was the past. The Age of Aquarius has now dawned. "Exactly when a new star age begins is difficult to predict. Each is supposed to last 2,200 years, and the best guess astrologers can give is plus or minus 100 years." Many New Age proponents, including Shirley MacLaine, believe we are already into the Aquarian Age—an age of "humanism, brotherhood, and occult happenings."[1]

From a sociological perspective, the New Age Movement differs significantly from the cults of the 1960s that were a refuge for rebellious youth turning their backs on their middle-class families and sacrificing all to live in dingy communes and to work long hours for the cause. The New Age Movement, on the other hand, attracts middle-aged people—primarily women—who are in many cases financially able to support their "addiction" and maintain a comfortable lifestyle at the same time. It is a movement in which "respectable" people can participate and solicit their friends without embarrassment. As such, it incorporates vast numbers of individuals who would otherwise shun any involvement in "cult" activity. "Part of the reason for this growth," writes Diane Salvatore, "may . . . be demographics. New Age has attracted the majority of its adherents from aging baby boomers—a group second only to the elderly in population growth."[2]

In seeking to understand the scope of the New Age Movement, it is important to recognize that New Age thinking permeates the theology of a wide range of alternative religions and cultic movements, many of which predated the contemporary New Age Movement by generations or even centuries. Mormonism is an example. Joseph Smith was deeply involved in spiritualism and had frequent communication with spirit guides. There is, likewise, considerable New Age philosophy in Christian Science, New Thought, Unity, the Children of God, the Unification Church, the Hare Krishnas, Scientolo-gy, and many lesser-known cultic movements such as Rosicrucianism, Swedenborgianism, est, Eckankar, the Church Universal and Triumphant, Silva Mind Control, Yoga, the Rajneesh Ashram, and the Divine Light Mission (See Appendix A). Broadly speaking, then, the New Age Movement encompasses many religious movements that would not generally be categorized as such.

But far beyond the influence of New Age philosophy on organized religious movements is the influence of New Age thinking in everyday society. According to Karen Hoyt, executive director of the Spiritual Counterfeits Project, "The New Age Movement influences can be seen in America's shifting religious beliefs. Currently, 23 percent of Americans believe in reincarnation; 23 percent believe in astrology; and 25 percent believe in a nonpersonal energy or life force."[3]

What is an objective definition and evaluation of New Age? In a cover-story article, *Time* magazine summed up the movement by saying, "All in all, the New Age does express a cloudy sort of religion, claiming vague connections with both Christianity and the major faiths of the East . . . plus an occasional dab of pantheism and sorcery." The article went on to emphasize the subjective and unorthodox nature of the religion, which only seems to add to its appeal: "The underlying faith is a lack of faith in the orthodoxies of rationalism, high technology, spiritual law and order. Somehow, the New Agers believe, there must be some secret and mysterious shortcut or alternative path to happiness and health. And nobody ever really dies."[4]

Another analysis of this movement portrays it as having a cohesiveness that is often overlooked. What is often seen by the casual observer is "a disjointed collection of stories and ideas—stories of UFOs, hauntings, predictions, premonitions, ghosts, mysterious happenings, psychic powers and ESP." But, "seen as a whole, the New Age rag bag of ideas displays an amazing unity. It is not a deliberately created system, but rather a pattern that is reinforced by sheer repetition."[5]

Historical Predecessors to New Age

Virtually every aspect of the New Age Movement (such as channeling and the use of crystals) has its historical antecedent in some practice that dates back centuries. But it is important to point out that the movement as a whole also has a heritage in movements that developed in the nineteenth century and earlier.

Spiritualism

Spiritualism is a religious tradition that has flourished in almost every age and is considered by some to be the world's oldest religious cult still alive. Like New Age ideologies, it generally does not require exclusivity. Spiritualists are often members of major denominations, as is true in Brazil, for example, where millions of Roman Catholics are practicing various forms of spiritualism. Spiritualism, by its simplest definition, is simply a belief that people are able to communicate with the spirits of the dead.

Spiritualism in America reached a fever pitch in the mid-nineteenth century when Kate and Margaret Fox, the adolescent daughters of a Methodist farmer in the "burned-over district" of Western New York state, began hearing rappings in the old "haunted" house they were living in. They insisted that they were communicating with the spirit of Charles Rosma, who had been murdered some years earlier. They would ask his spirit questions, and the spirit responded through curious rapping sounds. In many ways their form of spiritualism appeared to be simplistic and juvenile. They would contact the "rapper" by calling out "Hear, Mr. Splitfoot, do as I do," and then they would proceed with their verbal questions and rapping answers. Word quickly spread through the neighborhood, and curious onlookers began gathering at the Fox home to witness this peculiar phenomenon. The excitement spread beyond the neighborhood after an older sister volunteered to serve as an agent of sorts, charging admission fees for those who wished to observe. In 1949, less than two years after the rappings began, P. T. Barnum signed them up, and they soon became celebrities.[6]

Spiritualism soon became a popular pastime for Americans. "Seances and spiritualist societies became a common phenomenon all across the country. . . . Mesmerists, magicians, and fortune-tellers also discovered an important opportunity, with the result that a whole new era in American roadshow entertainment was opened." The simplistic rappings of Kate and Margaret soon seemed very rudimentary as "table turnings, slate writings, mysterious appearances, and great feats of clairvoyance" were demonstrated.

But spiritualism was far more than a Barnum circus event. "There were always the bereaved and the remorseful who desperately needed and wanted to make contact with the departed—a fact that stimulated interest in spiritualism after each of the country's major wars." Mary Todd Lincoln is an example of those who in grief took spiritualism seriously.[7]

There have been efforts over the generations to develop a spiritualist denomination, but these have never been successful. Tiny groups here and there have formed, but nothing that would bring them together on a large scale. In this sense the movement parallels the New Age Movement, which remains too diverse to organize into one unified religion.

Theosophy

In many ways Theosophy, as a historical movement, more closely parallels New Age than does spiritualism. It was a more diverse movement than spiritualism—"a mixture of spiritualism, hypnotism, Eastern and Egyptian myth and mysticism, speculative astronomy, and exotic anthropology." It differed from New Age and spiritualism in that it was a far more cohesive movement than either of the former; and it had a founder, the "immensely fat, often foul-mouthed Madame Blavatsky."[8]

Helena Petrovna was born in Russia in the early 1830s. As a teenager she married N. B. Blavatsky, a military general, and two months later she deserted him and began a twenty-five-year pilgrimage that took her West as far as America and East to India. During this time she studied various religious philosophies and became a channeler for a spirit-guide who called himself King John. In 1875, she founded the Theosophical Society in New York, and served as that movement's leader until 1891, when she died. Annie Besant, one of her followers, picked up the mantle and led the movement well into the twentieth century. Besant's "outstanding claim was that her adopted son Kirshnamurti . . . was the new Messiah, or the reincarnation of the World Teacher."[9]

In many ways Theosophy was a precursor to the New Age Movement of today. Madame Blavatsky outlined the basic philosophy of the Society in her book *The Secret Doctrine*:

(1) An Omnipresent, Eternal, boundless and Immutable PRINCIPLE, on which all speculation is impossible, since it transcends the power of human conception. . . . (2) The Eternity of the Universe in toto as a boundless plane. . . . The absolute universality of that law of periodicity, of flux and reflux, ebb and flow, which physical science has observed and recorded in all departments of nature. (3) The fundamental identity of all Souls with the Universal Over-soul, the latter being itself an aspect of the Unknown Root; and the obligatory pilgrimage for every soul. . . . The pivotal doctrine of the Esoteric Philosophy admits no privileges or special gifts in man, save those won by his own Ego through personal effort and merit throughout a long series of metempsychoses and reincarnations.

The movement also has some close parallels to Scientology, a new age religion. For example, in Theosophy, an "Adept" (in Scientology, an OT—Operating Thetan) is one "who has reached the power and degree and also the purification which enables him to 'die' in his physical body, and *still live and lead* a conscious life in his Astral body."[10]

Contemporary Distinctions

Is New Age merely an age-old form of the occult that will taper off in popularity as the fad loses its luster, or is it truly a movement that has only barely begun to make its all-encompassing mark on the world? The answer to this question is one of the very few things the most ardent religious critics and the devoted disciples of the movement agree on. Both sides envision a future one-world-religion united under the banner of New Age, and both speak of the enormous impact the movement is making on every aspect of modern life. In making these claims, it is easy to make sweeping generalizations about various influences in society, labeling them all "New Age." It would seem that neither the critics nor the disciples duly acknowledges other forces such as secularism, rationalism, and humanism that have long had a powerful influence in society but have little connection with New Age per se. It has become all too easy for some writers uncritically to label the movement a massive conspiracy and to lump such things as modern trends in psychology, concern for world hunger, and "secular humanism" under the same New Age banner.

Conspiracy Theories

Conspiracy theories are the stuff of political intrigue and corporate scandals, and they often find their way into religious speculations—especially those focused on eschatology and the coming one-world church. In many situations involving government, business, and religion, conspiracy theories are warranted, but in other instances they are utterly without foundation. There is often a fine line between the truth and the falsehood of one theory or another, and thus it is sometimes difficult for ordinary church-goers to sort out what is fact and what is fantasy. Several years ago, many Christians were duped by the alarming speculations of one John Todd, who warned of ominous underworld conspiracies of a group composed of an odd assortment of world political, financial, and religious leaders called the Illuminati. His evidence turned out to be fabricated, and what many people blindly accepted as a well-founded and thorough investigation turned out to be little more than a grand hoax. Students of the New Age Movement need to exercise caution in blindly accepting conspiracy theories. It is a field of study open to such speculation and it is all too easy to become caught up in popular notions that are impossible to verify.

Constance Cumbey

Of all the New Age observers espousing a conspiracy theory, Constance Cumbey, in her book *The Hidden Dangers of the Rainbow*, has made some of the most grandiose charges. She approaches her subject from a very personal perspective, and her writing is often flavored with the jargon of fear and anger: "Near-horror gripped me as I read . . . ," "Listening to Creme in horrified fascination . . . ," "Calling upon the Lord to spare me from this man's evil influence . . . ," and "I was scarcely able to contain my anger."[11]

In arguing her conspiracy case, Cumbey maintains that the New Age Movement is in essence a rebirth of Nazism. She refers to the movement as "the Fourth Reich," and associates it with the Third Reich which "practiced unmatched barbarity towards its Jewish population." This same form of barbarism, sustained by the occult and mysticism, characterizes the New Age Movement. "Painstakingly I collected every available scrap of information on the mystical roots of Nazism and compared it all to the data in my possession of the New Age Movement. I sought the assistance of political science experts who concurred that what I was showing them was indeed Nazism revived—in the purest sense."[12]

According to Cumbey, one of the most shocking parallels between New Age and Nazism is militarism. She maintains that the New Age Movement has a "police/military arm" that will aid in its effort to achieve "world domination"—the most well-publicized branches of which are the Guardian Angels, a tightly organized group of young adults who seek to curb crime in inner-city neighborhoods, and the First Earth Battalion, which is an official part of the United States military. "Even more startling," she contends, "is another parallel to Nazism—attempts to swell their ranks with prisoners, especially convicted felons." She writes of the "literally dozens of New Age prisoner recruiting efforts," which are advertised to "help curb recidivism," but "are actually designed to give ex-con-

victs the mystical experiences that help enhance their desired solidarity with other rank-and-file New Agers."[13]

Cumbey's conspiracy theory about New Age goes far beyond paramilitary organizations and convict rehabilitation. Indeed, she maintains that some evangelical Christians have been promoting New Age concepts. Speaking of Ron Sider and his widely acclaimed *Rich Christians in an Age of Hunger*, she writes:

> The first thing noticeable about Sider's book to one versed in New Age lore is his use of a vocabulary prevalent among New Agers. Words such as Spaceship Earth, vanguard, holistic, New Age, and global village are a common part of his vocabulary.
>
> The very same form of New World Order as that proposed by prominent New Agers and the Alice Bailey books is urged upon the readers. In fact, they are told it would be a sin for them not to support this "New World Economic Order" and "New World Order."[14]

Stanley Mooneyham of World Vision and David Bryant of InterVarsity Christian Fellowship are also cited as promoting New Age philosophy, primarily because of the terminology they use. For example, Bryant is suspect, in part, because he uses such words as "global village," "global cause," "global scale," "interlinked," and "inter-dependent."[15]

In Appendix G of her book, Cumbey offers a more complete list of what she refers to as "code words," "signals," and "buzz-words" by those involved in the New Age conspiracy "to communicate between themselves":

1. Holistic;

2. Transformation;

3. Spaceship Earth;

4. Global village;

5. Interdependent or interdependence;

6. Manifestation or manifest;

7. Initiation or Initiate;

8. Crowded planet;

9. Transcendent;

10. Consciousness-raising;

11. Paradigm or "new paradigm";

12. Vision or "new vision";

13. Global thread;

14. New Consciousness;

15. Planetary vision;

16. Global vision;

17. Transpersonal.[16]

Texe Marrs

Another New Age observer who writes about the conspiracy aspect of New Age is Texe Marrs, in his book *Dark Secrets of the New Age: Satan's Plan for A One World Religion*. In speaking of this One World Religion, Marrs writes:

> Even now, a man is perhaps being groomed to be this world ruler. I do not know when he will come forth, though the time must surely be drawing near, based on current events. However, after years of research into the objectives of the New Age Movement, I am convinced of one thing: this man of Satan, called the Beast with the number 666 in Revelation, will find already in place a popularly acclaimed One World Religion perfectly suited for his style of leadership. The Antichrist will therefore find great satisfaction in assuming the reigns of the New Age World Religion.[17]

The Aquarian Conspiracy and Earth at Omega

But it has not only been the opponents of New Age who have claimed the movement is a conspiracy. One of the most well-known New Age authors, Marilyn Ferguson, speaks candidly about this in her book *The Aquarian Conspiracy: Personal and Social Transformation in the 1980s.* Unlike the dark conspiracies of political or military intrigue, this, she maintains, is a "benign conspiracy" that "has triggered the most rapid cultural realignment in history." It is not merely a "new political, religious or philosophical system. It is a new mind—the ascendance of a startling worldview that gathers into its framework break-through science and insights from earliest recorded thought." It is a massive networking that brings together "schoolteachers and office workers, famous scientists, government officials and lawmakers, artists and millionaires, taxi drivers and celebrities, leaders in medicine, education, law, and psychology" all under one umbrella.[18]

A similar conspiracy theme is presented in a New Age volume by Donald Keys, *Earth at Omega*. Although he does not use the term "conspiracy," and while he concedes the movement is decentralized, he refers to a massive flow of activity of which the outside world is largely unaware:

> We mentioned earlier how the dominant straight "society" has apparently not recognized the strength and pervasiveness of the new consciousness culture. Perhaps this is just as well, as so far a polarization between the old culture and the new one has been

avoided. If the New Age movement does become a target of alarmed forces and defenders of the *status quo ante*, however, it will offer a widely dispersed and decentralized target, very hard to identify and impossible to dissuade or subvert from its life-serving values.[19]

An Objective Analysis

Is there then an underlying conspiracy, albeit a decentralized one, which is subverting the Western mind and bringing society into its vast web of New Age consciousness? For those who enjoy plotting suspense dramas with covert complicity and intrigue, the New Age Movement offers an abundance of raw material on which to fashion the scheme. But whether such a scenario would resemble the reality of a diffuse and ever-changing movement filled with self-serving profiteers, is another matter. Douglas Groothuis has made a thoughtful observation regarding the conspiracy that places the issue in proper perspective:

> Much Christian interest in the New Age has centered around various conspiracy theories. Because of the pervasiveness and influence of New Age ideas, it would not be unnatural to assume that some level of conspiracy was afoot. But we must keep in mind that conspiracy theories of all shapes, styles and sizes have been crisscrossing the planet throughout history. Any group that has transnational allegiances (such as Freemasons, Jews, Roman Catholics and international bankers) has been targeted as the elite conspirators plotting world takeover. New Age conspiracy charges simply transfer this thinking into a more modern context.[20]

But if the New Age Movement is not a conspiracy in the classical sense, it should not be dismissed as "an essentially harmless anthology of illusions," as *Time* magazine has suggested. Even the view of the highly respected J. Gordon Melton, who is the director of the Institute for the Study of American Religion, indicates a failure to fully acknowledge the movement's potential for harm: "It's important to point out the moral imbecility of what the New Age people are trying to do," he insists. "But at the same time, I wouldn't see it as a threat."[21]

Channeling

One of the most publicized aspects of New Age has been that involving channeling (also referred to as trans-channeling). This practice is a variation of spiritualism that involves more than simply communication with the dead (necromancy), but allowing the spirit of a deceased individual to speak through a living individual—the channeler. In most instances, this spirit is claimed to be from an individual who is not known to have actually existed.

J. Z. Knight and Ramtha

One of the most highly publicized channelers has been J. Z. Knight, a housewife from Yelm, Washington, who claims that her body is taken over by a thirty-five-thousand-year-old warrior from Atlantis named Ramtha. She has channeled his "wisdom," which is superficial at best, before crowds of thousands who have paid hundreds of dollars each for the experience. Her influence over her followers is as commanding as that of the "mind-control" cult leaders of the 1960s. Indeed, Knight and her New Age channeling colleagues "are often charismatic types who inspire absolute devotion and claim they are the sole source of revelations from God." Painful accounts of this have been told by family members and disillusioned ex-followers who relate stories of how they themselves or loved ones almost without warning abandoned everything to follow their guru/channeler. At Knight's urging many people have become involved in financial scams wiping out their life savings. Knight advertised one such investment opportunity in the early 1980s which involved the sale of Arabian horses to people who based their decision on personal advice from Ramtha. A government investigation terminated the scheme, but not before millions of dollars were lost.[22]

According to Knight, Ramtha first appeared to her in 1977. Having been raised as a strict Baptist, she became involved in metaphysical activities and was at the time experimenting with pyramids. Suddenly, she saw a seven-foot man in a robe standing in her kitchen hallway. He identified himself as Ramtha the Enlightened One, and promised to teach her the truth. He later explained that she had been one of his daughters, and that he had come to use her body to deliver his message for this age.[23]

Ramtha teaches through Knight that there is no such thing as a "judgmental God that you could never please" and that guilt is a false sentiment because sin does not exist. Ramtha also delivers specific messages for people of modern America, including an ominous apocalyptic forecast of earthquakes, pollution, and tidal waves which would so devastate the country that the only safe place to live would be the Pacific Northwest. As a result, "hundreds of Americans have pulled up stakes around the country and moved to rural areas in Washington, Oregon, Idaho, Montana and northern California. In some cases, the decision to move has divided families and led to divorces."[24]

Lazaris

Another spirit guide who has gained celebrity status is Lazaris, who speaks on the "mysteries, magick, and muses of Love." Although Lazaris purportedly had already "touched the whole planet," large crowds continued to come to hear him at nearly four hundred dollars per person. According to the promotional advertising, "Once we have met Lazaris, he is like an old friend who somehow we have always known. His joy, his insight, his love makes us realize he has always known us, too."[25] Lazaris speaks through Jack Pursel, a Los Angeles art dealer who previously earned his living selling insurance, and who says of his channeling: "It's not a business; it's a labor of love."[26]

Lazaris, like the other highly promoted spirit guides, "is a commercial entity as well as a spiritual one." A weekend seminar offered to hundreds of people at a time can collect as much as two hundred thousand dollars. "Lazaris has a two-year waiting list for private consultations, at $93 per hour. Or you can reach out and touch Lazaris by phone at $53 per half-hour, billed to your Visa or MasterCard account. Audio tapes of Lazaris are available at $20 per set, videotapes at $60."[27]

Private Practice and Historical Precedents

Channeling is not a new concept among spiritualists. Indeed, it has a long history, but it has only been in very recent years that the practice has been widely publicized and offered to mass audiences. While previously channeling was done largely in private, it is now not only used by celebrity figures who command high fees for their services, but by individuals for their own fulfillment who practice privately or in small groups. Maxine Hondema, a bookstore proprietor from Grand Rapids, Michigan, is an example. Although she would not consider herself a professional, her credentials indicate that she is deeply involved in New Age: Aurovoyant, Teacher, Lecturer, Author, Licensed Minister, Reiki First Degree, Academic with intensive training in many related fields of Parapsychology, and the local chairperson of Spiritual Frontiers Fellowship.[28]

Hondema, like most channelers, places great faith in spiritual guides: "They try to explain to us both what Cosmic Law is (or God's law if you prefer that term) and how if we try to understand and use that knowledge it will eliminate most of the difficulties that beset us. . . . If we choose to misuse, ignore or scoff at their message . . . the responsibility is ours." In regard to her own experience, Hondema writes: "I personally was and am a channel for a beautiful guide who gave us his name as Obidiah. These messages came through within a group presence of seven people who met for prayer and meditation on a regular basis. We had been together for nearly one year when Obidiah appeared."[29]

Part of Hondema's New Age activity involves distribution and republication of Stuart White's writing. White, who died in 1946, published several books called "The Betty Books," on his wife Betty's channeling in the 1930s. Even after she died (after her "transition") she continued to channel through her friend "Joan," and from those messages came *Unobstructed Universe*. These books have obtained a new popularity in recent years, and many of them are now available in paperback.[30]

Inner Voices

With the new popularity of channeling there has been an effort to give the practice historical and religious credibility, and one means of doing that is to link it with testimonies of the Christian saints from ages past. Alfred Alschuler, who authored an article subtitled "Inner Voices Throughout History," includes such individuals as St. Teresa, Madame Guyon, and Martin Luther on his list of people who were influenced by inner voices. He does not distinguish between figures who represent a Christian tradition and individuals such as Socrates, "who was warned of dangerous situations in his life by an inner voice," and Hitler, who claimed to be warned by an inner voice that saved his life:

I was eating my dinner with several comrades. Suddenly a voice seemed to

An assortment of New Age magazines.

be saying to me, "Get up and go over there." It was so clear and so insistent that I obeyed automatically, as if it had been a military order. I rose at once to my feet and walked twenty yards along the trench carrying my dinner in its tin can with me. Then I sat down to go on eating, my mind being once more at rest. Hardly had I done so when a flash and deafening report came from the part of the trench I had just left. A stray shell had burst over the group in which I had been sitting, and every member of it was killed.[31]

Alschuler writes of Hitler's inner voices in the same sense that he writes of St. Francis, Joan of Arc, and Moses: "Saint Francis was told to rebuild the Church. Saint Joan was authorized to throw the English out of France by raising the siege at Orleans. . . . Authorizations often are sudden, surprising and ask for outcomes that defy the odds. . . . A voice

in a vision of a burning bush authorized Moses to liberate the Israelites." How do proponents of the New Age Movement today compare to these saints of old? "In her autobiography Alice Bailey explained how she was given 19 Arcane books in as many years by a master living in a Tibetan monastery. . . . Bailey echoes Saint Teresa: 'I have never changed anything the Tibetan has given me. If I once did so, he would never dictate to me again.'"[32]

The most ambitious and controversial religious figure in history to depend on inner voices was probably Emmanuel Swedenborg, born of Swedish parents in 1688. Unlike Moses and the Roman Catholic saints, his "revelations" were often outside the boundaries of biblical orthodoxy, but nevertheless he has had a powerful impact on the Christian world. In 1742, he claimed to have heard a voice: "He said that he was the Lord God, the creator of the world and the redeemer, and that He had chosen me to explain the spiritual sense of the scripture, and that He, Himself would explain to me what I should write on the subject."[33]

Inner Space

While claiming to hear inner voices is still considered somewhat odd by most people, getting in touch with one's inner self has certainly come into vogue and is now a prominent theme in New Age literature and seminars. This "development and transformation of the human consciousness" is explained by Brian O'Leary, a former astronaut:

Seven years ago I took a Lifespring training in Philadelphia and it awakened parts of me that I never knew existed. Then I took an Insight training and began studying MSIA (Movement of Spiritual Inner Awareness) discourses about two years ago, and I've been sailing ever since! . . .

During a spiritual retreat, I reconnected with a feeling . . . which I knew had to come from inside myself . . . . I just *knew* that outer space was a manifestation of inner development. . . .

Outer space for me is a physical metaphor for inner space. . . . There is so much . . . we can do to accelerate the new age. . . .[34]

Finding one's inner space may involve seeking one's origins by extracting submerged memories so deeply embedded that a group leader or personal guide is often required. This exercise, sometimes referred to as "regressing," can draw on the belief in reincarnation or in evolu-

tion, as is the case in psychologist Jean Houston's sessions:

"Remember when you were a fish," Houston suggested in Sacramento. Nearly a thousand people . . . dropped to the floor and began moving their "fins" as if to propel themselves through water.

"Notice your perceptions as you roll like a fish. How does your world look, feel, sound, smell, taste?"

"Then you came up on land," Houston recalled, taking us through the amphibian stage. . . .

Then Houston suggested, "Allow yourself to fully remember being a reptile. . . . Then some of you flew. Others climbed trees" . . . . We became a zoo of sounds and movements made by early mammals, monkeys, and apes.

Houston then called us to remember being "the early human" who loses his/her "protective furry covering" and . . . evolves into the modern human.

The climax of the already intense exercise that had taken us more than an hour followed: "Now I want you to extend yourselves even further—into . . . the next stage of your own evolution." We became a room of leaping, joyous, sometimes alone, often together human beings who eventually joined hands and voices. The impact was electric. . . .

We had become a wriggling sea of bodies—nearly a thousand housewives, therapists, artists, social workers, clergy, educators, health professionals. . . [who] had crawled over and under each other, enjoying ourselves and re-learning what was deep within our memories.[35]

Visualization

Formulating visual images of a desirable situation or condition (such as the healing of a wound or the loss of weight) is a popular technique used among New Age therapists. It is a technique that has close association with occult magic, as David Conway, in his book *Magic: An Occult Primer*, explains:

... The technique of visualization is something you will gradually master, and indeed must master if you are to make any progress at all in magic. . . . It is our only means of affecting the etheric atmosphere.

It enables us to build our own thought forms, contact those already in existence and channel the elemental energy we need down onto the physical plane.[36]

Visualization has been popularized by therapists in the fields of psychology and counseling and has been employed as a form of meditation technique for self-improvement. Adelaide Bry guides the reader into this procedure in her book *Directing the Movies of Your Mind: Visualization for Health and Insight:* "Choose a time and place for your visualizations in which you won't be disturbed and you can let yourself relax," she advises. "Put aside, for the moment, your everyday activities and concerns. Allow yourself the heavenly pleasure of letting go of your thoughts and tensions in your body. . . . Once you are relaxed, focus your inner eye on your inner movie screen"[37]

Bry describes several types of visualizations, including those that would simply recreate a past experience and "programmed visualization"—"the deliberate use of the power of your mind to create your own reality." She offers an example of creating one's own reality: "My friend

Margot visualizes taxis emerging from dark, empty streets when she's returning home late at night. She has no conflict about wanting to get home quickly and safely, and, invariably, taxis appear where taxis are rarely known to cruise." Weight loss is another common goal for people who use visualization, and so is financial success, as a chapter subheading in her book indicates: "Money-Making and Mind Expansion."[38]

Reincarnation

Until recently it was uncommon to hear anyone in Western culture speak seriously of reincarnation. The belief that individuals transmigrate from one life to another—their souls never dying—has been viewed largely as part of the Hindu caste system that served to excuse the ill treatment and poverty of the lower castes, outcastes, and women. Though incorporated into such movements as the Unity School of Christianity, reincarnation had aroused little attention in the West until recent decades, with the advent of the New Age Movement and the corresponding penetration of Eastern mysticism into Western thought. New Age reincarnation concepts involve the channeling of past lives through spirit guides, but more commonly they focus on therapy that purports to guide an individual through past lives.

Advertisements for reincarnation seminars proliferate in New Age magazines and journals. One such seminar is directed by Carole Carbone, the founder of Sixth Sense Discover Workshops and Past Life Odyssey

Workshops, as well as an ordained Metaphysical minister. Her seminar includes Saturday morning and afternoon sessions and a "gourmet luncheon," all for fifty-five dollars. In the sessions, students take part in "exploring your past lives."

Embark on a remarkable journey of self discovery into the fascinating world of your past lives. You will be gently guided through a past-life regression, see first-hand where many of your current fears, judgments and hang-ups originated and clearly understand the reasons you have chosen certain relationships for yourself in this lifetime. Opportunity will then be given to free yourself from past life negativity and restructure your current life to your best advantage.[39]

In recent years reincarnation has been utilized extensively by professional therapists. One of the most widely-read individuals in this field is Dr. Helen Wambach, a licensed hypnotherapist and the author of *Reliving Past Lives: The Evidence Under Hypnosis*. She has "hypnotically regressed" more than two thousand people in her therapy sessions. Her method is to hypnotize individuals, and once they have reached a trance-like state, she queries them about life at a particular stage in their development—requesting, for example, that they retrieve data and "describe impressions" from a thousand years ago. Sometimes she uses a geographical rather than a chronological approach: "We're going to float back all around the world, back into past time. When I call out the name of a place, let the images come into your mind. An image for the Far East . . . an image for Central Asia . . . an image for Europe . . . an image for the Near East and Africa . . . or an image for North, Central or South America. . . . Now choose your character."[40]

Crystals and Stones

The most sacred object in the minds of many New Age believers is the crystal. It is believed to have healing powers not present in other objects, and many New Age therapists use crystal to treat their patients. Crystal is also widely worn as jewelry and is used as home decoration in the belief that it will provide a healthful energy field. Miraculous cures have been claimed by believers. According to *Time* magazine, one woman found a crystal wand to be the solution to her physical maladies: "I healed a fungus under my toenail with my wand, and I had a stomach problem that doesn't bother me anymore. The energy is subtle. It's not like you're being zapped."[41]

The power of crystals is maximized through meditation. "As we meditate, we begin to find that we are limitless," writes Uma Silbey, author of *The Complete Crystal Guidebook*. "Add quartz crystals with your meditation and you will find that the meditative process is tremendously amplified and the results experienced more quickly." What is the unique quality in crystal that causes it to function this way?

. . . . As we work with quartz crystals, we work on the level of subtle vibration which, in turn, affects the physical to do things which before were physically impossible. With quartz crystals we can develop a sense for and/or physically feel this subtle vibration. Then we use our focussed attention to manipulate this vibration in some way to make physical changes.

For example, we can shift the vibratory rate associated with "illness" to one of "wellness." In the same way we can change subtle vibrations to heal, we can energize and shift our unsatisfying thoughts and emotions to those that are satisfying. . . . The mind, heart and focused-will interact with the crystal to create change. . . . There is no limit to what can be done. The only limits are self-imposed: lack of focus, lack of will and doubt.[42]

Silbey moves from theory to the actual exercises that bring out the full potential of quartz crystals. The four-step "Pendulum Exercise" involves the suspension of a crystal, and through "strong intention" getting "the crystal to move in clockwise circles." Once that is accomplished, "use your mind to change the direction of the spin to counter-clockwise. . . . Do not move your hands while doing this." The purpose of this exercise is to train the mind to "interact with physical matter" and to "strengthen the will you need to empower your intention." The most complicated and advanced of the exercises is the twelve-step "Exercise to Open the Third Eye," which builds on another routine known as the "Heart Center Exercise." This exercise involves gazing into a large crystal ball while holding a quartz crystal on the navel point, approximately two inches below the belly button, and asking the question, "Who am I?" This meditation exercise is gradually increased in time over a forty-day period. Part of step eleven involves deep breathing and sounds: "Silently to yourself, say the sounds 'RA' on the inhale and 'MA' on the exhale."

The climax is step twelve: "Finally inhale completely and then shout out or say loudly on the exhale: 'HA.' Do this 3 times."[43]

What is accomplished through opening the "third eye"? The third eye energy center "in the middle of your forehead" is opened up. "As the third eye opens, it will increase your intuition, increase your abilities of concentration and focus, stimulate creativity and originality, and increase psychic abilities. Combined with the open heart, it will bring you wisdom."[44]

Crystals are not the only sacred objects utilized by New Age believers. The list is extensive, and includes such things as Tibetan bells, exotic herbal teas, Viking runes, solar energizers, and colored candles for chromotherapy. Some New Age gurus have their own personalized products such as "gem elixirs," stones exposed to water and sunlight which have been sold by a profiteer from Colorado by the name of Gurudas. In addition to these relics, there are countless books and tapes that promise to offer a new consciousness for self-fulfillment.[45]

Best-selling Books

The popularity and publicity surrounding the New Age Movement has been heightened by the publication of best-selling books and subsequent motion pictures. Shirley MacLaine's *Out on a Limb* has been one of the most popular of recent books dealing with the New Age Movement and channeling. For fifteen weeks it was on the New York *Times* best-seller list. It tells the story of MacLaine's spiritual pilgrimage from her doubts

Shirley MacLaine, "high priestess" of the New Age Movement.

about Christianity to her encounters with people who believe in reincarnation. Finally, she herself experienced an out-of-body episode that changed her life. She describes this incident in detail:

I was silent. I wanted to think. I wanted not to think. I wanted, above all, to rest. I breathed deeply. A kind of bile rose to my throat. I stared at the flickering candle. My head felt light. I physically felt a kind of tunnel open in my mind. It grew like a cavern of clear space that was open and free to jumble. It didn't feel like thought. It felt actually physical. The flame of the candle slowly melted into the space in my mind. Once again I felt myself *become* the flame. I had no arms, no legs, no body, no physical form. I became the space in my mind. I felt myself flow in to the space, fill it, and float off, rising out of my body until I began to soar. . . . My spirit or mind or soul, or whatever it was, climbed higher into space . . . until I could see the mountains and the landscape below me and I recognized what I had seen during the day.

And attached to my spirit was a thin, thin silver cord that remained stretched though attached to my body in the pool of water. I wasn't in a dream. No, I was conscious of everything, it seemed. I was even conscious that I didn't want to soar too high. I was conscious that I didn't want to soar too far away from my body. I definitely felt connected. What was certain to me was that I felt two forms . . . my body form below and my spirit form that soared. I was in two places at once, and I accepted it completely. I was aware, as I soared, of vibrational energy around me. I couldn't see it, but I felt a new sense of "sensing" it. It felt like a new dimension of perception, somehow, that had nothing to do with hearing or seeing or smelling or tasting or touching. I couldn't describe it to myself. I knew it was there—physically—yet I knew my body was below me.[46]

What was unique about this book was that "for the first time in contemporary publishing history, people who would not ordinarily pick up a book about the unseen and unknown were reading Shirley's adventures."[47] She has since written two sequels, including another best-seller, *Dancing in the Light*, and the more recent, *It's All in the Playing*. Through these books, a film ("Out on a Limb"), and her frequent appearances on television talk shows, MacLaine has done more than any other single individual to make the New Age Movement respectable.

Another best-seller heavily influenced by New Age thought was *Jonathan Livingston Seagull*, which was supposedly dictated to Richard Bach by a being that came to him in the form of a bird. He maintains that he was simply the channel through which this entity worked. The small volume was at the top of the best-seller list for more than two years,

and broke publishing records set decades earlier.[48]

Philosophical Foundations

As diverse as New Age is, there are certain religious beliefs and philosophical concepts that are generally held to be true by adherents of the movement, no matter what their particular specialty interest in the movement might be. Still, it is very difficult to make generalizations, because proponents approach the "faith" from such a vast array of perspectives. Reincarnation, for example, may have entirely different connotations for one individual in the movement than for another, and some connect New Age concepts to their traditional Christian values and beliefs while others look to Eastern religions. Many take a completely secular approach.

A New Age Dawning

New Age is named for its core doctrine—the belief that a new age is dawning. This is summed up in Robert Mueller's book, *The New Genesis*, which looks to the year 2000 to usher in a New Order—"A Bimillennium Celebration of Life, the advent of an Era of Peace, a Golden Age, and the First Millennium of World Harmony and Human Happiness."[49]

Precise date-setting for end-time calamity or salvation is not outside the scope of New Age eschatology. In his book *The Mayan Factor: Path Beyond Technology*, Jose Arguelles "argued that his studies of ancient Mayan calendars showed that the 'materialistic' world would end on August 16 [1987]—when three

Harmonic Convergence . . . Westport, Ct. — Believers of the Harmonic Convergence assembled Aug. 16th at a sunrise ceremony at Compo beach overlooking Long Island Sound. It was one of many ceremonies held throughout the world to ring in a new age of peace and harmony. Courtesy Religious News Service.

planets line up with the new moon—unless 144,000 true believers gathered in various 'sacred sites' around the world and 'resonated' sufficiently to bring on a new age of peace and harmony." In accordance with his prophecy, thousands of New Age enthusiasts met on beaches and at Indian burial grounds, but otherwise the day was uneventful.[50]

Some New Age thought reflects a grandiose version of postmillennialism. Lola Davis writes of the progressive improvement of mankind until people "will have developed god-like qualities and sufficient knowledge and wisdom to cooperate with God (the universal energy force) in materializing the Kingdom of God on earth."[51]

Lord Maitreya

There will be a messiah to welcome in this new age, according to many New Age theorists. Some call him Lord Maitreya. His identification was revealed by "the Tibetan" through channeler Alice Bailey, who maintains that he will bring about a New World Order. His coming was first made public in 1982, when advertisements were placed in newspapers proclaiming a New Age Messiah prepared to install "a new world government and new world religion." Some years later, another full-page advertisement promoting Lord Maitreya appeared in *USA Today*, with the headlines, "THE CHRIST IS IN THE WORLD."[52]

The individual who paid the two hundred thousand dollars for the newspaper advertisements in 1982 was Benjamin Creme, a Scottish-born writer and artist. While touring the United States and publicizing his beliefs in 1986, Creme revealed that for thousands of years Maitreya lived

THE WORLD HAS HAD *enough...* OF HUNGER, INJUSTICE, WAR.

IN ANSWER TO OUR CALL FOR HELP, AS WORLD TEACHER FOR ALL HUMANITY,

THE CHRIST IS NOW HERE.

HOW WILL WE RECOGNIZE HIM?

Look for a modern man concerned with modern problems—political, economic, and social. Since July, 1977, the Christ has been emerging as a spokesman for a group or community in a well-known modern country. He is not a religious leader, but an educator in the broadest sense of the word— pointing the way out of our present crisis.

We will recognize Him by His extraordinary spiritual potency, the universality of His viewpoint, and His love for all humanity. **He comes not to judge, but to aid and inspire.**

WHO IS THE CHRIST?

Throughout history, humanity's evolution has been guided by a group of enlightened men, the Masters of Wisdom. They have remained largely in the remote desert and mountain places of earth, working mainly through their disciples who live openly in the world. This message of the Christ's reappearance has been given primarily by such a disciple trained for his task for over 20 years.

At the center of this "Spiritual Hierarchy" stands the World Teacher, *Lord Maitreya*, known by Christians as the *Christ*. And as Christians await the Second Coming, so the Jews await the *Messiah*, the Buddhists the fifth *Buddha*, the Moslims the *Imam Mahdi*, and the Hindus await *Krishna*. These are all names for one individual. **His presence in the world guarantees there will be no third World War.**

WHAT IS HE SAYING?

"My task will be to show you how to live together peacefully as brothers. This is simpler than you imagine. My friends, for it requires only the acceptance of sharing."

"How can you be content with the modes within which you now live: when millions starve and die in squalor; when the rich parade their wealth before the poor; when each man is his neighbor's enemy; when no man trusts his brother?"

"Allow me to show you the way forward into a simpler life where no man lacks; where no two days are alike; where the Joy of Brotherhood manifests through all men."

"Take your brother's need as the measure for your action and solve the problems of the world."

WHEN WILL WE SEE HIM?

He has not as yet declared His true status, and His location is known to only a very few disciples. One of these has announced that soon the Christ will acknowledge His identity and within the next two months will speak to humanity through a worldwide television and radio broadcast. His message will be heard inwardly, telepathically, by all people in their own language. From that time, with His help, we will build a new world.

WITHOUT SHARING THERE CAN BE NO JUSTICE;
WITHOUT JUSTICE THERE CAN BE NO PEACE;
WITHOUT PEACE THERE CAN BE NO FUTURE.

THE TARA PRESS	TARA CENTER	INFORMATION CENTER AMSTERDAM
59 DARTMOUTH PARK ROAD	P.O. BOX 6001	P.O. BOX 41877
LONDON NW5 1SL	N. HOLLYWOOD, CA 91603	1009 DB AMSTERDAM
ENGLAND	U.S.A.	HOLLAND

in a mountain village in the Himalayas, but that on July 8, 1977, he "descended" in "a self-created body." Since then he has been living "in the Asian-Indian community in the east end of London in what's called the Brick Lane area, a very down-trodden, slummy area." Creme claims that his own role is to create a "climate of hope and expectancy for the return of the Christ. . . . I'm showing the mode of appearance and the methods by which we will recognize the Christ, because when he came 2,000 years ago he was not recognized as the Christ. In fact, he was condemned to death."[53]

What will Maitreya do when he makes himself known as the Christ? He will "appeal for sharing, justice and the transformation of the political and economic structures of the world. At the same time there will be a mass healing." Through Maitreya's leadership the world will enter into a new era:

Depending on the quality of our response, the world will begin to be transformed. He will not do it, but he will inspire, guide and counsel humanity to do it for themselves—he along with about 40 masters over the next 20 years. We shall, in a very short time, transform the political, economic and social conditions of the world, which will bring us into correct spiritual relationships.[54]

A Messiah Within

Some New Age philosophers believe that the messiah will not be an individual but rather a "messiah within" who will lead the world into a new consciousness. In her book *The Evolutionary Journey*, Barbara Marx Hubbard offers an optimistic messianic outlook: "At this moment of our planetary birth each person is called upon to recognize that the 'Messiah is within.' Christ consciousness or cosmic consciousness is awakening in millions of Christians and non-Christians."[55]

All Is One

New Age has been called a religion that is not a religion, and that definition is based in part on the fact that the foundational belief of the movement is *monism*—the belief that all is one. "Any perceived differences between separate entities—between Joe and Judy or between Joe and a tree or between God and Judy—are only apparent and not real."[56]

The significance of this doctrine is summed up by Jonathan Stone, who sees it as an essential facet of the New World Order:

I feel that there is coming a World Order in which science will merge with monistic philosophy and all the world will be swept up in a new consciousness.

The one distinguishing feature in the World Order will be the credo: "All is one."[57]

We Are All God

This concept of *monism*, while blurring all of humanity into one singular essence, at the same time deifies the individual. There is no God outside the individual, for the individual is God. This is clearly articulated in the writing of Betty Galyean:

Once we begin to see that we are all God, that we all have the attributes of God, then I think the whole purpose of human life is to reown the Godlikeness within us; the perfect love, the perfect wisdom, the perfect understanding, the perfect intelligence, and when we do that, we create back to that old, that essential oneness which is consciousness.[58]

This foundational doctrine that every individual is God is not hidden in the pages of profound philosophical volumes. It is a conspicuous teaching and a central focus of the New Age Movement in its most popular form. When Shirley MacLaine portrayed herself in her television rendition of "Out On A Limb," this doctrine was central. "In one breathtakingly blatant scene, MacLaine is initiated into the understanding that Divine Being and the Human Soul are one. She and her spiritual adviser stand on Malibu Beach with their arms flung open to the cosmos, shouting, 'I am God! I am God! I am God!'" The same message was given by Ramtha when he spoke through J. Z. Knight on the "Merv Griffin Show." When asked what the most important message he had for the planet was, he responded, "What is termed God is within your being. . . . And that which is called Christ is within your being. . . . And when you know you are God, you will find joy."[59]

Counterfeit Christianity

Given the fact that the New Age assault has been focused on the

West, it is no accident that there are numerous efforts to make it compatible with Christianity. References to biblical passages are common, and the term "Christ-consciousness" is well-worn in New Age literature. Another common biblical topic is that of miracles—a subject that is often combined with New Age phenomena. Cindy Saul, the editor of *Phenome-NEWS*, illustrates this in an editorial entitled "Expect A Miracle."

> In her latest book, *Star Signs*, Linda Goodman relates the story of how she was in her hotel room one night and a turbaned man appeared at her door. She invited him in and they talked for quite a while. During that time, he revealed things to her that she would be doing in the future. After he "disappeared," just as mysteriously as he had appeared, Linda noticed a small card he had left behind with three simple words imprinted on it, "expect a miracle."

Saul goes on in the editorial to counsel that "If we will just keep on being our true beautiful selves and doing what we know in our hearts is ours to do, all else will be taken care of for us. Our 'miracles' will occur daily."[60]

A Course in Miracles

An even more obvious attempt to tie the biblical concept of miracles to New Age ideology is found in a widely distributed volume entitled *A Course in Miracles*. The course "is among the most popular and influential of all contemporary 'channeled' documents: Over 300,000 copies of the Course have been sold since it was published in 1975." The most controversial aspect of the volume is that the author, Helen Schuc-man, a New York psychologist, claims that it is a message from Jesus and that she served only as a channel. Christian terms such as "Christ," "Holy Spirit," and "Atonement," are used frequently—a factor making it even more offensive to Christians. According to Richard Smoley, "Conventional Christianity regards it as a heresy and dismisses it out of hand, while those who believe in it treat it virtually as scripture."[61]

Schucman began writing the book in the 1960s, after being assured by a colleague that the inner voices she heard were not signs of schizophrenia, and that she should obey the voice and write down its dictates. When she finished she had some twelve hundred pages, which she divided into three separate sections: the text itself, the workbook, and the Teacher's guide. The overall message is typical New Age philosophy—finding truth, "which is the awareness that in reality we are not separate from God or from each other. In fact, the collective reality of all human beings past and present is known as the Sonship; we are all Sons of God—or, more accurately, the Son of God, since, in the Course's view, there is ultimately no difference between me and you."[62]

Aquarian Gospel of Jesus Christ

Another book which counterfeits Christianity is *Aquarian Gospel of Jesus Christ*, "edited" by Eva Dowling. The source of the book is purportedly a channeler from Ohio, by the name of "Levi," who claimed to have received its message in 1911 from an angel. The contents include over 170 chapters on the life of Jesus, including His trip to India to learn from Hindu gurus. An example is when Jesus affirmed the doctrine of reincarnation after listening to "a band of wandering singers and musicians," none of whom had apparently enjoyed the luxury of musical training.

Among the high-breed people of the land we hear no sweeter music than that these uncouth children of the wilderness bring here to us. From whence this talent and this power? In one short life they surely could not gain such grace of voice, such knowledge of the laws of harmony and tone. Men call them prodigies. There are no prodigies. All things result from natural law. These young people are not young. A thousand years would not suffice to give them such divine expressiveness, and such purity of voice and touch. Ten thousand years ago these people mastered harmony. In days of old they trod busy thoroughfares of life, and caught the melody of birds, and played on harps of perfect form. And they have come again to learn still other lessons from the varied notes of manifests.[63]

Revival of Pagan Religions

New Age has not only drawn from Hinduism and Christianity, but also from ancient pagan religions and tribal spiritism. Indeed, it has become vogue in recent decades to research ancient pagan beliefs and to travel to exotic locations and study under tribal witch doctors and shamans. These concepts are then reinterpreted to fit the New Age framework for contemporary issues and lifestyles.

The Goddess Movement

One aspect of New Age philosophy is goddess worship combined with witchcraft—a religious ideology that has had a particular appeal among feminists who shun the masculine images of God found in traditional Christianity. Those involved claim to be reviving ancient traditions, such as the Babylonian Goddess Mystery Religion. One such individual is Miriam Starhawk, a self-described witch and the president of a church in California known as the Covenant of the Goddess. Though focused specifically on worshiping a Mother God, the philosophy of the movement is typical of New Age belief, as Starhawk explains:

Mother Goddess is reawakening and we can begin to recover our primal birthright, the sheer intoxicating joy of being alive. We can open our eyes and see that there is nothing to be saved from . . . no God outside the world to be feared and obeyed.[64]

According to Starhawk, "The Goddess . . . is the world. Manifest in each of us, she can be known by every individual, in all her magnificent diversity."[65]

Although some feminist scholars, such as Rosemary Ruether of Garrett Evangelical Seminary, downplay the prevalence of goddess worship in ancient history, there are many other feminists who are researching manuscripts for the sole purpose of trying to find historical continuity in feminist spirituality. The worship of Isis is only one example of revived ancient goddess worship. It is described by Kathleen Alexander-Berghorn, an activist in the movement, as a healing faith:

Today women are rediscovering
Isis. . . . The reawakening of Isis as a
source of inspiration for contemporary
women is exemplified by the healing
ministry of Selena Fox, co-founder and
High Priestess of Circle Sanctuary near
Madison, Wisconsin. Every month at
the New Moon, Selena holds a Spiritual
Healing Circle centered around an Isis
Healing Altar. . . . Each of us can personally experience the healing presence of the Goddess within us. All
women are Isis and Isis is all women.[66]

Shamanism

Goddess worship is but one "neo-
pagan" practice now popular in the
New Age Movement. Another is
shamanism—a spiritistic methodology that became widely publicized
through Michael Harner's book, *The
Way of the Shaman*. In primitive tribal
groups, the shaman served as the
"medicine man" or "witch doctor."
The modern shaman carries out that
tradition as a " 'technician of ecstacy,'
whose purpose is to reconnect people with the sacred, as mystic mediator, guide and healer." Harner conducts seminars that offer his students the techniques he first learned
while researching shamanism as an
anthropologist, and then while practicing as a shaman himself.[67]
What is a shaman in modern-day
New Age terminology? According to
Harner: "A shaman is a man or
woman who enters an altered state of
consciousness—at will—to contact
and utilize an ordinarily hidden reality in order to acquire knowledge,
power and to help other persons.
The shaman has at least one, and
usually more, 'spirits' in his personal
service." The term "shaman" is used
"because it lacks the prejudicial over-

tones and conflicting meanings associated with the more familiar labels"
such as "witchdoctor," "medicine
man," and "sorcerer."[68]
In some instances, shamanism, like
the goddess movement, has been
linked with feminism. Lynn Andrews
is the subject of a newspaper article
entitled "She's A Pathfinder in Post-
feminist Era." For fifteen years Andrews studied shaman women
throughout the world, and out of her
research has come five books, including *Medicine Woman* and *Crystal
Woman*.

On her often grueling road to enlightenment, she learned such things
as living directly off the earth (finding
and cooking larvae over coals in one
instance), tracking prey, butchering a
freshly slain deer and eating it raw (an
assignment designed to teach her to
deal with her emotions), ridding herself
of all peripheral habits and using
stones and crystals as tools for healing
(which she frequently does in working
with the hundred or so clients she now
privately counsels).[69]

As a practicing shaman, Andrews is
known by many as the "Beverly Hills
medicine woman." She began her
work after a divorce and a long
struggle with depression. Through
shamanism, she became convinced
she could help others with similar
problems. She now counsels clients
on a private basis, charging them
$150 per hour, carries on a lucrative
writing career, and maintains a home
in Beverly Hills, a studio in New
Mexico, and drives a Mercedes-Benz.
She views her work as "a bridge
between the primal mind and white
consciousness . . . taking what I've
learned about the spirit and power of

women back to our patrilineal society."[70]

Worship of Lucifer

Another attempt to borrow from ancient religious practices among certain segments of the New Age Movement is the revival of interest in worshiping Lucifer. This cultic worship was practiced in ancient Babylon and in Gnostic mystery religions in the second century, and it was later revived in the fourteenth century by a movement known as the Luciferians. The worship of Lucifer, or Satan, has continued throughout history in the occult, but has not been accepted in "respectable" circles—until the advent of the New Age Movement. One of the first to revive this aspect of the occult was Eklal Kueshana in his best-selling book *The Ultimate Frontier*, in which he maintains that "Lucifer is the head of a secret Brotherhood of Spirits, the highest order to which man can elevate himself."[71]

Other New Age writers have also blatantly glorified Lucifer in such a way as to make his worship not only acceptable but removed from Satan worship as it is generally regarded. David Spangler, in *Reflections of the Christ*, writes:

> Christ is the same force as Lucifer. . . . Lucifer prepares man for the experience of Christhood. . . . Lucifer works within each of us to bring us to wholeness, and as we move into a new age . . . each of us in some way is brought to that point which I term the Luciferic initiation . . . that many people now, and in the days ahead, will be facing, for it is an initiation into the New Age.[72]

Astrology

Many modern-day astrologists would argue that astrology is not a religion. They would seek to place it into a scientific category on the par of psychology. But the history of astrology clearly places it in the category of religion that began in ancient Babylonia some two thousand years before Christ. The stars were believed to be "gods of the night," who were involved in the affairs of human beings. "Early astrology," according to Howard Van Til, "was but part of a vast collection of omens from lunar eclipses to animal entrails that were thought to betoken either warnings or encouragement." It was a primitive form of astrology that prevailed until approximately the sixth century B.C. when Zodiacal astrology was developed by the Chaldeans. Initially, this more complex view of the heavens (which focuses on the precise location of the sun, moon, and planets within the zodiac) was applied "only to affairs of the state and its rulers," but "was later expanded by the Greeks and Romans to the affairs of all individuals."[73]

It was out of this religion of astrology that astronomy developed. The more important these gods in the heavens became, the more people wanted to know about their patterns of movement. Thus astrology/astronomy became one of the most developed of the early sciences. It became the subject of keen interest on all levels of society, and many Roman emperors and medieval popes had their own personal astrologers. Pope Julius II went so far as to postpone for several weeks his coronation in 1503, until a "lucky day" was ascertained by his astrologer.[74]

The Reformation church was also infected by a belief in astrology. Churchmen and politicians alike depended heavily on the advice of astrologers. Philip Melanchthon argued that there was a true Christian form of astrology that was based on an accurate examination of God's divine order in the heavens. He placed great faith in horoscopes and was convinced that he would have prohibited his daughter's marriage had he been wise enough to read her fiance's horoscope. "Sabinus is headstrong and will not listen to advice," he wrote; "this is due to the conjunction of Mars and Saturn at his nativity, a fact which I ought to have taken into account, when he asked the hand of my daughter."[75]

That astrology was accepted in past centuries by secular rulers is not surprising, but that it was accepted by those who based their faith on Scripture is perplexing, as is the continued interest in astrology today despite the scientific advances that have shown it to be utterly untenable. Indeed, the acceptance of astrology has been growing in recent decades and has corresponded with the growth of New Age thought. From the most generalized and simplistic newspaper horoscopes to sophisticated individualized and computerized charts, astrology has become a multibillion-dollar business in the United States. New books appear each week that emphasize some new angle of astrology with titles for every taste: *Your Dog's Astrological Horoscope*, *Cat Horoscope Book*, *Your Baby's First Horoscope*, *The Teenager's Horoscope Book*, *Find Your Mate Through Astrology*, *Sex Signs*, *Homosexuality in the Horoscope*, *The Astrologers Guide to Counseling*, *Cooking with Astrology*, *Medical Astrology*, *Stock Market Predictions*, and even *Astrology and the Bible*.

Popularity of these books and the more than one hundred astrology magazines have a ready market. Studies indicate that more than thirty million Americans believe in some form of astrology, and that figure is likely to increase due to the avid interest among young people. A 1984 Gallup poll indicated that 55 percent of teenagers believed in astrology, an increase of fifteen percent in just six years. A similar poll in 1988 revealed that ten percent of evangelical Christians believed in astrology.[76] Although it has long been regarded as folly and utterly without foundation in the scientific community, astrology gained worldwide attention and a measure of credibility when it was disclosed in May of 1988 that presidential schedules had been correlated with astrological charts. *Time* magazine featured a cover story entitled "Astrology in the White House" and spoke of "Nancy Reagan's obsession with astrology."[77]

The Reagan White House

It was Donald Regan's book, *For the Record*, that offered the first public revelations about a reliance on astrology on the part of the Reagans. He writes that another presidential aide first told him "that Mrs. Reagan's dependence on the occult went back at least as far as her husband's governorship, when she had relied on the advice of the famous Jeanne Dixon. Subsequently, she had lost confidence in Dixon's powers. But the First Lady seemed to have absolute faith in the clairvoyant talents of the woman in San Francisco." This woman in San Francisco, according to Regan, "believed that the zodiac controls events and human behavior and that she could read the secrets of the future in the movements of the planets." He maintained that "virtually every major move and decision the Reagans made during [his] time as White House Chief of Staff was cleared in advance" with this woman, "who drew up horoscopes to make certain that the planets were in a favorable alignment for the enterprise."[78]

Who was this unknown woman from San Francisco? According to *Time* magazine, "the First Lady's oracle is San Francisco Heiress Joan Quigley, author of three books on astrology, including *Astrology for Teens*," who "was first introduced to Nancy Reagan by TV Talk Show Host Merv Griffin in the early 1970s, and has provided the Reagans with suggestions about the timing of various political events ever since." The daughter of a wealthy hotelier, she graduated from Vassar in 1947 and then served as an apprentice of sorts under an elderly astrologer who advised her mother in earlier years. Quigley, like many astrologers, takes her "profession" seriously. She maintains that a horoscope "can tell you more about yourself than a psychiatrist can tell you after many hours of consultations on his couch," and she predicts that some day astrology "will be taught in the schools and colleges and will be considered a profession on a par with medicine and law."[79]

According to some observers, the California culture giving credence to forms of the occult and New Age thinking such as astrology has had a powerful impact on the Reagans for decades. Out of this California culture emerged one of the nation's most influential astrologers, Carroll Righter, who gave counsel to many film stars, including Nancy Reagan.

When Ronald Reagan and Nancy Davis were first making their way in Hollywood, it was quite in fashion to see an astrologer. And no astrologer was more fashionable than Carroll Righter, the self-styled "gregarious Aquarius" who counted Marlene Dietrich, Cary Grant and Princess Grace among his clients. Storefront gypsy he was not. A Philadelphia lawyer, Righter had moved to Hollywood in 1937 on the advice of a horoscope, and soon became a true believer. . . . By the time of his self-predicted death . . . at the age of 88, Righter was one of the deans of American astrology, his columns syndicated in 166 newspapers.

A dapper, lifelong bachelor, Righter was in a way the society "walker" of his day, confidante of the rich and famous, who saw him less as a backdoor soothsayer than as social equal. . . .

As an astrologist, Righter was a stickler for exact timing. He once informed Susan Hayward that the most auspicious time to sign a movie contract was 2:47 a.m., so she obediently arranged for a 2:45 wake-up call. Righter himself took calls at all hours, keeping the charts of most-favored clients in a file by his bed for late-night consultations. "They need me here," he said. "Just like they need a doctor."[80]

When the Reagans married in the early 1950s, both were consulting with Righter, and Nancy "ranked high enough on Righter's roster to

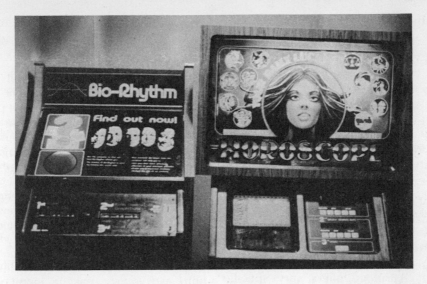

Bio-Rhythm and Horoscope machines that are commonly found in hotels and airport terminals.

merit a mention in his celebrity column for *Horoscope* magazine." During the 1960s "Reagan's interest had turned to politics, and his stable of advisers had widened to include Jeane Dixon.... When Reagan did gain the Governor's mansion, however, it was likely the time-conscious Righter, not Dixon, who prevailed upon him to schedule the inauguration for the ungodly hour of 12:10 a.m.—which caused much merriment among the astrologically hip in California."[81]

Attraction of Astrology

What is the attraction of astrology for so many millions of people—including the nation's top leaders—in a computerized age of high technology and rapid scientific and medical advances? What is it that makes an astrologer more appealing than a trained therapist or consultant? Perhaps it is the mystery involved in trying to glimpse the one frontier that will forever remain an unknown, the future; and perhaps it is the security of believing that through this knowledge an individual has an opportunity to impact the unknown events of the future. For some, astrology provides the security of believing that one's fate is determined in the heavens and is entirely beyond human control.

Astrology is as simple or as complicated as anyone desires to make it, though with the advent of computer technology it tends to be more and more complex and intricate. Simply defined, astrology is the belief that the planets and stars and universe beyond—the heavens—have a direct and personal influence on individuals. The nature of the impact depends on the various "signs" within the twelve "houses" (divisions) of the zodiac which represent twelve consecutive periods of the calendar year. An individual's "sign" is determined by their date of birth—for example, an "Aries" has a birth date between March 21 and April 19, and a "Scorpio" from October 24 to November 22.

Simplistic Horoscopes

In its simplistic form, astrology is utterly superficial and devoid of originality. This form of astrology is published in the "Horoscope" section of daily newspapers everywhere and in books such as *Instant Astrology*. Unlike daily horoscopes, however, which are often so generalized that they cannot be entirely wrong, *Instant Astrology* offers very specific descriptions of individuals born under a particular sign. Here the authors tell their readers that if, for example, they were born under the sign of Leo (between July 22 and August 23), they like "to be at the hub of things," have "a sense of the dramatic and a tendency towards display," and that "they have a natural authority which makes them good leaders, although this quality can appear overbearing at times." Moreover, "like children, their basic nature is open and trusting. Craftiness is alien to them."[82] Despite such utterly unproven conclusions, many people buy these books and are caught up in the astrology game.

Complex Horoscopes

To avoid such simplistic dogmatism as is illustrated in the above description of a Leo, many astrologers seek to devise complex qualifications to the standard sign descriptions. However, in doing so, the reader is sometimes caught in a zodiac jungle difficult to untangle.

The following is an example of a more complex and vague reading on Leo.

> The house on which you find Leo shows the potential fulfillment of ego needs and describes the sense of purpose. In the matters of this house you need to dramatically express your Aries identity, Taurus values, Gemini knowledge and Cancer feelings in everything you do in order to see the reflection of yourself of your inner ideals. Making an impression on your environment is your way of proving to yourself that you are a distinct individual. . . .[83]

Many other complex qualifiers help astrologers make a significant impact on an individual's astrological chart, qualifiers that daily newspaper horoscopes make no effort to consider. For example, in the book *Moon Signs*, Sasha Fenton, an astrologer, palmist and tarot card reader, presents her case for the effects of the moon on an individual's personality: "Lunar Leo's," for example, "can be surprisingly self-sacrificing towards loved ones but heaven help them if the loved one doesn't appreciate the sacrifices." The moon even affects the individual's tastes and personal appearance. "The Moon is associated with the home, therefore, yours will be attractive with an interesting sort of decor. You are very fussy about your own appearance and may even be vain. . . . The one thing which is the bane of your life is your hair."[84]

Modern Astrology vs. Traditional Astrology

With the advent of the New Age Movement, astrology, according to many of its proponents, has come of age. It is a new astrology that avoids the fatalism of the past and maximizes its therapeutic power. This is the theme of Steven Forrest's book, *The Changing Sky: A Practical Guide to the New Predictive Astrology*. In this volume he illustrates the differences between the new astrology and the old through the suicidal death of the famous American author Ernest Hemingway. He maintains that Hemingway took his life when Mars was coming to the ascendant on his birthchart, which signals "an ominous astrological event." If he had visited a traditional astrologer before his suicide, Forrest conjectures, "he would have heard that a hard time was coming, that he was likely to have an accident involving fire and blood, and that he had better batten down the hatches for a short but intense period of conflict and stress. For a person in his psychological condition at the time, that would have been like handing a drowning man a tire iron." But had Hemingway instead visited "a truly modern astrologer," he would have been told "that he would soon face a fundamental spiritual challenge. A set of events and attitudes were about to coalesce around him, testing his bravery, his will to live, and his elemental human dignity. His task was to show unflinching determination and self-control *for a few days* until Mars moved into less sensitive territory."[85]

Forrest challenges readers to "use astrology yourself. This magnificent tool is your natural ally. It will not subjugate you or bind you. Let the signs and planets guide you, but let them guide you gently, not as tyrants, but as trusted friends. Let astrology

be part of your freedom, assisting it, illuminating it." What about the old concepts of astrology? "Leave prediction to the fortune-tellers and gypsies. Let them make their prophecies. Let them hunger for the events they foresee, or cringe before them. Our task is not to foresee events. It is to create them."[86]

But despite Forrest's efforts to equate prediction with older concepts of astrology, prediction is very much alive and well today. In her 1987 book, *Astro-Focus Your Future*, Mary Coleman begins with a question that strikes at the very heart of this issue:

Can anyone learn to forecast the future? And get it right?

Those are questions many people ask nowadays and the answer is quite simply—"Yes." To both. In a sense, it's just like the way meteorologists can forecast weather for weeks, months, or even years ahead by the plain, scientific method of studying maps and local conditions. Modern astrological science shows you how to do the same for your own life.[87]

Holistic Health

The popularity of holistic health in recent years has developed in part out of a disillusionment with the medical profession, which to many overemphasizes short-term textbook remedies for specific maladies with little concern for maintaining the overall physical, emotional, and spiritual well-being of people. Holistic health focuses attention on positive notions of "wellness" rather than simply preventing illness, which has been the perceived goal of modern medicine. For these reasons its champions have soared in numbers.

But for all its positive features, holistic health also has a negative side. "While many involved in holistic health may not follow the idea that all is one and all is god," writes Douglas Groothuis, "this is what is most often meant by *holistic*. The emphasis on 'universal energy' betrays the world view."[88]

Many of the concepts of New Age holistic health have been drawn from a long tradition of healing arts in Eastern mysticism. In some instances, the concepts can be utterly mind-boggling to the Western mind. An example is Ayurveda, a holistic system of medicine that claims to be the "Science of Life," as the term indicates in Sanskrit. Ayurveda has been practiced in India for more than five thousand years and has only recently come to the West. The major obstacle to its widespread proliferation outside India is the difficult terminology in which it is clothed.

> According to Ayurveda, the first requirement for healing oneself and others is a clear understanding of the three doshas or tridosha (the balance of kapha, pitta, and vata). The concept of vata-pitta-kapha is unique to Ayurveda and it holds the potential for revolutionizing the healing systems of the West. . . . The basic premise of the philosophy is that "A balance among the tridosha is necessary for health."
>
> Vata is a principle of movement. That which moves is called vata. Therefore, vata may be translated as the bodily air principle. However, the element of Air in the external atmosphere is not the same as the air in the body. Bodily air, or vata, may be characterized as the subtle energy that governs biological movement. . . .

> Pita is translated as fire. . . . Pita governs digestions, absorption, assimilation, nutrition, metabolism, body temperature, skin coloration, the luster of the eyes, and also intelligence and understanding. . . .
>
> The translation of kapha is biological water. . . . Kapha lubricates the joints, provides moisture to the skin, helps to heal wounds, fills the spaces in the body, gives biological strength, vigor, and stability, supports memory retention, gives energy to the heart and lungs. . . .[89]

As complicated as the concept seems to be, the method appears to be incredibly simple. "You don't have to watch Star Trek to see a doctor diagnose a patient's illness simply by checking his pulse," writes Hugh McCann, in reference to Rajvaidya Brihaspati Dev Triguna, "one of Ayurveda's most skilled practitioners," who has a reputation for "diagnosing anything within a few seconds by taking the pulse of the individual." Ayurveda is a medical philosophy that utilizes "many therapies, including transcendental meditation and yoga, to achieve balance and harmony among mind, body and environment. Treatments included herbal preparations, food supplements, dietary approaches, behavioral advice, educational advice, music and . . . 'approaches on the level of consciousness.' " What is perhaps most amazing about this ancient medical philosophy is its growing popularity in the West. "Since the Ayurvedic medical organization was formed in 1985, about 150 American MDs have trained in the philosophy. The association, which has set its sights on recruiting 10,000 members, boasts a membership of 600 members" with medical centers in Los Angeles, Washington, D.C., Lancaster, Mass., and Fairfield, Iowa.[90]

Eastern Influence on Science

Science and technology are often considered to be largely the outgrowth of Western thought and research. New Age scientists and scholars, however, seek to correct that assumption. *The Tao of Physics*, *The Dancing Wu Li Masters*, and *The Eye of Shiva* may be unusual titles for popular books on science. Yet, these and a host of similar best-sellers crowd the shelves at bookstores across the country, heralding the convergence of Western science and Eastern mysticism. But the interest in Eastern thought among scientists not only appears in so-called popular books. The highly-acclaimed British astronomer and physicist Arthur Edington, the author of *The Nature of the Physical Universe*, argues that consciousness is the most basic part of reality.

> The one undisputable fact about the universe we know is human consciousness, which is known to us by direct and immediate self-knowledge. Physics now accepts the fact that we have to restore consciousness to the fundamental position in the universe, rather than see it simply as a secondary material. . . . The background of the world is mind-stuff. This mind-stuff is not spread out in time and space; on the contrary, it is time and space that are spun out of it.[91]

In describing the situation in the scientific community today, which appears to be a union of East and West, Douglas Groothuis contends that "religion and science have come together in a new way; instead of a stand-off, we see a new partnership, even a wedding. After centuries of warfare peace breaks out. Science grasps hands with the spiritual, and together they follow the same path." Groothuis summarizes some of the sentiment that has grown out of this union:

> Without going into detail, the upshot for many New Age thinkers is that all knowledge is potentially contained in consciousness. Pribram has speculated that "maybe the *world* is a hologram!" Leonard speculates that "in such a universe, information about the whole is available at its every point." According to Michael Talbot, "the new physics suggests that the consciousness contains a "reality structurer," some neurophysiological mechanism which psychically affects reality itself."[92]

Human Potential in Secular Life

The publicity about New Age is most commonly presented from a religious perspective, but in recent years there has been a greater emphasis on its impact on business and education. Articles appearing in major newspapers and news magazines report that business management is in many instances utilizing New Age principles of self-actualization for its own benefit. Training programs have been developed to encourage meditative activity, which often decreases the worker's critical reasoning and which makes for a more pliable workforce. One opponent of these programs charges that "for a company to concentrate on developing the 'inner selves' of their employees for the sake of higher performance seems manipulative."[93]

It is through self-actualization training programs more than anything else that New Age has infiltrated business and industry. Paul Rondina of Digital Equipment has written that this is a serious problem which should not be allowed to go uninvestigated: "I see the training industry being used to proselytize New Age religion under the deceptive marketing of increased productivity, self-actualization and self-improvement. As trainers, we must sound the alarm to this covert missionary work."[94]

How extensive these New Age training programs are and how many businesses and industries they have infiltrated is impossible to verify, but Jerry Main, writing in *Fortune Magazine*, maintains that the impact is enormous. Giant corporations such as General Motors of Canada, Scott Paper, and Dupont have spent large sums of money utilizing the services of such organizations as Werner Erhard's Transformed Technologies, World Institute of Scientological Enterprises (WISE—sponsored by Scientology), and Movement of Inner Spiritual Awareness (MISA).[95]

The message these programs offer is essentially the same. Executives and engineers at Hughes Aircraft in Southern California, who were enrolled in a company sponsored self-improvement course, were offered a "wonderful 'secret' . . . known and practiced by all the great teachers of the truth"—that being the ability to make a "mental picture" on the "screen of the mind" in order to transform their lives into something better. In a similar vein, The Rockwell California Chapters of the National Management Association offered a course entitled, "Visualization Training to Expand Life's Potential."[96]

According to a 1988 article in *Christianity Today* entitled "Karma for Cash: A 'New Age' for Workers?" the New Age influence in employee training seminars had dramatically increased over the previous five years. This training employs a vast array of New Age techniques, "which are based on a mixture of Eastern, cultic, pantheistic, and human-potential philosophies" and "include meditation, hypnosis, encounter groups, chanting, biofeedback, and isolation, as well as tarot cards, psychic healing, channeling, fire walking, flotation tubs, and intervention of spirit guides."[97]

New Age Music

New Age music is often described as having nothing to do with the philosophy of the New Age Movement. It is probably true that its listeners, in a majority of cases, do not hold to New Age ideology, but that is certainly not to say that there is not a religious philosophy that is associated with the sounds that are heard. "In the beginning was the Word, the sound of the mighty Aum, the first vibration: creator and sustainer of the universe," writes Joanne Crandall in *Self-Transformation Through Music*. An underlying principle of the New Age Movement is that everything has a vibration, and that this vibration is the divine energy of Aum that holds the universe together. *True* New Age music is produced by someone who is in touch with the great Aum or Om—someone who has tapped into this vibration and has thus assimilated a higher consciousness into the music. The listener then will also be lifted into a higher consciousness, which can bring about healing and self-actualization.[98]

New Age music was first introduced in 1964, when Tony Scott recorded "Music for Zen Meditation." In the years that followed this "impressionistic" music became popular in California, but was not sold nationally until the 1980s. Windam Hill is the largest producer of New Age music, grossing some thirty million dollars in 1987, but many competitors have recently come into the market. There is a wide variety in style of New Age music, but very often it is dreamy music associated with nature. Typical would be that of Paul Winter who on his saxophone accompanies the sounds of humpback whales, timber wolves, and eagles—letting them "create" the melody. Other New Age music features the sounds of waterfalls, ocean waves, and crickets.[99]

Reflection and Assessment

Because it is such a decentralized movement, it is difficult to assess the impact of New Age. There is no doubt that it has already had a powerful influence on Western society, but its future is impossible to predict. Is it a passing fad that will be largely forgotten in decades to come, or is it a movement that has only just begun to gain momentum? In reference to channeling, Brooks Alexander writes in *Christianity Today:* "Is this just another diversion for New Age dabblers, or is it something more enduring?"[100] Their are many "faddish" characteristics of the movement, but

fads have sometimes developed into time-honored traditions.

Indeed, there are many signs that New Age on the whole is gaining a powerful foothold in society that will not quickly pass away. This position is gaining credibility among secular scholars. According to Carl A. Raschke, a religion professor at the University of Denver and a student of the movement, New Age is "the most powerful social force in the country today." Nor does he view it strictly in a religious framework:

> I think it is as much a political movement as a religious movement and it's spreading into business management theory and a lot of other areas. If you look at it carefully you see it represents a complete rejection of Judeo-Christian and bedrock American values.[101]

The mounting influence of the New Age Movement is documented in the December 16, 1988 issue of *Publishers Weekly*, which is devoted to the subject, with such articles as "New Age: Still Glowing," "Getting New Age into the Marketplace," and "The Latest in New Age." The fact that the New Age Movement is still rapidly expanding is very apparent from a marketing standpoint—especially among book sellers. "Behind all the efforts of the New Age publishers, distributors and booksellers to develop the field into a long-term enterprise is the New Age Publishing and Retailing Alliance," writes John Bethune. "Numbering about 30 when the organization was formed in 1987 .... NAPRA's membership is now approaching 300." The purpose of the organization, according to Bethune, is to promote a distinct philosophy. "The organization's goals are a mixture of business, spiritual and social aims, from improving communications among New Age publishers, distributors and booksellers, to encouraging 'understanding, awareness and acceptance of the notions of human and global transformation and ultimately [assisting] in the expansion of peaceful human and more responsible stewardship of our planet.' "[102]

Many people are nonchalant about New Age, reasoning that religion is a personal matter and what others believe will not hurt them. Such naive thinking can be dangerous. Any philosophical system making inroads as rapidly as has New Age in recent years has the potential to drastically change society. The future of Western culture may be in jeopardy, and every individual concerned about maintaining traditional Christian values should be apprehensive about the potential negative effect the New Age may have on the coming generations.

Robert J. L. Burrows of the Spiritual Counterfeits Project in Berkeley, California, has spoken to this very issue:

> Humans are essentially religious creatures, and they don't rest until they have some sort of answer to the fundamental questions. Rationalism and secularism don't answer those questions. But you can see the rise of the New Age as a barometer of the disintegration of American culture. Dostoevsky said anything is permissible if there is no God. But anything is also permissible if everything is God. There is no way of making any distinction between good and evil.[103]

In fact, this very mindset, that anything is permissible, is supported by the messages that frequently come from spirit guides through their channelers. Moral issues are to be determined by the truth each individual knows from the inner self. An example is the message that comes from Soli, an "off-planet being" who speaks through Neville Rowe before crowds of people who have paid to hear his truth for earthlings. "You are here to search for yourself. The highest recognition you can make is that I am what I am. All that is, is. You are God. You are, each and every one, part of the Second Coming." When an antagonist in the crowd shouted out asking if murderers were God too, Soli responded, "Your truth is your truth. My truth is my truth."[104]

Such a statement which is reflective of much of New Age thinking is entirely opposed to biblical teaching. Among other absolutes of Christianity is the fact that Jesus is "the way, the *truth*, and the life," and no one comes to God the Father except through him. But besides this refusal to acknowledge absolute truth, New Age thinking is at odds with Scripture at many points. One of the strongest warnings given by God regarding much of what today would relate to New Age thinking was directed at the children of Israel:

> When you enter the land the LORD your God is giving you, do not learn to imitate the detestable ways of the nations there. Let no one be found among you who sacrifices his son or daughter in the fire, who practices divination or sorcery, interprets omens, engages in witchcraft, or casts spells, or who is a medium or spiritist or who consults the dead. Anyone who does these things is detestable to the LORD. . . (Deut. 18:9–12a).

Elsewhere Scripture deals with specific aspects of divination, such as astrology. "All the counsel you have received has only worn you out!" writes the Prophet Isaiah. "Let your astrologers come forward, those star-gazers who make predictions month by month, let them save you from what is coming upon you. . . . Each of them goes on in his error; there is not one that can save you" (Isa. 47:13, 15b). This last sentence could well sum up the biblical warning against the New Age Movement, and against all the alternative religions claiming to worship the true God.

New Age Influence on Christianity

The New Age Movement has not only made its mark on culture and business and education, but it has also influenced Christianity—so say some of the harshest critics of the movement. In their best-selling book *The Seduction of Christianity*, Dave Hunt and T. A. McMahon maintain that New Age concepts have penetrated evangelical Christianity at an alarming rate. They give numerous examples of this and implicate many well-known Christian leaders such as Paul Yonggi Cho and Robert Schuller because of their emphasis on visualization and positive thinking (or possibility thinking). "Through visualization and dreaming," exhorts Cho, "you can incubate your future and hatch the results." Schuller's message is reminiscent of Norman Vincent Peale: "You don't know what power you have within you! . . . You make the world into anything you choose. Yes, you can make your world into whatever you want it to be."[105]

However one evaluates this philosophy, the suggestion that it is reflective of New Age thinking is an extreme charge that can be very misleading and destructive. It is attaching guilt to association, even as Constance Cumbey has done in her supposition that those who use New Age "buzz words" are influenced by the movement itself. Hunt and McMahon do this in their citing a five-year evangelism plan in the Presbyterian Church (U.S.A.), the title of which is "New Age Dawning." "It is difficult to understand," write Hunt and McMahon, "how the committee responsible could work for two years on this 'Plan' without realizing that the words *New Age* already had an accepted meaning that would make their adoption by a Christian denomination confusing at best."[106] However difficult that may be to understand, it is utterly unfair to assume that this plan reflects in any way the New Age Movement itself.

That is not to say, however, that there is no New Age thinking in Christian circles today. Hunt and McMahon do point to some individuals who may be influenced by the New Age Movement and whose writing significantly differs from biblical orthodoxy. An example is *Journey to Inner Space: Finding God-in-Us* by Rodney R. Romney, the pastor of the First Baptist Church in Seattle. In this volume he maintains that "To understand God is finally to realize one's own godhood," and that Jesus wanted His followers to "realize the Christ within their own consciousness." He further contends that "He [Jesus] meant to establish a world religion that would embrace every soul and synthesize every creed."[107]

Another example of New Age ideology—or Eastern religion—that seems to have crept into Christian thinking is found in the writing of Agnes Sanford. She speaks of concepts some would suggest are dangerously close to ideas of past-life regression, though she is careful to disassociate herself from the doctrine of reincarnation. "When it is good, when it has a purpose," she writes in *The Healing Gifts of the Spirit*, "God allows us to see both before and after what we call time. We can enter into the accumulated thought vibrations of the ages, and feel the feelings and think the thoughts of someone who lived long ago. Many take this as a proof of reincarnation but I do not so consider it. It is something both more simple and also more profound."[108]

Another Christian writer whose terminology is far more blatantly that of a New Age proponent is Morton Kelsey, the author of several books, including *The Christian and the Supernatural, Discernment: A Study in Ecstasy and Evil, Dreams: A Way to Listen to God, Afterlife: The Other Side of Dying,* and *Christo-Psychology.* "Jesus was a man of power. He was greater than all shamans," he writes in *The Christian and the Supernatural.* "My students begin to see the role Jesus was fulfilling when they read Mircea Eliade's *Shamanism* and Carlos Castaneda's *Journey to Ixtlan.* . . . This is the same kind of *psi* power Jesus himself had." He goes on to make a specific comparison between Jesus and a shaman: "Franc Newcomb's description in *Hosteen Klab* of how the Navajo shaman turned a tornado aside gives a modern-day example much like Jesus' calming of the storm."[109]

Have these Christian leaders been influenced by New Age thought, and if so, what is a responsible reaction? It is important to keep in mind that Christians in all walks of life are influenced by secular thought. The materialism that is so prevalent in the evangelical church certainly does not have its origins in Scripture. Yet there are some aspects of what Americans enjoy in a wealthy capitalist society that are not evil, and there are philosophical concepts that can be carried over to the Christian life without necessarily doing damage and perhaps offering benefits. The same could be said for particular aspects of Eastern mysticism and New Age ideas.

Not all Christians who appear to reflect New Age thinking have been influenced by such. There is a long history of mysticism in the Christian church, and Christians in every century have chosen to express their faith in a variety of ways. From the New Testament to the present the Christian church has encompassed a wide range of worship and expression—from ritualistic formalism to straight-laced legalism to contemplative mysticism to ecstatic spontaneity—and it is crucial to recognize that contemporary Christianity reflects these various traditions. Some of the most influential spiritual leaders and movements of the past have incorporated ideas that could be labeled New Age. Hannah Whitall Smith, author of *The Christian's Secret of a Happy Life,* and the entire "Deeper Life Movement" that she represented, are examples. Yet both have had a powerful influence for good in the Christian church.

It is unfortunate that such time-honored Christian traditions as meditation, mysticism, and inner healing are being lumped together with New Age thinking. It is to be expected that not all Christians are personally comfortable with certain types of worship and prayer. To point an accusing finger, however, at such individuals as Richard Foster, the author of *Celebration of Discipline*, as Hunt and McMahon do, and to suggest that his reference to visualized meditation is comparable to "an old occult practice"[110] is a very serious charge. The Christian community ought not passively permit the New Age Movement (or its opponents) to appropriate words and concepts and practices that historically belong to the church. Yes, there may be similarities between certain Christian teachings and New Age concepts, but it does not logically follow that these teachings should be abandoned simply because of the association. They may have great benefit for Christians. As in all areas, however, Christians must have discernment.

APPENDIX A

LESSER-KNOWN CULTIC MOVEMENTS

Religious groups such as the Mormons, the Jehovah's Witnesses, the Unification Church, and Scientology have been widely publicized and are known to virtually everyone, but there are hundreds of lesser-known unorthodox or "cultic" movements of recent generations that have also made an impact on the American religious environment. Some of these movements have decreased in size in recent years; others have grown and are significantly larger than well-known movements such as the Hare Krishnas and Unification Church (both of which are relatively small movements that have lost membership in America in recent years but have nevertheless retained high visibility). Yet, for various reasons, these lesser-known groups either have not gained the attention of the wider press or have lost their one-time highly visible image. Some of these movements had only a brief debut in the limelight, some have been decimated by internal dissention, others have been geographically limited, and still others have avoided any attention-getting publicity. The following pages offer brief summaries and insight on some of these movements in alphabetical order. Some groups are subcategories of others—such as the Church Universal and Triumphant and Eckankar, which are part of the "I AM" Ascended Masters Movement, but all three will be dealt with because they are often perceived as three different religions.

Alamo Christian Foundation

Like so many of the cultic movements of the 1960s and 1970s, the Alamo Christian Foundation, founded in 1969, has declined in size and significance in recent years. As is true of many other religious movements founded in the mid-twentieth century, its charismatic cofounder and copastor, Susan Alamo, has passed from the scene. That fact alone accounts for some of its lack of vitality. Furthermore, it was a movement which focused on the hippie culture, and with the passing of that era recruits were not as plentiful as before.

Unlike most movements deemed to be cultic, the Alamo Christian Foundation does not usually veer significantly in doctrine from historic orthodoxy. In practice, however, the movement reflects the characteristics of a modern cult. The charismatic leaders, Tony and Susan Alamo, lived in palatial splendor while the majority of their followers lived in squalor, worked long hours for the movement, adhered to strict rules and regulations, and dared not challenge Alamo authority or teachings.[1]

The Alamos have argued vehemently that their movement is not a cult and that such allegations are a product of "slander and malicious gossip" instigated by the devil. "If you believe the Tony and Susan Alamo Christian Foundation is a cult and not a church," their literature reads, "then you will have to say that the Baptist Church . . . and all fundamental churches are cults. You will also have to admit that Christ is an imposter and that all born again Christians are brainwashed."[2] Yet, the charge that the movement is a cult has persisted.

In his published testimony, Tony Alamo claims that while living in Los Angeles prior to his marriage he was a wealthy and highly successful promoter of celebrities—celebrities he chooses not to name: "I managed and promoted stars, top ones. I would pick up complete unknowns, manage and promote them to big stars." It was during this period of time that one day, while in the process of making a major financial deal, that Tony testifies, "suddenly I heard a voice; a voice that came from every direction." Twice the voice repeated, "I AM THE LORD THY GOD. STAND UP ON YOUR FEET AND TELL THE PEOPLE IN THIS ROOM THAT JESUS CHRIST IS COMING BACK TO EARTH, OR THOU SHALL SURELY DIE." After that experience, Tony developed a close relationship with Susan, who was at that time an itinerant evangelist. Soon after they were married they began working with youth, which according to Tony was the beginning of the Jesus Movement.

> So we went to the streets, me very reluctantly, and here is where the Jesus Movement began. You hear a lot today of where the Jesus Movement started. I can tell you all about it. Many people have tried to take the credit for the great revival that has swept the world, but believe me, there was no one else in the streets when Susan and I first went out there.[3]

In many ways the Alamo Christian Foundation is similar to evangelical Christianity, with its emphasis on evangelism and the born-again experience. But one significant point of departure from evangelicalism lies in its bent for exclusivism—the belief that the Alamo Christian Foundation is the only true standard-bearer for Christianity. An undated letter from Tony Alamo to potential supporters tells of the "commendations and praise from notables" the organization has received "for its outstanding work in rehabilitating people from lives of crime, drugs and narcotics through the gospel of the Lord Jesus Christ." The letter gives only a hint that the Foundation is different from other Christian groups. In speaking of the work in Europe, Alamo condemns the "false messages . . . about the great work that has been done for the Lord by Christians in these areas. . . ." To counter this ineffective version of Christianity, Alamo insisted he was bringing "the real message of the Lord"— a message that "cleaned up the 'red-light district' of Nice, France in less than three weeks."[4]

One of the most bizarre aspects of the movement has been the response to the death of its idolized preacher and cofounder. She was not buried, but rather left in a coffin waiting for a miraculous resurrection, which according to Tony Alamo, was simply exercising faith in God.

> After a 14 year old battle with terminal cancer, my darling, partner, my angel Susie, went to be with the Lord on April 8, 1982. Our church is currently praying for God to raise Susie from the dead as commanded in Matthew 10:8, "Heal the sick, cleanse the lepers, *raise the dead*, cast out devils: freely ye have received, freely give." These are commandments that we aim to keep. And while we are doing this, we are continuing in the compassion of the Lord, going into all the world to preach the gospel. . . .⁵

Susan has since been interred in a mausoleum in Dyer, Arkansas, where the movement continues on a much smaller scale under the leadership of Tony Alamo.

Association for Research and Enlightenment (A.R.E.)

The Association for Research and Enlightenment is a massive computerized organization located in Virginia Beach, Virginia, that offers "one of the largest and most impressive records of psychic perception ever to emanate from a single individual." Who was this single individual? Edgar Cayce, an uneducated man from Hopkinsville, Kentucky. For most of a half century until his death in 1945, Cayce was one of this nation's most celebrated clairvoyants. "He gained international attention by putting himself to sleep in a self-induced hypnotic trance and then talking in his sleep. What was particularly remarkable about Cayce's talking in his sleep was that he could diagnose illnesses of people thousands of miles away and prescribe effectively for their treatment while in a trance."⁶

But what seemed at times to be accurate diagnoses and treatments were at other times no more than idle speculation into supposed past lives. Such was his evaluation of a mongoloid individual: "Here we find a physical expression of wantonness and selfishness in the past manifested in the present in the lack of physical, mental and spiritual faculties. The entity (in high position of authority) turned away from those who were without hope, who were disturbed in body and mind . . . and what he has sown he is reaping." In the case of an individual with Multiple Sclerosis, his evaluation was similar: "The law of cause and effect is here being demonstrated. Karmic conditions are being met. For as given of old, each soul shall give an account of every idle word spoken. It shall pay every whit. The entity is at war with *itself*."⁷

The publicity that surrounded Cayce's "readings" (prophecies that he gave while in a trance) began at the age of twenty-one, when he claimed his throat was paralyzed and he was unable to speak. He cured himself while in a trance, and from that point on his reputation grew. Initially his work was done on a small scale, but in 1931 he founded the Association for Research and Enlightenment, which was directed by his son after Cayce's death. "The A.R.E. did not stagnate after its founder's death, but instead used his readings and experiences as a vast resource for reading the contemporary world."⁸

By the 1980s there were some twenty thousand members of the A.R.E., or people who were involved in study groups. Although the organization does not consider itself a religion, it does claim to "offer a contemporary and mature view of the reality of extrasensory perception, the importance of dreams, the logic of reincarnation, and a rational or loving personal concept of God, the practical use of prayer and meditation and a deeper understanding of the Bible."[9]

Had Cayce claimed only to be psychic and clairvoyant, his work would not have resulted in so much confusion among his followers. But in conjunction with his active involvement in the occult, Cayce considered himself a practicing Christian. He was a member of the "Christian" church, and claimed that he read the Bible from cover to cover every year for forty-six years.[10]

Despite his efforts to align himself with Christian orthodoxy, the prophecies and doctrines that emerged from Cayce's readings were frequently utterly false or biblically unfounded. The following are some examples:

—California would fall into the Pacific Ocean in the early 1970s.

—Jesus Christ was a reincarnation of Adam, Melchizedek, Joshua, and other figures who lived before Him.

—God has in His nature a male and female principle, making Him a Father-Mother God.

—Mary, the mother of Jesus, was virgin-born like her Son.

—God does not know the future.

—Salvation is something man does on his own. It is not a work of God alone.

—Reincarnation occurs in many human beings.

—Jesus was tutored in prophecy on Mt. Carmel while He was a teenager. His teacher was a woman named Judy, a leader of the Essenes.

—Jesus grew up in Capernaum, not Nazareth.

—Luke did not write the Acts of the Apostles as traditionally believed by the Church. The true author was Cayce himself in a previous life as Lucius, Bishop of Laodicea.[11]

Church of the Living Word

The Church of the Living Word, also known as The Walk, is a relatively small, secretive, and dangerous movement that has come to the attention of many people in recent years through an extraordinary film called "Vain Glory."[12] Produced by Tony Cox, the ex-husband of Yoko Ono and a former member of The Walk, this film traces his journey from his marriage to Yoko to his custody battle for daughter Kioko. He then details his subsequent marriage and his involvement in the cult, which provided what initially seemed to be an ideal escape from authorities who sought to return his daughter to the mother she hardly knew. On the surface, the movement appeared to be a branch of evangelical Christianity, and those involved seemed to be deeply committed Christians. But behind the facade Cox discovered a violent and authoritarian cult.

The resemblance of the Church of the Living Word to evangelical Christianity is not surprising, considering the background of John Robert Stevens, the founder of the movement. His father was a pastor in the Foursquare Gospel Church, and Stevens followed in his father's footsteps. However, in 1949, at the age of thirty, his ordination was revoked due to unorthodox beliefs which came to the attention of denominational leaders. For two years following that he became affiliated with the Assemblies of God, until 1951, when that denomination also terminated its association with him. This rejection only spurred Stevens on, and in 1954 he founded his own movement—a decision he claims was prompted by a vision similar to the apostle Paul's on the Damascus Road.[13]

The heyday of the Church of the Living Word was in the 1970s, when some one hundred churches were a part of the movement, the largest concentration of which were in California. The headquarters of the organization, however, was located at Shiloh, a large tract of farm land near Washington, Iowa. Here Stevens' followers were required to work from dawn to dark at the saw mill, or doing other types of manual labor. Their contact with the outside world was limited, and news reports always had a ring of conspiracy attached to them. The Kennedys and Rockefellers were viewed as the enemy, and prayer was invoked to destroy them. Indeed, Robert Kennedy's assassination was viewed as a direct answer to prayer. Stevens mesmerized his following to the point of evoking worship from them. Such activity distressed some of the members, but there was no easy way out. Dissidents were regarded as enemies, and their lives were often threatened.[14]

Like Joseph Smith, Herbert W. Armstrong, and many other cult leaders, Stevens considered himself God's mouthpiece and apostle for this age. He claimed to depend on the Bible for his authority, but his followers were expected to accept the biblical message only as it was offered through his own divine interpretation. He viewed his role both in terms of an Old Testament military leader and a New Testament prophet:

> God is moving for us to go in to conquer with the sharp two-edged sword ministry under the Captain of the Lord's hosts, spoken of in Joshua 5. He is saying to us, "I am the Captain. I have come to lead you. You shall not cease to meditate upon my word. You shall listen to it until it is not only written on the tablets of your heart, but until you become God's mouthpiece to speak the Word of the Lord as did the early Church."[15]

Stevens' interpretation of the Bible departs significantly from the doctrinal position of the Pentecostal churches out of which he came, and certainly it differs from orthodox Christianity in general. "When you ask the Lord Jesus to come into your heart," Stevens wrote, "something must first be wrought in your nature so that you will want to be a child of God and not a human being. Therefore, the Lord puts you through a process that will bring you into sonship, into deity. . . . God becoming man means nothing unless we become God. . . ."[16]

If the doctrine of God the Father has been distorted, so has the orthodox view of Christ. "Christ is not one individual any longer, but Christ is composed of a many-membered Body," according to Stevens. "Christ is not one Man, one Person: Christ is a many-membered Body. . . . Everything that He is, we are. Everything that He will be, we will be. Everything over which He has dominion and authority, throughout the ages, we share in, because we are a part of the Christ."[17]

Stevens' message embraces doctrines from established orthodoxy, occultism, Eastern religions, and gnosticism. But it is more a religion of experience than one of doctrine. Believers are encouraged to seek "deification, tongues, prophecy, healings, auras, and 'transference of powers' in noisy and emotional meetings."[18] The movement has remained small despite the fact that its message was disseminated widely through literature and tapes. Stevens' death in the early 1980s was a setback for the cult—especially after his bodily resurrection did not occur as anticipated.[19]

Church Universal and Triumphant

The Church Universal and Triumphant, previously known as the Summit Lighthouse, is similar in some ways to nineteenth-century Theosophy, especially so in its eclectic religious philosophy. It is properly categorized within the "Ascended Masters" movement which has developed in recent decades. The Church Universal and Triumphant was founded in 1958 by Mark Prophet, who testified that he received messages from a Tibetan spirit guide who "ascended" just before the turn of the century. When Prophet died in 1973, his wife Elizabeth Clare Prophet, now known as "Guru Ma," claimed that "the ascended masters of the Great White Brotherhood had summoned her late husband and herself to be the messengers of God releasing the sacred Scriptures of the Aquarian age to the world. The Great White Brotherhood are spirit guides who use Guru Ma as a mouthpiece." She is not reluctant about interpreting the Bible through her spirit guides: "We see all around us," she wrote in 1977, "the signs of the end times which Jesus described in chapter twenty-four of the book of Matthew, signifying that the end of the age of Pisces is upon us, and the rising sun of a new order of the ages is about to appear." In the book *The Chela and the Path*, which consists of a message from the spirit guide El Morya, there are more than one hundred Scripture references.[20]

Mrs. Prophet's book *The Lost Years of Jesus* is purportedly based on long-lost manuscripts found in the Himalaya Mountains, that tell of how Jesus traveled East with a caravan and studied with gurus in India and neighboring countries.[21]

Jesus did not die on the cross as an atonement for sin, according to the Prophets. That "pagan" doctrine, they insist, had nothing to do with His earthly ministry:

The erroneous doctrine concerning the blood sacrifice of Jesus—which he himself never taught—has been perpetuated to the present hour, a remnant of pagan rite long refuted by the Word of God. God the Father did not require the sacrifice of His Son Christ Jesus, or of any other incarnation for the sins of the world.[22]

The doctrinal stance of the movement contains a ring of biblical terminology, but the content itself is easily distinguished from historic Christian orthodoxy:

We acknowledge and adore the one supreme god, the Creator of heaven and earth, and the individualization of the God flame in the I AM Presence as the I AM THAT I AM, the Source of life for each individual soul. We give allegiance to the Word that was made flesh, the only begotten of the Father, the eternal Logos, who is the universal Christ individualized as the Christed Self of the sons and daughters of God and the children of God.[23]

Like many other Eastern-oriented religious movements that originated in America, the Church Universal and Triumphant combines a variety of world religions. According to promotional literature, "Summit University is sponsored by Gautama Buddha and assisted by . . . the World Teachers, Jesus and Kuthumi. The teachers at Summit University are the individual I AM Presence and Christ Self, the ascended masters, and the messengers. . . ." Some course offerings include such titles as "Consciousness of the Cosmic Christ and Planetary Buddha," "Mother Mary's Scriptural Rosary for the New Age," and "Meditations for the Conception of New-Age Children."[24]

Another religion that the Church Universal and Triumphant draws from is Animism—particularly in its belief that spirits inhabit nonliving elements of nature. The sun is an example: "Our sun, giant hub of activity, aggregate focus of the Creator's Self-expression in all planes of Spirit and Matter, is governed and ensouled by Helios and Vesta, the highest representatives of the Godhead in this system of worlds."[25]

Like the Unity School of Christianity and other movements emphasizing Christ Consciousness, the Church Universal and Triumphant makes a sharp distinction between Jesus and the Christ. "The Universal Christ is the universal consciousness of God." Jesus merely possessed this Consciousness, which is the same Consciousness available to all mankind. Indeed, according to Mark and Elizabeth Prophet, it is utter heresy promoted by fallen angels to worship Jesus:

Not at all content in having caused the rape of a planet, the fallen angels had as their goal the thorough indoctrination of the people . . . so that when the Christ should come to save their souls from perdition, they would no longer recognize him as the archetype of their own God-identity and the exemplar of that mission which they had failed to fulfill. They would either reject him totally or worship his personality as one who could do for them that which they had no right to do for themselves.[26]

Besides its decidedly non-Christian doctrine, one of the most cultish aspects of the movement is that followers are cut off from the world around them. This practice is particularly noticeable at Summit University, which is located in the Santa Monica Mountains of California and offers accredited courses on the teachings of the movement. It uses isolation as the major aspect of a restructuring process. Robert Burrows writes that "The university discourages communication with the outside world, except with immediate relatives when necessary. . . . Forbidding talk of the past has a disorienting effect that tends to undermine the student's identity. A set of all-encompassing and highly detailed regulations governing student conduct also serves to diminish one's sense of autonomy. . . ."[27]

In recent years there have been law suits brought against the movement by disgruntled former members, but the movement continues to grow, according to Robert Burrows: "It has ten teaching centers, five of which are in California, plus study groups in 100 American cities. Members can be found in over 50 foreign countries, particularly in Ghana and Sweden."[28]

Divine Light Mission

The heyday of the Divine Light Mission was in the early 1970s when its teenage founder and leading guru, Maharaj Ji, claimed to have some sixty thousand followers in the United States and several million worldwide. The movement might have gone virtually unnoticed but for the publicity the youth achieved through his lavish and worldly lifestyle. Publicity was also generated by some of Maharaj Ji's celebrated followers. In 1973, Rennie Davis, who had gained notoriety as a member of the Chicago Seven for his antiwar violence and activism, proclaimed at a news conference that he had become a devotee. "There is now a practical way to fulfill all the dreams of the movement of the early sixties and seventies," he insisted. "There's a practical method to end poverty, racism, sexism, imperialism." The answer was in the teachings of Maharaj Ji, for whom Davis confessed: "I would cross the planet on my hands and knees to touch his toe."[29]

Born in India in 1957, Maharaj Ji grew up under the teachings of his father, who founded the movement, and as a very young child showed promise as a successor to his guru father as the new Perfect Master. Indeed, before he died, his father reportedly encouraged worship of his son by saying, "He is so great I can but prostrate myself in front of him." He also prophesied that his son "would one day shine over the whole world as brightly as the sun shines in the sky." Following his father's death, Maharaj Ji's mother named him the successor, and by the time he was twelve years old he had thousands of converts.[30]

In 1971, an American businessman encouraged Maharaj Ji to bring his teachings to America. He was immediately caught between his mission as a Hindu guru and his taste for Western materialism. He "declared himself to be the incarnation of God for this age," writes Kenneth Boa, "yet his tastes were remarkably like those of a young teenager (ice cream, squirt guns, grade B horror movies)." He quickly gained converts and attracted tens of thousands of devotees and spectators at his widely publicized festivals. But his newly acquired taste for wealth and worldliness were viewed with disgust by his family and his followers in India. "His mother, Mataji, who used to kiss his 'lotus feet' whenever in his presence, began to denounce him because of his materialistic way of life. She charged him with becoming a playboy, drinking alcoholic beverages, and eating meat." In 1974 his ties were entirely severed both from his mother and his ashrams (religious communes) in India when, at the age of seventeen, he married his American secretary who was eight years his senior.[31]

Devotees of Maharaj Ji are called "premies," and as was true of other cultic movements of the 1960s and 1970s, they have been largely young people disillusioned with traditional values. Initiation is the most important step of a devotee, and that comes only when the individual is deemed ready to receive the true Knowledge. The ceremony of initiation, which takes place in a darkened room, is lengthy and complicated. After a lecture on the significance of this Knowledge, the initiate receives the knowledge through four avenues: the divine light, the divine music, the divine nectar, and the divine word. The light is seen through the "third eye," when the leader squeezes the initiates temples and presses on the center of the forehead—the location of the "third eye." The "divine music" is heard with the "third ear," when the leader "places his fingers in the initiate's ears long enough for the recipient to be conscious of the sounds of his own internal organs and systems."

Tasting divine nectar isn't as easy. The substance is said to be a fluid flowing from the brain, the very elixir which sustained Christ forty days in the wilderness. With the devotee's mouth open, the *mahatma* (teacher or master) places his fingers in the *premie's* throat and forces his tongue backward until it rests against the uvula. The resulting mucous of postnasal drip is interpreted as being "sweeter than honey."

Finally, John 1:14 is quoted to justify the theory that God's Word is in man's flesh. The candidate is told that a repetitive pattern of rhythmic breathing actually constitutes a mantra. In reality, this experience of the "primordial vibration of the divine word" is a hyperventilative technique which leaves the *premie* in an altered state of consciousness much like a drug-induced high. This concluding experience conveys a sense of omnipotence producing a feeling of oneness with the universe. Followers of the Guru refer to this ultimate high as being "blissed out."[32]

Since the mid 1970s, the American wing of the Divine Light Mission has significantly declined. The Denver headquarters closed its doors in 1979, and since then Maharaj Ji, who continues to regard himself as the head of the movement, has been publishing two periodicals (*Divine Times* and *Elan Vital*) from his residence in Miami. In 1980, the movement claimed to still have more than ten thousand active American members.[33]

Eckankar

Eckankar is a religious philosophy that emphasizes the experience known as "soul travel" or "bilocation." While it is the invention of Paul Twitchell, it claims to be the oldest religion in the world. As such, this "Ancient Science of Soul Travel" is deemed to be "the Path of Total Awareness," by which the soul can become "God realized." Unlike other New Age movements, Eckankar is highly exclusivistic. Twitchell maintains that "it is not possible to enter into the Kingdom of Heaven except through the teachings of ECKANKAR." He has also said that "belief in anything except ECK is false." What is this Kingdom of Heaven? It is "a cosmic layer cake of eleven different realms or planes. Strictly speaking, only the upper six planes are heavenly. The lower five are ruled by the negative God-forces, especially by a cruel buffoon named Kal Niranjan who causes all the woes and confusion we experience here on the earth plane, or first realm."[34]

Twitchell was born in Kentucky in 1908 and died in 1971. However, these dates, according to Twitchell's way of calculating existence, are of little significance. He claims that he was a mineral some eight million years ago, and then through a series of reincarnations worked his way through plant life and on to animal life. Then, in his final reincarnation, he became a Mahanta who would be "translated" into another realm beyond the cycle of paying off his debt of karma. It is a process through which all souls pass. "The only shortcut in the process," according to William Petersen, "is by meeting an Eck Master or if you are living at the right time a Mahanta. . . . A Mahanta is in effect an incarnation of God. No one can "be higher in this world and other worlds than the Mahanta, the Divine One."[35]

After Twitchell's death, Darwin Gross "received the rod of power and was acknowledged as the 972nd ECK Master." Under his leadership, he authored several books and the movement acquired new headquarters in Menlo Park, California, and more than doubled in size. Nevertheless, his tenure was controversial, in part because of his marriage to and subsequent divorce of Gail Twitchell, his predecessor's widow. In 1981, he was succeeded by Harold Kemp as ECK Master, though he continued for a time to maintain influence in the movement. He later was "officially cut off from the ECKANKAR organization." Kemp, like his predecessors, testifies to his own experiences of soul travel, which are recorded in his autobiography, *The Winds of Change.* [36]

Through soul travel, an individual can progress to the point of attaining Christ Consciousness. "These travelers," writes Twitchell, "are what we know as the supermen of the universe . . . an agent of God, or what we might call a *Sat Guru*"—one whose teachings "lead to the most complete religious experience, and the most happy."[37]

Eckankar, like Scientology, draws the adherent deeper and deeper into its esoteric and classified levels of knowledge. For the individual who progresses upward, there are ten separate initiation ceremonies—each one promoting the devotee onto a higher plane of understanding. In the process of attaining this highest level of enlightenment, individuals enjoy the benefits their religion offers them.

> The primary spiritual exercise is soul travel or out-of-the-body experiences. Five of the major techniques used are imaginative projection, meditation, projection via the dream state, trance, and direct projection or intentionally willing one's consciousness to be in another location. Mantras are frequently chanted, and contact

with spirit guides is practiced. In fact, almost all forms and types of occult mystical consciousness-alteration come into play.[38]

Like other Eastern-oriented religions, Eckankar encourages a close relationship between the Master and the disciple. Without the Master, the disciple is unable to progress. There is no personal relationship, as such, with God. Indeed, in his book *Eckankar—The Key to Secret Worlds*, Twitchell speaks of God in impersonal terms, one who is "unconcerned about any living thing in this universe. He is detached and unconcerned about man."[39]

est

Like many other "new" religious movements, est (Erhard Seminars Training) is not a new religion. It has drawn heavily from other religious philosophies—especially Zen, one of the oldest religions still practiced today. Werner Erhard, the founder of the movement, concedes that he studied Zen, as well as Scientology and Silva Mind Control. "Est might, in fact, be considered a sort of ultimate, demythologized simplification and rationalization of the whole popular self-transformation process into a few easy steps and concepts (or rather non-concepts)," writes Robert Ellwood. "It could be seen as the ultimate Americanization of Zen, for, as far as I can see, the gist of it is Zen, but the language is wholly American—as is the junior executive atmosphere of the seminars—and there are no exotic trappings."[40]

Est was developed in 1971, after Erhard had spent several years in California experimenting with various mind-altering forms of meditation and therapy. He had come to California in 1960, leaving behind him his wife, four children, and job as a used car salesman. He was looking for a new life and new identity, and the first step he took in that direction was to change his name—from Jack Rosenberg to Werner Erhard (said to be taken from Werner Heisenberg, a noted physicist and Ludwig Erhard, an economic advisor to Hitler). Soon after he experienced enlightenment he initiated his seminars. He "got it," i.e., enlightenment, while driving his Mustang on a California freeway. The message or knowledge he received was hardly profound: "What is, is," and "What isn't, isn't." His attempt to further expand on this insight was similarly vague: "What I recognized is that you can't put it together. It's already together, and what you have to do is experience it being together."[41]

Perhaps the most amazing aspect of Erhard's seminars has been their popularity—popularity enhanced by the laudatory testimonies of famous celebrities, including John Denver, Valerie Harper, Joanne Woodward, Cloris Leachman, Jerry Rubin, Diana Ross, and Yoko Ono. In one single decade, between 1971 and 1981, more than three hundred thousand people enrolled in the seminar training. As many as three hundred participate at the same time, a lucrative venture considering the fact that each participant pays some four hundred dollars to attend. There are no est churches and the movement is not an organized religion, but individuals may participate in seminars on a continuing basis and there is a continuing flow of literature to be purchased.

The result of this training is amazing, according to satisfied customers who report that "they have rid themselves of medical problems, can lose weight without trying, are getting better jobs and forming better relationships, and feeling better about money, sex and God."[42]

The seminars—billed as "60 hours that transform your life"—are held on two consecutive weekends in a hotel ballroom. There are rigid rules of conduct that strictly limit such things as interaction with others, eating, bathroom breaks, and relaxation. "Pen, paper, watches, tape recorders, and cigarettes must be left outside." What happens inside elicits mixed reviews. Believers laud the value of the exercises, insisting their money was well spent. Critics, however, condemn the harsh treatment, arguing that it can be very emotionally harmful.

> An est seminar is a calculated process of breaking down the inductee's personality and then rebuilding it by harassment and intimidation. A trainer begins immediately to abuse the audience verbally with repeated obscenities. All ego defenses are ridiculed by means of demeaning epithets hurled at anyone who resists the tactics of the trainer. Eyewitnesses report that scores of people urinate, defecate, convulse, sob, scream, and vomit (in specially provided, silver-colored est bags). The only relief comes in the form of "meditation practices" (to acquire an altered state of consciousness), and exercises of lying on the floor to "find one's space." The latter practice has its relaxing effect quickly ended by the trainer who proceeds to create feelings of fear and danger, causing some to respond hysterically.[43]

Interspersed with the verbal abuse and military tactics are lectures and mind exercises. Participants are instructed to imagine themselves inside a flower or a vegetable and told that they are every atom and every atom is part of them, and that "We are all gods who created our own worlds." The climax of the seminar comes at the end when the participants receive enlightenment. "Then came the miracle," one such "estian" testified. "In that instant, you became exactly what you always wanted to be! . . . The light dawned slowly . . . and then one and another acknowledged eagerly that, yes, they got it, and gradually a swell of exultant revelation swept the place. It was amazing to behold. They were perfect exactly the way they were."[44]

One of the most basic beliefs of est is summed up by Erhard in a simple statement of fact: "Belief is a disease." Beliefs are what prevent individuals from living life in the fullest and most satisfying way. "The truth believed is a lie," according to Erhard. "If you go around preaching the truth, you are lying. The truth can only be experienced. . . . The horrible part about it is that the truth is so damn believable, people usually believe it instead of experiencing it." The purpose of est, like Zen, is to rid the mind of beliefs and rational thought. According to promotional literature, the seminar training "is not like group therapy, sensitivity training, encounter groups, positive thinking, meditation, hypnosis, mind control, behavior modification, or psychology." According to Erhard, est is "definitely a way past the mind. It transcends the mind. Actually, what I would really say—because I think it communicates better than anything, although it is not totally accurate—is that it *blows the mind.*"[45]

Erhard has insisted from the beginning that est is not a religion itself but is compatible with true religion. What is true religion? In the estian context it is acknowledgement of self as god and complete reliance on experience. "Belief in God is the greatest single barrier to God in the Universe," Erhard argues. "It is almost a total barrier to the experience of God. When you *think* you have experienced God, you haven't. Experiencing God is experiencing God, and that is true religion."[46]

In 1985, Erhard changed the name of est to "the Forum" and repackaged his seminar to be more appealing to large businesses and corporations. "The Forum," he insisted, "promises to produce an extraordinary advantage in your personal effectiveness and decisive edge in your ability to achieve." Much of the philosophy of the Forum seems vague, especially its emphasis on getting in touch with "being"—"that one essential ingredient that makes the difference, which gives one human being a decisive edge, a personal advantage." Another concept of the Forum is that of "finding the questions." An individual must abandon the idea that the solution is better than the problem or the answer is better than the question. "The Forum is about living in the question," maintains Sharon Sinclair, an area director of the Forum. It is "Much more powerful than having *an* answer—which closes possibilities. If you look, when you get *the* answer to something, you notice how that closes down any other possibility. So, the inquiry of the Forum allows people to begin to live in a question."[47]

How is the Forum different than est? "Est has changed cosmetically, but not philosophically," writes J. Yutaka Amano. "Several of the est and Forum graduates interviewed confirmed that there were no essential differences between est and its heir apparent. The Christian businessman, and all Christians, should be wary of the Forum and other similar self-motivation type training. Such training has cleverly disguised its wolverine fangs of Eastern thought under the sheepskin of business seminars."[48]

"I AM" Ascended Masters

The "I AM" Movement is most properly categorized as a New Age religion which consists of more than one single group or organization. The religion began in 1930, following a life-changing experience of one Guy Ballard—a mining engineer who was hiking the snow-covered volcanic Mount Shasta in northern California. He testified that while he was stopping to drink from a mountain stream, he sensed an "electrical current" run through his body. He then encountered "a remarkable man who gave him a vitalizing drink superior to spring water and discoursed on philosophical matters"—an experience not unlike that of the woman at the well in Samaria who talked with Jesus. This experience, according to Ballard, altered his life "so completely that I could almost believe I were on another planet."[49]

Ballard identified his visitor as one Saint Germain, who he claimed taught him about the "Great Creative Word" (I AM) and the Law of Life, which is similar in some respects to the Hindu law of karma. Following this encounter, Ballard wrote books, published a magazine, and held rallies across the country. Following his sudden death in 1939, his wife Edna led the movement, and by the early 1940s claimed a membership of over three million.[50]

Since Ballard's mountain-top experience, others have testified to similar encounters, and the various groups that have developed from such encounters have become known as the "I AM" Ascended Masters, or simply the "I AM" Movement. What these groups have in common is that "ascended masters" have appeared in recent generations to offer receptive individuals new truth, preparing them for the coming Age of Aquarius. These "masters" are individuals who have lived and died and returned to communicate this new truth.[51]

The Love Family

The Love Family, officially known as the Church of Armageddon, like The Way International, the Children of God, and the Alamo Christian Foundation, grew out of the Jesus Movement of the 1960s and 1970s. The movement was founded by Paul Erdman, a salesman who in 1969 moved from California to Seattle, where he established a commune "based on love and truth, based on God and Jesus Christ . . . a home for everyone who loves." Erdman took the name Love Israel, and began teaching that Israel is the name of God's people and that all true Christians are Israelites. He insisted that the end was near and that his community was properly preparing for that event.[52]

The emphasis on love turned out to be a sham, after it was discovered that members of the group—especially children—had been physically abused and deprived of necessary food and clothing. An example of this mistreatment came through the testimony of a young woman who lived with the "family" for several months. "One child repeatedly wet the bed and so they made him sleep on the floor, in a corner, with no clothing in the dead of winter," she related. "He cried and cried until I wanted to cry myself. It was so pitiful. One of the women gave him a blanket, but an elder came in and took it away and locked him in a closet." The most shocking scandal to make the newspaper headlines was the death of two men in 1972, caused by their sniffing the chemical toluene during a religious ceremony known as the "rite of breathing." The response of Erdman was that God had caused the men's deaths because of sin in their lives.[53]

Why would people continue to live under such conditions? The term "brainwashing" has often been used in reference to such cults, and in the case of the Love Family, the accusation of brainwashing may have justification. Newspapers, magazines, television, and radio were forbidden, and members were not allowed to hold jobs outside the community unless they worked in groups. When an individual joined the movement, there were immediate attempts to eradicate personal identity and the ability to relate to the world outside. The following testimony is one of many that bears this out:

> Everyone was given biblical names or virtue names, like Strength, Courage, or Serendipity. When you joined the group, you were baptized into the Love Family, not the church or Christ. They used the word "Christ" interchangeably with "the Family." They had different names for everything. The days of the week were named after the seven churches in the Book of Revelation; the months were named after the twelve tribes of Israel. Even their calendar was slightly different: each month had thirty days, with the extra days at the end for a Passover celebration. We also had different ages, which were computed according to the book of Matthew.[54]

Like some of the other lesser-known cults, the Love Family was known far more by the publicity it created than by the numbers of recruits it drew into its clutches. Its membership was numbered in the hundreds during the peak of its popularity and has since declined.[55]

The Peoples Temple

The Peoples Temple was a tiny and obscure religious movement until November 19, 1978, when headlines around the world told the gruesome story of a mass suicide ordered by Jim Jones at the Jonestown compound in Guyana. More than nine hundred people—a large percentage of them children—drank Kool-Aid laced with cyanide, and their bloated bodies provided a ghastly spectacle for newsmen who photographed the atrocity. The incident occurred after horror stories of the abuse prompted Leo Ryan, a Congressman from California, to investigate. In the aftermath he and four others were gunned down on a nearby airstrip by Jim Jones' henchmen.[56]

Jim Jones grew up in a poor family in Indiana during the Great Depression, and he determined as a young man that he would enter the ministry. At first he was associated with mainline and Pentecostal churches, but his denial of the Trinity—and his refusal to baptize in the name of the Trinity—caused controversy that led to his forming an independent church in Indianapolis, which later became known as Peoples Temple. "With great fanfare he opened Peoples Temple to all races," writes Jack Sparks, "making a distinct effort to especially bring in poor people. As time went on and his resources grew, he opened and widely publicized a free clothing store, free restaurant, and free grocery. He and Marceline [his wife] also opened the first of a series of nursing homes." Despite his unitarian views, he sought membership for his church in a reputable denomination, "and by 1960 he succeeded in getting Peoples Temple listed by the Disciples of Christ as a member congregation. That relationship still existed on the day of the Jonestown massacre."[57]

In 1965, Jones and his congregation moved to California, claiming Indianapolis was not only too racist for his tastes, but that it would be destroyed by a thermonuclear war in 1967. Despite this bizarre prediction, along with accusations of sexual immorality and fake healings, Jones quickly gained respect in certain political circles even as he had in Indianapolis. As his congregation grew, he expanded into other communities. When word came that his idol, Father Divine (the founder of the Peace Mission Movement, who claimed to be God incarnate), had died, he convinced members of Divine's Philadelphia congregation that he was God's chosen successor. Many of them moved to California to join him. By the early 1970s, Jones was claiming to have some twenty thousand followers. Accusations of abuse and sexual misconduct continued to surround Jones, prompting him in 1973 to move his congregation to Guyana to establish a socialist colony that would be free from the critical eye of the press.[58]

It was in Guyana that the tyrannical control Jones exercised over his following became more blatant and insidious. "He began to direct the sex lives of his followers, using the principle that he was the only one allowed to have any. He forced couples apart and used the Temple members, male and female, as his harem. He became addicted to pills. He used beatings to discipline his followers; for unruly children, he used electric shocks."[59]

How he sustained such domination over his followers has been a mystery to researchers, but the two factors most evident in the testimonies of survivors and dissidents were those of fear and gullibility. Threats and blackmail were used to intimidate those showing signs of disloyalty, but it was Jones' ability to beguile his followers that proved to be the most effective means of control. Jack Sparks describes the duplicity that frequently accompanied Jones' public preaching. Once he faked his own violent death and subsequent resurrection.

> There were other such staged dramatics. On one occasion, as Jones was telling the congregation that he was the reincarnation of Christ, he held up his hands, saying, "See them bleed!" Sure enough, they appeared to be bleeding, though a former aide said the "blood" was from capsules he had hidden in his fists. At another time, he dropped pills into containers of water to make it appear he had turned it into wine. . . .
>
> There are still greater lengths to which Jones would go to be worshiped! In the services, he would cry out, "I am God! I am God!"[60]

Jones' diabolical ability to influence his followers is unexplainable and is one of the mysteries that will ever remain with Jonestown. There is evidence, however, that on the fateful day in November of 1978, when 913 people died, they did not all die willingly. They did not all passively submit to his orders. Although initial news stories lent credence to the belief that they calmly drank the poison and then laid down and died, later evidence indicated otherwise. This was not the message Jones wanted the world to hear. "In his last moments," Mark Lane conjectures, "Jones wanted the world to believe that all of his followers voluntarily took the final step with him."[61]

Rajneesh Ashram

The religion of Bhagwan Shree Rajneesh illustrates the extreme contrast that may exist between various Hindu sects. His philosophy and lifestyle are far removed from the philosophy of the Hare Krishnas, and neither are very similar to those who practice Transcendental Meditation. Claiming that a movement is an offshoot of Hinduism or is characterized by Eastern mysticism is little more precise than saying a movement is a variant of Christianity. Rajneesh is utterly unique among the more well-known founders of Hindu sects. "The message is simple—anything goes," writes Bob Larson. "He preaches indiscriminate premarital sex, open marriages, and the abolition of the family, which he says is 'the biggest threat to human progress.' In his perception of religion, Christianity is a 'cult,' and even the Pope and Mother Teresa receive his castigation."[62]

In his major written work, entitled *The Book*, Rajneesh offers his perspective on a multitude of subjects, including that of God and worship:

God is not a person. That is one of the greatest misunderstandings, and it has prevailed so long that it has become almost a fact. Even if a lie is repeated continuously for centuries it is bound to appear as if it is a truth.

God is a presence, not a person. Hence all worshiping is sheer stupidity. Prayerfulness is needed, not prayer. There is nobody to pray to; there is no possibility of any dialogue between you and God. Dialogue is possible only between two persons, and God is not a person but a presence—like beauty, like joy.

God simply means godliness. It is because of this fact that Buddha denied the existence of God. He wanted to emphasize that God is a quality, an experience—like love. You cannot talk to love, you can live it. . . .

The theist is wrong, the atheist is wrong, and man needs a new vision so that he can be freed from both the prisons.

God is the ultimate experience of silence, of beauty, of bliss, a state of inner celebration. . . .[63]

Rajneesh was virtually unknown to Americans until 1981 when he arrived in New York from India with more than ten tons of personal belongings and soon thereafter relocated to a remote tract of land in Oregon that his followers had purchased. A settlement consisting of tents and temporary housing facilities was quickly erected. Among other features, the settlement developed an eighty-acre truck farm, a poultry and dairy business, and a gigantic greenhouse—on the surface a demonstration of productivity in an area that otherwise might have been characterized as a dry wasteland.[64]

As is true with many cultic movements, the Rajneesh organization misrepresented its claims of humanitarian outreach to an often unsuspecting public. In a brochure entitled "Rajneesh Medical Corporation," Ma Anand Sheela praised the community services that the movement was offering to nearby residents in Oregon. "According to the teaching of Bhagwan Shree Rajneesh," she wrote, "the body is a temple and the residence of a deity. This very body has the potential to become a Buddha, an enlightened one, the greatest potential of human consciousness. It needs and deserves tremendous love and care, both medical and psychological." As a response to that need, the movement offered "treatment and counselling programs for all" that included the services of "health professionals," "two fully equipped ambulances," a "technically superb research facility," and a proposed "36-bed skilled nursing facility and ambulatory surgery center." Such "medical services," however, were certainly not within the framework of traditional medicine. Much of it consisted of "educational" programs, such as the "Rajneesh Vision Course," designed to improve eyesight.

> Vision happens from a state of let-go—it is not something we do. The tensions in our bodies are reflected in our eyes. We have become conditioned to strain to see, and have lost the ability to allow light to enter our eyes and illuminate our vision. With glazed, staring eyes, we appear to be hypnotized. . . . Using the Rajneesh Meditations, relaxation breathing, visualization and sunning, and by sharing our ways of seeing and expanding our awareness, we can joyfully and playfully remember how to see.[65]

The religious philosophy of Rajneesh is a mixture of Eastern mysticism, the occult, and New Age self-actualization. "There is only one search—to find yourself," according to the Bhagwan. "Whatsoever you are, you are beautiful as you are. Those who have gathered around me are not my followers, not my imitators—just fellow companions, fellow celebrants, dance partners!" He insisted that "existence . . . is a carnival; it is just a festival."[66]

Although he claimed that his followers were mere companions, Rajneesh referred to an initiated devotee as a *sannyasin*, a Sanskrit word meaning "one who is under a vow of renunciation." The ritual of initiation was serious business—"a powerful experience . . . often spoken of as a spiritual rebirth," according to one observer. "In the ceremony, Rajneesh gives his kneeling disciple a *mala* (a necklace of wooden beads with a locket displaying Rajneesh's photograph). . . . Then he presses the initiate's forehead with his thumb and 'opens his third eye,' an experience that often elicits a strong physical response, said to be 'cosmic energy.' " After that the initiate receives a Hindu name, giving the individual a new identity.[67]

Prior to his coming to America, Rajneesh encouraged some very destructive forms of "therapy" in his Indian ashram at Poona. A former devotee filmed episodes that showed "beatings, bones being broken, and an attempted rape during a therapy session." Another former member testifies of rampant demonstrations of sex: "I witnessed an English-born group leader having sexual intercourse in the presence of the group with a sannyasin who was mourning the death of her parents. His comment to her was, 'All you need is sex.' During the same month, I saw two men in the group have sexual relations with a woman."[68]

In Antelope, Oregon, local residents strongly opposed the incursion into their quiet and sparsely populated community, but to no avail. Within months after the city of Rajneeshpuram was founded, cult members were seeking to gain political control in local elections. To outsiders, Rajneesh pretended to be an easy-going optimist. He insisted his followers wear red clothing, proclaimed his motto to be "Live, Laugh, and Love," and required that his city council meetings be opened with a joke.[69]

But Rajneesh's philosophy or lifestyle was no joke. He owned and drove dozens of Rolls-Royces, while his devotees worked twelve hour days in the ranch. Local residents were threatened and some fled for their lives. In the fall of 1985, evidence surfaced that large sums of money had been embezzled by the organization's president and that there had been plots to murder uncooperative members and Rajneesh himself. Soon after these schemes were uncovered, he was arrested and jailed for attempting to leave the country.[70]

Rajneesh has since returned to India, where he continues to lead his followers, but under a restylized religious movement. "The wearing of red garb and the mala [beaded necklace with a Rajneesh photo] is no longer obligatory, the Gachchhamis [ritual bowing before Rajneesh or his picture] have been discontinued, work has replaced worship. . . ." The communal lifestyle has been phased out and replaced by a "looser disciple-type of organization."[71]

His return to India did not take him out of the international limelight. As reported in *Time* in January of 1989, he announced to his ten thousand followers "that he no longer wanted to be called Bhagwan (God). His body, he proclaimed, was host to the ascetic soul of Gautama Buddha." Within days, however, Rajneesh declared that he had kicked Gautama out because he had disapproved of his jacuzzi. "Four days are enough," he insisted. "I say goodbye to you." Rajneesh later claimed that he had taken on the identity of "Zorba the Buddha." who as *Time* magazine cynically described, is "a pleasure-loving divinity who travels the 1,200 ft. between home and work in a Rolls-Royce equipped with TV, fridge and bar."[72]

Reorganized Church of Jesus Christ of Latter-Day Saints

Only a month before he died, Joseph Smith made an exaggerated claim that utterly distorted the reality of the previous dozen years and would, likewise, not reflect the events to come: "I have more to boast of than ever any man had. I am the only man that has ever been able to keep a whole church together since the days of Adam. A large majority of the whole have stood by me. Neither Paul, John, Peter, nor Jesus ever did it. I boast that no man ever did a work as I."[73]

Even Mormon historians themselves admit that the early years of Mormonism were torn by dissension. Indeed, the most grievous problems Smith endured were those involving "apostates"—some of them who were at one time his very closest associates and confidants.

Following Smith's death, his followers split into many factions, the largest being those who acknowledged Brigham Young as their prophet and who settled in the Great Basin. The second largest segment of Mormons, including Joseph Smith's widow Emma, later immigrated to Missouri and became known as the Reorganized Church. The remaining Mormons were split into a number of factions, each with a prophet claiming God's blessing.

Of all the Mormon factions that sprang up after the death of Smith, it was the Reorganized Church that has been the most successful in terms of long-range growth. Headquarters for this group are in Independence, Missouri, but its membership of a quarter million is spread out throughout the world, due largely to an intense missionary endeavor. The Reorganized Church shuns identification with the Utah Mormons, claiming that it is the only true mouthpiece of Joseph Smith. Brigham Young is seen as a false teacher who led the Latter-day Saints astray. This faction has also separated itself from some of the most heretical and controversial teachings of Joseph Smith. The church disavows Mormon doctrines such as those associated with plural marriage, temple rites, and the plurality of gods. Yet, the church reveres Joseph Smith, and reveres his descendants as its prophet-presidents.[74]

The Reorganized Church is much closer in style to Protestantism than is the Utah Mormon church. Indeed, the church services have many similarities to evangelical church services. In doctrine, however, a large segment of the church is closer to churches proclaiming a more liberal theology. The Bible is viewed as being filled with contradictions, and the *Book of Mormon* is viewed as a work that reflects nineteenth-century "thought and ethics" and "medieval theology," the historicity of which "cannot be proven." The validity of these scriptures do not "depend upon truth or error." *The Pearl of Great Price* is not accepted as scripture by the Reorganized Church, and the *Doctrine and Covenants* "remains an open canon, with additions currently being made after a formal vote of the church's conference."[75]

This "liberal" teaching affects other areas of belief and is not universally endorsed by Reorganized Church members. This became very evident in 1984 when Wallace B. Smith, church prophet and president, proclaimed a new revelation opening the priesthood to women. Opponents charged that this "was the latest liberal step of the leadership to upset the more fundamentalist members"—evidenced previously in "a movement away from literal interpretations of scriptural teachings." Although church officials acknowledge that "many members have left the church, creating splinter groups," the ordination of women is well established. By 1987, less than three years after the revelation, more than six hundred women had been admitted to priesthood.[76]

The RLDS is diverse for its small size, and in recent years there has been a movement in some circles toward evangelical Christianity, with an emphasis on salvation by faith alone and a de-emphasis on the role of Joseph Smith.

Rosicrucianism

Although Rosicrucians deny that their movement constitutes a religion, insisting that it is simply a fraternal order, there is considerable evidence that would indicate otherwise. The movement has obscure origins, but it dates back at least to the fifteenth century when one Christian Rosencreutz allegedly made a pilgrimage to Egypt where he ascertained the secret of the "rose cross," for which the movement has been named. The symbol of a rose in the center of a Christian cross represents "the body of man" (the cross) with "man's soul unfolding and evolving" (the rose). The "mystery" then of the rose cross (mankind's evolutionary past and future) is "the only means of mastership of life"—"an understanding of natural, cosmic laws." There are two principal Rosicrucian organizations in the United States, both with headquarters in California: The Rosicrucian Fellowship, which openly disseminates its beliefs, and the Ancient and Mystical Order of Rosae Crucis (AMORC), a highly secret order founded in 1915 by H. Spencer Lewis. Although Rosicrucians deny it, "some evidence indicates they exchanged ideas with Freemasonry," according to Bob Larson. "Freemasonry does include a Rosicrucian degree, and there appears to be a strong historical link between these two closed societies."[77]

In many ways Rosicrucianism is similar to New Age philosophy in that it offers a cosmic optimism regarding the evolutionary development of mankind—the belief that humans are evolving into gods. Unlike most New Age ideologies, however, Rosicrucianism builds on a race-oriented scenario. The various races developed during "epochs" or stages of human history. "We find that there have been various epochs or great stages of unfoldment in the earth's history, and that the negro was the humanity of the third of these epochs, the Lemurian. The whole human race of that time was black-skinned. Then came a time, called the Atlantean Epoch, when humanity was red, yellow, except one race which was white." The white race, whose heritage lies in the mythical continent of Atlantis, was originally Semitic—"people . . . chosen to become the progenitors of our present Aryan race."[78]

Who is this man—this human being—who has been evolving through the various races throughout human history? In Rosicrucianism, answers are offered through symbols. Indeed, as is true in Freemasonry, symbolism is a crucial aspect of the esoteric tenets—tenets that are never expressed in simple straightforward language.

> The upper limb of the Cross is the symbol of man, because the life currents of the human kingdom pass downward from the sun through the vertical spine. Thus man is the inverted plant, for as the plant takes its food through the root, passing it *upward,* so does the man take his nourishment by way of the head, passing it *downward.* The plant is chaste, pure and passionless, and stretches its creative organ, the flower, chastely and unshamed *toward the sun,* a thing of beauty and delight. Man turns his passion-filled generative organ *toward the earth. . . .*[79]

How can this man find his full potential and overcome his "selfish" and "dominating" qualities? "To keep him steadfast and true through adversity," wrote Rosicrucian spokesman Max Heindel, "the Rose Cross holds aloft, as an inspiration, the glorious consummation in store for him that overcometh, and points to Christ as the Star of Hope, the 'first fruits,' who wrought that choicest of all gems, the Philosopher's Stone while inhabiting the body of Jesus." More than Jesus or the cross, however, it is the rose that stands as a symbolic reminder of purity:

> The rose, like any other flower, is the generative organ of the plant. Its green stem carries the colorless, passionless plant blood. The blood-red rose shows the passion-filled blood of the human race, but in the rose the vital fluid is not sensuous; it is chaste and pure. Thus it is an excellent symbol of the generative organ in the pure and holy state to which man will attain when he has cleansed and purified his blood of desire, when he has become chaste, pure and Christ-like.[80]

The most basic concept of Rosicrucianism is that of man's evolutionary struggle, and it is in this realm that Christianity—or rather Christ—becomes an important factor:

> The mission of the Lord Jesus Christ in rosicrucian theology was to manifest Himself for the aid of mankind in the evolutionary struggle. Rosicrucian theology relegates Him to the highest manifestation or initiate of the Son. And He, along with Buddha and other great leaders, was revealed to facilitate human progress. . . .[81]

Satanism

Satanism, perhaps more than any other cultic or occultic movement, is permeated with horror stories and hearsay media reports that are very difficult to substantiate. As a result, the authenticity of the subject matter—rather than the nature of it—has become the most heated focus of controversy, as a 1988 report in *Christianity Today* indicates: "Within the past five years, ritualistic child abuse has become an emotionally charged issue that has rocked communities and divided parents, social workers, therapists, and law enforcers—some who charge a growing conspiracy of satanic worship, others who cry witch-hunt."[82]

Those who perpetuate these stories, according to J. Gordon Melton, are journalists who are looking for sensational copy and fundamentalist Christians who are perpetuating the myth of Satanism through their "imaginative literature." This literature focuses on "the manifestations of ritual remains in graveyards, church break-ins and vandalism, and mutilated bodies of animals and humans." Melton does not deny that such satanic rituals have occurred, but, like others, he questions how widespread they actually are.[83]

The most widely publicized news story of alleged satanic crime was in 1969 when actress Sharon Tate and six others were killed by Charles Manson and some of his followers. Manson, it was believed, had connections with The Power, a satanic movement that originated in London in the 1960s.[84]

Since the Manson murders, there have been numerous other chilling accounts of satanic ritual that have made the headlines, and many of these were recounted in a two-hour television documentary by Geraldo Rivera in the fall of 1988. His report tied satanism with heavy metal rock music and indicated that satanism was far more prevalent among teenagers than previously suspected. It also indicated that police departments around the country have been seeing an increased number of incidents that appear to be directly associated with satanic ritual. Among those interviewed in the documentary were those associated with the Church of Satan, who strongly objected to being in any way identified with alleged ritual crimes by "free-lance" satanists. They insisted that satanism as an organized religion opposes criminal activity and that as such the religion has been unfairly attacked.

The "father" of modern satanism is considered by many to be Aleister Crowley, a British cult leader who founded a utopian community in Sicily in the 1920s and who promoted a variety of occultic and satanic rituals. In the 1960s, many of his ceremonies and symbols were appropriated and popularized by Anton LaVey, the author of *The Satanic Bible* and high priest and founder of San Francisco's First Church of Satan. In his *Satanic Bible*, LaVey begins with nine statements of faith:

1. Satan represents indulgence, instead of abstinence!
2. Satan represents vital existence, instead of spiritual pipe dreams!
3. Satan represents undefiled wisdom, instead of hypocritical self-deceit!
4. Satan represents kindness to those who deserve it, instead of love wasted on ingrates!
5. Satan represents vengeance, instead of turning the other cheek!
6. Satan represents responsibility to the responsible, instead of concern for psychic vampires!
7. Satan represents man as just another animal, sometimes better, more often worse than those that walk on all fours, who because of his divine and spiritual and intellectual development has become the most vicious animal of all!
8. Satan represents all of the so-called sins, as they lead to physical or mental gratification!
9. Satan has been the best friend the church has ever had, as he has kept it in business all these years![85]

LaVey first gained nation-wide attention when he performed a satanic wedding in January of 1967 and several months later conducted a satanic funeral with full Navy colorguard. The movement spawned other churches around the country but has remained small. Estimates range from a few hundred to two thousand, and today, the San Francisco-based church has lost much of its influence due to numerous schisms. The most prominent of these splinter groups is the Temple of Set, founded in 1975 by Michael Aquino from Spotswood, New Jersey. The teaching of this movement comprises a more "sophisticated" form of satanism and "views itself as elitist and selective in taking in new members for initiation." For that reason, in part, the membership throughout the United States has not exceeded five hundred. It is a highly secretive organization, with most teaching done through private tutoring and networking carried out through a newsletter entitled *Scroll of Set.* [86]

One of the most nefarious facets of satanic ritual is the so-called Black Mass, a tradition that is repudiated by some so-called Satanists. It is a ceremony that is purposefully aimed at blaspheming the Roman Catholic Mass. Such ceremonies are typically held in an abandoned church before an inverted cross. A young woman (preferably a virgin) lies naked on an altar, as a symbolic sacrifice to Satan. The bread and wine is then defiled with urine or semen—or worse, and then placed on the woman as those present partake. As part of the ritual, the Lord's Prayer is recited backwards and an animal sacrifice is made. In some cases this sacrifice has been known to be a human infant. The blood is then poured over the woman on the altar. A sexual orgy may follow. The purpose of the Black mass is in part a "magical attainment. . .of power."[87]

Silva Mind Control

Silva Mind Control, like est, appears on the surface to be a psychology seminar more than a religion. Promotional materials promise that "In 48 hours you can learn to use your mind to do anything you wish." How is this accomplished? "The key is a relaxed level of thinking called Alpha. At Alpha, the intuitive right hemisphere of the brain is activated and functions more in balance with the logical left hemisphere. . . . But education has largely ignored the right hemisphere. Enter the Silva Method." The method has startling results according to testimonies of individuals who have utilized it:

> I took a deep breath and as I exhaled I visualized a light around me. I saw it extending five or six feet around me. I programmed that everyone who came within that range would become more positive and more receptive to my working with them. It happened every time. I could see a person coming down the hall just "loaded for bear," his emotional guns blazing. As soon as he reached me, he would calm down. I could talk with him, reason with him. He would go away feeling better. He would react to my "space" in a positive way.
>
> If we had a deadline to meet, I would go to the Alpha level and imagine everyone working as a team to meet it. And they did. I would see us doubling our quotas and reaching them. And we did. I would see myself being congratulated by my peers and getting promotions. And it would happen.[88]

Silva Mind Control was developed by Jose Silva, who was born in 1914 into a very poor family in Laredo, Texas. He did menial labor as a youth to help support his family, and learned to read and write through the tutoring of his brother and sister. From that informal educational experience he went on to educate himself by reading books on psychology and metaphysics.[89]

Silva proudly reveals that he "never attended a day of school in his life—as a student," but despite that is "serving as chairman or president of five corporations" and has developed a mind control method that "has been taught to millions of people in fifty-five countries around the world." If that is not enough to establish his credibility, he has credentials indicating he was appointed "an honorary Ambassador-at-large for the territory of Guam."[90]

There is very little overt religion intertwined in the Silva Mind Control Method, but what religion there is does not coincide with orthodox Christianity. The method is "based on the assumption that everything is, ultimately, 'energy,' or 'mind,' and that therefore an individual can get in touch with this 'energy' within him, and have access to all knowledge. Everything is energy. . . . There is nothing that is not energy, including you and me and everything we think."[91]

The Silva Mind Control Method teaches that graduates of the program who continue to progress in the technique "eventually will have so balanced all the proper levels and frequencies that they . . . will have mastered earth and become the Masters they are called to be. They then have attained what might be called *Supra-Consciousness* . . . ofttimes referred to as illumination and enlightenment." This is a "permanent state" that is "perfectly self-controlled"—a state called *Christ Awareness* . . . "open to all alike—Christian,

Jew, Moslem, Hindu, Atheist." It is available to all because, according to Silva's philosophy, "we are from the same Ultimate Source and we all live within the same system of law. We all call only One our Father. And the Father is within each of us."[92]

Many of the Silva techniques are common to those associated with the New Age Movement, and thus the method ought to be categorized as part of New Age. Meditation, listening to the "inner voice," and visualization are essential aspects of the method. "Visualization and imagination are two faculties that contribute to clairvoyance," writes Jose Silva. "You may feel that holding simple pictures in your mind is a waste of time. It smacks of daydreaming. Why picture this or that? This erroneous universal concept about visualization and imagination is the reason more people are not clairvoyant."[93]

Swedenborgianism

The Church of the New Jerusalem, more commonly known as Swedenborgianism, like Rosicrucianism, is a precursor of the New Age Movement. And like Rosicrucianism it is centuries old. Its founder Emmanuel Swedenborg, born in Sweden in 1688, was a brilliant government scientist and author of more than thirty scientific treatises, who resigned his post and spent the last twenty-five years of his life writing and speaking on spiritual matters. He considered his calling to be that of bringing revival to Christianity. But in his attempt to do so, he veered far from the course of the traditional orthodoxy of his father, who was a Lutheran bishop. Swedenborg wanted his Christianity to be more than the cold formalism he found in the state church, a desire that led him into an extreme form of mysticism. His writings were based on alleged communication from spirit guides who offered new biblical interpretations and extrabiblical revelations.[94]

Swedenborg, like Joseph Smith and others, was convinced that he had been chosen by God to be a messenger for this age:

> I went to my room, but that night the same man revealed himself to me again. I was not frightened then. He said that He was the Lord God, the Creator and Redeemer of the world, and that He had chosen me to declare to men the spiritual contents of Scripture; and that He Himself would declare to me what I should write on this subject.
>
> Then, on the same night, the world of spirits, hell, and heaven were opened to me with full conviction. I recognized there many acquaintances of every condition in life. And from that day on I gave up all practice of worldly letters and devoted my labor to spiritual things.
>
> I have written entire pages, and the spirits did not dictate the words, but absolutely guided my hand, so that it was they who were doing the writing . . . as flowed from God Messiah. . . .[95]

The messages these spirits gave Swedenborg included a denial of the historic doctrine of the Trinity and an entirely new interpretation of such doctrines and practices as the bodily resurrection, the second coming of

Christ, life after death, baptism, and communion. He sought to counter virtually every point of doctrine in his own Protestant heritage, including justification by faith. Indeed, "he was quite convinced that he, Swedenborg himself, had succeeded after many efforts, to bring the spirit of Martin Luther to peace at last by causing that spirit to repent of Luther's nefarious doctrine of justification by faith."[96]

Today Swedenborgianism survives mainly in the United States and Western Europe, with an estimated one hundred thousand adherents worldwide. They are divided into three principal factions, but all view their leader's writings as divinely inspired by God.[97]

Transcendental Meditation

An imported variant of Hinduism to be widely marketed in the United States in recent decades has been Transcendental Meditation. The appeal of TM over other forms of Hinduism is its simplicity and its availability to people for "recreational use." Unlike the sacrificial commitment expected of a Hare Krishna, the individual who practices TM is expected to set aside just twenty minutes twice a day. Of course there are opportunities to become more engrossed in the movement, but the vast majority of adherents maintain their previous lifestyle, with no pressure to adopt Indian garb or communal living arrangements.

TM, which is advertised as a meditative method of obtaining "serenity without drugs," was brought to the West in 1959 by Maharishi Mahesh Yogi, who had been a devotee of Swami Brahmanand Saraswati Maharij, a well-known and highly respected Indian guru. From his master he not only acquired a distinctive outlook on life and meditation technique, but he also was inspired to take the message abroad.[98]

From Maharishi's perspective, his master, who was known by his followers as Guru Dev, was one of the great teachers of India, whom he credits with bringing a great revitalization of Hinduism to northern India. Maharishi spent twelve years as his disciple and became his "favored student." After his master's death, Maharishi spent two years in seclusion in the Himalayas, and then began traveling from city to city in India teaching the technique of Transcendental Meditation. By 1958, he was drawing large crowds in India, and after that he began taking his message throughout the world.[99]

Maharishi's first big break came after he had inaugurated the "Dawn of the Age of Enlightenment" in 1975 and then appeared on the "Merv Griffin Show," where he announced this new era to some thirty million viewers. Griffin introduced his guest by divulging that he himself had begun practicing TM through the encouragement of actor Clint Eastwood, and that since he began he felt better than he ever had before. In addition to Maharishi, Griffin interviewed three other guests—a well-known actress, a psychiatrist, and a California state senator—who lauded the effects of TM on their lives. And if these testimonies were insufficient to convince the viewers, Griffin reported that "the Transcendental Meditation Program is being taught in many public school systems. It's being used by businesses, by hospitals, by athletic teams, by the military. It's being funded for various projects by the state governments of Pennsylvania, Massachusetts and New Jersey." But the clincher in his flattering review was that "last week in Detroit, a judge sentenced a young drug offender to four years on the TM Technique. Twice a day."[100]

Despite the efforts to promote TM as a nonreligious technique to attain a higher level of physical and emotional health, the initiation ceremony is a blatant form of worship to Hindu gods. Most initiates are not fully aware of this because Sanskrit is used, rather than the English language. The initiate is required to bring an offering (flowers, fruit, and a handkerchief) and stand before the picture of Guru Dev while the "Puja" is sung. The religious nature of this ceremony is obvious upon an English reading of the Puja.

PUJA

Whether pure or impure, whether purity or impurity is permeating everywhere, whoever opens himself to the expanded vision of unbounded awareness gains inner and outer purity.

Invocation

To Lord Narayana, to lotus-burn Brahma the Creator, to Vashishta, to Shakti, and to his son, Parashar, to Vyasa, to Shukadava, to the great Gaudapada, to Govinda, ruler among yogies, to his disciple, Shri Trotika and Vartika-Kara, to others, to the tradition of our masters I bow down. To the abode of the wisdom of the Shrutis, Smritis, and Paranas, to the abode of kindness, to the personified glory of the Lord, to Shankara, emancipator of the Lord, I bow down. To Shankaracharya, the redeemer, hailed as Krishna and Badarayana, to the commentator of the Brahma Sutras, I bow down again and again. At whose door the whole galaxy of gods pray for perfection day and night, adorned with immeasurable glory, preceptor of the whole world, having bowed down to him, we gain fulfillment. Skilled in dispelling the cloud of ignorance of the people, the gentle emancipator, Bramananda Saraswati— the supreme teacher, full of brilliance, him I bring to my awareness.

Offering

Offering the invocation to the lotus feet of Shri Guru Dev, I bow down.

Offering a seat to the lotus feet of Shri Guru Dev, I bow down.

Offering an ablution to the lotus feet of Shri Guru Dev, I bow down.

Offering a cloth to the lotus feet of Shri Guru Dev, I bow down.

Offering sandalpaste to the lotus feet of Shri Guru Dev, I bow down.

Offering rice to the lotus feet of Shri Guru Dev, I bow down.

Offering a flower to the lotus feet of Shri Guru Dev, I bow down.

Offering incense to the lotus feet of Shri Guru Dev, I bow down.

Offering light to the lotus feet of Shri Guru Dev, I bow down.

Offering water to the lotus feet of Shri Guru Dev, I bow down.

Offering fruits to the lotus feet of Shri Guru Dev, I bow down.

Offering water to the lotus feet of Shri Guru Dev, I bow down.

Offering betel leaf to the lotus feet of Shri Guru Dev, I bow down.

Offering coconut to the lotus feet of Shri Guru Dev, I bow down.

Offering camphor light.

White as camphor, kindness incarnate, the essence of creation, garlanded with the Brahman, ever dwelling in the lotus of my heart, the creative impulse of cosmic life, to that in the form of Guru Dev, I bow down.

Offering camphor light to the lotus feet of Shri Guru Dev, I bow down.

Offering water to the lotus feet of Shri Guru Dev, I bow down.

Offering a handful of flowers.

Guru in the glory of Brahma, guru in the glory of Vishnu, guru in the glory of the great Lord Shiva, guru in the glory of personified transcendental fullness of Brahman, to him Shri Guru Dev, adorned with glory, I bow down. The unbounded, like the endless canopy of the sky, by whom the moving and unmoving universe is pervaded, by whom the sign of That has been revealed to him to Shri Guru Dev, I bow down. Guru Dev, Shri Brahmananda, bliss of the absolute, transcendental joy, the self-sufficient, the embodiment of pure knowledge, which is beyond and above the universe like the sky, the goal of "thou art That" and other such expressions which unfold eternal truth, the one, the eternal, the pure, the immovable, to the very being of that which is the witness of all intellects, whose status transcends thought, the transcendent along with the three gunas, the teacher of the truth of the Absolute, to Shri Guru Dev, I bow down. To him to whom the blinding darkness of ignorance has been removed by applying the balm of knowledge; the eye of knowledge has been opened by him and therefore, to him, to Shri Guru Dev, I bow down.

Offering a handful of flowers to the lotus feet of Shri Guru Dev, I bow down.[101]

Following the Puja, the initiate receives his own personal and secret mantra, which is his to repeat over and over again in daily meditation involving two twenty-minute sessions. The "purpose of transcendental meditation," writes Jack Forem, "is to connect the outer field of activity with the unbounded potentiality of the inner man, for the purpose of enriching all aspects of life." The ideal, according to Maharishi, is to reach perfection: "Man is born to live a perfect life, encompassing values of the transcendental Absolute—unlimited energy, intelligence, power, peace and bliss—together with the unlimited values of the world of multiplicity in relative existence."[102]

United Pentecostal Church

The United Pentecostal Church (also known as "Jesus Only" Pentecostals) is rarely discussed among cultic groups, but doctrinally the group purposely determined to depart from traditional orthodoxy—not in a slow slide toward liberalism as many mainline denominations. It has maintained its distinctive heresy for more than a half century. The United Pentecostal Church developed out of a controversy in the infant Assemblies of God during the second decade of the twentieth century. The belief that people should be baptized in the name of "Jesus only" was brought before ministers at a Los Angeles camp meeting in 1913. There was immediate opposition from leading ministers, but the issue was not settled. "One preacher, John G. Scheppe, 'spent the night in prayer' and toward morning 'was given a glimpse of the power of the name of Jesus.' Awakening the campers, he ran through the camp shouting about his discovery." That led to a conflict "which was to shake the Pentecostal movement from coast to coast."[103]

Those who adhered to the "oneness" doctrine were initially fragmented into many small groups, but after a series of mergers and further splits, the United Pentecostal Church emerged in 1945 as the largest of the unitarian Pentecostal movements, and in the decades that followed the church spread out around the world through a massive missionary endeavor.[104]

Except for the denial of the doctrine of the Trinity, the United Pentecostal Church is not significantly different from other Pentecostal groups. On that point, they maintain that there is only one person in the Godhead, and that person is Jesus Christ. This "oneness" doctrine is based largely on the statement of Jesus: "I and my Father are one" (John 10:30). God the Father and the Holy Spirit are merely "manifestations" of Christ. In light of that conviction, converts are baptized only in the name of Jesus.[105]

This doctrine of "oneness" is emphasized most notably in the rite of baptism. When the movement first arose, many of the adherents were claiming that miracles were taking place "in the name of Jesus," which convinced some that God had given a new "revelation" concerning "the name"—the name of Jesus, which almost had a magical aura about it. Baptism, it was believed, was invalid, unless it was done in the name of "Jesus only," as John Nichol explains:

> To be sure, the "revelation" impressed many, and they hastened to examine the Bible for what teaching it contained regarding the "name of Jesus." Their research produced a revolution within Pentecostalism, for they fastened upon two texts— Acts 2:38 and John 3:5—and asserted that *true* baptism *must* be only "in the name of Jesus" rather than "in the name of the Father, and of the Son, and of the Holy Ghost."[106]

The United Pentecostal Church, with headquarters in Hazelwood, Missouri, has seen steady growth since its founding in the early years of the twentieth century. American membership in 1986 was nearly a half million, and worldwide membership was approximately twice that much.[107]

Yoga

Yoga is a Hindu system of mental and physical exercises, the goal of which is to separate the soul from the body and mind in order to release the soul from the endless cycle of reincarnation. It is an avenue that unites the soul with God. Yoga can be used as a general term to describe various forms of Hindu meditation, including the meditation used in Transcendental Meditation, the Divine Light Mission, and the Hare Krishnas. However, the school of

Yoga that has become best known in the West is *Hatha* Yoga, which emphasizes breathing exercises and various Yoga postures, with a corresponding deemphasis on philosophical and religious dogma. The objective is to bring the body in control of what are generally perceived to be involuntary functions such as "body temperature, the pulse rate, and the reflexes that cause erection and ejaculation, besides an over-all stamina to fit it [the body] for the strains of tantric sexual practices, with the ultimate aim of achieving supernatural powers and making the body perfect and immutable."[108]

Like Zen Buddhism, Yoga, according to its proponents, cannot be understood by anyone who does not practice it. "Yoga has to be known by Yoga. Yoga manifests through Yoga." Yoga, it is argued, is not primarily a philosophy. "In Yoga metaphysical questions play a minor role. To the yogin, philosophy is never the final object; his aim is to actually 'experience' . . . the reality beyond the phenomenal world."[109]

As is true of many other Eastern meditative religions that emphasize the master-disciple relationship, Yoga is practiced with the assistance of a guru. The disciple must go through eight stages in his process of separating the soul from the body. These include 1) nonviolent and disciplined behavior, 2) ritual cleansing and dietary restrictions, 3) posture techniques, particularly the lotus position, 4) controlled breathing, 5) withdrawing from the world through the control of the senses, 6) concentration for long periods on a fixed object, 7) deep meditation on consciousness, and 8) the realization of self-collectedness, or oneness with God.[110]

The deep concentration and meditation are deemed crucial for reaching the final stage, and various forms of meditation are employed. The following is an example of one:

> Let [the yogin] imagine that there is a great sea of nectar in his own heart; and in the middle that there is an island of precious stones, the sand of which is pulverised gems; that on all sides if it are nipa-trees laden with sweet flowers; that next to these trees, like a rampart, there is a row of flowering trees . . . and that the fragrance of these flowers is spreading all round in every quarter. In the middle of this garden, let the yogin imagine that there rises a beautiful kalpa-tree with four branches, representing the four Vedas, and that it is laden with flowers and fruits. Beetles are humming there and cuckoos are singing. Beneath that let him imagine a great platform of precious gems. Let the yogin imagine that in its middle there is a beautiful throne inlaid with jewels. On that let the yogin imagine his particular deity as taught by the teacher [who will teach him] the appropriate form, adornment and vehicle of that deity. Such a form constantly meditated upon—know this to be *sthula-dhyana* [course meditation].[111]

The true religious nature of Yoga is frequently disguised in the West, and individuals frequently practice the exercises without, they claim, becoming involved in the actual religion. But the two are deeply entwined and ought to be viewed in that light. The Tantra tradition of Yoga, sometimes described as sexual Yoga, is an example of how completely the physical and the spiritual are combined. Mantras are recited and various postures and exercises are followed during the act of sexual intercourse. Instructions for this routine are accompanied by assurances of spiritual results: "Touch your right hand to her forehead, eyes, nostrils, mouth, arms, and thighs. Then touch her vulva with your right thumb and mutter *aim* one-hundred times," at which time "you have already reached union with the goddess." The next step is even more explicit Hindu worship: "Now begin copulation, the ritual sacrifice to Sakti. Keep in mind at all times that your partner is the goddess; your penis, according to the Tantric texts, is a sacred ladle, an instrument of sacrificial oblation."[112]

Is Yoga truly a religion? Many people practice it simply as a means of relaxation, but according to Irving Hexham, "as time passes, such people very gradually and imperceptibly begin to accept other concepts which involve definite religious convictions." He argues that, "despite claims to the contrary . . . yoga cannot be practiced in isolation from other Indian beliefs. The whole concept of yoga is based upon a carefully worked out theory of beliefs about the human condition. The terminology used to explain the practice itself involves acceptance of pre-suppositions with religious origins."[113]

Zen

Zen, or Zen Buddhism, has been characterized as the world's most difficult religion to understand. It is so utterly esoteric that it cannot be rationally understood or explained through language. It can only be understood by those who experience it. It is a religion wholly different than any other, its adherents say, because it avoids creeds and doctrines and any attempts to otherwise explain the truth. Instead, it "moves in a direct line to the Goal." Zen does not present ideas *about* truth, but rather "is a vigorous attempt to come into direct contact with the truth itself without allowing theories and symbols to stand between the knower and the known."[114]

Only decades ago Zen was virtually unknown in America, but today dozens of books on the religion are often on public library shelves to satisfy the curiosity of young intellectuals in their search to discover an identity deep inside themselves. Zen is a form of meditation first popularized by Bodhidharma in the late fifth century A.D., after returning to China following a lengthy residence in India. His method became known as "wall meditation," a technique he himself perfected. "To prove his diligence at Zen, Bodhidharma sat in a cave while staring at a wall for nine years. He eventually lost the use of his legs through atrophy and even had to cut off his eyelids so he could sustain open-eye meditation."[115]

Centuries following Bodhidharma's death, Zen split into two major schools—the *Rinzai* sect, which teaches that enlightenment can be obtained in a momentary flash, and the *Soto* sect, which teaches that enlightenment is reached through a slow and determined process. Bodhidharma himself emphasized three main aspects of the meditation: 1) the goal was to "see into the nature of one's own being" in order to acquire a "peaceful settling of the mind"; 2) the method to be used was "wall-gazing," described as "an inner state of mind in which all disturbing and entangling chains of ideas are cut asunder"; and, 3) the ethic is that of "no merit," meaning that "deeds performed with any idea of merit accruing from them have no moral value whatever."[116]

Alan Watts, a writer who has done much to popularize Zen in the West, summarizes the technique of the meditation:

> The method of Zen is to baffle, excite, puzzle and exhaust the intellect until it is realized that intellection is only thinking *about*; it will provoke, irritate and again exhaust the emotions until it is realized that emotion is only feeling *about*, and then it contrives, when the disciple has been brought to an intellectual and emotional impasse, to bridge the gap between second-hand, conceptual contact with reality, and first-hand experience. To effect this it calls into play a higher faculty of the mind, known as intuition or *Buddhi*, which is sometimes called the "Eye of the Spirit." In short, the aim of Zen is to focus the attention on reality itself, instead of on our intellectual and emotional reactions to reality—reality being that ever-changing, ever-growing, indefinable something known as "life," which will never stop for a moment for us to fit it satisfactorily into any rigid system of pigeon-holes and ideas.[117]

The highest goal of practicing Zen is to reach *satori*, a point of ultimate insight and enlightenment that may come in a momentary flash. To attain this state of mind one must meditate in a manner that will clear the mind of all encumbrances of language and logic. This is done through techniques known as the *mondo* and the *koan*. "The Mondo is a question-and-answer method between the Zen Master and the disciple . . . that often seems presented in nonsense-riddles. The *koan* is a statement which the student must fathom by himself." The most oft-quoted Zen nonsense-riddle is, "What is the sound of one hand clapping?" The question is either impossible to answer rationally, or the answer has nothing to do with the question. "A Zen Master was asked by a monk: 'What is Buddha?' And he replied: 'The cat is climbing up the post.' When the monk confessed that he could not understand the Master, the latter said: 'You go and ask the post.'" The following is an example of Master/disciple interaction:

> Question: "In what way do my hands resemble the Buddha's hands?"
> Answer: "Playing the lute in the moonlight."
> Question: "In what way do my feet resemble the feet of a donkey?"
> Answer: "When the heron stands in snow, its color is not the same."[118]

Through such questions and nonthought patterns, a disciple is in the proper frame of mind to obliterate all rational thinking and dependence on language and knowledge in preparation for *satori*.

Not surprisingly, Zen has found most of its adherents in the West among intellectuals who are willing to discipline themselves enough to change their thought patterns—or eradicate their thought patterns, if possible. Like other religions that require serious discipline, it is more talked about in the West than seriously practiced. One of the most noted proponents of Zen in recent years has been the one-time governor of California, Jerry Brown.[119]

APPENDIX B

CULTIC STATEMENTS OF BELIEF

This section is limited in some instances by the fact that certain of the alternative religious movements, for philosophical or for other reasons, do not publish a statement of belief. In other instances, this material is limited by the fact that the statement which is included is incomplete and may give the reader a false impression of the particular set of doctrinal tenets. This is true, for example, in the case of "The Articles of Faith" of the Mormon church. In other literature, the Mormon doctrine of the plurality of gods is clearly enunciated, and many would consider it significant enough to be included in the church's doctrinal statement. But it is not. Why? Perhaps, as some have suggested, because that particular doctrine is one better left more obscure since it deviates so significantly from historic Christian orthodoxy. Another reason why these doctrinal statements cannot be taken at face value in all cases is that they can be very vague. For example, this is true in the case of Unity—particularly in the affirmative response the statement makes to the question, "Does Unity believe in the Divinity of Jesus?"

But while many of the following statements of belief are incomplete or vague, they nevertheless are helpful because they present the doctrines for which the movement wishes to be known. And in contrast to the Mormons' very incomplete statement of belief, the Jehovah's Witnesses' is very detailed, with each point supported by scripture references. In each case, the style and the content of the statements offer insight into the fabric and essence of the movement.

The Articles of Faith of the Church of Jesus Christ of Latter-Day Saints History of the Church, vol. 4, 535–41

1. We believe in God, the Eternal Father, and in His Son, Jesus Christ, and in the Holy Ghost.

2. We believe that all will be punished for their own sins, and not for Adam's transgression.

3. We believe that through the Atonement of Christ, all mankind may be saved, by obedience to the laws and ordinances of the Gospel.

4. We believe that the first principles and ordinances of the Gospel are: first, Faith in the Lord Jesus Christ; second, Repentance; third, Baptism by immersion for the remission of sins; fourth, Laying on of hands for the gift of the Holy Ghost.

5. We believe that a man must be called of God, by prophecy, and by the laying on of hands by those who are in authority, to preach the Gospel and administer in the ordinances thereof.

6. We believe in the same organization that existed in the Primitive Church, namely, apostles, prophets, pastors, teachers, evangelists, and so forth.

7. We believe in the gift of tongues, prophecy, revelation, visions, healing, interpretation of tongues, and so forth.

8. We believe the Bible to be the word of God as far as it is translated correctly; we also believe the Book of Mormon to be the word of God.

9. We believe all that God has revealed, all that He does now reveal, and we believe that He will yet reveal many great and important things pertaining to the Kingdom of God.

10. We believe in the literal gathering of Israel and in the restoration of the Ten Tribes; that Zion (the New Jerusalem) will be built upon the American continent; that Christ will reign personally upon the earth; and, that the earth will be renewed and receive its paradisiacal glory.

11. We claim the privilege of worshipping Almighty God according to the dictates of our own conscience and allow all men the same privilege, let them worship how, where, or what they may.

12. We believe in being subject to kings, presidents, rulers, and magistrates, in obeying, honoring, and sustaining the law.

13. We believe in being honest, true, chaste, benevolent, virtuous, and in doing good to all men; indeed, we may say that we follow the admonition of Paul—We believe all things, we hope all things, we have endured many things, and hope to be able to endure all things. If there is anything virtuous, lovely, or of good report or praiseworthy, we seek after these things.

Joseph Smith

Beliefs of the Seventh-day Adventists

The Trinity

There is one God, the Father, Son, and Holy Spirit, a unity of three coeternal Persons commonly called the Trinity. God the Father is the Creator, Source, Sustainer, and Sovereign of all creation. God the eternal Son became incarnate in Jesus Christ, through Whom all things were created, the character of God is revealed, the salvation of humanity is accomplished, and the world is judged. God the Holy Spirit draws men and women to Himself and extends spiritual gifts to the Church.

Christ Our Hope

In Christ's life of perfect obedience to God's will, His suffering, death, and resurrection, God provided the only means of atonement for human sin, so that those who by faith accept this atonement may have eternal life.

Christ's Return

The second coming of Christ is the blessed hope of the Church, the grand climax of the gospel. His coming will be literal, personal, visible, and worldwide. When He returns the righteous dead will be resurrected and together with the righteous living will be glorified and taken to heaven. The unrighteous—those who have rejected divine grace—will die.

The Church

The Church is the community of believers who confess Jesus Christ as Lord and Saviour. In it men and women join together for worship, fellowship, instruction in the Word, with celebration of the Lord's Supper, service to our neighbors and the worldwide proclamation of the gospel.

The Holy Scriptures

The Old and New Testaments are the written Word of God, given by divine inspiration through holy men of God who spoke and wrote by the Holy Spirit. The Scriptures are the infallible revelation of God's will.

Baptism

Baptism by immersion is a symbol of our union with Christ, the forgiveness of our sins, and our reception of the Holy Spirit.

Ten Commandments

The Ten Commandments, the great principles of God's law are exemplified in the life of Christ. They express God's love, will, and purpose concerning human conduct and relationships. Salvation is all of grace and not of works, but its fruitage is obedience to the Commandments, not in hopeless effort to earn salvation, but in grateful harmony with the life and will of Him Whose perfect obedience has brought us confidence and acceptance as His sons and daughters.

The Sabbath

The seventh day of the week, Saturday, is observed as the day of rest, worship, and ministry in harmony with the teaching and practice of Jesus, the Lord of the Sabbath. The Sabbath is a day of delightful communion with God and one another. We joyfully observe this holy time from Friday evening to Saturday evening, from sunset to sunset, as a celebration of God's creative and redemptive acts.

The New Earth

On the new earth, in which righteousness dwells, God will provide a glorious home for the redeemed with a perfect environment for everlasting life, love, joy, and learning. God Himself will dwell with His people, and suffering and death will exist no more.[1]

What Jehovah's Witnesses Believe

Bible is God's Word and is truth (2 Tim. 3:16, 17; 2 Pet. 1:20, 21; John 17:17)

Bible is more reliable than tradition (Matt. 15:3; Col. 2:8)

God's name is Jehovah (Ps. 83:18; Isa. 26:4; 42:8, AS; Ex. 6:3)

Christ is God's Son and is inferior to him (Matt. 3:17; John 8:42; 14:28; 20:17; 1 Cor. 11:3; 15:28)

Christ was first of God's creations (Col. 1:15; Rev. 3:14)

Christ died on a stake, not a cross (Gal. 3:13; Acts 5:30)

Christ's human life was paid as a ransom for obedient humans (Matt. 20:28; 1 Tim. 2:5, 6; Titus 2:14; 1 Pet. 2:24)

Christ's one sacrifice was sufficient (Rom. 6:10; Heb. 9:25–28)

Christ was raised from the dead as an immortal spirit person (1 Pet. 3:18; Rom. 6:9; Rev. 1:17, 18)

Christ's presence is in spirit (John 14:19; Matt. 24:3; 2 Cor. 5:16; Ps. 110:1, 2)

Kingdom under Christ will rule earth in righteousness and peace (Isa. 9:6, 7; 11:1–5; Dan. 7:13, 14; Matt. 6:10)

Kingdom brings ideal living conditions to earth (Ps. 72:1–4; Rev. 7:9, 10, 13–17; 21:3, 4)

Earth will never be destroyed or depopulated (Eccl. 1:4; Isa. 45:18; Ps. 78:69)

God will destroy present system of things in the battle of Har-Magedon (Rev. 16:14, 16; Zeph. 3:8; Dan. 2:44; Isa. 34:2)

Wicked will be eternally destroyed (Matt. 25:41–46; 2 Thess. 1:6–9)

People God approves will receive eternal life (John 3:16; 10:27, 28; 17:3; Mark 10:29, 30)

There is only one road to life (Matt. 7:13, 14; Eph. 4:4, 5)

We are now in the "time of the end" (Matt. 24:3–14; 2 Tim. 3:1–5; Luke 17:26–30)

Human death is due to Adam's sin (Rom. 5:12; 6:22)

The human soul ceases to exist at death (Ezek. 18:4; Eccl. 9:10; Ps. 6:5; 146:4; John 11:11–14)

Hell is mankind's common grave (Job 14:13, Dy; Rev. 20:13, 14, AV margin)

Hope for dead is resurrection (1 Cor. 15:20–22; John 5:28, 29; 11:25, 26)

Adamic death will cease (1 Cor. 15:26; Rev. 21:4; Isa. 25:8; 1 Cor. 15:54)

Only a little flock of 144,000 go to heaven and rule with Christ (Luke 12:32; Rev. 14:1, 3; 1 Cor. 15:40–53; Rev. 5:9, 10)

The 144,000 are born again as spiritual sons of God (1 Pet. 1:23; John 3:3; Rev. 7:3, 4)

New covenant made with spiritual Israel (Jer. 31:31; Heb. 8:10–13)

Christ's congregation is built upon himself (Eph. 2:20; Isa. 28:16; Matt. 21:42)

Prayers must be directed only to Jehovah through Christ (John 14:6, 13, 14; 1 Tim. 2:5)

Images must not be used in worship (Ex. 20:4, 5; Lev. 26:1; 1 Cor. 10:14)

Spiritism must be shunned (Deut. 18:10–12; Gal. 5:19–21; Lev. 19:31)

Satan is invisible ruler of world (1 John 5:19; 2 Cor. 4:4; John 12:31)

A Christian must have no part in inter-faith movements (2 Cor. 6:14–17; 11:13–15; Gal. 5:9; Deut. 7:1–5)

All human laws that do not conflict with God's laws should be obeyed (Matt. 22:20, 21; 1 Pet. 2:12; 4:15)

Taking blood into body through mouth or veins violates God's laws (Gen. 9:3, 4; Lev. 17:14; Acts 15:28, 29)

Bible's laws on morals must be obeyed (1 Cor. 6:9, 10; Heb. 13:4; 1 Tim. 3:2; Prov. 5:1–23)

Sabbath observance was given only to the Jews and ended with Mosaic law (Deut. 5:15; Ex. 31:13; Rom. 10:4; Gal. 4:9, 10; Col. 2:16, 17)

A clergy class and special titles are improper (Matt. 23:8–12; 20:25–27; Job 32:21, 22)

Man did not evolve but was created (Isa. 45:12; Gen. 1:27)

Christ set example that must be followed in serving God (1 Pet. 2:21; Heb. 10:7; John 4:34; 6:38)

Baptism by complete immersion symbolizes dedication (Mark 1:9, 10; John 3:23; Acts 19:4, 5)

Christians must give public testimony to Scriptural truth (Rom. 10:10; Heb. 13:15; Isa. 43:10–12)[2]

Religious Tenets of Christian Science

1. As adherents of Truth, we take the inspired Word of the Bible as our sufficient guide to eternal life.

2. We acknowledge and adore one supreme and infinite God. We acknowledge His Son, one Christ; the Holy Ghost or divine Comforter; and man in God's image and likeness.

3. We acknowledge God's forgiveness of sin in the destruction of sin and the spiritual understanding that casts out evil as unreal. But the belief in sin is punished as long as the belief lasts.

4. We acknowledge Jesus' atonement as the evidence of divine, efficacious Love, unfolding man's unity with God through Christ Jesus the Way-shower; and we acknowledge that man is saved through Christ, through Truth, Life, and Love as demonstrated by the Galilean Prophet in healing the sick and overcoming sin and death.

5. We acknowledge that the crucifixion of Jesus and His resurrection served to uplift faith to understand eternal Life, even the allness of Soul, Spirit, and the nothingness of matter.

6. And we solemnly promise to watch, and pray for that Mind to be in us which was also in Christ Jesus; to do unto others as we would have them do unto us; and to be merciful, just, and pure.[3]

[Three of] "Twenty Questions About Unity"

1. What is Unity?

Unity is the practical application in everyday life of the principles of Truth taught and exemplified by Jesus Christ, as interpreted in the light of modern-day experience by Unity School of Christianity. Unity is a way of life that leads to health, prosperity, happiness, and peace of mind. The Association of Unity Churches, in cooperation with Unity School of Christianity, has established centers of study and worship throughout the world where people study and practice the Unity way of life.

2. What are the basic tenets of the Unity teaching?

First: God, Divine Mind, is the source and Creator of all. There is no other enduring power. The nature of God is absolute good; therefore, all manifestations partake of good. What is called "evil" is a limited or incomplete expression of God or good. Its origin is ignorance.

Second: We are spiritual beings, ideas in the Mind of God, created in His image and after His likeness. Ideal man is the perfect man, the Christ the pattern every person is seeking to bring forth. Manifest man is the idea of perfection brought into expression according to the degree of understanding in the individual consciousness.

Third: Jesus was a person in history who expressed perfection and thereby became the Christ, or Jesus Christ. He was a Teacher who demonstrated the importance of thoughts, words, and deeds in shaping the life and world of the individual.

Fourth: Jesus' teaching was based on prayer, which to Him was conscious communion with God. Preparation for prayer involves the use of the spoken word, the creative power of God, which is made practical through denials and affirmations. Unity teaches that through the daily repetition of statements of Truth until they become established as habitual patterns of thinking, feeling, and acting, we attain the ability to take dominion over mind, body and affairs.

3. Does Unity believe in the divinity of Jesus Christ?

Yes. Unity teaches that the Spirit of God dwelt in Jesus, just as it indwells every person; and that every person has the potential to express the perfection of Christ, as Jesus did, by being more Christ-like in everyday life.[4]

Doctrines and Beliefs of the Worldwide Church of God

The Church of God believes in one God, the Creator, who is Spirit, of supreme Mind, Power, and Authority; that God is a Family consisting of more than one personage; that Jesus of Nazareth was the Son of God and the Son of man, conceived by the Holy Spirit, born of the Virgin Mary; that He founded and is the living Head of the Church of God; that He brought the true Gospel from God for mankind; that He was the promised Messiah; that He died for the sins of the world, and that repentant and believing sinners are justified and reconciled to God by His shed blood; that God raised Him from the dead the third day; that He ascended to heaven and was glorified; that He is the living Christ at the right hand of God as our High Priest.

The Church of God believes this is not the only day of salvation. We believe that the living Christ will soon return to earth, this time in all the power and glory of the Creator GOD, as King of kings and Lord of lords. He will solve the now fast-mounting world problems, establish world peace, end poverty, ignorance, and disease, and set His hand to save the world. Christ commissioned His Church to proclaim the Gospel—which is the good news of the Kingdom of God—"as a witness," NOT to convert the world. Those whom God calls and converts at this time are called "the firstfruits" of salvation.

God has allotted 7000 years (seven millennial days, II Pet. 3:8) to accomplish the spiritual creation of mankind. The Creator's plan for humanity is typified by the seven-day week, which was established at man's creation (Gen. 2:1-3). Man has been given six days in which to work, followed by a day of rest (Ex. 20:9-11). On the seventh day, man is to rest from his normal routine of daily activites. The Sabbath begins with sunset at the end of the sixth day (Friday) and ends with sunset of the seventh day (Saturday) each week. God's master plan is also pictured by seven annual Holy Days and festivals, each pointing to a great event in God's plan for humanity. The weekly Sabbath and the annual Holy Days and festivals are a sign of identity between the Creator God and His people.

We believe the Holy Bible is the inspired revelation from God to man; it is the "instruction book" which the Maker designed for the finest and most complicated mechanism ever produced (the human being). It reveals the PURPOSE of human life and the WAY of life God set in motion to bring peace, happiness, and abundant well-being. We believe true Christians should, as Jesus said, actually *live by* every word of this divine "instruction book" as THE WAY to every good thing all humans desire; and that blessings are the result of obedience to this *way of life*.

Statement of Beliefs
The Way International

1. We believe the scriptures of the Old and New Testament were Theopneustos, "God-breathed," and perfect as originally given; that the Scriptures, or the Word of God, are of supreme, absolute and final authority for believing and godliness.

2. We believe in one God, the creator of the heavens and earth; in Jesus Christ, God's only begotten Son our lord and savior, whom God raised from the dead; and we believe in the workings of the Holy Spirit.

3. We believe that the virgin Mary conceived Jesus Christ by the holy spirit; that God was in Christ, and that Jesus Christ is the "mediator between God and men," and is "the man Christ Jesus."

4. We believe that Adam was created in the image of God, spiritually; that he sinned and thereby brought upon himself immediate spiritual death, which is separation from God, and physical death later, which is the consequence of sin; and that all human beings are born with a sinful nature.

5. We believe that Jesus Christ died for our sins according to the Scriptures, as a representative and substitute for us, and that all who believe that God raised him from the dead are justified and made righteous, born again by the Spirit of God, receiving eternal life on the grounds of His eternal redemption, and thereby are the sons of God.

6. We believe in the resurrection of the crucified body of our Lord Jesus Christ, his ascension into heaven and his seating at the right hand of God.

7. We believe in the blessed hope of Christ's return, the personal return of our living lord and savior Jesus Christ and our gathering together unto him.

8. We believe in the bodily resurrection of the just and the unjust.

9. We believe in the receiving of the fullness of the holy spirit, the power from on high, plus the corresponding nine manifestations of the holy spirit, for all born-again believers.

10. We believe it is available to receive all that God promises us in His Word according to our believing faith. We believe we are free in Christ Jesus to receive all that he accomplished for us by his substitution.

11. We believe the early Church flourished rapidly because they operated within a Root, Trunk, Limb, Branch and Twig setup, decently and in order.

Unification Theology

Unification Theology is based on the teachings of the Old and New Testaments as clarified by the revelations found in the *Divine Principle*. Central to the Divine Principle is the conviction that: "The ultimate purpose of God's providence of salvation is to establish the Kingdom of God on earth." (*Divine Principle*, p. 13.) Unification Theology can be categorized into three major sections: The Principle of Creation, The Principle of the Fall, and The Principle of Restoration.

Principles of Creation

God created the universe for joy—the joy of experiencing love, life and ideal reflected in God's creation, especially in humankind as God's children. Human beings were created to bring joy to God by fulfilling the "three great blessings" of individual perfection, the love of family, and dominion over creation (Gen. 1:28).

The blessing of individual perfection means that each person can relate to God so closely and so intimately as to feel God's heart and emotions as his or her own. Such a person would not harm others, lest he feel the pain that such an act would cause God.

The blessing of family life means to express every quality of love in the family and to extend that love to embrace others, thus participating with God in creating one human family.

The blessing of dominion over the creation means to take responsibility for the creation and, as co-creator with God, to build the most comfortable, harmonious and beautiful world.

Principles of the Fall

However, our first human ancestors fell away from God. The fall was not merely disobedience, but the misuse of love. Love is the power that binds human beings to God and binds the human family together; but by the fall, the bond between God and His children was broken. God lost His children and became a grieving, sorrowful God.

Without God, human beings lost their true selves. They became lonely and miserable, and in their desperation to find love, they became selfish. People were originally intended to freely give love to others, but since the fall they have tended first to seek love for themselves. In the world of God's original ideal, people would have put the welfare of others ahead of their own. But in this fallen world, selfish desires have taken precedence over the purpose of the whole.

The fall of our first ancestors represented both a loss of faith and a perversion of love. Nevertheless, God gave humankind free will, and therefore He cannot use force to compel people to become good, since that would deprive them of the potential to ever love truly. Instead, self-sacrifice and unconditional love have been the tactics of God and God's people to win over a hostile world.

Principles of Restoration

Salvation means the restoration of the fallen world back to its original state. In order to accomplish this task the Messiah, a man without any sin, must come. Since the fall resulted from the failure to constitute the first human family expressing the love of God, the Messiah must be born fully human, conquer sin as a man and, united with God, manifest God's masculine nature. Then he must find a bride to manifest God's feminine nature.

Jesus came as the Messiah and called people to follow him. But tragically, he was misunderstood, rejected and crucified. Only after his death and resurrection did his disciples unite with him completely and become reborn into his spiritual family.

The Kingdom of Heaven has yet to be established on earth. Christ must come again to save this physical world. Christianity now has the responsibility to show faith and love sufficient to receive the Messiah at the Second Coming.

According to *Divine Principle*, that time is today. As at the time of Jesus, humankind once again has the choice of whether to accept the Messiah or to reject him. When they receive him and cooperate with him on earth, the world will enter a new age of heavenly love, worldwide peace, universal prosperity, and unparalleled creativity.[5]

Basic Beliefs
International Society for Krishna Consciousness

1. The Absolute Truth is contained in all the great Scriptures of the world, the Bible, the Koran, Torah, etc. However, the oldest known revealed Scriptures in existence are the Vedic literatures, most notably *Bhagavad-gita* which is the literal record of God's actual words.

2. God, or Krsna, is eternal, all-knowing, omnipresent, all-powerful and all-attractive, the seed-giving father of man and all living entities. He is the sustaining energy of all life, nature and the cosmic situation.

3. Man is actually not his body, but is eternal soul, part and parcel of God, and therefore eternal.

4. That all men are brothers can be practiced only when we realize God as our common father.

5. All our actions should be performed as a sacrifice to the Supreme Lord: ". . . all that you do, all that you eat, all that you offer and give away, as well as all austerities that you may perform, should be done as an offering unto Me." (*Bhagavad-gita*, 9.27)

6. The food that sustains us should always be offered to the Lord before eating. In this way He becomes the offering, and such eating purifies us.

7. We can, by sincere cultivation of bona fide spiritual science, attain to the state of pure, unending blissful consciousness, free from anxiety, in this very lifetime.

8. The recommended means to attain the mature stage of love of God in the present age of Kali, or quarrel, is to chant the holy name of the Lord. The easiest method for most people is to chant the Hare Krsna *mantra:* Hare Krsna, Hare Krsna, Krsna, Krsna, Hare, Hare/ Hare Rama, Hare Rama, Rama, Rama, Hare, Hare.

Our basic mission is to propagate the *sankirtana* movement [chanting of the holy names of God] all around the world, as was recommended by the incarnation of the Lord Sri Caitanya Mahaprabhu. . . .

It is not recommended that a Krsna conscious devotee go into seclusion to chant by himself and thereby gain salvation for himself alone. Our duty and religious obligation is to go out into the streets where the people in general can hear the chanting and see the dancing. . . .

It is hoped that the government authorities will cooperate with our *sankirtana* parties enabling us to perform *sankirtana* on the streets. To do this it is necessary that we be able to chant the names of Krsna, dance, play *mrdunga* drum, request donations, sell our society's journal, and on occasion sit down with the *mrdunga* drum. As devotees of Lord Krsna, it is our duty to teach the people how to love God and worship Him in their daily life. This is the aim and destination of human life.[6]

Basic Facts of the Baha'i Faith

The word *Baha'i* comes from the name of the Founder of the Faith—Baha'u'llah (*The Glory of God*). Baha'i simply means a follower of Baha'u'llah. . . .

Baha'is believe in one God, even though men have called Him by different names. God has revealed His Word in each period of history through a chosen Individual whom Baha'is call "the Manifestations of God." He restates in every age God's purpose and will. His teachings are a revelation from God. Abraham, Moses, Krishna, Buddha, Zoroaster, Christ, and Muhammad were Manifestations of God. Each gave men divine teachings to live by. Baha'is believe that true religion is the real basis of civilized life.

Since there is one God, these Manifestations of God have each taught the same religious faith. They have developed and adapted it to meet the needs of the people in each period of history. This unfoldment of religion from age to age is called "progressive revelation." Baha'u'llah, the founder of the Baha'i Faith, is the Manifestation of God for our time.

This is the basis of Baha'i Belief: one God has given men one Faith through progressive revelations of His will in each age of history, and Baha'u'llah reveals the will of God for men and women of the present age. This basic belief enables Baha'is to unite and work together in spite of different religious backgrounds.

The oneness of mankind is like a pivot around which all the Teachings of Baha'u'llah revolve. This means that men and women of all races are equal in the sight of God and equal in the Baha'i community. People of different races must have equal educational and economic opportunity, equal access to decent living conditions—and equal responsibilities. In the Baha'i view, there is no superior race or superior nation.[7]

APPENDIX C
MAJOR TENETS OF ORTHODOX CHRISTIANITY

There is considerable confusion today as to what constitutes orthodox Christianity and what constitutes heresy. The terms, by their very nature, can only be defined in the final analysis by the individual who is using them because there are so many variables. Does it constitute heresy, for example, if an individual rejects the literal creation account in Genesis 1? Does it constitute heresy if an individual accepts the word of a present day "prophet" as being in some way inspired or dictated by God? Does adherence to orthodoxy require that an individual believe in salvation by faith alone? Can an individual who believes baptism is necessary for salvation be considered orthodox?

These questions and others are crucial to many Christians, and yet they could each be answered in the extreme affirmative or in the extreme negative by individuals who are faithful adherents of denominations within the framework of historic orthodox Christianity. For this reason, there are serious problems attempting to offer a detailed delineation of exactly what constitutes Christian orthodoxy.

Much of what has become known as orthodoxy was carefully defined by scholars during the early centuries of the church, based on their painstaking and systematic study of Scripture. In many cases these doctrines were taken for granted until a heresy arose, such as that of Arianism in the fourth century. The central perpetrator of this heresy was Arius, a presbyter of Alexandria, who denied the concept of the Trinity by insisting that only the Father was truly God and that Jesus, the Son, was a created being. His position was widely debated and then condemned at the Council of Nicea, a council that was a landmark in the framing and systematizing of orthodox theology. There were other ecumenical or universal councils during the fourth and fifth centuries that also contributed to the delineating of doctrine—The Council of Constantinople, the Council of Ephesus, and the Council of Chalcedon, being the most noteworthy.

Proponents of various alternative religions have claimed for generations (and more) that true Christianity was corrupted by Emperor Constantine at the Council of Nicea and by other "heretics" at other church councils. The problem with that argument is that the doctrines formulated at these councils were (and are) based on the Bible and the doctrines were widely held long before the Council of Nicea in 325. Indeed, creeds containing the essence of orthodoxy which were enunciated by church fathers as early as 170 A.D. and used at baptismal services as early as 215 A.D. are similar in many respects to the Apostles' Creed which came into use more than a century later. This creed, which is accepted as orthodox by all three major branches of Christendom, illustrates the unity to be found in orthodoxy. The old Roman version of this creed read as follows:

I believe in God Almighty
And in Christ Jesus, his only Son, our Lord
Who was born of the Holy Spirit and the Virgin Mary
Who was crucified under Pontius Pilate and was buried
And the third day rose from the dead
Who ascended into heaven
And sits on the right hand of the Father
Whence he comes to judge the living and the dead.
And in the Holy Ghost
The holy church
The remission of sins
The resurrection of the flesh
The life everlasting.

Through the centuries the various church councils and creeds, as well as the independent work of great theologians have combined to build the structures and define the boundaries of orthodox theology. What is perhaps most significant about this process that has continued most of nineteen centuries is not that there are differences of opinion as to precisely what constitutes heresy and what constitutes orthodoxy, but that there is such uniformity of belief in this realm—and that cults or alternative religions in the vast majority of cases are easily recognized as beyond the boundaries of orthodoxy.

The following doctrines of God, Christ, man, the atonement, the church, the Scriptures, and of future things are ones that are generally deemed critical to Christians within the three major branches of Christendom (Catholic, Protestant, and Orthodox) and they are the ones that are most often cited in a test for orthodoxy.

Doctrine of God

Notwithstanding the accusations of adherents to most alternative religions that Trinitarianism was a concoction of the fourth century, the doctrine of the Trinity is deeply rooted in the Bible. Although the word *trinity* itself is not found in Scripture, the doctrine is derived from numerous biblical references and has become the focal point of Christian belief. Even the Old Testament presents strong support for a concept of God which does not always fit the radical monotheism of Jewish theologians. Indeed, the oft-quoted *Shema* itself—"Hear O Israel, the Lord our God is one Lord" (Deut. 6:4)—could be rendered, "Hear O Israel, Yahweh our Gods (Elohim) is Yahweh a unity." The term *Elohim* is plural and the Hebrew word *Echod* that indicates the oneness of God is a word that often denotes a *composite* unity, such as in Genesis 2:24, when a man and his wife become one (Echod) flesh. This composite unity of God is also seen in Genesis 1:26 ("Then God said, 'Let *us* make man in *our* image. . . .' ") and in other Old Testament passages.

Once the composite unity of God is established, it follows that the make-up of the unity must be established. That God the Father is truly God is not really an issue among those in alternative religions who would argue against the Trinity. They would generally accept the teachings of such Scriptures as Exodus 3:14 ("God said to Moses, 'I AM WHO I AM.' This is what you are to say to the Israelites: 'I AM has sent me to you.' "), Isaiah 43:10 ("Before me no god was formed, nor will there be one after me.") and 1 Corinthians 8:6 (". . . there is but one God, the Father, from whom all things came and for whom we live.").

That Jesus is truly God and one with the Father is frequently challenged even though it is clearly taught in many familiar New Testament passages such as John 1:1, 18; John 5:18; John 10:30; John 20:28; Colossians 2:9; Titus 2:13; Hebrews 1:8, 10. Here we learn that Jesus (the Word or *Logos*) *was* God, that he was "God the One and Only," that he was "calling God his own Father, making himself equal with God," that Thomas acknowledged him as "My Lord and my God!," that the "Deity lives in bodily form," that we wait for "the glorious appearing of our great God and Savior, Jesus Christ," and that God the Father himself says to Jesus, "Your throne, O God, will last for ever and ever."

The deity of the Holy Spirit is also taught in the Bible in such passages as Genesis 1:2; Mark 3:22–30; Luke 12:12; John 14:26; John 15:26; John 16:7–15; Acts 5:3–4; and Acts 13:2–3. Here we learn that the Holy Spirit does very specific things that are characteristic of a person and not of an "influence." These passages indicate that he was involved in creation, that he can be blasphemed, that he teaches individuals what to say, that he testifies of Christ, that he convicts people of guilt and guides them into all truth, that Ananias lied to him, and that he sent Barnabus and Saul on their way to Seleucia.

But not only does the Bible teach the deity of the Father, the Son, and the Holy Spirit, it brings them together in a Trinity. God is a unity subsisting in three Persons: the Father, the Son, and the Holy Spirit, all three of whom are one God. This is taught most notably in Matthew 28:19, where the disciples are instructed to baptize "in the name of the Father and of the Son and of the Holy Spirit," and in 1 Corinthians 12:3–6:

> Therefore I tell you that no one who is speaking by the Spirit of God says, "Jesus be cursed," and no one can say, "Jesus is Lord," except by the Holy Spirit.
>
> There are different kinds of gifts, but the same Spirit. There are different kinds of service, but the same Lord. There are different kinds of working, but the same God works all of them in all men.

Through the study of the Scripture the church fathers developed a systematic theological approach to the Trinity that was argued in treatises and formulated into creeds and has weathered the test of time. The Athanasian Creed of the fourth century, accepted by all branches of

Christendom, clearly enunciates the trinitarian doctrine of the Godhead and has stood as a glorious monument over the centuries in defense of this pivotal doctrine of orthodox Christianity.

1. Whosoever will be saved, before all things it is necessary that he holds the catholic faith.

2. Which faith except every one do keep whole and undefiled, without doubt he shall perish everlastingly.

3. But this is the catholic faith: That we worship one God in trinity, and trinity in unity;

4. Neither confounding the persons; nor dividing the substance.

5. For there is one person of the Father: another of the Son: another of the Holy Ghost.

6. But the Godhead of the Father, and of the Son, and of the Holy Ghost is all one: the glory equal, the majesty co-eternal.

7. Such as the Father is, such is the Son, and such is the Holy Ghost.

8. The Father is uncreated: the Son is uncreated: the Holy Ghost is uncreated.

9. The Father is immeasurable: the Son is immeasurable: the Holy Ghost is immeasurable.

10. The Father is eternal: the Son is eternal: the Holy Ghost is eternal.

*   *   *

15. So the Father is God: the Son is God: and the Holy Ghost is God.

16. And yet there are not three Gods; but one God.

*   *   *

25. And in this Trinity none is before or after another: none is greater or less than another.

26. But the whole three Persons are co-eternal together, and co-equal.

27. So that in all things, as aforesaid, the Unity in Trinity, and the Trinity in Unity is to be worshipped.

28. He therefore that will be saved, must thus think of the Trinity.[1]

Doctrine of Christ

Jesus is God incarnate. This is the core of the doctrine of Christ—not simply that the Word (the *logos*) in John 1:1 *was* God and that "He was with God in the beginning," but that "The Word became flesh and lived for a while among us" (John 1:14). That Jesus was fully human and fully divine is a settled matter for most twentieth-century trinitarians, but it was an issue of great magnitude in the early church and not fully settled until the Council of Chalcedon in 451. Here the effort to separate the two natures of Christ, to the point of almost making him two separate persons, something Nestorius had done, was rejected. So too was the Monophysite concept of deemphasizing the humanity of Jesus to the point that it was almost entirely overshadowed by his divinity. The Council offered a new confession that was drawn largely from the remarkable work of Leo the Great, who did more than any other individual to establish the doctrine of the two natures of Christ that has been accepted by orthodox Christianity in the centuries that followed.

> We all with one voice confess our Lord Jesus Christ one and the same Son, at once complete in Godhead and complete in manhood, truly God and truly man, consisting of a reasonable soul and body; of one substance with the Father as regards his Godhead, of one substance with us as regards his manhood, like us in all things, apart from sin; begotten of the Father before the ages as regards his Godhead, the same in the last days, for us and for our salvation, born from the Virgin Mary, the God-bearer (*theotokos*), as regards his manhood; one and the same Christ, Son, Lord, Only-begotten, to be acknowledged in two natures, without confusion, without change, without division, or without separation; the distinction of natures being in no way abolished because of the union, but rather the characteristic property of each nature being preserved, and coming together to form one person (*prosopon*) and one entity (*hypostasis*), not as if Christ were parted or divided into two persons. . . .[2]

The significance of the doctrine of the two natures of Christ is emphasized in 1 John 4:2–3, which would seem to give a very clear test of orthodoxy: "This is how you can recognize the Spirit of God: Every spirit that acknowledges that Jesus Christ has come in the flesh is from God, but every spirit that does not acknowledge Jesus is not from God. This is the spirit of the antichrist, which you have heard is coming and even now is already in the world." The one verse that perhaps most powerfully establishes belief in Christ as both God and man is Colossians 2:9: "For in Christ all the fullness of the Deity lives in bodily form."

Doctrine of Man and Sin

The orthodox doctrine of man is summed up very simply in the Westminster Shorter Catechism in a statement that reflects orthodox belief: "God created Man, male and female, after his own image, in knowledge, righteousness, and holiness, with dominion over the creatures." This statement is derived largely from Genesis, recording the fall of man, which resulted in a depraved nature manifested by sin.

The doctrine of sin was summarized in a succinct statement that reflects the orthodox position at the sixteenth-century Roman Catholic Council of Trent:

> Adam, when he had transgressed the commandment of God in Paradise, immediately lost the holiness and justice wherein he had been constituted; and . . . he incurred through the offense of that prevarication, the wrath and indignation of God, and consequently death . . . and that the entire Adam, through that offense of prevarication was changed, in body and soul, for the worse. . . . This sin of Adam . . . [is] transfused into all by propagation, not by imitation. . . .[3]

The sinfulness of man is one of the most significant points of issue between orthodoxy and alternative religions. The Bible does not teach that "Man is incapable of sin," as Christian Science, for example, teaches. There are many scriptural passages that would counteract this view, Jeremiah 17:9 and Romans 5:12 being two of the most familiar: "The heart is deceitful above all things and beyond cure;" "Therefore, just as sin entered the world through one man, and death through sin, and in this way death came to all men, because all have sinned."

Doctrine of the Atonement

The term *atonement* literally means "at-onement"—indicating the restoration of oneness between God and man that was broken at the time of man's fall in the Garden of Eden. This separation is clearly enunciated in Isaiah 59:2: "But your iniquities have separated you from your God; your sins have hidden his face from you so that he will not hear." It was Christ's atonement on the cross that provided the way of salvation, a truth that is summed up in 1 Peter 2:24: "He himself bore our sins in his body on the tree, so that we might die to sins and live for righteousness." Unlike other doctrines, however, the doctrine of the atonement was not clearly formulated in the early church. While there are many points of agreement on this doctrine, there are also some significant points of differences, as Leon Morris has pointed out.

> We can detect three broad trends in the multiplicity of theories of atonement emerging during nineteen centuries of church history.
>
> The first trend . . . leans heavily on those biblical passages which speak of the Atonement as a ransom. It sees sinners as justly belonging to Satan because of their sin. But in the death of His Son God paid the price of their redemption. Satan accepted Jesus in place of sinners but he could not hold Him. On Easter Day Jesus rose triumphant, leaving Satan without either his original captives or their ransom. . . .
>
> The second group of theories may be said to have originated with Anselm of Canterbury, who saw sin as dishonor to the majesty of God. On the cross the God-man rendered satisfaction for this dishonor. Along similar lines the Reformers thought that Christ paid the penalty sinners incurred when they broke God's law. The strong points of this theory are its agreement with biblical teaching (e.g., on justification) and its insistence that the moral law cannot be disregarded in the process of forgiveness.
>
> The third group of theories (especially linked with the name Abelard) sees the Atonement in the effect on man of what Christ did. When we contemplate the love of God shown in the death of his Son we are moved to repent and to love Him in return. We are thus transformed. All is subjective.
>
> All three theories have something to say to us. Each is inadequate by itself (especially the third, for it sees Christ as doing nothing except setting an example; the real salvation is worked out by sinners themselves). But taken together they help us to see a little of Christ's great work for men.[4]

Doctrine of the Church

After Simon Peter's glorious confession of who Jesus was—"You are the Christ, the Son of the living God—Jesus blessed him and said, "I tell you that you are Peter, and on this rock I will build my church, and the gates of Hades will not overcome it." In Colossians 2, the apostle Paul speaks of Christ as the "head of the body, the church," made up of "saints" whom "God has chosen to make known among the Gentiles the glorious riches of this mystery, which is Christ in you, the hope of glory." This "invisible" church is made up of individuals who acknowledge Christ as Savior.

The Westminster Confession of Faith summarizes the doctrine of the church—a statement which reflects the orthodox view:

> The catholic or universal Church, which is invisible, consists of the whole number of the elect, that have been, are, or shall be gathered into one, under Christ the head thereof, and is the spouse, the body, the fullness of Him that filleth all in all. The visible Church, which is also catholic or universal under the gospel (not confined to one nation, as before under the law), consists of all those, throughout the world, that profess the true religion, and of their children, and is the kingdom of the Lord Jesus Christ, the house and family of God, out of which there is no ordinary possibility of salvation.

This concept of the invisible church flies in the face of those alternative religions such as the Jehovah's Witnesses and The Worldwide Church of God who would claim that they alone have the true gospel for this age.

Doctrine of the Scriptures

As is true of the doctrine of the Atonement, the doctrine of the Scriptures (also referred to as the doctrine of revelation, the doctrine of authority, or the doctrine of the Bible) varies within Christendom. All branches of orthodoxy accept the sixty-six books of the Old and New Testaments as the fully inspired Word of God. (Of course, as is true with other doctrines, some denominations or representatives of denominations have been influenced by modernism and reject this doctrine of historic orthodoxy.) In addition to these sixty-six books, the Roman Catholic Church accepts the Apocrypha as inspired of God and part of the canon. The Roman Catholic and Orthodox churches also recognize church tradition as a high source of authority—some would say equal to that of the Bible itself. Protestantism, rooted in the Reformation, rejects tradition as authoritative with the motto *sola scriptura*. Within Protestantism, however, there are some churches and individuals—particularly segments within the Pentecostal and charismatic wing of the church—who would emphasize "continuing revelation" or prophecy on a near par with Scripture. In this respect, they would be bordering on the position held by many alternative religions concerning continuing revelation.

The three branches of orthodoxy strongly agree on the point that there are no new scriptures to be added to the canon, and this clearly sets them apart from alternative religions that look to such writings as the *Book of Mormon*,

Science and Health, and the *Divine Principle*, as God's inspired word for this age.

Scripture references supporting a high view of the Bible are numerous. Some of the more familiar verses include Isaiah 40:8 ("The grass withers and the flowers fall, but the word of our God stands forever"), 2 Timothy 3:16 ("All Scripture is God-breathed and is useful for teaching, rebuking, correcting and training in righteousness, so that the man of God may be thoroughly equipped for every good work"), and 2 Peter 1:21 ("For prophecy never had its origin in the will of man, but men spoke from God as they were carried along by the Holy Spirit").

Doctrine of Future Things

Eschatology, the study of the last or future things, is an area of theology that is more often associated with divisiveness than with harmony. But there are some major areas of agreement among Christians in this area, such as the belief in a place known as heaven, where those who truly follow Christ will live eternally in the presence of God and his angels. Those who reject the teachings of Christ will be relegated to hell, a place of eternal punishment. Roman Catholics maintain there is a third place called purgatory, where the souls of Christians with unforgiven sins remain until those sins are absolved.

The belief in the Second Coming—that Christ will come in glory at the end of this present world to judge those who are alive as well as those who have died—is central to the doctrine of future things. The biblical basis for these beliefs are found throughout Scripture—particularly in Daniel, Isaiah, Zechariah, the synoptic Gospels, 1 and 2 Thessalonians, and Revelation. The teaching on the Second Coming is symbolic and often difficult to comprehend, but such verses as 1 Thessalonians 4:15–17 constitute important pieces of this difficult puzzle:

> According to the Lord's own word, we tell you that we who are still alive, who are left till the coming of the Lord, will certainly not precede those who have fallen asleep. For the Lord himself will come down from heaven, with a loud command, with the voice of the archangel and with the trumpet call of God, and the dead in Christ will rise first. After that, we who are still alive and are left will be caught up together with them in the clouds to meet the Lord in the air. And so we will be with the Lord forever.

While not stated in denominational creeds per se, most orthodox churches would reject the practice of date-setting in regard to apocalyptic events—a trait very common among cultic movements (and not entirely foreign to some on the extreme fringe of dispensational premillennialism).

NOTES

INTRODUCTION

[1] E. Stanley Jones, *The Christ of the Indian Road* (New York: Abingdon, 1925), 8, 49.

[2] Joseph Fielding Smith, *Doctrines of Salvation*, I, 188–89, quoted in Tanners, *The Changing World of Mormonism* (Chicago: Moody, 1979), 26.

CHAPTER 1

[1] "Why Cults Succeed Where the Church Fails," *Christianity Today* (March 16, 1984), 14.

[2] Ibid.

[3] James W. Sire, *Scripture Twisting* (Downers Grove, Ill.: InterVarsity Press, 1980), 20.

[4] Brooks Alexander, "What is a Cult," *Spiritual Counterfeits Newsletter*, (January/February 1979).

[5] John T. Biermans, *The Odyssey of New Religious Movements: Persecution, Struggle, Legitimation: A Case Study of the Unification Church* (Lewiston, N.Y.: Edwin Mellen, 1986), 7.

[6] Ronald Enroth et al., *A Guide to Cults and New Religions* (Downers Grove, Ill.: InterVarsity Press, 1983), 12.

[7] Jim Quinn and Bill Zlatos, "52 Deaths Tied to Sect," *News-Sentinel*, Fort Wayne (May 2, 1983).

[8] Jim Quinn and Bill Zlatos, "Faith Assembly Rejects Dissent," *News-Sentinel*, Fort Wayne (May 3, 1983).

[9] Bruce Barron, *The Health and Wealth Gospel: What's Going On Today in A Movement That Has Shaped the Faith of Millions?* (Downers Grove: InterVarsity Press, 1987), 30.

[10] Ronald Enroth, "Churches on the Fringe," *Eternity* (October 1986), 17–22.

[11] Enroth et al., *A Guide to Cults and New Religions*, 23.

[12] Jay Cocks, "Why He's a Thriller," *Time* (March 19, 1984), 59.

[13] Ellen K. Coughlin, "Alternative Religions or Dangerous Scams? Scholars Assess the Problem of Cults," *The Chronicle of Higher Education* (March 9, 1983), 6.

[14] "The Children of Cults," *Christianity Today* (March 4, 1983), 61.

[15] *Grand Rapids Press* [Michigan] (January 14, 1981).

[16] Walter Martin, *The Kingdom of the Cults* (Minneapolis: Bethany, 1985), 248, 250.

[17] Robert B. Mitchell, *Heritage and Horizons: The History of Open Bible Standard Churches* (Des Moines: Open Bible Publishers, 1982), 47.

[18] "Why Cults Succeed," 17.

[19] Jack Sparks, *The Mindbenders: A Look at Current Cults* (Nashville: Thomas Nelson, 1979), 309–10.

[20] Jan Karel Van Baalen, *The Chaos of Cults: A Study in Present-Day Isms* (Grand Rapids: Eerdmans, 1962), 390–92.

[21] "Why Cults Succeed," 18.

[22] Ibid., 20–21.

[23] David G. Bromley and Anson D. Shupe, Jr., *Strange Gods: The Great American Cult Scare* (Boston: Beacon, 1981), ix.

[24] Thomas S. Brandon, Jr., *New Religions, Conversions and Deprograming: New Frontiers of Religious Liberty* (Oak Park, Ill.: The Center for Law & Religious Freedom, 1982), 1.

[25] James R. Spencer, "Who is the god of Mormonism?," *Through the Maze* (No. 19), 1, 3.

[26] Jerald and Sandra Tanner, "Covering Up Sin," *Salt Lake City Messenger* (April 1988), 1–18.

[27] Bromley and Shupe, *Strange Gods*, 208.

[28] Stephen Neill, *A History of Christian Missions* (New York: Penguin, 1964), 42.

CHAPTER 2

[1] Robert S. Ellwood, Jr., *Alternative Altars: Unconventional and Eastern Spirituality in America* (Chicago: Univ. of Chicago Press, 1979), 90.

[2] John Ahmanson, *Secret History: A Translation of Vor Tids Muhamed*, trans. Gleason L. Archer (Chicago: Moody Press, 1984), 26.

[3] Harold O. J. Brown, *Heresies: The Image of Christ in the Mirror of Heresy and Orthodoxy from the Apostles to the Present* (Garden City, N.Y.: Doubleday, l984), 118–19.

[4] 1 Tim. 1:3–4, 4:1; 2 Tim. 2:17.

[5] F. F. Bruce, *The Spreading Flame: The Rise and Progress of Christianity from its First Beginnings to the Conversion of the English* (Grand Rapids: Eerdmans, 1979), 218.

[6] *The Ecclesiastical History of Eusebius Pamphilus* (Grand Rapids: Baker, 1955), 196.

[7] Bruce, *The Spreading Flame*, 219.

[8] Ted A. Campbell, "Charismata in the Christian Communities of the Second Century," *Wesleyan Theological Journal* 17:2 (Fall 1982): 13, 15–16.

[9] Ibid., 14.

[10] Philip Schaff, *Ante-Nicene Christianity*, A.D. *100–325*, vol. 2 in *History of the Christian Church* (Grand Rapids: Eerdmans, 1979), 484.

[11] W. Ward Gasque, "Marcion," in J. D. Douglas, *The New International Dictionary of the Christian Church* (Grand Rapids: Zondervan, 1978), 629.

[12] "Margaret of Antioch" in Douglas, ed., *Dictionary of the Christian Church*, 630.

[13] John Clare, "The Cathars," in Tim Dowley, ed., *Eerdmans Handbook to the History of Christianity* (Grand Rapids: Eerdmans, 1977), 319.

[14] Brown, *Heresies*, 254–55.

[15] Ronald A. Knox, *Enthusiasm: A Chapter in the History of Religion* (New York: Oxford Univ. Press, 1961), 124.

[16] Henry Osborn Taylor, *The Medieval Mind*, vol. 1 (Cambridge: Harvard Univ. Press, 1949), 390.

[17] Ibid., 1, 391.

[18] Ibid.

[19] Ibid., 1, 393.

[20] Quoted in Taylor, *The Medieval Mind*, 395–96.

[21] Larry D. Shinn, *The Dark Lord: Cult Images and the Hare Krishnas in America* (Philadelphia: Westminster, 1987), 154.

[22] Lina Eckenstein, *Woman Under Monasticism* (New York: Russell & Russell, 1896), 467.

[23] Knox, *Enthusiasm*, 153.

[24] George Allen Turner, *The Vision Which Transforms: Is Christian Perfection Spiritual?* (1964), 175.

[25] Knox, *Enthusiasm*, 150.

[26] Ibid., 173.

[27] Ibid., 141.

[28] Lawrence Foster, *Religion and Sexuality: The Shakers, the Mormons, and the Oneida Community* (Chicago: Univ. of Illinois Press, 1984), 27.

[29] Robley Edward Whitson, ed., *The Shakers: Two Centuries of Spiritual Reflection* (New York: Paulist Press, 1983), 137.

[30] Foster, *Religion and Sexuality*, 28.

[31] Edward Andrews, *The People Called Shakers* (New York: Oxford Univ. Press, 1953), 232–36.

[32] Robert S. Ellwood, Jr., *Alternative Altars: Unconventional and Eastern Spirituality in America* (Chicago: Univ. of Chicago Press, 1979), 70.

[33] Ibid., 70.

[34] Fawn Brodie, *No Man Knows My History: The Life of Joseph Smith* (New York: Alfred A. Knopf, 1945), 12.

[35] Robert Thomas, *The Man Who Would be Perfect: John Humphrey Noyes and the*

NOTES

Utopian Impulse (Philadelphia: Univ. of Pennsylvania Press, 1977), 23.

36 James E. Johnson, "Charles G. Finney and Oberlin Perfectionism," *Journal of Presbyterian History* (March 1968), 42–57.

37 Timothy L. Smith, "The Doctrine of the Sanctifying Spirit: Charles G. Finney's Synthesis of Wesleyan and Covenant Theology," *Wesleyan Theological Journal* (Spring 1978), 92–113.

38 Thomas, *The Man Who Would Be Perfect*, 45.

39 Elmer T. Clark, *The Small Sects in America* (Nashville: Abingdon, 1965), 143.

40 Thomas, *The Man Who Would Be Perfect*, 48.

41 Ibid., 56.

42 Ibid., 88.

43 Ibid., 107.

44 Foster, *Religion and Sexuality*, 120.

45 Stanley P. Hirshon, *The Lion of the Lord: A Biography of Brigham Young* (New York: Alfred A. Knopf, 1969), 57–58.

46 Linda K. Newell and Valeen T. Avery, *Mormon Enigma: Emma Hale Smith: Prophet's Wife, "Elect Lady," Polygamy's Foe, 1804–1879* (Garden City, N.Y.: Doubleday, 1984), 232.

47 Hirshon, *The Lion of the Lord*, 58, 100–101, 287–88.

48 Latayne Colvett Scott, *The Mormon Mirage* (Grand Rapids: Zondervan, 1979), 149.

49 Wesley P. Walters, "The Return of the Christadelphians," *Personal Freedom Outreach Newsletter* (Jan.–Mar. 1984), 1.

50 Ibid., 1, 7.

51 Ibid., 1.

CHAPTER 3

1 Donna Hill, *Joseph Smith: The First Mormon* (Garden City, N.Y.: Doubleday, 1977), 45–46.

2 Ibid., 44.

3 Fawn M. Brodie, *No Man Knows My History: The Life of Joseph Smith, the Mormon Prophet* (New York: Alfred A. Knopf, 1945), 19.

4 Hill, *Joseph Smith*, 61–65.

5 "Joseph Smith—History," 1:14–17, in *Pearl of Great Price*.

6 Ibid., 1:19.

7 Ibid., 1:30–34.

8 Linda King Newell and Valeen Tippetts Avery, *Mormon Enigma: Emma Hale Smith, Prophet's Wife, "Elect Lady," Polygamy's Foe, 1804–1879* (Garden City, N.Y.: Doubleday, 1984), 19.

9 Brodie, *No Man Knows My History*, 40.

10 Hill, *Joseph Smith*, 73.

11 Quoted in Newell and Avery, *Mormon Enigma*, 25.

12 Ibid., 28.

13 Hill, *Joseph Smith*, 86–87.

14 Quoted in Newell and Avery, *Mormon Enigma*, 25.

15 Hill, *Joseph Smith*, 90.

16 "The Testimony of Three Witnesses," *Book of Mormon*, vi.

17 *Doctrine and Covenants*, 19:15, 26.

18 2 Nephi 5:15–28.

19 Gleason Archer, *A Survey of Old Testament Introduction* (Chicago: Moody, 1971), 501–4.

20 2 Nephi 5:21–23.

21 Helaman, 16:4; 3 Nephi 12.

22 Brodie, *No Man Knows My History*, 62–63.

23 Richard L. Bushman, *Joseph Smith and the Beginnings of Mormonism* (Urbana: Univ. of Illinois Press, 1984), 115.

24 Many "liberal" Mormons also question its source, but "have faith" that it is still somehow from God, no matter what the evidence proves.

25 Wayne L. Cowdrey, Howard A. Davis, and Donald R. Scales, *Who Really Wrote the Book of Mormon?* (Santa Anna, Calif.: Vision House, 1977), passim.

26 Ibid., 167–76.

27 Brodie, *No Man Knows My History*, 46–47.

28 Lucy Mack Smith, *Biographical Sketches of Joseph Smith the Prophet and His Progenitors for Many Generations* (Liverpool, 1853), 87.

29 *Doctrine and Covenants*, 21:1–5.

30 Hill, *Joseph Smith*, 108.

31 "The Articles of Faith of the Church of Jesus Christ of Latter-Day Saints," *History of the Church*, vol. 4, 535–41.

32 *Doctrine and Covenants*, 25:1–4.

33 Quoted in Newell and Avery, *Mormon Enigma*, 30.

34 *Doctrine and Covenants*, 89.

35 Newell and Avery, *Mormon Enigma*, 47.

36 *Doctrine and Covenants*, 38:18, 32.

37 Hill, *Joseph Smith*, 140–41.

38 Francis M. Gibbons, *Joseph Smith: Martyr, Prophet of God* (Salt Lake City: Deseret Book Co., 1977), 113–14.

39 Newell and Avery, *Mormon Enigma*, 65.

40 Ibid., 39–40.

41 Klaus J. Hansen, *Mormonism and the American Experience* (Chicago: Univ. of Chicago Press, 1981), 31.

42 Joseph Smith, Jr., *History of the Church of Jesus Christ of Latter-Day Saints*, 2 (Salt Lake City: Deseret News, 1902–1912), 428.

43 Quoted in Newell and Avery, *Mormon Enigma*, 59.

44 Ibid., 62–63.

45 Gibbons, *Joseph Smith*, 140.

46 Fawn Brodie, *No Man Knows My History*, 131.

47 Hill, *Joseph Smith*, 161–67.

48 *Doctrine and Covenants*, 103:15–20.

49 Hill, *Joseph Smith*, 169–72, 180, 183–84.

50 Hill, *Joseph Smith*, 199–203.

51 Newell and Avery, *Mormon Enigma*, 67–69.

52 Hill, *Joseph Smith*, 223–25.

53 Newell and Avery, *Mormon Enigma*, 73–77.

54 Brodie, *No Man Knows My History*, 265.

55 Ibid., 277–78; "The Articles of Faith."

56 Newell and Avery, *Mormon Enigma*, 65–66.

57 Quoted in Newell and Avery, *Mormon Enigma*, 66.

58 Newell and Avery, *Mormon Enigma*, 67.

59 *Doctrine and Covenants*, 132:52–54.

60 Gibbons, *Joseph Smith*, 303, 307–8.

61 Hill, *Joseph Smith*, 348.

62 Newell and Avery, *Mormon Enigma*, 134–35, 164, 171.

63 Ibid., 98.

64 Fawn Brodie, *No Man Knows My History*, 354.

65 Quoted in Hill, *Joseph Smith*, 368.

66 Klaus J. Hansen, *Quest for Empire: The Political Kingdom of God and the Council of Fifty in Mormon History* (Lansing: Michigan State Univ. Press, 1967), 53–54.

67 Newell and Avery, *Mormon Enigma*, 180–81.

68 Ibid., 181–83.

69 Quoted in Hansen, *Mormonism and the American Experience*, 106.

70 Quoted in Newell and Avery, *Mormon Enigma*, 203.

71 Hansen, *Mormonism and the American Experience*, 107.

72 Newell and Avery, *Mormon Enigma*, 204–6.

73 Stanley P. Hirshon, *The Lion of the Lord: A Biography of Brigham Young* (New York: Alfred A. Knopf, 1969), 85.

74 Lawrence Foster, *Religion and Sexuality: The Shakers, the Mormons, and the Oneida Community* (Chicago: Univ. of Illinois Press, 1984), 184.

75 Leonard J. Arrington, *Brigham Young: American Moses* (New York: Alfred A. Knopf, 1985), 198.

76 Hirshon, *The Lion of the Lord*, 177–81.

77 Ibid., 164–65.

78 *Deseret News*, February 8, 1857; cited in Hirshon, *The Lion of the Lord*, 157, 164–65.

79 Hirshon, *The Lion of the Lord*, 3.

80 Robert Gottlieb and Peter Wiley, *America's Saints: The Rise of Mormon Power* (New York: Harcourt Brace Jovanovich, 1986), 48.

81 Gottlieb and Wiley, *America's Saints*, 53.

82 Foster, *Religion and Sexuality*, 223.

83 *Deseret News*, November 14, 1855; cited in Jerald and Sandra Tanner, *The*

Changing World of Mormonism (Chicago: Moody, 1980), 266.

[84] Gottlieb and Wiley, *America's Saints*, 50–51.

[85] Ibid., 54–55.

[86] Latayne Colvett Scott, *The Mormon Mirage: A Former Mormon Tells Why She Left the Church* (Grand Rapids: Zondervan, 1979), 216–17.

[87] Jan Shipps, *Mormonism: The Story of a New Religious Tradition* (Urbana: Univ. of Illinois Press, 1985), 131–32.

[88] Tanners, *The Changing World*, 442.

[89] *Doctrine and Covenants*, 13.

[90] Jerald and Sandra Tanner, "Mormonism" in David J. Hesselgrave, ed., *Dynamic Religious Movements* (Grand Rapids: Baker, 1978), 202.

[91] Scott, *The Mormon Mirage*, 249.

[92] Gottlieb and Wiley, *America's Saints*, 187, 207–8.

[93] Abraham 1:24, 26.

[94] Gottlieb and Wiley, *America's Saints*, 180.

[95] *Deseret News*, June 9, 1978; cited in Tanners, *The Changing World of Mormonism*, 308–9.

[96] Scott, *The Mormon Mirage*, 241.

[97] Shipps, *Mormonism*, 133.

[98] *Doctrine and Covenants*, sec. 89.

[99] Scott, *The Mormon Mirage*, 154, 221.

[100] Joseph Fielding Smith, *Doctrines of Salvation*, vol. 2: 44, 61, 62.

[101] Tanners, *The Changing World*, 526–27.

[102] Hansen, *Mormonism and the American Experience*, 76–77.

[103] *Journal of Discourses*, vol. 19, 229.

[104] Tan, *Encyclopedia of 7770 Illustrations*, 414.

[105] Hansen, *Mormonism and the American Experience*, 108–9.

[106] *Times and Seasons*, vol. 5, 613–14. Cited in Tanners, *The Changing World*, 173.

[107] *Journal of Discourses*, vol. 7, 333.

[108] Ibid., vol. 3, 93; vol. 10, 223.

[109] Bruce R. McConkie, *Mormon Doctrine* (Salt Lake City: Bookcraft, 1979), 257, 577.

[110] *Doctrine and Covenants*, 130:22.

[111] *Journal of Discourses*, vol. 1, 50.

[112] Milton R. Hunter, *The Gospel Through the Ages* (Salt Lake City: Deseret, 1958), 98.

[113] James Talmage, *The Articles of Faith* (Salt Lake City: The Church of Jesus Christ Latter Day Saints, 1952), 466–67.

[114] Orson Pratt, *The Seer* (Washington, D.C., 1953–54), 158, quoted in Tanners, *The Changing World*, 182.

[115] Joseph Fielding Smith, Jr., *Religious Truths Defined* (Salt Lake City: Bookcraft, 1959), 44.

[116] Tanners, *The Changing World*, 188–89.

[117] Joseph Fielding Smith, *Doctrines of Salvation* (Salt Lake City: Bookcraft, 1960), vol. 1, 76.

[118] Moses 3:5.

[119] Abraham 3:21–22.

[120] Joseph Fielding Smith, *Man: His Origin and Destiny*, 351, 355.

[121] Talmage, *Articles of Faith*, 193.

[122] *Doctrine and Covenants*, 84:1–4.

[123] Ibid., 29:9; 76:33–34, 44–45, 62, 77, 87, 92, 99.

[124] Scott, *The Mormon Mirage*, 208.

[125] John Ahmanson, *Secret History: A Translation of Vor Tids Muhamed*, trans. Gleason L. Archer (Chicago: Moody, 1984), 16, 18.

[126] Ruth A. Tucker, "Foreign Missionaries With A False Message," *Evangelical Missions Quarterly* (October 1984), 329.

[127] James Warner and Styne M. Slade, *The Mormon Way* (Englewood Cliffs, N.J.: Prentice Hall, 1976), 122, 130.

[128] R. Lanier Britsch, "Mormon Missions: An Introduction to the Latter-Day Saints Missionary System," *Occasional Bulletin*, (January 1979), 23.

[129] Ruth A. Tucker, "Nonorthodox Sects Report Global Membership Gains," *Christianity Today* (June 13, 1986), 50.

[130] Kenneth Woodward, "Onward Mormon Soldiers," *Newsweek* (April 17, 1981), 88.

[131]Cited in Jerald and Sandra Tanner, "Salamandergate," *Salt Lake City Messenger* (June 1985), 1.

[132]Ibid.

[133]Marjorie Hyer, "Amazing Case of Forged Documents Still Puzzles Mormon Community," *Grand Rapids Press* (Michigan), August 16, 1987.

[134]"Polygamist Mayor Frowns On Practice—By Others," *Grand Rapids Press* (Michigan), January 2, 1984.

[135]*Improvement Era*, June 1945, 354.

[136]Jerry P. Cahill to Ruth A. Tucker, June 30, 1986.

[137]"Mormons and Christ," *Christianity Today*, (July 16, 1982).

[138]Sheila Garrigus, Saints Alive meeting, audio tape.

[139]Della Olson, *A Woman of Her Times* (Minneapolis: Free Church Press, 1977), 54–57.

[140]Jack Houston, "The Jerald Tanners vs. Mormonism," *Power for Living* (June 14, 1970), 2–3.

[141]John Gutman, "Jerald and Sandra Tanner: An Unpopular 'Mission,'" *The Salt Lake Tribune* (January 27, 1985), 6S.

[142]"Fighting Mormonism in Utah," *Christianity Today*, (July 16, 1982).

CHAPTER 4

[1]William Miller, "Memoir of William Miller" in *Views of the Prophecies and Prophetic Chronology* (Boston: Joshua V. Himes, 1842), 7, 8, 11, 12.

[2]Quoted in James White, *Sketches of the Christian Life and Public Labors of William Miller* (Battle Creek, Mich.: Steam Press, 1875), 55–57.

[3]Ibid., 57, 65, 68.

[4]Ibid., 93, 94, 102, 118, 119.

[5]Sydney E. Ahlstrom, *A Religious History of the American People* (Garden City, N.Y.: Doubleday, 1975), I, 580.

[6]Mark A. Noll et al., *Eerdmans' Handbook to Christianity in America* (Grand Rapids: Eerdmans, 1983), 179.

[7]White, *Sketches of the Christian Life*, 173, 176.

[8]Ibid., 278–79, 282, 283.

[9]Ibid., 295, 300.

[10]Ibid., 310.

[11]Quoted in Francis D. Nichol, *The Midnight Cry* (Washington: Review and Herald, 1945), 458.

[12]Anthony A. Hoekema, *Seventh-day Adventism* (Grand Rapids: Eerdmans, 1972), 13–14.

[13]Ibid., 15–16.

[14]Ibid.

[15]Walter Martin, *The Kingdom of the Cults* (Minneapolis: Bethany House, 1985), 438.

[16]Cited in William Edward Biederwolf, *Seventh Day Adventism: The Result of A Predicament* (Grand Rapids: Eerdmans, 1950), 9.

[17]Rene Noorbergen, *Ellen G. White: Prophet of Destiny* (New Canaan, Conn.: Keats Publishing, 1972).

[18]Ronald L. Numbers, *Prophetess of Health: A Study of Ellen G. White* (New York: Harper & Row, 1976), 8–10.

[19]Numbers, *Prophetess of Health*, 1–4.

[20]Noorbergen, *Ellen G. White*, 28.

[21]Numbers, *Prophetess of Health*, 14.

[22]Ibid., 15.

[23]James White, *Life Sketches of James and Ellen White*, quoted in Noorbergen, *Ellen G. White*, 31.

[24]Numbers, *Prophetess of Health*, 17.

[25]Quoted in Numbers, *Prophetess of Health*, 18–20.

[26]Numbers, *Prophetess of Health*, 28–29.

[27]Noorbergen, *Ellen G. White*, 37–38.

[28]Ellen G. White, *Testimonies for the Church* (Oakland: Pacific Press, n.d.), II, 526–27.

[29]Ibid., II, 337–38, 455.

[30]Ibid., II, 391.

[31]Ibid., II, 472–75.

[32]Numbers, *Prophetess of Health*, 181–82.

[33]Godfrey T. Anderson, "Sectarianism and Organization, 1846–1864," in Gary Land, ed., *Adventism in America: A History* (Grand Rapids: Eerdmans, 1986), 46.

[34]Ibid., 63.

[35] Emmett K. Vandevere, "Years of Expansion, 1865–1884," in Land, ed., *Adventism in America*, 67.

[36] Ibid., 91.

[37] Richard W. Schwarz, "The Perils of Growth, 1886–1905," in Land, ed., *Adventism in America*, 96–97.

[38] Ibid., 99–101.

[39] Ibid., 105–6.

[40] Ibid., 106–7.

[41] Ibid., 108–9.

[42] Gary Land, "Shaping the Modern Church, 1906–1930," in *Adventism in America*, 154.

[43] Ibid., 155–56.

[44] Ibid., 156–57.

[45] Ibid., 159.

[46] Walter T. Rea, *The White Lie* (Turlock, Calif.: M & R Publications, 1982), 50.

[47] Richard N. Ostling, "The Church of Liberal Borrowings," *Time* (August 2, 1982), 49.

[48] D. M. Canright, *Seventh-day Adventism Renounced* (Grand Rapids: Baker, 1961), 135.

[49] James C. Hefley, "Adventist Teachers Are Forced Out In A Doctrinal Dispute," *Christianity Today* (March 18, 1983), 23–24.

[50] Appendix 1, in Land, ed., *Adventism in America*, 249.

[51] Ellen White, *The Great Controversy Between Christ and Satan* (Mountain View: Pacific Press, 1911), 483.

[52] *Questions on Doctrine* (Washington D.C.: Review and Herald, 1957), 441.

[53] White, *The Great Controversy*, 442, 485–86.

[54] Anthony Hoekema, *The Four Major Cults* (Grand Rapids: Eerdmans, 1963), 122.

[55] Gary Land, "Coping With Change, 1961–1980," in *Adventism in America*, 224.

[56] Keld J. Reynolds, "The Church Under Stress, 1931–1960," in *Adventism in America*, 187.

[57] *Questions on Doctrine*, 154–58.

[58] Martin, *The Kingdom of the Cults*, 485.

[59] *Questions on Doctrine*, 166–69.

[60] Jan Karel Van Baalen, *The Chaos of Cults: A Study in Present-Day Isms* (Grand Rapids: Eerdmans, 1962), 245–46.

[61] Carlyle B. Haynes, *Life, Death, and Immortality* (Nashville: Southern Publishing, 1952), 202.

[62] *Questions on Doctrine*, 543.

[63] Ellen G. White, *Fundamentals of Christian Education* (Nashville: Southern Publishing Association, 1923), 201.

[64] Gary Land, "Shaping the Modern Church, 1906–1930," in *Adventism in America*, 140.

[65] George E. Knowles, "When People Seek Answers," *These Times*, SDA Services Annual Report, 15.

[66] Clarence W. Hall, *Adventurers for God* (New York: Harper & Row, 1959), 178–93.

[67] Neal Wilson, "Time for Reaping," *Adventist Review* (September 2, 1982), 3.

[68] Chris Meehan, "Defenders of Their Faith," *Grand Rapids Press* (Michigan), November 1, 1986.

CHAPTER 5

[1] Stanley N. Gundry, "Hermeneutics or *Zeitgeist* as the Determining Factor in the History of Eschatologies?" *Journal of the Evangelical Theological Society* (March 1977), 50, 54.

[2] Alan Rogerson, *Millions Now Living Will Never Die: A Study of Jehovah's Witnesses* (London: Constable, 1969), 6.

[3] Barbara Grizzuti Harrison, *Visions of Glory: A History and a Memory of Jehovah's Witnesses* (New York: Simon and Schuster, 1978), 42–43.

[4] Sydney E. Ahlstrom, *A Religious History of the American People* (Garden City, N.Y.: Doubleday, 1975), II, 276.

[5] M. James Penton, *Apocalypse Delayed: The Story of the Jehovah's Witnesses* (Toronto: Univ. of Toronto Press, 1985), 7.

[6] J. J. Ross, *Some Facts and More Facts about the Self-Styled Pastor Charles T. Russell* (New York: Charles C. Cook, 1912), 4.

[7] Edmond C. Gruss, *Apostles of Denial: An Examination and Exposé of the History,*

Doctrines and Claims of the Jehovah's Witnesses (Phillipsburg, N.J.: Presbyterian and Reformed Publishing Co., 1970), 39.

[8] Penton, *Apocalypse Delayed,* 17–23.

[9] Rogerson, *Millions Now Living,* 8–13.

[10] Penton, *Apocalypse Delayed,* 26, 32.

[11] Herbert H. Stroup, *The Jehovah's Witnesses* (New York: Columbia Univ. Press, 1945), 7.

[12] Penton, *Apocalypse Delayed,* 34.

[13] Ibid., 35–36.

[14] Ibid., 36–38.

[15] Ibid., 38–39.

[16] Rogers, *Millions Now Living,* 25–27.

[17] Cited in William J. Whalen, *Armageddon Around the Corner: A Report on Jehovah's Witnesses* (New York: John Day, 1962), 40.

[18] Walter Martin, *The Kingdom of the Cults* (Minneapolis: Bethany House, 1985), 39.

[19] *Watchtower* (September 15, 1910.)

[20] Raymond Franz, *Crisis of Conscience: The Struggle Between Loyalty to God and Loyalty to One's Religion* (Atlanta: Commentary Press, 1983), 147.

[21] Watch Tower Bible & Tract Society, *The Truth That Leads to Eternal Life* (New York: Watch Tower Bible & Tract Society, 1968), 86.

[22] Franz, *Crisis of Conscience,* 343–44.

[23] *Studies in the Scriptures* (New York: Watchtower Bible & Tract Society, 1891), 342.

[24] Leonard and Marjorie Chretien, *Witnesses of Jehovah: A Shocking Exposé of What Jehovah's Witnesses Really Believe* (Eugene, Ore.: Harvest House, 1988), 30–31.

[25] C. J. Woodworth and George H. Fisher, eds., *The Finished Mystery,* vol. 7 in *Studies in the Scriptures* (Brooklyn: International Bible Students Association, 1917), 57.

[26] *Watch Tower* (December 1917), quoted in Stroup, *The Jehovah's Witnesses,* 13.

[27] James A. Beckford, *The Trumpet of Prophecy: A Sociological Study of Jehovah's Witnesses* (Oxford: Basil Blackwell, 1975), 22–23.

[28] Rogerson, *Millions Now Living,* 32–39.

[29] Beckford, *The Trumpet of Prophecy,* 28–29.

[30] Heather and Gary Botting, *The Orwellian World of Jehovah's Witnesses* (Toronto: Univ. of Toronto Press, 1984), 40–41.

[31] William J. Schnell, *Thirty Years a Watch Tower Slave* (Grand Rapids: Baker, 1959), 16–19.

[32] Penton, *Apocalypse Delayed,* 72.

[33] Ibid., 48, 73–74.

[34] Ibid., 58.

[35] Rogerson, *Millions Now Living,* 46–47.

[36] Penton, *Apocalypse Delayed,* 58.

[37] "A Time to 'Lift Up Your Head' in Confident Hope," *Awake!* (October 8, 1968), 1.

[38] Penton, *Apocalypse Delayed,* 60–63.

[39] Beckford, *The Trumpet of Prophecy,* 47.

[40] Penton, *Apocalypse Delayed,* 78–79.

[41] Beckford, *The Trumpet of Prophecy,* 49, 52.

[42] Timothy White, *A People for His Name* (New York: Vantage Press, 1967), 385–86.

[43] Penton, *Apocalypse Delayed,* 87.

[44] Harrison, *Visions of Glory,* 143.

[45] Franz, *Crisis of Conscience,* 205–7.

[46] *1979 Yearbook of the Jehovah's Witnesses* (New York: Watchtower Bible and Tract Society, 1978), 30–31.

[47] Richard N. Ostling, "Witness Under Prosecution," *Time* (February 22, 1982), 66.

[48] Penton, *Apocalypse Delayed,* 108–9.

[49] Susan C. Cowley, "Persecution in Malawi," *Newsweek* (May 10, 1976), 106–7.

[50] Franz, *Crisis of Conscience,* 116–26.

[51] Penton, *Apocalypse Delayed,* 143.

[52] *The Truth That Leads to Eternal Life,* 167–68.

[53] "Woman Dies After Faith Ruled Out New Blood," *Grand Rapids Press* (Michigan), June 23, 1980.

[54] John E. Molder and Marvin Comisky, "Jehovah's Witnesses Mold Constitutional Law," *Bill of Rights Review* (Summer 1942), vol. 2, 262.

55 Whalen, *Armageddon Around the Corner*, 177–80.

56 Heather and Gary Botting, *The Orwellian World*, 95.

57 Franz, *Crisis of Conscience*, passim.

58 Penton, *Apocalypse Delayed*, 280.

59 Harrison, *Visions of Glory*, 144.

60 "Witnesses Build Halls in a Jiffy," *Grand Rapids Press* (Michigan), October 23, 1982.

61 Charles Taze Russell, *Studies in the Scriptures*, 410; quoted in Wilton M. Nelson and Richard K. Smith, "Jehovah's Witnesses: The Background," in David J. Hesselgrave, *Dynamic Religious Movements* (Grand Rapids: Baker, 1978), 181.

62 Gordon E. Duggar, *Jehovah's Witnesses: Watch Out for the Watchtower!* (Grand Rapids: Baker, 1985), 11–12.

63 *Watchtower* (February 15, 1951; March 15, 1960.)

64 Harrison, *Visions of Glory*, 72–74.

65 Cited in Duggar, *Jehovah's Witnesses*, 27–28.

66 Walter Martin, *The Kingdom of the Cults* (Minneapolis: Bethany House, 1985), 86.

67 Joseph Franklin Rutherford, *The Harp of God: Proof Conclusive That Millions Now Living Will Never Die* (New York: Watch Tower Bible and Tract Society, 1921), 101; *The Harp of God* (New York: Watch Tower Bible and Tract Society, 1952), 106.

68 Nelson and Smith, "Jehovah's Witnesses," 179.

69 *Make Sure of All Things; Hold Fast to What Is Fine* (New York: Watch Tower Bible and Tract Society, 1965), 319.

70 Duggar, *Jehovah's Witnesses*, 73–74.

71 *Let God Be True*, 202.

72 Duggar, *Jehovah's Witnesses*, 74.

73 Franz, *Crisis of Conscience*, 199.

74 Gruss, *Apostles of Denial*, 97.

75 Anthony A. Hoekema, *The Four Major Cults* (Grand Rapids: Eerdmans, 1963), 309.

76 Gruss, *Apostles of Denial*, 101–2.

77 *Let God Be True*, 98–99.

78 *This Means Everlasting Life* (New York: Watch Tower Bible and Tract Society, 1950), 137, 181.

79 Heather and Gary Botting, *The Orwellian World*, 107.

80 *New World Translation of the Christian Greek Scriptures* (New York: Watchtower Bible and Tract Society, 1950), 10–12.

81 Robert H. Countess, *The Jehovah's Witnesses' New Testament: A Critical Analysis of the New World Translation of the Christian Greek Scriptures* (Phillipsburg, N.J.: Presbyterian and Reformed Publishing Company, 1982), 33.

82 *New World Translation*, 11.

83 Heather and Gary Botting, *The Orwellian World*, 99.

84 Countess, *The Jehovah's Witnesses' New Testament*, 1, 89.

85 Heather and Gary Botting, *The Orwellian World*, 29, x–xi.

86 *1984 Yearbook of the Jehovah's Witnesses* (New York: Watchtower Bible and Tract Society, 1983), 24, 28.

87 *1988 Yearbook of the Jehovah's Witnesses* (New York: Watchtower Bible and Tract Society, 1987), 34–40.

88 *Let God Be True*, 9.

89 *The Truth that Leads to Eternal Life*, 183–84.

90 *Christianity Today* (September 3, 1982), 37–39.

91 Franz, *Crisis of Conscience*, 96.

92 Morey, "A Jehovah's Witness?" 37.

93 Martin, *Kingdom of the Cults*, 62.

94 *New World Translation*, 283.

95 Ibid., 351.

96 Ibid., 296–97, 317.

CHAPTER 6

1 Robert Peel, *Mary Baker Eddy: The Years of Discovery* (New York: Holt, Rinehart and Winston, 1966), 84.

2 Robert Peel, *Mary Baker Eddy: The Years of Trial* (New York: Holt, Rinehart and Winston, 1971), 251.

3 Peel, *Mary Baker Eddy: The Years of Discovery*, 4–6.

4 Ibid., 31.

5 Julius Silberger, Jr., *Mary Baker Eddy: An Interpretive Biography of the Founder of Christian Science* (Boston: Little, Brown and Company, 1980), 22.

6 Silberger, *Mary Baker Eddy*, 25, 27.

7 Peel, *Mary Baker Eddy: The Years of Discovery*, 32.

8 Sydney E. Ahlstrom, *A Religious History of the American People*, 2 vols. (Garden City, N.Y.: Image Books, 1975), 2:531.

9 Sibyl Wilbur, *The Life of Mary Baker Eddy* (New York: Concord Publishing Company, 1907), 30.

10 Peel, *Mary Baker Eddy: The Years of Discovery*, 132–33.

11 Ibid., 121.

12 Silberger, *Mary Baker Eddy*, 39.

13 Ernest Sutherland Bates and John V. Dittemore, *Mary Baker Eddy: The Truth and the Tradition* (Alfred A. Knopf, 1932), 41–42, 151, 445.

14 Peel, *Mary Baker Eddy: The Years of Discovery*, 109.

15 Silberger, *Mary Baker Eddy*, 53.

16 Richard Quebedeaux, *By What Authority: The Rise of Personality Cults in American Christianity* (New York: Harper & Row, 1982), 40–41.

17 Cited in Silberger, *Mary Baker Eddy*, 62.

18 Ibid., 64.

19 Ibid., 67.

20 Peel, *Mary Baker Eddy: The Years of Discovery*, 163, 180.

21 Wilbur, *The Life*, 132.

22 Silberger, *Mary Baker Eddy*, 86.

23 Ibid., 85–87.

24 Ibid., 25.

25 Wilbur, *The Life*, 130–32.

26 Edwin F. Dakin, *Mrs. Eddy: The Biography of a Virginal Mind* (New York: Scribner's, 1930), 61–62.

27 Silberger, *Mary Baker Eddy*, 94.

28 Ibid., 102.

29 Dakin, *Mrs. Eddy*, 70–71.

30 Silberger, *Mary Baker Eddy*, 111.

31 Wilbur, *The Life*, 189-190.

32 Silberger, *Mary Baker Eddy*, 119

33 Quoted in Silberger, *Mary Baker Eddy*, 124.

34 Peel, *Mary Baker Eddy: The Years of Discovery*, 287.

35 Ibid., 290.

36 Dakin, *Mrs. Eddy*, 120.

37 Silberger, *Mary Baker Eddy*, 129.

38 Dakin, *Mrs. Eddy*, 133.

39 Silberger, *Mary Baker Eddy*, 133.

40 Ibid., 134.

41 Dakin, *Mrs. Eddy*, 153.

42 Silberger, *Mary Baker Eddy*, 136.

43 Ibid., 143.

44 Ibid., 149.

45 Georgine Milmine, *The Life of Mary Baker G. Eddy and the History of Christian Science* (Grand Rapids: Baker, 1971), 234.

46 Peel, *Mary Baker Eddy: The Years of Trial*, 70.

47 Silberger, *Mary Baker Eddy*, 207.

48 Ibid., 213.

49 Peel, *Mary Baker Eddy: The Years of Trial*, 270.

50 Stephen Gottschalk, *The Emergence of Christian Science in American Religious Life* (Berkeley: Univ. of California Press, 1973), 187.

51 Silberger, *Mary Baker Eddy*, 233–36.

52 Gottschalk, *The Emergence of Christian Science*, 102–3.

53 Ibid., 100, 109, 117.

54 Ibid., 127.

55 Ibid., xvi.

56 Ibid., xv–xvi.

57 Silberger, *Mary Baker Eddy*, 4.

58 Ahlstrom, *Religious History*, 2:532.

59 Robert Peel, *Mary Baker Eddy: The Years of Authority* (New York: Holt, Rinehart and Winston, 1977), 223.

60 Gottschalk, *The Emergence of Christian Science*, 168.

61 Ibid., 169.

62 Ibid.

63 James A. Logwood, "A Trip to the Rockies," *Christian Science Journal*, XVIII (May 1900), 81.

64 Clara Knox McKee, "With Sandals on and Staff in Hand," in *We Knew Mary Baker Eddy* (Boston: Christian Science Publishing Society, 1950), 71.

65 Gottschalk, *The Emergence of Christian Science*, 172.

[66] Ahlstrom, *Religious History*, 2:533.

[67] Silberger, *Mary Baker Eddy*, 240.

[68] Ibid., 240.

[69] Gottschalk, *The Emergence of Christian Science*, 176.

[70] Ibid., 176.

[71] Ibid., 175, 179–85.

[72] *Science and Health*, 20.

[73] Ibid., 34–35.

[74] Gottschalk, *The Emergence of Christian Science*, 191–92.

[75] John Dart, "Christian Science's Health Shows Signs of Decline," *St. Petersburg Times*, January 10, 1987.

[76] Gottschalk, *The Emergence of Christian Science*, 192–93.

[77] *The New York Times*, July 10, 1904, cited in Martin, *The Kingdom of the Cults*, 128–29.

[78] *Science and Health*, 107, 110.

[79] Gottschalk, *The Emergence of Christian Science*, 27.

[80] *The First Church of Christ, Scientist, and Miscellany* (Boston: Christian Science Publishing Society, 1941), 115; *Science and Health*, 139.

[81] Gottschalk, *The Emergence of Christian Science*, 19.

[82] Ibid., 20–22.

[83] *Science and Health*, 123.

[84] Mary Baker Eddy, *Miscellaneous Writings, 1883–1896* (Boston: The First Church of Christ, Scientist, 1896), 62–63.

[85] *A Century of Christian Science Healing* (Boston: Christian Science Publishing Society, 1966), 239.

[86] Ibid., 240.

[87] *Science and Health*, 256, 331.

[88] Gottschalk, *The Emergence of Christian Science*, 56–57.

[89] *Science and Health*, 332, 517.

[90] Gottschalk, *The Emergence of Christian Science*, 83.

[91] *Science and Health*, 29.

[92] Ibid., 23.

[93] Mary Baker Eddy, *Christian Science: No or Yes* (Boston: Christian Science Publishing Society, 1887), 96.

[94] Eddy, *Miscellaneous Writings*, 15.

[95] *Science and Health*, 55, 471.

[96] Ibid., 86.

[97] Gottschalk, *The Emergence of Christian Science*, 141–42, 148.

[98] "Two Students Succumb Despite Prayer, Medicine," *Grand Rapids Press* (Michigan), February 17, 1985.

[99] Quoted in *Christian Science Is for Sharing* (Boston: The Christian Science Publishing Society, 1972), 5.

[100] John DeWitt, *The Christian Science Way of Life* (Boston: Christian Science Publishing Society, 1962), 71–72.

[101] Dart, "Christian Science's Health," January 10, 1987.

CHAPTER 7

[1] Quoted in Richard Quebedeaux, *By What Authority: The Rise of Personality Cults in American Christianity* (San Francisco: Harper & Row, 1982), 43.

[2] Quebedeaux, *By What Authority*, 41.

[3] Horatio W. Dresser, *History of the New Thought Movement* (New York: Crowell, 1919), 211.

[4] Stephen Gottschalk, *The Emergence of Christian Science in American Religious Life* (Berkeley: Univ. of California Press, 1973), 128.

[5] Ibid., 152.

[6] D. R. McConnell, *A Different Gospel: A Historical and Biblical Analysis of the Modern Faith Movement* (Peabody, Mass.: Hendrickson, 1988), 184–85.

[7] James Dillet Freeman, *The Story of Unity* (Unity Village, Mo.: Unity Books, 1978), 14.

[8] Freeman, *The Story of Unity*, 24.

[9] Ibid., 31–33.

[10] Jan Karel Van Baalen, *The Chaos of Cults: A Study in Present-Day Isms* (Grand Rapids: Eerdmans, 1962), 131.

[11] Hugh D'Andrade, *Charles Fillmore: Herald of the New Age* (New York: Harper & Row, 1974), 21.

[12] Freeman, *The Story of Unity*, 41–42.

[13] Ibid., 44–45.

[14] Ibid., 47–48.

[15] Taken from photographic reproduction, Unity Village, Missouri.

[16] Walter Martin, *The Kingdom of the Cults* (Minneapolis: Bethany House, 1985), 279.

[17] Freeman, *The Story of Unity*, 60.

[18] Marcus Bach, *The Unity Way of Life* (Englewood Cliffs, N.J.: Prentice-Hall, 1962), 158.

[19] Freeman, *The Story of Unity*, 70.

[20] Winthrop Hudson, *Religion in America: An Historical Account of the Development of American Religious Life* (New York: Scribner's, 1973), 290.

[21] Russell P. Spittler, *Cults and Isms: Twenty Alternates to Evangelical Christianity* (Grand Rapids: Baker, 1962), 74.

[22] *Unity's Statement of Faith*, (Lee's Summit, No.: Unity School of Christianity, n.d.) pts. 1, 16, 17.

[23] H. Emilie Cady, *Lessons in Truth* (Lee's Summit: Unity School of Christianity, 1962), 8–9.

[24] Fillmore, *Christian Healing*, 162–63, 226.

[25] Charles Fillmore, "The Atomic Prayer," *Unity* (November 1945).

[26] Freeman, *The Story of Unity*, 11.

[27] Elizabeth Sand Turner, *What Unity Teaches* (Lee's Summit, Mo.: Unity School of Christianity, n.d.), 8–9.

[28] Charles Fillmore, *Mysteries of John* (Lee's Summit, Mo.: Unity School of Christianity, 1954), 172–73.

[29] *Unity's Statement of Faith* (Lee's Summit, Mo.: Unity School of Christianity, n.d.), pt. 22.

[30] Bach, *The Story of Unity*, 159.

[31] Ibid., 159–60, 162.

[32] Ibid., 161.

[33] D'Andrade, *Charles Fillmore*, 133–34.

[34] Charles Fillmore, *Christian Healing*, 28, 31.

[35] Cady, *Lessons in Truth*, 36.

[36] Freeman, *The Story of Unity*, 204.

[37] D'Andrade, *Charles Fillmore*, 133.

[38] Ibid.

[39] Freeman, *The Story of Unity*, 199–200.

[40] Ibid., 200.

[41] Charles Fillmore, *Twelve Powers of Man*, quoted in Van Baalen, *The Chaos of Cults*, 136–37.

[42] Charles Fillmore, *Prosperity* (Kansas City, Mo.: Unity, 1936), 69.

[43] Ibid., 103–4.

[44] Harold J. Berry, "Unity School of Christianity in the Light of the Scriptures," *Good News Broadcaster* (October 1964), 18.

[45] "Twenty Questions About Unity" (Lee's Summit, Mo.: Association of Unity Churches), 2–3.

CHAPTER 8

[1] Herbert W. Armstrong, *The Autobiography of Herbert W. Armstrong* (Pasadena: Ambassador College Press, 1957), I, 11.

[2] Armstrong, *Autobiography*, I, 17, 29, 30, 34.

[3] Joseph Hopkins, *The Armstrong Empire: A Look at the Worldwide Church of God* (Grand Rapids: Eerdmans, 1974), 27.

[4] Armstrong, *Autobiography*, I, 286.

[5] Ibid., I, 282.

[6] Ibid., I, 284.

[7] Ibid., I, 289.

[8] Ibid., I, 292.

[9] Ibid., I, 296–97.

[10] Ibid., I, 207–8.

[11] Ibid., I, 208–9.

[12] Herbert W. Armstrong, "Personal from the Editor," *The Good News* (August 1969), 4.

[13] Stanley R. Rader, *Against the Gates of Hell* (New York: Everest House, 1980), 49–53.

[14] Armstrong, *Autobiography*, I, 344–49.

[15] Ibid., I, 468.

[16] Paul N. Benware, *Ambassadors of Armstrongism: An Analysis of the History and Teachings of the Worldwide Church of God* (Philadelphia: The Presbyterian and Reformed Publishing Co., 1975), 25.

[17] Armstrong, *Autobiography*, I, 400, 407.

[18] Ibid., I, 336.

[19] Herbert W. Armstrong, "Autobiography," *The Plain Truth* (September 1963), 17.

[20] Hopkins, *The Armstrong Empire*, 50.

21 Rader, *Against the Gates of Hell*, 106–8.

22 Ibid., 109.

23 Robert L. Sumner, "The Incredible Armstrong Duo," *Faith for the Family* (September/October 1975), 8–9.

24 William C. Martin, "Father, Son, and Mammon," *Atlantic Monthly* (March 1980), 60.

25 Rader, *Against the Gates of Hell*, 109–10.

26 "A Mellowed Garner Ted Starts Over," *Grand Rapids Press* (Michigan), June 13, 1981.

27 Kenneth L. Woodward, "Apocalypse Now?" *Newsweek* (January 15, 1979).

28 "Death Takes Founder of Controversial Sect," *Grand Rapids Press* (Michigan), January 17, 1986.

29 Ibid.

30 Martin, "Father, Son, and Mammon," 59.

31 Armstrong, *Autobiography*, I, 36.

32 Hopkins, *The Armstrong Empire*, 22.

33 Ibid., 14.

34 Ibid., 187–90.

35 Martin, "Father, Son, and Mammon," 59.

36 Ibid., 60.

37 Roger R. Chambers, *The Plain Truth About Armstrongism* (Grand Rapids: Baker, 1972) 11.

38 Martin, "Father, Son, and Mammon," 60.

39 Ibid.

40 Ibid., 61.

41 Ibid., 63.

42 Ibid.

43 Armstrong, *Mystery of the Ages*, (New York: Dodd, Mead and Company, 1985), 55, 198.

44 Armstrong, *Autobiography*, I, 338.

45 Ibid., I, 322.

46 Ibid., I, 321.

47 Hopkins, *The Armstrong Empire*, 115.

48 Bill McDowell, "Keep God's Sabbath Holy!" *The Good News* (March 1968), 17.

49 Armstrong, *Autobiography*, I, 344–45.

50 Hopkins, *The Armstrong Empire*, 67–68.

51 Ibid., 68.

52 Herbert W. Armstrong and Garner Ted Armstrong, *The Wonderful World Tomorrow* (Pasadena: Ambassador College, 1966), 57–58.

53 Ibid., 3.

54 Armstrong, *Autobiography*, I, 407–8.

55 Herbert W. Armstrong, *The Incredible Human Potential* (Pasadena: Worldwide Church of God, 1978), 1.

56 Ibid., 5.

57 Herbert W. Armstrong, *The United States and Britain in Prophecy* (Pasadena: Worldwide Church of God, 1980), 123–28.

58 Ibid., 153.

59 Ibid., 9, 154.

60 Ibid., 9, 10.

61 Ibid., 168–69.

62 Ibid., 170, 176–77.

63 Armstrong, *Autobiography*, I, 400, 407–8.

64 Ibid., I, 408.

65 Armstrong, *The Incredible Human Potential*, 123.

66 Ibid., 32, 123.

67 David Jon Hill, "Why is God the Father Called a Father?" *Tomorrow's World* (September 1970), 27.

68 Cited in Bob Withers and Paul Benware, "Armstrongism from the Inside," *Moody Monthly* (October 1978), 73.

69 Herbert W. Armstrong, *Mystery of the Ages* (New York: Dodd, Mead & Company, 1985), 57, 210.

70 Chambers, *The Plain Truth*, 10.

71 Armstrong, *Mystery*, 56.

72 Ambassador College Correspondence Course, Lesson 9 (1956, 1966), 9, cited in Hopkins, *The Armstrong Empire*, 112.

73 Armstrong, *Mystery*, 46–47.

74 Hopkins, *The Armstrong Empire*, 135.

75 Ibid., 135–36.

76 Herbert W. Armstrong, "Is All Animal Flesh Good Food?" (Pasadena: Ambassador College, 1958), 2.

77 Armstrong, *The Incredible Human Potential*, 114, 121.

78 Ibid., 114–20.

79 Hopkins, *The Armstrong Empire*, 51.

[80]"This Is the Worldwide Church of God" (Pasadena: Worldwide Church of God, 1979), 21.

[81]Isaiah A. Issong, "The Missionary Outreach of the Worldwide Church of God in Nigeria," unpublished paper, Grand Rapids School of the Bible and Music, (May 16, 1983), 4.

[82]Herbert W. Armstrong, *Autiobiography of Herbert W. Armstrong*, II (Pasadena: Worldwide Church of God, 1987), 651–653.

[83]Michael A. Snyder to Ruth A. Tucker, personal correspondence, February 1, 1989.

[84]Snyder to Tucker, February 1, 1989.
[85]Armstrong, *Autobiography*,II, 640–647.

[86]Snyder to Tucker, February 1, 1989.
[87]Armstrong, *Mystery of the Ages*,(New York: Dodd, Mead and Company, 1985), 134, 247.

[88]Snyder to Tucker, February 1, 1989
[89]Ibid.
[90]Armstrong, *Autobiography*, II, 65.
[91]Snyder to Tucker, February 1, 1989.
[92]Ibid.

CHAPTER 9

[1]J. L. Williams, *Victor Paul Wierwille and The Way International* (Chicago: Moody, 1979), 17–19.

[2]Walter Martin, *The New Cults* (Santa Anna, Calif.: Vision House, 1980), 38–39.

[3]Victor Paul Wierwille, *Power For Abundant Living* (New Knoxville, Ohio: American Christian Press, 1972), 3.

[4]Ibid., 120.

[5]William J. Petersen, *Those Curious New Cults in the 80s* (New Canaan, Conn.: Keats, 1982), 273.

[6]Jack Sparks, *The Mind Benders* (Nashville: Thomas Nelson, 1979), 189–90.

[7]Williams, *Victor Paul Wierwille*, 28.

[8]Victor Paul Wierwille, *How to Speak in Tongues* (New Knoxville, Ohio: American Christian Press, n.d.), 102.

[9]"Profile—The Way International," printed and distributed by The Way International, n.d.

[10]"Frequent Questions" (New Knoxville, Ohio: The Way International, n.d.)

[11]Joseph M. Hopkins, "The Way Founder Wierwille Announces Plan to Retire," *Christianity Today* (March 13, 1981), 57.

[12]Wierwille, *Power For Abundant Living*, 82.

[13]Martin, *The New Cults*, 47.

[14]Wierwille, *Power For Abundant Living*, 207–10.

[15]Williams, *Victor Paul Wierwille*, 71–72.

[16]Ibid., 49–50.
[17]Ibid., 61.
[18]Victor Paul Wierwille, *Jesus Christ Is Not God* (New Knoxville: American Christian Press, 1975, 3–5.
[19]Ibid., 89.
[20]Ibid., 115.
[21]Victor Paul Wierwille, *The Word's Way*, vol. 3 of *Studies in Abundant Living* (New Knoxville, Ohio: American Christian Press, 1971), 161, 164.
[22]Ibid., 166–67, 174.
[23]Victor Paul Wierwille, *Receiving the Holy Spirit Today* (New Knoxville, Ohio: American Christian Press, 1972), 4.
[24]Wierwille, *Receiving the Holy Spirit Today*, 39–40.
[25]Victor Paul Wierwille, *The New Dynamic Church* (New Knoxville, Ohio: American Christian Press, 1971), 104.
[26]Wierwille, *Receiving the Holy Spirit Today*, 41.
[27]Wierwille, *The New Dynamic Church*, 123.
[28]Wierwille, *Receiving the Holy Spirit Today*, 254.
[29]Elena S. Whiteside, *The Way: Living in Love* (New Knoxville, Ohio: American Christian Press, 1974), 178.
[30]Ibid., 180–81.
[31]Williams, *Victor Paul Wierwille*, 21.
[32]Victor Paul Wierwille, *The Bible Tells Me So*, vol. 1 in *Studies in Abundant Living* (New Knoxville, Ohio: American Christian Press, 1971), 119, 124.
[33]Ibid., 141.
[34]Wierwille, *The Word's Way*, 235.

35 Ibid., 235, 242.

36 Ibid., 187, 198.

37 Wayne Clapp to Jimel Aumann, March 22, 1983.

38 Williams, *Victor Paul Wierwille*, 38–39.

39 "International WOW Scene," *The Way Magazine* (November–December 1985), 31.

40 Ibid., 31.

41 Wierwille, *Power For Abundant Living*, 109.

42 Hopkins, "The Way Founder," 57.

43 Keith Tolbert, "Infighting Trims Branches of Way International," *Christianity Today* (February 19, 1988), 44.

44 Hopkins, "The Way Founder," 57; Tolbert, "Infighting," 44.

45 Tolbert, "Infighting," 44.

CHAPTER 10

1 Walter Martin, *The New Cults* (Santa Ana: Vision House, 1980), 144–45.

2 Roy Wallis, "Observations On the Children of God," *The Sociological Review*, 24 (November 1976): 811.

3 Moses David, *The Disciple Revolution* (London: The Children of God, 1975), 7–8.

4 Ronald Enroth, *Youth, Brainwashing and the Extremist Cults* (Grand Rapids: Zondervan, 1977), 37.

5 Deborah (Linda Berg Davis with Bill Davis), *The Children of God* (Grand Rapids: Zondervan, 1984), 79, 83–86.

6 Moses David, *He Stands in the Gap* (London: Children of God, 1971), 1, 5.

7 Moses David, *The Spirit World*, 4–5; cited in Walter Martin, *The New Cults*, 193.

8 Davis, *The Children of God*, 6, 88–89.

9 Martin, *The New Cults*, 147.

10 Davis, *The Children of God*, 108–9.

11 Ibid., 111–12.

12 Jack Sparks, *The Mindbenders: A Look at Current Cults* (Nashville: Thomas Nelson, 1979), 161.

13 Davis, *The Children of God*, 116.

14 *New York Times*, October 1974; cited in Enroth, *Youth, Brainwashing and the Extremist Cults*, 48–49.

15 Enroth, *Youth, Brainwashing and the Extremist Cults*, 49–50.

16 Sparks, *The Mindbenders*, 173.

17 Martin, *The New Cults*, 161.

18 Enroth, *Youth, Brainwashing and the Extremist Cults*, 45.

19 Martin, *The New Cults*, 152–53.

20 Ibid., 153.

21 Moses David, *The Revolutionary Rules* (London: Children of God, March 1972), 1; cited in McDowell and Stewart, *Understanding the Cults* (San Bernadino, Calif.: Here's Life Publishers, 1982), 130.

22 Moses David, *A Prayer for the Poor!* (Rome: Family of Love, Mar. 19, 1978, Dfo., No. 681), 1–10; cited in Martin, *The New Cults*, 178.

23 Davis, *The Children of God*, 119.

24 Ibid., 120.

25 Moses David, "The Flirty Little Fishy!" (London: Children of God, 1974), 2340–47.

26 Davis, *The Children of God*, 122–23.

27 Moses David, "God's Whores?" (Rome: Children of God, April 26, 1976), 3.

28 Martin, *The New Cults*, 168.

29 William J. Peterson, *Those Curious New Cults in the 80s* (New Caanan, Conn.: Keats, 1982), 268.

30 Moses David, *Islam* (Rome: Children of God, May 18, 1975, Dfo., No. 631), 14; cited in McDowell and Stewart, *Understanding the Cults*, 129.

31 Peterson, *Those Curious New Cults*, 268.

32 Sparks, *The Mindbenders*, 166.

33 David G. Bromley and Anson D. Shupe, Jr., *Strange Gods: The Great American Cult Scare* (Boston: Beacon, 1981), 29–30.

34 John Butterworth, *Cults and New Faiths* (Elgin, Ill.: David C. Cook, 1981), 6.

35 Davis, *The Children of God*, 4, 7.

36 Ibid., 9–13.

37 Ibid., 13, 127–43.

38 Ibid., 145.

39 Ibid., 201.

40 Una McManus, *Not for a Million Dollars* (Nashville: Impact Books, 1980), passim.

[41] Ruth Gordon, *Children of Darkness* (Wheaton: Tyndale House, 1988), 304–5.
[42] Ibid., 304.

CHAPTER 11

[1] *Divine Principle* (New York: The Holy Spirit Association for the Unification of World Christianity, 1973), 16.
[2] Max Weber, *The Theory of Social and Economic Organization* (New York: Free Press, 1964), 398.
[3] Ronald Enroth, *Youth, Brainwashing and the Extremist Cults* (Grand Rapids: Zondervan, 1977), 108.
[4] J. Isamu Yamamoto, *The Puppet Master: an Inquiry into Sun Myung Moon and the Unification Church* (Downers Grove, Ill.: InterVarsity Press, 1977), 16.
[5] Mose Durst, *To Bigotry, No Sanction: Reverend Sun Myung Moon and the Unification Church* (Chicago: Regnery Gateway, 1984), 63.
[6] "Sun Myung Moon, A Biography," Berkeley, Calif.: Unification Church, n.d., 1–2.
[7] Durst, *To Bigotry, No Sanction*, 64.
[8] Sun Myung Moon, *Message to the World Unification Family* (Washington, D.C.: The Holy Spirit Association for the Unification of World Christianity, 1964), 4.
[9] Yamamoto, *The Puppet Master*, 17.
[10] Quoted in Yamamoto, *The Puppet Master*, 17–18.
[11] Frederick Sontag, *Sun Myung Moon and the Unification Church* (Nashville: Abingdon, 1977), 79.
[12] Won Pil Kim, "Father's Early Ministry in Pusan," *Today's World* (May 1982), 12.
[13] Sebastian A. Matczak, *Unificationism: A New Philosophy and World View* (Jamaica, N.Y.: Learned Publications, 1982), 9–10.
[14] David G. Bromley and Anson D. Shupe, Jr., *"Moonies" in America: Cult, Church, and Crusade* (Beverly Hills: Sage Publications, 1979), 36–37.
[15] Ibid., 37.
[16] Durst, *To Bigotry, No Sanction*, 64.

[17] William J. Petersen, *Those Curious New Cults in the 80s* (New Canaan, Conn.: Keats, 1982), 165–66.
[18] Bromley and Shupe, *"Moonies" in America*, 48–49.
[19] Sontag, *Sun Myung Moon*, 199.
[20] Peterson, *Those Curious New Cults*, 166.
[21] Quoted in James Bjornstad, *The Moon Is Not the Sun* (Minneapolis: Bethany House, 1976), 33–34.
[22] Yamamoto, *The Puppet Master*, 21.
[23] Robert Boettcher with Gordon L. Freedman, *Gifts of Deceit: Sun Myung Moon, Tongsun Park, and the Korean Scandal* (New York: Holt, Rinehart and Winston, 1980), 37.
[24] Young Oon Kim, *Unification Theology* (New York: The Holy Spirit Association for the Unification of World Christianity, 1980), 132–33, 164.
[25] Ibid., 185.
[26] Ibid., 197.
[27] Ibid., 183.
[28] Ibid., 151.
[29] Sun Myung Moon, "On Bible Understanding," *The Master Speaks* (Washington, D.C.: Unification Church, 1965).
[30] *Divine Principle*, 348.
[31] Ibid., 9–10.
[32] Ibid., 348.
[33] Kim, *Unification Theology*, 230.
[34] Ibid., 231.
[35] Durst, *To Bigotry, No Sanction*, 100.
[36] Kim, *Unification Theology*, 53–54, 72.
[37] Ibid., 116–18.
[38] Bromley and Shupe, *"Moonies" in America*, 99.
[39] Kim, *Unification Theology*, 118.
[40] Ibid., 124–25.
[41] *Divine Principle*, 148.
[42] Durst, *To Bigotry, No Sanction*, 101.
[43] Bromley and Shupe, *"Moonies" in America*, 98.
[44] Ibid., 98–99.
[45] David G. Bromley and Anson D. Shupe, Jr., *Strange Gods: The Great American Cult Scare* (Boston: Beacon, 1981), 35.
[46] Durst, *To Bigotry, No Sanction*, 101.
[47] *Divine Principle*, 520–21.

[48]"11,674 Say 'I dos' at Big Moonie Wedding" *Grand Rapids Press* (Michigan), October 14, 1982.

[49]"With Rev. Moon, Who Needs Cupid?" *Chicago Tribune*, October 31, 1988, 14.

[50]Yamamoto, *The Puppet Master*, 21–23.

[51]Bromley and Shupe, *"Moonies" in America*, 64, 71.

[52]Ibid., 72.

[53]Ibid., 113, 175.

[54]Ibid., 104–5.

[55]Ibid., 97–98.

[56]*Divine Principle*, 461, 463.

[57]Sun Myung Moon, "God's Hope for America" in *Christianity in Crisis* (Washington, D.C.: Holy Spirit Association for the Unification of World Christianity, 1974), 60.

[58]Sun Myung Moon, *New Hope: Twelve Talks*, vol. 2 (New York: The Holy Spirit Association for the Unification of World Christianity, 1984), 10.

[59]Bromley and Shupe, *"Moonies" in America*, 153–55.

[60]Ibid., 161.

[61]Ibid., 179.

[62]"*Playboy* Interview with Ted Patrick," *Playboy* (March 1979), 120.

[63]Ted Patrick, *Let Our Children Go!* (New York: E. P. Dutton, 1976), 97.

[64]Kim, *Unification Theology*, 84–85.

[65]Bromley and Shupe, *"Moonies" in America*, 180.

[66]John Whaley, "Moon's Son Reincarnated?" *Watchman Expositor* (vol. 5, no. 4, 1988), 1.

[67]"Insights from the Spirit World?" *Christianity Today* (May 13, 1988), 54.

[68]Chung Hwan Kwak, "World Missions," *Today's World* (May 1983), 24.

[69]"Serving the Needy: IRFF Projects Around the World," *Today's World* (July 1983), 26–29.

[70]Bob Jones, Letter to the Editor, *Christianity Today* (July 5, 1974), 24.

[71]Bromley and Shupe, *"Moonies" in America*, 157.

[72]Kim A. Lawton, "Unification Church Ties Haunt New Coalition," *Christianity Today* (February 5, 1988), 46–47.

[73]"The Moonies Seek a Niche in American Religion," *Christianity Today* (March 5, 1982), 44–45.

[74]Lawton, "Unification Church Ties," 46.

[75]Biermans, John T., *The Oddyssey of New Religions Today: A Case Study of the Unification Church* (Lewiston, N.Y.: Edwin Mellen, 1988), 191.

[76]Ibid., 225.

[77]"Shocking Reversal in California Court Case," *Unification News* (December 1988), 7.

CHAPTER 12

[1]Marvin H. Harper, *Gurus, Swamis, and Avataras: Spiritual Masters and Their American Disciples* (Philadelphia: Westminster, 1972), 8–9.

[2]Larry D. Shinn, *The Dark Lord: Cult Images and the Hare Krishnas in America* (Philadelphia: Westminster, 1987), 9–10.

[3]Garuda Dasa, "Sankirtana: The Perfection of Glorifying God," *Back to Godhead* 16, no. 11 (1981), 6.

[4]Satsvarupa dasa Goswami, *Planting the Seed: New York City, 1965–1966* (Los Angeles: Bhaktivedanta Book Trust, 1980), 7.

[5]Shinn, *The Dark Lord*, 35.

[6]Faye Levine, *The Strange World of the Hare Krishnas* (Greenwich, Conn.: Fawcett, 1974), 30.

[7]Shinn, *The Dark Lord*, 35–37.

[8]Satsvarupa dasa Goswami, *Prabhupada-lila* (Potomac, Md.: Gita-nagari Press, 1987), 76.

[9]Levine, *The Strange World*, 31.

[10]Goswami, *Planting the Seed*, 256–57.

[11]William J. Petersen, *Those Curious New Cults in the 80s* (New Canaan, Conn.: Keats, 1982), 108.

[12]Shinn, *The Dark Lord*, 106.

[13]"Srila Prabhupada Speaks Out on Responsibility," *Back to Godhead* 16, no. 11 (1981), 14.

[14]Shinn, *The Dark Lord*, 111–12.

15 Jack Sparks, *The Mindbenders* (Nashville: Thomas Nelson, 1979), 95–97.

16 "Brahma, Vishnu, Siva: Clearing up some Misconceptions about 'the Hindu trinity,' " *Back to Godhead* 17, no. 6 (June 1982), 27.

17 *The Krsna Consciousness Handbook: for the Year 848, Caitanya Era* (March 24, 1970–March 12, 1971), 108–9.

18 A. C. Bhaktivedanta Swami Prabhupada, *The Science of Self-Realization* (Los Angeles: Bhaktivedanta Book Trust, 1977), 126, 136.

19 Prabhupada, *The Science*, 126, 135.

20 Sparks, *The Mindbenders*, 96.

21 Shinn, *The Dark Lord*, 103.

22 Ibid., 103, 107.

23 "Reincarnation: The Soul's Secret Journey," *ATMA* 1 (1983): 6.

24 Ibid.

25 Shinn, *The Dark Lord*, 101.

26 A. C. Bhaktivedanta Swami Prabhupada, *Bhagavad-gita As It Is* (New York: Bhaktivedanta Book Trust, 1972), xxv–xxvi.

27 Ibid., xx–xxiv, 273.

28 Ibid., 270–71.

29 Shinn, *The Dark Lord*, 28.

30 Prabhupada, *Bhagavad-gita As It Is*, 14.

31 John Hubner and Lindsey Gruson, "Dial Om for Murder," *Rolling Stone* (April 9, 1987), 58.

32 Ibid., 78.

33 Shinn, *The Dark Lord*, 160.

34 Ibid., 95, 140.

35 Ibid., 86.

36 Ibid., 13–14.

37 Ibid., 133, 153.

38 Michael W. Ross, "Clinical Profiles of Hare Krishna Devotees," *American Journal of Psychiatry* 140 (April 1983): 417–18.

39 Frank Trippet, "Troubled Karma for the Krishnas," *Time* (September 1, 1986).

40 Hubner and Gruson, "Dial Om for Murder," 58.

41 Ibid.

42 Goswami, *Prabhupada-lila*, 85.

43 "A Remote Spiritual Disneyland," *Time* (September 15, 1980), 71.

44 *The Krsna Consciousness Handbook* (March 24, 1970–March 12, 1971), 108–9.

45 "Hare Krishna Movement Expands Spiritual Leadership," *Back to Godhead* (June 1982), 19.

46 "New Spanish Book A Best-Seller in Latin America," *Back to Godhead*, vol. 16, no. 11, n.d., 19.

47 "Govinda's Restaurant in Teheran: 'Down to Earth and Up to God,' " *Back to Godhead* (June 1981), 19.

48 Dasa, "Sankirtana," 7.

49 "Govinda's Restaurant," 19.

50 Shinn, *The Dark Lord*, 110.

51 Visakha-Devi Dasi, "Sailing Back to Godhead," *Back to Godhead* (June 1981), 7.

52 Ibid., 8–9.

53 Ibid., 12.

CHAPTER 13

1 Richard N. Ostling, "Slow Death for Iran's Baha'is," *Time* (February 20, 1984), 76.

2 Ibid.

3 J. E. Esslemont, *Baha'u'llah and the New Era* (Wilmette, Ill.: Baha'i Publishing Trust, 1980), 2–3.

4 Ibid., 4.

5 Ibid., 4–5.

6 William S. Hatcher and J. Douglas Martin, *The Baha'i Faith: The Emerging Global Religion* (New York: Harper & Row, 1984), 3–5.

7 William McElwee Miller, *The Baha'i Faith: Its History and Teachings* (Pasadena: William Carey Library, 1974), 14–15.

8 Esslemont, *Baha'u'llah*, 14–15, 20.

9 Ibid., 15–18.

10 Ibid., 23, 30.

11 Ibid., 31–32.

12 Ibid., 42.

13 Miller, *The Baha'i Faith*, 139.

14 Adib Taherzadeh, *The Revelation of Baha'u'llah: Baghdad, 1853–63* (Oxford: George Ronald, 1974), 59.

15 Esslemont, *Baha'u'llah*, 46–47.

16 *Baha'i Scriptures*, ed. Horace Holley (New York: Brentano's, 1923), 241, 243.

17 Baha'u'llah and Abdu'l-Baha, *Baha'i World Faith: Selected Writings of Baha'u'llah and Abdu'l-Baha* (Wilmette, Ill.: Baha'i Publishing Trust, 1943), 205.

18 Hatcher and Martin, *The Baha'i Faith*, 52–54.

19 Ibid., 59–61.

20 Esslemont, *Baha'u'llah*, 131.

21 Hatcher and Martin, *The Baha'i Faith*, 170.

22 Esslemont, *Baha'u'llah*, 93.

23 *Baha'i Prayers: A Selection of Prayers Revealed by Baha'u'llah, the Bab and Abdu'l-Baha* (Wilmette, Ill: Baha'i Publishing Trust, 1982), 4.

24 Hatcher and Martin, *The Baha'i Faith*, 157.

25 Esslemont, *Baha'u'llah*, 202.

26 Miller, *The Baha'i Faith*, 355.

27 Esslemont, *Baha'u'llah*, 234–36.

28 Miller, *The Baha'i Faith*, 356.

29 Ibid.

30 Abdu'l-Baha, *Some Answered Questions*, comp. and trans. Laura C. Barney (Wilmette, Ill.: Baha'i Publishing Trust, 1981), 215.

31 Baha'u'llah, *Gleanings from the Writings of Baha'u'llah*, 217.

32 "Basic Facts of the Baha'i Faith" (Wilmette, Ill.: Baha'i Publishing Trust, n.d.)

33 Esslemont, *Baha'u'llah*, 78–79.

34 Ibid., 82–83.

35 Ibid., 85.

36 Ibid., 86.

37 Ibid., 201.

38 Abdu'l-Baha, *The Promulgation of Universal Peace, Talks Delivered By Abdu'l-Baha During His Visit to the United States and Canada in 1912*, comp. Howard MacNutt (Wilmette: Baha'i Publishing Trust, 1922–1925), 181.

39 Esslemont, *Baha'u'llah*, 161.

40 Ibid., 161.

41 Hatcher and Martin, *The Baha'i Faith*, 90.

42 Miller, *The Baha'i Faith*, 193–94.

43 Ibid., 195–96.

44 Abdu'l-Baha, *Questions*, 30.

45 Robert H. Stockman, *The Baha'i Faith in America, 1892–1900* (Wilmette, Ill.: Baha'i Publishing Trust, 1985), 41.

46 Hatcher and Martin, *The Baha'i Faith*, 171.

47 Ibid., 202–3.

CHAPTER 14

1 "L. Ron Hubbard: The Current Scene" (Tampa: Dianetics, 1984), 1.

2 Bent Corydon and L. Ron Hubbard, Jr., *L. Ron Hubbard: Messiah or Madman?* (Secaucus, N.J.: Lyle Stuart, 1987), 11–14.

3 L. Ron Hubbard, *Mission into Time* (Los Angeles: American Saint Hill Organization, 1973), 4.

4 Hubbard, *Mission into Time*, 5–6; "What Scientology Teaches," *Christianity Today* (September 17, 1982), 33.

5 Hubbard, *Mission into Time*, 9–11.

6 "Mystery of the Vanished Ruler," *Time* (January 31, 1983), 65.

7 Harriet Whitehead, *Renunciation and Reformulation: A Study of Conversion in an American Sect* (Ithaca, N.Y.: Cornell Univ. Press, 1987), 49.

8 Hubbard, *Mission into Time*, 11–12.

9 Whitehead, *Renunciation and Reformulation*, 21.

10 Ibid., 66.

11 L. Ron Hubbard, *Dianetics: The Modern Science of Mental Health* (Los Angeles: Bridge, 1985), 10–11, 102, 113, 220.

12 Ibid., 148.

13 Omar V. Garrison, *Playing Dirty: The Secret War Against Beliefs* (Los Angeles: Ralston-Pilot, 1980), 18.

14 *Freedom* (February 1985), 12–15.

15 Hubbard, *Dianetics*, 68–69.

16 Ibid., 70, 113.

17 Ibid., 182–83, 190.

18 Ibid., 216–17.

19 Whitehead, *Renunciation and Reformulation*, 62; Hubbard, *Dianetics*, 202.

20 Hubbard, *Dianetics*, 217.

21 Hubbard, *Mission into Time*, 16.

22 Whitehead, *Renunciation and Reformulation*, 52, 69.

23 Roy Wallis, *The Road to Total Freedom: A Sociological Analysis of Scientolo-*

gy (New York: Columbia Univ. Press, 1977), 88–89, 98.

[24] L. Ron Hubbard, *Dianetics: The Evolution of a Science* (London: F. E. Bording, 1966), 14–15.

[25] Garrison, *Playing Dirty*, 23.

[26] Corydon and Hubbard, Jr., *L. Ron Hubbard*, 89–90.

[27] Whitehead, *Renunciation and Reformulation*, 194.

[28] Wallis, *The Road to Total Freedom*, 104.

[29] Ibid., 104.

[30] Hubbard, *Mission into Time*, 100.

[31] "Mystery," *Time*, 65.

[32] Wallis, *The Road to Total Freedom*, 116.

[33] "What Scientology Teaches," *Christianity Today*, 33.

[34] "Mystery," *Time*, 64; Hubbard, *Mission into Time*, 27.

[35] Hubbard, *Mission into Time*, 34.

[36] Ibid., 34–40.

[37] Garrison, *Playing Dirty*, 205.

[38] Jay Mathews, "Scientology on a Roll," *Grand Rapids Press* (Michigan), January 11, 1986.

[39] Whitehead, *Renunciation and Reformulation*, 31, 36–37.

[40] "Your Bridge to Full OT," *Source: Magazine of the Flag Land Base* (Issue 50), 7–9.

[41] L. Ron Hubbard, "Cause and Effect: Part Two," *Source: Magazine of the Flag Land Base* (Issue 50), 4.

[42] Wallis, *The Road to Total Freedom*, 87.

[43] Mathews, "Scientology on a Roll," January 11, 1986.

[44] Whitehead, *Renunciation and Reformulation*, 33.

[45] Hubbard, *Dianetics*, 444–45.

[46] Whitehead, *Renunciation and Reformulation*, 34.

[47] Price List Insert, *Source: Magazine of the Flag Land Base*, Issue 50.

[48] Joseph M. Hopkins, "Is L. Ron Hubbard Dead?," *Christianity Today* (February 18, 1983), 31.

[49] Wallis, *The Road to Total Freedom*, 131, 155.

[50] Ibid., 144–45.

[51] Corydon and Hubbard, *L. Ron Hubbard*, 116.

[52] Ibid., 119.

[53] Mathews, "Scientology on a Roll," January 11, 1986.

[54] Garrison, *Playing Dirty*, 25–27.

[55] Ibid., 34–35.

[56] Trevor Meldal-Johnsen and Patrick Lusey, *The Truth About Scientology* (New York: Grosset & Dunlap, 1980), 1, 4.

[57] Garrison, *Playing Dirty*, 44–45.

[58] Corydon and Hubbard, *L. Ron Hubbard*, 13–14.

[59] Whitehead, *Renunciation and Reformulation*, 34–35.

[60] Garrison, *Playing Dirty*, 81.

[61] Hubbard, *Dianetics*, 508–12.

[62] Meldal-Johnsen and Lusey, *The Truth About Scientology*, 19.

CHAPTER 15

[1] Irving Hexham and Karla Poewe-Hexham, "The Soul of the New Age," *Christianity Today* (September 2, 1988), 20.

[2] Diane Salvatore, "The New Victims of Cults," *Ladies' Home Journal* (August 1987), 48.

[3] Karen Hoyt, *The New Age Rage* (Old Tappan, N.J.: Fleming H. Revell, 1987), 11.

[4] Otto Friedrich, "New Age Harmonies," *Time* (December 7, 1987), 64.

[5] Hexham and Poewe-Hexham, "The Soul of the New Age," 19.

[6] Sydney E. Ahlstrom, *A Religious History of the American People* (Garden City, N.Y.: Doubleday, 1975), I, 590.

[7] Ibid., I, 591.

[8] Stephen Gottschalk, *The Emergence of Christian Science in American Religious Life* (Berkeley: Univ. of California Press, 1973), 156.

[9] Jan Karel Van Baalen, *The Chaos of Cults* (Grand Rapids: Eerdmans, 1962), 63.

[10] H. P. Blavatsky, *The Secret Doctrine* (New York, 1895), I, 27, 42–45.

[11] Constance E. Cumbey, *The Hidden Dangers of the Rainbow: The New Age*

Movement and Our Coming Age of Barbarism (Shreveport: Huntington House, 1983), 92, 95, 97.

12 Ibid., 92–99.

13 Ibid., 85.

14 Ibid., 157.

15 Ibid., 157–59.

16 Ibid., 258.

17 Texe Marrs, *Dark Secrets of the New Age: Satan's Plan for A One World Religion* (Westchester, Ill: Crossway Books, 1987), viii.

18 Marilyn Ferguson, *The Aquarian Conspiracy: Personal and Social Transformation in the 1980s* (Los Angeles: J. P. Tarcher, 1980), 23–24.

19 Donald Keys, *Earth at Omega: Passage to Planetization* (Boston: Branden Press, 1982), 88.

20 Douglas R. Groothuis, *Unmasking the New Age* (Downers Grove, Ill.: InterVarsity Press, 1986), 33.

21 Friedrich, "New Age Harmonies," 72.

22 Salvatore, "The New Victims of Cults," 46, 48, 146.

23 Thomas French, "Ramtha: Ancient Teacher or Fraud?" *St. Petersburg Times*, February 16, 1987.

24 Robert Lindsey, "Reincarnated Spirit 'Ramtha' Urges Followers to Go West," *Detroit Free Press*, December 15, 1986.

25 Marrs, *Dark Secrets*, 110.

26 Friedrich, "New Age Harmonies," 66.

27 Brooks Alexander, "Theology from the Twilight Zone," *Christianity Today* (September 18, 1987), 22.

28 Maxine P. Hondema, "Channeling the Spirits," *Co-op Times* (September 1986), 20.

29 Maxine Hondema, "Introduction" to the *Seven Steps Edition* of the *Gaelic Manuscripts* (Grand Rapids, 1983), iii.

30 Ibid., i.

31 Alfred S. Alschuler, "Recognizing Inner Teachers: Inner Voices Throughout History," *Gnosis: A Journal of Western Inner Traditions* (Fall 1987), 8–10.

32 Ibid., 10–11.

33 Cited in Alschuler, "Recognizing Inner Teachers," 10.

34 Cited in Dave Hunt and T. A. McMahon, *The Seduction of Christianity: Spiritual Discernment in the Last Days* (Eugene, Ore.: Harvest House, 1985), 69–70.

35 Shepherd Bliss, "Jean Houston: Prophet of the Possible," *Whole Life Times* (Oct./mid-Nov. 1984), 24–25; cited in Hunt and McMahon, *The Seduction of Christianity*, 76.

36 David Conway, *Magic: An Occult Primer*, 59; cited in Hunt and McMahon, *The Seduction of Christianity*, 142.

37 Adelaide Bry, *Directing the Movies of Your Mind: Visualization for Health and Insight* (New York: Harper & Row, 1978), 32–33.

38 Ibid., 40–41, 57.

39 Advertisement, *Meditation* ('87 Winter '88), 13.

40 Cited in Mark Albrecht, *Reincarnation: A Christian Appraisal* (Downers Grove, Ill.: InterVarsity Press, 1982), 54.

41 Friedrich, "New Age Harmonies," 64.

42 Uma Silbey, "Meditation and Quartz Crystals," *Meditation* ('87 Winter '88), 39.

43 Ibid., 39–42.

44 Ibid., 42.

45 Friedrich, "New Age Harmonies," 64.

46 Shirley MacLaine, *Out on a Limb* (New York: Bantam Books, 1983), 332–33.

47 Hondema, "Channeling the Spirits," 20.

48 Brooks Alexander, "Entities in Print," *Christianity Today* (September 18, 1987), 26.

49 Robert Mueller, *The New Genesis: Shaping A Global Spirituality* (New York: Image Books, 1984), 186.

50 Martha Smilgis, "A New Age Dawning," *Time* (August 31, 1987), 63.

51 Lola Davis, *Toward A World Religion for the New Age* (Farmingdale, N.Y.: Coleman, 1983), 180.

52 Alice Bailey, *The Externalization of the Hierarchy* (New York: Lucis, 1957), passim; *USA Today*, (January 12, 1987).

53 Interview with Benjamin Creme, "'New Age' Leader Contends Christ Resides in London," *Grand Rapids Press* (Michigan), August 18, 1986.

[54] Ibid.

[55] Barbara Marx Hubbard, *The Evolutionary Journey* (San Francisco: Evolutionary Press, 1982), 157.

[56] Groothuis, *Unmasking the New Age*, 18.

[57] Jonathan Stone, *SPC Journal* (July 1977.)

[58] Cited in Francis Adeney, "Educators Look East," *Spiritual Counterfeits Journal* (Winter 1981), 28.

[59] Alexander, "Theology from the Twilight Zone," 25.

[60] Cindy Saul, "Expect A Miracle," *PhenomeNEWS* (April 1988), 2.

[61] Richard Smoley, "Pitfalls of A Course in Miracles," *Gnosis: A Journal of the Western Inner Traditions* (Fall 1987), 17.

[62] Ibid.

[63] Levi, *Aquarian Gospel of Jesus* (Los Angeles: DeVorss, 1970), 76.

[64] Miriam Starhawk, *Yoga Journal* (May–June 1986), 59.

[65] Miriam Starhawk, *The Spiral Dance* (San Francisco: Harper & Row, 1979), 9.

[66] Kathleen Alexander-Berghorn, "Isis: the Goddess as Healer," *Woman of Power* (Winter 1987), 20.

[67] Groothuis, *Unmasking the New Age*, 137.

[68] Michael Harner, *The Way of the Shaman* (San Francisco: Harper & Row, 1980), 20.

[69] "She's A Pathfinder in Post-feminist Era," *Grand Rapids Press* (Michigan), February 15, 1988.

[70] "She's A Pathfinder."

[71] Marrs, *Dark Secrets*, 74, 77, 79.

[72] David Spangler, *Reflections of the Christ* (Morayshire, Scotland: Findhorn Press, 1977), 40–45.

[73] Howard J. Van Til, *The Fourth Day: What the Bible and the Heavens Are Telling Us About the Creation* (Grand Rapids: Eerdmans, 1986), 36.

[74] Philip Schaff, *History of the Christian Church*, vol. VI, *The Middle Ages* (Grand Rapids: Eerdmans, 1979), 616.

[75] Clyde L. Manschreck, *Melanchthon: The Quiet Reformer* (Nashville: Abingdon, 1958), 104.

[76] John Ankerberg and John Weldon, *The Facts on Astrology* (Eugene, Ore.: Harvest House, 1988), 8–9.

[77] *Time* (May 16, 1988), 4.

[78] Donald T. Regan, *For the Record: From Wall Street to Washington* (New York: Harcourt, Brace, Jovanovich, 1988), 3, 74.

[79] Laurence Zuckerman, "The First Lady's Astrologer," *Time* (May 16, 1988), 41.

[80] Joyce Wadler et al., "The President's Astrologers," *People* (May 23, 1988), 108.

[81] Ibid.

[82] Mary Orser and Rick and Glory Brightfield, *Instant Astrology* (San Diego: ACS Publications, 1984), 10.

[83] Joanne Wickenburg and Virginia Meyer, *The Spiral of Life: Unlocking Your Potential with Astrology* (Reno: CRCS Publications, 1987), 91.

[84] Sasha Fenton, *Moon Signs: Discover the Hidden Power of Your Emotions* (Wellingborough, Northamptonshire: The Aquarian Press, 1987), 67–68.

[85] Steven Forrest, *The Changing Sky: A Practical Guide to the New Predictive Astrology* (New York: Bantam Books, 1986), 12.

[86] Forrest, *The Changing Sky*, 12–13.

[87] Mary E. Coleman, *Astro-Focus Your Future* (Wellingborough, Northamptonshire: The Aquarian Press, 1987), 9.

[88] Groothuis, *Unmasking the New Age*, 66.

[89] Vasant Lad, "Ayurveda: Life Knowledge," *The Harmonist Magazine* (Summer 1986), 21, 24.

[90] Hugh McCann, "Alternative Medicine Sheds Image of Quackery," *The Detroit News*, June 25, 1987.

[91] Cited in Michael Dolan, "The World is in the Mind," *The Harmonist Magazine* (Summer 1986), 37–38.

[92] Groothuis, *Unmasking the New Age*, 99.

93 Richard Watring, "New Age Training in Business: Mind Control in Upper Management?" *Eternity* (February 1988), 30.

94 Ibid.

95 Robert Burrows, "Corporate Management Cautioned on New Age," *Eternity* (February 1988), 33.

96 Hunt and McMahon, *The Seduction of Christianity*, 142.

97 Steve Rabey, "Karma for Cash: A 'New Age' for Workers?" *Christianity Today* (June 17, 1988), 71, 74.

98 Joanne Crandall, *Self-Transformation Through Music* (Wheaton: Theosophical Publishing House, 1986), 7.

99 John Topp, "New Age Music: Yuppie Musak, or Wolf in Sheep's Clothes?," unpublished paper, Calvin College (January 27, 1989), 3.

100 Alexander, "Theology from the Twilight Zone," 22.

101 Cited in Marrs, *Dark Secrets of the New Age*, 32.

102 John Bethune, "New Age: Still Glowing," *Publishers Weekly* (December 16, 1988), 22.

103 Friedrich, "New Age Harmonies," 72.

104 Ibid., 66.

105 Cited in Hunt and McMahon, *The Seduction of Christianity*, 24–25.

106 Ibid., 80.

107 Rodney R. Romney, *Journey to Inner Space: Finding God-in-Us* (Nashville: Abingdon, 1980), 26, 29, 31; cited in Hunt and McMahon, *The Seduction of Christianity*, 70–71.

108 Sanford, *The Healing Gifts of the Spirit* (New York: J. B. Lippincott, 1966), 165.

109 Morton T. Kelsey, *The Christian and the Supernatural* (Minneapolis: Augsburg, 1976), 93, 133.

110 Hunt and McMahon, *The Seduction of Christianity*, 145.

APPENDIX A

1 Ronald Enroth, *Youth, Brainwashing, and the Extremist Cults* (Grand Rapids: Zondervan, 1977), 56–64.

2 Undated Foundation flyer.

3 Tony and Susan Alamo, "Signs of the Times" (Alma, Ark.: Tony and Susan Alamo Foundation, 1984), 3.

4 Tony Alamo, undated publicity letter.

5 Alamo, "Signs of the Times," 7.

6 William J. Petersen, *Those Curious New Cults in the 80s* (New Canaan, Conn.: Keats, 1982), 44–45.

7 Case # 2319-P-1 and Case # 3124-P-1 in Lytle W. Robinson, *Edgar Cayce's Story of the Origin and Destiny of Man* (New York: Coward, McCann and Geoghegan, 1972), 183.

8 Josh McDowell and Don Stewart, *Handbook of Today's Religions* (San Bernadino, Calif.: Campus Crusade for Christ, 1983), 169.

9 Peterson, *Those Curious New Cults*, 45.

10 McDowell and Stewart, *Handbook of Today's Religions*, 169.

11 Ibid., 170.

12 Available now in video through Word Publishing in Waco, Tex.

13 Walter Martin, *The New Cults* (Santa Ana, Calif.: Vision House, 1980), 269–70.

14 "Vain Glory," video distributed by Word, Inc.

15 John Robert Stevens, *Beyond Passover* (Living Word, 1977), 137.

16 John Robert Stevens, *Plumb Perfect* (Living Word, Jan. 16, 1977), 13.

17 John Robert Stevens, *The ManChild* (Living Word, 1972), 6–7.

18 Martin, *The New Cults*, 269.

19 "Vain Glory."

20 Peterson, *Those Curious New Cults*, 282–83.

21 Elizabeth Clare Prophet, *The Lost Years of Jesus* (Malibu, Calif.: Summit Univ. Press, 1984), passim.

22 Ibid.; Mark and Elizabeth Clare Prophet, *The Science of the Spoken Word* (Colorado Springs: Summit Univ. Press, 1974), 73.

23 *Tenets of Church Universal and Triumphant* (n.p.: Church Universal and Triumphant, 1975), 1.

24 Dave Hunt, *The Cult Explosion* (Irvine, Calif.: Harvest House, 1980), 153.

25 Mark and Elizabeth Prophet, *Climb the Highest Mountain* (Los Angeles: Summit Lighthouse, 1975), 332.

26 Ibid., 71.

27 Robert Burrows, "Church Universal and Triumphant: The Summit Lighthouse," *SCP Journal* (Winter 1984), 65.

28 Burrows, "Church Universal and Triumphant," 63.

29 A. James and Marcia R. Rudin, *Prison or Paradise? The New Religious Cults* (Philadelphia: Fortress, 1980), 62.

30 Petersen, *Those Curious New Cults*, 147–48.

31 Kenneth Boa, *Cults, World Religions, and You* (Wheaton: Scripture Press, 1979), 188–89.

32 Bob Larson, *Larson's Book of Cults* (Wheaton: Tyndale, 1982), 210.

33 J. Gordon Melton, *Encyclopedic Handbook of Cults in America* (New York: Garland, 1986), 144.

34 Mark Albrecht, Brooks Alexander, and Woodrow Nichols, "Eckankar," in Ronald Enroth et al., *A Guide to Cults and New Religions* (Downers Grove, Ill.: InterVarsity Press, 1983), 63–64.

35 Petersen, *Those Curious Cults*, 288–89.

36 Melton, *Encyclopedic Handbook of Cults*, 147.

37 Paul Twitchell, *Eckankar—The Key to Secret Worlds* (Menlo Park, Calif.: Illuminated Way Press, 1969), 72–73.

38 Albrecht et al., "Eckankar," 66–67.

39 Twitchell, *Eckankar*, 42.

40 Robert S. Ellwood, Jr., *Alternative Altars: Unconventional and Eastern Spirituality in America* (Chicago: Univ. of Chicago Press, 1979), 165.

41 Flo Conway and Jim Siegelman, *Snapping: America's Epidemic of Sudden Personality Change* (New York: J. B. Lippincott, 1978), 25–26.

42 John Weldon, "est" in Ronald Enroth, et al., *A Guide to Cults and New Religions* (Downers Grove: InterVarsity Press, 1983), 76.

43 Larson, *Larson's Book of Cults*, 276–77.

44 Weldon, "est," 82.

45 Bry, *est: 60 Hours That Transform Your Life* (New York: Harper & Row, 1976), 2, 8, 31.

46 Ibid., 153–54.

47 Cited in J. Yutaka Amano, "Bad for Business," *Eternity* (March 1986), 55–56.

48 Amano, "Bad for Business," 57.

49 Robert S. Ellwood, Jr., *Alternative Altars: Unconventional and Eastern Spirituality in America* (Chicago: Univ. of Chicago Press, 1979), 42.

50 Martin, *The New Cults*, 208–9.

51 Ibid., 203–5.

52 Enroth, *Youth, Brainwashing, and the Extremist Cults*, 82–83.

53 Carroll Stoner and Jo Anne Parke, *All God's Children: The Cult Experience— Salvation or Slavery* (New York: Penguin Books, 1977), 175, 178.

54 Conway and Siegelman, *Snapping*, 157.

55 Larson, *Larson's Book of Cults*, 374.

56 Louis Stewart, *Life Forces: A Contemporary Guide to the Cult and Occult* (New York: Andrews and McMeel, 1980), 283.

57 Sparks, *The Mindbenders*, 260–61.

58 Ibid., 264–65.

59 Stewart, *Life Forces*, 282.

60 Sparks, *The Mindbenders*, 269–70.

61 Mark Lane, *The Strongest Poison* (New York: Hawthorn, 1980), 50.

62 Larson, *Larson's Book of Cults*, 191.

63 Bhagwan Shree Rajneesh, *The Book: An Introduction to the Teachings of Bhagwan Shree Rajneesh* (Rajneeshpuram, Ore.: Rajneesh Foundation, 1984), 576.

64 Julie Sterling, "The Big Bhag's Commune: Enlightened View of Spending," *Chicago Tribune*, May 1, 1983.

65 "Rajneesh Medical Corporation" (Rajneeshpuram, Oregon, 1984), 3, 13.

66 Sterling, "The Big Bhag's Commune," May 1, 1983.

67 Eckart Floether with Eric Pement, "Bhagwan Shree Rajneesh," in Ronald Enroth, et al., *A Guide to Cults and New Religions* (Downers Grove, Ill.: InterVarsity Press, 1983), 48.

[68] Floether, "Bhagwan Shree Rajneesh," 49–50.

[69] Sterling, "The Big Bhag's Commune," May 1, 1983.

[70] "Murder Manuals, Poison Lab Found At Home of Rajneesh's Fugitive Aide," *Grand Rapids Press* (Michigan), September 18, 1985; "Customs Agents Nab Guru Trying to Flee Country," *Grand Rapids Press* (Michigan), October 28, 1985.

[71] Susan Palmer, "Community and Commitment in the Rajneesh Foundation," *Update* (December 1986), 14.

[72] "Butt Out, Buddha!," *Time* (January 16, 1989), 78.

[73] Joseph Smith, *History of the Church*, vol. 6, 408–9.

[74] M. Kurt Goedelman, "Sizing up the Saints," *The Quarterly Journal: Watchman Fellowship*, (January–March, 1988), 5–7.

[75] Ibid., 6.

[76] William Robbins, "Reorganized Church of Latter Day Saints Battles New Split," *St. Petersburg Times*, January 31, 1987.

[77] Larson, *Larson's Book of Cults*, 306–7, 310.

[78] Max Heindel, *The Rosicrucian Philosophy in Questions and Answers*, 54.

[79] Ibid., 202.

[80] Max Heindel, *The Rosicrucian Cosmo-Conception or Mystic Christianity*, (n.p.: Conkey, 1929), 519, 534.

[81] Walter R. Martin, *The Kingdom of the Cults* (Minneapolis: Bethany House, 1985), 508

[82] Katherine Kam, "Ritual Killings Have Satanic Overtones," *Christianity Today* (September 2, 1988), 52.

[83] Melton, *Encyclopedic Handbook of Cults*, 78.

[84] William Sims Bainbridge, *Satan's Power: A Deviant Psychotherapy Cult* (Berkeley: Univ. of California Press, 1978), 2, 119–24.

[85] Anton LaVey, *The Satanic Bible* (New York: Avon, 1969), 25.

[86] Melton, *Encyclopedic Handbook of Cults*, 78–79.

[87] Thomas Wedge, *The Satan Hunter* (Canton, Ohio: Daring, 1988), 117.

[88] Jose Silva, *The Silva Mind Control Method for Business Managers* (New York: Prentice-Hall, 1983), 17–19.

[89] Martin, *The New Cults*, 237–38.

[90] Silva, *The Silva Mind Control Method for Business Managers*, 7–8.

[91] Jose Silva and Philip Miele, *The Silva Mind Control Method* (New York: Simon and Schuster, 1977), 84.

[92] Harry McKnight, *Silva Mind Control: Key to Inner Kingdoms through Psychorientology* (Laredo, Tex.: Institute of Psychorientology, 1972), 77–78.

[93] Silva, *The Silva Mind Control Method for Business Managers*, 100.

[94] J. K. Van Baalen, *The Chaos of Cults: A Study in Present-Day Isms* (Grand Rapids: Eerdmans, 1962), 177–80.

[95] Cyriel O. Sigstedt, *The Swedenborg Epic: The Life and Works of Emmanuel Swedenborg* (New York: Bookman, 1952), 198, 211.

[96] Van Baalen, *The Chaos of Cults*, 180–81.

[97] Larson, *Larson's Book of Cults*, 397.

[98] Gordon R. Lewis, *What Everyone Should Know About Transcendental Meditation* (Glendale, Calif.: Regal, 1975), 3.

[99] Harold Bloomfield, Michael Cain, and Dennis Jaffe, *TM: Discovering Inner Energy and Overcoming Stress* (New York: Delacorte Press, 1975), 32–34.

[100] Robert Oates, Jr. *Celebrating the Dawn: Maharishi Mahesh Yogi and the TM Technique* (New York: G. P. Putnam's Sons, 1976), 16–18.

[101] Cited in Sparks, *The Mindbenders*, 30–32.

[102] Jack Forem, *Transcendental Meditation: Maharishi Mahesh Yogi and the Science of Creative Intelligence* (New York: E. P. Dutton, 1974), 35–36.

[103] Vinson Synan, *The Holiness-Pentecostal Movement in the United States* (Grand Rapids: Eerdmans, 1971), 154.

[104] John T. Nichol, *The Pentecostals* (Plainfield, N.J.: Logos, 1966), 118–19.

[105] Donald C. Palmer, "Jesus Only: The United Pentecostal Church," in David J. Hesselgrave, ed., *Dynamic Religious Movements* (Grand Rapids: Baker, 1978), 228–29.

[106] John T. Nichol, *Pentecostalism* (New York: Harper & Row, 1966), 90.

[107] Constant H. Jacquet, Jr., *Yearbook of American and Canadian Churches, 1986* (Nashville: Abingdon, 1986), 112.

[108] B. Walker, *Tantrism* (Wellingborough, Northamptonshire: Aquarian Press, 1982), 37.

[109] Georg Feuerstein and Jeanine Miller, *Yoga and Beyond: Essays in Indian Philosophy* (New York: Schocken Books, 1972), xii.

[110] Stewart, *Life Forces*, 4.

[111] Feuerstein and Miller, *Yoga and Beyond*, 33.

[112] Stewart, *Life Forces*, 15.

[113] Irving Hexham, "Yoga, UFOs, and Cult Membership," *Update* (September 1986), 6.

[114] Alan W. Watts, *The Spirit of Zen: A Way of Life, Word and Art in the Far East* (New York: Grove Press, 1958), 18.

[115] Larson, *Larson's Book of Cults*, 92.

[116] Daisetz Teitaro Suzuki, *The Awakening of Zen* (Boulder, Colo.: Prajna Press, 1980), 16–17.

[117] Watts, *The Spirit of Zen*, 19.

[118] Joseph Gaer, *What the Great Religions Believe* (New York: New American Library, 1963), 178.

[119] Martin, *Kingdom of the Cults*, 261.

APPENDIX B

[1] "A Quick Look at Seventh-day Adventists."

[2] "Jehovah's Witnesses in the Twentieth Century," 13.

[3] Mary Baker Eddy, *Science and Health*, 497.

[4] "Twenty Questions About Unity" (Lee's Summit, Mo.: Association of Unity Churches).

[5] "The Unification Church: People of the Quest" (New York: Unification Church).

[6] *The Krsna Consciousness Handbook: For the Year 484, Caitanya Era* (March 24, 1970–March 12, 1971), 108–9.

[7] "Basic Facts of the Baha'i Faith" (Wilmette, Ill.: Baha'i Publishing Trust).

APPENDIX C

[1] Philip Schaff, *Nicene and Post-Nicene Christianity*, vol. 3 in *History of the Christian Church* (Grand Rapids: Eerdmans, 1979), 690–92.

[2] Taken from Tim Dowley, ed., *Eerdman's Handbook to the History of Christianity* (Grand Rapids: Eerdmans, 1977), 175.

[3] John H. Gerstner, *The Theology of the Cults* (Grand Rapids: Baker, 1960), 124.

[4] Leon Morris, "Atonement," in J. D. Douglas, ed., *The New International Dictionary of the Christian Church* (Grand Rapids: Zondervan, 1978), 83–84.

BIBLIOGRAPHY

General Works

Adair, James R. and Miller, Ted. *We Found Our Way Out*. Grand Rapids: Baker, 1964.

Atkins, G. *Modern Religious Cults and Movements*. New York: Fleming H. Revell, 1923.

Bach, Marcus. *Major Religions of the World*. New York: Abingdon, 1959.

————. *Strangers at the Door*. Nashville: Abingdon, 1971.

————. *They Have Found a Faith*. New York: Bobbs-Merrill, 1946.

Biermans, John T. *The Odyssey of New Religions Today: A Case Study of the Unification Church*. Lewiston, N.Y.: Edwin Mellen, 1988.

Bjornstad, James. *Counterfeits at Your Door*. Glendale, Calif.: Regal Books, 1979.

Boa, Kenneth. *Cults, World Religions, and You*. Wheaton: Victor Books, 1979.

Braden, Charles. *These Also Believe*. New York: Macmillan, 1951.

Breese, Dave. *Know the Marks of Cults*. Wheaton: Victor Books, 1975.

Bromley, David G. and Shupe, Anson D., Jr. *Strange Gods: The Great American Cult Scare*. Boston: Beacon, 1981.

Brown, Harold O. J. *Heresies: The Image of Christ in the Mirror of Heresy and Orthodoxy from the Apostles to the Present*. New York: Doubleday, l985.

Burrell, Maurice C. and Wright, J. Stafford. *Today's Sects*. Grand Rapids: Baker, 1983.

Burstein, Abraham. *Religion, Cults, and the Law*. Dobbs Ferry, N.Y.: Oceana Publications, 1980.

"Butt Out, Buddha!" *Time* (January 16, 1989): 78.

Caplovitz, David and Sherrow, Fred. *Religious Drop-outs*. Beverly Hills: SAGE Publications, 1977.

Cinnamon, Kenneth and Farson, Dave. *Cults and Cons*. Chicago: Nelson-Hall, 1979. 00B1 Clark, Elmer T. *The Small Sects in America*. Nashville: Abingdon, 1965.

Clements, R. D. *God and the Gurus*. Downers Grove, Ill.: InterVarsity Press, 1975.

Cohen, Daniel. *The New Believers*. New York: M. Evans, 1975.

Conway, Flo and Siegelman, Jim. *Snapping: America's Epidemic of Sudden Personality Change*. Philadelphia: J. B. Lippincott, 1978.

Davies, Horton. *The Challenge of the Sects*. Philadelphia: Westminster, 1961.

Ellwood, Robert S., Jr. *Alternative Altars: Unconventional and Eastern Spirituality in America*. Chicago: University of Chicago Press, 1979.

Enroth, Ronald. *The Lure of the Cults*. Chappaqua, N.Y.: Christian Herald Books, 1979.

————. *Youth, Brainwashing and the Extremist Cults*. Grand Rapids: Zondervan, 1977.

Enroth, Ronald and Melton, J. Gordon. *Why Cults Succeed Where the Church Fails*. Elgin, Ill.: Brethren Press, 1985.

Enroth, Ronald Enroth, et al. *A Guide to Cults and New Religions*. Downers Grove, Ill.: InterVarsity Press, 1983.

Evans, Chris. *The Cults of Unreason*. New York: Dell, 1973.

Ferguson, Charles. *New Books of Revelation*. Garden City, N.Y.: Doubleday, 1929.

Ferm, Vergilius, ed. *Religion in the Twentieth Century.* New York: Philosophical Library, 1948.

Fichter, Joseph H. ed. *Alternatives to American Mainline Churches.* Barrytown, N.Y.: Unification Theological Seminary, 1983.

Forrest, Alistair and Sanderson, Peter. *Cults and the Occult Today.* London: Marshalls, 1982.

Gerstner, John H. *The Theology of the Major Sects.* Grand Rapids: Baker, 1960.

Glock, Charles Y. and Bellah, Robert N., eds. *The New Religious Consciousness.* Los Angeles: University of California Press, 1976.

Greenfield, Robert. *Spiritual Supermarket.* New York: Saturday Review, 1975.

Gruss, Edmond C. *Cults and the Occult.* Grand Rapids: Baker, 1982.

Guinness, Os. *The East: No Exit.* Downers Grove, Ill.: InterVarsity Press, 1974.

Hefley, James C. *The Youth Nappers.* Wheaton: Victor Books, 1977.

Hesselgrave, David J. *Dynamic Religious Movement: Case Studies of Rapidly Growing Religious Movements Around the World.* Grand Rapids: Baker, 1978.

Hexham, Irving and Poewe, Karla. *Understanding Cults and New Religions.* Grand Rapids: Eerdmans, 1986.

Hoekema, Anthony A. *The Four Major Cults.* Grand Rapids: Eerdmans, 1963.

Hudson, Winthrop. *Religion in America: An Historical Account of the Development of American Religious Life.* New York: Scribners, 1973.

Hultquist, Lee. *They Followed the Piper.* Plainfield, N.J.: Logos, 1977.

Hunt, Dave. *The Cult Explosion: An Expose of Today's Cults and Why They Prosper.* Irvine, Calif.: Harvest House, 1978.

Igleheart, Glenn A. *Church Members and Nontraditional Religious Groups.* Nashville: Broadman, 1985.

Lane, Mark. *The Strongest Poison* New York: Hawthorn Books, 1980.

Larson, Bob. *Larson's Book of Cults.* Wheaton: Tyndale House, 1982.

Lewis, Gordon R. *Confronting the Cults.* Grand Rapids: Baker, 1966.

Loymeyer, Ernst. *Lord of the Temple: A Study of Relations Between Cult and Gospel.* Geneva, Ala.: Allenson-Brekenridge, 1961.

McBeth, L. *Strange New Religions.* Nashville: Broadman, 1977.

McDowell, Josh and Stewart, Don. *Understanding the Cults.* San Bernardina, Calif.: Campus Crusade for Christ, 1982.

Martin, Walter. *The Kingdom of the Cults.* Minneapolis: Bethany, 1985.

————. *The New Cults.* Santa Anna, Calif.: Vision House, 1980.

————. *The Rise of the Cults.* Santa Ana, Calif.: Vision House, 1980.

Marty, Martin. *A Nation of Behavers.* Chicago: University of Chicago Press, 1976.

Mathison, Richard R. *Faiths, Cults and Sects of America.* Indianapolis: Bobbs-Merrill, 1960.

Mayer, F. E. *The Religious Bodies of America.* St. Louis: Concordia, 1956.

Mead, Frank S. *Handbook of Denominations in the United States.* 8th ed. Nashville: Abingdon, 1985.

Means, Pat. *The Mystical Maze.* San Bernadino, Calif.: Campus Crusade for Christ, 1976.

Melton, J. Gordon. *Encyclopedia of American Religions.* Wilmington, N. C.: McGrath, 1978.

Needleman, Jacob. *The New Religions.* New York: E. P. Dutton, 1977.

Neve, J. L. *Churches and Sects in Christendom.* Minneapolis: Augsburg, 1952.

Passantino, Robert and Gretchen. *Answers to the Cultists at Your Door.* Eugene, Ore.: Harvest House, 1981.

Petersen, William J. *Those Curious New Cults in the 80s.* New Canaan, Conn.: Keats, 1982.

Quebedeaux, Richard. *By What Authority: The Rise of Personality Cults in American Christianity.* San Francisco: Harper & Row, 1982.

Robbins, Thomas and Anthony, Dick, eds. *In Gods We Trust: New Patterns of Religious Pluralism in America.* New Brunswick, N.J.: Transaction Books, 1981.

Robertson, Irvine. *What the Cults Believe.* Chicago: Moody, 1983.

Rhodes, A. B., ed. *The Church Faces the Isms.* New York: Abingdon, 1958.

Rosten, Leo, ed. *Religions in America.* New York: Simon and Schuster, 1962.

Rudin, James and Marcia. *Prison or Paradise: The New Religious Cults.* Philadelphia: Fortress, 1980

Sanders, J. Oswald. *Cults and Isms.* Grand Rapids: Zondervan, 1962.

"Shocking Reversal in California Court Case." *Unification News* (December 1988): 7.

Sire, James W. *Scripture Twisting.* Downers Grove, Ill.: InterVarsity Press, 1980.

Sparks, Jack. *The Mindbenders: A Look at Current Cults.* Nashville: Thomas Nelson, 1979.

Spittler, Russell P. *Cults and Isms: Twenty Alternates to Evangelical Christianity.* Grand Rapids: Baker, 1962.

Stoner, Carroll and Parke, Jo Anne. *All Gods Children: The Cult Experience–Salvation or Slavery?* Radnor, Pa.: Chilton Book Company, 1977.

Thielmann, Bonnie. *The Broken God.* Elgin, Ill.: David C. Cook, 1979.

Ungerleider, J. Thomas. *The New Religions: Insights into the Cult Phenomenon.* New York: Merck, Sharp and Dohme, 1979.

Van Baalen, Jan Karel. *The Chaos of Cults: A Study in Present-Day Isms.* Grand Rapids: Eerdmans, 1962.

Wedge, Thomas. *The Satan Hunter.* Canton, Ohio: Daring Books, 1988.

Whalen, William J. *Minority Religions in America.* Staten Island, N.Y.: Alba House, 1981.

Wuthnow, Robert. *Experimentation in American Religion: The New Mysticisms and Their Implications for the Churches.* Berkeley: University of California Press, 1978.

Wyrick, Herbert M. *Seven Religious Isms.* Grand Rapids: Zondervan, 1940.

Zaretsky, Irving and Leone, Mark P., eds. *Religious Movements in Contemporary America.* Princeton: Princeton University Press, 1974.

Mormonism

Ahmanson, John. *Secret History: A Translation of Vor Tids Muhamed.* Trans. by Gleason L. Archer. Chicago: Moody, 1984

Anderson, Nels. *Desert Saints—The Mormon Frontier in Utah.* Chicago: University of Chicago Press, 1966.

Andrus, Hyrum L. *Doctrines of the Kingdom.* Salt Lake City: Bookcraft, 1973.

————. *God, Man, and the Universe.* Salt Lake City: Bookcraft, 1968.

————. *Joseph Smith, the Man and the Seer.* Salt Lake City: Deseret News Press, 1965.

Arrington, Leonard J. *Brigham Young: American Moses.* New York: Alfred A. Knopf, 1985.

Bailey, Jack Stephan. *Inside A Mormon Mission.* Salt Lake City: Hawkes Publishing Company, 1976.

Britsch, R. Lanier. "Mormon Missions: An Introduction to the Latter-day Saints Missionary System." *Occasional Bulletin* (January 1979), 22–27.

Brodie, Fawn M. *No Man Knows My History: The Life of Joseph Smith, the Mormon Prophet.* New York: Alfred A. Knopf, 1945.

Bushman, Richard L. *Joseph Smith and the Beginnings of Mormonism.* Urbana: University of Illinois Press, 1984.

Cannon, Frank J. *Brigham Young and His Mormon Empire.* New York: Fleming H. Revell, 1913.

Clark, James R. *The Story of the Pearl of Great Price.* Salt Lake City: Bookcraft, 1962.

Cowdrey, Wayne L., Davis, Howard A. and Scales, Donald R. *Who Really Wrote the Book of Mormon?* Santa Anna, Calif.: Vision House, 1977.

Foster, Lawrence. *Religion and Sexuality: The Shakers, the Mormons, and the Oneida Community.* Chicago: University of Illinois Press, 1984.

Geer, Thelma. *Mormonism, Mamma, and Me.* Chicago: Moody Press, 1985.

Gibbons, Francis M. *Joseph Smith: Martyr, Prophet of God.* Salt Lake City: Deseret Book Company, 1977.

Gibbs, Josiah F. *The Mountain Meadows Massacre.* Salt Lake City: Salt Lake Tribune, 1910.

Gottlieb, Robert and Wiley, Peter. *America's Saints: The Rise of Mormon Power.* New York: Harcourt Brace Javanovich, 1986.

Gutman, John. "Jerald and Sandra Tanner: An Unpopular 'Mission.'" *The Salt Lake Tribune,* January 27, 1985.

Hansen, Klaus J. *Mormonism and the American Experience.* Chicago: University of Chicago Press, 1981.

————. *Quest for Empire: The Political Kingdom of God and the Council of Fifty in Mormon History.* Lansing: Michigan State University Press, 1967

Hesselgrave, David J., ed., *Dynamic Religious Movements.* Grand Rapids: Baker, 1978.

Hill, Donna. *Joseph Smith: The First Mormon.* Garden City, N.Y.: Doubleday, 1977.

Hinckley, Gordon B. *Truth Restored—A Short History of the Church of Jesus Christ of Latter Day Saints.* Salt Lake City: Deseret News Press, 1969.

Hirshon, Stanley P. *The Lion of the Lord: A Biography of Brigham Young.* New York: Alfred A. Knopf, 1969.

Hougey, Hal. *Archaeology and the Book of Mormon.* Concord, Calif.: Pacific Publishing, 1976.

Houston, Jack. "The Jerald Tanners vs. Mormonism." *Power for Living.* June 14, 1970.

Howe, E.D. *Mormonism Unveiled.* Painsville, Ohio: E. D. Howe, 1834.

Hunter, Milton R. *The Gospel Through the Ages.* Salt Lake City: Deseret, 1958.

Journal of Discourses, by Brigham Young, President of the Church of Jesus Christ of Latter-day Saints, His Two Counsellors, the Twelve Apostles, and Others. 26 vols. Liverpool, 1854–1886.

Lee, Hector. *The Three Nephites: The Substance and Significance of the Legend in Folklore.* Albuquerque, N. M.: University of New Mexico Press, 1949.

Lee, John Doyle. *A Mormon Chronicle.* San Marino: Huntington Library, 1955.

Linn, William A. *The Story of Mormons.* New York: Macmillan, 1902.

McConkie, Bruce R. *Mormon Doctrine.* Salt Lake City: Bookcraft, 1966.

McGavin, E. Cicil. *Mormonism and Masonry.* Salt Lake City: Bookcraft, 1956.

Thomas McGowan. "Mormon Millennialism," in M. Darrol Bryant and Donald W. Dayton, eds. *The Coming Kingdom: Essays in American Millennialism and Eschatology.* Barrytown, N.Y.: International Religious Foundation, 1983.

Newell, Linda King and Avery, Valeen Tippetts. *Mormon Enigma: Emma Hale Smith, Prophet's Wife, "Elect Lady," Polygamy's Foe, 1804–1879.* Garden City, N.Y., 1984.

Nibley, Hugh. *An Approach to the Book of Mormon.* Salt Lake City: Deseret News Press, 1957.

————. *The Myth Makers.* Salt Lake City: Bookcraft, 1961.

O'Dea, Thomas F. *The Mormons.* Chicago: University of Chicago Press, 1957.

Olson, Della. *A Woman of Her Times.* Minneapolis: Free Church Press, 1977.

Richards, LeGrand. *A Marvelous Work and A Wonder.* Salt Lake City: Deseret Book Company, 1963.

Roberts, Brigham H. *A Comprehensive History of the Church of Jesus Christ of Latter-day Saints.* 6 vols. Salt Lake City, 1930.

Scott, Latayne Colvett. *The Mormon Mirage: A Former Mormon Tells Why She Left the Church.* Grand Rapids: Zondervan, 1979.

Shipps, Jan. *Mormonism: The Story of a New Religious Tradition.* Urbana: University of Illinois Press, 1985.

Smith, Joseph, Jr. *Book of Mormon.* Church of Jesus Christ of Latter-day Saints, first published in Palmyra, N.Y., 1830.

————. *The Doctrine and Covenants of the Church of Jesus Christ of Latter-Day Saints.* Church of Jesus Christ of Latter-day Saints, first published in Kirkland, Ohio, 1935.

————. *History of the Church of Jesus Christ of Latter-day Saints.* 6 vols. Salt Lake City: Deseret News, 1902-1912.

————. *Inspired Version of the Holy Scriptures.* Independence, Mo.: Reorganized Church of Jesus Christ of Latter Day Saints, 1965.

————. *Pearl of Great Price.* Church of Jesus Christ of Latter-day Saints, first published in Liverpool, 1851.

Smith, Joseph Fielding. *Doctrines of Salvation.* 3 vols. Salt Lake City: Bookcraft, 1954-1956.

————. *Essentials in Church History.* Salt Lake City: Deseret News Press, 1942.

————. *Teachings of the Prophet Joseph Smith.* Salt Lake City: Deseret News Press, 1949.

————. *The Way to Perfection.* Salt Lake City: Genealogical Society of Utah, 1931.

Smith, Joseph Fielding, Jr. *Religious Truths Defined.* Salt Lake City: Bookcraft, 1959.

Smith, Lucy Mack. *Biographical Sketches of Joseph Smith the Prophet and His Progenitors for Many Generations.* Liverpool, 1853.

Tanner, Jerald and Sandra. *The Changing World of Mormonism.* Chicago: Moody, 1980.

————. *Did Spaulding Write the Book of Mormon?* Salt Lake City: Modern Microfilm, 1974.

————. *Joseph Smith and Polygamy.* Salt Lake City: Modern Microfilm, 1966.

————. *Joseph Smith's Strange Account of the First Vision.* Salt Lake City: Modern Microfilm, 1965.

————. *Mormonism—Shadow or Reality?* Salt Lake City: Modern Microfilm, 1972.

————. *Mormon Scriptures and the Bible.* Salt Lake City: Modern Microfilm, 1970.

————. *Mormons and Negroes.* Salt Lake City: Modern Microfilm, 1970.

————. "Salamandergate," *Salt Lake City Messenger,* June 1985.

————. *3,913 Changes in the Book of Mormon.* Salt Lake City: Modern Microfilm, 1965.

Terry, Keith and Whipple, Walter. *From the Dust of Decades: A Saga of the Papyri and Mummies.* Salt Lake City: Bookcraft, 1968.

Todd, Jay M. *The Saga of the Book of Abraham.* Salt Lake City: Deseret News Press, 1969.

Tucker, Ruth A. "Foreign Missionaries With A False Message." *Evangelical Missions Quarterly* (October 1984), 326-342.

Turner, Wallace. *The Mormon Establishment.* Boston: Houghton Mifflin, 1966.

Walters, Wesley P. "Joseph Smith Among the Egyptians." *The Journal of the Evangelical Theological Society,* 16 (Winter 1973).

_____. *New Light on Mormon Origins from the Palmyra (N.Y.) Revival*. LaMesa, Calif.: Utah Christian Tract, 1967.

Warner, James and Slade, Styne M. *The Mormon Way*. Englewood Cliffs, N.J.: Prentice Hall, 1976.

Whalen, William J. *The Latter-day Saints in the Modern-day World*. South Bend, Ind.: Notre Dame Press, 1967.

Woodward, Kenneth. "Onward Mormon Soldiers," *Newsweek*. April 17, 1981.

Young, Kimball. *Isn't One Wife Enough? The Story of Mormon Polygamy*. New York: Holt, 1954.

Seventh-day Adventism

Ahlstrom, Sydney E. *A Religious History of the American People*. Garden City, N.Y.: Doubleday, 1975.

Anderson, Godfrey T. *Outsider of the Apocalypse: The Life and Times of Joseph Bates*. Mountain View, Calif.: Pacific Press, 1972.

_____. "Sectarianism and Organization, 1846-1864," in Gary Land, ed., *Adventism in America: A History*. Grand Rapids: Eerdmans, 1986.

Andross, Matilda. *Story of the Adventist Message*. Washington, D.C.: Review and Herald, n.d.

Baker, Alonzo L. *Belief and Work of Seventh-Day Adventists*. Mountain View, Calif.: Pacific Press, 1938.

Ball, B. W. *The English Connection: The Puritan Roots of Seventh-day Adventist Belief*. Cambridge: James Clarke, 1981.

Barnhouse, Donald Grey. "Are Seventh-day Adventists Christian?" *Eternity*. September, 1956.

Biederwolf, William Edward. *Seventh Day Adventism: The Result of A Predicament*. Grand Rapids: Eerdmans, 1950.

Brinsmead, Robert D. *Judged by the Gospel*. Fallbrook, Calif.: Verdict Publications, 1980.

Canright, D. M. *Seventh-day Adventism Renounced*. Grand Rapids: Baker, 1961.

Carson, D. A., editor. *From Sabbath to Lord's Day*. Grand Rapids: Zondervan, 1982.

Craven, Joan. "The Wall of Adventism," *Christianity Today*. October 19, 1984.

Douty, Norman F. *Another Look at Seventh-day Adventism*. Grand Rapids: Baker, 1962.

Froom, LeRoy Edwin. *The Prophetic Faith of Our Fathers*. 4 vols. Washington, D.C.: Review and Herald, 1950.

Hall, Clarence W. *Adventurers for God*. New York: Harper & Row, 1959.

Haynes, Carlyle B. *The Christian Sabbath*. Nashville: Southern Publishing Association, 1949.

_____. *Life, Death, and Immortality*. Nashville: Southern Publishing, 1952.

Hefley, James C. "Adventist Teachers Are Forced Out In A Doctrinal Dispute." *Christianity Today*. March 18, 1983.

Hoekema, Anthony A. *Seventh-day Adventism*. Grand Rapids: Eerdmans, 1972.

Land, Gary. "Coping With Change, 1961-1980," in Gary Land, ed., *Adventism in America: A History*. Grand Rapids: Eerdmans, 1986.

_____. "Shaping the Modern Church, 1906-1930," in Gary Land, ed., *Adventism in America: A History*. Grand Rapids: Eerdmans, 1986.

Loughborough, J. N. *The Great Second. Advent Movement: Its Rise and Progress*. Washington, D.C.: Review and Herald, 1905.

Martin, Walter R. *The Kingdom of the Cults*. Minneapolis: Bethany House,1985.

_____. *The Truth About Seventh-day Adventism*. London: Marshall, Morgan & Scott, 1960.

Maxwell, C. Mervyn. *Tell It To The World: The Story of Seventh-day Adventists*. Mountain View, Calif.: Pacific Press, 1976.

Meehan, Chris. "Defenders of Their Faith," *Grand Rapids Press*. November 1, 1986

Miller, William. "Memoir of William Miller" in *Views of the Prophecies and Prophetic Chronology*. Boston: Joshua V. Himes, 1842.

Nichol, Francis D. *The Midnight Cry*. Washington, D.C.: Review and Herald, 1945.

Noll, Mark A. et al. *Eerdmans' Handbook to Christianity in America*. Grand Rapids: Eerdmans, 1983.

Noorbergen, Rene. *Ellen G. White: Prophet of Destiny*. New Canaan, Conn.: Keats Publishing, 1972.

Numbers, Ronald L. *Prophetess of Health: A Study of Ellen G. White*. New York: Harper & Row, 1976.

Numbers, Ronald L. and Butler, Jonathan M. *The Disappointed: Millerism and Millenarianism in the Nineteenth Century*, Bloomington: Indiana University Press, 1987.

Olsen, M. Ellsworth. *A History of the Origin and Progress of Seventh-day Adventists*. Washington, D.C.: Review and Herald, 1925.

Ostling, Richard N. "The Church of Liberal Borrowings." *Time*. August 2, 1982.

Paxton, Geoffrey J. *The Shaking of Adventism*. Grand Rapids: Baker, 1977.

Questions on Doctrine. Washington, D.C.: Review and Herald, 1957.

Rea, Walter T. *The White Lie*. Turlock, Calif.: M & R Publications, 1982.

Robertson, John J. *The White Truth*. Mountain View, Calif.: Pacific Press, 1981.

Schwartz, Richard W. *Lightbearers to the Remnant*. Mountain View, Calif.: Pacific Press, 1979.

_____. "'The Perils of Growth, 1886–1905," in Gary Land, ed., *Adventism in America: A History*. Grand Rapids: Eerdmans, 1986.

Van Baalen, Jan Karel. *The Chaos of Cults: A Study in Present-Day Isms*. Grand Rapids: Eerdmans, 1962.

Vandevere, Emmett K. "Years of Expansion, 1865–1884," in Gary Land, ed., *Adventism in America: A History*. Grand Rapids: Eerdmans, 1986.

Walker, Allan. *The Law and the Sabbath*. Nashville: Southern Publishing Association, 1953.

White, Ellen G. *The Desire of Ages*. Mountain View, Calif.: Pacific Press, 1898.

_____. *Fundamentals of Christian Education*. Nashville: Southern Publishing Association, 1923.

_____. *Gospel Workers*. Washington, D.C.: Review & Herald, 1892.

_____. *The Great Controversy Between Christ and Satan*. Mountain View: Pacific Press, 1911.

_____. *The Ministry of Healing*. Mountain View, Calif.: Pacific Press, 1905.

_____. *The Sanctified Life*. Washington, D.C.: Review and Herald, 1937.

_____. *Testimonies for the Church*. 9 vols. Oakland: Pacific Press, 1855-1909.

White, James. *Life Incidents in Connection with the Great Advent Movement*. Battle Creek: Seventh-day Adventist Publishing Association, 1880.

_____. *Sketches of the Christian Life and Public Labors of William Miller*. Battle Creek, Mich.: Steam Press, 1875.

Wilson, Neal. "Time for Reaping," *Adventist Review*. September 2, 1982.

Jehovah's Witnesses

Adair, James R. and Miller, Ted. *We Found Our Way Out*. Grand Rapids: Baker, 1964.

Axup, Edward J. *The Jehovah's Witnesses Unmasked*. New York: Greenwich, 1959.

Ahlstrom, Sydney E. *A Religious History of the American People*. Garden City, N.Y.: Doubleday, 1975.

Beckford, James A. *The Trumpet of Prophecy: A Sociological Study of Jehovah's Witnesses*. Oxford: Basil Blackwell, 1975.

Biederwolf, William E. *Russellism Unveiled*. Grand Rapids: Eerdmans, 1949.

Botting, Heather and Gary. *The Orwellian World of Jehovah's Witnesses*. Toronto: University of Toronto Press, 1984.

Bowman, Robert M., Jr. *Jehovah's Witnesses, Jesus Christ, and the Gospel of John*. Grand Rapids: Baker, 1988.

Cole, Marley, *Jehovah's Witnesses*. New York: Vantage Press, 1955.

————. *Triumphant Kingdom*. New York: Criterion Books, 1957.

Countess, Robert H. *The Jehovah's Witnesses' New Testament: A Critical Analysis of the New World Translation of the Christian Greek Scriptures*. Phillipsburg, N.J.: Presbyterian and Reformed Publishing Company, 1982.

Cowley, Susan C. "Persecution in Malawi," *Newsweek*. May 10, 1976.

Cratt, Milton. *The International Bible Students: Jehovah's Witnesses*. New Haven: Yale University Press, 1933.

Dencher, Ted. *The Watchtower Heresy Versus the Bible*. Chicago: Moody, 1961.

Duggar, Gordon E. *Jehovah's Witnesses: Watch Out for the Watchtower!* Grand Rapids: Baker, 1985.

Franz, Raymond. *Crisis of Conscience: The Struggle between Loyalty to God and Loyalty to One's Religion*. Atlanta: Commentary Press, 1983.

Gruss, Edmond C. *Apostles of Denial: An Examination and Exposé of the History, Doctrines and Claims of the Jehovah's Witnesses*. Phillipsburg, N.J.: Presbyterian and Reformed Publishing Co., 1970.

Harrison, Barbara Grizzuti. *Visions of Glory: A History and a Memory of Jehovah's Witnesses*. New York: Simon and Schuster, 1978.

Hoekema, Anthony A. *The Four Major Cults*. Grand Rapids: Eerdmans, 1963.

Lewis, Gordon R. *The Bible, the Christian, and Jehovah's Witnesses*. Phillipsburg, N.J.: Presbyterian and Reformed, 1976.

McKinney, George D., Jr. *The Theology of the Jehovah's Witnesses*. Grand Rapids: Zondervan, 1962.

Make Sure of All Things; Hold Fast to What is Fine. New York: Watch Tower Bible and Tract Society, 1965.

Martin, Walter R. *Jehovah of the Watchtower: A Thorough Exposé*. Grand Rapids: Baker, 1953.

————. *The Kingdom of the Cults*. Minneapolis: Bethany House, 1985.

Mayer, F. E. *Jehovah's Witnesses*. St. Louis: Concordia, 1957.

Metzger, Bruce. "The Jehovah's Witnesses and Jesus Christ," *Theology Today*. Vol. 10, April 1953.

Molder, John E. and Comisky, Marvin. "Jehovah's Witnesses Mold Constitutional Law," *Bill of Rights Review*. Vol. 2, Summer 1942.

Morey, Robert. "A Jehovah's Witness At Your Door?" *Christianity Today*. September 3, 1982

Nelson, Wilton M. and Smith, Richard K. "Jehovah's Witnesses: The Background," in David J. Hesselgrave. *Dynamic Religious Movements*. Grand Rapids: Baker, 1978.

New World Translation of the Christian Greek Scriptures. New York: Watchtower Bible and Tract Society, 1950.

Ostling, Richard N. "Witness Under Prosecution," *Time.* February 22, 1982.

Penton, M. James. *Apocalypse Delayed: The Story of the Jehovah's Witnesses.* Toronto: University of Toronto Press, 1985.

————. "The Eschatology of Jehovah's Witnesses: A Short, Critical Analysis," in M. Darrol Bryant and Donald W. Dayton, eds. *The Coming Kingdom: Essays in American Millennialism and Eschatology.* Barrytown, N.Y.: International Religious Foundation, 1983.

Reasoning from the Scriptures. Brooklyn: Watch Tower Bible and Tract Society, 1985.

Rogerson, Alan. *Millions Now Living Will Never Die: A Study of Jehovah's Witnesses.* London: Constable, 1969.

Ross, J. J. *Some Facts and More Facts about the Self-Styled "Pastor" Charles T. Russell.* New York: Charles C. Cook, 1912.

Russell, Charles Taze. *The Divine Plan of the Ages.* Brooklyn: Dawn Publishers, 1937.

————. *Studies in the Scriptures.* 7 vols. Brooklyn: International Bible Students Association, 1917

Rutherford, Joseph Franklin. *Creation.* Brooklyn: Watch Tower Bible and Tract Society, 1927.

————. *Deliverance.* Brooklyn: Watch Tower Bible and Tract Society, 1926.

————. *Government.* Brooklyn: Watch Tower Bible and Tract Society, 1928.

————. *The Harp of God: Proof Conclusive That Millions Now Living Will Never Die.* Brooklyn: Watch Tower Bible and Tract Society, 1921.

————. *Religion.* Brooklyn: Watch Tower Bible and Tract Society, 1940.

————. *Salvation.* Brooklyn: Watch Tower Bible and Tract Society, 1939.

Schnell, William J. *Thirty Years a Watch Tower Slave.* Grand Rapids: Baker, 1959.

Stroup, Herbert H. *The Jehovah's Witnesses.* New York: Columbia University Press, 1945.

The Truth That Leads to Eternal Life. New York: Watch Tower Bible & Tract Society, 1968.

This Means Everlasting Life. New York: Watch Tower Bible and Tract Society, 1950.

Thomas, Stan. *Jehovah's Witnesses and What They Believe.* Grand Rapids: Zondervan, 1967.

Whalen, William J. *Armageddon Around the Corner: A Report on Jehovah's Witnesses.* New York: John Day, 1962.

White, Timothy. *A People for His Name: A History of Jehovah's Witnesses and an Evaluation.* New York: Vantage Press, 1967.

1988 Yearbook of the Jehovah's Witnesses. New York: Watchtower Bible and Tract Society, 1987.

Christian Science

A Century of Christian Science Healing. Boston: Christian Science Publishing Society, 1966.

Ahlstrom, Sydney E. *A Religious History of the American People.* 2 vols. Garden City, N.Y.: Image Books, 1975.

Bates, Ernest Sutherland and Dittemore, John V. *Mary Baker Eddy: The Truth and the Tradition.* Alfred A. Knopf, 1932.

Beasley, Norman. *The Cross and The Crown: The History of Christian Science.* New York: Duell, Sloan & Pearace, 1952.

Braden, Charles S. *Christian Science Today: Power, Policy, Practice.* Dallas: Southern Methodist University, 1958.

Christian Science is for Sharing. Boston: The Christian Science Publishing Society, 1972.

Dakin, Edwin F. *Mrs. Eddy: The Biography of a Virginal Mind.* New York: Scribner's, 1930.

Dart, John. "Christian Science's Health Shows Signs of Decline." *St. Petersburg Times,* January 10, 1987.

DeWitt, John. *The Christian Science Way of Life.* Boston: Christian Science Publishing Society, 1962.

Dickey, Adam. *Memoirs of Mary Baker Eddy.* England: Robert G. Carter, 1927.

Eddy, Mary Baker. *Christian Healing.* Boston: Christian Science Publishing Society, 1936.

————. *Manual of the Mother Church.* Boston: Christian Science Publishing Society, 1895.

————. *Miscellaneous Writings, 1883–1896.* Boston: The First Church of Christ, Scientist, 1896.

————. *No and Yes.* Boston: Christian Science Publishing Society, 1891.

————. *Pulpit and Press.* Boston: Christian Science Publishing Society, 1895.

————. *Retrospection and Introspection.* Boston: Christian Science Publishing Soceity, 1891.

————. *Rudimental Divine Science.* Boston: Christian Science Publishing Company, 1891.

————. *Unity of Good.* Boston: Christian Science Publishing Company, 1887.

————. *Science and Health With Key to the Scriptures.* Boston: Christian Science Publishing Society, 1918.

Fisher, H. A. L. *Our New Religion: An Examination of Christian Science.* New York: J. Cape and H. Smith, 1930

Gottschalk, Stephen. *The Emergence of Christian Science in American Religious Life.* Berkeley: University of California Press, 1973.

————. "Spiritual Healing On Trial: Christian Scientist Reports," *The Christian Century.* June 22–29, 1988.

Leishman, Thomas L. *Why I am a Christian Scientist.* New York: Nelson, 1958.

Logwood, James A. "A Trip to the Rockies," *Christian Science Journal,* XVIII (May 1900).

McKee, Clara Knox. "With Sandals on and Staff in Hand," in *We Knew Mary Baker Eddy.* Boston: Christian Science Publishing Society, 1950.

Milmine, Georgine. *The Life of Mary Baker G. Eddy and the History of Christian Science.* Grand Rapids: Baker, 1971.

Peel, Robert. *Christian Science: Its Encounter with American Culture.* New York: H. Holt, 1958.

————. *Mary Baker Eddy: The Years of Authority.* New York: Holt, Rinehart and Winston, 1977.

————. *Mary Baker Eddy: The Years of Discovery.* New York: Holt, Rinehart and Winston, 1966.

————. *Mary Baker Eddy: The Years of Trial.* New York: Holt, Rinehart and Winston, 1971.

Powell, Lyman P. *Christian Science: The Faith and Its Founder.* New York: G. P. Putnam, 1909.

————. *Mary Baker Eddy: A Life-Size Portrait.* New York: Macmillan, 1930.

Quebedeaux, Richard. *By What Authority: The Rise of Personality Cults in American Christianity.* New York: Harper & Row, 1982.

Sheldon, Henry C. *Christian Science So-called.* New York: Eaton and Mains, 1913.

Silberger, Julius, Jr. *Mary Baker Eddy: An Interpretive Biography of the Founder of Christian Science.* Boston: Little, Brown and Company, 1980.

Snowden, James H. *The Truth about Christian Science: The Founder and the Faith.* Philadelphia: Westminster, 1920.

The First Church of Christ, Scientist, and Miscellany. Boston: Christian Science Publishing Society, 1941.

Tomlinson, Irving C. *Twelve Years with Mary Baker Eddy: Recollections and Experiences.* Boston: Christian Science Publishing Soceity, 1945.

Twain, Mark. *Christian Science.* New York: Harper, 1907.

Wilbur, Sibyl. *The Life of Mary Baker Eddy.* New York: Concord Publishing Company, 1907.

New Thought and Unity

Allen, A. L. *Message of New Thought.* New York: n.p., 1914.

Anderson, John B. *New Thought, Its Lights and Shadows.* Boston: Sherman, French, 1911.

Bach, Marcus. *The Unity Way of Life.* Englewood Cliffs, N.J.: Prentice-Hall, 1962.

Barron, Bruce. *The Health and Wealth Gospel.* Downers Grove, Ill.: InterVarsity Press, 1987.

Berry, Harold J. "Unity School of Christianity in the Light of the Scriptures," *Good News Broadcaster.* October, 1964.

Braden, Charles S. *Spirits in Rebellion.* Dallas: Southern Methodist University Press, 1963.

Cady, H. Emilie. *Lessons in Truth.* Lee's Summit, Mo.: Unity School of Christianity, 1962.

D'Andrade, Hugh. *Charles Fillmore: Herald of the New Age.* New York: Harper & Row, 1974.

Dresser, Horatio W. *A History of the New Thought Movement.* New York: Crowell, 1919.

————. *On the Threshold of the Spiritual World.* New York: G. Sully, 1919.

————. *Spiritual Health and Healing.* New York: Crowell, 1922.

————. *The Philosophy of the Spirit.* New York: G. P. Putnam's Sons, 1908.

Fillmore, Charles. *Mysteries of John.* Lee's Summit, Mo.: Unity School of Christianity, 1954.

————. "The Atomic Prayer," *Unity.* November, 1945.

————. *Prosperity.* Kansas City, Mo.: Unity Schol of Christianity, 1936

————. *Twelve Powers of Man.* Lee's Summit, Mo.: Unity School of Christianity, 1943.

————. *Christian Healing.* Lee's Summit, Mo.: Unity School of Christianity, 1954.

Fillmore, Lowell. *New Ways to Solve Old Problems.* Kansas City: Unity School of Christianity, 1939.

Fillmore, Myrtle. *Healing Letters.* Lee's Summit, Mo.: Unity School of Christianity, 1936.

Fox, Emmet. *Make Your Life Worthwhile.* New York: Harper, 1946.

Freeman, James Dillet. *The Story of Unity.* Unity Village, Mo.: Unity Books, 1978.

Gottschalk, Stephen. *The Emergence of Christian Science in American Religious Life.* Berkeley: University of California, 1973.

Hudson, Winthrop. *Religion in America: An Historical Account of the Development of American Religious Life.* New York: Scribners, 1973.

McConnell, D. R. *A Different Gospel: A Historical and Biblical Analysis of the Modern Faith Movement.* Peabody, Mass.: Hendrickson, 1988.

Martin, Walter. *The Kingdom of the Cults.* Minneapolis: Bethany House, 1985.

Quebedeaux, Richard. *By What Authority: The Rise of Personality Cults in American Christianity.* San Francisco: Harper & Row, 1982.

Spittler, Russell P. *Cults and Isms: Twenty Alternates to Evangelical Christianity.* Grand Rapids: Baker, 1962.

Turner, Elizabeth Sand. *What Unity Teachers.* Lee's Summit, Mo.: Unity School of Christianity, n.d.

Unity's Statement of Faith. Lee's Summit, Mo.: Unity School of Christianity, n.d.

Van Baalen, Jan Karel. *The Chaos of Cults: A Study in Present-Day Isms.* Grand Rapids: Eerdmans, 1962.

Worldwide Church of God

Anderson, Stanley E. *Armstrongism's 300 Errors Exposed by 1300 Bible Verses.* Nashville: Church Growth Publications, 1973.

Armstrong, Herbert W. *The Autobiography of Herbert W. Armstrong.* Vol. 1. Pasadena: Ambassador College Press, 1957.

————. *The Book of Revelation Unveiled at Last.* Pasadena: Worldwide Church of God, 1959.

————. *Does God Exist?* Pasadena: Worldwide Church of God, 1957.

————. *The Incredible Human Potential.* Pasadena: Worldwide Church of God, 1978.

————. *Mystery of the Ages.* New York: Dodd, Mead & Company, 1985.

————. *The Plain Truth About Christmas.* Pasadena: Worldwide Church of God, 1952.

————. *The Plain Truth About Healing.* Pasadena: Worldwide Church of God, 1979.

————. *The Seven Laws of Success.* Pasadena: Worldwide Church of God, 1961.

————. *The United States and Britain in Prophecy.* Pasadena: Worldwide Church of God, 1980.

————. *Which Day is the Christian Sabbath?* Pasadena: Worldwide Church of God, 1962.

————. *Why Were You Born?* Pasadena: Worldwide Church of God, 1957.

Armstrong, Herbert W. and Garner Ted Armstrong. *The Wonderful World Tomorrow.* Pasadena: Ambassador College, 1966.

Benware, Paul N. *Ambassadors of Armstrongism: An Analysis of the History and Teachings of the Worldwide Church of God.* Philadelphia: The Presbyterian and Reformed Publishing Co., 1975.

Chambers, Roger R. *The Plain Truth About Armstrongism.* Grand Rapids: Baker, 1972.

DeLoach, Charles F. *The Armstrong Error.* Plainfield, N.J.: Logos, 1971.

Grant, Robert G. *The Plain Truth About the Armstrong Cult.* Glendale, Calif.: United Community Church, 1969.

Hill, David Jon. "Why is God the Father Called a Father?" *Tomorrow's World.* September 1970.

Hoeh, Herman L. *A True History of the True Church.* Pasadena: Ambassador College, 1959.

Hopkins, Joseph. *The Armstrong Empire: A Look at the Worldwide Church of God.* Grand Rapids: Eerdmans, 1974.

Issong, Isaiah A. "The Missionary Outreach of the Worldwide Church of God in Nigeria." Unpublished paper, Grand Rapids School of the Bible and Music, May 16, 1983

Kirban, Salem. *The Plain Truth About the Plain Truth.* Huntington Valley, Pa.: Salem Kirban, 1970.

Lowe, Harry. *Radio Church of God.* Mountain View, Calif.: Pacific Press, 1970.

Marson, Richard A. *The Marson Report Concerning Herbert W. Armstrong.* Seattle: Ashley-Calvin Press, 1970.

Martin, William C. "Father, Son, and Mammon," *Atlantic Monthly.* March 1980.

Martin, Walter R. *Herbert W. Armstrong and the Radio Church of God.* Minneapolis: Bethany, 1968.

McDowell, Bill. "Keep God's Sabbath Holy!" *The Good News.* March 1968.

Meredith, Roderick C. *The Ten Commandments.* Pasadena: Ambassador College, 1968.

Rader, Stanley R. *Against the Gates of Hell.* New York: Everest House, 1980.

Smith, Noel. *Herbert W. Armstrong and His World of Tomorrow.* Springfield: Bible Baptist Tribune, 1964.

Sumner, Robert L. *Herbert W. Armstrong: False Prophet.* Murfreesboro, Tenn.: Sword of the Lord, 1961.

————. "The Incredible Armstrong Duo," *Faith for the Family.* September/October 1975.

This Is the Worldwide Church of God. Pasadena: Worldwide Church of God, 1979.

Wilson, Paul. *The Armstrong Heresy: A Brief Examination.* Denver: Wilson Foundation, n.d.

Withers, Bob and Benware, Paul. "Armstrongism from the Inside," *Moody Monthly.* October 1978.

Woodward, Kenneth L. "Apocalypse Now?," *Newsweek.* January 15, 1979.

The Way International

Cummins, Walter J. *Fruit of the Spirit.* New Knoxville, Ohio: American Christian Press, n.d.

Frequent Questions. New Knoxville, Ohio: The Way International, n.d.

Hopkins, Joseph M. "The Way Founder Wierwille Announces Plan to Retire," *Christianity Today.* March 13, 1981.

"International WOW Scene." *The Way Magazine.* November-December 1985.

MacCollam, Joel A. "The Way," in Ronald Enroth et al., ed. *A Guide to Cults and New Religions.* Downers Grove, Ill.: InterVarsity Press, 1983.

————. *The Way of Victor Paul Wierwille.* Downers Grove, Ill.: InterVarsity Press, 1978.

McDowell, Josh and Stewart, Don. *Understanding the Cults.* San Bernardino, Calif.: Campus Crusade for Christ, 1982.

Martin, Walter R. *The New Cults.* Santa Anna, Calif.: Vision House, 1980.

Petersen, William J. *Those Curious New Cults in the 80s.* New Canaan, Conn.: Keats, 1982.

Profile—The Way International. New Knoxville, Ohio: The Way International, n.d.

Robertson, Irvine. *What the Cults Believe.* Chicago: Moody, 1983.

Sparks, Jack. *The Mind Benders.* Nashville: Thomas Nelson, 1979.

Tolbert, Keith. "Infighting Trims Branches of Way International," *Christianity Today.* February 19, 1988.

Whiteside, Elena S. *The Way: Living in Love.* New Knoxville, Ohio: American Christian Press, 1974.

Wierwille, Victor Paul. *Are the Dead Alive Now?* Old Greenwich, Conn.: Devin-Adair, 1971.

————. *The Bible Tells Me So.* Vol. 1 in *Studies in Abundant Living.* New Knoxville, Ohio: American Christian Press, 1971.

————. *God's Magnified Word.* New Knoxville, Ohio: American Christian Press, 1977.

_____. *How to Speak in Tongues.* New Knoxville, Ohio: American Christian Press, n.d.

_____. *Jesus Christ Is Not God.* New Knoxville, Ohio: American Christian Press, 1975.

_____. *The New Dynamic Church.* New Knoxville, Ohio: American Christian Press, 1971.

_____. *Power For Abundant Living.* New Knoxville, Ohio: American Christian Press, 1972.

_____. *Receiving the Holy Spirit Today.* New Knoxville, Ohio: American Christian Press, 1972.

_____. *The Word's Way.* Vol. 3 of *Studies in Abundant Living.* New Knoxville, Ohio: American Christian Press, 1971.

Williams, J. L. *Victor Paul Wierwille and The Way International.* Chicago: Moody, 1979.

The Children of God

Berg, David Brandt ("Moses David"). *The Disciple Revolution.* London: Children of God, 1975.

_____. "The Flirty Little Fishy!" London: Children of God, 1974.

_____. "God's Whores?" Rome: Children of God, April 26, 1976.

_____. *He Stands in the Gap.* London: Children of God, 1971.

Bromley, David G. and Shupe, Anson D., Jr. *Strange Gods: The Great American Cult Scare.* Boston: Beacon, 1981.

Butterworth, John. *Cults and New Faiths.* Elgin, Ill.: David C. Cook, 1981.

Davis, Deborah (Linda Berg), with Bill Davis. *The Children of God.* Grand Rapids: Zondervan, 1984.

Enroth, Ronald. *Youth, Brainwashing and the Extremist Cults.* Grand Rapids: Zondervan, 1977.

Gordon, Mark and Ruth. *Children of Darkness.* Wheaton: Tyndale House, 1988.

Hopkins, Joseph. "Children of God: Disciples of Deception," *Christianity Today.* February 28, 1977.

Larson, Bob. *Larson's Book of Cults.* Wheaton: Tyndale House, 1982.

Lefkowitz, Lewis. "Final Report of Children of God." Charity Frauds Bureau, World Trade Building, New York, New York.

Martin, Walter. *The New Cults.* Santa Ana: Vision House, 1980.

McDowell, Josh and Stewart, Don. *Understanding the Cults.* San Bernadino, Calif.: Here's Life Publishers, 1982.

McManus, Una. *Not for a Million Dollars.* Nashville: Impact Books, 1980.

Petersen, William J. *Those Curious New Cults in the 80s.* New Caanan, Conn.: Keats, 1982.

Sparks, Jack. *The Mindbenders: A Look at Current Cults.* Nashville: Thomas Nelson, 1979.

Wallis, Roy. "Observations On the Children of God," *The Sociological Review.* Vol. 4. November 1976.

The Unification Church

Bjornstad, James. *Sun Myung Moon and the Unification Church.* Minneapolis: Bethany House, 1984.

RL(5,360.) *The Moon Is Not the Sun.* Minneapolis: Bethany House, 1976.

Boettcher, Robert with Gordon L. Freedman. *Gifts of Deceit: Sun Myung Moon, Tongsun Park, and the Korean Scandal.* New York: Holt, Rinehart and Winston, 1980.

Bromley, David G. and Shupe, Anson D., Jr., *"Moonies" in America: Cult, Church, and Crusade.* Beverly Hills: Sage Publications, 1979.

————. *Strange Gods: The Great American Cult Scare.* Boston: Beacon, 1981.

Bryant, David and Hodges, Susan, eds. *Exploring Unification Theology.* Barrytown, N.Y.: Rose of Sharon Press, 1978.

Durham, Deanna. *Life Among the Moonies: Three Years in the Unification Church.* Plainfield, N.J.: Logos, 1981.

Durst, Mose. *To Bigotry, No Sanction: Reverend Sun Myung Moon and the Unification Church.* Chicago: Regnery Gateway, 1984.

Edwards, Christopher. *Crazy for God: The Nightmare of Cult Life.* Englewood Cliffs, N.J.: Prentice-Hall, 1979.

Elkins, Chris. *Heavenly Deception.* Wheaton: Tyndale House, 1980.

————. *What Do You Say to A Moonie?* Wheaton: Tyndale House, 1981.

Enroth, Ronald. *Youth, Brainwashing and the Extremist Cults.* Grand Rapids: Zondervan, 1977.

Horowitz, Irving Louis, ed. *Science, Sin and Scholarship: The Politics of Reverend Moon and the Unification Church.* Cambridge, Mass.: Massachusetts Institute of Technology Press, 1978.

James, Gene G., ed. *The Family and the Unification Church.* Barrytown, N.Y.: Unification Theological Seminary, 1983.

Jones, W. Farley, ed. *Unification Church: As Others See Us.* Washington, D.C.: Holy Spirit Association for the Unification of World Christianity, 1974.

Kemperman, Steve. *Lord of the Second Advent.* Ventura, Calif.: Regal Books, 1981.

Kim, Won Pil. "Father's Early Ministry in Pusan," *Today's World.* May 1982.

Kim, Young Oon. *Unification Theology.* New York: The Holy Spirit Association for the Unification of World Christianity, 1980.

Kwack, Chung Hwan. "World Missions," *Today's World.* May, 1983.

Levitt, Zola. *The Spirit of Sun Myung Moon.* Irvine, Calif.: Harvest House, 1976.

Matczak, Sebastian A. *Unificationism: A New Philosophy and World View.* Jamaica, N.Y.: Learned Publications, 1982.

Moon, Sun Myung. *America in God's Providence.* New York: Unification Church of America, 1976.

————. *Christianity in Crisis.* Washington, D.C.: Holy Spirit Association for the Unification of World Christianity, 1974.

————. *Divine Principle.* New York: The Holy Spirit Association for the Unification of World Christianity, 1973.

————. *Message to the World Unification Family.* Washington, D.C.: The Holy Spirit Association for the Unification of World Christianity, 1964.

————. *New Hope: Twelve Talks.* 2 vols. New York: The Holy Spirit Association for the Unification of World Christianity, 1984.

————. "On Bible Understanding," *The Master Speaks.* Washington, D.C.: Unification Church, 1965.

Patrick, Ted with Dulack, Tom. *Let Our Children Go!* New York: E. P. Dutton, 1976.

Petersen, William J. *Those Curious New Cults in the 80s.* New Canaan, Conn.: Keats, 1982.

Quebedeaux, Richard. *Lifestyle: Conversations with Members of the Unification Church.* Barrytown, N.Y.: Unification Theological Seminary, 1982.

Quebedeaux, Richard and Sawatsky, Rodney, eds. *Evangelical-Unification Dialogue.* New York: Rose of Sharon Press, 1979.

Sontag, Frederick. *Sun Myung Moon and the Unification Church.* Nashville: Abingdon, 1977.

Sun Myung Moon, A Biography. Berkeley, Calif.: Unification Church, n.d.

Whaley, John. "Moon's Son Reincarnated?," *Watchman Expositor.* Vol. 5, No. 4, 1988.

Wood, Allen Tate with Vitek, Jack. *Moonstruck: A Memoir of My Life in a Cult.* New York: William Morrow, 1979.

Yamamoto, J. Isamu. *The Puppet Master: an Inquiry into Sun Myung Moon and the Unification Church.* Downers Grove, Ill.: InterVarsity Press, 1977.

————. "Unification Church," in Ronald Enroth et al., *A Guide to Cults and New Religions.* Downers Grove, Ill.: InterVarsity Press, 1983.

The Hare Krishnas

Bartel, Dennis. "Who's Who in Gurus," *Harper's.* November 1983.

"Brahma, Vishnu, Siva: Clearing up some Misconceptions about the Hindu Trinity," *Back to Godhead.* Vol. 17, no. 6, June 1982.

Dasa, Garuda. "Sankirtana: The Perfection of Glorifying God," *Back to Godhead.* Vol. 16, no. 11, 1981.

Dasi, Visakha-Devi. "Sailing Back to Godhead," *Back to Godhead.* June 1981.

Goswami, Satsvarupa dasa. *Planting the Seed: New York City, 1965–1966.* Los Angeles: Bhaktivedanta Book Trust, 1980.

"Govinda's Restaurant in Teheran: 'Down to Earth and Up to God,' " *Back to Godhead.* June 1981.

Harper, Marvin H. *Gurus, Swamis, and Avataras: Spiritual Masters and Their American Disciples.* Philadelphia: Westminster, 1972.

Hubner, John and Gruson, Lindsey. "Dial Om for Murder," *Rolling Stone.* April 9, 1987.

Judah, J. Stillson. *Hare Krishna and the Counterculture.* New York: John Wiley & Sons, 1974.

————. "The Hare Krishna Movement," in Irving I. Zarestsky and Mark P. Leone, eds. *Religious Movements in Contemporary America.* Princeton: Princeton University Press, 1974.

The Krsna Consciousness Handbook: For the Year 848, Caitanya Era. March 24, 1970– March 12, 1971.

Levine, Faye. *The Strange World of Hare Krishnas.* New York: Fawcett, 1974.

Kennedy, Melville T. *The Chaitanya Movement: A Study of Vaishnavism of Bengal.* New York: Oxford University Press, 1925.

"New Spanish Book A Best-Seller in Latin America," *Back to Godhead.* Vol. 16, no. 11, n.d.

Petersen, William J. *Those Curious New Cults in the 80s.* New Canaan, Conn.: Keats, 1982.

Prabhupada, A. C. Bhaktivedanta Swami. *Beyond Birth and Death* Los Angeles: Bhaktivedanta Book Trust, 1972.

————. *Bhagavad-gita As It Is.* New York: Bhaktivedanta Book Trust, 1972.

————. *Easy Journey to Other Planets.* Los Angeles: Bhaktivedanta Book Trust, 1970.

————. *Krsna Consciousness: The Topmost Yoga System.* Los Angeles: Bhaktivedanta Book Trust, 1970.

————. *Krsna: The Reservoir of Pleasure.* Los Angeles: Bhaktivedanta Book Trust, 1970.

————. *Krsna: The Supreme Personality of Godhead.* 3 vols. Los Angeles: Bhaktivedanta Book Trust, 1970.

_____. *The Nectar of Devotion*. New York: Bhaktivedanta Book Trust, 1970.

_____. *The Science of Self-Realization*. Los Angeles: Bhaktivedanta Book Trust, 1977.

_____. *Teachings of Lord Chaitanya*. Los Angeles: Bhaktivedanta Book Trust, 1968.

"Reincarnation: The Soul's Secret Journey," *ATMA*. Vol. 1, 1983.

"A Remote Spiritual Disneyland," *Time*. September 15, 1980.

Ross, Michael W. "Clinical Profiles of Hare Krishna Devotees," *American Journal of Psychiatry*. Vol. 140, April 1983.

Shinn, Larry D. *The Dark Lord: Cult Images and the Hare Krishnas in America*. Philadelphia: Westminster, 1987.

Sparks, Jack. *The Mindbenders*. Nashville: Thomas Nelson, 1979.

"Srila Prabhupada Speaks Out on Responsibility," *Back to Godhead*. Vol. 16, no. 11, 1981.

Trippet, Frank. "Troubled Karma for the Krishnas," *Time*. September 1, 1986.

Yamamoto, J. Isamu. *Hare Krishna, Hare Krishna*. Downers Grove, Ill.: InterVarsity Press, 1978.

The Baha'i Faith

Abdu'l-Baha, *The Promulgation of Universal Peace, Talks Delivered By Abdu'l-Baha During His Visit to the United States and Canada in 1912*. Compiled by Howard MacNutt. Wilmette: Baha'i Publishing Trust, 1922–1925.

Abdu'l-Baha, *Some Answered Questions*. Compiled and translated by Laura C. Barney. Wilmette, Ill.: Baha'i Publishing Trust, 1981.

Bach, Marcus. "Bahai, A Second Look," *Christian Century*. April 10, 1957.

Baha'i Scriptures, ed. by Horace Holley. New York: Brentano's, 1923.

Baha'i Prayers: A Selection of Prayers Revealed by Baha'u'llah, the Bab and Abdu'l-Baha. Wilmette, Ill: Baha'i Publishing Trust, 1982.

Baha'u'llah, *Gleanings from the Writings of Baha'u'llah*. Wilmette, Ill.: Baha'i Publishing Trust, 1952.

_____. *The Seven Valleys and the Four Valleys*. Wilmette, Ill.: Baha'i Publishing Trust, 1952.

Baha'u'llah and Abdu'l-Baha, *Baha'i World Faith: Selected Writings of Baha'u'llah and Abdu'l-Baha*. Wilmette, Ill.: Baha'i Publishing Trust, 1943.

"Basic Facts of the Baha'i Faith." Wilmette, Ill.: Baha'i Publishing Trust, n.d.

Beckwith, Francis. *Baha'i*. Minneapolis: Bethany House, 1985.

Boykin, John. "The Baha'i Faith," in Ronald Enroth et al., *A Guide to Cults and New Religions*. Downers Grove, Ill.: InterVarsity Press, 1983.

Effendi, Shoghi. *God Passes By*. Wilmette: Baha'i Publishing Trust, 1970.

_____. *The World Order of Baha'u'llah*. Wilmette, Ill.: Baha'i Publishing Trust, 1955.

Esslemont, J. E. *Baha'u'llah and the New Era*. Wilmette, Ill.: Baha'i Publishing Trust, 1980.

Hatcher, William S. and Martin, J. Douglas. *The Baha'i Faith: The Emerging Global Religion*. New York: Harper & Row, 1984.

Martin, Walter R. *The Kingdom of the Cults*. Minneapolis: Bethany House, 1985.

Miller, William McElwee. *The Baha'i Faith: Its History and Teachings*. Pasadena: William Carey Library, 1974.

Ostling, Richard N. "Slow Death for Iran's Baha'is," *Time*. February 20, 1984.

Stockman, Robert H. *The Baha'i Faith in America, 1892–1900*. Wilmette, Ill.: Baha'i Publishing Trust, 1985.

Taherzadeh, Adib. *The Revelation of Baha'u'llah: Baghdad, 1853–63.* Oxford: George Ronald, 1974.

Scientology

Alexander, Brooks and Halverson, Dean C., eds. *Scientology: The Technology of Enlightenment.* Berkeley: Spiritual Counterfeits Project, 1982.

Cooper, Paulette. *Scandal of Scientology.* New York: Tower Publishers, 1971.

Corydon, Bent and Hubbard, L. Ron, Jr. *L. Ron Hubbard: Messiah or Madman?* Secaucus, N.J.: Lyle Stuart, 1987.

Evans, Chris. *The Cults of Unreason.* New York: Dell, 1973.

Gardner, Martin. *Fads and Fallacies in the Name of Science.* New York: Dover, 1957.

Garrison, Omar V. *Playing Dirty: The Secret War Against Beliefs.* Los Angeles: Ralston-Pilot, 1980.

Hopkins, Joseph M. "Is L. Ron Hubbard Dead?" *Christianity Today.* February 18, 1983.

Hubbard, L. Ron. "Cause and Effect: Part Two," *Source: Magazine of the Flag Land Base.* Issue 50.

―――――. *Dianetics: The Evolution of a Science.* London: F. E. Bording, 1966.

―――――. *Dianetics: The Modern Science of Mental Health.* Los Angeles: Bridge, 1985.

―――――. *Mission into Time.* Los Angeles: American Saint Hill Organization, 1973.

Kaufman, Robert. *Inside Scientology.* New York: Olympia Publications, 1972.

L. Ron Hubbard: The Current Scene. Tampa: Dianetics, 1984.

Mathews, Jay. "Scientology on a Roll," *Grand Rapids Press* (Michigan). January 11, 1986.

Mendal-Johnsen, Trevor and Lusey, Patrick. *The Truth About Scientology.* New York: Grosset & Dunlap, 1980.

Methvin, Eugene H. "Scientology: Anatomy of a Frightening Cult," *Readers Digest.* May, 1980.

Robertson, Irvine, *What the Cults Believe.* Chicago: Moody, 1983.

Wallis, Claudia. "Mystery of the Vanished Ruler," *Time.* January 31, 1983.

Wallis, Roy. *The Road to Total Freedom: A Sociological Analysis of Scientology.* New York: Columbia University, 1977.

"What Scientology Teaches," *Christianity Today.* September 17, 1982.

Whitehead, Harriet. *Renunciation and Reformulation: A Study of Conversion in an American Sect.* Ithaca: Cornell University Press, 1987.

"Your Bridge to Full OT," *Source: Magazine of the Flag Land Base.* Issue 50.

The New Age Movement

Adeney, Francis. "Educators Look East." *Spiritual Counterfeits Journal,* Winter 1981.

Albrecht, Mark. *Reincarnation: A Christian Appraisal.* Downers Grove, Ill.: InterVarsity Press, 1982.

Alexander, Brooks. "Entities in Print." *Christianity Today,* September 18, 1987.

―――――. "Theology from the Twilight Zone," *Christianity Today,* September 18, 1987.

Alexander-Berghorn, Kathleen. "Isis: the Goddess as Healer." *Woman of Power,* Winter 1987.

Alschuler, Alfred S. "Recognizing Inner Teachers: Inner Voices Throughout History." *Gnosis: A Journal of Western Inner Traditions,* Fall 1987.

Bailey, Alice. *The Externalization of the Hierarchy.* New York: Lucis, 1957.

―――――. *Problems of Humanity.* New York: Lucis Publishing, n.d.

―――――. *The Rays and the Initiations.* New York: Lucis Publishing, 1960.

Bennett, John G. *The Masters of Wisdom.* England: Turnstone Press, 1980.

Blavatsky, H. P. *The Secret Doctrine*. New York, 1895.

Bliss, Shepherd. "Jean Houston: Prophet of the Possible." *Whole Life Times*, Oct./mid–Nov. 1984.

Bry, Adelaide. *Directing the Movies of Your Mind: Visualization for Health and Insight*. New York: Harper & Row, 1978.

Bry, Adelaide and Bair, Marjorie. *Visualization*. New York: Barnes and Noble, 1979.

Burrows, Robert. "Corporate Management Cautioned on New Age." *Eternity*, February 1988.

Capra, Frijof. *The Tao of Physics*. New York: Bantam Books, 1984.

————. *The Turning Point*. New York: Simon and Schuster, 1982.

Coleman, Mary E. *Astro-Focus Your Future*. Wellingborough, Northamptonshire: The Aquarian Press, 1987.

Cox, Harvey. *Turning East*. New York: Simon and Schuster, 1977.

Creme, Benjamin. " 'New Age' Leader Contends Christ Resides in London." *Grand Rapids Press* (Michigan), August 18, 1986.

————. *The Reappearance of the Christ and the Masters of Wisdom*. London: The Tara Press, 1980.

Cumbey, Constance E. *The Hidden Dangers of the Rainbow: The New Age Movement and Our Coming Age of Barbarism*. Shreveport: Huntington House, 1983.

————. *A Planned Deception: The Staging of A New Age Messiah*. East Detroit, Mich.: Pointe Publishers, 1985.

Davis, Lola. *Toward A World Religion for the New Age*. Farmingdale, N.Y.: Coleman, 1983.

Dolan, Michael. "The World is in the Mind." *The Harmonist Magazine*, Summer 1986.

de Parrie, Paul and Pride, Mary. *Unholy Sacrifices of the New Age*. Westchester, Ill.: Crossway, 1988.

Fair, Charles. *The New Nonsense*. New York: Simon and Schuster, 1974.

Fenton, Sasha. *Moon Signs: Discover the Hidden Power of Your Emotions*. Wellingborough, Northamptonshire: The Aquarian Press, 1987.

Ferguson, Marilyn. *The Aquarian Conspiracy: Personal and Social Transformation in the 1980s*. Los Angeles: J. P. Tarcher, 1980.

Forrest, Steven. *The Changing Sky: A Practical Guide to the New Predictive Astrology*. New York: Bantam Books, 1986.

French, Thomas. "Ramtha: Ancient Teacher or Fraud?" *St Petersburg Times*, February 16, 1987.

Friedrich, Otto. "New Age Harmonies." *Time*, December 7, 1987.

Gottschalk, Stephen. *The Emergence of Christian Science in American Religious Life*. Berkeley: University of California Press, 1973.

Groothuis, Douglas R. *Confronting the New Age*. Downers Grove, Ill.: InterVarsity Press, 1988.

————. *Unmasking the New Age*. Downers Grove, Ill.: InterVarsity Press, 1986.

Harner, Michael. *The Way of the Shaman*. San Francisco: Harper & Row, 1980.

Hexam, Irving and Poewe-Hexham, Karla. "The Soul of the New Age." *Christianity Today*, September 2, 1988.

Hondema, Maxine P. "Channeling the Spirits." *Co-op Times*, September 1986.

————. "Introduction to the *Seven Steps Edition* of the *Gaelic Manuscripts*. Grand Rapids, 1983.

Hoyt, Karen. *The New Age Rage*. Old Tappan, N.J.: Fleming H. Revell, 1987.

Hubbard, Barbara Marx. *The Evolutionary Journey*. San Francisco: Evolutionary Press, 1982.

Hunt, Dave and McMahon, T. A. *The Seduction of Christianity: Spiritual Discernment in the Last Days.* Eugene Ore.: Harvest House, 1985.

Jaki, Stanley. *The Road of Science and the Ways to God.* Chicago: University of Chicago Press, 1980.

Kelsey, Morton T. *The Christian and the Supernatural.* Minneapolis: Augsburg, 1976.

Keys, Donald. *Earth at Omega: Passage to Planetization.* Boston: Branden Press, 1982.

Korem, Dan. *Powers: Testing the Psychic and Supernatural.* Downers Grove, Ill.: InterVarsity Press, 1988.

Kueshana, Eklal. *The Ultimate Frontier.* Chicago: The Stelle Group, 1970.

Lad, Vasant. "Ayurveda: Life Knowledge." *The Harmonist Magazine,* Summer 1986.

Larson, Bruce. *The Whole Christian.* Waco: Word, 1978.

Levi, *Aquarian Gospel of Jesus.* Los Angeles: DeVorss, 1970.

Lindsey, Robert. "Reincarnated Spirit 'Ramtha' Urges Followers to go West." *Detroit Free Press,* December 15, 1986.

MacLaine, Shirley. *Out on a Limb.* New York: Bantam Books, 1983.

Marrs, Texe. *Dark Secrets of the New Age: Satan's Plan for A One World Religion.* Westchester, Ill: Crossway Books, 1987.

McCann, Hugh. "Alternative Medicine Sheds Image of Quackery." *The Detroit News,* June 25, 1987.

McWaters, Barry. *Conscious Evolution: Personal and Planetary Transformation.* San Francisco: Evolutionary Press, 1982.

Matrisciana, Caryl. *Gods of the New Age.* Eugene, Ore.: Harvest House, 1984.

Michaelson, Johanna. *The Beautiful Side of Evil.* Eugene, Ore.: Harvest House, 1982.

Montgomery, Ruth. *A Gift of Prophecy: The Phenomenal Jeanne Dixon.* New York: Bantam Books, 1966.

————. *Strangers Among Us.* New York: Ballantine/Fawcett Crest Books, 1979.

————. *A World Beyond.* New York: Ballantine/Fawcett Crest Books, 1972.

Morey, Robert A. *Battle of the Gods: Exposing the Foundations of the New Age Movement.* Nashville: Wolgemuth and Hyatt, 1988.

Mueller, Robert. *The New Genesis: Shaping A Global Spirituality.* New York: Image Books, 1984.

"Nancy Reagan's Obsession with Astrology." *Time,* May 16, 1988.

Orser, Mary and Brightfield, Rick and Glory. *Instant Astrology.* San Diego: ACS Publications, 1984.

Ponder, Catherine. *The Millionaire from Nazareth: His Prosperity Secrets for You.* Marina del Rey, Calif.: DeVorss, 1979.

Price, John Randolph. *The Planetary Commission.* Austin: Quartus Books, 1984.

Rabey, Steve. "Karma for Cash: A 'New Age' for Workers?" *Christianity Today,* June 17, 1988.

Regan, Donald T. *For the Record: From Wall Street to Washington.* New York: Harcourt, Brace Javanovich, 1988.

Reisser, Paul C. and Teri K. and Weldon, John. *The Holistic Healers.* Downers Grove: InterVarsity Press, 1983.

Romney, Rodney R. *Journey to Inner Space: Finding God-in-Us.* Nashville: Abingdon, 1980.

Ruether, Rosemary. "Goddesses and Witches: Liberation and Countercultural Feminism." *The Christian Century,* vol. 10, September 1980.

Salvatore, Diane. "The New Victims of Cults." *Ladies' Home Journal,* August 1987.

Sanford, Agnes. *The Healing Gifts of the Spirit.* Old Tappan, N.J.: Revell, 1966.

Saul, Cindy. "Expect A Miracle." *PhenomeNEWS,* April 1988.

Schucman, Helen. *A Course in Miracles*. New York: Foundation for Inner Peace, 1975.

"She's A Pathfinder in Post-feminist Era." *Grand Rapids Press* (Michigan), February 15, 1988.

Sikking, Sue. *Seed of the New Age*. New York: Doubleday, 1970.

Silbey, Uma. "Meditation and Quartz Crystals." *Meditation*, '87 Winter '88.

Smilgis, Martha. "A New Age Dawning." *Time*, August 31, 1987.

Smoley, Richard. "Pitfalls of a Course in Miracles." *Gnosis: A Journal of the Western Inner Traditions*, Fall 1987.

Spangler, David. *Reflections of the Christ*. Scotland: Findhorn, 1977.

————. *Revelation: The Birth of A New Age*. Middleton, Wis.: Lorian Press, 1976.

Starhawk, Miriam. *The Spiral Dance*. San Francisco: Harper & Row, 1979.

Timms, Moira. *Prophecies and Predictions: Everyone's Guide to the Coming Changes*. Santa Cruze: Unity Press, 1980.

Tucker, Robert. "Back to Basics: The New Age Conspiracy." *New Age Source*, February 1983.

Walder, Joyce et al. "The President's Astrologers." *People*, May 23, 1988.

Watring, Richard. "New Age Training in Business: Mind Control in Upper Management?" *Eternity*, February 1988.

Weldon, John and Levitt, Zola. *Psychic Healing: An Exposé of an Occult Phenomenon*. Chicago: Moody, 1982.

Wickenburg, Joanne and Meyer, Virginia. *The Spiral of Life: Unlocking Your Potential with Astrology*. Reno: CRCS Publications, 1987.

Zuckerman, Laurence. "The First Lady's Astrologer." *Time*, May 16, 1988.

Lesser-Known Alternative Religions

Bartley, William Warren, III. *Werner Erhard: The Transformation of a Man, The Founding of est*. New York: Clarkson N. Potter, 1978.

Bloomfield, Harold, Cain, Michael and Jaffe, Dennis. *TM: Discovering Inner Energy and Overcoming Stress*. New York: Delacorte Press, 1975.

Bry, Adelaide. *est: 60 Hours That Transform Your Life*. New York: Harper & Row, 1976.

Burrows, Robert. "Church Universal and Triumphant: The Summit Lighthouse." *SCP Journal*, Winter 1984.

Cameron, Charles, ed. *Who is Guru Maharaj Ji?* New York: Bantam, 1973.

Clements, R. D. *God and the Gurus*. Downers Grove, Ill.: InterVarsity Press, 1975.

Conway, Flo and Siegleman, Jim. *Snapping: America's Epidemic of Sudden Personality Change*. New York: J. B. Lippincott, 1978.

Ellwood, Robert S., Jr. *Alternative Altars: Unconventional and Eastern Spirituality in America*. Chicago: University of Chicago Press, 1979.

Feuerstein, Georg and Miller, Jeanine. *Yoga and Beyond: Essays in Indian Philosophy*. New York: Schocken Books, 1972.

Forem, Jack. *Transcendental Meditation: Maharishi Mahesh Yogi and the Science of Creative Intelligence*. New York: E. P. Dutton, 1974.

Forrest, Alistair and Sanderson, Peter. *Cults and the Occult Today*. London: Marshalls, 1982.

Greene, William. *Est: Four Days to Make Your Life Work*. New York: Simon and Schuster, 1976.

Heindel, Max. *The Rosicrucian Cosmo-Conception or Mystic Christianity*. Oceanside, Calif.: The Rosicrucian Fellowship, 1929.

_____. *The Rosicrucian Philosophy*. Oceanside, Calif.: The Rosicrucian Fellowship, 1922.

Hunt, Dave. *The Cult Explosion*. Irvine, Calif.: Harvest House, 1980.

King, Godfre Ray. *The "I AM" Discourses*. Chicago: St. Germain Press, 1936.

Larson, Bob. *Larson's Book of Cults*. Wheaton: Tyndale House, 1982.

Lewis, Gordon R. *What Everyone Should Know About Transcendental Meditation*. Glendale, Calif.: Regal, 1975.

Lewis, H. Spencer. *Rosicrucian Questions and Answers With Complete History of the Rosicrucian Order*. San Jose: Supreme Grand Lodge of AMORC, 1981.

McKnight, Harry. *Silva Mind Control: Key to Inner Kingdoms through Psychorientology*. Laredo, Texas: Institute of Psychorientology, 1972.

Means, Pat. *The Mystical Maze*. San Bernadino, Calif.: Campus Crusade for Christ, 1976.

Melton, J. Gordon. *Encyclopedia of American Religions*. Wilmington, N.C.: McGrath, 1978.

Miller, Calvin. *Transcendental Hesitation: A Biblical Appraisal of TM and Eastern Mysticism*. Grand Rapids: Zondervan 1977.

Oates, Robert, Jr. *Celebrating the Dawn: Maharishi Mahesh Yogi and the TM Technique*. New York: G. P. Putnam's Sons, 1976.

Palmer, Donald C. "Jesus Only: The United Pentecostal Church," in David J. Hesselgrave, ed. *Dynamic Religious Movements*. Grand Rapids: Baker, 1978.

Petersen, William J. *Those Curious New Cults in the 80s*. New Canaan, Conn.: Keats, 1982.

Porter, Donald and Taxson, Diane. *The est Experience*. New York: Award Books, 1976.

Prophet, Mark and Elizabeth Clare. *The Science of the Spoken Word*. Colorado Springs: Summit University Press, 1974.

Prophet, Elizabeth Clare. *The Lost Years of Jesus*. Malibu, Calif.: Summit University Press, 1984.

Prophet, Mark and Elizabeth. *Climb the Highest Mountain*. Los Angeles: Summit Lighthouse, 1975.

Rajneesh, Bhagwan Shree. *I Am the Gate*. New York: Harper & Row, 1977.

Rhinehart, Luke. *The Book of est*. New York: Holt, Rhinehart and Winston, 1976.

Rudin, James and Marcia. *Prison or Paradise: The New Religious Cults*. Philadelphia: Fortress, 1980.

Sparks, Jack. *The Mindbenders: A Look at Current Cults*. Nashville: Thomas Nelson, 1979.

Shields, Steven L. *Latter Day Saint Beliefs: A Comparison Between the RLDS Church and the LDS Church*. Independence, Mo.: Herald Publishing House, 1986.

Sigstedt, Cyriel O. *The Swedenborg Epic: The Life and Works of Emmanuel Swedenborg*. New York: Bookman, 1952.

Silva, Jose. and Miele, Philip. *The Silva Mind Control Method*. New York: Simon and Schuster, 1977.

_____. *The Silva Mind Control Method for Business Managers*. New York: Prentice-Hall, 1983.

Smyth, Julian K., and Wunsch, William. *The Gist of Swedenborg*. Philadelphia: J. B. Lippincott, 1920.

Sterling, Julie. "The Big Bhag's Commune: Enlightened View of Spending." *Chicago Tribune*, May 1, 1983.

Stevens, John Robert. *Beyond Passover*. n.p.: Living Word, 1977.

_____. *Plumb Perfect*. n.p.: Living Word, Jan. 16, 1977.

_____. *The ManChild*. n.p.: Living Word, 1972.

Stewart, Louis. *Life Forces: A Contemporary Guide to the Cult and Occult.* New York: Andrews and McMeel, 1980.

Suzuki, Daisetz Teitaro. *The Awakening of Zen.* Boulder, Colo.: Prajna Press, 1980.

Twitchell, Paul. *Eckankar—The Key to Secret Worlds.* Menlo Park, Calif.: Illuminated Way Press, 1969.

Walker, B. *Tantrism.* Wellingborough, Northamptonshire: Aquarian Press, 1982.

Watts, Alan W. *The Spirit of Zen: A Way of Life, Work and Art in the Far East.* New York: Grove Press, 1958.

Yogi, Maharishi Mahesh. *Maharishi Mahesh Yogi on the Bhagavad-Gita.* Baltimore: Penguin, 1969.

————. *Meditations of Maharishi Mahesh Yogi.* New York: Bantam Books, 1968.

————. *Science of Being and Art of Living.* Los Angeles: International SRM Publications, 1967.

INDEX

INDEX

Another Gospel
was typeset by the Composition Department
of Zondervan Publishing House, Grand Rapids, Michigan
on a Mergenthaler Linotron 202/N.
Compositor: Nancy Wilson
Editor: Leonard George Goss

The text was set in 10 point Zaph,
a face designed for ITC by Hermann Zapf in 1976.
Conceived of as an all-purpose text and display type,
it also provides warmth and personality uncommon
to many typefaces.
This book was printed on 50-pound Antique Book paper
by R. R. Donnelley & Sons, Harrisonburg, Virginia.